SALLY YOUNG'S HISTORY OF AUSTRALIAN NEWSPAPERS

The first volume in Sally Young's history of Australian newspapers is *Paper Emperors: The Rise of Australia's Newspaper Empires*. It covers the period 1803 to 1941. *Media Monsters: The Transformation of Australia's Newspaper Empires* is the second volume, covering from 1941 to 1972.

Paper Emperors was awarded the Colin Roderick Literary Award 2020 and the Australian Political Studies Association (APSA) Henry Mayer Book Prize 2021. It was also longlisted for the Stella Prize 2020.

PRAISE FOR *PAPER EMPERORS*

An 'exceptional book ... Sally Young tells the story beautifully'.
Michael Cannon, *Inside Story*.

'A magisterial account' that 'brings dead documents to life'.
Kosmas Tsokhas, *Business History*.

'Meticulously researched ... and as gripping as *Citizen Kane*'.
**Australian Political Studies Association,
Henry Mayer Book Prize judges' report.**

A 'brilliant exposé of the Australian newspaper industry ... compulsively readable'. **Foundation for Australian Literary Studies,
Colin Roderick Award judges' report.**

'Weaves the best of storytelling devices and academic research into a highly readable history.' **Stella Prize 2020 judges' report.**

'The best narrative of the power of the press seen for a long time.'
Jim Sullivan, the *Otago Daily Times*.

PRAISE FOR *MEDIA MONSTERS*

Whether striding imperiously across the land like feudal lords, quietly pulling strings behind the scenes, or brawling violently over control of a suburban printing press like bar room drunks, Australia's media bosses and their companies have been among the most influential players in the nation's business and politics. One of them would in time become the most powerful media magnate in the world. Sally Young tells the remarkable story of these mid-twentieth-century media monsters, drawing on formidable industry knowledge, meticulous original research, and a gifted, witty story-teller's eye for telling detail and play of personality. This absorbing book is essential reading for anyone with a serious interest in how power has been exercised in this country.

**Frank Bongiorno AM, Professor of History,
The Australian National University**

A masterful account of the rise and rise of Australia's newspaper dynasties, as the Fairfax, Murdoch and Packer families extended their tentacles into radio and television while waging corporate and propaganda warfare, and stalking the corridors of power.

Bridget Griffen-Foley, Professor of Media, Macquarie University

The good news about Sally Young's second volume on the history of the Australian press is that it is just as interesting, just as revealing, just as wise, as the first volume. The research is original and deep, and provides a rich source of fresh information and analysis to the history of the Australian press.

**Rodney Tiffen, Emeritus Professor of Government
and International Relations, University of Sydney**

MEDIA MONSTERS

SALLY YOUNG is professor of political science at the University of Melbourne. She is the author of six previous books on Australian politics and media, including the prequel to this book (*Paper Emperors*, 2019), plus works on political journalism (*How Australia Decides*, 2011), press photography (*Shooting the Picture*, with Fay Anderson, 2016) and political advertising (*The Persuaders*, 2004).

To Jay, Abi and Megan.

And with my love and thanks always to Kathy, Harold, Frances and Joe.

MEDIA MONSTERS

THE TRANSFORMATION OF AUSTRALIA'S NEWSPAPER EMPIRES

SALLY YOUNG

UNSW PRESS

A UNSW Press book

Published by
NewSouth Publishing
University of New South Wales Press Ltd
University of New South Wales
Sydney NSW 2052
AUSTRALIA
https://unsw.press/

© Sally Young 2023
First published 2023

10 9 8 7 6 5 4 3 2 1

This book is copyright. Apart from any fair dealing for the purpose of private study, research, criticism or review, as permitted under the *Copyright Act*, no part of this book may be reproduced by any process without written permission. Inquiries should be addressed to the publisher.

A catalogue record for this book is available from the National Library of Australia

ISBN   9781742235707 (paperback)
        9781742238753 (ebook)
        9781742239699 (ePDF)

Internal design Josephine Pajor-Markus
Cover design Hugh Ford
Cover image Newspapers off the presses at the *Sydney Morning Herald* Broadway building in Jones Street, Ultimo in November 1973. Nine Publishing.
Printer Griffin Press

All reasonable efforts were taken to obtain permission to use copyright material reproduced in this book, but in some cases copyright could not be traced. The author welcomes information in this regard.

This book is printed on paper using fibre supplied from plantation or sustainably managed forests.

This research was supported under the Australian Research Council's Future Fellowship scheme (project number FT130100315). A Future Fellowships Establishment Grant and a Faculty of Arts Publication Subsidy Scheme were provided by the University of Melbourne.

CONTENTS

List of figures	ix
List of tables	xii
List of textboxes	xiii
Acknowledgments	xiv
Abbreviations	xvii
Introduction	1

PART ONE: THE 1940s — 5

1	At their peak	7
2	Curtin's circus	33
3	The press and the 'Cocky' go to war	54
4	New beginnings	78
5	Banking on the press	98

PART TWO: THE 1950s — 121

6	Newspapers fight the Cold War	123
7	Death and betrayal in Melbourne	142
8	Jack Williams: Empire builder, *Argus* killer?	158
9	On the move in Adelaide and Sydney	175
10	Taking over television	196
11	A licence to print money	219

PART THREE: THE 1960s — 241

12	Brawling in the suburbs	243
13	Old and new tricks	261
14	The realm of the Black Prince	292

| 15 | The quiet baron of Flinders Street | 316 |
| 16 | The new world | 340 |

PART FOUR: THE EARLY 1970s — **367**

17	The magic garden of computers	369
18	A new *Age*	396
19	Frank plays politics	419
20	The Whitlam experiment	441

Postscript	462
Notes	465
Bibliography	510
Index	524

LIST OF FIGURES

1.1 The front page of the *Sun News-Pictorial* announces the outbreak of war, 2 September 1939 8

1.2 A newsboy sells copies of a special edition of the *Sun News-Pictorial* during Victory in the Pacific celebrations outside Flinders Street Station, Melbourne, 15 August 1945 9

1.3 Although it had a half-finished clock tower with no clock, the *Argus* building on the corner of Elizabeth and La Trobe streets, Melbourne, was one of the grand newspaper buildings built in the 1920s, shown here circa 1950 29

2.1 Prime Minister John Curtin meets the Canberra Press Gallery (known as 'the Circus'), 1945 36

2.2 Sir Keith Murdoch, with his wife Elisabeth and son Rupert, pictured around 1950 39

3.1 The number one enemy of the press, Arthur Calwell, photographed by Max Dupain, November 1945 57

3.2 What all the fuss was about: The *Sunday Telegraph* publishes blank spaces indicating censorship, 16 April 1944 62

3.3 The famous photograph of a Commonwealth peace officer, gun drawn, stopping a truck from leaving the dock at Consolidated Press' Castlereagh and Elizabeth streets building, Sydney, 1944 68

3.4 A Commonwealth peace officer draws his revolver at the *Daily Mirror* office in Sydney in 1944 69

3.5 *Sydney Morning Herald* cartoonist John Frith represents Arthur Calwell as a cockatoo because of his raspy voice and repetitive complaints against the press 75

4.1 The historic use of four mastheads on the owners' strike-breaking combined newspaper, Sydney, 9 October 1944 80

5.1 The *Sydney Morning Herald* shows Ben Chifley and HV Evatt blowing up the banks with their nationalisation plans, 1947 107

5.2 The Liberal Party used, with permission, a John Frith–*Sydney Morning Herald* cartoon on its election campaign pamphlet, 1949 116

6.1 A newsboy takes a break, 16 June 1954 128

8.1 A rare photograph of the HWT's post-Murdoch empire builder, Sir John Williams, 1972 159

8.2 The HWT building in Flinders Street, Melbourne, circa 1956–60; note the HSV-7 van and 3DB studios, indicating the empire's span across print, radio and television 161

9.1 The *Sydney Morning Herald* heir who once rode a bus, Warwick Fairfax, 1953 189

9.2 Rupert Henderson, the business brain and managing director of the Fairfax company, in his office, Sydney, 7 March 1962 191

11.1 The *Daily Telegraph* hypes up the opening night of television and its TCN-9 station, 17 September 1956 220

12.1 Frank Packer with his sons Clyde (left) and Kerry, pictured in 1962. The caption to the photograph helpfully pointed out that, 'Clyde is 6 feet 3 inches and 240 pounds; Kerry is 6 feet 2 inches and 215 pounds'. 251

12.2 Clyde Packer throws the general manager of Anglican Press into the street during an infamous brawl over Sydney's suburban newspapers, *Daily Mirror*, 8 June 1960 253

13.1 Packer's newspaper ridicules Warwick Fairfax and Rupert Henderson for their antipathy to Menzies in a Les Tanner cartoon in the *Daily Telegraph*, 29 September 1961 265

13.2 The *Daily Telegraph* was amused by Fairfax's reconciliation with Menzies. Calwell is shown being thrown out of the boardroom while the *Financial Review* and the *Sydney Morning Herald*'s finance editor, Tom Fitzgerald, have been caned and sent to the naughty corner, 25 November 1963. 279

13.3 Alan Reid kills Labor's election hopes with his 'faceless men' scoop in the *Daily Telegraph*, 22 March 1963 282

LIST OF FIGURES   xi

14.1 The scale of the Fairfax company after Rupert Henderson retired, 1965 303

16.1 Labor leader Gough Whitlam reads the *Sun-Herald* at his Cabramatta home with his daughter, Catherine, the day after the 1969 federal election, 26 October 1969 356

17.1 These linotype operators, working at the HWT building, Melbourne, in 1964, could produce about six lines a minute 371

17.2 *Sydney Morning Herald* compositors preparing the paper on the stone, 1944. This was the first edition with news, rather than advertisements, on the front page. 372

17.3 A pneumatic tube delivery system used for *Sun* telegrams, Sydney, circa 1929. It is unclear if this image is showing the tubes at Associated Newspapers' building or the GPO. 377

17.4 The Herald and Weekly Times' Linotron 606 phototypesetter was capable of setting up to 3000 lines of type a minute 389

17.5 After three decades of transition, computers in the newsroom at the Herald and Weekly Times' Flinders Street building, 1986 394

18.1 Ranald Macdonald, the great-grandson of David Syme, and managing director of David Syme and Co, 1979. Behind him is a statuette of Mercury, the Roman messenger god which symbolised *The Age*'s role in communication. 399

18.2 The old *Age* building in Collins Street on the left in 1957, and on the right as it was when *The Age* moved out in 1969. After a new tower was built, the famous roof-top statue of Mercury was moved to the older building. 406

18.3 The ugliest building in Melbourne? The new *Age* building in Spencer Street, 1969. 408

19.1 Packer's man, William (Bill) McMahon, on the left, deposed Murdoch's man, John Gorton, on the right, in 1971. They are shown here outside (old) Parliament House in 1969. Gorton was Murdoch's first prime minister but Murdoch had abandoned him by 1971. 423

LIST OF TABLES

1.1 Australia's daily metropolitan newspapers, 1945 14

5.1 Newspaper and bank links, 1940s–early 1950s 101

10.1 The Menzies government's award of metropolitan commercial television licences in Sydney and Melbourne, 1955 (and station ownership until 1987) 214

11.1 The Menzies government's award of metropolitan commercial television licences, 1958–60 (and station ownership until 1987) 232

13.1 The partisan support of major newspapers, 1943–72 266

13.2 Newspaper groups abandoned: The Menzies government's allocation of new commercial television licences, 1963–64 277

14.1 Rupert Henderson's regional media empire, 1968–69 307

16.1 The financial strength of the major newspaper groups, 1969 361

16.2 The size of the media monsters: Their major interests and assets, 1969 362

17.1 The transition from hot metal to cold type, 1977–84 393

19.1 Daily metropolitan newspaper ownership after the *Daily Telegraph* sale, 1972 438

20.1 Australia's daily national and metropolitan newspapers, December 1972 442

LIST OF TEXTBOXES

1.1   Radio 10
1.2   Magazines 11
1.3   Opinion polls 17
1.4   Columns 25
1.5   Women in the newspaper office 26
6.1   Back to the butterfly department 124
6.2   Family newspapers 126
6.3   Paper problems 130
8.1   Keeping the *Herald* on top 161
9.1   Another Sydney strike, 1955 185
9.2   Magazines in the 1950s 187
10.1   Australia's two major commercial radio networks, 1954–55 200
11.1   Early television 221
11.2   Stars, opinions, images: Newspapers respond to television 226
15.1   Colour on the page 326
16.1   Radio in the 1960s 359
16.2   A new paper: The *Canberra News* 359
16.3   Taking over the country (papers) 364
17.1   The future of printing 374
17.2   Pneumatic tubes 376
20.1   Television switches on in 1972 444

ACKNOWLEDGMENTS

This book would not have been possible without the support of a Future Fellowship grant from the Australian Research Council (ARC), a Coral Thomas fellowship provided by the State Library of NSW and the support of the University of Melbourne in providing research time, resources and small grants.

I am grateful to Rod Kirkpatrick who read every chapter, checked facts and suggested changes that polished my grammar and punctuation. Rod's own scholarship is a gift to every newspaper historian and I was very fortunate to have his assistance. Helen Bones sent me images of archived papers from Sydney when Covid lockdowns in Victoria prevented me from travelling. Jessica Megarry located newspaper editorials. Claudia Talon found material in *AdNews*. And Leon Gettler conducted two interviews. Some of the background research performed by Maria Rae, Tom Roberts and Amanda McKittrick for *Paper Emperors* was drawn on for this book. My thanks to all.

I also owe a special thank you to several others. Rod Tiffen read all of *Media Monsters* and *Paper Emperors* and provided very helpful suggestions. Rod's research has always been an inspiration and his support and encouragement over the years have been invaluable. John Dahlsen generously provided me with boxes of important documents, sat for several interviews, sent me information, and read the chapter on Jack Williams. Ranald Macdonald was a very generous interviewee who also patiently answered all of my random questions by email and telephone. Bob Murray gave me a great deal of his time and shared his incredible knowledge with me. Denis Muller kindly read the chapter on computers and suggested improvements. David Dunstan generously provided important material and answered questions. John Bednall kindly gave me permission to quote from his father's manuscript papers and helped me understand more about Colin Bednall.

Many other people helped me in one way or another for this book, including providing information, source material, encouragement, or relating their experiences in interviews with me. I wish to thank Eric Beecher, John Bowie Wilson, the late Moss Cass, Judith Cook, Mark Day, John B Fairfax, Geoff Gallop, Peter Gardener, Michael Gawenda, Peter Gill, Julia Gillard, Jock Given, Murray Goot, Michelle Grattan, Bridget Griffen-Foley, the late Ian Hamilton, John Howard, Paul Keating, Sally Laming (John Curtin Prime Ministerial Library), Geoff Lomman, the late Stuart Macintyre, Gary Morgan, Bryan Mowry, Joan Newman, Laurie Oakes, Henry Rosenbloom, Kevin Rudd, Gavin Souter, Max Suich, Shannon Sutton (National Library of Australia), Anastasia Symeonides (Fairfax Syndication/Nine Publishing), Mark Tanner, Jamie Trew (Newspix), Jim Usher, and others who wished to remain anonymous.

The usual disclaimer applies – my interviewees would not necessarily agree with my interpretations, and any errors or omissions that remain in the book after all the help I have received are my responsibility alone.

At UNSW Press/NewSouth Publishing, I would like to gratefully acknowledge the support of Kathy Bail, Elspeth Menzies, Joumana Awad, Emma Hutchinson and Fiona Sim, as well as Phillipa McGuinness, as a smaller project grew into a monster.

I also wish to thank Rob Thomas, who established the Library's Coral Thomas Fellowship in honour of his mother. And at the Mitchell Library, Rachel Franks, who looked after me so well during my time as a fellow, and Richard Neville and John Vallance. For help with images and copyright, thank you to Linda Brainwood, Philippa Stevens, Gosia Bojanowski and Scott Wajon.

Finally, my family deserve more thanks than I could ever convey here for living with this endeavour over many years and for sacrificing so much to make it possible. Jay, thank you – for everything.

***

Estimates of historical currency into present-day equivalents were calculated using the website 'Measuring Worth': https://www.measuringworth.com/australiacompare/.

Small sections on press reporting of the Petrov affair and the Vietnam War were adapted from *Shooting the Picture*, and on 1972 from *How Australia Decides*.

A note on gender-neutral language: I have used 'newsboy', 'copy boy' and 'copy girl' because those dated terms have no modern equivalent, and I have also retained the use of 'chairman' where that was someone's formal job title.

ABBREVIATIONS

AAP	Australian Associated Press
ABC	Australian Broadcasting Commission (today known as the Australian Broadcasting Corporation)
ABC	American Broadcasting Company (US)
ABCB	Australian Broadcasting Control Board
ACP	Australian Consolidated Press
ACTU	Australian Council of Trade Unions
AIF	Australian Imperial Force
AMP	Australian Mutual Provident Society
ANC	Australian Newspapers' Council
ANM	Australian Newsprint Mills Ltd
ANPA	Australian Newspaper Proprietors' Association
ANZUS	Australia, New Zealand and United States Security Treaty
AP	Associated Press (US)
ATS	Amalgamated Television Services Pty Ltd
ATV	Associated Television Corporation Ltd (UK), had an Australian subsidiary called ATV (Australia) Pty Ltd
AWA	Amalgamated Wireless (Australasia) Ltd
AWU	Australian Workers' Union
BBC	British Broadcasting Corporation (originally called the British Broadcasting Company until 1 January 1927)
BHP	Broken Hill Proprietary Ltd
CBS	Columbia Broadcasting System (US)
CSR	Colonial Sugar Refining Company
CUB	Carlton and United Breweries Ltd
DLP	Democratic Labor Party
ES&A	the English, Scottish & Australian Bank Ltd
FCC	Federal Communications Commission (US)
GE	General Electric
GPO	General Post Office

HWT	Herald and Weekly Times Ltd
IBM	International Business Machines Co. (US)
IPA	Institute of Public Affairs
ITA	Independent Television Authority (UK)
ITV	Independent Television (UK)
MP	Member of Parliament
NAB	National Australia Bank
NBC	National Broadcasting Company (US)
PIEUA	Printing Industry Employees' Union of Australia (1915–66)
PKIU	Printing and Kindred Industries Union (1966–95)
PMG	Postmaster-General's Department
RCA	Radio Corporation of America
SMH	*Sydney Morning Herald*
TTS	teletype setting
UAP	United Australia Party
UNICEF	United Nations International Children's Emergency Fund
VFL	Victorian Football League
VRC	Victoria Racing Club
WAN	West Australian Newspapers Limited

A NOTE ON COMPANY NAMES

The company that is called **Consolidated Press** in this book was previously called Sydney Newspapers. Between 1936 and 1956, it was formally called Consolidated Press Ltd, and from 1956 to 1994, Australian Consolidated Press Ltd (ACP).

The company called **News Limited** (founded 1923) became News Corp Australia on 1 July 2013.

The company originally owned and controlled by the Fairfax family is mostly called 'the Fairfax group' or **Fairfax & Sons** to cover the minor variations in name it underwent between 1856 and April 1956 (from John Fairfax & Sons, to John Fairfax & Sons Ltd and John Fairfax & Sons Pty Ltd). From April 1956 to January 1992, it was incorporated as a public holding company called **John Fairfax Ltd** (one of its subsidiary companies was John Fairfax & Sons Pty Ltd, publisher of its newspapers). Between January 1992 and January 2007, it was called **John Fairfax Holdings Ltd**, and from January 2007, it was **Fairfax Media** until it was taken over and absorbed into the **Nine group** on 10 December 2018.

I use 'the **Daily Mirror group**' (non-italicised) for the British company that owned London's *Daily Mirror* to indicate the name of the larger company but also to help differentiate it from Sydney's *Daily Mirror*.

INTRODUCTION

Colin Bednall was a gifted journalist and respected media manager. In the early 1970s, he dubbed Australia's largest newspaper groups 'media monsters' to convey a sense of their extraordinary size, wealth and power.[1] This book describes how they got to that point.

It begins in 1941. Robert Menzies had just resigned as prime minister, two years after announcing the beginning of Australia's involvement in World War II. Bednall was a war correspondent in Europe reporting for Australian Associated Press.

Bednall soon became the aviation correspondent for Lord Rothermere's mass-circulation British newspaper, the *Daily Mail*, in 1942. Bednall's vivid accounts of accompanying allied flying missions and bombing raids as a qualified gunner made him famous in the United Kingdom. His reports helped lift the profile of the air war so that it became prominent in British strategic planning and the public's understanding of the war.[2]

Journalists considered Fleet Street 'the hardest street in the world', but Bednall's reputation was so high in London's newspaper industry that he was made assistant editor of the *Daily Mail* in 1944.[3] Arthur Christiansen, the fabled editor of its even higher-selling rival, the *Daily Express*, considered Bednall 'one of the best journalists he had ever known, one he would have employed on his "perfect newspaper staff"'.[4]

But Bednall did not stay in Fleet Street because his potential had already been recognised years earlier by Keith Murdoch when 'Sir Keith' was head of the Herald and Weekly Times (HWT), and the undisputed leader of Australia's newspaper industry. Bednall had first come to Murdoch's attention when he was working at the Adelaide *News* where he had started as a copy boy and then became a cadet in 1932. Bednall was called to Melbourne where he worked under Murdoch at the *Sun News-Pictorial* and the *Herald* before he went to the United Kingdom, in 1938, with his mentor's blessing.

Murdoch lured Bednall back to Australia in 1946 by making him the managing editor of Brisbane's *Courier-Mail* and head of its allied radio stations. Later, Bednall became the managing editor of the Melbourne *Argus*, and then a television pioneer as the managing director of GTV-9 television station in Melbourne. Bednall ascended to some of the highest positions that a salaried employee could reach in Australian media. But by 1972, when this book ends, it had all come undone.

Bednall had been displaced in the 1950s by the deaths of two of his newspaper owners, Keith Murdoch and John Wren, and then sacked by another, British press baron Cecil Harmsworth King. In the 1960s, Bednall had his house burned down (he alleged 'a gangster' did it as payback after Bednall refused to make GTV-9's female television performers available to a prostitution ring). Bednall resigned from Frank Packer's employment after that incident, and after pressure over cost-cutting and 'telephone calls from the boardroom to disreputable persons'.[5] He was blacklisted in the Australian media industry.

At the time, some media owners had a standing agreement that, as a way of discouraging disloyalty and salary increases, they would refuse to hire anyone who had left the other's employment.[6] But Bednall had an added disadvantage; he was considered annoyingly independent, and principled. After his break with Packer in 1965, Bednall never worked as a media executive in Australia again. In the early 1970s, he finished writing a sharp, engaging and illuminating autobiography, but to his great disappointment it was never published as a book. Today, Bednall's manuscript lies in a manilla folder languishing inside a box of his private papers held at the National Library of Australia.

Bednall's autobiography was probably judged too hot to handle. In some parts, it was quite bitter, justifiably so. In other parts, Bednall included harsh criticism of press barons, and some racy anecdotes about them. He wrote that one (unnamed) proprietor kept a gun in his top drawer and was rumoured to be involved in bribery, prostitution and shady underworld businesses. According to Bednall, another (also unnamed) press magnate had shocked New York film executives by bragging that he sometimes bugged the telephones in the hotel bedrooms of foreigners who came to Australia to do business with him.[7]

Bednall said that the proprietors he worked for – including Keith Murdoch, Frank Packer and the British press magnates, Lord Rothermere and Cecil Harmsworth King (Bednall called them 'my millionaires') – all had in common that they 'loved their money', were 'often fickle' and 'untrustworthy'.[8] But he also said that Murdoch had a 'greatness' about him and some very admirable qualities, and that Packer and Murdoch both had an 'intimidating capacity for mental arithmetic'.[9]

Bednall was a seasoned observer of press barons and press executives in the mid-20th century. He witnessed the rise of his nemesis, John (Jack) Williams, who was Murdoch's successor at the HWT, and its second grand reformer. Bednall also saw the reign of the patrician Warwick Fairfax, custodian of the *Sydney Morning Herald*, and his right-hand man and chief executive, Rupert Henderson (who he thought was 'vulgar' and 'a nasty squirt of a man'). And Bednall never forgot seeing Ezra Norton, the maverick owner of Sydney's *Daily Mirror*, show up drunk to a meeting of proprietors, and then dance around the boardroom table singing a nursery rhyme and waving an imaginary fairy wand over their heads.[10]

Because Bednall was a perceptive insider and an eyewitness throughout the period covered in this book, some of his story, memories and views are dotted throughout its pages. But he especially appears in chapters on the 1950s, because he played an important role at a crucial moment for Australian newspapers.

Bednall was appointed to the Royal Commission on Television in 1953. He was still working in service of newspaper proprietors then, and he used the opportunity to lobby for commercial television and for the already powerful newspaper groups to be able to gain television licences. Bednall did everything he could behind the scenes to make that possible. And when it happened, it was a transformative moment.

Television turned the paper emperors into multimedia giants. By the early 1970s, a now sidelined Bednall could see that the main newspaper groups in Australia had become 'immensely wealthy and powerful', and in a way that was unique in the western world.[11] The role he had played in that transformation became one of his greatest regrets. But in 1941, that sense of bitter regret lay 30 years in the future. Newspapers were king. Television was 15 years away. And Australians were reading news of the war over breakfast, including a stirring account by Bednall of being an observer on a 15-hour RAAF flight over the heart of the Atlantic hunting for a German submarine.[12]

PART ONE

THE 1940s

CHAPTER 1
AT THEIR PEAK

Australians were buying newspapers in record numbers during World War II, just as they had during World War I. Newspaper executives knew that no wartime sales boom could last forever, but few could have imagined that Australia's 140-year-old newspaper industry was hitting its sales peak. The fortunes of individual papers would continue to wax and wane, but on a collective and per capita basis, Australia's metropolitan daily newspapers would never sell more printed copies than they did in the mid-1940s.

Morning newspapers were being delivered to more than a million Australian homes before breakfast. Australians were then buying over a million more afternoon papers after lunch from newspaper kiosks, city intersections and train stations, and into the evening from vendors outside theatres, stadiums and racetracks. Dramatic wartime events, such as the D-day Normandy landings, boosted sales considerably, and helped Melbourne's *Sun News-Pictorial* become the first Australian paper to sell more than 300 000 copies.[1]

Even some of the more conservative newspapers began placing news, instead of advertisements, on their front page during the war, and newsprint rationing and postwar shortages caused several to move from their traditional broadsheet size to a smaller tabloid size.[2] Newspapers were trying out new features, including lighthearted front-page columns and regular public opinion polls that promised to reveal 'what the public thinks'. They were publishing more photographs and drawings within the bounds of censorship restrictions that limited what could be said – and shown – about the progress of the war.

Daily papers were also publishing more comic strips, despite concerns they were an American medium 'Yankeefying the daily press' and threatening Australian jobs.[3] Comics were extremely popular among adults as well as children (up to 87 per cent of readers read the comics),

FIGURE 1.1 The front page of the *Sun News-Pictorial* announces the outbreak of war, 2 September 1939

SOURCE Australian War Memorial.

FIGURE 1.2 A newsboy sells copies of a special edition of the *Sun News-Pictorial* during Victory in the Pacific celebrations outside Flinders Street Station, Melbourne, 15 August 1945

SOURCE Australian War Memorial.

so even during newsprint rationing, space was found to include 'Blondie', 'Mickey Mouse' and 'Wally and the Major'.[4] Ignoring parent groups who complained that comics were 'corrupting the minds of children' by depicting 'crime, mysticism, war, sex, [and] bad English', even formerly resistant papers such as the *Sydney Morning Herald* were publishing comic strips and cartoons by the war's end.[5]

Australians had already been enthusiastic newspaper readers when the war began, but between 1941 and 1946 there was a spectacular 53 per cent increase in newspaper sales.[6] Over 2.6 million copies were sold each day at a

TEXTBOX 1.1 Radio

Newspapers had two main competitors in the 1940s: radio and magazines. In the United Kingdom and United States, radio was a greater threat to newspapers because it played an important role as a news medium. In Australia, radio was more of an entertainment medium that left the provision of news and information to newspapers. This was no accident.

In the 1930s, major newspaper groups had shaped the development of radio by lobbying the Lyons government to restrict the news capacity of the national public broadcaster, the Australian Broadcasting Commission (ABC), and also by securing commercial radio licences and becoming influential broadcasters themselves.[7] The result of these efforts was captured in a 1945 Gallup poll survey that found 61 per cent of Americans preferred radio news over daily newspapers, but only 21 per cent of Australians did.[8]

Although held back in the past, radio was forging ahead during World War II. Nearly three-quarters of Australian homes had a radio receiver.[9] For the first time, many families were hearing war news in real time. And despite newspaper complaints, the ABC was breaking free of its restrictions and gathering its own news.

The ABC's news coverage became more popular and respected as the war went on. It was broadcasting news more frequently, including delivering up to seven national broadcasts a day, plus state services and commentaries. Some of its news broadcasts were being relayed on commercial stations, which encouraged them to develop independent news bulletins by 1945.[10]

Radio was broadcasting news – and also sporting events – at a speed and level of intimacy that newspapers could not match. And advertisers were following the audience, with 1941 a record year for commercial radio advertising. Newsprint rationing drove even more advertisers across to radio once papers had to turn them away due to lack of space.[11]

Radio's gain was not entirely newspapers' loss, of course, because by 1942 newspapers owned or controlled 44 per cent of Australia's 99 commercial radio stations.[12] This was unevenly spread though. Fairfax and Consolidated Press had no radio assets, whereas the Herald and Weekly Times Ltd (HWT) and Associated Newspapers had extensive interests.

The HWT owned the popular 3DB in Melbourne and held interests (through its affiliated companies) in the *Advertiser*'s 5AD Adelaide, Queensland Newspapers' 4BK Brisbane and 4AK Oakey, plus nine other radio stations across Victoria, South Australia, Queensland and Western Australia.

Associated Newspapers was extensively involved in radio. It controlled Sydney's popular 2UE, and through a major shareholder, Denison Estates, controlled the major radio network in Australia, the Macquarie Network, which included the top Sydney station, 2GB, plus 2CA (Canberra) and four other stations, with a wide reach through 19 stations across Australia.

In Victoria, *The Age*'s parent company, David Syme and Co, held shares in 3AW (Melbourne) and owned 3HA (Hamilton), 3SH (Swan Hill) and 3TR (Sale). The *Argus* had shares in 3UZ and owned 3SR (Shepparton), 3UL (Warragul) and 3YB (Warrnambool). In Western Australia, WAN owned 6IX Perth, 6WB Katanning and 6MD Merredin. News Limited owned 2BH Broken Hill. The Hobart *Mercury* was connected with 7HO.

TEXTBOX 1.2 Magazines

Magazines provided fierce competition to newspapers in the 1940s. Magazines made much less arduous demands on limited paper supplies than a daily newspaper, and had a much better ability to be printed in colour using offset printing.

Sales of the *Australian Women's Weekly*, founded in 1933, soared during the war from an average of 400 000 per issue to nearly 700 000.[13] It began publishing glamourous front covers with colour photographs in 1942. It would take another ten years before one newspaper could publish colour photographs on its front page (see Chapter 8), and another ten years before other papers would occasionally print colour covers for special editions (see Chapter 15).

Although ostensibly a women's magazine, the *Women's Weekly* was often read by the whole family, making it a true competitor for newspapers. But, as with radio, newspapers were not necessarily victims of rival media. Consolidated Press owned the money-spinning *Women's Weekly*. And several other newspaper groups also published magazines, although with less success.

Associated Newspapers published a less popular rival, *Woman*, plus *Radio and Hobbies* and a photojournalism magazine called *Pix*. The HWT published the monthly *Australian Home Beautiful*. Fairfax & Sons had a lavish *Home* magazine but had to suspend its publication in 1942 due to newsprint scarcity. The *Argus* went the other way and transformed its weekly paper, the *Australasian*, into a pictorial magazine in 1940.

When the war was over, and supplies and equipment were no longer an issue, newspaper companies would keep trying to capitalise on the growing magazine market. The *Argus*'s *Australasian* was given another makeover and became the *Australasian Post* in April 1946. The HWT launched *Australian Woman's Day* in August 1947 and Fairfax re-launched *Home* as a colour magazine in 1948. Still, none could touch the *Women's Weekly*.

time when Australia's population was only 7.5 million, and readership was two or three times higher than sales because a purchased newspaper was usually shared between family members and co-workers.[14]

It was no coincidence that newspaper circulation was peaking at the same time as the use of public transport in Australian cities.[15] Most city workers were travelling to and from work by train, bus, tram or ferry, so they had the time and motivation to read a newspaper on the journey. Australians were not only buying newspapers to read dramatic stories about the war, but also to read local news, sports results, the horse racing form guide, stock market reports, fiction serials, comics and radio program lists. And some people – perhaps many – bought a newspaper not for the journalism at all but for the advertisements, so they could find a job or accommodation, buy goods or services, or find out about the latest department store sales.

NEWSPAPERS AND THEIR OWNERS

In the mid-1940s, there were 16 capital city newspapers sold daily (usually from Monday to Saturday) (Table 1.1).[16] A period of rapid growth in the 1920s had been followed by an era of consolidation after the Depression and only the largest cities of Sydney and Melbourne still sustained direct competition between rival papers (and only in the morning in Melbourne, not in the afternoon).

Most of the daily papers were already over 60 years old and the enormous advantages of an early start – in terms of capital, printing equipment, advertising revenue and popularity – were so strong that 12 of them had begun before 1888, and half could trace their lineage back before 1860. The *Sydney Morning Herald* was the oldest (1831), and the youngest was the *Daily Mirror*, freshly launched during the war (1941).

Around half of the 12 separate owners were family businesses. The Fairfax, Syme and Davies families especially were carrying on a long tradition of family ownership. Other companies – including the Herald and Weekly Times Ltd (HWT), Advertiser Newspapers Ltd, News Limited and West Australian Newspapers (WAN) – were large public companies. Technically, they were owned by hundreds – or even thousands – of individual shareholders. In reality, there were usually a small number of dominant shareholders. These were wealthy individuals who either owned shares in their own name or through a company, or even via a trustee company which managed and invested funds on their behalf (and masked their identity in the process).

Ownership was becoming even more complicated in the 1940s as the HWT was at the forefront of using a strategy of interlocking shareholdings to expand and fortify itself against takeover. By the 1940s, that interlocking structure meant the HWT was the dominant shareholder in Adelaide's Advertiser Newspapers Ltd. In turn, Advertiser Newspapers owned a controlling interest in News Limited. Completing the circle, Advertiser Newspapers was on its way to becoming the HWT's largest shareholder.

The HWT dominated in Melbourne and Adelaide as a result, but it also had a presence in Brisbane and at least the ghost of a presence in

TABLE 1.1 Australia's daily metropolitan newspapers, 1945

Location	Title	Year launched	Circulation*	Type of newspaper	Owner and major shareholders
Sydney	Sydney Morning Herald	1831 (as the Sydney Herald)	282 000	Morning broadsheet	John Fairfax & Sons Pty Ltd (Fairfax family)
	Daily Telegraph	1879	276 000	Morning tabloid	Consolidated Press Ltd (Frank Packer and EG Theodore)
	Sun	1910 (launched from the Australian Star, founded 1887)	262 000	Afternoon broadsheet (tabloid from 1947)	Associated Newspapers Ltd
	Daily Mirror	1941	(estimated) 300 000	Afternoon tabloid	Truth and Sportsman Ltd (Ezra Norton)
Melbourne	Argus	1846	120 000	Morning broadsheet (tabloid from 1950)	Argus and Australasian Ltd
	The Age	1854	112 000	Morning broadsheet	David Syme and Co (Syme family)
	Sun News Pictorial	1922	327 000	Morning tabloid	Herald and Weekly Times Ltd
	Herald	1840	313 000	Afternoon broadsheet	Herald and Weekly Times Ltd
Brisbane	Courier-Mail	1933 (descended from the Moreton Bay Courier, 1846)	157 000	Morning broadsheet	Queensland Newspapers Ltd (Keith Murdoch and John Wren)
	Telegraph	1872	123 000	Afternoon broadsheet (tabloid from 1948)	Telegraph Newspaper Company Ltd
Adelaide	Advertiser	1858	128 000	Morning broadsheet	Advertiser Newspapers Ltd (Herald and Weekly Times Ltd)
	News	1923	78 000	Afternoon broadsheet (tabloid from 1948)	News Limited (Advertiser Newspapers Ltd - Herald and Weekly Times Ltd)
Perth	West Australian	1879 (although it claims lineage to 1833)	94 000	Morning broadsheet (tabloid from 1949)	West Australian Newspapers Ltd
	Daily News	1882	64 000	Afternoon tabloid	Perth Newspapers Ltd (subsidiary of West Australian Newspapers Ltd)

Location	Title	Year launched	Circulation*	Type of newspaper	Owner and major shareholders
Hobart	*Mercury*	1854	29 000	Morning tabloid	Davies Brothers Ltd (Davies family)
Canberra	*Canberra Times*	1926	(estimated) under 10 000	Morning broadsheet	The Federal Capital Press of Australia Ltd (Shakespeare family)

NOTE The *Herald* and *Weekly Times*' (HWT) newspapers are shaded. The two WAN (Perth) newspapers are partly shaded because WAN and the HWT had key common shareholders. Paper size changes are shown for the period from 1945-1950. The Northern Territory did not have a daily newspaper at this time.
* Average daily paid circulation figures are from Murray Goot, 'Newspaper circulation in Australia, 1932-1977', Media Centre Paper no.11, Centre for the Study of Educational Communication and Media, La Trobe University, Melbourne, 1979, p. 5.

Perth. In Brisbane, the HWT held shares in the company that owned the *Courier-Mail*. Keith Murdoch, in his own right, was one of Queensland Newspapers' two major shareholders. In Perth, HWT shareholders also owned shares in WAN, owner of the *West Australian* and the *Daily News*. These common owners were connected to the mining industry.

Murdoch's rise in the 1920s and 1930s had been supported by some of the largest of the HWT's shareholders, William Lawrence (WL) Baillieu, members of his family, and companies associated with their industrial empire, Collins House (named after its headquarters in Melbourne). Collins House had made a fortune during World War I from its domination of mining, especially of iron ore, and in the interwar period had diversified into a stunning array of manufacturing interests. It was also involved in shipping, banking, insurance, aircraft production, breweries, real estate and agriculture. The group had developed some of Australia's most famous brands, including Consolidated Zinc (now Rio Tinto), Carlton and United Breweries (CUB), Dunlop Rubber and Dulux.

Collins House was still a formidable corporate and political presence. A Labor politician in 1940 called it 'the centre which really controls Australia'.[17] But it was on the cusp of decline after the extraordinary highs of the interwar years. And although members of the Baillieu family and

Collins House companies still had links with the HWT in the 1940s, and even into the 1960s and 1970s, these were not as close or controlling as they had been in the 1920s.

Ownership and control of the HWT had become more dispersed, and the HWT had become a big business in its own right, among the 20 largest companies in Australia in 1940.[18] Other newspaper groups that were small, tired or on the verge of collapse in the 1940s, looked to the HWT for inspiration. It had grown from a single Melbourne newspaper, the *Herald*, into the most powerful media organisation in the country.

THE HERALD AND WEEKLY TIMES AT HOME

The HWT's board and management were thoroughly dominated by its chairman, Keith Murdoch. A star journalist during World War I and the *Herald*'s editor in the 1920s, even those who were critical of Murdoch acknowledged he had a 'talent that at times approached genius'.[19] Murdoch was not a major owner of the HWT – he held only a small shareholding – but as a manager and executive, he had been the driving force behind the company's expansion. Murdoch had become chairman only recently, in 1942, after a long internal power struggle against the Fink family, leading Catherine Fink (a HWT shareholder and sister-in-law of the previous chairman), to lament that 'Keith Murdoch is [now] in sole command!'[20]

Command was exercised out of the HWT's base in Melbourne, a grand, five-storey building in Flinders Street, where it published the *Herald* and the *Sun News-Pictorial*. Both papers were thriving during the war, and by November 1945 were selling over 320 000 copies each, making them the two highest-selling daily newspapers in the country.[21]

The *Herald* was the foundation of the empire and Melbourne's monopoly afternoon paper. It was a broadsheet with strong news and sports coverage printed between lots of Myer department store advertisements. The *Herald* had a more serious reputation than Australia's other afternoon papers. It tried to combine the solid reporting and accuracy of a morning paper with the liveliness of an afternoon one.[22] The paper's late deadline and its rapid processing of cable news from around the world made it the breaking news medium of the day. The *Herald* spectacularly scooped the newspaper world with news of Germany's invasion of Poland in 1939, and again with a special late edition revealing news of Britain's – and therefore Australia's – involvement in the war.

Australia's best-selling paper, the *Sun News-Pictorial*, was a morning tabloid known for its light, bright style, vivid photographs and easy-to-digest news coverage. Instantly popular when it had launched in 1922 as Australia's first pictorial newspaper, the *Sun News-Pictorial* was still the newspaper that many others tried to imitate. During the war, its circulation rose by an extraordinary 38 per cent.[23]

Trying to find enough paper for high-circulation papers like the *Herald* and the *Sun News-Pictorial* posed a problem in wartime. Newsprint was mostly imported from overseas and had been affected by restricted supply lines and shipping, as well as newsprint rationing. The only local newsprint manufacturing mill, Australian Newsprint Mills Ltd (ANM), was jointly owned by the major newspaper groups. It averted complete disaster but could not produce enough.

HWT executives made an important choice to set strict limits on advertising so they could save space for news and popular features and keep the papers' circulations growing. The company's advertising revenue dropped painfully, by 60 per cent, but when the war ended, the HWT was able to charge advertisers more for reaching a larger audience.[24] This contributed to the company's emergence as a big winner from World War II. Its profits had more than doubled and its reserves nearly tripled.[25]

TEXTBOX 1.3 Opinion polls

Opinion polls were another American innovation to hit Australian newspapers in the 1940s. On a trip to the United States in 1936, Keith Murdoch had been impressed by the work of pollster George Gallup. That year, Gallup upended traditional methods of sampling public opinion when he correctly predicted a presidential victory for Franklin D Roosevelt. Other pollsters had used expensive, large-scale mail-outs but failed to predict the result. Gallup used a much smaller sample but one selected using more scientific techniques and with an emphasis on personal interviews.

In April 1940, Murdoch dispatched a young freelancer and consultant, Roy Morgan, to the United States to study opinion polling from Gallup. Morgan had developed a reputation as a financial whizz who could read between the lines of company balance sheets. He had been performing that work for the Stock Exchange but also for Murdoch and MH 'Jac' Baillieu, as well as working as a freelance financial writer for the *Herald* since 1936.[26]

Morgan had ambitions to become the paper's finance editor and move up the ranks of the HWT.[27] There was a slight sense of destiny involved in this as Morgan had a family connection to the *Herald* – his grandfather, the printer William Williams, had worked at the paper with its founder, George Cavenagh.

Roy Morgan quickly impressed Murdoch and proved his value to the HWT by convincing every major company in Australia to release their balance sheets in the morning, before the Stock Exchange opened, rather than in the afternoon so they could be printed in the first edition of the *Herald*, rather than the morning papers. This coup boosted the *Herald*'s popularity and influence, especially among the business community.[28]

Morgan returned to Australia in October 1940 and became managing director of 'Australian Public Opinion Polls (The Gallup Method)'. The company set up 300 interviewing centres throughout Australia.[29] Murdoch wanted the poll to be nation wide and syndicated through newspaper chains (as in the United States). The new polling company was therefore jointly owned by newspapers from each of the state capitals, but effectively controlled by the HWT.[30]

Morgan reported to the HWT's general manager and worked out of the *Herald* building (in the office next to Murdoch's). Murdoch insisted that the subscribing papers had the right to veto any of the questions Morgan submitted to them in advance.[31] The ability to influence what questions would be asked of the public, and when, but also which results, if any, would be made public, always has an impact on polls and what they reveal.

The results of Roy Morgan's first Gallup poll were published in the *Herald* in October 1941. The topic was equal pay and 59 per cent of those surveyed said they favoured equal pay for women doing the same work as men. This result was reported on a page alongside advertisements for silk pantihose, clothes, lipstick and curtain sets.[32]

> For the next three decades, Morgan's company was the only one doing nationwide polling in Australia.[33] Rival newspaper groups attempted only some small-scale studies during the war years to try to capitalise on the public interest in, and news value of, opinion polls.[34]

RULING BY PROXY IN ADELAIDE

The HWT had a dominant stake in Advertiser Newspapers but that was kept quiet in Adelaide, where any notion of Melbourne control of an Adelaide institution would be unwelcome. Lloyd Dumas, the chairman and managing director of Advertiser Newspapers, was a Keith Murdoch protégé and confidant. Keith's son, Rupert Murdoch, later claimed that Dumas had been appointed by his father to head the *Advertiser* as Keith's 'nominee' and had accepted the job on that basis, with the two men 'work[ing] together ... in the running of the *Advertiser*'.[35]

The *Advertiser* had enjoyed the benefits of a monopoly position in the morning market in Adelaide since 1931. It was a conservative and influential paper in South Australia, with a large number of classified advertisements (as its name suggested). Its excellent profits and high per capita circulation increased even further during the war and the *Advertiser* building was even busier than usual as 120 women were producing munitions parts for shells and mortar bombs in a fireproof annex constructed in the composing room.[36]

Four blocks away, Adelaide's afternoon paper, the *News*, was produced from North Terrace. The *News* had been launched in 1923 by Collins House consultant Gerald Mussen and former *Herald* editor (and Murdoch nemesis) James Edward Davidson.[37] After the Depression had severely weakened the paper, Murdoch had overseen Advertiser Newspapers (and thus the HWT) gaining a majority shareholding of its parent company, News Limited, in 1931. News Limited was still struggling financially in the 1940s.

Sales of the *News* rose from 42 000 to 80 000 during the war, but the company's profits fell.[38] The paper was on the verge of entering the kind of death spiral feared throughout the industry. This was where a newspaper's circulation increased, so it had to spend more on newsprint and labour, but its advertising revenue did not increase enough to match those higher costs. Every additional copy that was sold would be costing its publisher money, not making it money.

POWERING AHEAD IN PERTH

In 1926, the *West Australian* had been purchased by a public company called West Australian Newspapers Ltd (WAN). Keith Murdoch had led the takeover on behalf of Collins House leader William Sydney (WS) Robinson, who became one of WAN's directors.[39] After a backlash against 'Eastern state' control, WAN was reported to have been returned to local ownership in the early 1930s but Labor politicians and left-wing newspapers in the 1940s were not convinced and still sometimes referred to WAN as part of the 'Murdoch press'.[40] Although Murdoch was no longer a WAN owner, there were still common owners between WAN and the HWT. These included Baillieu family members and Collins House companies who remained invested in WAN even after the eastern state retreat. This was the cause of the confusion – and suspicion – about how separate WAN and the HWT really were.

The circulation of WAN's *West Australian* was at an all time high by the end of the war and its financial stability was becoming the envy of the industry.[41] A lack of competition and a mining and population boom were the solid foundations of its growth but the conservative paper was also proud it had grown its circulation and profits without resorting to gimmicks such as competitions, or even front-page news (which the *West Australian* did not adopt until 1949).

WAN also owned the afternoon tabloid *Daily News*, giving it a monopoly over both the morning and afternoon markets in Perth. The *Daily News*' editor, James Macartney, exercised a strong editorial hand and shifted it to a more dynamic format with 'stop press' updates and breaking sports results. The *Daily News* was selling an extra 40 000 copies per day by the end of the war.[42] In case Japanese air raids disrupted production of either paper, WAN had purchased a property away from the city, in Maylands, and stocked it with enough equipment to produce an eight-page newspaper at an hour's notice. Unneeded, the building was sold after the war.[43]

A SECRET PARTNER IN BRISBANE

The other paper that critics considered part of the 'Murdoch press' was the *Courier-Mail* in Brisbane. The HWT owned some shares in Queensland Newspapers, the *Courier-Mail*'s parent company, but it was primarily an independent project for Keith Murdoch. Since 1933, Murdoch had secretly co-owned the *Courier-Mail* with John Wren. Regularly described as a 'gangster' or 'crime boss', Wren had built his immense fortune from illegal gambling in Melbourne, and then investments in mining, racetracks and many other businesses.[44]

The *Courier-Mail* was produced out of a glamourous cream-coloured Art Deco building in Queen Street, opposite Brisbane's GPO. It became the centre of great activity when American General Douglas MacArthur set up his command in the AMP building across the road and the *Courier-Mail* acted as a base for international news agencies. In 1937, Murdoch had sent one of his most impressive protégés to make the *Courier-Mail* more lively and lift its circulation. John (Jack) Williams was a journalist, accountant and financial prodigy who had formerly been the *Herald*'s chief financial writer. After the *Courier-Mail*'s circulation rose from 76 000 in 1939 to 157 000 in 1945, Williams returned to Melbourne, a rising star at the HWT.[45]

SYDNEY'S GRANNY

No other newspaper company could rival the assets or reach of the HWT, but the most likely contenders for future media empires were located in Sydney, the nation's largest, toughest and most competitive newspaper market. Four Sydney companies owned one daily newspaper each, and unlike in Melbourne, there was competition in both the morning and afternoon markets.[46]

The oldest and wealthiest Sydney newspaper company was Fairfax & Sons. The jewel in its crown, the *Sydney Morning Herald*, was a serious and earnest morning broadsheet published out of a 12-storey building in Sydney's CBD stacked with sandbags during the war. The paper was the oldest in the country and known for its gravitas, self-declared 'old-fashioned' values and its conservative political stance (leading critics to refer to it as 'Granny' *Herald*). Styled as a 'paper of record', the *Sydney Morning Herald*'s coverage was thorough, sometimes to the point of exhaustive, and this depth was underwritten by the lucrative returns from pages of classified advertising.

The *Sydney Morning Herald* had been owned by the wealthy Fairfax family, the blue bloods of the Australian newspaper industry, for four generations. Warwick Fairfax had been in charge of Fairfax & Sons since 1930 as managing director, but the paper's general manager since 1938, Rupert Albert Geary (RAG) Henderson (nicknamed 'Rags' behind his back), was emerging as the business brain who would expand the company. Fairfax & Sons had already invested in new and cooperative ventures, including ANM and Australian Associated Press (AAP), jointly with the HWT, but the *Sydney Morning Herald* remained the company's overwhelming focus. (It was not involved in the vulgarity of commercial radio.)

The Fairfax family considered the *Sydney Morning Herald* to be no ordinary newspaper but a force for public good, with a moral and educative purpose, and they felt a deep sense of responsibility to act as the paper's guardians and custodians. Henderson encouraged these perceptions. As he saw it, part of his role in managing the company was to manage the Fairfax family and he was fortunate that the family's control of the company was vested in relatively few hands and among individuals who were committed to the paper and willing to invest in it.[47]

In the forced choice that newsprint rationing demanded between sales or advertising revenue, the *Sydney Morning Herald*'s executives took the opposite approach to the HWT – they chose advertising – and it worked equally well for them. Fairfax & Sons deliberately sold fewer copies of the *Sydney Morning Herald* during the war, and even for several years after it ended, so the paper could publish as many classified and display advertisements as possible.[48] This policy of maintaining goodwill with Sydney's advertisers, along with Henderson's investment in new printing presses and raising of advertising rates, drove a boom in profits that could be put to use in the future.[49]

SYDNEY'S BUCCANEERS

A few blocks away from the *Sydney Morning Herald*, Frank Packer lorded it over his staff at the *Daily Telegraph* office in Castlereagh Street. Rivals griped that Packer had pushed his company into being through a series of 'unsavoury' business manoeuvres at the expense of Associated Newspapers and with some traitorous inside help from his father, Robert Clyde (RC) Packer, who was Associated Newspapers' managing editor in the early 1930s.[50] Father and son were both considered tough, energetic and ruthless men. Frank was said to have been aggressive as a child and to have been expelled from his North Shore school, aged nine, for possessing a revolver.[51] In his early twenties, he was an amateur heavyweight boxing champion.

Frank had also teamed up with Edward Granville (EG) Theodore, a former Labor treasurer who had become a Fijian gold mining magnate. Using 'no compete' money coerced out of Associated Newspapers, Packer and Theodore had started the *Women's Weekly* and used that as a springboard to advance on Associated Newspapers' neglected *Daily Telegraph*.

In 1936, Packer and Theodore had gone into a 70–30 partnership with Associated Newspapers as the minor partner. They brought new energy to revitalising the *Daily Telegraph*, and editor Brian Penton shaped it into a passionate, irreverent and non-conformist paper. Its sales doubled between 1936 and 1945.[52] Consolidated Press was still a small player – and saddled with some large debts after Packer launched the *Sunday Telegraph* in 1939 – but Packer was a shrewd, ambitious and unpredictable force.

The other brash newcomer to Sydney's daily paper industry was the cantankerous Ezra Norton, son of the notorious John Norton, a crusading journalist, wildly behaved MP and a violent drunk who was the proprietor of the muck-raking scandal sheet, *Truth*. Ezra had begun the tabloid *Daily Mirror* in 1941 and was publishing it out of a building behind Central railway station that one journalist described as a 'poorly lighted and ventilated sweatshop'.[53] The new paper published news from its independent cable news service and wartime scoops obtained by its European editor, Eric Baume, who was using his social contacts and operating out of the Savoy Hotel in London. The *Daily Mirror* quickly made inroads into the afternoon market by focusing on attracting lower-income readers, and by 1946 was selling more copies than its rival, the once-mighty *Sun*.[54]

Measured against the solid conservatism of other daily metropolitan papers, the *Daily Mirror* was the closest thing Australia had to a left-wing paper for a working-class readership. This was not saying much though, because the *Daily Mirror* was still firmly anti-socialist and its politics tended to be as erratic as Norton's. It advocated a vote for the conservatives as much as for Labor during federal elections in the 1940s and 1950s. The Communist Party's *Tribune* sniped that the *Daily Mirror* only wears a 'mask of sympathy for the labor movement'.[55]

THE FAILED EMPIRE

The final Sydney player, Associated Newspapers, had been wounded by Packer and Norton, as well as by its own directors' miscalculations. Back in the early 1920s, the enormous success of its popular, retail advertisement-filled flagship, the *Sun*, had led to an interstate excursion in Melbourne that had ended in expensive retreat. That was followed by a newspaper buying spree in Sydney that nearly brought the company down when the Depression hit.

In 1930–31, Associated Newspapers owned four daily newspapers in Sydney, but by World War II, the *Sun* was the only daily left in the stable (plus the company's 30 per cent interest in Consolidated Press' *Daily Telegraph*). And the *Sun* was no longer the prize it had once been. Its lucrative monopoly had been shattered by Ezra Norton's launch of the *Daily Mirror*. During the war, the two papers were locked in an intense and expensive competition, and after it ended Associated Newspapers' profits

> **TEXTBOX 1.4** Columns
>
> In February 1946, the first regular front-page column in an Australian newspaper made its debut. 'Town Talk' was published in the *Daily Telegraph* and written by David McNicoll. Frank Packer had poached him from the *Sydney Morning Herald* in 1944 after promising to help McNicoll get out of the army.
>
> The son of a brigadier, McNicoll was a dapper, well-connected, upper-class conservative. Known for his charm and fondness for the good life, including nightclubs and the racetrack, McNicoll soon became a favourite of Frank Packer's.
>
> Packer sent him to the United States to meet the big American columnists, and when McNicoll returned to Sydney, he modelled 'Town Talk' on columns in Washington and New York papers, including Walter Winchell's show-business column, 'On Broadway', Drew Pearson's 'Washington Merry-Go-Round' on political insiders, and Earl Wilson's chronicle of New York's night life, 'It Happened Last Night'.
>
> The popularity of McNicoll's chatty, light-hearted front-page column led other papers to quickly follow suit. A column called 'Contact' appeared in the *Sun* only weeks later, in March 1946, written by Jim Macdougall.[56] In January 1947, the *Sydney Morning Herald* introduced a column of short paragraphs on its front page called 'Column 8', written by Syd Deamer. Signed 'Granny' in an elderly hand, 'Column 8' signalled a new level of self-deprecating playfulness for the usually sombre paper.[57] Other columns to spring forth included, in 1949, the *Courier-Mail*'s 'Day by Day' column by Arthur Richards, taken over by Keith Dunstan in 1954.[58]
>
> Columns were given a new prominence in the 1940s but they were not entirely new to Australian journalism. 'Town Talk' revived the name of a regular column published in the *Daily Telegraph* in 1925–26 and the *Sun News-Pictorial*'s famous column, 'A Place in the Sun', dated back to its first edition in 1922. Wit, humour and lightness had long been part of the mix that newspapers offered to readers. What was new was the star billing on the front page and the emphasis on named columnists who became well known in their cities. Earlier columns had been anonymous.

rose by only a measly £182 between 1945 and 1946.⁵⁹ It ended the 1940s reporting high costs, very low profits and facing an uncertain future.

A COUNTRY PAPER IN THE CAPITAL

No paper was doing it tougher during the war years than the *Canberra Times*. It had been founded in 1926 in the nation's new capital and was a real family venture. Arthur Thomas (AT) Shakespeare, eldest son of the paper's founder, was its managing editor. His brothers, uncle, cousin and future wife had all helped keep the paper going. It had struggled from the beginning because projections of Canberra's population growth did not eventuate, and then, during the Depression, Canberra's development was put on hold. The paper was barely able to pay wages during that period.

In 1936, ten years after it began, the newspaper finally managed to balance its revenue and expenditure for the first time, mainly due to advertising revenue from a new cinema.⁶⁰ By 1941, Canberra's population had risen to 13 000 and the paper's prospects were improving.⁶¹ It was set back again when many of its staff were taken for the war effort. The Shakespeare family again filled the gaps, with family members working multiple jobs and re-using envelopes to write advertisements on. One of the staff who contributed enormously was Heather Cameron. She had begun as a secretary to the paper's founder, Thomas Mitchell (TM) Shakespeare, but also did the banking, wages and office work. Cameron became the company's secretary in 1938, and started attended board meetings, a rare event for a woman in the world of 1940s newspapers.

TEXTBOX 1.5 Women in the newspaper office

Women who were employed as journalists at metropolitan newspapers before the war were in the minority. They were usually on the lowest pay, and were mostly confined to writing for the 'women's pages' about fashion, shopping, homecraft, society gossip and social events.⁶²

The war changed things dramatically. Newspapers lost about half of their male staff due to enlistment and 'manpower' requirements, and newsprint rationing meant the 'women's pages' were reduced or temporarily discontinued.[63]

This meant some women were given the chance to perform general reporting, including political, industrial and war news. This included 21 female journalists who worked as war reporters. They were still expected to report on the war from a 'woman's perspective' and keep well away from operational areas but many challenged those restraints.[64]

Some women were also promoted to positions they would have been overlooked for in peacetime. For example, Elizabeth Riddell was sent to run the New York bureau of the *Daily Mirror* when labour restrictions meant Ezra Norton could not hire a man to do the job.[65]

The chauvinistic *Smith's Weekly* despaired at all of this war-induced 'growing feminisation of employment', saying it was creating 'a newspaper Press of tea-table and cocktail gossip – the gush Press, the rag Press, the sissy Press' and this was 'sap[ping] virility'.[66] In fact, women had played an important role in newspapers since their earliest days, not only as writers and journalists, but also as owners, editors and managers.

An early example was Ann Howe, the daughter-in-law of Australia's first newspaper publisher, George Howe. She ran the *Sydney Gazette* between 1829 and 1836 after the deaths of her father-in-law and husband.[67] Another example was the *Perth Gazette*, which was edited by the owner's widow between 1846 and 1847, and again from 1871 to 1874.[68]

At country newspapers, women more regularly took on leadership roles.[69] By the 1880s, that was rare at the capital city dailies. Once they became large public and private companies, women were not considered suitable for senior roles involving editing, managing staff, or acting as directors on company boards. A century later, even in the 1980s and 1990s, women in senior roles were still rare. Two women were forging a pathway toward it in the 1940s though.

One was Heather Cameron, company secretary for the *Canberra Times* at a time when it was more a family-run country paper than a big-city daily. In the 1950s, Cameron would become a director of the paper's parent company, but resigned when she became engaged to AT Shakespeare in 1962, as married women were expected to give up work.

The other trailblazer was Kathleen Syme at *The Age* in Melbourne. David Syme's granddaughter was a journalist, an advocate of women's liberation, a formidable presence in *The Age* office, and rode racehorses under a man's name. When the new Parliament House opened in Canberra in 1927, Syme was not part of the official press contingent but she motored from Melbourne to Canberra and camped out in a paddock so she could report on it.[70]

Women were told they could not become subeditors because they lacked the 'dirty mind' required to spot double entendres lurking in copy, but during World War II, Syme performed an editing role at *The Age*.[71] In 1943, she retired from that position to take up her father's place as a trustee of the David Syme Trust. She became a director of David Syme and Co when it became a public company in 1948, and stayed on the board until her 75th birthday in 1971.[72] Syme's journalism skills and her input were respected on the board. Her family connection had provided an extraordinary opportunity that was not available to other women at the time, or even decades later.

Aside from journalism, women performed other vital roles in newspaper offices. One of the largest areas of employment for girls and young women was as binders who finished off newspapers by collating, folding, stacking and wrapping them. Secretaries acted as crucial repositories of corporate knowledge and gatekeeping, and some worked for the industry's leaders for decades. Women were also employed as telephonists and cashiers. They took the details of retail and classified advertisements and collected the revenue. Without that essential work, newspapers would not have been able to publish at all.

GENTEEL DECAY

The four remaining newspapers were run by family companies or trusts, and the war years were exposing their struggle to adapt and modernise. Two of these companies were in Melbourne, where the bright, easy-to-read *Sun News-Pictorial* had taken away readers from its morning competitors when

FIGURE 1.3 Although it had a half-finished clock tower with no clock, the *Argus* building on the corner of Elizabeth and La Trobe streets, Melbourne, was one of the grand newspaper buildings built in the 1920s, shown here circa 1950

SOURCE State Library of Victoria.

it arrived, back in the 1920s, and neither the *Argus* nor *The Age* had made much of an attempt to win them back since.

Once a radical friend of oppressed gold miners in the early 1850s, the *Argus* had morphed into a staunch defender of capital, the voice of the city's business class, and a profitable outlet of commercial intelligence – a sort of '*The Times* of the Southern Hemisphere'.[73] In the late 1800s and early 1900s, the *Argus* had a reputation for being the best newspaper in Australia due to its extensive news coverage. It had built an expensive six-storey building on the corner of Elizabeth and La Trobe streets (Figure 1.3). But by the end of the 1920s, the paper's appeal had narrowed – journalist and editor Cecil Edwards described the *Argus* as being 'produced by the Melbourne Club for the Melbourne Club'.[74] After it moved to La Trobe Street, it lost classified advertising to *The Age*, which was located in the busier part of the city and easier to walk to in the days when advertisements were lodged in person. The *Argus*'s fortunes had then declined dramatically after the Depression, and in a rather desperate move, had tried to revive itself by starting an afternoon paper, the *Evening Star*, to take on the *Herald*.

By the time the failed *Star* was closed in 1936, it had dragged the *Argus* to the edge of financial ruin. Eight years later, the *Argus*'s parent company was still making only small profits, just £3000 in 1944.[75] Its major shareholder was a trust, the Edward Wilson Trustees, representing the descendants of its old proprietors. There was no dynamic leadership able to change course or willing to inject the necessary funds for new equipment and building modifications so it could compete with rivals. Without the capacity to sell off a portion of its newsprint ration throughout the rationing period, the *Argus* would have gone bankrupt.

Melbourne's other morning daily, *The Age*, was published a few blocks away, in a cramped old building in Collins Street. Under owner David Syme, *The Age* had been a highly influential paper in Victoria from the 1860s to the 1890s that had pushed social liberal causes, including workers' rights, the eight-hour week, and especially protectionism. Historian Frank Bongiorno pointed out that, even under Syme, *The Age* was wary of class distinctions, opposed to working-class candidates, and used loyalty to the King as a way to mobilise anti-Labor sentiment.[76] But by comparison with its competitors, *The Age* was considered a progressive force in Victoria. Uniquely, it combined a reputation as the 'worker's paper' with a large, lucrative share of classified advertising.

After Syme's death in 1908, *The Age* was carried on by his sons as trustees under the terms of his complicated will but it stagnated in both editorial outlook and physical design. From 1938, even the troubled *Argus* had been outselling it, and by 1940, *The Age*'s circulation was less than it had been in 1900.[77] David Syme's only surviving son, Oswald, was 64 years old when he reluctantly became chairman in 1942 (Chapter 18).

Where other papers – including its competitor, the *Sun News-Pictorial* – saw a wartime sales boom, *The Age*'s circulation lifted by only 16 000 copies.[78] But *The Age* still had the very important financial advantage of its classified advertising. It was printing over 25 000 individual classified ads every week in 1947, more than twice the number published by the three other Melbourne daily papers combined.[79] When Roy Morgan conducted survey research in the mid-1940s, *Age* readers nominated the paper's classified ads as its major virtue, not its news coverage! But *Age* readers were also unusually loyal to their paper and its ethos. It retained a reputation for upholding liberal and democratic values, and an aura of being the 'worker's paper' by comparison with Melbourne's other conservative dailies.[80] During the 12 federal elections between 1922 and 1949, *The Age* advocated a vote for the Labor Party only three times, but that was three more times than the *Herald*, *Sun News-Pictorial* or the *Argus*.

In Brisbane, unlike *The Age*, the *Telegraph* was enjoying a wartime boom. Its circulation doubled between 1939 and 1945.[81] The *Telegraph* was published in a stunning, but dated, Italianate building in Queen Street that had been erected in 1891. This reflected the company's tendency to hold on to things for a long time. The *Telegraph* had the same editor for 31 years (1885 to 1916), and during World War II its directors were descendants of the company's original 1870s owners, the Brentnall, Cowlishaw and Edwards families. Some of the descendants had sat on the board for over two decades.[82]

Hobart's *Mercury* had an even longer pedigree. It had been co-founded in 1854 by a former convict, John Davies. Ninety years later, the Davies family was still in charge. A grandson of the founder was managing director when the war began. Another grandson was the managing editor, and other family members were on the board and in management roles. Although the *Mercury*'s four-storey building in Macquarie Street had been given an impressive Art Deco façade in the 1930s, inside, the paper was still being printed on an old Goss rotary press that limited its capacity.[83]

FACING THE FUTURE

The newspaper groups were facing the future from very different starting points in the 1940s. Already a multimedia giant, the HWT was starting from a position of strength. Fairfax & Sons was overwhelmingly focused on the *Sydney Morning Herald* but was also increasingly prosperous and primed for expansion. A slimmed-down Associated Newspapers was no longer a burgeoning empire and finding it difficult to adapt to competition. Several old, family companies were living off a genteel past and in need of substantial capital to modernise. In Sydney, Frank Packer and Ezra Norton were unknown quantities – small, feisty and independent players in an industry that had already seen consolidation focused on building larger publishing companies.

Whatever their points of difference, the newspaper companies faced some common challenges during wartime, including staffing, censorship and newsprint supply. A different sort of challenge arose in October 1941 when the Curtin Labor government took office, but Australia's normally anti-Labor newspapers gave it a surprisingly warm welcome.

CHAPTER 2
CURTIN'S CIRCUS

Robert Menzies, prime minister when the war began, faced a party revolt in August 1941 and resigned. Menzies had fallen out of favour with his colleagues but also with newspaper owners, especially Warwick Fairfax, but also Keith Murdoch and Frank Packer. Country Party leader Arthur Fadden served only 40 days as prime minister after two independents withdrew their support. Labor Party leader John Curtin then formed a minority government with a Labor Cabinet in October 1941.

Although the vast majority of daily newspapers were traditionally anti-Labor, there was a sense of relief in newspaper offices that a Curtin Labor government looked to be more stable, unified and focused on the war than Menzies' government had been. There was also a high degree of personal respect for Curtin. The conservative *Sydney Morning Herald* welcomed him to office by saying that Curtin lacked an independent majority but he 'possesses much else – the present trust of his whole party, the liking and respect of the Opposition, and the hopeful goodwill of the nation'.[1]

Even the *Argus*, normally hostile to the Labor Party, supported the Curtin government 'loyally, though not uncritically'.[2] Its managing director, Errol Knox, even worked as director-general of public relations and undertook several overseas missions for Curtin. The *Daily Telegraph* explained the surprising degree of press support for Curtin by concluding that 'Menzies was a failure; Curtin was a success', and where the 'newspapers prodded, pushed, hammered Menzies …', they admired Curtin's 'dignity', his non-partisan approach, his work ethic and determination to win the war.[3]

The Murdoch newspapers were the exception. Three days before the government was sworn in, the Melbourne *Herald* warned it not to target business in its Budget.[4] But the Curtin government ignored the special pleading and increased company taxation dramatically to pay for the war effort. Curtin argued companies making large wartime profits should 'give back to the nation' and that the Budget put 'the largest burden on the broadest shoulders'.[5] Higher taxation affected all the newspaper companies, but as the largest war profiteer, the HWT especially felt the impact. In 1938, the HWT had paid only £43 000 in tax (15 per cent of its profits). By 1944, it was paying a record tax bill of £197 745 (51 per cent of profits).[6]

Within a month of taking office, the Curtin government had already inflicted a tax hike on business. Curtin was once an avowed international socialist and, officially, the Labor Party still had socialisation of industry as its stated aim – an objective that Curtin had supported. Despite this, he managed to build good relations with the majority of the commercial press, and his background as a journalist was key to this.

CURTIN THE JOURNALIST

When Boris Johnson became British prime minister in 2019, the *Guardian* called him 'the first British prime minister with genuine journalistic experience, having been a reporter, columnist and editor'.[7] Such was the centrality of newspapers to Australian politics and society when Curtin took office 79 years earlier, he was not even Australia's first prime minister with a background in 'genuine' journalism. That had been Alfred Deakin in 1903, followed by Andrew Fisher, Billy Hughes and James Scullin, and two other prime ministers before Curtin had worked in non-journalism roles at newspapers (Chris Watson and Joe Lyons).

Curtin had been a 'printer's devil' (someone who runs errands for printers), a copy boy at *The Age* in Melbourne, and a journalist and labour newspaper editor before entering parliament. He edited the weekly *Westralian Worker*, the official organ of the Western Australian Labor Party, in Perth from 1917 until 1928.[8] The paper was part of the labour movement's long-held ambition to create a daily labour paper in each capital city as an antidote to the capitalist press.[9] The *Westralian Worker* never managed to become a daily, although Curtin had written stirring editorials in the 1920s advocating for that.[10] Even as a weekly, it struggled financially and had to close in 1951. It had lasted nearly 50 years though, and when

Curtin was editing it, had commanded attention among Labor and union leaders.

Not surprisingly given his background, Curtin believed the commercial press was biased against Labor, a sentiment that many Labor MPs shared. He said in parliament in 1941 that 'there, is hardly a great newspaper in Australia which is not grossly and unfairly partisan in its political outlook'.[11] Privately, he was scathing about some outlets, and not just in terms of bias. He once described the *Daily Telegraph* as a 'nitwit' paper.[12] But where Curtin's fellow Labor MP, Arthur Calwell, believed that many journalists were the unscrupulous and unthinking tools of their capitalist bosses, and Menzies privately admitted he 'loathed' the press and had a reputation for being rude to journalists, Curtin had warm feelings for journalists.[13] He identified with them and respected their work. Curtin was a former state president of the Australian Journalists Association (AJA) and famously wore his AJA badge on his watch chain even when prime minister.

Curtin was unusually accessible to journalists and cultivated excellent relations with them, aided by Don Rodgers, a former *Labor Daily* journalist who Curtin appointed as the first full-time prime ministerial press secretary. Initially, Curtin held two press conferences a day, during which he confided off-the-record information, including about his fears and worries, to a select group of senior press gallery journalists (Figure 2.1). Curtin gave them sensitive and classified information about the progress of the war which they could confide to their editors and superiors but not publish, an arrangement they respected. The *Herald*'s Canberra bureau chief, Joe Alexander, said the journalists were like 'a travelling circus which went everywhere with Curtin' and 'shared his confidence to an extent previously unknown in the history of the press in Australia'.[14]

There was a great deal of affection for Curtin among the circus journalists, who saw him carrying out the heavy responsibilities of wartime leadership with sensitivity and gravity and at the expense of his health. Despite the *Sydney Morning Herald*'s steadfast conservatism, one of its key journalists, Ross Gollan, was said to 'idolise' Curtin.[15] The head of the *Daily Mirror*'s Canberra bureau, Allan Fraser, quit journalism to follow in Curtin's footsteps and became a Labor MP himself.[16] Edgar Holt, chief

FIGURE 2.1 Prime Minister John Curtin meets the Canberra Press Gallery (known as 'the Circus'), 1945. Curtin is seated. Standing, from left to right, are Don Whitington (*Daily Telegraph*), Ross Gollan (*Sydney Morning Herald*), John Corbett (*Argus*), Frederick Smith (Australian United Press), Richard Hughes and Norman Kearsley (Brisbane *Telegraph*), TL Thomas (Australian United Press), Ted Waterman and Joe Alexander (Melbourne *Herald*), Jack Commins (Australian Broadcasting Commission) and smiling on the far right is Don Rodgers (Curtin's press secretary).
SOURCE John Curtin Prime Ministerial Library.

editorial writer for the *Daily Telegraph*, recalled Curtin inviting him to sit in his car where they discussed poetry for an hour, with not a word of politics. Holt said he voted Labor that year even though his own politics were conservative and he later joined the Liberal Party.[17] Journalists' attitudes towards Curtin fed into their reporting of him and his government, which helped win Curtin public popularity and the respect of newspaper owners – with one notable exception.

MURDOCH ON THE OUTER

Keith Murdoch had been politically well connected and influential for decades, including being close to Billy Hughes (prime minister, 1915–23), and to the powerful Baillieu family and their political allies. He had also developed a reputation as a kingmaker for helping to entice Joe Lyons from the Scullin Labor government in 1931, precipitating its downfall. Murdoch threw the full weight of his media outlets behind Lyons, whose new United Australia Party (UAP) won the 1931 election. Lyons then served as prime minister until his death in 1939.

With a Labor government in office, Murdoch was a much less powerful figure. Curtin, Calwell and other Labor MPs despised Murdoch for his role in the downfall of the Scullin government. When the UAP government had been languishing under Menzies' leadership in 1939, Murdoch had loudly and publicly called for a British-style all-party ministry in which Labor would join with the conservatives in a national government. Curtin had resisted because the conservatives were unstable and he hoped Labor might be able to rule in its own right. Once Labor did, from October 1941, Murdoch continued to press for a national government. Right up to the 1943 election, Murdoch vehemently and repetitively called on Curtin to include conservatives in his Cabinet. For four years, Curtin ignored his demands.

Murdoch's counterpart at Fairfax, the wily Rupert Henderson, later said that Murdoch had an extraordinary ability to be unable to 'face facts and reality. The Curtin Government would not have a bar of Murdoch, and Murdoch never realised it.'[18] The less influence Murdoch had, the more loudly he expressed his frustrations in his newspapers. Murdoch not only wanted an all-party national government, he also called for an amalgamation of the Australian Imperial Force (AIF) and militia, and renewed his demand for conscription for overseas military service. Murdoch was just as keen to have men sent to war against their will as he had been during World War I, when he was a key propagandist for the conscription cause.

One of Murdoch's more critical biographers, Michael Ward, said Murdoch's support for conscription and all-party government were based on 'commercial motives'. Ward argued that Murdoch's call for all-party government was, at first, based on trying to 'delay or frustrate the formation of a Labor government', but once Labor was in office, it was motivated by the prospect of having at least some friendly conservative politicians involved in government decision making so that Murdoch could exercise some influence on newsprint rationing, 'manpower' labour restrictions and price rises for newspapers.[19]

With no conservative friends in Cabinet, and a very poor relationship with Curtin and most of Labor's ministers, Murdoch was firmly on the outer. As backroom channels of influence were closed off, Murdoch used the multiple papers under his control to lobby for his pet policies. For the first time in more than a decade, he was back writing long articles for the HWT's chain of newspapers and signing them with his own name. The Labor government generally ignored them, and Curtin wondered aloud why a man with Murdoch's executive responsibilities did not have 'more things to do' than to write two or three columns a week.[20]

In a signed column in 1943, Murdoch went too far and Curtin threatened to sue for libel.[21] Murdoch had implied that Curtin was a coward in shirking service in World War I and had only opposed conscription because he did not want to fight.[22] This was quite an insult coming from Murdoch, who never undertook military service himself but used his typewriter to demand it of others. The next day, Murdoch published a retraction saying he accepted the comments he reported were 'incorrect' but he still slipped in a sledge that Curtin had been 'fanatical' in his anti-conscription stance during World War I.[23] This too was quite a statement given Murdoch's zealous devotion to the conscription cause during both world wars.

Murdoch's columns continued to lambast the Curtin government, but in prose that suggested his best writing days were behind him. Murdoch wrote about how 'minds steeped in isolation policies and appeasement move under pressure to defence-mindedness but are late in reaching the full tide of martial-mindedness'.[24] He sometimes took a spiritual, or oddly metaphorical, turn. Reflecting on the possibility of Japanese invasion, Murdoch wrote:

> To me, the most hateful aspect of defeat is that the children of Australia would be corrupted in mind and soul by the compulsory schools of the new rulers. What happens to their elders from the swords and the lusts of bestial conquerors is of less account than the mental befoulment of our next generation and its issue. The beautiful flowers that grow now in fresh fertile and free soil would wither ...[25]

Murdoch's eccentric and pessimistic articles were so out of touch with wartime patriotism and general public support for the government – but also so politically ineffective – that his staff were losing respect for him. Joe Alexander was privately dismayed because Murdoch's articles were 'extremely hostile to Curtin ... [which] made a painful impression on me, because the country was at war and in grave danger, and certainly there was no one else who could conceivably [take] Curtin's place'.[26] Alexander observed that the *Herald* 'had made enemies everywhere' for no gain, but Murdoch seemed oblivious and unable to temper his behaviour.[27]

Cecil Edwards, who was subediting the *Herald* and had to find space for Murdoch's lengthy columns, wrote in his diary in 1942 that Murdoch had 'risen to his most Messianic mood' and was writing 'long exhortatory articles' with 'peculiar phrases' describing the military as 'dear brown robins' (army), 'brave blue fliers' (air force) and 'spray boys' of the seas (navy).[28] Murdoch (whose father and both grandfathers had been Presbyterian ministers) called for the nation to unite and say a prayer he

FIGURE 2.2 Sir Keith Murdoch, with his wife Elisabeth and son Rupert, pictured around 1950
SOURCE Author.

had composed. He talked about 'the beauty of the universe' and the 'glory of death for victory'.²⁹

Murdoch's biographer, Tom Roberts, said a diplomat, Frederic Eggleston, was reading through back copies of the *Herald* in Chungking and concluded that a 'panic-stricken' Murdoch had 'gone nuts'.³⁰ A briefing note prepared for General MacArthur described Murdoch as 'a little fanatical' and MacArthur was so incensed by some of Murdoch's censor-challenging articles that he described the HWT chairman as 'an Australian Quisling' (a traitor who collaborates with the enemy).³¹

Murdoch was proving such an irritant to authorities and the government that the attorney-general, Dr Herbert Vere (HV) Evatt, asked a senior *Herald* journalist to find out whether Murdoch could be tempted to leave newspapers and take up a public post such as high commissioner.³² Murdoch was not interested. His only foray into public administration as the Menzies government's director-general of information in 1940 had been the greatest mistake of his career. Murdoch had tried to introduce tighter censorship regulations that led his fellow proprietors to publicly attack him as out of touch and 'dictatorial'. Murdoch was forced into a humiliating backdown, then resigned after only five months in the job.³³

Murdoch's prestige and self-esteem had been severely damaged and, probably overcompensating, he had refashioned himself as an anti-censorship warrior. He was keeping the censors busy as a result. About a dozen of the *Herald* articles he wrote in 1942 and 1943 'were amended by censorship or resulted in reprimand, and four were prohibited before publication'.³⁴ Murdoch felt he was championing freedom of expression. The censors – and sometimes MacArthur – felt he was endangering national security.

His fellow newspaper owners were again wary. The *Argus* described an article that Murdoch had written as 'unseemly' and contravening the 'great responsibility' that newspapers had during wartime.³⁵ Rupert Henderson complained to the chief censor that one of Murdoch's columns had revealed details of fighting in the Coral Sea that other papers had been forbidden from publishing.³⁶ Henderson's complaint was probably directed more at inconsistent application of the censorship rules than at Murdoch personally, but it was significant that when newspapers did make a dramatic stand against censorship in 1944, the Sydney papers led the battle and Murdoch the censorship warrior was conspicuously absent (Chapter 3).

Curtin believed that what Murdoch really wanted was to exercise control over Australian public opinion. In private, Curtin called him a 'bastard'.[37] At one point, Curtin showed other journalists some of Murdoch's censored articles, including one where Murdoch had defended the Japanese after they had attacked and sunk an Australian hospital ship, the *Centaur,* in May 1943, killing 268 on board.[38] One of the journalists present, Fred Smith of Australian United Press (AUP), wrote in his notes that Murdoch's words were 'remarkable' and had implied 'the Japanese did not intend to sink the *Centaur,* because they were kind, considerate foes who had treated their prisoners, the Red Cross and everybody else very well indeed'.[39]

There was speculation about whether the animosity between Curtin and Murdoch stemmed from their having crossed paths at *The Age* many years before. But Curtin's brief stint as an *Age* copy boy ended several years before Murdoch began working there in 1903.[40] Curtin's hostility instead reflected Murdoch's reputation within Labor circles as an anti-Labor propagandist for big business, as well as his role in the downfall of the Scullin Labor government. There was also a strangely specific cause of offence. Curtin's press secretary, Don Rodgers, later revealed that Curtin never forgave a cartoon the *Herald* had published during the Scullin government that depicted Scullin as Bill Sikes robbing the Commonwealth Bank.[41] (Sikes was a fictional character in Charles Dickens' *Oliver Twist*, a malicious criminal, vicious robber and murderer.) Ten years after that cartoon was published, Rodgers witnessed Curtin 'cutting dead in public an executive, a very high executive, of the Melbourne *Herald*'. When Rodgers asked Curtin whether he failed to recognise the man, Curtin replied, 'I remember, but I haven't forgotten that cartoon'.[42]

It was again on a colleague's behalf that Curtin was infuriated in October 1942 after Murdoch wrote a column attacking the army minister. During one of Curtin's off-the-record briefings to 'the circus', he launched into a character assessment of Murdoch that the journalists considered an 'amazing outburst'. Curtin said Murdoch's article was 'silly and unfair'.

Then he said, 'I do not like Sir Keith Murdoch. I do not trust him. He is utterly unscrupulous in the way he conducts his newspapers.' Curtin even brought up the painful cartoon, saying it depicted 'Mr Scullin ... getting away with the nation's wealth and assets [and] was infamous and utterly unscrupulous'. Curtin said Murdoch 'is full of hot air and witlessness ... [and] should leave [reporting and writing] to the men under him who are more competent'.[43]

Off the record, Curtin also told journalists that he felt Murdoch's behaviour stemmed from frustration, that Murdoch was upset he could not find a leader to attach himself to 'even from our camp. He had hopes of me for a while, and then Evatt – but Evatt had two trips to the United States and was not accessible.'[44] Leaders within the newspaper industry had their own views on Murdoch's behaviour. Rupert Henderson was becoming the more widely regarded newspaper industry leader and when he clashed with his company's proprietor, Warwick Fairfax, in early 1945, Henderson pointed to Murdoch as a salutary warning to his boss.

The cause of the disagreement was that Fairfax was undergoing a period of Christian fervour and had published a signed article in the *Sydney Morning Herald* conveying his religious views. Henderson wrote to Fairfax that this attempt to lead 'a spiritual revival' had damaged the paper's 'good will' and 'was a departure from the office and family tradition of anonymity'. Henderson said, 'I am not questioning your right to ... change the [*Sydney Morning*] *Herald* from a great public organ to a personal journal, as Northcliffe did with *The Times* and Murdoch has done with the Melbourne *Herald*. But that is not my conception of the [*Sydney Morning*] *Herald*.'[45] Henderson tendered his resignation, but the crisis was averted after Fairfax backed down and agreed to keep his religious enthusiasm off the *Sydney Morning Herald*'s pages.

No-one was standing up to Murdoch in this way at the HWT, nor advising him to keep his personal passions out of the paper for the sake of its reputation and his own.

CENSORSHIP AND OTHER SKIRMISHES

Overall, there was a high level of cooperation and dependence between government and the press during World War II on issues of censorship. Unless a newspaper was specifically directed to submit copy for clearance by the censor, it operated under a voluntary system of self-regulation. Most newspapers, most of the time, voluntarily suppressed information due to military security or to minimise bad news in order to keep up public morale. For example, photographs of the wrecked American fleet at Pearl Harbor on 8 December 1941 were not published in Australia until 6 February 1942, and photographs of the Japanese bombing of Darwin on 19 February 1942 were not published until two months later.[46]

Censorship became more of an issue once fears of an imminent wartime attack on Australia had subsided and the newspapers began to be more critical of the government on familiar partisan and domestic grounds. Changes in policy and personnel also increased the likelihood of tension over censorship.

Edmund Garnet (EG) Bonney had been appointed by the Menzies government in April 1941 as chief publicity censor. Bonney filled that role after the resignation, due to illness, of Percy Jenkin. Like many appointed to censorship roles during the Menzies era, Bonney had worked closely with Murdoch. In Bonney's case, he had worked under Murdoch for 12 years as chief of staff for the *Herald* (1926–32), then editor-in-chief of the *News* (1932–38).[47] But Bonney was no Murdoch lackey. He believed the stress that Jenkin had suffered from Murdoch's interference, and the media harassment he had faced, had caused his premature death.[48]

A tribute posted by an anonymous 'friend' in *Newspaper News* described Jenkin as 'temperamentally out of tune' with the job of censor. It said he lacked the harsh quality required.[49] Bonney was not lacking that quality. A toughened former drover, sailor and experienced journalist, to his admirers Bonney was a brave man of integrity and 'a superb administrator'.[50] He neither feared nor revered newspaper proprietors and he had a reputation among his staff of immense loyalty and 'a high sense of public duty'.[51] By his critics in the newspaper industry, including those he took on over censorship, Bonney was considered a ruthless, ambitious and devious bureaucrat.

When Labor had been in opposition, Evatt had complained in 1941 that the Menzies government was carrying out 'political censorship', and provided examples from left-wing outlets.[52] Bonney, as chief censor, had argued those cases of censorship were necessary for national security. He would say the same when he was working under the Curtin government and the proprietors of the *Daily Telegraph* and the *Sydney Morning Herald* began to join Keith Murdoch in complaining about censorship.

After the outbreak of war with Japan in December 1941, the likelihood of tension over censorship had increased because it was also being applied as a way to keep up public morale at home and to protect Australia's reputation overseas in order to maintain good relations with its allies, especially the United States once it entered the war. This meant that even stories about domestic industrial disputes or complaints about government decisions were being censored. For Bonney, reports of industrial strife or harsh criticism of military leadership were harmful to national security because they were 'bad for morale' and Australia's reputation.[53] The newspapers viewed such information as posing no threat to national security and it was important in making their evolving case against the Labor government and its failure to quash industrial activism and its 'red tape', 'socialism-by-stealth' approach to governing. The newspapers were making these charges more frequently from mid-1942 – Curtin's press honeymoon was over – and they believed censorship was occurring for political reasons, to suppress criticism and protect government ministers from embarrassment.

Curtin managed these tensions by sharing confidential information with 'the circus' that they would pass on to their editors to keep them informed and help secure their adherence to censorship regulations. When disputes became more robust, Curtin assumed personal responsibility for censorship on 1 March 1942.[54] In April, he announced the formation of a Press Censorship Advisory Committee so that newspapers could present their concerns. He appointed as chair the former Labor prime minister James Scullin (subject of that never forgotten cartoon). The press members of the committee were Warwick Fairfax, Keith Murdoch, HAM Campbell (*Age* editor), and GE Sparrow (general president of the AJA).[55]

The first meeting in June 1942 discussed a seven-page analysis written by Warwick Fairfax about five cases of censorship he argued were unsatisfactory. In August, Fairfax resigned from the committee in protest at further cases of what he called 'rank political censorship'.[56]

Frustrated by increased press sniping, Curtin lashed out in August 1942 and said the press was criticising the government because they were 'very afraid' that Labor would continue in office after the war and 'the capitalist wolf will not be able to feed on the lambs in the factories and workshops as it has done in the last 50 years in this country'.[57] That statement would normally have provoked a fierce backlash from the daily press but such was the level of support for Curtin that the *Daily Telegraph* defended him, saying he was usually 'temperate and so dignified in his polemical style'. They put the outburst down to tiredness and hoped Curtin would soon 'recover his urbanity. For he is too big a man to remain petulant'.[58]

Fairfax re-joined the committee in September after personal discussions with Curtin, but he continued to argue that censorship policy was being abused.[59] In November, Scullin resigned from chairing the committee due to ill-health. Bonney believed that, yet again, self-centred proprietors had driven a man to stress-induced illness. Curtin proposed that Bonney now chair the meetings but the press members wanted a minister in charge. Relations between Bonney and the press members broke down. Bonney described Murdoch as a 'dangerous propagandist' and the Australian Newspaper Proprietors' Association (ANPA) sent a telegram to Curtin saying they had no confidence in Bonney.[60]

In late 1942 and early 1943, newspaper criticism of the Curtin government hardened, illustrated by the treatment of John Dedman. As minister for war organisation of industry, Dedman was responsible for reorganising non-essential industries to free up workers and resources for military needs and essential services, a task that made him an unpopular figure in business circles, including at newspapers.

In July 1942, Dedman had introduced a wartime limit on clothing that restricted the sizes and styles of women's dresses to avoid wasting material. When the rule was introduced, the Sydney *Sun* reported that: 'The new skirt lengths are ideal'.[61] But the newspaper industry was now finding Dedman difficult to deal with. He had presented the newspapers with proposals to cut their staff, newsprint and transport. At a meeting between Dedman, Eddie Ward (the federal minister for labour) and ANPA members, Rupert Henderson gave a long speech pledging the newspapers' willingness to bear 'sacrifices' for the war effort, before arguing that newspapers were an essential service that could not be rationalised much further. Dedman said he was considering forcing newspapers to merge in order to save labour and costs. He argued that multiple newspapers were unnecessary because the news was 'all the same' anyway. Henderson expressed his absolute 'shock'. Ward responded: 'I am not satisfied the industry has given the greatest contribution it can'.[62]

By late 1942, there was increased talk that Dedman would demand metropolitan newspapers reduce their resources and staff and the *Sun* began to ridicule him over the earlier 'ideal' clothing regulation. On 3 January 1943, the paper published two photographs. The first showed a tall woman wearing a too-short dress; the other was of a short woman wearing a dress that was too long, down to her ankles. The paper claimed Dedman's rules forced women to wear unsuitable dresses and even 'SHOW KNEES' because the length of their dresses had to correspond to their bust measurements. Dedman responded this was false and 'ridiculous'.[63]

Both women in the photographs later made affidavits. They said the *Sun* photographer gave them the dresses and then stood six steps below the tall woman to make the dress look even shorter, and climbed a stepladder to photograph the shorter woman to make her dress look even longer. Dedman's department lodged an official protest, saying the women were never obliged by the regulation to wear those dresses, and it asked the *Sun* to publish its letter to the editor. The paper refused. The letter had said: 'I charge you with deliberately faking these photographs in order to mislead the public ... [They were] barefaced deception.'[64]

THE 1943 ELECTION

By mid-1943, the tide of the war had begun to turn in the Allies' favour. There was still a high degree of support for Curtin personally but press complaints were mounting that the government was using the war as a pretext to introduce socialism and was too soft on striking unionists and too bureaucratic. During the 1943 election, the *Sydney Morning Herald* and *The Age* advocated a vote for 'new blood' regardless of party. The other daily metropolitan newspapers endorsed the conservatives, some with notable reluctance because there was obvious disarray in conservative ranks, but the Murdoch-controlled papers with enthusiasm.

The UAP had been formed with the enthusiastic support of the commercial daily press in 1931 as a compromise party that had melded disparate factions and groups. It was beset by tension and policy stagnation and had been in electoral decline since 1937. Menzies' tenure as UAP leader had been marked by discord, including the Country Party's departure from the Coalition, and Menzies' own resignation in 1941. He had said, 'I have been done … I'll lie down and bleed awhile', but by March 1943, Menzies was back making a statement of fresh leadership intentions. He led 17 colleagues to form a 'National Service Group'. They did not formally resign from the UAP but refused to attend party and joint Opposition meetings.[65]

At the federal election in September 1943, Country Party leader Arthur Fadden and UAP leader Billy Hughes led the joint campaign for the Coalition parties but Menzies was seen by many – including himself – as an alternative leader. Tensions between Hughes and Menzies, and also between Fadden and Menzies, threatened to boil over during the campaign. The Opposition parties were also in dispute over policies, including on income tax.

The dissent in the Opposition's ranks did not affect Murdoch's loathing for the Curtin government and he used his outlets to vigorously campaign against it. In June and July 1943, the *Herald* published seven of Murdoch's columns. In August, across the three weeks before polling day, it published another nine, including columns in which Murdoch said Curtin was running a 'class government' and was a 'bamboozler' who was 'hesitant and apologetic about global war'. Murdoch now wanted not just a national government, but one that would extend the war and fight across the globe rather than just being 'defence-minded'.[66]

Cecil Edwards later described Murdoch's contributions during the election as including 'a number of incoherent and venomous articles, accusing Labor of being defeatist and pacifist'. Edwards believed Murdoch was 'scared' of a Labor victory and was misusing the *Herald* as a platform to 'shout' his personal views, even when they contradicted the paper's more reasoned stance and embarrassed its staff.[67]

Murdoch had never accepted that Curtin had a level of public popularity and stature, and in 1943 he seemed especially unable to read the public mood. People who observed Murdoch at this time – including Edwards, but also Frank Packer and others – described him as being cut off from people. His world had become more insular, materialistic and defensive.[68]

Although Murdoch ensured his columns were given prominent space in the papers under his control, those papers were still in the news business and the *Sun News-Pictorial* gained a scoop that helped damage the election prospects of Murdoch's preferred UAP–Country Party Coalition. One of the *Sun News-Pictorial*'s reporters, Frank Chamberlain, was new to political reporting and rather than relying on a handout of a Menzies speech (as more weary, seasoned reporters tended to), he went along to Menzies' town hall meeting at Camberwell to hear it in person. The hall was packed so Chamberlain pretended to be a young Nationalist in order to gain entry and was shown to a seat on stage behind Menzies. Part-way through his speech, Menzies suddenly paused, leaned forward and checked that the press table was empty, then launched into some intemperate remarks about taxation policy and what he really thought of his Coalition colleague and leader of the joint Opposition parties, Arthur Fadden.[69]

The *Sun News-Pictorial* published the story, although as Chamberlain noted, not as prominently as its news value seemed to warrant. After all, this was the story of a divided party with two party leaders criticising each other in the middle of a war and an election campaign. Country Party leader Arthur Fadden was dragged out of bed and informed of what Menzies had said. He told reporters that it was a 'typical Menzian stab in the back'. That colourful quote was buried in the second column of a page three story in the *Herald*, and barely mentioned in other HWT papers.[70]

The stinging quotes were not given the emphasis they seemed to deserve (or would have been given had they been made by Labor's leaders), but the articles were still published, and Chamberlain knew his scoop went against the political stance of his boss. He was called into Murdoch's office the next day. Chamberlain was thinking, 'Well, here's the sack, I've only been on the paper six weeks'. Instead, Murdoch told him: 'It's a scoop I would have preferred not to have had politically, but as a newspaperman I regard it as an outstanding scoop'. He gave Chamberlain a bonus in his pay that week.[71]

Over at the *Daily Telegraph*, Frank Packer was not interested in journalistic initiative or integrity. He told the paper's Canberra bureau head, Don Whitington, 'I don't care what you say about the other politicians, but I have a terrific respect for Menzies'. During the election campaign, Whitington was called into a conference and Packer asked him who would win the election. Whitington replied, 'Labor are a stone dead certainty. They've been in office for two years and haven't put a foot wrong. The UAP are divided.' Packer warned, 'Well, I don't think you want to be too enthusiastic. I want whoever accompanies Curtin to write some criticism of him.' Whitington replied that he would criticise anyone if it was warranted but would not 'be disposed to ... just for the sake of knocking him'. Packer then announced the paper would send someone else on tour with Curtin and Whitington spent the month stationed at a hotel instead, doing very little at the office's expense.[72]

Over at the *Sydney Morning Herald*, Warwick Fairfax was contributing articles to his paper, but unlike Murdoch's columns, Fairfax's were published under a pseudonym ('A Political Observer'). Fairfax noted the conservative parties were beset by 'intrigues, disputes, and incoherence'.[73] He was particularly scathing about Menzies, their 1941 feud over newsprint rationing still smarting. Before that feud, Menzies had been a regular visitor to the Fairfax homes and lunch guest at the *Sydney Morning Herald* office.[74] But in a lively column in August 1943, Fairfax presented a venomous portrait of 'The Bewildering Mr Menzies'. It compared Menzies to Hamlet for his indecision ('to be or not to be'), his 'dislike of having to face great and dangerous issues' and even his figure ('He's fat and scant of breath'!). The column also included a 'candid' observation that 'Menzies is an unbelievably self-centred person' who was also lazy.[75] These were extraordinary personal attacks.

The *Sydney Morning Herald* declared the UAP and Country Party 'contain much dead wood which ... must be ruthlessly pruned away', and the paper renewed its appeal (first made in 1940 when Menzies was already out of favour) for 'newcomers' and the best candidates to be elected regardless of party. One column argued the Curtin Labor government had shown itself to be 'unexpectedly superior' to the Menzies government in the 'vigour and efficiency of its war administration'.[76] The *Sydney Morning Herald*'s editorial recommended the election of six Labor members in New South Wales (including Evatt and Ben Chifley) plus 13 conservative members. Privately, Fairfax even sent Curtin a cheque for £50 for use in his Fremantle electorate. Curtin politely returned it with the suggestion that it be forwarded on to the Labor Party rather than him personally. There is no indication it ever was.[77]

The *Sydney Morning Herald* was not abandoning its long tradition of solid support for free enterprise nor its unyielding anti-socialism. Its 1943 election endorsement was less a full embrace of Labor than rejection of the disorderly UAP, and especially Menzies. The company attempted to soften the blow when Henderson – not Fairfax – sent Menzies a cheque for £25 towards his Kooyong election campaign funds – but Menzies also politely returned it.[78]

Labor's HV Evatt was so emboldened by the extraordinary support for him in the pages of the *Sydney Morning Herald* that he seemed to feel it unnecessary to actively campaign in his Sydney seat of Barton, and especially because he also had the support of Sydney's other morning paper, the *Daily Telegraph*. In 1940, the *Daily Telegraph* had encouraged Evatt to enter politics in the hope he would form part of a national government. Packer had even provided secretarial assistance.[79] In 1943, Evatt spent the crucial part of the election campaign at home, reportedly in bed with a case of influenza. Others believed he had gone to ground in order to position himself as a potential leader of a national government should Curtin fall. Despite his absence, the vote for Evatt was so high that it broke records for the highest primary votes recorded in a NSW seat since Federation.[80]

Curtin's government also achieved an overwhelming victory – a 49-seat majority in the lower house. The *Sydney Morning Herald* called it the 'most convincing parliamentary majority in history'.[81] Murdoch was stunned, even though the polling produced for his papers had indicated that Labor would win (and even from afar, British newspapers were expecting that too).[82] The *Herald*'s bias in reporting the election had been widely noted. Some HWT journalists had complained to the AJA that anti-government comments had been interjected into their factual accounts of meetings and speeches.[83] The *Herald*'s campaign against the government had been so harsh that when Murdoch attended the Monday morning news conference after the election result, his chief of staff, Frank Murphy, opened with the cheeky question 'Well, what will we do today? Print or sprint? Are we going to continue publishing in the open or go underground?'[84]

Joe Alexander was also worried the government might retaliate against the Murdoch papers.[85] A week before polling day, Senator Keane, minister for trades and customs, had told a Labor rally at Yarra Bank that the Australian newspapers had treated the government in a 'brutal' manner, suppressing information on its achievements and magnifying its missteps even though the Curtin government had bent over backwards to help them on newsprint. The minister for air, Arthur Drakeford, suggested the *Herald* was the worst offender, and the next day, Keane had called the Murdoch press unfair, one-sided, dirty and disgraceful.[86]

This was all increasing Murdoch's anxiety about the implications of his election crusade. Two days after Labor's victory, Murdoch added a postscript to a letter he sent to the *Advertiser*'s chairman and managing director, Lloyd Dumas. 'Do you have any complaints that my articles "overdid it"?'[87] Dumas soothed Murdoch by focusing only on Adelaide, replying he detected 'no noticeable bitterness towards the *Advertiser* at the Trades Hall' and had 'only heard strong objection taken to one of your articles, and that was the one on Dedman'. Three days later, Dumas wrote that he had now detected some 'upsetting' levels of bitterness in Labor ranks, but it 'would be contrary to human nature if these people did not feel rather bitter' and as 'the Caucus will not meet for nearly a month, tempers will have cooled …'. Another three days passed before Dumas wrote again to reassure Murdoch that 'the heat is dying out' and he felt they need not fear retribution. But even into September 1943, Dumas and Murdoch were keeping an eye on Trades Hall and Labor MPs, and worrying about proposals that the labour movement should establish a daily Labor newspaper in each state.[88]

The *Herald* conceded on the Monday after the election that there was no 'prospect of a national or composite party government'.[89] Murdoch's years of advocacy had been in vain and neither Curtin nor Labor ministers such as Arthur Calwell would ever forget Murdoch's rugged campaign against them. When Murdoch fell badly in November 1943, Calwell sent him a wickedly ambiguous telegram: 'Very sorry to hear you have broken your ankle. It could have been worse.'[90] If Murdoch detected the spite, he ignored it and replied with courtesy.[91]

Murdoch had endured multiple health problems since the 1930s, which may have contributed to his declining influence and judgement. One of Murdoch's sympathetic biographers said the 1943 election loss 'personally wounded' him.[92] A less sympathetic biographer said this was because Murdoch 'was of the opinion that he could force Labor from office'.[93] Murdoch considered Labor's sweeping victory a disaster. He was more subdued for a time, and travelled extensively overseas. He was not the only one shocked and disappointed. Frank Packer had thrown a dinner party he thought would be a conservative 'victory dinner'.[94]

POLITICS AND THE PRESS

Australians had voted the Labor government back into office despite contrary advice by nearly every daily metropolitan newspaper in the country and an especially strong anti-Labor campaign waged in the Murdoch papers. The presumed power of the press was coming into question. As the editor of Brisbane's *Telegraph* noted, there were five Labor governments in seven Australian parliaments in 1944 despite 'almost universal press opposition to Labor'.[95]

The anti-Labor side of politics was obviously in dire need of renewal and Menzies would be the one to lead that project. He had been successfully courting Frank Packer's support and also re-established cordial relations with Murdoch. Following the party's poor showing in the 1943 election, Menzies was again elected UAP leader following the resignation of 80-year-old Hughes. Despite taunting him with insults during the campaign, Fairfax sent Menzies a note that said:

Whatever political differences we have had in the past, or may have in the future, I cannot but congratulate you upon attaining the leadership of the Opposition ... Whatever one may think of the Government it will be necessary to bring the light of parliamentary and public discussion fully upon their actions, in a way which was certainly not adequately done in the last eighteen months.[96]

One of Curtin's first actions upon being returned would send the newspapers into a frenzy of 'shining light' on the government and a fresh embrace of the anti-Labor side of politics. Curtin was about to unleash a known press-hater upon them.

CHAPTER 3
THE PRESS AND THE 'COCKY' GO TO WAR

Most elected politicians try very hard to avoid offending newspaper proprietors, but not Arthur Calwell. Labor's federal member for Melbourne from 1940 to 1972 relished fighting with the press, and no other government minister ever gave newspaper owners so much trouble. When Calwell was minister for information between 1943 and 1949, the newspapers faced an energetic opponent and tough political brawler, who had an acerbic tongue and a legendary ability to hold a grudge. The conflict reached its peak in 1944 in one of the most dramatic incidents in Australian press history when Sydney's newspapers were suppressed at gunpoint.

THE MINISTER FOR INFORMATION

After Labor was re-elected in 1943, Curtin appointed Calwell as minister for information, in charge of censorship. Only when Labor was safely in office in its own right did Curtin unleash him on the press. Calwell's loathing of the commercial press was well known. In November 1941, he had said the Australian press was 'owned for the most part by financial crooks and is edited for the most part by mental harlots'.[1]

Curtin disliked Calwell but the Victorian MP had won the last place in the new ministry, and by giving him the troublesome portfolio of censorship, Curtin may have hoped to keep a rival and known troublemaker busy. Perhaps Curtin also enjoyed the prospect of making a man who despised the newspapers have to deal with them daily. Privately, Curtin said that Calwell had 'been fighting with the newspapers all this time, and now he can learn to live with them' – but Curtin was overestimating Calwell's interest in appeasement.²

Since Labor had formed in the 1890s, many Labor MPs had felt the 'capitalist press' was working against them, but Calwell felt this more deeply than most, and for him, it was personal. Calwell's biographer, Colm Kiernan, noted that Calwell's political career began and ended with a libel action against a newspaper.³ The first action, in 1935, was against the *Herald*. When Calwell was a Treasury official, the paper had reported with seeming approval the comments of a political rival who said Calwell's public service role dealing with confidential documents was incompatible with his party political activities. The HWT settled out of court, paid Calwell £150 damages, and published an apology which said the imputation about Calwell's integrity had 'escaped our notice'.⁴ Not much at the *Herald* escaped Keith Murdoch's notice though, and Calwell's hatred of Murdoch grew from then.

Calwell also despised the *Daily Telegraph*'s editor, Brian Penton. In May 1942, Calwell told parliament that Penton was a debt evader, a publisher of 'indecent pictures' and a malicious liar.⁵ Calwell said a visa should not be provided 'to a creature' like Penton for a lecture tour of the United States until it was determined whether the trip had been set up so Penton could avoid his military responsibilities.⁶ Penton dared Calwell to repeat these accusations without the cover of parliamentary privilege and called him 'a blackguardly coward' in the *Daily Telegraph*.⁷

Calwell also clashed regularly with Penton's boss, Frank Packer, as well as Rupert Henderson at Fairfax. Calwell believed Australia's major daily newspapers were 'the appendages and organs of big business', dedicated to misleading the public and keeping Labor out of office.⁸ He saw no reason to be polite to such men.

Calwell grew up in inner-city Melbourne, conscious of the poverty and misery around him. He worked hard to educate himself at school and was a political insider in Victorian politics for 20 years before entering federal parliament in 1940. A devout Catholic with a battered face and distinctive husky voice, Calwell had a talent for using rich, blunt and evocative language. He was outspoken, determined and courageous –

some said reckless. To his friends, Calwell was a man of wit and charm, who was steadfastly loyal. To his newspaper enemies, he was a dangerous socialist with an authoritarian streak. Calwell hated his enemies with a passion that was unusual even in the hard world of Australian politics. He enjoyed provoking them and called it 'stirring the possum'.[9]

Journalist Frank Chamberlain, who observed Calwell over a long period, thought there was something 'sinister' about Calwell's hatred of his opponents.[10] But Calwell's deep feelings could run either way. Calwell could hate a journalist and not speak to him for years but be the first to offer sincere condolences when a family tragedy struck. He could despise enemies purely on matters of politics and principle, but quickly forgave and offered to help a disturbed young man who shot him in the face in a botched assassination attempt in 1966.

Calwell's relationship with the press was equally complicated. From the earliest days of his career, Calwell had played the press game as hard as any other politician, and possibly harder. He was well known among journalists as a confidential source and valuable Cabinet leak. On one occasion, Calwell stood up in parliament and condemned Chamberlain as an unethical journalist for printing details that Calwell had provided to him in secret. Then Calwell went straight back to his office, rang Chamberlain and asked him round for tea.[11]

Calwell built up a friendship with Ezra Norton even though he thought Norton published 'indecent pictures' and immoral stories, but he reserved a special hatred for Keith Murdoch. Calwell said in his autobiography, published in 1972:

> When I became a member of the Federal Parliament in 1940,
> I despised Murdoch for his exploitation of human misery. I despised
> him for having destroyed the Scullin Government in 1931–32 and
> I despised him for the manner in which he sought to take over
> control of our national affairs and censorship when he was appointed
> Director-General of Information.[12]

In March 1941, when Menzies was still prime minister, Calwell had called Murdoch a 'sinister figure'.[13] He believed Murdoch's grandstanding

FIGURE 3.1 The number one enemy of the press, Arthur Calwell, photographed by Max Dupain, November 1945

SOURCE Mitchell Library, State Library of New South Wales (IE19411785).

on censorship was unpatriotic and dangerous. He thought Murdoch 'suffered from megalomania' and aspired to be like Murdoch's former employer and idol, Lord Northcliffe, the British newspaper baron who had been a ruthless propagandist and power player.[14]

A BREAKDOWN IN RELATIONS

When Calwell took up his post as minister for information, press complaints about censorship were simmering. Curtin advised him that, rather than hearing appeals on individual cases of censorship, Calwell should either back the chief censor, EG Bonney, and his decisions or sack him.[15] Calwell not only backed Bonney but also immediately increased his power by bringing the separate Department of Information and Publicity Censorship under one control – Bonney's. Bonney was now responsible for censoring information and for maintaining public morale. Combining these two previously distinct functions made Bonney more likely to use censorship to maintain public morale.

The enlarged Department of Information included men who knew Murdoch well – not just Bonney but also other former HWT journalists. Some shared Calwell's harsh views on the HWT chief. A brutal dossier, written anonymously from within the Department and kept in Calwell's private papers, described Murdoch as 'an evil influence' and 'crazy extremist'. The paper argued that '[Murdoch's] success as a money maker and little dictator in his own newspaper offices' stood in contrast to his failure as director-general of information, an experience that had made him 'a puzzled and embittered man ever since'.[16]

When press complaints about Bonney's censorship rulings reached Calwell, he dismissed them as the griping of over-privileged newspaper barons. The censors operating under Bonney and Calwell felt emboldened to wield their blue pencils more liberally. Newspapers believed censorship was being applied in a heavy-handed, inconsistent and politically motivated manner. They argued that public morale could withstand frank reports of military losses and casualty figures, and that there was no justification for preventing newspapers from reporting on matters such as public transport strikes, which was information citizens needed to know if only to prevent them waiting in vain for a train that would never arrive.[17]

Left-wing critics – including Calwell – responded that the newspapers were the biggest censors of all and routinely censored opposing political views or news that criticised any of their large advertisers, their businesses, friends, family and club colleagues.[18] Calwell gave an example of how US President Roosevelt's broadcast on 12 October 1943 was reported. Roosevelt had said Allied war planning was 'not being decided by the typewriter strategists who expound their views in the Press', and wryly added that all the best generals seemed to be working for the newspapers instead of the army. This jibe must have been too close for comfort for Murdoch, Australia's leading typewriter strategist, as those lines were deleted from reports of the speech, not by the censors, but by the editors of the *Herald* and the *Sun News-Pictorial*.[19]

Meanwhile in Sydney, Packer and Penton continued to challenge the censors. On 30 November 1943, they published comments on coal shortages and strikes, in defiance of censorship instructions. Calwell responded by authorising Bonney to place the paper under an order to submit all copy to the censors before publication. This was the first order-to-submit since 1940.[20] Curtin backed Bonney and Calwell, describing the *Daily Telegraph* as a 'deliberate and persistent offender'.[21]

A few weeks later, Penton submitted an article as a direct challenge to the censor, headed 'WE INVITE MR CALWELL TO PROSECUTE'. The censor allowed it to be published but deleted several sentences, including one that described Calwell as 'Australia's would-be Goebbels'.[22] On 31 January 1944, the censorship row intensified when Murdoch, Warwick Fairfax and Eric Kennedy threatened to withdraw from the Censorship Advisory Committee. Not yet showing any sign of desiring conciliation, Calwell replied on 7 February that the newspapers just regarded all censorship, 'no matter how important to the safety of the nation', as 'unwarranted interference in their money-making activities'.[23]

Without Curtin's leadership, the Censorship Advisory Committee was being rendered useless as a way of navigating disputes, and the press began to criticise censorship more openly.[24] In March 1944, ANPA published a report citing examples of rulings on censorship that it argued were political. When Murdoch's criticisms of censorship were raised in parliament, Calwell replied he had not seen them because 'I have not much time these days to read the drivellings of Sir Keith Murdoch ... this anti-Australian newspaper magnate'.[25]

Warwick Fairfax had continued to document cases of what he believed to be political censorship. One example was a report of a protest against rationing in Townsville. The speaker had said of Calwell, 'it is fitting that I pay him tribute with a Nazi salute'. The censor cut that line. The newspapers argued that there was no national security purpose for that and censorship was instead being used to protect the minister from harsh criticism.[26]

The *Sydney Morning Herald* was arguing with the censor and the government against particular censorship rulings but it still complied with them if it lost the argument.[27] The *Daily Telegraph*, under Packer and Penton, was becoming more aggressive in pushing the boundaries. The Sydney papers had recognised that Calwell would neither back down nor 'live with' them on their terms. They were regularly consulting with their lawyers and had come to the conclusion that the best way to achieve reform was to overtly challenge the censor and the government. Timing would be crucial.

SUPPRESSION AND REBELLION: APRIL 1944

In early April 1944, Curtin set sail for the United States. Before he had even arrived, the Sydney daily papers had been suppressed at gunpoint. The newspapers would later claim that Calwell was 'itching for a fight' and had initiated the crisis once Curtin left.[28] But, as combative as Calwell was, the incident did not benefit him and was not of his design. It was the executives of the Sydney papers – principally, the *Daily Telegraph* and the *Sydney Morning Herald* – who engineered it. They waited until Curtin was out of the country because they still had strong respect for him personally, but also because they understood, as Penton wrote later in his account of the incident, that Curtin had a 'genius for evading crises by compromise'. Penton said the papers knew from experience that, if Curtin were there, he would have 'steered the parties around and around ... [and] soothed everyone ... Nothing would have been solved'.[29] The papers wanted a solution, not just on censorship, but also on Calwell, something that would diminish and restrain him in his future dealings with the newspapers.

When the newspaper proprietors banded together to manufacture a showdown, Joe Alexander of the *Herald* was 'disgusted' by what he viewed as an attempt to damage the Curtin government. But Edgar Holt of the *Daily Telegraph*, who was closer to the action, believed the newspaper owners timed the challenge in order to specifically target Calwell – not the government.[30] The *Daily Telegraph* acknowledged as much after the crisis was over when it said: 'Calwell is the enemy ... The Australian Press is fighting a Calwell dictatorship not the Labor government'.[31]

The pretext the Sydney papers used to spark their challenge to censorship was a decision the government had made in October 1943 to bring back some Australian troops to assist with food production and postwar preparation. The number to be returned was 20 000 service personnel, but when reports were cabled from Sydney newspapers to American correspondents in early April 1944, the number reported was

90 000 (a figure that erroneously included routine discharges and natural attrition). On the basis of the inaccurate report, three US senators had criticised Australia's commitment to the war. This was precisely the sort of incident the government and censors had wanted to avoid – an important ally gaining a damaging impression of Australia based on false information. On 13 April, Calwell criticised the Sydney papers for the misunderstanding and said they had published 'partisan and inaccurate editorials' that distorted information and gave a misleading impression to the Americans.[32]

That day, Rupert Henderson, as chairman of the ANPA, replied, making the exaggerated claim that censorship was so bad most American correspondents had been withdrawn from Australia. Calwell responded by accusing Henderson of being inaccurate and untruthful. Henderson then made another statement in his own defence. Instead of providing evidence to prove his claim about American correspondents, he focused on the issue of censorship itself, and included examples of what he called political censorship. Under censorship regulations, it was forbidden to reveal that censorship had taken place by disclosing instances of it or showing where any alterations to copy had been made at the direction of a censor. Giving examples in public was a transgression that Henderson and Packer knew the censors could not ignore.

Reports of Henderson's statement were submitted to the censorship authorities on the night of Friday 14 April. As expected, the censor used his blue pencil to cut all but a few paragraphs. All of the references to examples of censorship were deleted, while Calwell's original statement was not touched. At this point, Packer rang Henderson and encouraged him to join the *Daily Telegraph* and publish blank spaces in the *Sydney Morning Herald* in order to challenge the censor. Henderson decided not to take that course of action. He was willing to challenge but the complicating factor was that the *Sydney Morning Herald* was due to launch its first edition with front page news, instead of advertising, the next day, Saturday 15 April. The *Sydney Morning Herald* had been planning the shift for months and did not want readers to see areas of blank space and think the paper had botched its new-look front page.[33]

Packer decided to challenge alone. He was assured by his legal counsel

FIGURE 3.2 What all the fuss was about: The *Sunday Telegraph* publishes blank spaces indicating censorship, 16 April 1944

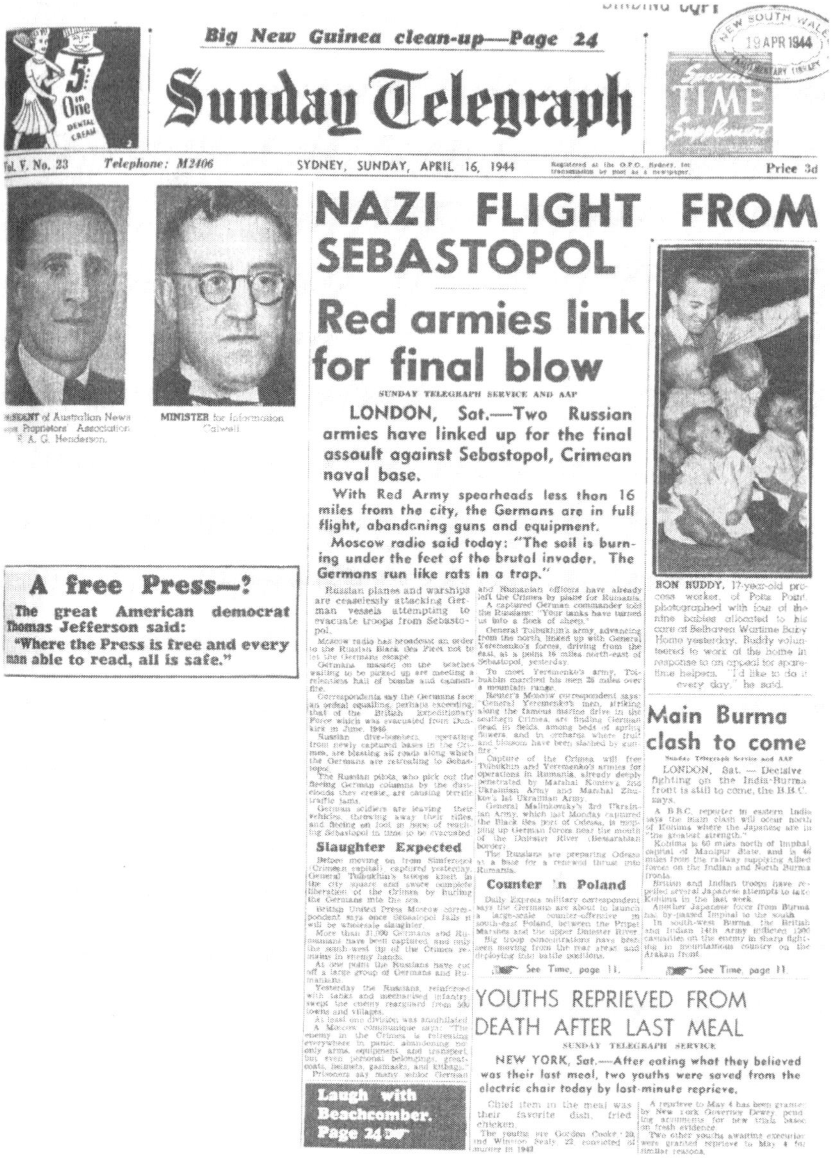

SOURCE State Library of New South Wales.

that the censor had overstepped. He also consulted with his Consolidated Press partner, EG Theodore, who agreed that the newspapers should 'push to have the matter brought before the High Court'.[34] Packer authorised Penton to publish the *Daily Telegraph* on the morning of Saturday 15 April with Henderson's statement on page three containing blank spaces to make it obvious where long passages had been deleted by the censor. Consolidated Press was quickly served with another order to submit all publication matter to the censor for review. That night, executives from Consolidated Press gathered in the company's boardroom with Rupert Henderson, Eric Kennedy (chief executive of Associated Newspapers), Consolidated Press's solicitor and two constitutional lawyers, to discuss their next course of action.[35]

After the visitors left, the editor of the *Sunday Telegraph*, Cyril Pearl, prepared copy for the next day's edition. It included Henderson's new statement plus an editorial decrying the censor's abuse of power. The paper submitted its copy to the censor at 9.16 pm that Saturday. Henderson's statement was banned because of its reference to acts of censorship, but by 9.45 pm the censor had still not made a final decision on the planned editorial.[36] With Packer's encouragement, Pearl defied the censor's directions by publishing the first edition of the *Sunday Telegraph* with two empty columns on its front page where the editorial would have been, and a blank column on page three where Henderson's statement would have been. This was a clear breach of censorship rules. The editorial was returned from the censor in time for later editions but had been heavily cut, so Pearl left the two columns of empty space on the front page but added photographs of Henderson and Calwell along with a quote from Thomas Jefferson on the value of a free press (Figure 3.2).

'ONE IN ALL IN': BAITING THE CENSOR

One of the main reasons the censorship dispute arose in Sydney was because of the NSW state publicity censor, Horace Mansell. Unlike the previous state censor, Mansell had been put into the job by Bonney and was firmly on board with Bonney's hard-line approach. Mansell was a former editor of the *Labor Daily*, 'a sincere Labor man', and a campaign director for HV Evatt.[37] On the night of Saturday 15 April, Mansell warned Consolidated Press that unless the blank spaces were filled with type, he would take action to confiscate the paper. When his order was ignored, Mansell instructed Commonwealth peace officers (an early version of federal police) to go to the *Daily Telegraph* office and prevent distribution of the paper. Peace officers arrived around 11.15 pm. As Packer bamboozled and bluffed them to stall for time, his staff managed to carry a few thousand copies out the front door. But the rest were seized without violence when peace officers stood in front of the trucks loaded with papers ready for delivery.[38]

When the *Sunday Telegraph* did not appear on the streets on the morning of 16 April, by prior agreement the rival Sunday papers did not take advantage of the situation by increasing their print runs. Around 300 000 readers had to go without a Sunday paper.[39] At 2.30 pm that day, senior representatives from Sydney's major newspaper groups met again in the Consolidated Press boardroom. This time, Ezra Norton joined them so representatives from all four Sydney daily papers were there.[40]

Nine barristers, including five King's Counsel, were also present.[41] The barristers gave their view that no breach had been committed by the *Sunday Telegraph* because the act of censorship lay outside the defence powers validated by the Constitution. They recommended applying for an injunction in the High Court.[42] Henderson and Fairfax agreed to take a collective approach to fighting censorship. This was crucial because even the pugnacious Frank Packer feared that, without a group effort, the government might put his papers off the street, confiscate his plant and keep him in court for months.[43]

Ezra Norton was the other crucial player because if Norton would not join his *Daily Mirror* to the fight, then his rival, Associated Newspapers' *Sun*, could not either, and two morning papers fighting the government would not be as effective as all four. Norton was worried the public might not support the newspapers. He pointed out that the papers had been editorialising for months that coal miners needed to follow the law and take their grievances to the relevant tribunal rather than strike. How would it look if the papers now set about deliberately breaking the law?

But Norton was finally persuaded when one of the King's Counsel assured him that they would be testing the law rather than just breaking it, and it was not possible to test any other way. The High Court needed a specific example to rule on.

According to the meeting notes, Rupert Henderson then said: 'Our desire is to get the regulations tested. We need to bowl up something which we know he will censor, and we know by our advice that he has no right to do so.'[44] When Norton asked what would happen if the government picked on only one or two papers, Henderson replied, 'Then there is an undertaking by each of us (as in a case of strike). If he suppresses you and does not suppress us, we publish for you. The point is that all have to stand or fall together.' After obtaining the agreement of Dr Waddell (acting chairman of Associated Newspapers) for this approach, Norton said, 'So long as it is "One in all in", and that is perfectly clear, I will be there'.[45]

Until now, the *Sydney Morning Herald* had been notorious for standing apart from other newspapers, even on matters of common interest. But now the paper was fighting shoulder to shoulder with its rivals in a battle that was later melodramatically characterised by the *Daily Telegraph* as a moment when 'the Press risked its very existence'.[46]

The meeting participants agreed that the task of baiting the censor should go to the *Daily Telegraph*'s editor Brian Penton. He was perfect for the job. Considered one of the great editors of the 1940s, Penton was a nonconformist provocateur known for his gall and his gift for bold, forthright language (he was also a poet and novelist). His colourful and direct writing style – which he insisted *Daily Telegraph* staff follow – had carried the paper to new heights of popularity. He also had a very personal reserve of emotion to draw upon for this particular writing exercise due to his earlier stoushes with Calwell.

After the meeting broke up that Sunday afternoon, Penton prepared a joint statement to be published in all of the Sydney daily papers the next day, Monday 17 April. It included the background to the suppression of the *Sunday Telegraph* and Henderson's two original (banned) statements. Penton knew just what sort of language to 'bowl up' to make the censors act. A reference to Calwell as Joseph Goebbels, the hated Nazi propagandist, had already been censored and was bound to do the trick if repeated.

(Bonney believed it 'very destructive to public morale to have Ministers of State ... given the names or attributes of the enemy'.)[47]

The statement that Penton drafted for all the Sydney dailies to publish included provocative lines such as: 'Mr Calwell's ambition to be Australia's No.1 Censor and Newspaper Dictator ... is rooted in a small-time politician's hatred of the Press. This hatred ... became more bitter when newspapers revealed how he had bungled his job, wasted time on vicious little feuds, instead of making Australia and her war effort better known.' The censor did not actually cut any of those words, but he did cut a section that stated: 'Mr Calwell has abused his Ministerial powers to persecute a newspaper because it has found it necessary to criticise him as a public man ... The latest and most scandalous example of Mr Calwell's methods shows how important it is to defend our free institutions against tin-pot dictators.'[48] This cut was more than enough for the papers to argue that there were no military secrets involved here and censorship was instead being used to protect a minister's reputation and save him from embarrassment.

Once the joint statement was ready, at 8.30 pm on Sunday 16 April, the papers' executives and lawyers reassembled. As soon as Penton's statement and the newspapers' separate editorials were approved by their counsel, the *Sydney Morning Herald* and *Daily Telegraph* went to work preparing their morning papers for 17 April. In defiance of the censor, both would be publishing Penton's full statement plus Henderson's, complete with its examples of censorship. Penton's colourful statement stood out in the usually sedate *Sydney Morning Herald*, and the *Daily Telegraph*'s editorial gave full vent to rallying against 'Australia's Would-Be Goebbels', stating that 'Mr Calwell [is] using censorship to further a personal vendetta against newspapers'.[49]

An officer from the censor's department arrived at the *Daily Telegraph* at midnight wanting two copies of the first edition for review. They kept him waiting about 40 minutes, trying to stall for time so the *Sydney Morning Herald* could get its first edition out. But an official had already arrived at the *Sydney Morning Herald*.[50] When he saw a copy of the paper, he hurried back to his office, a few blocks away.

PISTOLS AND PROTESTS

Bonney became aware of the newspapers' plan for rebellion in the early hours of Monday 17 April.[51] He contacted Calwell. Rather than prosecuting the papers for breaches of censorship rulings (a strategy that likely would have been more successful), Bonney decided to seize the papers. Calwell checked that Bonney had been assured by the solicitor-general the government had the power to do it, then he replied, 'Well, if you go ahead, I will support you in all you do and accept full ministerial responsibility for everything you do'.[52]

Commonwealth peace officers were sent to seize the newspapers. At the *Sydney Morning Herald*, about 100 000 copies had already been printed. Henderson initially told the driver of a truck loaded with papers to proceed, but an 'officer placed his hand on the shoulder of the driver and threatened him with arrest', so Henderson told the driver to stop and ordered the presses to stop.[53] No guns were drawn at the *Sydney Morning Herald*.

At Consolidated Press, a Commonwealth peace officer was photographed brandishing a pistol at the loading dock to stop a truck loaded with papers leaving (Figure 3.3). This became the defining image of the conflict and it helped the newspapers win the public relations battle. It was used as strong evidence to support the papers' claim that censorship was being applied in a heavy-handed manner. Packer and his staff well understood the symbolism and had a hand in producing it. They had a photographer at the ready, and as historian Bridget Griffen-Foley recounts:

> Alec Boyd, the paper's police roundsman, asked an officer what he would do if a driver tried to leave the loading dock. After receiving a hesitant response, Boyd insisted 'Show us what you'd do, you know. Get your gun out and show us'. A photographer captured the image of the hapless officer pointing his gun at the lorry, which was used to great effect in the final edition of the [*Daily*] *Telegraph*.[54]

After printing was stopped at Consolidated Press's Castlereagh building, staff tried to print an emergency four-page issue at the old *Labor Daily/Daily News* plant at Brisbane Street (which Consolidated Press had

FIGURE 3.3 The famous photograph of a Commonwealth peace officer, gun drawn, stopping a truck from leaving the dock at Consolidated Press's Castlereagh and Elizabeth streets building, Sydney, 1944
SOURCE *Daily Telegraph*, 18 April 1944, p. 3; State Library of Victoria.

acquired in 1940). A skeleton crew struggled for four hours with 'dusty, cob-webbed machines', but Commonwealth peace officers arrived there too and seized all of the copies, except for some that staff managed to smuggle out under their coats.[55]

When Sydney woke up on Monday 17 April, there were no morning newspapers. People were baffled. The only indication of what had happened were street posters: 'TELEGRAPH BANNED: POLITICAL CENSORSHIP'.[56] In the afternoon, Commonwealth peace officers arrived at the *Sun* and *Daily Mirror* offices to seize their early editions. At the *Sun* office, photographers captured colourful scenes of copies of the paper floating down from the windows after being thrown to people gathered below in Elizabeth Street. Union leaders later claimed this was a press beat-up, that these were not crowds of people clamouring for a paper (as the

FIGURE 3.4 A Commonwealth peace officer draws his revolver at the *Daily Mirror* office in Sydney in 1944
SOURCE Newspix (NPX125907).

press reported the next day), but just city workers making their way home as usual.[57]

At the *Daily Mirror* office, press photographers were also waiting when a peace officer drew a gun to stop a truck leaving. The photograph published in the paper showed a dramatic close-up of the officer brandishing his gun, but a wider angle view showed an employee laughing in the foreground (Figure 3.4). So unintimidating was the peace officer, he 'was brushed aside by a crowd of onlookers and workmen, and the van left with its load for the city'.[58] Many vans managed to leave the *Daily Mirror* office that day to distribute their papers.

The four Sydney daily papers were acting in concert so they were always going to win the part of the battle that was fought in the court of public opinion. There was no other source of daily print news in the city. And publicity was their turf. They fanned that day's spectacle and drama to maximum effect. Rowdy university students who the *Sydney Morning Herald* and *Daily Telegraph* would normally condemn for disturbing the peace were suddenly celebrated as freedom fighters after they mobilised surprisingly quickly that day and started demonstrating against censorship. The papers estimated that 2000 students advanced upon the city centre and called for Calwell outside the censor's office.[59] Unions again claimed this was all stage managed. Melbourne's Trades Hall Council said the student demonstrations were 'pre-arranged by the newspapers concerned', then passed off as a 'spontaneous demonstration'.[60]

At one surreal point in the afternoon, the demonstrators paused outside the *Sydney Morning Herald* building – normally considered a reactionary opponent – chanting, 'We want the press', and singing, 'The freedom of the press lies a mouldering in the grave, but its soul goes marching on'. Warwick Fairfax and Rupert Henderson – two men who normally avoided both the limelight and rowdy demonstrations – even made an appearance on the balcony to acknowledge the applause of demonstrators. The national president of the Communist Party, Lance Sharkey, mocked that 'Granny' *Herald* had joined a sit-down strike with the *Daily Telegraph* and 'broke the law'.[61]

The drama of that day overshadowed how, for most of the war, relations between the censors and the newspapers had been cosy, and outside of Sydney, they still were. Censors were often journalists closely connected to the newspapers they were scrutinising and keen to return to the industry once their official role was over. The HWT joined in the Sydney papers' fight only in a marginal way. The final editions of the *Herald* in Melbourne and *News* in Adelaide were seized when they tried to publish Henderson's statement. But the censors had taken great care to make sure that only the last editions were seized to avoid affecting advertising revenue. In fact, relations were so good that the Victorian censor, Tom Hoey, retired to the pub for a drink with some of the *Herald*'s staff after he had just officially banned their paper.[62] They were his colleagues: Hoey had been a subeditor at the *Herald* for nearly ten years before he was seconded to the role of censor.

South Australia's censor, Gilbert Mant, was said to be 'horrified' by the NSW censor's heavy-handed approach.[63] Mant quietly agreed with Hoey's assessment that this was 'a private Sydney gang war. Let them fight it out there'.[64] That fight had now become a legal battle.

AT THE HIGH COURT

The five High Court justices had been warned that they might be required to urgently consider the matter of newspaper suppression, so the full bench sat on the morning of 17 April to hear an application by Consolidated Press for an injunction restraining the Commonwealth from preventing publication of the censored material. Some of the judges were carrying a morning paper when they took their seats. Packer had arranged for smuggled copies to be delivered to their homes early that morning.

The hearing was supposed to be confined to procedural matters but justices Starke and Williams were keen to inquire about the validity of the censor's actions. Justice Starke pushed the Crown's legal representative to defend the censor's approach even though that was outside the realms of the injunction hearing. Spreading out his copy of the *Sydney Morning Herald* in front of him, Starke remarked: 'I can see nothing in this that justifies censorship'. He went further and stated: 'It is intolerable for the citizens of New South Wales that because of two small articles the whole paper is censored and not allowed to be published'.[65] By a majority of three to two, the High Court granted an interim injunction restraining censorship authorities from interfering with the papers' publication.

One of the other judges who voted for the injunction was Justice Dudley Williams, who was related to the Fairfax family by marriage. (Williams' wife was a great-granddaughter of John Fairfax, the original Fairfax owner of the *Sydney Morning Herald*.[66]) Calwell does not seem to have been aware of this or he would surely have added it to his complaint, made in parliament months later, that:

> Mr Justice Starke and Mr Justice Rich threw away their wigs when they took their seats on the High Court bench and openly barracked for the press ... Mr Justice Starke said, 'Why can't I read what I want to read in my morning newspaper?' He presumed to usurp the

function of the Chief Publicity Censor. The issue he had to decide was whether the Chief Publicity Censor had acted within the law.[67]

Calwell had mistakenly identified Justice Rich when he meant Justice Williams, an error he later dismissed by saying 'I made a mistake. It was not Rich, it was another shell back ingrate.'[68]

The newspapers presented the injunction as a clear win for 'freedom'. It was not the end of the legal action but it was an important win in public relations terms because it allowed the newspapers to keep publishing their side of the story.

Calwell was not receiving much support from his colleagues. No-one else was keen to take on the papers. A national Cabinet meeting scheduled to make a statement, possibly supporting Calwell's action, was cancelled after the High Court injunction. The NSW Labor premier, William McKell, who was facing an election, condemned Calwell's approach as 'rash and ill-considered', in a telegram to Calwell that was leaked to the press.[69] McKell had not allowed the New South Wales police force to be used to seize the newspapers. That was why Commonwealth peace officers were used. Because they were unaccustomed to routine police work, the peace officers had been unnerved when goaded or when the newspapers had shown signs of resisting (including staff throwing bundles of newspapers at them), and so had drawn their pistols.[70]

In legal terms, the injunction was just the opening gambit, not the end of the matter, and the case was not quite the clear-cut victory the newspapers claimed it to be. Previous High Court cases on the powers of the government at a time of war had generally widened the Commonwealth's powers and suggested the government had absolute discretion in matters such as censorship during wartime. When the High Court hearing on the matter began on 21 April and continued into May, Chief Justice Latham made a statement strongly encouraging the two sides to resolve the matter out of court and 'hinted that Censorship was on fairly strong legal ground'.[71]

One person who had exceptional legal training to interpret the issues was Evatt, then attorney-general but previously a leading barrister and High Court justice. He was considered 'one of the greatest Constitutional authorities in the Commonwealth'.[72] Calwell had avoided contacting Evatt the night he authorised Bonney's decision though, because, as he later told Evatt, 'you would have tried to prevent me seizing the newspapers'.[73] Consolidated Press must have suspected this as well because its senior executives tried desperately to contact Evatt on the night the *Sunday Telegraph* was seized. They were bitterly disappointed that Evatt, who the company had championed during the 1940 and 1943 elections, and who was strongly critical of censorship under the Menzies government, gave them only a tepid response, suggesting they just fill in the blank spaces and avoid a censorship row.[74]

After Latham suggested mediation to resolve the case, it was Evatt who tried to broker peace between Calwell and the newspaper proprietors. He arranged a meeting between Calwell, Henderson, Packer and Norton. Calwell made a point of not shaking hands with any of them, then sat in silence, and left long before any agreement was arrived at.[75] Evatt continued negotiating with Henderson, including at Henderson's home in Wahroonga, and negotiated an agreement over Calwell's head.[76] The result was a 'code of censorship principles' added to the Press and Broadcasting Censorship Order.

The acting prime minister, Francis Forde, announced the new principles on 18 May, stating that censorship would be 'exclusively for reasons of defence security', but at the same time maintained that censorship under the Curtin government had always been 'strictly non-political'.[77] In the United States, Curtin also told American reporters at a press conference on 20 April, 'There has not been any political censorship'.[78]

Despite Forde's and Curtin's protestations that nothing had changed, something had. There was now a specific undertaking that censorship would not be imposed merely to keep up morale. Again, though, the press victory was not as total or straightforward as the newspapers claimed. The legal result was a compromise, with each party paying its own legal costs, and in practice, the Attorney-General's Department told Bonney that 'the powers of the Censor have not been greatly affected by the new code'.[79]

The real victory was that newspapers had sent a message about their joint political power that would serve as a warning to politicians for decades to come. The newspapers portrayed the sense of a colossal victory and did not spare the hyperbole. The *Daily Telegraph* positioned the victory as part of a 350-year battle for press freedom since Henry VIII.[80] The *Sydney Morning Herald* said the suppression of the papers had represented a 'drift to fascism in Australia'.[81] The industry publication *Newspaper News* celebrated the 'HISTORIC FIGHT FOR PRESS FREEDOM'.[82] At the ANPA meeting in June, all of the daily newspapers – even those not directly affected by the seizure or prosecution – offered to share the costs connected with the censorship fight.[83]

THE AFTERMATH

The censor's blue pencil was used less liberally after the fightback, but the newspapers had only partly hobbled an enemy. Both Calwell and Bonney retained their positions through to the end of the war. Bonney consistently defended his actions, including under lengthy cross-examination, arguing he was acting in the public interest. He did make an important concession, though, on 28 April 1944. When asked about censoring the passage that claimed Calwell had 'abused his Ministerial powers', Bonney said 'I admit if I had to do that over again I probably would not cut out those words'.[84]

Calwell was not subdued. In June 1944, he took to Cabinet a dramatic seven-point plan for 'urgent and necessary ... reform of the daily press'. The plan was a catalogue of nightmares for the newspapers. It wanted newspaper advertisements taxed; newspaper staff, cover prices and newsprint supplies reduced; and newspapers prohibited from owning or operating broadcasting stations. The plan also argued the ABC should expand its independent news service. While that point was reasonable – and later implemented – others were unworkable and extraordinary, including a proposal that any person 'attacked or misrepresented by any newspaper' should have 'a right to an equal amount of space in an equally prominent position in the next edition' to defend themselves.[85] The newspapers viewed Calwell's proposals as clearly motivated by revenge and his colleagues were in no hurry to adopt the more extreme or impractical ideas.

Of course, the papers were not above enacting some vengeance themselves. In December 1944, John Frith joined the *Sydney Morning*

Herald as its first staff cartoonist. Frith suspected he was hired specifically because the paper's executives knew 'I had no particular love for Arthur Calwell'. They asked Frith to work out a way to 'shut up' Calwell because the minister spent so much time attacking the press that their paper had to respond and this all 'took up space … [that] could be used for advertising or for a news item'. Frith came up with the idea of drawing Calwell as a cranky cockatoo sitting on a perch shrieking 'Curse the press'. Calwell's opponents took to mimicking the cry throughout the House and Frith's delighted employers gave him a huge pay rise of £500 a year.[86]

Hostilities continued to erupt periodically. In November 1944, Calwell criticised Packer and the *Daily Telegraph* for publishing, in defiance of the censor, details of the deaths of Japanese prisoners of war following the Cowra detention centre breakout.[87] The *Daily Telegraph* responded with a front page article calling Calwell 'a dishonest calculating liar' and again inviting him to sue.[88] Calwell did sue Penton for £25 000 in damages but the High Court ruled that, due to Calwell's prior verbal attacks on him, Penton could plead qualified privilege. Calwell withdrew his action because the ruling meant the newspaper could win even if what it said was untrue.[89]

FIGURE 3.5 *Sydney Morning Herald* cartoonist John Frith represents Arthur Calwell as a cockatoo because of his raspy voice and repetitive complaints against the press
SOURCE *Sydney Morning Herald*, circa 1945.

He also said privately, 'I cannot afford to fight this rich press combine. The obvious intention of this newspaper is to destroy me financially.'[90]

Calwell also continued to verbally spar with Henderson and said in parliament in March 1946 that, if the Japanese had landed in Australia:

> the first persons to fling up their greasy hands and surrender would have been the members of the editorial boards of the *Sydney Morning Herald* and the Sydney *Sun*. I know that Quilp-like creature, Henderson, and I know that had Australia been overcome the *Sydney Morning Herald* would not have ceased publication. It would have come out the following day as the *Sydney Morning Shimbun*, with Henderson still as editor.[91]

'Quilp' was a reference to the short, grotesque and vicious villain of Dickens' *The Old Curiosity Shop*. The *Sydney Morning Herald* reported Calwell's speech on its front page, adding an editor's note at the bottom that said Calwell was 'deliberately and maliciously lying'.[92]

For the rest of his career, Calwell believed that his speeches and statements were deliberately suppressed by the press.[93] Murdoch replied to one of Calwell's many complaints of suppression with just one line: 'I note that you still greatly exaggerate the public interest in, and public importance of, your statements'.[94] Calwell responded: 'I shall hold [this] against you for use when I deem the occasion a suitable one'.[95] Standing up to press barons was one thing but Calwell was also notorious among journalists for threatening to have them sacked.

Calwell used his confrontations with the capitalist press as a way to demonstrate his Labor credentials but he also relished the conflict. When the *Sydney Morning Herald* gave him a rare compliment for making a sensible decision, Calwell complained to journalist Ross Gollan that 'In no circumstances did he wish to see himself praised by the *Sydney Morning Herald*'.[96] Calwell said in 1945 that 'I have done my best to defend democracy against its enemies in the editorial chairs of certain newspapers'.[97]

Unlike many other politicians, Calwell at least had the courage to express in public what he thought in private about press owners and executives. Whether this was wise for an ambitious politician is another matter. After 1944, the newspapers did all they could to damage Calwell's public image by minimising his achievements, ridiculing him and portraying him as melodramatic and unhinged. According to historian Colm Kiernan, this denied Calwell his chance of leading the Labor Party after the death of Curtin's successor, Ben Chifley, in 1951.[98] But Calwell's time would come, and politics makes such strange bedfellows that one of his press enemies would become a strong supporter in 1961 (Chapter 13).

CHAPTER 4
NEW BEGINNINGS

After the censorship dispute, through the final days of the war, came a new lobby group aimed at bringing down the Curtin government, a fresh start for Menzies as head of a new political party, and a new Labor prime minister, Ben Chifley. Remarkably, Menzies' new political party was founded with the consent of the country's press barons secured over dinner. Probably no other mature, liberal democracy could claim such a close involvement by the press in the formation of one of their country's two major political parties.

By then, the wartime truce with the Labor government was over. Calwell and censorship had been two factors behind the compact fraying, but the newspapers also wanted an end to central planning and had been sending direct warnings that the government should tread carefully when planning for reconstruction.[1] There was also a growing view in the business community that the Curtin government had proven itself incapable of managing labour demands and industrial disputes. In September 1944, the *Sydney Morning Herald* lamented a 'wave of strikes' that had hit transport, the waterfront, coal mines, munitions, meat works and manufacturing.[2] Now, the issue of industrial relations was about to hit home at the Sydney newspapers, turning them even more sharply away from the Labor government.

STRIKES HIT THE PAPERS

The prospect of a strike always caused genuine fear among newspaper owners and managers. Unlike other businesses, newspapers could not store up a supply of product in case of industrial action. They had a product for only one day, then had to make an entirely new one the next day. The newspaper business also depended upon creating a daily buying habit in readers. If a paper ceased publishing, even for only a day, readers might switch to a rival, or might discover that missing out on their daily paper was not so bad after all and break their buying habit. Worst of all, if retail and other sales continued as normal, then advertisers might start to question why they were spending so much on newspaper advertising.

For all these reasons, management usually assiduously avoided strikes through conciliation. When a strike occurred in Sydney in October 1944, it was the first serious one by daily newspaper printers since the 19th century.[3] It started at Associated Newspapers' *Sun* where printers, like workers in other industries, were pressing industrial claims they had held back during the emergency days of the war. The printers' claim for a 40-hour week and four weeks' annual leave was denied. When they read a report about the Industrial Court proceedings in their own paper, a report which they considered unfair, they stopped work on 7 October, backed by the Printing Industry Employees' Union of Australia (PIEUA).

The *Sun* management sent all its copy to Norton's *Daily Mirror* office so a joint *Sun-Daily Mirror* afternoon paper could be printed but *Daily Mirror* production staff stopped work in solidarity. Consolidated Press employees then refused to publish Norton's *Truth* jointly with the *Sunday Telegraph*, and *Sydney Morning Herald* employees refused to publish a *Sunday Sun* for Associated Newspapers at their office.[4]

As the strike spread to all four of Sydney's daily newspapers, the proprietors activated their 'one-in, all-in' principle and decided to publish a composite paper carrying all four mastheads. Journalists and the AJA now became involved. The AJA was normally considered a conciliatory white-collar union that cooperated with management and owners. It had not participated in strike action since 1912 in Perth.[5] The AJA declared the composite paper to be illegal and, after a vote at a large general meeting, journalists joined production staff on strike.[6]

The owners used non-union labour and executives from the four papers to publish a four-page composite at the *Sydney Morning Herald* office from 9 to 20 October (Figure 4.1). The presses at the other three papers remained silent. The broadsheet composite paper most resembled the *Sydney Morning Herald* but included features from the other papers,

FIGURE 4.1 The historic use of four mastheads on the owners' strike-breaking combined newspaper, Sydney, 9 October 1944
SOURCE State Library of New South Wales.

such as cartoons. (Noting its audience was not scandalised by them, the prim *Sydney Morning Herald* introduced its own cartoons once the strike was over, including hiring the Calwell-baiting John Frith.)[7]

Within 48 hours, the AJA and PIEUA strikers published their own ten-page tabloid called *The News*. It was printed at the Communist Party's *Newsletter* printery without the benefit of trials or dummy runs. A volunteer editorial team worked firstly out of the cramped Journalists' Club, then took up an offer to work out of the Communist Party's headquarters, Green Coupon House (known as Marx House). *The News* was the first paper produced solely by the AJA and run independently of proprietors. It sold out its 100 000 copies each day of its nine-day run. It had the advantage of better distribution than the owners' hybrid because railway staff and the Road Transport Union refused to carry a 'scab' paper and the Newsboys'

Association refused to sell it. Even so, the owners still managed to sell about three times more copies of their composite paper than the strikers' paper.[8]

Newspaper workers were shocked by the bitterness of the dispute. At one newspaper office, it pitted father against son. At the *Daily Telegraph*, hundreds of staff assembled in an untidy queue on 9 October waiting to be called into the chief-of-staff's office. One by one, he wearily asked if they would work for the composite paper. If they replied 'no', he told them they were sacked. This process was repeated at other papers, including the *Daily Mirror* where Ezra Norton asked his managers how many staff refused to work for the composite. 'All but three', he was told. According to legend, Norton was unimpressed by their lack of solidarity with their colleagues and replied, 'Miserable bastards, sack them too'. At the *Sydney Morning Herald*, Henderson told the father of the printers' chapel to get 'your bastard mob ... out of here'. And at the *Sun*, the chief executive of Associated Newspapers, Eric Kennedy, made a notorious offer that any journalist who stood against their union would have a job for life.[9]

At a time of growing fear that communism had infected the union movement and was spreading throughout the nation, the strikers' use of Communist Party headquarters and equipment provoked intense reactions. Rupert Henderson argued the strike was not a normal industrial dispute but 'part of a comprehensive Communist newspaper' plot to take control of public utilities and start up a daily newspaper. He said communists in the New South Wales branch of the AJA were involved and that communists had stolen several thousand copies of the employers' composite paper and thrown them into Sydney Harbour.[10]

It took a case before the full bench of the Industrial Commission, and then consultation between newspaper representatives and the Labour Council, to work out settlement terms for the strike. These were accepted at a mass meeting of the unions on 19 October. The principles of a 40-hour week and four weeks' leave were broadly accepted, although it was some time before they were fully adopted. The strikers had demonstrated strong resistance by publishing *The News* and it helped them win concessions from their employers, but hopes that the paper would morph into an Australian version of London's left-wing *Daily Herald* were unrealistic. *The News* had enjoyed the benefits of no wages and no overheads but that could not last.[11]

And although the proprietors had been startled by the emergence of a well-distributed independent rival, they had managed to jointly publish a better-selling composite paper throughout the 13 days. The owners had served notice that they could withstand industrial action and would band together to do so, which helped discourage future claims and actions.

As part of the settlement terms, owners and executives had agreed to refrain from victimisation but Penton made sure that activist staff felt they had no option but to leave the *Daily Telegraph*. He also sacked two cartoonists who refused to sign anti-union cartoons.[12] Some of the key figures involved in the strike, such as Don Whitington of the *Daily Telegraph*, who acted as chief-of-staff on the strikers' paper, spent years doing freelance work before he was able to get back into the industry.[13] On the other side of the dispute, some of the 'scabs' who worked for the owners' composite paper were ostracised by the strikers, and in some cases, not spoken to for years afterward.

The strike hardened the newspaper owners' attitudes to the Labor government, especially because they felt that Labor ministers Arthur Calwell and Eddie Ward appeared to be cheering on the strikers. The proprietors became even more concerned about industrial conflict and the influence of communism and extremism.[14] In January 1945, the *Sydney Morning Herald* published a full page on the dangers of communism, warning of 'chaos', 'violence' and a 'dictatorship of the proletariat' achieved by 'forcible overthrow'. It said communists had captured the unions and infiltrated the education system.[15] In late 1944 and early 1945, the *Daily Telegraph* ran multiple articles warning of the '"THREAT" TO PRIVATE ENTERPRISE', of communism in the coal industry, universities and even high schools.[16] The Melbourne *Herald* and other papers also warned of the dangers of the 'RED MENACE'.[17]

A NEW LOBBY GROUP

A belief that the Labor government was too close to communists, and too invested in policies that were holding back private enterprise, was motivating the emergence of new political coalitions. New groupings were needed because the UAP's electoral defeat in 1943 had been so comprehensive that the *Daily Telegraph* had declared the party 'dead'.[18] Aside from the public brawling, policy inertia and organisational inefficiency, the UAP had also been damaged by public revelations about its shadowy finance committees, the Consultative Council in Sydney and the Melbourne-based National Union. Warwick Fairfax had contributed to this by writing columns in the *Sydney Morning Herald* that helped disclose the UAP was highly dependent on a small number of wealthy backers who tried to dictate party policy. He had broken ranks with wealthy friends in Sydney to make those revelations.

When Menzies had taken up the leadership of the UAP again in September 1943, it was on condition that his colleagues give him the right to develop a new party.[19] Menzies recognised the UAP was discredited beyond resurrection and he set about uniting the non-Labor side of politics under a new banner. Politically active businessmen had also assumed responsibility for transforming the depleted conservative forces into a new party.

The *Herald* announced in May 1943 that a 'group of leading Melbourne business men' had established the Institute of Public Affairs (IPA) to promote 'political freedom' and 'economic freedom'.[20] The newspaper noted that its own chairman, Keith Murdoch, was an IPA founder and serving as one of 14 members of its inaugural Council. For Murdoch, the war years under Labor had been a period of 'agony' and 'disappointment'.[21] The IPA was a step beyond journalistic criticism into political activism.

The idea for the IPA had come from a report commissioned by Sir Herbert Gepp, an industrial chemist, and written by his assistant, the economist Charles Kemp, for the Victorian Chamber of Manufactures in 1942. Gepp had worked for Collins House for 20 years, in mining and metals and then in paper making.[22] Kemp's report concluded that the position of business in 'the political sphere ... was dangerously weak' as a result of the UAP's decline.[23]

Fearing that socialist ideas had gained force during World War II and that private enterprise was under threat, the unambiguous purpose of the IPA was to 'combat socialism' and its major promoters in the Labor Party and the trade unions.[24] None of this was mentioned in the group's publicity, nor in the *Herald*'s promotional announcement. Instead, the IPA was disingenuously said to be a 'non-political' group formed to 'support and assist the government in the prosecution of the war', promote employment and study 'post-war reconstruction problems'.[25]

The first chairman of the IPA in Victoria was George Coles, chairman of the Coles retail group, which was one of the HWT's largest advertisers. Coles and his brothers had built a chain of more than 80 Coles stores nationwide, modelled on American 'five and dime' stores. But clothing rationing enforced by the Curtin government was hurting business. The company's sales had fallen by £1 million in 1943 and two stores had closed.[26] Like other industrialists, Coles was looking forward to pent-up demand for goods creating a postwar sales boom but worried the Labor government would put the brakes on that by continuing with wartime controls even after the war had ended.[27]

Another inaugural IPA council member was Harold Darling, the publicity-shy chairman of Australia's most profitable public company, the mining giant and steel producer, Broken Hill Proprietary Ltd (BHP). Darling was a former leader of the National Union, the body which held the purse strings of the UAP in Victoria. He too had many gripes with the Curtin government. Despite BHP's rapid growth during the early years of the war when Australian steel was in high demand, BHP had recently had to reduce its dividend. It had been beset by industrial stoppages and strikes affecting productivity, and it was paying more in taxes than it was making in final profits. In December 1943, industrial disputes took a turn for the worse and Curtin invoked the *National Security Act* to compel BHP to reopen its Newcastle steelworks after stoppages led to a lockout of more than 6000 workers. BHP was planning for peace and saw the expansion of manufacturing – without government interference – as a key to postwar profits.[28]

Sitting alongside Murdoch, Coles and Darling on the IPA council was Leslie McConnan, chief manager of the National Bank of Australasia. The National Bank was a Collins House- and BHP-connected bank (Darling was on its board from 1934 to 1959). It was also the HWT's banker. Banking was one of the industries that was considered most under threat from Labor's policies. McConnan had been worried since the 1930s that a 'socialist government' would try to 'nationalise banking'.[29] The Labor government's wartime controls and its emphasis on central banking were viewed as heading in that direction, and by 1943 they had caused private bank deposits and profits to decline. The National Bank had closed branches, and like other private banks, was less independent and less important than previously.[30]

The vice-chairman of the HWT, Harold Giddy, was chairman of the National Bank (he had been elected to the position in March 1943, just as the IPA was starting). Giddy was a pillar of commercial life in Melbourne and, like his fellow National Bank directors, Darling and McConnan, he was strongly opposed to Labor's nationalised banking policy.[31] Giddy had sat on the HWT board for more than ten years with Murdoch and was also Murdoch's confidant and personal banker.

In New South Wales, an IPA was also established in 1943 by prominent businessmen. Many of them were former members of the secretive Consultative Council which had funded the UAP, and some were members of the Old Guard, a 1930s paramilitary group that had trained to use force to prevent a socialist revolution.[32]

The *Sydney Morning Herald* introduced the IPA as a group that would wage a 'FIGHT AGAINST BUREAUCRACY' and had 'No political ties'.[33] But where Murdoch was so supportive of the IPA that he was a founding member, Warwick Fairfax wrote under his pseudonym, 'A Political Observer', in the *Sydney Morning Herald* that the IPA was 'the consultative council with a new façade'. He said it was 'no more public than the College of Cardinals, and is chosen in the same way – by co-option'. Fairfax acknowledged the IPA was formed to represent the interests of big business. He said at least business was well run generally, but it 'is just a tragedy that [the IPA founders] do not see that a healthy political system is not a thing that you can go out and buy with money ...'.[34]

British media emperor Lord Beaverbrook once said, 'The big draper is the biggest customer of the press.'[35] Here Fairfax was criticising two of the biggest drapers in Sydney – Charles Lloyd Jones and Sydney Snow – who were both founding members of the IPA.

Charles Lloyd Jones, chairman of the David Jones department store group, became chairman of the IPA in New South Wales. His grandfather, David Jones, was a close friend and financial backer of Warwick's great-grandfather, John Fairfax, in the 1850s–1870s. The two families were still close, and David Jones was a very important advertiser for the *Sydney Morning Herald*. Jones was another who had concerns about the government's impact on business. Profits from the three David Jones stores had been affected by higher taxation and rationing.[36] Jones had a lot of backroom influence on conservative politics as a fundraiser and influential voice, including previously as chairman of the UAP's Consultative Council.[37]

Sydney Snow, of the Snow's soft goods emporium, was also a former chairman of the UAP's Consultative Council and key figure in the UAP. As a director of Broken Hill South Ltd, Snow was connected with Collins House and had once been a deputy chairman of Associated Newspapers. Snow had been rallying against John Dedman, the minister for war organisation of industry, for years, and had fought against labour transfers from retailing firms to war production, as well as clothing rationing, company taxation and price controls.[38]

Like the Victorian IPA, the New South Wales IPA also had a newspaper director on its inaugural council – Septimus Rowe, a director of Associated Newspapers and AMP. Among the other men Warwick Fairfax was implicitly criticising as founders of the IPA were Norman Kater, a director of CSR and Newcastle-Wallsend Coal (which had been affected by industrial stoppages); TH Kelly, a director of the Bank of New South Wales; Cecil Hoskins, manager and director of Australian Iron and Steel (a BHP subsidiary also affected by strikes in the coal industry) and Cecil Scott Waine, chairman of Woolworths chain stores.[39]

Directors of some of Australia's largest companies were involved in founding the IPA. Its goal of fighting socialism was so popular that the IPA's coffers were soon well filled. It paid for a series of anti-government advertisements in the lead-up to the 1943 election as well as advertisements supporting the 'no' campaign for the August 1944 referendum. At that referendum, the federal government sought enlarged powers to facilitate postwar rebuilding.[40]

Many business leaders believed the '14 powers' referendum was a leap towards socialism. Unusually for such an important issue, the daily newspapers were divided. The *Daily Telegraph* enthusiastically supported a 'yes' vote. Murdoch personally advocated a 'yes' vote and the *Herald* followed his lead. *The Age* also supported the 'yes' case. But other papers were strongly opposed, especially the *Argus* and the *Sydney Morning Herald*, but also the *Sun*, *Advertiser*, *Courier-Mail*, *West Australian* and *Mercury*. This division was a sign of just how fragmented and ineffective the non-Labor side of politics had become after the UAP's 1943 election loss. The referendum was defeated.

Warwick Fairfax was critical of the IPA, despite his family and business links to some of its founders, but the momentum was building to revitalise the conservative side of politics and Fairfax and the *Sydney Morning Herald* would not long stand apart.

A NEW POLITICAL PARTY

Menzies had continued cultivating a better relationship with newspaper proprietors but, like many in the business community, Murdoch needed convincing that the public would support Menzies after the failure of his first stint as prime minister.[41] Packer's support was also crucial. A Liberal Party official later wrote that the *Daily Telegraph* 'is the most important [newspaper] to us because it has the largest circulation in [NSW] and undoubtedly is read by more swinging voters than any other paper'.[42] At a dinner in July 1942, Menzies tried to convince Packer and Theodore to support his efforts to resurrect his career and build a new party. Murdoch and Henderson were also there.[43]

Hoping to imitate the success achieved by Don Rodgers with Curtin's press relations, in March 1944 Menzies hired his own press secretary, a former *Age* Canberra reporter, Charles Meeking.[44] During August 1944, Meeking promoted Menzies' vigorous opposition to the '14 powers' referendum. The failure of the referendum gave the non-Labor side a morale boost and Menzies seized the momentum. He organised a Canberra conference for October 1944 aimed at uniting the many non-Labor groups that had sprung up following the disintegration of the UAP into a new political party.

At some point during the second half of 1944, possibly in August when he was visiting from London, WS Robinson, the influential Collins House leader and managing director of the Zinc Corporation, organised an important dinner party in Melbourne. It was held at the home of James Fitzgerald, a senior executive of New Broken Hill Consolidated. Over dinner and drinks, Robert Menzies sought the blessing of the country's most powerful press owners and managers. Keith Murdoch (HWT), Rupert Henderson (Fairfax), Frank Packer (Consolidated Press) and Eric Kennedy (Associated Newspapers) were all present.[45] The *Sydney Morning Herald* historian, Gavin Souter, wrote that, by the end of the dinner, 'It was agreed that all would do what they could to bring the new party into existence'.[46]

The attendees vowed to do everything they could to make sure the new party would appeal to the public and could win elections. Given their combined hold over newspapers, magazines and radio, there was a considerable amount they could do.[47] Of course, none of this secret compact was disclosed in the attendees' respective newspapers, and nor is the remarkable dinner mentioned in official accounts of the Liberal Party's history.[48]

Frank Packer eagerly took up the chance to play a role alongside Menzies. On 31 August, the *Daily Telegraph*'s headline was 'TIME FOR A NEW PARTY'.[49] Through September and October, Menzies was lauded for his 'outstanding' parliamentary performance and for bringing 'a new cohesion and vigor to the Opposition parties', a 'new fighting spirit which has been lacking'.[50]

When the Canberra conference was held from 13 to 16 October 1944, it was attended by 18 different anti-Labor groups. Newspaper groups were especially interested because it was held right in the middle of the Sydney newspapers' strike, just when they were most despairing of Labor's record on industrial issues, its harbouring of socialists in its ranks, and the growing threat of communist influence. Menzies impressed the conference with his intellect and oratorical flair. His position as the only realistic contender to resuscitate the conservative side of politics was shored up.

On the final day of the conference, the name 'Liberal Party of Australia' was adopted, a revival of the name used by Alfred Deakin for his party in the early Federation years. This was reported with approval by the newspapers whose support had been pledged at the Melbourne dinner: 'LIBERALS APPEAL TO ALL' (*Sun*); 'NEW LIBERALISM WILL TAKE A POSITIVE LINE' (*Herald*).[51] The owners' strike-breaking combined paper called the October convention 'highly successful' and applauded the 'NEW PARTY'S "POSITIVE" PROGRAMME'.[52]

A later meeting aimed at further cementing newspaper support for the Liberal Party was held in Sydney at the T & G Building, owned by Frank Packer's brother-in-law, Anthony Hordern. At this time, Menzies was so keen to involve the press barons that he asked Rupert Henderson to suggest a federal president for the party and to nominate a chairman for the NSW branch.[53]

Just weeks after the October newspaper strike in Sydney, when the *Sun* was asking 'CAN CURTIN HALT LABOR'S MOVE TO SOCIALISM?', the Labor government announced that it planned to nationalise the airlines. Internationally, this was not all that unusual at the time as a way to develop the new industry of consumer aviation.[54] But in Australia, there were two major airlines, Australian National Airways Ltd (ANA) and Qantas, and ANA strenuously opposed the nationalisation of aviation. It was a donor to the Liberal Party, and its shareholders included Adelaide Steamship Co, an important South Australian company that was linked to the *Advertiser*'s board of directors.[55]

The *Daily Telegraph* argued strongly against 'government intervention' in the airlines by a process of nationalisation.[56] The HWT papers were also firmly against it. The *Argus* chastised Labor for its 'foolish' policy, declaring it 'one of the most serious attempts' ever made to 'tamper with the free enterprise system of this country'.[57] The *Sydney Morning Herald* approvingly quoted Menzies that the Commonwealth takeover of interstate air services was 'the first shot in the socialist war' and a 'confiscation' of private property.[58] There were fears that shipping could be the next industry nationalised.[59]

Coal strikes continued into December. At the Albury conference that month, Menzies quoted at length from 'Looking Forward', a manifesto for a postwar liberal agenda published by the IPA. The text had been approved by a small committee of the IPA that included Keith Murdoch and Harold Darling.[60] The manifesto focused on protecting and promoting free enterprise but it also embraced progressive elements such as national development, full employment and social security.[61] 'Looking Forward' gave Menzies positive policies just when he needed them most. Kemp told Gerard Henderson in 1989 that Menzies had been:

> rather frightened ... He felt that one of the problems in getting a progressive policy for the Liberal Party could be the opposition of business. And the fact that the IPA had come out with these ideas and had been supported by all the big business people [meant] he was absolutely delighted.[62]

The Liberal Party was provisionally constituted at the Albury conference. The Melbourne HWT papers gave their blessing. In Sydney, the *Sydney Morning Herald* put aside its long held reservations about Menzies and approvingly declared 'A FRESH START AT ALBURY'.[63] The *Sun* editorialised on 'THE NEED FOR LIBERALISM' 'against the growing evils of Communism, bureaucratic control and pressure politics'. It declared simply that 'MENZIES IS RIGHT'.[64] The *Daily Telegraph* supported the new party's 'positive programme'.[65]

The Liberal Party was formally launched at the Sydney Town Hall on 31 August 1945. Menzies was determined it should be a broad-based political movement focused on garnering the support of a wide constituency. He characterised them as 'the forgotten people'. Historian Stuart Macintyre noted that these were the salaried workers and self-employed who identified neither with the 'company boardrooms nor the tribal solidarity of the manual workers'.[66]

Fairfax & Sons directors were so convinced they started sending donations to the Liberal Party.[67] As Keith Murdoch's biographer, Ronald Younger, noted, Murdoch 'took a deep and special interest in the public standing of the Liberal party from its formation'.[68] In other words, he backed and promoted it to the hilt after the bitter disappointment of being on the outer during the Curtin government years.

A NEW LABOR LEADER

As the new Liberal Party was being created in late 1944, Curtin's health was failing. He had once been a heavy smoker and drinker, and was working 'at least a 16-hour day every day' during the war.[69] Curtin's staff and members of the circus noticed he was deeply affected by the suffering of troops, the decisions he had to make, and the stress of travelling. He carried the burdens of the war in a way that ran down his mental and physical health. Journalists privately confided to their superiors that Curtin was not well during particular stages of the war, but they did not publicly report how sick he was until the final days of Curtin's life.[70]

Sydney Morning Herald directors continued to hold Curtin in high esteem but had become far more critical of government decisions during 1944. Henderson wrote to Curtin on 1 April 1944, 'you have displayed qualities of statesmanship unsurpassed in the history of the Commonwealth', and although the *Sydney Morning Herald* disagreed with policy decisions, 'never have I doubted your sincerity ... or the complete dedication of your work'.[71]

On 3 November 1944, Curtin suffered a serious heart attack in Melbourne and was hospitalised for nearly two months. On 15 November, Henderson wrote to Curtin that 'in my opinion this country can never repay you for what you have done for it during these difficult years'.[72] But on the day Curtin started back at work in late January 1945, a *Sydney Morning Herald* article welcomed him back by listing all of the 'political troubles' the paper wanted Curtin to urgently deal with.[73]

Curtin's health remained poor and he was back in hospital in April 1945 with congestion of the lungs. He never recovered enough to resume his duties. In March, when Curtin was noticeably ill, he had asked the news editor of the *Sydney Morning Herald*, Angus McLachlan, 'Mac, when you get back to the office see if you can't get them to lay off me a bit'.[74] It was too late for that. The *Sydney Morning Herald* and other newspapers had begun implying that new leadership was needed, although they stopped short of demanding his resignation.

Two days before Curtin's death, Ross Gollan's column in the *Sydney Morning Herald* published details of his medical conditions and suggested he was unlikely to recover enough to resume his duties. It then speculated about who would replace him.[75] Henderson told Fadden, leader of the Country Party, that he had lost confidence in Curtin and Fadden duly passed this message on to the prime minister. Curtin then telephoned Henderson. The two men yelled at each other over the phone, using what Henderson later admitted was 'gutter language'. Soon afterwards, Curtin's press secretary Don Rodgers, crossed paths with Henderson in Parliament House. When Henderson offered a handshake in greeting, Rodgers ignored the outstretched hand, looked Henderson up and down, then turned on his heel and left. Curtin died early the next morning, 5 July 1945, just six weeks before victory in the Pacific.[76] Rodgers told press gallery reporters that he believed 'Henderson had killed Curtin'.[77]

It was a mark of journalists' respect for Curtin that almost every member of the press gallery took the long journey on the Trans-Continental Express to attend his funeral in Perth.[78] Curiously insensitive to the situation, Warwick Fairfax wrote a petty letter of complaint to the acting prime minister, Francis Forde, complaining that Rodgers had delivered an 'insult' to the *Sydney Morning Herald* by refusing to shake Henderson's hand.[79]

Curtin's treasurer and close friend, Ben Chifley, was sworn in as Australia's sixteenth prime minister. For the next four years, Chifley held the dual roles of prime minister and treasurer, a daunting workload even in those days. Although Harold Cox of the *Herald* privately judged that Chifley did not have Curtin's grasp of detail, 'impressiveness or mastery of the House', the pipe-smoking Chifley had a friendly nature and was known for his integrity, extraordinary calm and lack of pretension.[80] He was a popular figure with his colleagues, the public and even his political opponents, especially Menzies, who regarded Chifley as a friend.

The son of a blacksmith, Chifley had sought out educational opportunities and become a first-class locomotive engine driver before his grounding in the tough world of union and Labor politics. As wartime treasurer, Chifley was applauded by one of his biographers for his efficiency and frugality, which ensured that Australia's war effort was financed without the nation becoming 'burdened with overseas debt, as it had been after World War I'.[81] To achieve that, Chifley had used central planning, increased taxation, and introduced controls on production, trade and consumption, as well as price controls and central bank credit.

Chifley's taxes were deeply unpopular in the business community but he would not tolerate appeals for special favours, including from Murdoch's *Courier-Mail* partner, John Wren, on behalf of himself and EG Theodore, Packer's Consolidated Press partner.[82]

Chifley was yet another Australian prime minister who had a background in newspapers. On a very modest scale, he was a newspaper owner himself. He was a co-owner and director of one of his hometown's two newspapers, the Labor-leaning *National Advocate*, a Bathurst daily (1889–1963). Chifley held about 15 per cent of the company's shares.[83] His father Patrick had been a director of the paper, and after his death, Chifley was appointed to the board in 1922 in his place.[84] Unlike Curtin, whose journalism was central to his identity and experiences, Chifley had done some writing but focused more on the management side of running a regional paper.

Through the *National Advocate*, Chifley had been able to exercise significant influence on politics in Bathurst. It was not a great money earner though, securing him only £26 in dividends in 1948.[85] One of Chifley's biographers, LF Crisp, argued that Chifley undertook the role more out of a sense of community service than financial gain.[86] Unlike other politicians who were involved in newspapers, Chifley paid surprisingly little attention to the public relations side of politics – and this would be to his party's detriment over the next few years.

In the months immediately after the war's end, Chifley had to deal with growing industrial unrest. Steelworkers at BHP went on strike, joined by miners in the New South Wales coalfields and the Seamen's Union, which refused to crew ships carrying coal or steel in four states. The strikes led to severe transport and lighting restrictions in New South Wales, and affected industries that had strong links to newspapers, especially coal mining, steelworks and shipping.

Some newspaper companies had directors sitting on the boards of affected companies. For example, John Butters, chairman of Associated Newspapers, was also a director of coal company Hetton Bellbird Collieries. Lloyd Dumas, managing director of the *Advertiser*, was also a director of Elder Smith and Co, a woolbroking and pastoral finance company on whose board sat directors from BHP and Adelaide Steamship.[87] Large shareholders in several newspaper groups (such as the National Bank, AMP and the Baillieu family) were also major shareholders in BHP, Melbourne Steamship, Adelaide Steamship and other companies heavily affected by the strikes.

The newspapers attributed the industrial chaos to the influence of communists in leadership positions in trade unions, including unions that Labor relied upon for electoral and political support. The Melbourne *Herald* editorialised that communists were seeking to 'seize control of trade unionism in Australia and to establish a communist dictatorship over Australian industry'.[88] The *Sydney Morning Herald* and *Daily Telegraph* also described an ongoing 'battle against Communist infiltration' of trade unions.[89]

THE 1946 ELECTION AND AN INDUSTRY SPLIT

When the war's end finally released the 'pent-up demand' for goods and services that industrialists had been hoping for, it led to a shortage of housing and household goods.[90] Chifley asked Australians to be patient as the country converted from a war economy, based on centralised planning and austerity, to peacetime conditions. But business and newspaper owners keen to take up the commercial opportunities were in no mood to wait.

Menzies opened the Liberal Party's 1946 election campaign by offering better conditions, more individual freedom and a 20 per cent reduction in income tax. Chifley's speech was austere by comparison. He refused to make new promises, said that further income tax reductions would not be prudent and instead asked voters to re-elect the government based on its record.

Packer's *Daily Telegraph* strongly endorsed the new Liberal Party, applauded Menzies' promised tax reductions, and said that married couples waiting for a home, women who had to wait in queues at the shops, and 'businessmen shackled with heart-breaking restrictions' would all benefit from being 'rid of' the Labor government.[91] The *Daily Telegraph* said Liberal Party policies were the best way to end years of shortages and lift the 'dismal burden' of taxation.[92]

The *Sydney Morning Herald* was also won over by Menzies' proposed tax cuts, declaring that 'beyond any doubt this is a "tax election"'.[93] Unusually, the Melbourne *Herald* put its editorial advice on its front page, telling voters 'IT'S VERY SIMPLE'; the Liberals deserved victory because of their 'promise to lift some of the great tax burdens' and lead the 'revival of personal liberty'.[94] Other papers, such as the *West Australian* and the *Advertiser* took a similar stance and the *Mercury* opened its election eve editorial by saying that 'Reduction of taxes ... would be one of the most vital and beneficial acts of government in the history of the federation'.[95] The new Liberal Party had found a reliable way to win newspaper support – promise lower taxes. The *Daily Mirror* was the only metropolitan daily to advocate a vote for Labor.

Despite the lack of newspaper support and attractive new promises, Labor won the election. The Liberal Party gained several seats though, and throughout 1947 Labor's appeal was weakening. The public was growing weary of austerity, delays and strikes. Among the powerbrokers and business leaders who were concerned that Menzies was not electable, resistance eased. Menzies recalled in a 1972 interview that it was around 1946 when 'they began to swing around and by say 1949, I was the answer ... It took a long time.'[96]

Murdoch still had doubts. Impatient with the Liberal Party's failure to make significant gains in public opinion in 1946, and perhaps also with Menzies' lack of pliability (always a barrier between them), Murdoch was promoting his friend, the former MP and ambassador to the United States, Richard Casey, as an alternative leader of the Coalition. In August 1947, Murdoch's newspapers prominently reported a Gallup poll that found 18 per cent of Labor voters would vote for the Liberal or Country parties if Menzies was not the leader. The *Herald*'s report was headlined 'BIGGER VOTE FOR LIBERALS IF MENZIES NOT LEADER?' and the *Courier-Mail*'s report was even stronger. It was not framed as a question but a statement: 'LIBERAL-CP STRONGER IF MENZIES OUT'.[97]

A fed-up Menzies wrote to Murdoch accusing him of using the poll as a 'calculated blow'. In testy letters between them, Murdoch protested that the polls were well conducted and should not be suppressed just because they were against Menzies' interests. Menzies replied that the questions used in polls were not 'divinely inspired' but 'chosen by human beings' and he complained about a poll that was 'so unnecessary and so hostile'. He (correctly) suggested that Murdoch must usually have knowledge of, if not a hand in developing, the questions asked in Morgan's Gallup polls. Murdoch replied by saying that Menzies should have interpreted the poll as a reminder that he needed to 'build up a team around him' and said, 'I cannot help it' if instead 'you choose … to make yet another series of slurring statements about newspapers'. Menzies responded that he was not questioning the accuracy of the poll, but he believed the question about leadership was a 'loaded one' and 'completely misleading' because no other name was proposed as an alternative leader to him. Murdoch wrote a note to his pollster in the margin: 'Mr Morgan, There may be something in this point'.[98]

Two weeks after the poll was reported, Menzies took the chance to clear up the sniping and speculation about his leadership. He resigned from the parliamentary leadership at the second Liberal Party council on 1 September 1947, challenged the party to replace him, and was then unanimously endorsed. Labor government policy on newsprint then pushed the newspapers further into his corner.

Even after war's end, each newspaper was still being given a quota of newsprint based on the quantity it had used in the base year of 1938–39. And newsprint was still being administered through a voluntary newsprint pool. When importation of newsprint was temporarily suspended in 1942, the newspapers had banded together to form a pool of newsprint so no paper would be forced out of production. The voluntary pool worked so well that the newspapers retained it after the war had ended and shortages were still a problem.

The arrangement was upset towards the end of 1947 though, after the pound became convertible to dollars. Holders of sterling in Britain's trading partners converted their sterling to dollars so rapidly that it caused a monetary crisis. The Chifley government had to lower dollar expenditure quickly and one method it used was to force a drastic reduction in newsprint imports from the American dollar area, including Canada. The government decided to restrict consumption of newsprint to 90 000 tons a year for all Australian newspapers. This reduction approximated the deepest wartime cut.[99]

The newspaper groups started fighting among themselves over how to distribute the much-reduced allocation of newsprint. Two factions developed. The Murdoch and Packer groups joined forces and wanted revised quotas based on circulation. Since 1938, the HWT's best sellers, the *Sun News-Pictorial* and the *Herald*, had grown in circulation by more than 150 000 each, and Packer's *Daily Telegraph* had grown by 122 000. Meanwhile, other papers had less than half that growth. For instance, the *Sydney Morning Herald* and the *Argus* had grown by only 52 000 and 24 000 respectively.[100] Murdoch and Packer argued the basis for sharing newsprint had become unfair, and slow-growth papers with lots of advertisements and big broadsheet pages (like the *Sydney Morning Herald* and *The Age*) were receiving more paper than they could use and were hoarding it, while the most popular newspapers were not receiving enough. They wanted the formula changed. In August, Packer withdrew his company from the newsprint pool. He and Murdoch travelled to Canberra to lobby Chifley.[101]

The government soon grew tired of trying to mediate between squabbling press barons. In November 1947, Chifley lamented in parliament that the 'newspaper proprietors themselves [had not] been able to get together and recommend a system of distribution which would be accepted by all parties as reasonable and equitable …'.[102] The quota took effect on 1 January 1948. The newspapers reduced in size and circulation to wartime proportions and tensions boiled over. The Murdoch and Packer papers resigned from the ANPA in February 1948 and set up their own breakaway group, the Australian Newspapers' Council (ANC). After the paper situation eased internationally, newsprint rationing was lifted in November but Murdoch and Packer remained enraged at the government. Murdoch privately told staff that it was the most difficult year he had faced 'during 26 years of chief executive work' and that 'the newspapers had been deliberately trampled upon' by the government.[103]

CHAPTER 5
BANKING ON THE PRESS

Labor's plan to take on the banks in the 1940s meant taking on the newspapers too. In 1940, Curtin had declared Labor's policy was 'national control of banking and credit' to ensure full employment, control interest rates and keep down the costs of the war, industry and production. Curtin saw the Commonwealth Bank, which had been founded in 1911 as a government-owned trading and savings bank, as 'the logical instrument' for those measures and for 'providing the machinery of post-war reconstruction'.[1] This policy was going to devastate Australia's privately owned trading banks and had encouraged bank leaders to become active in the IPA (Chapter 4).

To manage postwar conditions, the Chifley government wanted to continue wartime restraints on the economy, including controlling the volume of credit, as a way to guide the transition from war to peace, and to create jobs, provide housing and stimulate trade and development. Labor MPs and supporters viewed the party's victory in the 1946 election as an endorsement of these policies, and Chifley was personally prepared to carry the fight for banking nationalisation whatever the result.

Chifley was haunted by memories of poverty and suffering during the Depression and he bitterly recalled the role that commercial banks had played in the Scullin government's downfall when they frustrated government policies for even mild economic stimulus measures aimed at alleviating unemployment. For Chifley, full employment and avoiding inflation were non-negotiable goals. He had strong views on banking and a grasp of financial matters that dated from his service as Labor's representative on the 1935 Royal Commission into banking and finance. Chifley had spent 18 months studying the issues before writing a minority report that advocated bank nationalisation.[2]

Labor's main complaints about the private trading banks were articulated by Eddie Ward, the federal minister for transport, who was often described in newspapers as 'the fiery socialist member for East Sydney'.[3] Ward argued there was no real competition between the banks, that they instead acted as a powerful cartel and had deeply entwined themselves with Australia's major companies – including BHP, Colonial Sugar Refining Company (CSR), breweries, shipping, insurance, woolbrokers and newspapers – as a way of controlling 'the financial policy of the country'.[4]

BANKS AND NEWSPAPERS

It was true that bank directors sat on the boards of many of Australia's largest companies, and had connections to major newspaper groups (Table 5.1). Connections between banks and newspapers dated back to the early days of both industries. George Howe, owner of the first newspaper in Australia, the *Sydney Gazette* (established 1803), was simultaneously one of the first 14 shareholders of the Bank of New South Wales when it began in 1817.[5] In the 130 years since then, banks had passed through a period of growth and competition, followed by rounds of consolidation and takeovers, similar to the trajectory of the metropolitan newspapers.

By the mid-1940s, only nine private trading banks were left. The Bank of New South Wales was by far the largest bank in the country. Left-wing activists called it, and the Commercial Banking Co of Sydney, the 'sugar banks' because of their connection with CSR.[6] CSR's major owner and chairman, Sir Edward Knox, sat on the board of the Commercial Banking Co for 37 years. His son also sat on that board, plus the Bank of New South Wales board. When the Chifley government began seriously considering bank nationalisation in the mid-1940s, Knox's grandson, Edward Ritchie Knox, was chairman of both CSR and the Commercial Banking Co.[7]

The Fairfax family had a long connection to the sugar banks and to CSR. Warwick Fairfax's great-grandfather, John Fairfax, was a trustee of the Bank of New South Wales. His grandfather, James Reading Fairfax, was on the Bank of New South Wales and the Commercial Banking Co boards, sitting alongside the Knoxes. In the mid-1940s, Warwick Fairfax still had two uncles who sat on the boards of the sugar banks (Table 5.1).[8] Associated Newspapers was also connected to the Bank of New South Wales. One of Australia's wealthiest men, Sir Frederick Tout, sat on both boards and became chairman of the Bank of New South Wales's board of directors, 1945–50.[9]

In Victoria, South Australia and Tasmania, the dominant banks were instead the National Bank, the English, Scottish & Australian Bank Ltd (ES&A) and the Commercial Bank of Australasia. These were dubbed the 'metal banks' because of their strong links with mining, and especially with BHP and Collins House.[10] The Baillieu family connected the HWT and the metal banks. One of the HWT's major shareholders and key directors between the 1890s and 1920s, WL Baillieu, had been a bank clerk, a bank loan defaulter, and then a bank investor who bought up cheap bank shares after the bank collapses of the 1890s. He bought a stake in the London Bank of Australia, arranged a merger with the ES&A, and collected a fortune that helped him wind his way back from bankruptcy and into mining.[11] Baillieu had been one of ES&A's biggest shareholders, and in the 1940s, ES&A was still Collins House's banker. WL's son, Clive (a friend of Murdoch's), was a director of ES&A, and from London very concerned about Labor's banking policy.[12]

The National Bank was the HWT's banker and one of its largest shareholders, and this helps explain Harold Giddy's dual role as chairman of the National Bank and deputy chairman and then chairman, of the HWT. Some of the HWT's top individual shareholders also had large shareholdings in the National Bank, including the children of Mark Schwarz, a former bookmaker. The Schwarz siblings had inherited their father's shares in the HWT, National Bank and Commercial Banking Co when he died in 1944.[13]

Banks were a powerful influence at the HWT but they had also become important to Murdoch personally during the 1940s. As he worked to build up a newspaper empire to hand on to his son, Rupert, Keith borrowed heavily from banks, life insurance and private lenders. He was in serious debt.[14] He had mortgages and a large overdraft with the National Bank, whose chairman sat alongside him on the HWT board.[15]

TABLE 5.1 Newspaper and bank links, 1940s–early 1950s

Newspaper group	Banks historically associated with	Bank name in 2022 (following mergers)	Key bank links through directors	Other finance company links through directors
HWT	National Bank	NAB	Harold Giddy (HWT deputy chairman and National Bank chairman).	AMP
	Bank of Adelaide	ANZ		Union Trustee Co
	English, Scottish & Australian Bank Ltd (ES&A)	ANZ		
Fairfax & Sons	Bank of New South Wales	Westpac	Vincent Fairfax (Fairfax & Sons director. Became Bank of NSW director in 1953).	AMP
	Commercial Banking Co of Sydney	NAB	John Hubert Fairfax (director of Fairfax & Sons (1929 to 1944) was a Bank of New South Wales and Commercial Banking Co director).	
	Australia and New Zealand Bank Limited*	ANZ		
Associated Newspapers	Bank of New South Wales	Westpac	Frederick Tout (Associated Newspapers director and chairman of the Bank of New South Wales).	AMP
				Union Trustee Co
				Colonial Mutual
				Royal Insurance

* Formed 1951 from the merger of the Bank of Australasia and the Union Bank of Australia Limited.

Aside from the banking links of Fairfax, Associated Newspapers and the HWT, there were also bank directors on the board of WAN and Queensland Newspapers. When Chifley's Cabinet began to implement its banking policy, Calwell said Labor would never receive a fair hearing from the country's commercial newspapers because 'When the press speaks, the banks speak'.[16]

They pushed ahead anyway. In 1945, Cabinet began to pursue two controversial bills that included a requirement for all public bodies, such as councils and state governments, to conduct their business with the government-owned Commonwealth Bank. The private banks recognised this was a direct challenge to their future existence. The 'urbane and smooth' but 'aggressive' McConnan, general manager of the National Bank, and a founder of the IPA, viewed himself as fighting for the survival of the private banks in a 'crusade against the government'.[17] In Sydney, the very wealthy Bank of New South Wales was also primed to fight.[18]

In Melbourne, the wealthy stockbroker and financier Ian Potter was another IPA founder. Potter originally had a close relationship with the Collins House group of mining companies, and was becoming the underwriter of choice for many companies, including newspaper groups.[19] In the financial world, Potter and his rival, Staniforth Ricketson of JB Were, were 'the two great field marshals who gaze[d] across at each other in Collins Street'.[20] Potter had ambitions to become a merchant banker and was a close confidant of Menzies.[21] Potter had been involved in the founding of the Liberal Party in 1944 and had become one of its inaugural trustees in January 1945.[22] Two months later, on 21 March 1945, Potter was in Canberra to brief Menzies on the government's banking bills. Other Sydney- and Melbourne-based financiers were also there doing the same thing.[23] That night, Menzies launched into a 108-minute speech before a packed visitors' gallery in the House of Representatives. Many of the bankers who had travelled to Canberra were sitting there. They heard Menzies' speech attacking Labor's bank legislation. Critics said the bankers had also helped write it.[24]

Menzies' performance that day was much like a job interview. At this time, he was still on probation as far as many in the business and press communities were concerned. The *Daily Telegraph*, for example, had said the previous week that the banking bills were an 'ELECTION TEST FOR MENZIES' who was no 'spell-binder like Lyons and Curtin' but was showing 'at last ... some fire and dash'.[25]

Menzies impressed with his parliamentary speech but the Chifley government had control over both houses of parliament so the legislation eventually went through with only minor amendments. This was far from the end of the matter. In August 1947, the High Court struck down part of the banking legislation. The trigger for the litigation was the clause requiring state and local governments to conduct their business with the Commonwealth Bank. Back in 1945, even Chifley had reservations about that clause and had obtained agreement from his more eager colleagues that it would only come into force in 1947. When it did, the wealthy Melbourne City Council (which banked with the National Bank) challenged the legislation in the High Court.

The court handed down its decision on 14 August 1947 and Cabinet met two days later on the Saturday morning. Chifley gave Cabinet two options. They could either accept the ruling and diminished oversight of banking, and await further attacks from the private trading banks, or they could head off any further erosion of the government's banking powers by nationalising the banks. Chifley asked each member present, in turn, what they wanted to do. All declared in favour of nationalisation. When one of the MPs then asked where Chifley stood on the issue, he replied 'With you and the boys, to the very last ditch.'[26]

Technically, nationalisation had been on Labor's platform for more than 25 years but it had never been seriously acted upon. Warwick Fairfax noted in editorials published in the *Sydney Morning Herald* that, for a quarter of a century, Labor governments 'in State and Commonwealth have been coming and going without nationalising a single industry'.[27] To decide to suddenly implement bank nationalisation after a two-hour Cabinet meeting, and with no real assessment of the consequences, was risky. Chifley then unintentionally inflamed the situation by putting out a brusque 42-word announcement that the government had decided to nationalise the banks.[28] The statement was handed out to the press at lunchtime on the Saturday as Chifley left the Cabinet room. It did not explain why the decision had been made and it was not until several days later that Chifley said anything more on the matter. In the meantime, bankers, business leaders and Opposition politicians had filled the void with dire predictions of socialist control that had been published in the press.[29]

Representatives from every trading bank met in Melbourne to work out how to fight the government.[30] With McConnan at the helm, and the IPA and daily press supporting, the major banks launched an unprecedented long-term publicity campaign involving protest meetings, direct mail, pamphlets, broadcasting and advertising. Historian Geoffrey Blainey and journalist Geoffrey Hutton said '[e]very bank customer was circularized, and every letter-box in the land received leaflets delivered by bank officers'.[31] Leaflets were dropped from aeroplanes.[32] Statements written on behalf of the banks were misleadingly published as news reports in some papers, especially the country press.[33] Radio programs were sponsored. Newspaper advertisements told readers to 'Make your protest now'.[34] Letters of protest starting pouring into Parliament House.

The banks did not want to be seen publicly as aggressive opponents of Labor's banking plans so they largely used front organisations and spokespeople to make their case. The IPA secretly bankrolled a number of these groups. As historians Warwick Eather and Drew Cottle noted, the IPA had used this tactic against Labor's 1944 referendum and in the 1946 election. Now, rival banks joined forces, pooled their capital, and '[n]o expense was spared'.[35] Labor MPs correctly suspected they were 'under attack from a host of seemingly unrelated and supposedly "non-political" organisations' that were actually funded or supported by the banks, the IPA and allied retailers, graziers, manufacturers and employer groups.[36]

The bank advocates argued that Labor's policy meant Australians could do their banking only at the Commonwealth Bank and a few state banks. Allan Fraser, then a Labor MP, said in an interview conducted nearly 30 years later that this was a misrepresentation because the policy allowed 'the existing banks to remain in operation' but they would have been required to include a Treasury official among their directors so that all banks would speak with one voice on matters of credit policy. Even this was, as Fraser acknowledged, 'an extreme measure for the government to take'.[37] But the newspapers reported an even more extreme version – that Chifley had said all directors of private banks would 'cease to hold office' on the day their bank was compulsorily acquired and the governor of the Commonwealth Bank would appoint new directors and a new chair.[38]

The directors of the trading banks were facing extinction and they, and the business community (which included newspapers), were not going to accept that level of government interference in private companies, nor in finance and banking, which were the foundations of a capitalist economy.

Chifley was equally unyielding. He advised colleagues to 'Always make your decision on moral grounds, and the details will fall into place' so at least 'if you go down, you go down on something you believe in'.[39] Contrary to the way politics is practised now, with electoral prospects front and centre in politicians' minds, Chifley firmly believed that it was more important to keep fighting for Labor principles and goals such as full employment than to try to win over sections of the public with watered-down policies or, worse, electoral bribes.

Chifley thought if the public was not ready for Labor's program, then it was better to go out of office and keep trying to persuade people of its value than to compromise the party's integrity.[40] Allan Fraser said Cabinet knew bank nationalisation would be unpopular and probably cause them to lose the next election but they went ahead with it anyway as a matter of principle, including marginal seat MPs who knew they would very likely lose their seats. Principled or not, as Fraser admitted, 'It was, of course, a debacle for the Labor Party.'[41]

Even Chifley's supporters considered the move hasty and politically ill-advised. It created enormous controversy and backlash. It supplied the Opposition with a strong case to further its attacks on the government. And it pushed the newspapers even closer to Menzies and the new Liberal Party. Nine days after what the *Sydney Morning Herald* called Chifley's 'curt' announcement of the bank nationalisation policy, Menzies held a public meeting at the Sydney Town Hall attended by 6000 people. His former nemesis, the *Sydney Morning Herald*, now commended Menzies' 'vigorous, fighting speech'.[42]

The daily press was absolutely outraged by the banking policy. The *Sydney Morning Herald*'s front-page report was headed 'BANK DECISION STAGGERS COMMUNITY'. It said the policy had 'shocked the business world'. The issue remained on the front page of the *Sydney Morning Herald* for another ten days and the paper called it the 'most revolutionary' legislation in the country's history.[43] The *Sun* and the HWT papers were also vehemently opposed, which was not surprising given that one of the *Sun*'s directors was the chairman of the Bank of New South Wales and the HWT chairman was the chairman of the National Bank. The *Argus*, the Brisbane *Telegraph*, the *West Australian*, the *Courier-Mail* and other papers considered the legislation 'totalitarian'.[44]

Lengthy columns and editorials blasted the government, and were published alongside infuriated letters to the editor and politically potent cartoons that showed Chifley breaking open bank vaults, interrogating bank customers about how they voted before granting them a loan, and refusing begging businessmen access to their money (Figure 5.1). One cartoon showed Chifley holding a gun labelled 'socialism' in the face of a bank customer.[45] Chifley was reported to have said that he could handle Menzies in the House, and the many advertisements placed by the banks in the press, but he had no answer to Frith's cartoons in the *Sydney Morning Herald*.[46] In fact, Chifley barely tried to answer back. He had neither laid the groundwork for winning public acceptance for the policy change in the first place, nor tried to mobilise a campaign to win public support for it once the banks had launched theirs.

In October 1947, the *Sydney Morning Herald* devoted an extraordinary nine columns across three broadsheet pages to reproducing one of Menzies' speeches against bank nationalisation. Under the headline 'A FINANCIAL MONOPOLY', the speech was broken up with sub-headings: 'attack on democracy', 'no freedom', 'totalitarian', 'echo of Marx', 'misleading', 'unjust, improper' and 'aspiring dictators'.[47] But the *Sydney Morning Herald* valued its reputation as a serious journal of record with a sense of fair play so it also published some opposing views, albeit far shorter and less prominent.[48] In 1946, the paper had even published a piece by Chifley. He twice refused to accept payment for it. When Henderson tried to insist, Chifley asked for the money to be sent to an orphanage in his home town instead.[49]

In Melbourne, where Giddy and Murdoch were vehemently opposed to bank nationalisation, the HWT papers were especially strident. In the *Herald*, Harold Cox called Chifley a 'financial dictator'.[50] Murdoch's

FIGURE 5.1 The *Sydney Morning Herald* shows Ben Chifley and HV Evatt blowing up the banks with their nationalisation plans, 1947
SOURCE *Sydney Morning Herald*, 18 August 1947, p. 2. Courtesy of the State Library of NSW.

opinion-poll push for an alternative Liberal leader had occurred three days before Cabinet's bank nationalisation decision, but now Murdoch's and Menzies' 'genteel hostility' receded as they joined forces to fight Labor's banking plans.[51]

Labor's ill-judged decision – 'probably the most controversial move by any Australian government in the history of the Commonwealth' – galvanised Labor's political opponents.[52] Aside from their massive public relations campaign, the banks also fought through litigation. They obtained an injunction to challenge the legislation in November 1947 and the High Court began hearing the challenge in February 1948. The verdict in favour of the banks was delivered in Sydney six months later and celebrated by cheering at the stock exchange.[53]

OWNERSHIP SHUFFLES

The next federal election was a crucial one that would have long-term implications for the major parties, the newspaper groups and the country. Before the election was held, there were three important changes in newspaper ownership. The first was a divorce between Packer and Associated Newspapers. Their uneasy partnership in the *Daily Telegraph* dated back to the mid-1930s. By 1946, Associated Newspapers still held about 160 000 shares in Consolidated Press. Its executives believed Packer was not looking after their interests as minority shareholders and withheld dividends from them.[54]

After some tense disagreements over this, Packer and Theodore bought out those shares. Associated Newspapers needed the cash and was glad to be rid of Packer. He again short-changed them by quickly selling their old shares at a higher price.[55] The profits enabled Consolidated Press to convert from a private to a public company at the end of 1948. Packer and Theodore were now an independent force in newspapers but Theodore was not able to enjoy it for long. He suffered a major heart attack in 1948, resigned the chairmanship of Consolidated Press in January 1949, and installed his elder son, John, as chairman.

Murdoch was also strengthening his position. He had been an independent owner of the *Courier-Mail* (in partnership with John Wren) since 1933, but Murdoch had long had his eye on the *News* in Adelaide. The Labor government and irritating press critics provided him with an opportunity.

Throughout the terms of both the Curtin and Chifley governments, newspaper leaders were concerned that Labor MPs and union leaders were undermining public confidence in the press through their constant criticism. Aside from 'Cocky' Calwell and Labor's federal president, Clarrie Fallon, who referred to 'the harlot press', other critics were also finding their voices.[56] Among many Australians, there was a sense that the Depression and the war had discredited capitalism and its major promoters. The expansion of secondary education and news sources also meant newspaper audiences were becoming more critical and were challenging journalism to cover the world more responsibly. In 1941, Lloyd Dumas of the *Advertiser* had written to journalist Jack Williams that 'newspapers today are unpopular and the subject of constant attack … I am absolutely certain [these attacks] are having an accumulative [sic] effect on the public mind.'[57]

The newspaper industry was also concerned that the 'first rumblings of a consumer movement [were] being felt in Australia', driven by housewives, students and 'thinking' adults. Australian newspaper executives feared this dissatisfaction could morph into an organised movement capable of boycotting newspapers or their products.[58] The newspaper industry's spokespeople had already been kept busy defending it against charges that newspapers were warmongers and war profiteers, as well as allegations of bias and unethical behaviour, particularly after the Murdoch papers' reporting of the 1943 election. A secret ANPA report in 1945 concluded that 'Faith in the press has been shaken'. The report warned its members that press critics had a point. They had documented: 'In black and white … justified criticism that [the] press distorts, makes careless errors, runs offensive political policies, often fails to correct errors.'[59]

Newspaper executives began to pay more attention to journalism training and to accuracy. Brian Penton established an impressive cadet training program at the *Telegraph*s. Murdoch appointed veteran war correspondent and known perfectionist, Geoffrey Tebbutt, to train HWT cadet reporters to be 'accurate, clear, fair, concise and quick – in that order'.[60] In 1943, the AJA drew up a code of ethics for the guidance of its members. Many proprietors refused to display the union's eight-point code in their newsrooms, and for decades the owners would oppose proposals for any external scrutiny of journalism ethics.[61]

The impact of press criticism became more concerning when Australian newspaper owners saw what was happening in the United Kingdom. In 1947, a Royal Commission on the press began holding a public investigation into whether large British newspaper groups had too much power. Its report came out in July 1949 and Australian newspaper owners were anxious it might add weight to calls by Labor MPs for an Australian inquiry and for greater regulation of the press. But Keith Murdoch found opportunity where others saw threat.

Since the 1930s, Murdoch had been focused on building up his own independent newspaper group. He had sold large parcels of his *Advertiser* and HWT shares so he could buy up shares in Queensland Newspapers, the company he co-owned with John Wren, but also in News Limited, publisher of the Adelaide *News*. Murdoch had pulled News Limited into the HWT orbit, joined its board as a director in 1931, and built up a personal interest in the company, but the majority of its shares were still owned by the HWT, with large parcels also owned by the Baillieu family.[62]

In 1948, Murdoch asked his talented protégé, Colin Bednall, managing editor of the *Courier-Mail*, to write a brief report for the HWT board on the British Royal Commission and its findings. In his report, Bednall made an impassioned case against media monopolies of the sort the British inquiry was concerned about. Murdoch used Bednall's report to persuade his colleagues on the HWT board that they should sell the company's News Limited majority stake cheaply to him in order to minimise the risk of government interference.

According to Cecil Edwards (then assistant editor of the *Herald*), Murdoch told the HWT board that people were talking unfavourably about the company's Adelaide monopoly, and with the Chifley government looking to rationalise – perhaps even merge – newspapers to stop labour shortages, the HWT was a target.[63] Decades later, Bednall summed up the manoeuvre by saying that Murdoch 'conned News Limited off [the HWT] for his son'.[64] When Murdoch told the annual meeting of shareholders in December 1949 that the HWT's shares in News Limited had been sold, he did not disclose that he was the purchaser.[65]

The third major ownership change was the most radical one of all, and it shook up the parochial Australian newspaper industry. The once influential *Argus* was put on the market in 1949. It had never recovered from its 1930s downturn and the managers of the Edward Wilson and Lauchlan Mackinnon estates – some of whom were now three generations removed from the old owners, plus another large *Argus* shareholder, trustee and director, Allan Spowers – were looking to sell out because the paper was not making money.

The British Daily Mirror group (not to be confused with Ezra Norton's Sydney *Daily Mirror*) was interested. The Daily Mirror group was the publisher of the saucy London *Daily Mirror*. It had been founded in 1903 by Keith Murdoch's mentor, Lord Northcliffe (then known as Alfred

Harmsworth). Northcliffe's brother, Harold Harmsworth (later Lord Rothermere) purchased the paper from him in 1914, when it was selling about a million copies a day. By 1949, the *Daily Mirror* was a powerhouse of profits under its chairman, the energetic Guy Bartholomew, and an ambitious director, Cecil Harmsworth King, who was the nephew of both Lord Northcliffe and Lord Rothermere. The left-leaning *Daily Mirror* had become the top-selling newspaper in the United Kingdom with a mammoth circulation of 4.5 million copies a day.[66] It was the largest circulation daily newspaper in the world.[67]

The Mirror group had ample cash reserves and was looking to expand. It had been sniffing around the Sydney market, where its scouts felt the quality of newspapers was poor and they could win a circulation war. They had been in talks with Ezra Norton to buy *Truth* and his *Daily Mirror*, and Chifley had quietly played a role in the background, hoping this could lead to a national chain of papers sympathetic to Labor, but the negotiations had failed.[68] The Mirror group instead went to Melbourne and paid over £550 000 for just under half the total shares in the *Argus*. This was paid significantly more than market value.[69]

To the Australian newspaper proprietors, this British invasion was a sensational development. The British *Daily Mirror* was known for its racy content, including its 'Jane' cartoons, starring a woman who kept losing her clothes and ending up in her underwear. Only three months before the Mirror group had bought the *Argus*, the *Daily Mirror*'s editor, Silvester Bolam, was jailed for three months in the United Kingdom for prejudicing the trial of a man alleged to have committed a series of murders it had dubbed the 'vampire killings', having described in grisly detail the acid-bath murder of a woman and the drinking of blood.[70]

Murdoch wrote to Colin Bednall that the HWT was 'going to meet very stiff competition' in Melbourne now because the Mirror group was backed by tremendous resources. It could afford to suffer much greater and more prolonged losses than the HWT could contemplate.[71]

The Mirror group's popular newspaper touch and its financial capacity were not the only worrying aspects of its arrival. King and Bartholomew had transformed the *Daily Mirror* into a left-wing paper for the working class during the 1930s and 1940s. It had supported the British Labour

Party for the first time at the general election of 1945. The prospect of a financially strong, Labor supporting, popular newspaper in Australia managed by the group behind the biggest daily circulation tabloid in the world rocked the local industry.[72]

The 'businessman's bible', the *Argus*, was now facing a very different future and editorial stance. Its new British owners put in two directors on the *Argus* board – Sydney Elliott, the political editor of the London *Daily Mirror*, and Jack Patience, a Sydney solicitor.[73] The inexperienced but cocky Elliot made an immediate impression when he arrived in Australia to take up the role of managing director. He declared himself 'a socialist' and chastised the Australian newspapers for being 'always pessimistic' and for neglecting people and 'the constructive, exciting things in human life'. Elliott also said Australia's newspapers were hypocritical in worrying about imported sensationalism because Melbourne's newspapers 'contained more sex and crime in one issue than the [London] *Daily Mirror* in a month'.[74]

The *West Australian* spoke for the newspaper industry when it wondered aloud 'what is the *Mirror* doing in Australia?'[75] There were rumours that it planned to launch a labour-focused evening newspaper and a new morning paper in Sydney. Neither eventuated but the British Daily Mirror group did quietly buy a chain of nine radio stations in 1951 from the family of Hugh Denison (the late founder of the Sydney *Sun* and Associated Newspapers), without the relevant minister's knowledge, causing controversy about weak foreign ownership rules. The British invader also bought up a 14 per cent stake in the HWT. Although the HWT shares had limited voting rights, they were still an indication of possible intent.

A 'POLL SENSATION': THE 1949 ELECTION

The new owner of the *Argus*, along with the new majority owner of the *News*, and the freshly unshackled Packer, were all in place for the 1949 election. For Labor, a more left-leaning *Argus* was a bonus but it in no way balanced out the hostility of the remaining daily newspapers or the increased power of Murdoch and Packer (who were stridently anti-Labor). In the past, Chifley's staff had worried that he was too easygoing about press criticism. His usual response when they showed him press attacks was to say 'Aw, forget it, there's nothing so hard to find tomorrow as yesterday's newspaper' and he had a policy of not worrying about 'half-truths' the papers published.[76]

Chifley believed *The Age* was admirably impartial in its presentation of news, but by mid-1948, he was disturbed that many other papers were blurring the line between news and editorial comment as part of their campaign to unseat him.[77] He was especially fed up with the Murdoch press. Chifley said publicly that quotes attributed to him in certain newspapers were false. He said that lies were being published, including claims of a huge government surplus that did not exist.[78] Chifley said the people who the press represented had wanted Labor in office during the war, but now they believed their property was safe, had gone back to worshipping wealth.[79] Calwell chimed in to inflame matters further by saying that one day he hoped to see 'the Editor of the Melbourne *Herald* in the dock facing a charge laid under the *Crimes Act*'.[80]

The *Herald* was drawing particular ire in Labor circles because it had become so noticeably committed to putting the Chifley government out of office. Murdoch had overcome his ambivalence and was now convinced that Menzies could lead the Liberal Party to victory so long as he had help from the media; help that Murdoch was determined to give.[81]

A sign of the rapprochement between the two had occurred in 1948 when Murdoch had the HWT fund a trip to the United States for Menzies by paying him to contribute articles on American politics. Menzies would not have been able to afford to go otherwise.[82] On that trip, Menzies observed the 1948 US presidential election that resulted in a surprise victory for underdog Harry S Truman. The American campaigning technique that impressed him most was how the communist issue could be used as a political weapon against an opponent. Menzies resolved to adopt this as part of his own electioneering strategies.[83] The theme would be amplified in most of the daily press, but the Murdoch press and the *Herald* were especially central.

In early 1949, a former communist organiser in Melbourne named Cecil Sharpley contacted Murdoch. The chairman of the HWT immediately grasped the opportunity the turncoat provided and arranged to buy

Sharpley's story of Communist Party intrigue for a large sum in cash.[84] Murdoch then assigned a journalist to craft Sharpley's revelations into a series of articles, and also a bodyguard to protect him.[85] The timing was perfect. On 7 April, eight months ahead of the federal election, the *Herald* reported the results of a Gallup poll that showed Labor and the Coalition had equal support and the 'FEDERAL ELECTION IS ANYBODY'S BET'.[86] On 9 April, the *Herald* added an important caveat that 'SWINGING VOTERS [ARE] WATCHING HOW LABOR DEALS WITH REDS'. The article said 'nationalisation and communism seem certain to be decisive issues with "swinging voters" at this year's election'.[87]

Seven days later, on Saturday 16 April, the *Herald* splashed its first exclusive front-page story on Sharpley's disclosures, headed 'RED SECRETS REVEALED BY LEADER WHO LEFT PARTY'. This was followed by another front-page story on the Monday. Over the next week, the *Herald* published another nine front-page articles focused on Sharpley's claims of 'RED-DOMINATED UNIONS USED AS STRIKE WEAPONS' and 'WE COULD TURN OUT EVERY LIGHT IN MELBOURNE'.[88]

Sharpley alleged that communists had undertaken ballot faking, corruption and industrial sabotage, and had manufactured strikes and committed treason. Sharpley described the communists he worked with as 'evil', said they wanted 'war' and 'revolution', and were taking their cues from Moscow.[89] The Sharpley disclosures caused a sensation. The HWT promoted them heavily, including on its 3DB radio station, conducting a prime-time interview with Sharpley that was relayed over radio stations in all states. They were the biggest radio hook-ups attempted in Australia at the time. The *Herald* even published the Sharpley articles as a red booklet with a hammer and sickle on the cover that sold for a shilling.[90]

Sharpley told the HWT that several of its staff were members of the Communist Party. A purge followed in which one journalist was sacked and a few others on Sharpley's list resigned.[91]

Historian Humphrey McQueen argued the *Herald* timed its publication of the Sharpley revelations to assist the industrial groups at the 1949 state conference of the Victorian Labor Party.[92] The industrial groups had been established to support Labor candidates who ran against communists in trade union elections. They worked closely with the Catholic Social Studies Movement (also known as 'the Movement'), led by the founding editor of the *Catholic Worker* newspaper, Bartholomew Augustine (BA) Santamaria. The industrial groups were a prelude to a major split in Labor and morphed into the Democratic Labor Party (DLP) (Chapter 6).

Following Sharpley's claims, a Royal Commission into the Communist Party's activities in Victoria was quickly announced. According to historian Stuart Macintyre, the Victorian government was '[t]ipped off in advance' by the *Herald*.[93] Sharpley was the star witness but the Commission found much of his evidence unreliable.[94] All but one of his allegations were dismissed as groundless but newspaper reporting focused on the sensational claims made during the inquiry, not on their veracity, nor that the Commission's final report was 'only a mild indictment of the Communist Party'.[95] McQueen argued that, by then, 'the *Herald* had poured out a constant stream of lies, half-truths and rumours about everyone connected with any progressive cause'. He said 'the *Herald*'s Sharpley campaign was particularly important in building up the atmosphere for Menzies' electoral victory in 1949'.[96]

Stories on 'Reds' continued to appear regularly in the *Herald* throughout 1949, and polling indicated they were making a difference to how people perceived the parties. The communist issue was also causing rifts within the labour movement and the Labor Party, and on this, Calwell's colourful rhetoric was now suddenly useful. In July 1949, he condemned communist leaders in the mining union as 'a band of standover men; industrial outlaws and political lepers, paranoiacs, degenerates, morons and ... scum'.[97] Putting aside the bitter Calwell–Murdoch feud, the *Herald* sought a special interview with Calwell and emphasised his words.

By this point, the newspapers were extremely frustrated with the Chifley government's economic controls. While the United States was experiencing a postwar consumer spending boom and advertising was taking off, in Australia, it was becoming difficult for the newspapers to convince advertisers of the value of advertising when government controls were dampening civilian demand and shortages meant that products tended to sell themselves anyway.

FIGURE 5.2 The Liberal Party used, with permission, a John Frith–*Sydney Morning Herald* cartoon on its election campaign pamphlet, 1949
SOURCE National Library of Australia.

The HWT papers and Murdoch's *News* and *Courier-Mail* gave Menzies unqualified editorial support in the lead-up to the 1949 election. All of the daily newspapers unequivocally backed Menzies except for Norton's *Daily Mirror* (which did not publish an editorial, although it did publish a lot of anti-socialist advertisements) and the re-branded *Argus* (which, despite expectations of a sharp left turn, said it would leave it up to readers to decide for themselves). The pro-Menzies newspapers used almost identical arguments and even particular phrases. They argued Chifley's Labor represented 'the deadening extension of socialism' (the *Herald*), 'a Socialist Master State' (*Sun News-Pictorial*) and was the party of 'Socialisation' (*Daily Telegraph*). The Liberal Party was instead the party of 'free enterprise' (*Daily Telegraph*) and prosperity that would allow Australians 'to be free' (*Sun News-Pictorial*).[98]

Since the dinner party pact in 1944, the major newspapers had helped rehabilitate Menzies in the eyes of the public after the failure of his first stint as prime minister. He was now portrayed as a strong, majestic and resolute leader who would soar above problems such as petrol rationing, communism and socialism (Figure 5.2).

In Queensland, Colin Bednall, who was running the *Courier-Mail* for Murdoch, made sure its anti-government stance was suitably vehement. Bednall received a major exclusive from the Archbishop of Brisbane when he called on Catholics to vote against Labor. This was widely understood to be responsible for a Catholic swing against Labor, especially in Queensland, which Calwell never forgave (Chapter 7).[99]

The Sharpley disclosures had elevated public concern about communism. By the time of the election in December, the Liberal and Country parties argued the Communist Party was so dangerous it needed to be outlawed. The Liberal Party's election slogan was, 'Halt socialism, end petrol rationing, prevent bank nationalisation, outlaw communism'.

Despite appeals from his worried advisers, Chifley again refused to make any new promises because he felt it would look rash or superficial.[100] He insisted on running a no-frills, 'judge us on our record' type campaign. As historian Ross McMullin pointed out, Chifley was 'jaded and in poor health … [and] Labor's campaign was complacent and lacklustre'.[101]

Labor also unwisely kept its unpopular banking policy prominent right up to the election by appealing the High Court's 1948 decision at the Privy Council in London. This meant the banks, the IPA and most of the daily metropolitan newspapers kept campaigning against bank nationalisation into the election year of 1949.[102] The National Bank's McConnan told a friend that he had become a 'cunning political organiser, and am spending my whole time trying to gather together our forces to defeat the government at the polls'. Menzies was keen for the bank issue to be kept alive, viewing it as a key to winning the election. McConnan said that he had made 'a bargain with Menzies that if he can at least hold the argument on the positive side we bank officers can defeat Chifley and his crowd on the Banking issue'.[103]

The Privy Council appeal again ended in a legal victory for the banks. Labor had spent political capital (again) for no tangible outcome and the business community was still concerned that Labor's nationalisation policy would be extended to shipping and insurance.[104] These were two more industries that had close links to the major newspaper groups (Table 5.1), especially with the Australian Mutual Provident Society (AMP), which was the largest insurer in the British Empire, a major shareholder in newspaper groups and well represented on newspaper boards.[105]

Because the Liberal Party's 1949 election campaign was extremely well funded by large donations from concerned businesses, it was able to marshal new techniques in political communication.[106] Labor's usual advertising agent, Solomon (Sim) Rubensohn of the advertising firm Hansen-Rubensohn, was so opposed to banking nationalisation that he moved across to the Liberal Party. On its behalf, he directed the most expensive election advertising campaign in Australian history. It included a fictional radio serial focused on John Henry Austral, an ordinary Australian confronted by the misfortunes of living under Labor, including rationing, high petrol prices, a lack of housing and strikes. There were 200 episodes spanning 20 months prior to the election.[107] The Liberals probably outspent Labor ten to one in 1949.[108]

Months of industrial unrest in 1948 and early 1949 had also led to greater public concern about communists exercising power in trade unions. A coal miners' strike called by the communist controlled Miners' Federation in winter 1949 caused widespread distress. It began in late June 1949, lasted seven weeks and affected all states except Western Australia. Labor speechwriter Graham Freudenberg said the strike 'threw half-a-million Australians out of work, cost £100 million in lost wages, devastated heavy industry and crippled the power and transport systems of the eastern capitals'.[109] Power shortages during a harsh winter added to a sense of hardship when people were still enduring rationing and other inconveniences from wartime restrictions.

Chifley viewed the industrial action as 'a direct communist challenge' and his government used drastic measures to try to break it, including rushing through emergency powers to freeze union funds, as well as prosecuting mining union officials (which resulted in prison terms for union leaders), and levying fines on unions.[110] The most drastic action, and one that damaged Chifley's standing among Labor's traditional supporters, was when Chifley called in the Army to work in open-cut mines. Two weeks later, the strike collapsed and miners returned to work, defeated. This was only four months before polling day.

The coal miners' strike boosted the Opposition's claim to be the only party capable of guarding against communism in industry. Along with a petrol crisis, it halted any sense that Labor might stage a comeback. The key newspapers mirrored Menzies' framing of the campaign, saying 'the real issue of the election is … Socialism versus Our Way of Life' (*News*) or whether 'Australia [is] to be a Socialist state' (*Courier-Mail*).[111]

Aside from Calwell, another Labor politician who had been formerly despised by the main newspaper groups but was now highly quotable was the former New South Wales premier, Jack Lang. Lang made sensational claims on the eve of the election that Chifley was a greedy money lender and exploitative landlord. Murdoch's papers publicised the allegations prominently as evidence that Chifley's attacks on banks were hypocritical. In the *Herald*, Lang's claims were headlined 'MONEYLENDING CHARGE: PM STILL SILENT'.[112] In the *Advertiser*, 'CHIFLEY CHARGED BY LANG: POLLING EVE SENSATION'.[113] The *Courier-Mail* made it even more personal: 'LANG … NAMES MRS. CHIFLEY' and 'CHIFLEY HIDING BEHIND WIFE'. The stories were stretched out over several days right up until polling day.[114] The attacks were a crude distortion of Chifley's role as a trustee and executor. The *Argus*, newly sympathetic to Labor, characterised them very differently as 'LANG MAKES BITTER ATTACK ON CHIFLEY' and 'LANG THE WRECKER'.[115]

The Coalition won the 1949 election decisively. Of the 121 seats in the newly enlarged House of Representatives, the Coalition won 74 to Labor's 47.[116] The Liberal Party's best results were in Victoria, where the HWT papers had the strongest influence, and in Queensland and South Australia, where Murdoch's papers were also influential. When Menzies wrote and thanked Murdoch for his support, Murdoch made sure Menzies was aware of this, saying he was gratified that the Liberal Party's best results were in the states 'in which we publish newspapers' and a fourth state 'in which we have some reflected influence' (presumably Western Australia).[117]

Despite the bitterness of the banking fight, many of the journalists and proprietors still had an appreciation for Chifley's wartime skill and the work he had done for them in solving problems over newsprint. And on a personal level, as opposed to a political one, there were still warm feelings towards Chifley. Rupert Henderson said he admired Chifley's 'steadfastness, honesty and courage' and told the Labor leader that 'Although we differ politically, I think you know that I have the highest regard and esteem for you personally'. Henderson thanked Chifley for his 'never failing courtesy and consideration'.[118] Ross Gollan of the *Sydney Morning Herald* called Chifley 'a human being of singular personal sweetness and dignity' who was thoroughly respected.[119] Even Murdoch, who did everything he could to get Chifley out of office, later described him as 'an able and kindly man, serene, severe but sincere'.[120]

PART TWO

THE 1950s

CHAPTER 6
NEWSPAPERS FIGHT THE COLD WAR

Change was a constant in the newspaper industry, but the 1950s was an especially important era and the last days of newspaper dominance before television, round-the-clock radio news and talkback. Newspaper editors were finding the public still had a 'ravenous appetite' for news but also more opportunity to obtain it elsewhere.[1] Even before television arrived in 1956, the growing use of private cars, and of lighter, portable radios, meant radio was 'flourishing' and commercial radio stations were broadcasting more news bulletins and sporting events.[2] Radio advertising revenue was boosting the coffers of newspaper companies that owned stations. The Fairfax group looked on in envy at how 'immensely powerful' the HWT's 3DB was in Melbourne and was inspired to acquire its own first shareholding in radio, a minority stake in Sydney's 2GB, at the end of 1952.[3]

The main newspaper groups would keep diversifying and growing in size over the next two decades. They were riding the wave of what historian Stuart Macintyre characterised as the 'long boom' of the 1950s and 1960s as Australia entered a period of relative affluence and domestic peace.[4] The economy grew and Australia's population increased rapidly through large-scale postwar immigration. Suburban development accelerated and unemployment was at minimum levels. Australians were working less labour-intensive jobs, living longer, and accruing more leisure time, home comforts and possessions.[5]

Newspapers had actively encouraged Australians to cast off austerity and leave behind the frugal ways of the war and reconstruction. Advertising roared back to life and people were encouraged to buy home appliances, machinery, fashion, cars, cigarettes, cosmetics, health and beauty products.[6] In 1955–56, there were nearly 12 million column inches of advertising, which *Newspaper News* declared the 'greatest [volume] in [Australian] newspaper history'.[7] Fittingly, private banks and financial institutions – which had won the fight against bank nationalisation with the help of the newspapers – were among the largest contributors to the press advertising boom.[8]

At a time when communism and the Soviet Union were viewed as real threats to national security, the consumerism of the 1950s was not just financially lucrative but also a way of waging the Cold War, as part of the ideological battle between American-style capitalism and Soviet-style communism. Simply by identifying with consumer culture and enjoying the benefits of capitalism, Australians were demonstrating freedom, choice and abundance.

Newspapers were a prime site in which Cold War politics played out and Australia's commercial daily press was firmly on the side of the United States, free enterprise and anti-communism. American journalism historian, David R Davies, said it was not surprising that daily newspapers in the United States 'reflected the anticommunism of their day' because they were 'politically conservative institutions whose editorials reflected the pro-business sentiments of their publishers'.[9] The same was true of the Australian metropolitan dailies, and as academic and author Julianne Schultz noted, 'The ideological fears of the Cold War imposed great restraint on the [Australian] mainstream press which generally shared and perpetuated the assumptions and fears of the dominant world view'.[10]

> **TEXTBOX 6.1 Back to the butterfly department**
>
> Many women who had been working during World War II lost their jobs after men returned from combat or national service. Newspapers and women's magazines encouraged readers to embrace this return to the home by heavily promoting ideals of feminine domesticity and conformity.
>
> At newspapers, female journalists who managed to keep their jobs after the war were mostly sent back to being segregated in the section of the office called the 'butterfly department' at some newspapers, and the 'hen coop' at others.[11] This was where women wrote up 'the women's pages'. Mostly, they wrote about who attended parties, weddings, balls, charity functions and the races, and what they were wearing.
>
> Even Elizabeth Riddell – who had covered politics and police rounds for

Norton's *Daily Mirror*, had started an overseas news bureau, and had written from Europe on the impact of World War II – was dispatched to *Woman* magazine by Associated Newspapers.[12] They sent her to cover the Queen's tour of New Zealand for the *Sun*, where she wrote descriptions of the Queen's 'dazzling gowns' and 'scenestealer' fringed tiara.[13] Riddell had to keep fighting her way back to more fulfilling reporting and commentary.[14]

Social news was 'the bread and butter of women journalists' work' in the 1950s.[15] Other topics judged suitable for women to read (and write) included homecraft, recipes and dress patterns. There were exceptions, such as Dulcie Foard, the chief state politics reporter at the *Argus* in the early 1950s, but women did not tend to have long careers in such roles.

In Sydney, Connie Robertson dominated women's journalism as editor of the *Sydney Morning Herald*'s women's supplement for 26 years (1936 to 1962). Robertson insisted her staff of female reporters were always correctly attired with hats, white gloves and bags that matched their shoes. She was back at work soon after having a baby, bringing her daughter to the office in a basket that was placed in an open drawer of a filing cabinet.[16]

In Melbourne, Pat Jarrett occupied a similarly dominant role at the *Sun News-Pictorial* where she was the women's editor for 25 years (1948 to 1973), despite being an accomplished sports reporter and war correspondent who had originally told Keith Murdoch that she wanted nothing of 'that piddling social stuff'.[17]

Robertson and Jarrett were given a level of autonomy to run their sections, manage their staff and edit others' work that was rare for women in journalism at the time. Although the women's pages of the 1950s mostly remained 'a world of intimate, chatty escapism varnished with a layer of social snobbery', managers such as Murdoch and Henderson had a solid respect for them. The pages were financially supported by department stores and were crucial to enticing female readers to buy the paper, and to keeping them in a mood where they were receptive to buying new products and fashions.[18]

Despite the strong social and media pressure to identify primarily as wives and mothers, employment rates for women continued to rise during the 1950s. At newspapers, the two main areas where women remained employed in larger numbers than men were as binders and telephonists.

When newspapers moved from requiring people to come into the office to place a classified advertisement to allowing telephone classified advertising, the *Sydney Morning Herald* hired an additional 70 telephonists.[19] Always referred to as 'girls', cheap wages were part of their appeal. For example, female binders were still paid less than 70 per cent of male wages.[20]

TEXTBOX 6.2 Family newspapers

As part of the Cold War ideal of domesticity, the family unit was celebrated and considered proof of the superiority of capitalist consumer societies. The family home symbolised peace, prosperity and security in contrast to Soviet poverty, oppression and aggression.

Respectable, wholesome papers committed to 'family values' prevailed in the 1950s.[21] Terms such as 'pregnant' and 'pregnancy' were frowned upon. Abortion was traditionally described as 'an operation designed to procure a certain event', and sexual assault was still often referred to as 'a capital offence'. The HWT papers were especially known for their puritanical approach to reporting when Jack Williams was in charge. Reporters at the *Sun News-Pictorial* were not allowed to use the word 'pyjamas' or to refer to 'false teeth'.[22] At the *Herald*, 'night-gown' was banned (it had to be 'night attire'), and toilets could not be mentioned.[23]

Muckraking and anti-establishment papers were out of place. The crusading, irreverent *Smith's Weekly* (which was also racist, sexist and jingoistic), was closed in 1950. The once prominent weekly – which Frank Packer's father had co-founded in 1919 – suffered an undignified end when Fairfax acquired it purely for its 897 tons of then-scarce newsprint and closed it down.[24]

After television arrived in 1956, American television shows such as *Leave it to Beaver* and *Father Knows Best* that reinforced traditional gender roles and the centrality of the family home became very popular in Australia.

The socially and politically conservative tone of the times was also apparent in the newspapers' heavy – and lucrative – promotion of the British Royal Family. The coronation of Queen Elizabeth II in June 1953 sold a record number of papers, and the Queen's tour of Australia in 1954 generated enormous boosts to newspaper and magazine circulation.[25]

COLD WAR POLITICS

Characteristic of what critics felt was Murdoch's slide into megalomania in his sixties, Murdoch believed that Menzies' 1949 victory was in no small measure due to his own efforts, and that Menzies would need his help to stay in office. Murdoch's sympathetic biographer, Ron Younger, phrased it kindly when he said, 'Murdoch knew that support for the new Menzies government could easily slip away' after the 1949 election (because the economy was not strong and Menzies was not personally popular) and Murdoch believed 'that in the adverse times immediately ahead Menzies would require sustained backing'.[26]

Murdoch was not acting as an independent press owner and executive but rather as an advocate and even propagandist. Despite the strong editorial support his papers gave to Menzies, their personal relationship was utilitarian rather than warm. Menzies did have friends among the other newspaper owners and managers though, including Packer, Dumas, and *The Age*'s editor, Harold Alfred Maurice ('HAM') Campbell.

In Queensland, Menzies was also friends with the managing editor of the *Courier-Mail*, Colin Bednall, who received a letter of gratitude from the prime minister in May 1953 after the half-Senate election. 'My dear Colin', Menzies wrote, 'I cannot go abroad without writing to let you know how much we have all appreciated the attitude of the *Courier-Mail* during the Senate campaign. No Government could have asked for its case to be better or more enthusiastically presented.'[27]

Menzies contested four House of Representatives elections during the 1950s and most of the newspapers supported him every time (Table 13.1). He skilfully exploited Cold War fears and the threat of communism, and in general, the newspapers supported this. The pressure for Cold War conformity was strong. Mainstream American newspapers felt it even more acutely, but the Australian newspapers had the added limitation of being owned by relatively few owners, most of whom were strongly anti-communist, and some obsessively so (especially Packer and Murdoch). The Australian owners were also notoriously cost conscious, to the point of 'meanness'. They relied on obtaining overseas news 'on the cheap' via

FIGURE 6.1 A newsboy takes a break, 16 June 1954
SOURCE Newspix.

second-hand agency news, which also left their newspapers ill-equipped to explain the complexities of Cold War politics to their readers.[28]

Unlike his first stint in office, Menzies so thoroughly dominated the Australian parliament, executive government and media relations in the 1950s, that Bednall said the major press groups were 'scared stiff of Menzies'. Bednall said he knew this from personal experience because 'I was frequently [their] Canberra emissary'.[29] The Australian newspapers generally adopted a fairly passive, unquestioning and uncritical approach to reporting the Menzies government, its actions and its worldview, although as journalist and historian Peter Gifford pointed out, there were 'glimmers of libertarian independence shown by some Australian journalists [and editors] during the Cold War'.[30]

ANOTHER CHANGE OF LABOR LEADER

In November 1950, Chifley suffered a heart attack. Although unwell, he was back campaigning for the April 1951 double dissolution election. All of the newspapers overwhelmingly supported Menzies at that election, except for the *Argus* (which made no formal endorsement) and the *Daily News* (which published a lightweight, non-directive election editorial).

Only six weeks after Labor's election loss, Chifley suffered a fatal heart attack at the Hotel Kurrajong in Canberra. Newspaper reporting was discreet, although some left it to readers to read between the lines by reporting that, on the night he died, 'Chifley had been reading in bed' at 10 pm when his 'personal typist', Phyllis Donnelly, brought him 'a cup of tea'.[31]

HV Evatt became the new Labor leader, and Arthur Calwell his deputy. Despite Evatt's brilliant legal mind, his leadership at a difficult time for Labor was not politically astute. His political judgement was unreliable. In political and journalistic circles, he was already known for his mood swings, phobias, outbursts of temper and for taking to his bed at times of stress. In later years, Evatt would suffer from what his biographers would speculate was either mental illness, dementia or the effects of arteriosclerosis (a thickening of the artery walls).[32]

> **TEXTBOX 6.3** Paper problems

Despite the economy roaring back, two familiar problems continued to haunt the newspapers – labour demands and newsprint shortages. Since the war, a 'steady upward trend in wages' had continued, including weekend penalties, shift and overtime rates.[33]

In 1951, newsprint supply became a serious issue due to a worldwide shortage. Power restrictions on the Tasmanian mills and a shortage of US dollar credits to purchase overseas aggravated the problem. This led to some skinny papers, as well as rounds of cost cutting and the closure of some suburban newspapers.[34]

Proprietors who had backed Menzies fulsomely in 1949 expected his attention and assistance. In March 1951, Murdoch sent the prime minister a telegram asking for a meeting to talk about newsprint.[35] In June, Henderson, as president of ANPA, asked Menzies to persuade the British government to allocate an export licence for newsprint and to make shipping space available. Menzies complied.[36]

In July, the Menzies government made dollars available to purchase newsprint and ensured that newspaper publishers received a quota of Canadian newsprint.[37] In August, Murdoch was back, asking Menzies to meet again, complaining, 'We are having a very bad time here'.[38]

As they had under the Chifley and Curtin governments, public servants found the proprietors' aggression, their special pleading, and insistence on going directly to the prime minister, 'most troublesome'.[39] An exasperated official briefed Menzies that, unlike other industries, 'it is impossible to get any unanimity out of' the newspapers because they were always focused on their own selfish concerns rather than the 'group as a whole'. The official also lamented that press owners invariably failed to recognise how generously they had been treated.[40] None of this would have been news to Menzies. He had been dealing with selfish and troublesome proprietors for decades. Future prime ministers would also find that, no matter how much they did for media barons, it was folly to expect either loyalty or any long-term gratitude.

In the early 1950s, Evatt was already exhibiting erratic behaviour. An ASIO officer reported suspicions that Evatt's mind had become 'unhinged and unbalanced'.[41] John Douglas (JD) Pringle, editor of the *Sydney Morning Herald*, 1952–57, later said his conversations with Evatt in 1954 convinced him the Labor leader had become irrational, was losing control of himself and 'already suffering from some mental imbalance'.[42] Evatt's behaviour certainly did not help Labor's cause, but in the Cold War atmosphere of the times, the metropolitan dailies were already firmly on the side of Menzies' free enterprise principles, even to the extent of willingly abandoning their long-held claim to be a leading light for freedom and civil rights.

THE COMMUNIST BAN BILL AND THE REFERENDUM

In 1950, Menzies turned his attention to delivering his signature 1949 election promise to ban the Communist Party. During his first, unsuccessful stint as prime minister between 1939 and 1941, Menzies had kept Murdoch at arm's length, which Murdoch resented. This time, Menzies tried to make Murdoch feel more involved. He invited him to Canberra about a month before the controversial bill was introduced and gave him an outline of what it would contain.[43] It was going to make it a criminal offence for an Australian to hold ties to the Communist Party.

Murdoch was enthusiastic about banning communists. They called him 'Australia's No. 1 newspaper monopolist' and had put a photograph of his Toorak home in a pamphlet to contrast its opulence with the dilapidated workers' cottages of inner-city Richmond.[44] Murdoch called them 'saboteurs, conspirators [and] enemies'. He genuinely feared that communists would target private wealth. His 36-year enthusiasm for warfare had not dimmed and Murdoch called for Australia to arm itself and wage a united war against Russia, death 'being no sweeter than by war'. He believed the Korean war 'may yet be the means to peace'.[45] Murdoch's friend and war correspondent, Douglas Brass, described this period as Murdoch's 'obsessive anti-Communist phase'.[46]

After being wined and dined by Menzies in Canberra, Murdoch went overseas and was returning to Melbourne when the bill was introduced. In his absence, the *Herald*'s Canberra bureau head, Harold Cox, had seen the bill and was 'absolutely horrified'. He told one of Murdoch's biographers, Desmond Zwar, that 'I regarded it as the most violently reactionary measure that had been introduced in a British parliament in two hundred years'. Jack Williams was acting for Murdoch and Cox told him on the phone that 'It's the biggest bitch of a bill I have ever seen'. He gave Williams 'a whole series of reasons why [he] thought so' and Williams asked him, 'Are you prepared to write what you told me?' Cox replied 'Are you prepared to publish it?'[47]

Among the HWT staff, Williams had a reputation for being editorially non-directive, especially compared to Murdoch. Cox's article was published. Murdoch saw it soon after his ship arrived in Port Melbourne. He phoned Cox and told him it was 'dreadful'. He asked, 'Young man, have you taken leave of your senses?' Cox replied that he thought his article was right and Murdoch would come to see that in the future. Murdoch fumed 'if I had been home you would never have got away with that'.[48]

The *Communist Party Dissolution Act* became law on 20 October 1950. A *Herald* editorial acknowledged the powers it granted were 'far-reaching and disturbing', but argued the denial of civil rights to communists was necessary.[49] The Communist Party and several unions quickly launched a challenge in the High Court. Evatt appeared for the Waterside Workers Federation and argued the Act would allow the government to do everything the Court had previously determined was beyond its power. In March 1951, the High Court ruled the legislation unconstitutional.

The Menzies government responded to this defeat by proposing a referendum that would give it the power to outlaw the Communist Party and to ban 'declared' communists from public office. The papers overwhelmingly advocated a 'yes' vote with the British Daily Mirror group's *Argus* the conspicuous exception.[50] Newspapers that declared freedom of thought, speech and expression to be keystones of a democracy – including during their fight against censorship – were now abandoning those principles because communism was judged to be too dangerous.

The *Herald* ran eight prominent editorials calling for a 'yes' vote in the four weeks before the referendum was held.⁵¹ The *News*, *West Australian* and the *Mercury* strongly advocated a 'yes' vote. So too did the *Sydney Morning Herald*, which said communists were not deserving of the rights of 'loyal citizens' because they were 'agents' of a foreign power. It concluded, 'We are under attack as a free nation. We must defend ourselves from enemies within no less than enemies without.'⁵² More bluntly, the *Daily Telegraph*'s front-page headline said 'VOTE "YES" AND HELP PM SMASH THE REDS'. To the *Daily Telegraph*, communists were 'traitors' who must be rooted out 'before they spread and cripple the nation'.⁵³ The *Age* also backed Menzies and said a ban would help resist 'the world-wide Communist attack on the free world'.⁵⁴

Evatt campaigned around the country calling for a 'no' vote and argued the proposal was a violation of civil rights. Despite the press's strong advocacy, the referendum was narrowly defeated.⁵⁵ Evatt's once friendly relationship with Packer and Australian Consolidated Press had cooled after the seizure of Sydney newspapers in the censorship row; it now deteriorated dramatically after Evatt campaigned against Menzies' Communist Party ban.⁵⁶ The *Daily Telegraph*'s coverage of Evatt between 1952 and 1954 was overwhelmingly negative. Typical headlines included 'EVATT CRITICISED', 'EVATT BITTER ON MIGRATION', 'EVATT MAY LOSE JOB', 'DR EVATT IS PLAYING POLITICS WITH RED-LIT FIRES', 'EVATT HECKLED', 'CRITICISM OF EVATT', 'EVATT'S "THREAT" TO AUST.', 'EVATT'S DAYS "NUMBERED"'. When Evatt complained about biased coverage, the *Daily Telegraph* mockingly published his complaint.⁵⁷

LOOKING TO THE UNITED STATES

Back in December 1941, Murdoch's *Herald* had missed a scoop that was published in its own pages. Curtin had written a piece for the Saturday magazine section (ghost-written by Don Rodgers) that articulated a realignment of Australia's national priorities.⁵⁸ The piece said Australia 'looks to America, free of any pangs as to our traditional links and kinship with the United Kingdom'. Cecil Edwards said the piece sat around the

Herald office for days and no one grasped its significance.[59] Once it was published, other outlets did though, and they emphasised Curtin's change of policy in their own papers.

The missed scoop was particularly embarrassing because Murdoch was one of the Australian businessmen who had lobbied for Australia to build closer ties with the United States. When he was director-general of the Department of Information, Murdoch had taken the lead in forming the Australian–American Co-operation Movement in 1941, and was its first president. Originally, the Movement was designed to entice the United States into the war, although this goal was not openly stated. Its more official goals included giving the Australian public 'a better understanding' of 'American affairs and point of view'.[60] Murdoch was in an excellent position to use his group's newspapers, radio stations and magazines to promote American views. In 1944, he travelled to the United States and was greatly impressed by its spirit of 'individualistic initiative' and focus on free enterprise.[61]

As the US economy grew through the postwar boom and it began developing into an economic superpower, Murdoch and other business leaders were even keener to entice American capital to Australia. Cold War tension heightened as the United States and the USSR both sought to extend their influence around the world and Murdoch and other Australian business leaders, including Frank Packer and Eric Kennedy (of Associated Newspapers), intensified their efforts.

In 1947, the Australian–American Co-operation Movement became the Australian–American Association. Murdoch remained its president from 1941 to early 1952. He was also a founding figure, in 1948, of the American–Australian Association in New York. Douglas Brass said Murdoch had 'a shrewd eye on the future' and was nurturing relationships with 'men of influence and talent in the United States'.[62] Murdoch had flown to the United States again in 1946, encouraging American oil company executives, bankers and businessmen to support the American–Australian Association. In the years following, he entertained visiting American bigwigs at his Toorak home.[63] Murdoch was also the recipient of leaked information from American intelligence services, and also the likely supplier of information to them.[64]

Murdoch lobbied for obstacles to American investment to be removed, particularly Australia's 'double taxation laws' which saw American investors pay tax on company profits once in Australia, and then again in the United States.[65] After the double taxation agreement was ratified, American investment sped up. By 1954, more than US$200 million was invested in Australian industry, particularly in cars, agricultural equipment, rubber tyres and petroleum refining and distribution.[66] Newspapers welcomed the new, big-spending advertisers to Australia, including General Motors, Heinz, Goodyear, Colgate-Palmolive, Kodak and General Electric. And Coca-Cola was promoted by an unprecedented worldwide selling campaign that boosted newspaper revenue.[67]

Murdoch and Packer sympathised with American expats' complaints about Australia's higher wages and more expensive working conditions. Frank Packer's heavy involvement with the Australian–American Association included promoting its perspectives in the pages of the *Daily Telegraph*. His company also printed its pamphlets and books. Packer even had his financial adviser speak to its members to explain how Americans living in Australia could manage their affairs to avoid paying tax (tax avoidance was always a point of pride for Packer).[68]

Familiar figures from the banking fight and the IPA were also prominent in the campaign to lure American investment, including Leslie McConnan's and Murdoch's friend Richard Casey, who had been Australia's first ambassador to the United States.[69] In its pro-American enthusiasm, the IPA expressed some wildly optimistic views. For example, Charles Denton (CD) Kemp, director of the IPA in Victoria, wrote in 1951 that the United States 'was the first nation which has brought within reach the possibility of completely abolishing poverty'.[70]

Murdoch too was almost evangelical about the United States. He wrote that the American way of life 'connects work with a man's inner balance and completeness. There is almost a religious aspect in this'.[71] In a syndicated piece written on his return from a 1951 visit to the United States, Murdoch wrote that the American free enterprise model was providing 'the present leadership of the world'.[72] In another piece prominently published in the *Herald*, Murdoch declared, 'There is no doubt that the Americans are today the best informed people in the world'. He called on Australians to do 'as America is doing', and especially for Australia's 'young men' to be America's 'willing friends at the door of the new Asia' (presumably referring here to the Korean war), so that Americans would bring their 'skills, products, men [and] money' to Australia. Veering into some of his more purple prose, Murdoch said Australia could then be 'strong in our manhood'.[73]

The Australian–American Association strengthened trade and business ties but it also promoted the United States as the cornerstone of Australia's defence policy, especially in South-East Asia. Collins House figures played key roles in the development of the ANZUS military pact, including Richard Casey, but also another Murdoch friend, mining magnate WS Robinson. Behind the scenes, Robinson was something of a grey eminence, diplomat and international problem solver for politicians on both sides of politics. He made around 40 trips to the United States in six years, including accompanying Evatt to the White House.[74]

Left-wing activists complained that Collins House leaders were 'opening Australian doors to the dollar kings of the US', and enticing 'Yankee big business' to Australia, aided by Menzies. The *Workers' Star* said that business leaders had a cheek to say that communists were foreign agents when they were the ones selling Australia cheaply to the United States.[75] But Murdoch felt Menzies did not understand how critical the United States and the American capitalist model were to Australia's future.[76] He was becoming frustrated and disappointed by Menzies just as he had been with Joe Lyons after helping him into office. In August 1952, Murdoch wrote to Bednall and said the Menzies 'government is not doing things well'. He felt it was not doing enough to get costs down by rejecting workers' claims for shorter hours, nor managing the risk of inflation.[77] Two months later, Murdoch was dead (Chapter 7).

THE PETROV AFFAIR AND THE 1954 ELECTION

In December 1953, Harold Cox privately told his HWT superiors that Labor MPs were convinced their hopes of winning the next election were 'rapidly evaporating' because the party was not strong or cohesive. Cox wrote that Evatt was 'on his final trial' and 'Calwell obviously realises this and is planning a bid for the leadership'. According to Cox, after the lavish 'high ceremonial' wedding of Evatt's daughter ten days previously, 'The whole caucus is now treating Evatt with complete ridicule'.[78]

Public perceptions were somewhat different. A March 1954 Gallup poll suggested a likely Labor victory in the upcoming election in May. It showed 47 per cent support for Labor and 41 for the Liberal–Country Party Coalition.[79] The prospect of Menzies losing office was of deep concern for the major newspaper groups, especially for those wanting commercial television licences (Chapter 10).

Matters took a sudden and dramatic turn for the worse for Labor in April after the defection of Soviet diplomat Vladimir Petrov. Press photographs taken on 19 April showed his wife, Evdokia Petrov, being forcibly escorted by two armed KGB agents to a waiting plane at Sydney airport, bound for Darwin and then Moscow. Thousands of demonstrators gathered at the airport, many of them Soviet and East European refugees who believed the KGB couriers were dragging Petrov to certain death.

Television was still two years away, so newspaper reporting provided the dominant interpretation of the Petrov affair. The vivid press photographs captured a shocked and crying Evdokia, one shoe missing, her foot bare, being forcibly pushed onto the plane. In the photograph, academic Robert Manne emphasised how '[t]he nation saw ... a durable visual image of what most Australians still believed the Cold War to be about – the struggle between the forces of Evil and Good' being acted out on Australian soil.[80]

After that, the issue of communism dominated the election campaign. In April, Cox told his HWT superiors that it 'had completely recast the background against which the election will be held and its prospective result'. About half the Caucus now believed Labor's chance at winning had 'been completely destroyed'.[81] The election was held six weeks after Evdokia was dragged across the tarmac. Labor lost. Banker and now HWT chairman, Harold Giddy, said there was 'great pleasure' on Wall Street at Menzies' victory.[82]

The presence of photographers and journalists at the airport on the crucial day was no accident. One journalist later said he was 'tipped off from Canberra' that Mrs Petrov was being driven to the airport.[83] Whether the timing of the Petrov defection was orchestrated by the Menzies government to help it win the election has been a matter of debate ever since. Harold Cox privately told his HWT bosses that Menzies was not as innocent in the matter of the Petrov disclosure as he was making out, and had timed matters to ensure maximum 'political bonus'.[84] An article written by Alan Reid, Canberra representative for the Sydney *Sun*, publicly suggested that Menzies 'framed' Evatt by deliberately timing his statement on the Petrov affair for a day when Evatt was absent from parliament. Menzies was highly offended and wanted Reid sacked.[85]

The Petrov Episode was widely covered in the press and acted as the catalyst for a Royal Commission on espionage, which kept the issue prominent. Labor already looked weak and divided on the issue of communism but Evatt's response to the Commission was so paranoid and politically inept that he lost credibility. In September 1954, the *News* published a damaging front-page story headlined 'IS DR EVATT FACING BREAKDOWN?' It reported that Labor colleagues were concerned Evatt was 'fanatically obsessed' with the Petrov affair, convinced that documents were fake, and that he was the victim of a plot. He was said to be shouting, 'white-faced and nervous', and 'badly needs a rest'.[86]

No other major paper, not even the Evatt-hating *Daily Telegraph*, reproduced the *News*' claims of a breakdown. The newspapers were highly critical of Evatt but the political reporting conventions of the time focused on public, not private behaviour, even if journalists and editors, including Pringle, had concerns about Evatt. A public incident in October 1955 dragged matters into the light though. Evatt's colleagues were mortified when he declared in parliament that he had tried to get to the bottom of the Petrov allegations by writing to the Soviet foreign minister, Molotov, to ask if the allegations of Soviet espionage were true. When Evatt said that Molotov – a known master of deception – had assured him they were not, there was a pause before incredulous laughter rang out in the parliament. Evatt's colleagues felt his performance was tragic and that Evatt was 'losing his grip of political matters'.[87] His colleagues observed him becoming more 'unstable', 'fanatical' and paranoid.[88] But Evatt remained Labor's leader for another four-and-a-half years, until February 1960. For the rest of his tenure, the Labor Party limped on in disarray over communism and his leadership.

THE LABOR SPLIT AND THE DLP

Evatt made such serious political errors over the report of the espionage Royal Commission that Menzies capitalised by calling an early election in 1955, which he won with an increased majority. The press was still overwhelmingly supportive of Menzies. The *News*, though, made no clear endorsement. After the death of his father, Rupert Murdoch was still finding his feet politically, but he was no fan of Menzies. The *Argus* was the other paper that stood out. Its main focus was on lambasting a new group of 'unofficial' Labor candidates.[89]

From 1954, Labor had been dealing with the emergence of a 'militantly anti-communist and predominantly Catholic faction' in the party influenced by BA Santamaria, who was supported by the powerful Archbishop of Melbourne, Daniel Mannix.[90] Evatt seemed unable to contain the feud, and sometimes inflamed it, including by denouncing 'disloyal' actors in the party.[91] In 1955, supporters of the Santamaria- and Catholic-aligned industrial groups formed a breakaway party called the Anti-Communist Labor Party (renamed the Democratic Labor Party [DLP] in 1957). This was the 'unofficial' Labor Party that the *Argus* was urging voters to avoid.

Like the previous Labor splits of 1916 and 1931, this one provoked intense reactions and divided political allies, friends, and even family members. The principal objective of the DLP was to keep Labor out of office until, in the eyes of DLP leaders, it faced up to the communist threat. Like Menzies and the conservative newspapers, the DLP portrayed Evatt as soft on communism and argued he was not doing enough to stamp it out within Labor and the unions. The DLP directed its supporters to preference the Liberal–Country Coalition ahead of Labor. This proved pivotal in keeping Labor out of office federally until 1972. Labor's opponents in the daily press were able to watch on contentedly as the party tore itself apart but also to help that process along by making regular (and sometimes exaggerated) reports on its 'disunity' and 'warring factions' (chapters 13 and 18).[92]

A COLD WAR PAPER IS BORN

Fear of communism was so strong in the 1950s that it motivated the launch of a new capital city newspaper. The *Northern Territory News* (*NT News*) began publishing in 1952 and became a daily in 1964. As the *NT News* later acknowledged, its founding was 'very much the result of a political game played in Canberra'. Two of its founders had never set foot in Darwin before.[93] They were Sydney business partners, journalist Don Whitington and former Liberal Party publicity officer Eric White. They teamed up with a Darwin printer named John Coleman and started their paper with help from the Menzies government and from businesses operating in Darwin, including, reportedly, BHP and Collins House's Zinc Corporation.[94]

The aim was to push Darwin's only newspaper, the pro-communist *Northern Standard*, out of business. Back in the early 1940s, a government letter had described the *Northern Standard* as 'subversive' and 'treasonable'.[95] By 1949, it was still the only paper in town. A weekly owned by the North Australian Workers' Union, it was run by George Brown, a 'well-known Communist'.[96] Members of the Chifley government had been concerned about the influence of the militant union in such a strategically important location for Australia's defence. On their behalf, the Secretary of the Department of External Affairs, Dr John Burton, had approached Whitington and suggested he start up a rival paper in Darwin. Since being sacked by the *Daily Telegraph* during the 1944 strike, Whitington had been a freelancer and with White had also launched a subscription newsletter called *Inside Canberra*.

When the Menzies government came to power in 1949, it was even more concerned about Darwin becoming a hotbed of communism and offered Whitington and White more concrete assistance, including accommodation for the newspaper and travel via the government-owned airline. The accommodation turned out to be essentially a tin shed. It housed the *NT News*' small staff, its one linotype machine and an ancient hand-fed press previously used for printing Arnott's Biscuits labels. But the *Northern Standard* did not pose strong competition. It was erratically published and sometimes did not appear at all. The *NT News* also made an immediate splash. As its staff were putting together its first edition, they heard radio reports of the death of King George VI and were able to lead on day one with that huge news story.[97] The *Northern Standard* struggled on for three years, but suddenly stopped publishing in February 1955. The *NT News* had fulfilled its purpose of 'materially assist[ing] to remove from the Northern Territory the influence of Communism'.[98]

CHAPTER 7
DEATH AND BETRAYAL IN MELBOURNE

When home-bound commuters picked up their copy of the *Herald* on Monday 6 October 1952, they learned from the front page that Keith Murdoch, aged 67, had died in his sleep on the Saturday night. The *Herald* made no mention though of the whispers circulating around its Flinders Street building. Murdoch's final days at the company, where he had spent 31 years at the top, had been marked by an internal power struggle, a sacking and the exposure of a traitorous plan.

Murdoch had suffered from heart trouble since the early 1930s, including two heart attacks from which he had never fully recovered. Murdoch found it difficult to relax or take time off work but operations and illness had kept him away from HWT board meetings, sometimes for weeks, during 1949.[1] At the end of that year, Murdoch had announced he was stepping back from day-to-day management after '46 years of strenuous daily journalism'.[2] He gave up his managing director title and even dictated a farewell message, but Murdoch did not withdraw into quiet retirement. He remained chairman of the HWT board and had installed a management structure designed to allow him to keep control and to restrain his successor, Jack Williams.

HOLDING ON

Williams had once been Murdoch's golden boy and protégé. The son of a watchmaker and jeweller, Williams had begun his career as an 18-year-old at the Sydney *Evening News*. Since joining the HWT in 1924, he had proven his skill and dedication to the company many times. Williams had been a star financial reporter and qualified as an accountant while working as a journalist. He was considered a 'genius' in the field of finance.[3]

In addition to all of his official newspaper roles, Williams had acted as a private financial adviser and strategist for Murdoch, including helping him gain a larger stake in News Limited. Williams knew a great deal about Murdoch's private financial affairs and strategies but was considered a master of discretion.

To the staff, Williams was a tough operator and a 'newspaperman's newspaperman', who had taught himself every aspect of the trade.[4] From 1933 to 1935, he had been Murdoch's man in Broken Hill, running the *Barrier Miner*. It was a tough assignment in a tough town but Williams loved it because he got to do everything, from journalism and editing to management and selling advertising. Impressed with his achievements there, Murdoch sent Williams to the *Courier-Mail* in 1937 where he worked directly for Murdoch as general manager, and then managing director, until 1945.[5] Again excelling, Williams was brought back to Melbourne as editor-in-chief of the *Herald* and *Sun News-Pictorial*. He grew their circulations and steadied the floundering *Woman's Day*.

Williams was highly capable and undertook the duties of chief executive in all but name in the five years leading up to Murdoch's death. But instead of giving Williams a clear, unqualified authority when he 'retired' from day-to-day management in 1949, Murdoch placed Williams' position as managing editor on an equal level with that of William Dunstan, the accountant general manager who was a Murdoch loyalist. Murdoch also appointed Archer Thomas (a 'one-hundred-percent [Murdoch] loyalist'), as editor of the *Herald* so that Murdoch's influence would still be paramount at the paper that was his 'life, his dreams'.[6]

Although he was no longer the managing director, and after August 1950, was past the retiring age of 65, Murdoch continued to go into the HWT office daily, and on many Saturdays. He was still trying to make decisions on staff appointments and giving opinions on matters that were now the responsibility of others. The HWT's top executives thought Murdoch was being unrealistic about his capacities. He was trying to retain overall command even though he was in poor health, especially after he underwent risky surgery for prostate trouble and removal of bowel cancer. For ten days after the bowel operation, it was not certain that Murdoch would survive.[7]

Murdoch had supposedly been casting around for a successor for years but none of the potential candidates had satisfied him. He favoured one aspirant, then another. His approach to staff relations had always been characterised by a paternalistic system of patronage in which he cultivated many 'bright young men' only to discard those who disappointed. To protect his own position, he also played staff off against each other – particularly Jack Williams, Colin Bednall and Lloyd Dumas. In Bednall's view, Murdoch deliberately kept his executives in 'fear and loathing' of each other.[8]

By 1949, Williams had fallen out of favour.[9] Perhaps Murdoch had never been fully set on him. In temperament and personality, they were very different men (Chapter 15). Murdoch came from a long line of Scottish Presbyterians while Williams was a practising Catholic. Murdoch was editorially interventionist, Williams was not. By 1948–49, Murdoch was being openly critical of Williams and often finding fault, and Williams was providing ammunition with his heavy drinking. He was spending most nights at the University Club, a private club in Collins Street, where he would get visibly drunk and talk indiscreetly. After one night out in 1948, Williams was arrested by police for urinating in Alfred Place.[10]

While running the *Courier-Mail*, Williams had also been known for indulging. (After Bednall arrived there to replace Williams in 1945, he discovered the *Courier-Mail* office was 'the biggest grog shop in Brisbane', with staff offices and lockers full of alcohol, and drunken executives and politicians in the boardroom.)[11] But Williams' supporters thought his excessive drinking in Melbourne was of a different magnitude and seemed to be a response to the strain of Murdoch's interference and unwanted advice.[12]

Williams was frustrated after years of outdated, overbearing and unnecessary supervision. He was also, according to Bednall, 'hurt and embittered' because Murdoch habitually made him promises that he did not keep.[13] The indecisive handover of power in 1949 had created conflict, especially when Williams did not defer to Murdoch on the running of the *Herald*. Murdoch had largely left him (and John Waters) alone to run the *Sun News-Pictorial*. They had built up its circulation to an unrivalled level but Murdoch was not happy even about that. He griped they only achieved it by lowering 'standards'. Murdoch wrote to his son Rupert in September 1950 complaining that the *Sun News-Pictorial* had become 'vulgarised, crimey [sic], badly printed and ill turned out'.[14] (Nearly three decades earlier, Murdoch had used crime to build up the *Herald*'s circulation, including through sensational – and some said, vulgar – coverage of the sexual assault and murder of a schoolgirl in 1921, known widely as the Gun Alley Murder.)

Colin Bednall was another highly capable Murdoch protégé who was favoured for a period. Bednall had used his friendship with Menzies to try to bolster his succession claim over that of Williams.[15] But Murdoch had come to reject Bednall, too.[16] His youth was against him (Bednall was only 39 at the beginning of 1952), and Murdoch seemed to fear he knew too much about the ownership of Queensland Newspapers in a way that could pose a threat to Murdoch's control of the company.

Rather than Williams or Bednall, who were both realistic candidates with suitable experience, Murdoch wanted his close friend, the former politician, diplomat and pro-American 'Cold-War warrior', Richard Casey, to succeed him as chairman of the HWT.[17] Since 1948, Murdoch had been pushing Casey to consider taking up the chairmanship. Casey wanted to return to politics, not go into newspaper management, but Murdoch had refused to take 'no' for an answer. In May 1949, he invited Casey to dinner at the Melbourne Club with Giddy and Dalziel Kelly of the HWT board, but still could not persuade Casey to consider the role. Even after Casey won a seat in the December 1949 election and joined Menzies' ministry, Murdoch persisted. He made the offer again in September 1950, and again Casey refused.[18]

Murdoch's insistence on Casey was odd. Casey was clearly not interested and he had no newspaper experience. His qualifications were in engineering. Although he had run businesses and chaired boards, he had never been a journalist or worked at a newspaper.

Toward the end of his life, Murdoch's connection to the HWT had changed. He was acutely aware that he had built up the company as a manager, not an owner. Murdoch held very few HWT shares. He was a salaried employee who could not pass on his managing director or chairman titles to Rupert. There was no guarantee of a place for his son at the HWT (and perhaps Murdoch's hope was that Casey as chairman would be more likely to create an opening for Rupert).

Murdoch (and his wife, Elisabeth) had also come to believe that the HWT had not properly rewarded him for his decades of exceptional service.[19] In 1946, Murdoch seems to have been earning a salary of around £7000 per year. This was roughly the same amount that Ezra Norton paid himself, and only £1000 more than Rupert Henderson made – and they were both in charge of considerably smaller companies.[20] Also, in retirement, Murdoch was due for what today would be considered a miserly remuneration package from the HWT.[21]

Murdoch had expanded the Herald group into a giant in the 1920s and 1930s, but since the 1940s, all of his major business moves had been for himself, not the HWT. Murdoch had focused on creating an independent newspaper chain, separate from the HWT, for his son Rupert and the rest of his family. He had given standing orders to buy on his behalf shares in News Limited and Queensland Newspapers whenever they were offered, and at premium price. Towards the end of his life, 'every penny he could raise was being channelled into News Limited' in particular.[22] Murdoch wanted to give Rupert a large shareholding and real power in one company rather than minority shareholdings in several companies.[23] The *News* was a small, tired paper but it had the best dynastic possibilities.

After convincing the HWT board to sell him the majority shareholding in News Limited in 1948–49, control of the company had passed from the HWT to Cruden Investments Pty Ltd, the Murdoch family company. But all of this dynasty building was expensive. Murdoch was carrying a massive overdraft, adding to his stress.[24] In 1951, after medical warnings, he rearranged his financial affairs and aimed for clear control of News Limited. In 1952, he bought more of its shares and raised his holding to 50 per cent.[25] Rupert later said his father borrowed so heavily, he 'cleaned himself out completely to buy the *News*'.[26]

Keith Murdoch had another project in mind as well. At the end of his life, he was secretly plotting the unthinkable, of joining up with a rival newspaper group and abandoning the HWT after more than three decades.

In 1951, Murdoch wrote to Lord Northcliffe's nephew, Cecil Harmsworth King, who had become chairman of the British Daily Mirror group after pulling off an internal coup. As noted in Chapter 5, the Daily Mirror group had acquired the *Argus* in 1949 and it competed against the HWT's *Sun News-Pictorial*. Despite the British invader's attempts to modernise and sensationalise the *Argus* – or perhaps because of them – it was not making money (Chapter 8).

Murdoch met with King in London in mid-1952 and began to negotiate with Jack Patience, a lawyer for the Daily Mirror group. Murdoch proposed a merger. The British would contribute the *Argus* and he would contribute the publications he personally controlled – the *News* and the *Courier-Mail*. Murdoch said that, with his newspaper experience and skills, all three papers would flourish, but the offer was neither very attractive nor realistic. It asked for King to put in a great deal of money and hand over 51 per cent of the new company to Murdoch, who was 65 and unwell.[27] Patience advised King to reject the offer because Murdoch was not up to the task and would have too much control.[28]

Like the Casey succession plan, the *Argus* negotiations seemed another sign of Murdoch's declining judgement. He did not have the energy to undertake such a big move at that point in his life and the *Argus*'s owners could see that. It would also have been a major betrayal because Murdoch would have had to run the *Argus* fiercely up against the *Sun News-Pictorial* and the HWT. Rupert Murdoch later claimed that the decision to abandon talks of a Murdoch–*Argus* merger was mutual and that his father backed away because he realised 'the people of Melbourne would never have believed he could leave the *Herald* of which he was so much a part; they might not accept what could possibly be seen as a breach of loyalty'.[29] Jack Williams at the HWT was one of those who definitely saw it as a breach of loyalty when he found out about Murdoch's secret plan.

DRAMATIC FINAL DAYS

Although the Murdoch family believed Keith's HWT service had not been properly rewarded, there were others who felt Murdoch had profited amply from the HWT over the years. Without HWT help, he would not have been able to branch out into Queensland to establish the *Courier-Mail*, and in more recent times, he had deprived the HWT of the *News*.

Some senior HWT executives believed Murdoch had a conflict of interest and had improperly used his position, and the HWT's resources, for personal gain.[30] Even the HWT's general manager, William Dunstan – who believed Murdoch to be a 'great man' – felt that Murdoch engineered 'outrageous' advantages for the *News* and *Courier-Mail* at the expense of the HWT, particularly over newsprint.[31] Cecil Edwards also noticed that Murdoch 'would select [the best] employees of the HWT and transfer them to his own papers', and that the '*News*, Adelaide often seemed to get the better of deals with the *Herald*, Melbourne'.[32]

Murdoch wrangled special deals for the *News*, including very cheap printing as well as access to the HWT's news services and its machinery. Those deals were at the expense of the *Advertiser*, much to the concern of its chairman, Lloyd Dumas.[33] In the early 1950s, Dumas was trying to break deals Murdoch had set up that gave the *News*, as Murdoch privately admitted, 'the far better side of the deal'.[34]

Even outsiders detected the breakdown in relations. In 1951, Christopher Chancellor, the general manager of Reuters, wrote to Rupert Henderson to fill him in on a dinner that Henderson had missed. Chancellor wrote:

> you have some terrible characters to deal with at your end ... Murdoch was appalling this time and left a very bad impression behind. He failed to conceal his jealousy of Lloyd Dumas ... tried to have Dumas put out of the chair for the joint meeting of the Directors and Trustees ... [but others] smacked him down and he failed to get his way on any point. Then during the banquet he spent his whole time denigrating and working at the Dumases ...[35]

Relations at Flinders Street were also strained at the end. Murdoch's 'retirement' plan had fuelled internal tension and office intrigue. Murdoch was still trying to exercise authority while Williams was doing the day-to-day hard work and had more staff loyalty, including from those who felt Murdoch should relinquish control and reduce his interference. After

Murdoch had had a second prostate operation in May 1952, his absence from the HWT office for nine weeks saw attitudes harden among Williams and his allies.

Murdoch had once prided himself on knowing all of the staff by name but now cut an increasingly lonely figure at the HWT. Williams had created his own team around himself and they answered to Williams, not Murdoch.[36] Murdoch felt there was a 'Catholic clique' developing.[37] Williams and Murdoch had offices on either side of the boardroom and kept a close eye on who was visiting the other.[38] Staff loyalty was seen as so important that HWT journalist Colin Fraser believed it was when the company's powerful advertising manager, Duncan (DJ) Riddle, started to join in Williams' social events that Murdoch decided to sack Williams.[39]

Murdoch had been considering sacking Williams since July 1952 but had ascribed the push to others. He wrote to Lloyd Dumas about the 'difficult problem I have been facing here since my return' (after his prostate operation). HWT board directors 'Harry [Giddy] and George [Caro] came to see me last week and told me that you all thought that the best thing that could happen was that Jack Williams should go.' (Dumas was also a director on the HWT board.) 'As you know I had come to that conclusion with some doubt and with great anxiety, and I fear we will just have to put it into effect.'[40]

In keeping with his technique of playing executives off against each other, Murdoch had shown Williams a letter that Dumas had written to him while he was recuperating. Dumas had said there was a 'bad drift' at the HWT and 'it was getting towards disintegration'. Murdoch showed this damning assessment to Williams who was 'confounded and surprised' by it.[41]

Murdoch conceded that Jack Williams had his good points. He was 'clear and good in mind', 'well-intentioned' and 'completely loyal' to the company. But Murdoch complained to Dumas that Williams was also brusque, sometimes hasty, and 'rude', and his editorial content 'tends towards the sensational'. Murdoch had already tried to coax Williams out of the driver's seat by asking him to go to London for a couple of years, but Williams had refused. Now, Murdoch wanted Williams to give 'an undertaking to abide by any instructions I would give him' but he was not confident Williams would agree to this and was worried he might quit and go and work for Packer, who had a close and lasting friendship with Williams and often tried to lure him to Sydney.[42]

Strangely, it was Arthur Calwell who triggered the final showdown. Murdoch and his partner in the *Courier-Mail*, John Wren, distrusted each other and were not close but Wren must have been aware that Murdoch was offering the paper up as part of his *Argus* merger proposal. Wren perhaps disclosed this to his close friend Calwell.

However he found out, the news infuriated Calwell as he did not want to see the pro-Labor *Argus* become part of the Murdoch press he despised. In September 1952, Calwell spotted Murdoch in Canberra at Parliament House. There for the Budget session, Murdoch was standing alone in King's Hall, gazing at a portrait of Joe Lyons, the man he thought he had made prime minister back in 1931. When Murdoch turned and smiled in greeting, Calwell yelled out, 'You bloody old scoundrel'. Murdoch was stunned.[43]

Someone else had also found out about Murdoch's *Argus* proposal – Colin Bednall – and he had tipped off his rival, Williams, probably in the hope of provoking a confrontation between Williams and Murdoch that would advance Bednall's ambition of leading the HWT.[44]

In early October 1952, Calwell ran into Bednall at Parliament House. Calwell beckoned him into Evatt's empty private office, then dramatically locked the door. He pocketed the key and told Bednall in a menacing tone, 'we will never forget nor forgive you for what you did in the 1949 elections'. He said when Labor got back into power, 'One of our first actions will be to have you shipped off for frontline duty in Korea'. Then Calwell softened and said, 'Perhaps I shouldn't be too hard on you. I know you and Jack Williams are plotting to get rid of old Murdoch and I expect things will be better for the Labor Party when you do so.'[45]

Calwell did not seem to realise that Williams and Bednall were rivals, not allies. Bednall's later account of his thinking that day was that he was gravely offended that 'Calwell could say I was party to some sordid palace revolution'. But he must also have feared that Calwell's interpretation of events might reach Murdoch's ears because Bednall cancelled a planned trip to Sydney and flew directly to Melbourne. He had lunch with Murdoch at his Toorak house and warned him that Williams knew about the failed

Argus plan. Bednall told Murdoch he would stay and help if Murdoch commenced 'a clean-up in Flinders Street' – in other words, if Williams was sacked – or otherwise he would return to Fleet Street.[46] When Bednall left that day, he was under the impression that he was about to be promoted to Williams' job.

Murdoch quickly called a special meeting of the HWT board for Friday 3 October. Williams was not sent his usual invitation to attend so he waited inside the building. Murdoch told the other four directors – Giddy, Caro, Dumas and Edward Richardson – that he had decided to terminate Williams' appointment. He obtained their approval to do so and to negotiate a settlement. Williams was then called in and told of his dismissal.[47] Murdoch had identified Bednall as Williams' replacement.[48]

After the meeting, Murdoch made his way to Cruden Farm, his weekend retreat. The next night – the night of 4–5 October 1952 – Murdoch died in his sleep. His wife Elisabeth believed the tense boardroom struggle was a factor in his heart attack and death.[49] Despite all that he had achieved in his long career, Murdoch had been vulnerable and fearful in his final days.

Just hours after being told of his dismissal, Williams was back in the office helping to write a glowing obituary of Murdoch and overseeing the memorial edition of the *Herald*.[50] Giddy had called an emergency meeting of the HWT board, the decision to sack Williams was overturned and all mention of it was erased from the minutes of the previous meeting.[51] Bednall was supposed to fly back to Melbourne on 5 October to discuss his new position with Murdoch but instead received a phone call telling him that Murdoch was dead.[52]

According to some HWT staff, Williams' dramatic return had happened because, upon learning of Murdoch's death, he had rushed back to the office in the early morning and had an employee from the engineering department use a drill to force open Murdoch's private safe. Inside, he found papers that he showed to the board. Whatever was in those papers convinced them to reinstate him.[53] Perhaps they included evidence of Murdoch's *Argus* plan or perhaps of how Murdoch had positioned his stake in Queensland Newspapers so that it – and his son – posed a threat to the HWT.[54]

MURDOCH'S LEGACY

Murdoch was survived by his wife (Dame) Elisabeth, his son Keith Rupert, and three daughters: Janet, Anne and Helen. Rupert missed his father's funeral because he was travelling back from the United Kingdom, where he was at university. Pallbearers included Giddy, Dumas and Williams, as well as Maurice H Baillieu representing the family that had been so crucial to Murdoch's rise.[55]

Keith's estate was sworn for probate at £358 852, equivalent to around $12 million today.[56] Unlike fellow media baron, Hugh Denison, Murdoch did not leave money to charity. He had revoked planned bequests to his children's schools, and despite his many suggestions of one day leaving his art and collections to the nation, he had left not one piece to a gallery or museum.[57] Cecil Edwards noted that Murdoch did not even leave a bequest for a legacy in journalism in his name, not even an annual lecture as 'the much less affluent and less important Arthur Norman Smith did'.[58]

When Murdoch died, his family trust owned 57 per cent of News Limited shares and he also had a large stake in Queensland Newspapers.[59] But Murdoch's estate had substantial debts, including money owed to Giddy's National Bank.[60] Once those debts, and the required death duties, had been paid, the family was left with very little in liquid assets. The executors of Murdoch's will, in consultation with his heirs, sold his Toorak home, his loss-making rural properties, most of his art and antiques collections, and his shares in Queensland Newspapers. This last sale left a legacy of bitterness within the family.

Upon Murdoch's death, Harry Giddy had become HWT chairman, and also the co-executor and trustee of Murdoch's will (along with Keith's widow, Elisabeth). The HWT had first option on the Queensland Newspapers shares under the terms of Murdoch's original purchase of them from the HWT. Rupert wanted to keep both the Queensland Newspapers and News Limited shares but his mother felt the family could not afford it. Once Rupert was back at Oxford, Harold Giddy and Lloyd Dumas convinced Elisabeth to sell the Queensland Newspapers shares to the HWT.

Rupert viewed Giddy's role in the matter as an appalling conflict of interest. Writing to Bednall from Oxford in December 1952, two months after his father's death, Rupert said the sale of the Queensland Newspapers shares to the HWT was 'a pretty bad shock' to him.[61] Much later, he told News Limited executive, Rodney Lever, 'They stole my inheritance. I could have raised the money in London.'[62] Others have pointed out that the family had little choice given Keith's debts, and that Rupert was involved in the transaction and helped squeeze a premium price out of Giddy that had helped eliminate the family's debt.[63] Nevertheless, the loss of the *Courier-Mail* was added to Rupert's grievances against the HWT even though Bednall and others viewed it more as a righting of wrongs because Keith Murdoch had 'conned' the HWT out of News Limited in the first place, and the company was just extracting what it could in return.[64]

The loss of the *Courier-Mail* hurt and not just because of its financial value, but also because it was the key to unlocking ownership of the HWT. In the 1930s, Keith Murdoch had used Williams' financial skill to establish the interlocking share arrangement (Chapter 1). All of the companies in the HWT group held a substantial interest in each other so any takeover bid would fail unless a corporate raider could manage to buy the group as a whole, which was beyond the means of nearly all local investors.[65] According to Lever, the scheme meant that '[i]f anyone wanted to take over the [HWT] they would need to know that they would first have to buy the *Courier-Mail* outright'.[66]

Lever's theory was that Keith Murdoch frantically bought up shares in Queensland Newspapers in his final years as a way of trying to give Rupert a long-shot chance of grasping the HWT.[67] And Williams and other directors on the board were reportedly 'horrified' at the prospect of Rupert Murdoch ever running the HWT. As a Geelong Grammar student, he would visit the HWT building 'arrogantly marching around the building giving orders to the staff. He was called "the brat"'.[68] Newspaper insiders said that the HWT treated Rupert like a pariah after his father's death.[69] If so, that may have been because they felt he was the intended beneficiary of treachery.

In his will, Keith had expressed his desire that Rupert should have the 'great opportunity' of 'ultimately occupying a position of high responsibility' in newspapers and broadcasting.[70] Although Rupert felt 'robbed' of the Queensland Newspapers shares, he still had the News Limited shares and was determined to be an independent force in newspapers just as his father had intended. He quickly turned down offers from Packer and Fairfax for a merger of assets. Bednall wrote to Rupert to express sympathy about the loss of Queensland Newspapers and commiserated that banker Giddy did not understand 'the difference between a newspaper and the normal sort of company. You do not just work for a newspaper. You have to live a newspaper – that is if it is going to be any good at all'.[71] Rupert Murdoch would 'live' newspapers for the next seven decades and well exceed the ambitions his father had for him.

THE *COURIER-MAIL*: FROM JOHN WREN TO JOHN WILLIAMS

When the HWT bought the Murdoch family's shares in Queensland Newspapers after Keith's death, it purchased an operating control. The major shareholding was still held by CWL Pty Ltd, the holding company owned principally by John Wren.[72] As part of Murdoch's and Wren's original deal in 1933, they had negotiated a split between control and financial profit. Murdoch exercised control of the newspaper, while Wren took most of the profits.[73] Aware of this set up, one senior HWT executive had said, 'Oh well, they've bought the right to wear Murdoch's harness and pull the cart for John Wren'.[74]

In 1945, when Keith Murdoch had offered Bednall the position of managing editor of the *Courier-Mail* and *Sunday Mail*, he had told him that, 'While I live I have complete control but after my death control will of course be divided'.[75] After Bednall took up the job, he discovered that Murdoch's partner was the notorious John Wren and was so shocked he stayed away from the office for days.

Wren's name never appeared on any company documents. He operated in the shadows through nominees, especially CWL Pty Ltd.[76] Although Wren had originally made his fortune from illegal bookmaking, by the early 1950s he was involved in mining, race tracks, restaurants and sporting stadiums, among many other legitimate businesses. Wren's reputation as an underworld figure and political manipulator was still well known though, and especially after the 1950 publication of Frank Hardy's book *Power Without Glory*. Its thinly veiled, fictitious account of Wren had him involved in sports rigging, political corruption, bombings, bashings and even murder.

Murdoch had told Bednall that he had made him a trustee of his estate to protect him and the paper in the event of his own death, but when Murdoch's will was read, Bednall discovered this was untrue.[77] Under the terms of the partnership, Murdoch had surrendered to Wren and his heirs the right to take over the *Courier-Mail* and its other assets in the event of Murdoch's death.

Soon after Murdoch's death, Bednall saw a small man sitting on a hard wooden bench in the foyer at the *Courier-Mail* office, swinging his legs like a child because they did not reach the floor. It was Wren, patiently waiting. (Unaware that he was the owner of the paper, staff had kept him waiting a long time.) Wren told Bednall that although the HWT had Murdoch's shares, they did not have control of the company. He pointed out that he had the right to appoint three new directors and take control, but 'as a gesture' to Bednall, would forfeit his right to do so. 'You run things', he said to Bednall.[78]

Bednall suddenly found himself 'one of [Wren's] team', which in Queensland, also included 'a Cabinet Minister, a police commissioner, a turf club chairman, sundry lawyers and [a] boxing promoter'. As promised, Wren did not interfere with Bednall's running of the paper, but he did ask for favours. He wanted stories in the paper promoting his boxing stadium in Brisbane, and promoting a beauty aid his son was selling. Bednall acquiesced to the first request but refused the latter, saying it was out of keeping with the tone of the paper. When Bednall ran an errand for him, Wren gave him a long-odds tip on a horse running at his race track. Naturally it won.[79]

Similar to how the mafia operates, Wren also kept pressing for Bednall to ask him for a favour. Finally, Bednall did ask a favour on behalf of Jack Williams. Williams asked Bednall to use his influence with Wren to stop a piece of legislation going through that would harm the HWT's control over newsagents and distribution in Victoria. Bednall went to Wren's office at Stadiums Limited in Flinders Lane, Melbourne, and then watched, fascinated, as Wren had his political friends block the bill from leaving the party room. Wren simply rang up a prominent MP, and in a quiet voice, asked, 'Is it true you're thinking of setting up a government board to run the newsagents? It is … Well, I don't care for that … please have it stopped.' Bednall sent a telegram to Williams telling him that Wren had taken action as requested but the more worldly Williams replied that he had no idea what Bednall was talking about as 'he would never dream of asking any favour of the likes of John Wren'.[80]

Over several months, Bednall also obtained a promise from Wren that he would support Bednall's dream of turning Brisbane's parochial *Courier-Mail* into a great national newspaper. Collingwood's win at the 1953 grand final dashed this plan. John Wren had a heart attack as he was fighting through the crowd to get behind his beloved Collingwood's goalposts for the last quarter. He died in hospital a month later. Bednall wrote in his unpublished autobiography, 'I had been so naïve'.[81] (A general, national paper would not be achieved for another decade, and not by Bednall [Chapter 13]).

Despite his reputation as a hard man, Wren had been a non-smoker and teetotaller who reportedly ate two whiting for breakfast, drank two glasses of water for lunch, and slept in an outdoor room.[82] He was possibly the wealthiest man in Australia when he died. His business empire was so vast, mysterious and complex, it took months for his heirs to work out an inventory of his assets. The total value of his estate was worth more than £4 million (equivalent to $155 million today).[83]

One of the first assets Wren's heirs sold was a part of the CWL holding in Queensland Newspapers.[84] And they sold it to the HWT. Williams understood the Queensland situation very well from his time in Brisbane running the *Courier-Mail* and he secured the purchase of the shares from Wren's estate. Added to the shares obtained from Murdoch's estate, the HWT now had clear control. The takeover was announced to the public in November 1953. Only Packer's *Daily Telegraph* rudely mentioned the involvement of the Wren family.[85] Other sources protected Keith Murdoch's reputation in death as in life.

Giddy wrote to Bednall and told him that the Queensland papers and their affiliated radio stations were now in Williams' domain. Bednall resigned. He did not think he could work under Williams.⁸⁶ Keith Dunstan later said, 'It was a mistake. Almost certainly Williams would not have been vindictive, and there was just a chance that Bednall might even have outlasted him to become [HWT] managing director himself.'⁸⁷

CHAPTER 8
JACK WILLIAMS: EMPIRE BUILDER, *ARGUS* KILLER?

Four years after Murdoch's death, the front page of the *Argus* reported its own death on 19 January 1957 with the heading 'YOUR LAST ARGUS'. A sketch below the headline showed a reader – or was it a journalist? – shedding tears.[1] After nearly 111 years, the *Argus* was gone. In the early 1920s, it was considered Australia's leading newspaper. When it closed, it was still a major employer and a Melbourne institution occupying a central place in the heart of the city (see Figure 1.3). Now, 1000 people were out of work and the wealthy British Daily Mirror group, which had 'swept into the Australian newspaper field roaring like a lion' seven years earlier, had 'left like a mouse'.[2] Conspiracy theorists asked: who killed the *Argus*? Jack Williams was the prime suspect but he was not the only one.

THE HWT AFTER MURDOCH

Williams was given the official title of managing director of the HWT in November 1953, a year after Murdoch's death. By then, it was becoming clear that an unleashed Williams was a godsend for the company. In 1954, the HWT nearly doubled the profit it had earned during Murdoch's last full year in charge.[3] As Keith Dunstan observed, 'the departure of Murdoch must [also] have relieved all kinds of pressure' personally, because 'I never saw or heard of Williams's being drunk, after 1952.'[4] And Williams remained a model of discretion. He made sure the HWT honoured Murdoch's memory, never spoke ill of him, nor revealed what had happened between them during Murdoch's final days.

Williams extended that discretion to the details of his own life. Unlike

FIGURE 8.1 A rare photograph of the HWT's post-Murdoch empire builder, Sir John Williams, 1972

SOURCE Newspix.

Murdoch, he never wanted to be a public figure. Williams was shy, aloof and introverted. He hated personal publicity and remarkably few words were ever written about him during his lifetime. Williams also hated being photographed (Figure 8.1 is one of only two known photographs and shows Williams when he was around 71). There is still no book-length biography of Williams, although historian David Dunstan has written several biographical entries and accounts. Dunstan had excellent inside knowledge of Williams because his grandfather, William Dunstan, was general manager of the HWT for 19 years, and his father, Keith Dunstan, was a prominent HWT journalist and columnist.

David Dunstan described Williams as being 'of medium height and dour expression ... [with] a gravelly voice and a twisted face'.[5] He was an intimidating figure in the office, with a 'glacial stare'.[6] As Murdoch had noted, Williams could be blunt but his supporters said that he at least criticised people to their face and took notice of people who contradicted him, whereas Murdoch was not often contradicted in his final years and that had contributed to his becoming out of touch.

Cecil Edwards said staff saw through Williams' gruff persona and knew that he was 'basically a just and kind man'.[7] Although he watched the company's pennies closely, Williams supported improved working conditions such as shorter hours, longer annual holidays and long-service leave. It pained him to sack anyone so he avoided doing it even when circumstances seemed to warrant it. Under Williams, the HWT was known as 'the best newspaper employer in Australia' and one that did not abandon loyal staff.[8]

Williams could be hard, though, and especially on staff he considered disloyal. When a columnist who had come over from the defunct *Argus* said he was thinking of resigning, Williams yelled, swore and threatened to blacklist and sue him.[9] Williams was complex, and according to Dunstan, 'a bit of a tortured man' and 'organisational obsessive' who, by today's standards, would be considered a 'control freak'.[10] Dunstan suspects that Williams was anxious and insecure, almost guilty. He seemed fearful of things falling apart.[11] Williams worked incredibly long hours and prided himself on being able to do every job in the organisation. He would suddenly appear at an editor's desk and take over. Or he would call up 3DB at 3 am because he had been listening and wanted to suggest a change. The HWT's chief of staff, Fred Flowers, kept a weekly summary of circulation figures on his person at all times in case he passed Williams in the corridor. If nine out of ten HWT publications were up in circulation, 'with unerring skill', Williams would always ask about the one that was down.[12]

In 1955, Williams negotiated another deal for the HWT in Queensland that cemented his reputation as a shrewd media manager. He managed to acquire from its owners virtually all of the ordinary shares of Telegraph Newspaper Company Ltd, publisher of Brisbane's only afternoon newspaper, the *Telegraph*.[13] Giddy tried to reassure Queenslanders who were nervous about a Melbourne-based media giant now owning both of Brisbane's daily papers. He publicly announced in May 1955 that it was not the HWT's 'intention to become permanent majority shareholders in the *Telegraph*. As soon as we can … it will be our aim to have the *Telegraph* shares spread over a wide range of Queensland and other Australian shareholders.'[14]

A year later, Williams led the formation of a new public company, Queensland Press, that joined together Queensland Newspapers (publisher of the *Courier-Mail* and the *Sunday Mail*) and Telegraph Newspaper Co

FIGURE 8.2 The HWT building in Flinders Street, Melbourne, circa 1956–60; note the HSV-7 van and 3DB studios, indicating the empire's span across print, radio and television
SOURCE Newspix.

TEXTBOX 8.1 Keeping the *Herald* on top

One way that Keith Murdoch made sure the *Herald* maintained its popularity was by keeping its cover price down. Under Murdoch, the *Herald* in October 1951 was the last capital city daily in Australia to lift its price to 3d, and this was a year after the other Melbourne dailies.

In July 1952, the three other Melbourne daily papers raised their price again, this time to 4d, as a way of dealing with rising costs. Murdoch again held the *Herald* back. He hoped its cheaper price would gain it an extra 10 000 sales.[15]

Williams also wanted to make sure the afternoon paper was affordable, especially when there were fewer commuters, and after 1956, people had television to go home to in the evening. Another 12 years passed before the *Herald*, in 1964, increased its cover price to 4d. Even then, it remained cheap compared to Sydney's afternoon papers, which both cost 6d.[16]

(publisher of the *Telegraph*). The official announcement again tried to stem disquiet. It said, 'No one interest will hold control in Queensland Press Ltd.'[17] Actually, at first, Queensland Press had only two shareholders – the HWT and CWL (Wren's heirs) – but in 1956, 1.5 million shares were opened up to the public. Confidence in the venture was so high that it was oversubscribed, and Williams' coup netted the HWT a handsome profit.

Contrary to promises made, though, the HWT did remain a majority shareholder, and it did exercise control. At first, the HWT controlled 33.7 per cent of Queensland Press Ltd, the Wren estate controlled 29.3 per cent, and the rest was held by members of the public.[18] But Williams was able to buy up more shares from the Wren holding because Wren's heirs were more interested in investing in the stock market than running newspapers or other businesses. John D'Arcy, who was later a director of Queensland Press, said the Wren family basically used 'the Queensland Press Share Register as a small bank to regularly renew their "petty cash"' and 'sold shares in Queensland Press Ltd monthly, over many years, until their holding became negligible'.[19]

Williams had cornered Queensland, and the new Queensland Press made excellent profits. He had also set the HWT on a renewed expansionist path with the 1950s later viewed as a golden era for the company. In 1956, it secured a television licence to launch HSV-7 (Herald-Sun TV Pty Ltd) in Melbourne, followed by the acquisition of television licences in other cities (Chapters 10 and 11). The HWT's net profit almost doubled again between 1957 and 1960.[20] Whenever large parcels of shares in the HWT became available, Williams directed them disproportionately towards Queensland Press to fortify the HWT's interlocking share structure and make Queensland Press the linchpin (where it had been Advertiser Newspapers Ltd in the 1940s).

THE CATHOLIC CONNECTION

When Williams began his career in 1919, his Catholicism might have ruled him out of a job at some newspapers. At a time when Protestant–Catholic sectarianism and hostility were rife, the Australian newspaper industry had developed from strong Protestant antecedents in the 1800s, including a high proportion of Scottish Presbyterian founders and editors. The sternly Protestant *Sydney Morning Herald* strongly opposed Catholics in its early years. John Fairfax, who was deeply religious, was a senior deacon at the Protestant Pitt Street Congregational Church. Along with David Jones, another Protestant bastion in Sydney, Fairfax & Sons was widely alleged to discriminate against Catholics when employing staff, although the claim that the *Sydney Morning Herald* hired its first Catholic editorial staff only in the 1950s, 120 years after its founding, is probably an exaggeration.

In Melbourne, it was *The Age* and the *Argus* that were considered 'blatantly anti-Catholic' in their formative years.[21] William Kerr, founder of the *Argus*, was 'an ardent Orangeman' who 'continually fomented Catholic/Protestant differences'.[22] Into the 1950s, Melbourne was still a city fractured by sectarian enmities, where real power lay in the Protestant-dominated Melbourne Club, and *The Age* still had staff who were reluctant to hire Catholics.[23]

The HWT was different, as Williams' ascension through the ranks in the 1930s and 1940s demonstrated. The Catholic Church had a long association with the *Herald* that dated from the 1840s. Although George Cavenagh, founder of the then-named *Port Phillip Herald*, was Protestant, his paper 'was sympathetic towards Roman Catholics', supported by the Irish community and promoted Irish Catholic journalists.[24] In 1871, Samuel Vincent Winter became a part-owner of the (re-named) *Herald*. Winter had first established the weekly Catholic journal, the *Advocate*, and was a leading figure within the Catholic community.[25]

For Williams, Catholicism was a key facet of his life. His mother and grandparents were devout Irish Catholics, and Williams was also a staunch churchgoer who regularly made the ten-minute walk from his house, or the HWT office, to St Patrick's Cathedral.[26] Significantly, Williams' local church was the site from which Archbishop Mannix acted as the centre of Catholic power in Melbourne for 45 years, from 1917 until his death in 1963, aged 99. For more than 30 years, Mannix, dressed in top hat and frock coat, walked nearly every day from his Kew home to St Patrick's.

Mannix was a fierce opponent of communism and a big factor in the 'Movement' which led to the formation of the DLP and the Labor split of 1954–55. Between 1955 and 1974, the Catholic-aligned DLP was able to command a significant vote in Victoria and Queensland, the two states where the HWT was most dominant. The HWT owned two of Melbourne's four daily papers (then two out of three after 1957), and both of Brisbane's dailies after 1955, plus key radio and television stations in those states.

Williams would have abhorred any suggestion that he used HWT assets to promote either Mannix or the DLP. Williams did not even want his Catholicism to be well-known among the HWT's staff lest 'perhaps he was thought complicit' in events around the Labor split.[27] His supporters believed Williams to be a man of integrity who did not dictate the editorial stance of papers under his control. Although the HWT newspapers remained steadfastly politically conservative under Williams, staff seemed to feel this occurred more organically than it had under Murdoch, who had been directly interventionist and had a propensity to run extreme campaigns (Chapter 15).

Journalist and HWT historian, Ron Younger, wrote that, although Williams continued the papers' editorial stance of criticising Labor, 'in the news columns [he] encouraged objective reporting [of] a range of political viewpoints'.[28] Critics felt the 'objective' news reporting was mere window dressing because the HWT papers always fell into line and solidly backed the conservatives at election time, but it mattered to the HWT staff who had lived through Murdoch's campaigns. Keith Dunstan wrote that Williams 'restored honesty to the *Herald* and the *Sun* [*News-Pictorial*]. To my mind he rid both newspapers of any suggestion of political bias.'[29]

The bitter Labor split and the formation of the DLP were particularly difficult issues for Williams, though. David Dunstan says Williams had 'strong sympathies for the cause of the DLP, which he kept very private'. And Williams' 'right-hand man [*Sun News-Pictorial* editor and later HWT editor-in-chief] Frank Daly was similarly inclined'.[30]

Williams may have tried to keep his views private, but somehow they tended to be very much in accordance with the public views expressed by the *Herald* and *Sun News-Pictorial*. The HWT papers argued that Labor was not ready to govern due to its failure to 'take effective action' on communism in trade unions and within its ranks. This was not an unusual stance among the daily papers in the 1950s, but the HWT papers tended to go further and to specifically call on Labor to cooperate with the DLP.[31] During the key years of the Labor–DLP split, between 1955 and the early 1970s, the HWT papers were notoriously hard on the Labor Party and kept up a running focus on any tensions, splits and divisions within Labor. When state DLP politician Frank Scully, a notorious industrial grouper and Santamaria supporter, lost his seat in the 1958 election, Williams reportedly rescued him from unemployment. (Scully became a newsagent in Sandringham.)[32]

Williams' personal beliefs and connections aside, there was one other important factor at play that was not widely known. In the 1950s, the Catholic Church was the HWT's eighth-largest shareholder.[33] It is unclear when the ownership link began (possibly in Winter's time), but by 1949 the Church held large shareholdings in the HWT through several different entities, including the Roman Catholic Trusts Corporation, the Catholic Church Property Insurance Company, and Daniel Mannix himself.[34] Yes, Archbishop Mannix was an HWT shareholder in a personal capacity, and had been since at least 1939, and probably earlier.[35]

The HWT newspapers devoted space to recording Mannix's activities and his views, including on state–federal relations, government funding for Catholic schools, and his remarks in 1953 that trends in women's dress were 'disgraceful' and 'women [were] degrading themselves by their dreadful immodesty'.[36] Was this attention justified because Mannix was a powerful and newsworthy figure, or had his connection with the HWT, and its sympathetic coverage, contributed to making Mannix a powerful and newsworthy figure?

During Williams' tenure, Mannix was both his parish priest and an important HWT shareholder. The archbishop was also linked to two other prominent Catholics mentioned in this book – John Wren and Arthur Calwell. *Courier-Mail* owner Wren was a major supporter of Mannix's and was rumoured to have bought him Raheen mansion in wealthy Kew because it was across the road from Wren's own home. Mannix lived there until his death in 1963. Mannix's determination to keep the Labor Party out of power meant Calwell was estranged from him on political matters but the Labor MP still treasured Mannix's friendship and religious counsel.

Calwell sat by Mannix's deathbed on his final day, and was a pallbearer at Wren's funeral.

After Mannix's death, the Catholic Church remained a major HWT shareholder. Not counting the HWT's interlocking shareholding arrangements, the Catholic Church was still the HWT's ninth-largest shareholder in the late 1960s.[37] It remained a major shareholder into the 1980s, and possibly longer.

WHO ELSE OWNED THE HWT?

The HWT's other important shareholders in the 1950s included banks, insurance companies and investment trusts. Collins House was on the decline after Zinc Corporation broke away from the rest of the group, but its long involvement with the HWT via the Fink and Baillieu families continued.[38] Descendants of both families still held HWT shares, albeit spread across multiple family members now, and directors connected with the Finks and other Collins House families – especially the Cohen family – were still on the HWT board in the 1970s.

Some of the other, large individual shareholders in the HWT in the 1950s were descendants of WL Baillieu's friends and contemporaries from the late 1800s, including Louise Dyer, a wealthy patron of the arts. Dyer was the daughter of Louis Lawrence Smith, a controversial medical 'entrepreneur' in the 1860s who charged £1 for a consultation by post, and later became an MP, newspaper owner and racehorse breeder.[39] Another large shareholder was Maud Hamilton Bowman. Although communist activists believed she was a 'front' for the Baillieus, Bowman was actually the great-niece of Thompson Moore who, like his friend WL Baillieu, was also a wealthy mining magnate, MP, *Herald* director, auctioneer and land boomer.[40]

None of the descendant-owners were particularly hands on. Bowman, for example, was a 'housewife' from South Australia who most HWT staff members had never heard of, and who rarely, if ever, visited the *Herald* office.[41] The ownership of the HWT was also becoming more dispersed. In 1955, it had 6000 shareholders, and by 1958, more than 7000.[42] There was no dominant, interfering owner looking over Williams' shoulder. He had an increasingly free hand in running the company so long as shareholders were kept happy, and this was something he took pains to ensure. Williams was a great believer in generous dividends.

THE MYSTERIOUS DEATH OF THE *ARGUS*

The wealthy British Daily Mirror group was considered the exemplar of a successful and modern popular-newspaper group when it took over the Melbourne *Argus* in 1949. In what was probably the most radical transformation of a daily newspaper in Australian history, the new owners took the stiff and staunchly conservative broadsheet newspaper and quickly turned it into a saucy, left-wing tabloid. It was not unusual for a once radical or left-wing paper to shift to the right over time (the *Argus* had done so in the past, as had the *Sydney Morning Herald* and *The Age*), but it was rare for a paper to turn from the right to the left, and with such dizzying speed.

Before 1949, the *Argus* had been known as an arch-conservative paper, so vehement in its convictions that most of its readers were probably never as conservative as the paper they were reading. One of the most successful Australian newspaper editors, Monty Grover (who had worked at the *Argus*), said the paper was living proof that people bought a newspaper 'not for its opinions, but its news'. He said the *Argus*'s views on politics were 'almost medieval' and it was 'hopelessly out of touch with public opinion … Probably not ten per cent of the population would support in their entirety the views which the *Argus* expressed … Even those who were most hostile to the Labor Party would repudiate the greater part of the abject Toryism of the *Argus*. Yet it had an immense circulation in its heyday because, Grover argued, the 'vast majority' of *Argus* subscribers 'held its views in utter detestation and [instead] bought it for the excellent, up-to-date and thorough handling of its news'.[43]

Even taking this into account, competitors thought the pace and scale of change imposed on the *Argus* in the early 1950s to be unwise. They thought the foreign owners were completely misjudging their market. Cecil

Edwards said the British owners tried to turn the *Argus* into the Fleet Street *Daily Mirror* but Melbourne was not London.⁴⁴ Historian David Dunstan said the *Argus*'s dramatic shift shocked its traditional audience in 'staid and suburban' Melbourne.⁴⁵ Clive Turnbull, editorial adviser to the *Argus* from 1949 to 1952, said the owners also 'much under-estimated the mental level of the Australian public' (see Chapter 16 on the *Daily Mirror–Sun* battle for some evidence to the contrary though).⁴⁶

The imported managing director, Sydney Elliott, was responsible for much of the hubris. Elliott was a neurotic, 'chain-smoking Scot' and 'Glasgow socialist', who proved to be erratic, overconfident and unwilling to listen to local advice.⁴⁷ Originally, it seems the Daily Mirror group planned 'to swing [the *Argus*] in behind' the Labor Party and extend its political influence (as they had done in the United Kingdom with the *Daily Mirror* and the British Labour Party), but they seemed to lose faith in Australian Labor rather quickly.⁴⁸ The 'byzantinely factional' politics of Victorian Labor at the time probably discouraged confidence.⁴⁹

At a sensitive time of Cold War politics and Labor division, Elliott had turned the *Argus* sharply to the left, then tried to make a formal alliance with Labor in the hope of gaining a big new audience among union members, then backed off that approach and left the paper with a tepid and confused editorial stance.⁵⁰ Elliott told some of the *Argus* staff that he was the illegitimate son of the Daily Mirror group chairman, Harry Guy Bartholomew, and they were inclined to believe him if only because it helped explain why Bartholomew showered favouritism on Elliott despite his lack of ability.⁵¹

The *Argus* was drawn into the divisive Labor politics of the time. In 1950, it was criticised by Labor staffers for fanning internal divisions in the party. Also that year, the *Argus*'s job-printing arm was contracted to cut the pages of communist Frank Hardy's book *Power Without Glory*. As noted, in fictional form the book was highly critical of John Wren, the Labor Party and the Catholic Church. Although the work seems to have been accepted innocently enough as a routine print job, Labor MP Stan Keon (who was smarting at the thinly-disguised fictional representation of him in *Power Without Glory*), claimed that 22 members of the *Argus* staff were known communists.⁵²

Journalist, author and historian, Robert Murray, notes that, at a time of Cold War concern and uncertainty about the new British owners and their aims, the accusation that the *Argus* was 'red' hurt the paper. In reality, it probably had about six staff who were Communist Party members (and some of them had come across from the HWT where they had been tolerated until the purge that followed Sharpley's revelations).[53]

In December 1951, the London board of the Daily Mirror group dismissed both Bartholomew and Elliott. Cecil Harmsworth King had used the example of the 'ailing, pathetic' *Argus* to help depose 'Bart' as chairman.[54] (Sent back to London, Elliott performed no better in his next role at the left-wing *Daily Herald* where his editorship was considered 'disastrous' and he caused 'nothing but trouble and friction with staff'.)[55]

Plenty of mistakes were made with the *Argus* but no-one could accuse the Daily Mirror group of not trying (to the contrary, some argued they chopped and changed far too much). They bought new expensive, high-speed printing presses. They changed the paper's size. They put pictures and general news on the back page so readers had as much news as possible before they needed to turn the page.[56] They introduced colour printing decades ahead of other newspapers. They raised the *Argus*'s cover price to try to increase revenue. Eventually, in 1954, they brought in a new and well-respected editor, Colin Bednall.

The printing presses were a solution that became a problem. In June 1950, the *Argus* had published an unusually frank 'letter from the editor' that admitted the paper was facing financial problems. It said the *Argus* was a victim of its own success because more people had been buying it, so there was more demand from advertisers for space, but the paper's pre-war presses could not print enough pages to accommodate them.[57] The paper's owners spent a fortune on new printing presses, including a pair of colour offset presses that were radically advanced for the time.

The massive presses were custom built in London in 1950 for the *Argus* by the famous Hoe and Crabtree firm. One press was exhibited at the British Industries Fair in London where King George VI pressed a button to set it in motion for the first time. The presses were then shipped to Melbourne and set up by engineers who had to sleep next to them because they took so long to assemble, fine-tune and test.[58]

The presses allowed the *Argus* to transform into a smaller size only weeks after the 'letter from the editor'. They were, as the *Argus* noted, 'one of the boldest newspaper experiments ever undertaken'.[59] When the presses worked, they were an asset. They meant the *Argus* was the only Australian daily that could offer advertisers colour printing on the news pages. And on 28 July 1952, the *Argus* became the first newspaper in the world to produce an action news photograph in colour within hours of the event. It managed this feat 'by synchronising offset on one side of the page with letterpress on the other in perfect register'.[60]

The *Argus* could not use colour on a daily basis because the technology was so expensive, but it used it regularly enough to make it the 'envy of the Australian newspaper world' and 'especially when it published colour photographs for the Olympics, the Melbourne Cup and the Queen's visit in 1954'. Circulation reportedly increased by up to 25 per cent for those special issues.[61] But the colour printing presses were horribly unreliable and often had to stop due to paper breaks in the machinery.[62] Sometimes the *Argus* missed all of its potential early morning sales because it was not out on the streets until after 10 am due to printing problems.[63]

When he saw the historic action photo in 1952, Keith Murdoch's private reaction was that the colour printing was 'well done and popular, but not truly effective without the backing of a really good newspaper – and the [*Argus*] has become a very poor newspaper'.[64] It was certainly causing its owners headaches. The *Argus* was costing a great deal of money – possibly more than £1 million had been lost.[65]

Cecil Harmsworth King visited Australia in April 1952 to investigate. Frank Packer memorably introduced himself by saying, 'I am interested in girls and horses. What are you interested in?'[66] Packer proposed forming a joint venture to save the *Argus*. The London company would put £1 million into the *Argus* and £1 million into Consolidated Press. Packer would lose some control of his Sydney assets but gain a foothold in Melbourne. Negotiations fell through after Packer greedily asked for £1.5 million for Consolidated Press.[67] The Daily Mirror group also considered (and rejected) proposals from Keith Murdoch, Rupert Murdoch, and also from Calwell who wanted to secure 'the paper for the Labor Party to run'.[68] For a time, Jack Williams – who was a 'drinking buddy' of Hugh Cudlipp's (the editorial director of the British *Daily Mirror*) – was also being touted as a possible executive saviour.[69]

In August 1952, about two months before he died, Murdoch had hosted Hugh Cudlipp at Cruden Farm and gained the impression that the *Argus*'s situation was 'critical'.[70] The Daily Mirror group's other Australian investments performed better. Its radio stations were thriving. By 1953, it had interests in 13 Australian radio stations, including 2GB (the leading station in Sydney) plus other stations in New South Wales, Victoria and Canberra. King and the Daily Mirror group also became involved with Australian television in 1955 as part of the group which obtained the Melbourne licence for GTV-9 and separately, as part of the group that obtained the Sydney television licence ATN-7 (see Chapter 10).

By 1953, however, the *Argus* was indeed critical. It lost more than £200 000 in 1952–53, and was unable to pay preference dividends (the Daily Mirror group had to step in and pay).[71] King flew Colin Bednall (who had left Queensland Newspapers after Williams took over) to London to meet him at the Savoy Hotel. Bednall found King to be the best informed of all the owners he worked for, but also 'cold and unbending'.[72]

King said he was determined to stem the losses and build the *Argus* back into one of the world's great newspapers. He invited Bednall to become managing director at a salary higher than any salaried Australian newspaper leader had ever been paid. (Bednall later quipped that 'it was [still] not enough to compensate for the problems I encountered'.)[73] In February 1954, Bednall became managing director. He was at the helm of the *Argus* for about 15 months and found problems at every turn.

Bednall discovered that the expensive printing presses were poorly designed and had a ruinous spoilage rate. Their colour units were 'something only Walt Disney could have dreamt up'. Sometimes, they worked brilliantly. Other times, Bednall wanted to send them to the scrap heap. The *Argus* was a more sensible, consistent paper under Bednall and he managed to get into profit 'for the first and only year' of the British Daily Mirror group's ownership.[74]

In April 1954, Hugh Cudlipp wrote from London to praise Bednall's approach: 'The whole paper is looking more dynamic, and I am certain that your news policy is dead right for Melbourne.'[75] Just a few months later,

King sacked him. According to Bednall, he was sacked over a 'relatively trivial' matter given the scale of the paper's much bigger problems. Bednall refused to publish a sales promotion stunt that claimed to give readers a chance at winning hundreds of thousands of dollars when he realised the fine print revealed 'the prizes were actually tickets in an illegal lottery'.[76]

Before being sacked, Bednall had passed on a proposition from Packer to the *Argus*'s owners that they start up an afternoon tabloid. Packer said he would put up £500 000 to form a joint company if the *Argus* would put in the same.[77] Again, the deal did not go through. The British owners had found the Australian newspaper scene much tougher than they had imagined, with its battle-scarred Australian owners and executives, its different cultural and political sensitivities, and its major newsprint and distribution challenges. (Bednall, who had experience of both worlds, said Fleet Street was genteel by comparison.)[78]

The *Argus* was on its knees by 1956. Its audience had grown, and so had its costs, but not its advertising revenue. The *Argus* had entered the dreaded death spiral where every additional copy it sold was costing the company money rather than making it money. Advertisers had shunned the bolshy, down-market, more left-wing paper. That was the deathblow, rather than a loss of readers. When the paper closed in 1957, it had 170 000 readers, and that was 42 000 more than *The Age*, and a higher circulation than five other capital city dailies had at that time.[79]

Many of the *Argus*'s new readers were in less affluent suburbs, and were not the lucrative 'A and B' demographic that advertisers paid more to reach.[80] And the new paper size was considered good for readers but not good for advertisers. Later, Rupert Murdoch would use the *Argus* as a cautionary tale. He said a lack of advertiser support killed it and only 5 per cent more advertising would have made a big difference to its future.[81]

The *Argus*'s owners made a deal with Jack Williams and the HWT. The *Argus* would be closed and the HWT would acquire the company's remaining assets – the *Argus*' plant, its three radio stations, its commercial printing arm, *Your Garden* magazine, and its successful weekly, the *Australasian Post*. The HWT paid for those assets by giving the British owners an issue of HWT shares worth £350 000 on face value but with an effective stock exchange value of about £1.6 million. The shares were in a special class, with no voting rights, to protect the HWT's autonomy. Once the sale was complete, HWT engineers quickly moved into the *Argus* building and dismantled the famous printing presses. As journalist Duncan Clarke noted, the HWT directors did not want 'to be bothered by the thought that a mighty battery of presses was in another part of the city, ready for action. So they were dismantled and sent across Bass Strait to Tasmania – out of the way.'[82]

David Dunstan's HWT informants said Williams 'agonised over the fate of the [*Argus*]' and was 'devastated' when the Mirror group insisted in the terms of the agreement that he close it. Williams had 'shed tears' over the paper's demise.[83] He was so 'anguished over the decision [that he] prayed for guidance for three hours in St Patrick's Cathedral'.[84] (Did he speak to Mannix while there? Mannix felt the Catholic Church was fighting for its existence against communism so he surely had some views on the 'red' *Argus*.) With significant misgivings, Williams complied with King's and Cudlipp's demand to close the paper.

In this version of events, the 'real villains' were the British owners, who had insisted the paper be closed and then fled Melbourne, leaving the 'tawdry fallout and frugal [staff] payouts' for the HWT to manage. There was no shortage of theories about why they had done so. Some speculated the British owners wanted the *Argus* destroyed so that no 'Colonial' would ever succeed with it where they had failed.[85] Others noted that the megalomaniac King could be very vindictive about anything that his rivals, 'Bart' and Elliott, had been associated with.[86] Former *Argus* journalist Jim Usher was convinced the Mirror group needed money because of a temporary financial squeeze resulting from the Suez crisis.[87] And some believed they killed the *Argus* because they needed the tax loss.[88] Cudlipp's later assessment was simply, 'wrong paper, wrong city'.[89] He might have added 'wrong owner'.

Williams made sure the HWT offered work to former *Argus* staff, but there was still some ill feeling among those who felt the HWT had played a subterfuge role in killing the paper. Among this group, there was a suspicion that the HWT and its executives were glad to see the back of a competitor and that the *Argus* closure was fully in keeping with the HWT's monopolistic method. At the December 1955 election, the *Argus* had also urged its readers to put the DLP last in every seat when Williams had known sympathies for the DLP. The Victorian district of the AJA produced a four-page leaflet titled 'Mystery and monopoly: The *Argus* story'. It argued, 'At the time of its closing, the *Argus* offered a greater threat [to its rivals] than at any other time.'[90]

There was also speculation that Melbourne's ruling class, including the city's largest advertisers, had starved the *Argus* of advertising revenue to stop a left-wing paper surviving in Melbourne although, in reality, the paper was much less radical than Melbourne's burghers had feared. During the four federal elections held when the paper was under Daily Mirror group ownership, it directly editorialised for Labor just once, and even then, it said the Menzies government's performance had been 'outstanding'.[91]

Whether it was poor decisions, the arrogance of British outsiders, the cunning of the HWT, suspicion from establishment Melbourne, or a combination of all of those factors, there was, as David Dunstan wrote, a sense that the closure of the *Argus* was 'tragic and probably avoidable'.[92] The *Argus* was part of Victorian history and its disappearance would have seemed impossible only a few years before.

When investors heard that the paper was about to be closed, shares in David Syme and Co jumped.[93] They knew that many *Argus* readers – and advertisers – would switch to *The Age* rather than the tabloid *Sun News-Pictorial*. When the Daily Mirror group had first turned the *Argus* to the left and down-market, *The Age* had turned to the right and promoted its credentials in journalistic responsibility to win over the respectable end of the market. The *Argus*'s death helped *The Age* solidify this new identity. It became even more solidly behind Menzies as a newspaper that prioritised a strong economy, low inflation and a US-based defence policy.

On the night Williams gave the final order that sealed the *Argus*'s fate, *Argus* staff had finished the last issue. Around 60 compositors – many of whom were weeping – performed a galley rattle to mark the passing of the paper, a long-held tradition in printing in which the long metal trays normally used to hold type are smashed against the compositors' metal benches.[94] The rhythmic sound echoed out into the dark of Elizabeth Street before the *Argus* presses fell silent.

CHAPTER 9
ON THE MOVE IN ADELAIDE AND SYDNEY

The balance of power was shifting in the turbulent Sydney newspaper world in the 1950s while sleepy, establishment Adelaide began stirring after Keith Murdoch's son, Rupert, arrived there to take up his inheritance of News Limited in September 1953. Rupert was 22 and had little experience of working at a newspaper, let alone running one. After completing his matriculation at Geelong Grammar in 1949 with marks that had not impressed his parents, Rupert had worked briefly as a cadet reporter at the Melbourne *Herald* under his father's watchful eye, spending a few months at the police courts with a friend from school before heading off to the United Kingdom.[1] Keith had accompanied him to London in early 1950 and introduced Rupert to leading figures in Fleet Street, helping his son land a summer stint as a junior reporter on the *Birmingham Gazette* – where Rupert made an impression when he tried to get the editor sacked by telling the proprietor the man was so incompetent he should be sacked.[2]

Rupert had then studied at Worcester College, Oxford. Again, he did not excel academically, but his contemporaries noticed that he was financially astute and a shrewd problem solver and risk taker. Like Rupert Greene, his namesake grandfather on his mother's side, Rupert dabbled in gambling and drinking beer more than his parents felt was good for him. And like his father had been as a young man, Rupert was attracted to labour politics. He famously kept a bust of Lenin in his room at Oxford.

Keith tolerated Rupert's excursion into left-wing idealism and even put him in touch with Ben Chifley, who always replied courteously to Rupert's letters. Keith told Chifley that his 18-year-old son 'is at present a zealous Laborite but will I think (probably) eventually travel the same course of his father'.³ In the last months of his life, Keith was confident that Rupert was on the right track and would outgrow his socialist ideals.

After finishing his studies at Oxford, Rupert worked on the subeditor's desk at Lord Beaverbrook's *Daily Express*, edited by the legendary Arthur Christiansen, considered one of Fleet Street's greatest editors. Christiansen was obsessed with detail and worked up to 18 hours a day for more than 20 years. His memorable instructions to staff were handed down through the ages, including his exhortation to 'Always, always tell the news through people'.⁴ The *Daily Express* was chosen for Rupert because it was one of the toughest and most prestigious schools in journalism. Keith had personally asked Beaverbrook to arrange this work experience for his son and Rupert trained as a down-table sub (a junior subeditor).⁵

When Rupert took up the reins at News Limited, that was the extent of his experience – a few months each at the *Herald*, the *Birmingham Gazette* and the *Daily Express*, plus all that he had picked up from his father's shop talk at home and the detailed letters that Keith sent Rupert during his school years.

THE BOY PUBLISHER

As part of the grandeur surrounding his rise, it is often said that Rupert built an empire out of just one tired Adelaide newspaper. To be pedantic, that is not quite true. When he inherited a controlling interest in News Limited, it published the *News*, the (Sunday) *Mail* in Adelaide and the *Barrier Miner* (in Broken Hill). It had a large stake in Southdown Press, which was housed in West Melbourne and published the national women's magazine *New Idea*.⁶ The company also controlled radio station 2BH Broken Hill and had a minor holding in 5DN Adelaide.⁷ Certainly, it was a small company by comparison with the HWT, but it was still a substantial start for a 22-year-old.

It is true that the *News* was a tired and insignificant paper. It had a stagnant circulation and was drained of resources and revenue.⁸ When Rupert arrived in Adelaide, he set about changing that and gave himself the unusual title of 'Publisher'. Old timers raised their eyebrows and expected

Rupert would sit in a corner at the *News* for a few years until he knew enough to have a say. They were misjudging him.

Rupert was a hands-on proprietor from the beginning. Editorially, he initially relied on, and gave a good deal of leeway to, Rohan Rivett, who had been editor of the *News* for almost two years. Rupert and Rivett were already close friends because Keith had sent Rivett to report from London between 1949 and 1951, with a side instruction to keep an eye on the boss's son.[9] Rivett, the grandson of Alfred Deakin, had been a war correspondent, and for three-and-a-half years a prisoner of war, including on the Burma–Thailand Railway.[10] From Keith's perspective, Rivett had some radical views but he was satisfied that Rivett was no communist, and in the early 1950s was a favourite Murdoch confidante. Rivett even named his son after Keith.

When Rupert arrived in Adelaide, Keith's older protégé turned nemesis, Lloyd Dumas, chairman of the *Advertiser*, gave Rupert a memorable welcome by trying to push him out of business before Rupert even got started. On 24 October 1953, the *Advertiser* launched the *Sunday Advertiser*. It was designed to crush News Limited's weekend paper, the *Mail*, which was the biggest circulation paper in the state and a solid earner. The intention was to force Murdoch's heirs to sell out so the HWT could reclaim the *News*.

Dumas was a knight, a pillar of Adelaide society, a city renowned for its 'luminous and eccentric' establishment, its British-style manored estates, and blueblood Adelaide Club members.[11] Rupert showed immediately that he was not going to play by the usual rules of conduct, though, including the unwritten rule that newspaper owners did not publish stories about each other. A month after the *Sunday Advertiser* launched, Rupert's *Mail* published a front-page story airing some industry dirty linen. It reported that, after Keith Murdoch's death, Dumas had gone to his widow, bound her to secrecy so she could not consult anyone, and told her to sell the family's controlling stake in the company to him. When Elisabeth refused, he gave her an alternative – either sell him the *Mail* or the *Advertiser* would start a new weekend paper and drive the *Mail* out of business. The article included excerpts from a private letter Dumas had sent to Elisabeth Murdoch.[12]

Dumas and Rupert fought a 'nasty circulation war'.[13] The challenger *Sunday Advertiser* was the better product but many of the *Mail*'s readers stayed loyal and it remained in front.[14] As Adelaide was not large enough to support two Sunday papers, both companies bled money for nearly two years before the opponents called a truce and agreed to merge. Both took 50 per cent of the newly merged *Sunday Mail* from December 1955. With no competition, it was very profitable. Rupert considered this co-venture a great victory and let it be known that Dumas had backed down.

RAPID EXPANSION

Rupert let Rivett develop the *News* into the most liberal daily paper in the country, one with a social conscience that published very different views to the establishment *Advertiser*. Murdoch learned all he could by working in various roles at the paper and developed a reputation for his overwhelming energy and for rolling up his sleeves and observing every phase of the production process. He was also becoming known for criticising and trying to make constant changes. One overwhelmed staff member called them 'Rupertorial interruptions'.[15]

Rivett focused on editorial while Murdoch focused on increasing advertising revenue, improving circulation, cutting costs and making production more efficient. Murdoch was particularly good at gaining retail and some new classified advertising for the *News*. News Limited's profits jumped from $62 000 when he began in 1953, to $432 000 in 1959.[16] Murdoch had his eye on expansion immediately. His first move was to expand News Limited's interest in magazine publisher Southdown Press. His next move, in October 1954, was to acquire Western Press Ltd, publisher of Western Australia's only Sunday paper, the *Sunday Times*, in Perth. (It also owned a Saturday publication called the *Mirror*, and 20 country newspapers.)[17]

The *Sunday Times* was where Murdoch honed his tabloid techniques. The paper was 'tawdry' even before Murdoch bought it, but he made it more 'sparkily so'.[18] Murdoch began flying to Perth every Friday to personally hammer the paper into a more sensational style to increase its sales.[19] Murdoch biographer, Thomas Kiernan, said the *Sunday Times* was the birthplace of Murdoch journalism, 'the exaggerated story filled with invented quotes; the slavishly sensationalised yarns; the eye-shattering, gratuitously blood-curdling headline'.[20] An infamous early one was 'LEPER RAPES VIRGIN, GIVES BIRTH TO MONSTER BABY'. He also used competitions and zealous promotion to sell the paper. These became some of the other hallmarks of Murdoch's tabloid approach.

The *Sunday Times* purchase was funded by a loan. Rupert had ditched the National Bank, which was associated with the HWT and Harold Giddy who had robbed him of his Queensland inheritance. Rupert's new bank was the Commonwealth Bank in Sydney. It was then relatively small and had become a trading bank only in June 1953. Its general manager, Alfred Norman 'Jack' Armstrong, and Vern Christie, who later became a managing director, thought Murdoch was a good risk, commercially savvy and always met his repayments.[21] The Commonwealth Bank's willingness to lend Murdoch huge sums would prove crucial to the growth of his media empire.

Rupert stayed in Adelaide for seven years, from 1953 to 1960. Aside from newspaper production, he was also learning everything he could about radio and television, including on trips to the United States. It was a crucial turning point when Murdoch's Southern Television Corporation Ltd (60 per cent owned by News Limited) was granted one of two commercial television licences in Adelaide in 1958 (see Chapter 10).[22]

After a visit to the Philadelphia office of the popular American magazine *TV Guide*, Murdoch launched an Australian weekly television magazine on returning home. Southdown Press began publishing *TV-Radio Week* in December 1957, 14 months after Australian television had begun (it was called *TV Week* from 1958).[23]

Murdoch was also buying up small papers in remote towns across the country. He acquired the Cold War–born *NT News* and the *Mount Isa Mail* from Don Whitington and Eric White at the end of 1959. Murdoch would fly into town in a DC-3 and haggle with the owner.[24] Former News Limited executive Rodney Lever said, 'His technique was simple: he would bully the owner into selling his paper with a threat that he would start a competing paper in the town.'[25] Murdoch soon turned the *NT News* into a tri-weekly, and the *Mount Isa Mail* into a bi-weekly. By 1965, both were daily papers.[26]

THE ESTABLISHMENT BITES BACK

Murdoch made two bold moves in Adelaide in 1958–59. One was political and the other commercial, and as journalist and author George Munster noted, these moves were not well coordinated; they ran in opposite directions.[27]

The *News* took a strong stance on the trial of Rupert Max Stuart, an Indigenous carnival worker who had been convicted in 1958 of the rape and murder of a nine-year-old girl. After a confession to police over which there hung significant doubt, Stuart was sentenced to death and his conviction was upheld by the Supreme Court of South Australia. Rivett was convinced that Stuart had not had a fair trial and the *News* campaigned fiercely for the case to be re-opened. The paper's attacks on authorities in South Australia's police force and courts were the talk of the city.

Murdoch supported Rivett 'wholeheartedly' and saw the case as a way to attack both the Adelaide establishment and the conservative Playford government which had been in office since 1938 as the beneficiary of a ruthlessly gerrymandered election system.[28] Labor politician Clyde Cameron, who was dining and socialising with Murdoch at this time, found Rupert 'was much further Left than me'. When the case was at its height, Murdoch said to him, 'I'm in a spot, Clyde. Myers [sic] have phoned to say that unless we drop our campaign in favour of Stuart, they are going to withdraw all of their advertising from the *News* and that means a lot to us ... I told them to go to hell.'[29]

Playford was forced to set up a Royal Commission to examine the Stuart case and the *News* ran fierce attacks on it, too, including lambasting royal commissioners for improperly sitting in judgement of their own earlier decisions. The *News*' coverage landed Rivett, Murdoch and other employees in court on a string of charges, including the archaic, rarely used charge of seditious libel, which could have seen them imprisoned. Rupert was said to be deeply shaken by the potential risks and how far matters escalated.

Eventually, the charges were dismissed and the *News* ran an editorial apologising and disavowing criticism of the judiciary members. There was speculation that Playford had dropped the charges in return for the *News* halting its campaign against his government.[30]

While the Adelaide establishment was still buzzing about the Stuart case, Murdoch made an audacious bid to gain control of the *Advertiser*. Backed by the Commonwealth Bank, Murdoch made an offer of more than £14 million in shares and cash to Advertiser Newspapers Ltd. At a time when News Limited had less than £1.8 million in shareholders' funds, it was one of the biggest corporate takeover bids in Australian history.[31]

Dumas quashed the bid. The *Advertiser* announced in its pages that its board rejected the takeover bid and Dumas announced that the holders of more than 50 per cent of *Advertiser* shares refused to accept Murdoch's offer.[32] Dumas added tartly that the South Australian community and the paper's shareholders have a 'real pride in the *Advertiser* and would never agree to its being modelled on the *News*', nor let Murdoch, as head of Cruden Investments, 'a Victorian company', exercise 'complete individual control' over the *Advertiser* as he did with the *News*.[33] The HWT's old hands had blocked Murdoch but he had made a strong impression and provided a bold declaration of his ambitions. He had also shown the business world that he could muster significant capital and it was becoming obvious that he would not easily be bought or driven out.

Five weeks after the last charges over the Stuart Royal Comission were withdrawn, Murdoch wrote a curt note from Sydney that 'summarily dismissed' Rivett as editor.[34] This was a man Murdoch had considered 'like the brother he never had'. Some speculated that Rivett's sacking may have been part of the deal with Playford.[35] Others believed it was inevitable because Murdoch was asserting himself more and his priorities were changing. Either way, it was strong evidence that Murdoch was not going to let friendship get in the way of business.

The Stuart case had happened at a formative time for Murdoch when his political views were still developing. Back in 1953, with a state election imminent in South Australia, he had written to Rivett, 'I implore you not to speak out too loudly on either side'.[36] Personally, Rupert had strong views on Menzies though. He was said to loathe the prime minister because he was part of the Melbourne business establishment that had rejected him after his father's death. Menzies had essentially chosen Jack Williams at the HWT over Murdoch.[37] Murdoch also thought Menzies was holding Australia – and himself – back.[38] In 1958–59, Murdoch had tried taking on the establishment in Adelaide by bringing on a showdown with the premier and the Adelaide Club but had to back down. The experience seemed to chasten him and turn him away from advocacy journalism for the moment, and toward safer forms that did not clash with his commercial goals.

PACKER'S INFLUENCE

In Sydney, Frank Packer started the 1950s on a low note. His talented editor, Brian Penton, died in 1951, aged only 47. Penton had given the *Daily Telegraph* new flair in the 1940s, driven up its circulation, and his active writing style had been parlayed into a much admired staff training program. Journalist Don Whitington described Penton as brilliant but also 'an evil genius who would go to any lengths to please Frank Packer'.[39]

Packer – who felt the Menzies government was not doing enough to stop inflation and wage growth – managed to squeeze one last sensation out of Penton. A journalist was sent to Penton's hospital bed where he was dying of cancer. Penton was barely conscious so the journalist left page proofs of an editorial beside the bed. When he came back, Penton was asleep but he had crossed out and re-written the first line. It now began, 'The Australian pound is bleeding to death'.[40]

A front page was devoted to this editorial and it got Menzies' attention as planned. Menzies wrote to Packer confiding that the Country Party was opposed to increasing the value of the pound and said:

> Your front page article this morning ... seems to declare war on me. If this is so, let's get on with it, while Chifley chuckles ... But I prefer understanding to dispute; and political good sense to brawling. Hence these lines to a man whose good sense I respect, and whose courage I have never publicly (or privately) impugned.[41]

Normally, Packer was firmly behind Menzies and used the *Telegraph*s to show uncompromising support, but this was one of the occasional flare-ups that happened if Packer felt his interests were not being looked after.

Another one occurred in 1952 when Treasurer Arthur Fadden introduced a bill to amend taxation law. It included a retrospective element that was going to give financial concessions to people affected by improper application of tax law, not tax them extra. But the *Telegraph*s savaged Fadden for the proposed changes. Norman Young, a corporate accountant who later became a director of News Limited, could not understand why the pro-government *Telegraph*s were using 'every known newspaper device to lampoon, discredit and embarrass' Fadden when the changes seemed so trivial. It was a campaign of 'hysterical bombardment' so severe that Menzies worried Fadden was 'cracking under the strain'.[42]

The working-class audience of the *Daily Telegraph* must also have wondered why their paper was so fixated on some obscure clauses dealing with the taxation of partnership assets. Packer's financial adviser, John Ratcliffe (a former deputy commissioner of taxation) was the reason. As Fadden explained to Cabinet, Ratcliffe was the 'master brain' behind an 'extremely ingenious' tax evasion scheme that had led to 'a very substantial avoidance of income tax'.[43] Although Ratcliffe's scheme was legal under current law, he was worried it was so audacious that a government might one day use retrospective law to rein it in. Ratcliffe had convinced Packer to campaign hard against the retrospective element of the proposal. Presumably, Packer was one of the beneficiaries of the scheme.

After Penton's death, the *Daily Telegraph* lacked the precision and vigour his editorship provided. An unleashed Packer – who had previously been restrained by his respect for the intimidating Penton – began interfering more and using his papers to express his pet projects and complaints.[44] The tax changes were one example. Another was when Packer commanded his staff to print a poster after Joseph Stalin's death in 1953: 'STALIN DEAD HOORAY'. The *Daily Telegraph*'s printing chapel thought that was in poor taste and complained. Packer stormed into a meeting with his printers. When they asked him to leave the room so they could confer, he told them he had more right to be there than they did, and they were the ones who should get out. The printers interpreted this as an order for them to leave the premises, so they left and did not finish printing editions of the *Daily Telegraph* on 7 March.

At a meeting of the PIEUA later that day, Packer insisted that he had the right to publish whatever he wanted in his papers. He risked a strike to prove his authority as proprietor.[45] In the afternoon, the Industrial Registrar ruled the poster instruction was lawful and ordered the men back to work. Some unfortunate journalist was tasked with writing a bizarre, fictitious front-page story interviewing Stalin's murdered comrades in heaven, illustrated by a crocodile shedding tears at Stalin's death.[46] Embarrassingly silly, it carried the byline 'Heaven Associated Reuter Cloud Service'. The cartoonist responsible for the weeping crocodile had drawn it under instruction but refused to sign it.[47]

The debonair David McNicoll became editor-in-chief of Australian Consolidated Press in 1953, and remained in the job until 1972. McNicoll was known for being good natured, unruffled and uncomplaining. Like Packer and Penton, he enjoyed the high life and womanising, and was even suspected of having a liaison with Princess Margaret.[48] The accommodating McNicoll was one of the few staff that Packer liked. McNicoll acknowledged that Packer was 'a very overpowering type of man' but said he also found him 'fair' and enjoyed his wicked sense of humour.[49]

One day in January 1957, Packer and McNicoll came back to the office after an enjoyable afternoon at the races. Packer opened an envelope on his desk, read the enclosed letter, then went white and slumped down in his chair. The letter was from John (Jack) Theodore, son of Packer's deceased business partner, EG Theodore. After Theodore had died in February 1950, his stake in the company had gone to his two sons, Jack and Ned. Packer did not have the respect for them that he had for their father.

According to McNicoll, since Jack Theodore had been made a director in 1947 and 'titular chairman' in 1949, he had sat in an office and 'twiddled his thumbs'. When the company entered television (Chapter 10), Packer gave Jack some responsibility and put him in charge of TCN-9 Sydney. The notoriously stingy Packer had been horrified to find that Jack was, in his view, 'throwing money around on lavish board tables and beautiful drapes ...'. Packer had scolded Jack, the two had fallen out, and then the letter arrived.[50]

The letter said that Jack and Ned 'wanted no more part of Consolidated Press' and were either going to buy out Packer or sell their shares (the HWT was a likely buyer). It was a takeover threat and Packer was vulnerable because he had just gained a television licence and his resources were stretched. Jack seems to have had a 'trojan horse' inside Consolidated Press who was feeding him sensitive financial information and he realised he had more power than he had thought.

McNicoll later recalled that Packer quickly 'had to lay hands on every bob he could beg, borrow or steal' to save his control over the company.[51] He had to 'mortgage everything' and change his lavish way of life. Frank and Clyde even broke into Jack Theodore's office one night 'to look through his desk', hoping to find incriminating information. They found none.[52] McNicoll said that after some 'appalling weeks, we managed to raise the money' to buy out the Theodores.[53] Packer had come close to losing the lot but his friend, stockbroker Ian Potter – a founding figure in both the IPA and the Liberal Party – had come to his rescue. Potter advanced money to the Theodore brothers to buy their shares while Packer scrimped and borrowed to pay out that debt to Potter.[54] Potter also became a substantial shareholder in Consolidated Press, a move that seemed designed to protect Packer's position rather than being a straightforward investment.[55] When the takeover attempt was averted, Packer became chairman and was more autonomous than ever.

> **TEXTBOX 9.1** Another Sydney strike, 1955
>
> With the economy booming and company profits high in the mid-1950s, printing workers began to seek higher wages and better conditions. In Sydney, the newspaper proprietors took a more ruthless and confrontational approach to industrial claims than in other cities, so it was again the city affected by a serious strike.
>
> This one began at the *Daily Mirror* office on 24 June 1955 when printers went on strike over a new industrial award that denied them the wage increases they were seeking. The newspaper owners had a joint interest in resisting higher wages and when they activated their agreement to band together and publish for a competitor in the event of a strike, printing staff at the *Sydney Morning Herald*, the *Daily Telegraph* and the *Sun* also went on strike.

As they had in 1944, the owners of the four papers joined forces to put out a composite edition printed at the *Sydney Morning Herald*. Again, the AJA and printing unions voted not to work for the proprietors' composite. More than 1400 Sydney newspaper employees were stood down without pay.

AJA members again published their own newspaper, this time called *The Clarion*. Volunteer workers first set up typewriters in their cars, then worked at the Federated Ironworkers' Association office, and finally at the Journalists' Club where the billiard tables were removed and journalists enjoyed the novelty – and convenience – of having a bar on the same floor as their editorial office.[56]

In 1944, the strikers' paper had been printed at the Communist Party printery, but in the Cold War environment of 1955 that would have been extremely provocative. *The Clarion* was printed at the Australian Workers' Union and the *Catholic Weekly*'s printing house.[57] The eight-page strikers' paper was printed on 13, 14 and 15 July. It reportedly sold up to 170 000 copies a day and made a small profit.[58]

The strike action went on longer than that. The *Daily Mirror* was not published for 19 days, the *Sun* for nine, and the *Daily Telegraph* and *Sydney Morning Herald* for six. No Sunday newspapers were published in Sydney for two weeks, and *Truth* did not publish for four Sundays.[59] The severest impact fell on the *Daily Mirror* and *Truth*, costing Ezra Norton a great deal of money and leading him to question his future in the industry.

The strike ended after a mass meeting of more than 3000 unionists voted to return to work.[60] Just a few months later, in October 1955, there was more industrial strife at Consolidated Press after Packer, who hated taking the stairs, sacked an assistant proofreader he thought had been messing around with the lift and kept him waiting.

The proofreader's colleagues went on strike and some journalists also left after they believed they had been sacked. The *Daily Telegraph* did not appear on the Saturday or Monday. Journalists on the *Sunday Telegraph* were told not to come to work and an issue of the *Women's Weekly* also failed to appear. Packer had to back down after he lost thousands of pounds in revenue and had dragged in two unions over such a petty incident. He reinstated the dismissed proofreader so work could resume.[61]

TEXTBOX 9.2 Magazines in the 1950s

The *Australian Women's Weekly*, with possibly the highest per capita penetration of any magazine in the world, was a profit-generating powerhouse for Consolidated Press. In 1950, a new plant and printing equipment enabled the *Women's Weekly* to move to glamorous full colour and circulation climbed to 800 000.[62]

David McNicoll, editor-in-chief of Consolidated Press, had to check with Packer on anything to do with the magazine and Packer regularly reminded him, 'The *Weekly*'s our milk cow, David ... Don't think that the bloody *Telegraph*s are paying your salary. It's the bloody *Weekly* that's paying your salary. That's the milk cow ... She's got to be very, very gently nurtured.'[63]

The *Women's Weekly* was a major contributor to the retail boom of the 1950s and an influential arbiter of Australian femininity (which was ironic given Frank Packer's boorish and misogynistic attitudes). Its editor, Esmé Fenston, shrewdly tapped into – and enhanced – the conservative tone of the 1950s. Stories about emancipated working women promoted during the war were out. The focus was now on family values, motherhood, home and the Royal Family, along with the staples of cooking and fashion.

In 1950, the HWT and Fairfax joined forces to try to make a dent in Packer's dominance of the women's magazine market. In September, Fairfax's *Home* magazine merged with the HWT's *Woman's Day*. The two magazines had a combined circulation of less than half the *Women's Weekly*'s.[64] Alice Jackson was poached from the *Women's Weekly*, which she had formally edited for 11 years (1939–50) but had effectively been in charge of for 16 years. Jackson was 62 but seems to have understated her age to her new employers.[65] She was in charge of the (weekly) *Woman's Day* for 15 months but it failed to create a strong demand and made heavy losses almost immediately.[66]

Keith Murdoch – who set up the venture – never had much success with magazines. Jack Williams was called in to try to save it. He reduced the magazine's losses, partly by making a deal with Consolidated Press and Associated Newspapers that all three of their women's magazines – *Woman's Day* (HWT–Fairfax), *Women's Weekly* (Consolidated Press) and *Woman* (Associated Newspapers) – would raise their advertising rates.

> In 1952, the Fairfax company wanted to cut its losses and asked to be released from the joint partnership. The HWT bought out Fairfax's shares and started to run *Woman's Day* on its own.[67] By 1956, the Fairfax company – now with more money at its disposal – was willing to try again. Henderson and Williams privately agreed there was room for only two women's magazines up against the *Women's Weekly*, not three, and also that neither of their companies was 'competent to run magazines successfully'.[68]
>
> Henderson was willing to try, though, and the Fairfax group bought back *Woman's Day* from the HWT for £200 000 and merged it with *Woman* (which Fairfax had obtained in 1953).[69] As part of their secret deal, the HWT agreed not to publish a women's magazine for the next ten years to avoid competition.[70] Even so, the *Women's Weekly* was still out-selling *Woman's Day* by more than 300 000 copies ten years later.[71]

FAIRFAX STEPS OUT

When Henderson had become managing director in 1949, Fairfax was a family company publishing only one daily newspaper, but that newspaper was one of the richest in the world. It had a near complete control of classified advertisements in Sydney and a cash flow that was the envy of other proprietors. The company had been content to focus on the *Sydney Morning Herald*, but in 1949 Fairfax & Sons demonstrated a new willingness to take on rivals and start expanding when it launched the *Sunday Herald* as a competitor to Packer's *Sunday Telegraph* and Associated Newspapers' *Sunday Sun*.

A further expansionist step occurred in 1951 when Fairfax launched a national weekly newspaper, the *Australian Financial Review*, aimed at 'investors, executives [and] businessmen [sic]'.[72] This was a defensive move, designed to prevent Associated Newspapers' from launching a rival product it was going to call the *Financial Times* but which was abandoned once Fairfax launched first.[73] Fairfax ran the *Financial Review* on a shoestring budget and it was a very modest publication in its early days, but it would become a bi-weekly in 1961, and a daily in 1963 (Chapter 13).

FIGURE 9.1 The *Sydney Morning Herald* heir who once rode a bus, Warwick Fairfax, 1953
SOURCE Mitchell Library, State Library of New South Wales.

The most dramatic leap forward for Fairfax came in 1953. For nearly a quarter of a century, Associated Newspapers had been 'short of liquid funds'.[74] It could not raise additional capital and had become – in the words of its chairman Sir John Butters – 'embarrassed' when debts for newsprint and machinery exceeded its capacity to pay.[75] In 1949, the company's production costs increased by a massive £480 000, mostly for newsprint and salaries, forcing Associated Newspapers to take out larger loans from AMP and its bank.[76] The company made only £2500 profit in 1950, and even less in 1951.[77] Shareholders' £1 shares plummeted and were worth only 10s 6d in 1952.[78]

James L Denison, grandson of the company's founder, Hugh Denison, noted that 'the *Sun* was finding the going hard against the lively tabloid [*Daily*] *Mirror*' and the *Sunday Sun* had been losing circulation for four years to Packer's *Sunday Telegraph*. Denison also pointed out that Associated Newspapers' board, led by Butters, 'did not have any directors with practical newspaper experience'.[79]

Butters was 67 and had been a prominent engineer and businessman. Competitors said Associated Newspapers' board was 'stiff', 'starchy' and 'elderly'. They described it as a slow and indecisive 'hydra-headed oligarchy'.[80] Rivals laughed at how Associated Newspapers hired a consultant to give advice on how to cut costs. The consultant reported that the company had 100 superfluous employees on its books. Management decided to keep the employees and sack the consultant.[81]

By 1951, it was costing more than £1 million a year to produce the *Sun*.[82] In order to be viable, Associated Newspapers needed a companion morning paper so its presses would not lie idle for half the day. Frank Packer had the same problem but he needed the opposite solution. He wanted an afternoon paper to keep his expensive presses running after they finished printing the morning *Daily Telegraph*. Packer wanted the *Sun*. He reduced advertising rates for the *Telegraph*s and hinted that he might lower their cover price in order to turn up the heat on the *Sun* and *Sunday Sun*.

In July 1953, Packer began approaching Associated Newspapers. Executives at Fairfax and the HWT learned of his overtures. Henderson was overseas but hurried back to Sydney.[83] In August, Giddy and Williams

FIGURE 9.2 Rupert Henderson, the business brain and managing director of the Fairfax company, in his office, Sydney, 7 March 1962

SOURCE Picture by Frank Burke. Fairfax Syndication/Nine Publishing (FXJ316880).

went to Butters and proposed partnering with the HWT through an exchange of shares.[84]

Henderson convinced Warwick Fairfax that, in order to 'protect the crown jewels' – that is, the advertising revenue of the *Sydney Morning Herald* – they needed to keep the HWT out of Sydney and stop Packer from becoming a more powerful force.[85] A merger with Associated Newspapers would also give the Fairfax group the huge advantage that Packer was seeking – an afternoon paper to maximise the use of morning paper presses.

Packer made a formal proposal to Associated Newspapers in August 1953.[86] Butters wrote up an account of this approach for his company's lawyers. He said Packer wanted to pay 20 shillings per share for the holdings of the board members and 'continue us in our directorships as puppets of Consolidated Press, in exchange for advice to our shareholders to sell their ordinary shares for £1 each'. Butters wrote, 'I need hardly say that I intensely resented this.'[87]

From Associated's perspective, Packer's proposal was not a merger, but a sellout to a company that Butters felt did not have 'the respect of the public'.[88] Consolidated Press certainly did not have the respect of Butters or his board. The way Packer and his father had exploited Associated Newspapers in the past still rankled.

When Associated Newspapers' negotiations with the HWT fizzled out because the two companies could not agree on the size of a share exchange, Butters and other board members met with Warwick Fairfax, Rupert Henderson, and their company solicitor. Henderson proposed a merger, not a takeover, and offered to match whatever price Packer offered.[89] Associated Newspapers' board members much preferred Fairfax, a prestigious company that valued its reputation for integrity. They agreed to sell Fairfax a 39 per cent holding and moved fast to head off Packer.[90] At 12.05 am on Monday 31 August (to avoid any allegation of illegal share trading on a Sunday), shares were quickly transferred between Fairfax and Associated Newspapers.[91]

The Fairfax company, usually known for its reticence and aloofness, had moved with speed, taken on the wily Packer, and won. Henderson was the driving force behind this and he and Packer would remain fierce commercial rivals for years to come. They respected each other and sometimes got on well – David McNicoll said both were 'tough, cunning, brilliant and hard working' – but Packer was very bitter about losing Associated Newspapers.[92] He backed legal challenges to the share sale that went on for two years but were unsuccessful.[93]

Sydney had lost one of its four daily newspaper publishers, but the Fairfax group was very sensitive about this, and wanted to avoid any appearance of diminished competition. Henderson insisted that even though the *Sydney Morning Herald*'s and the *Sun*'s management 'was unified under a common managing director' (him), there 'are four daily newspaper organisations in Sydney today just as there have been for many years'.[94] This fooled no-one. And although Associated Newspapers' directors thought the merger with Fairfax would guarantee their independence, with Fairfax more like a silent partner, that was never Henderson's intention.[95] He took immediate charge. Reportedly, one of the first things he did was sack the 100 excess employees.[96] Fairfax then quickly grew its shareholding. Within 12 months, it held more than 50 per cent, which made Associated Newspapers 'technically a subsidiary'.[97] In

October 1956, Butters announced that, because Fairfax held 98 per cent of Associated Newspapers' ordinary shares, all of its directors would now be filled from within the Fairfax organisation.⁹⁸

IN PRIME POSITION

The takeover of Associated Newspapers set the Fairfax company up for the future and positioned Henderson as a key figure in the industry. It gave Fairfax the *Sun* and *Sunday Sun*, as well as an extra printing plant. In October 1953, Fairfax merged its loss-making broadsheet *Sunday Herald* with the *Sunday Sun* to form a new tabloid, the *Sun-Herald*, as a super-competitor to Packer's *Sunday Telegraph*. Warwick Fairfax had agonised over what size the *Sun-Herald* should be. He thought people respected broadsheets more, but *Sunday Sun* editor Lindsay Clinch argued that tabloids were easier to read on the bus and at the beach. Warwick Fairfax finally decided saying, 'Yes, I think you're right – I took a ride on a bus.'⁹⁹

The *Sun-Herald* promised to combine the quality journalism of the *Sunday Herald* with the wide advertising reach of the *Sunday Sun*. Its bumper 88-page first edition broke sales records.¹⁰⁰ Although initially operating at a loss, the paper soon earned money. Before television, thick Sunday papers played a vital news and entertainment role – although not in Victoria (see Chapter 18). Within two years, the *Sun-Herald* was achieving a regular circulation of 600 000, making it the biggest selling newspaper in Australia.¹⁰¹

The *Sydney Morning Herald* was also being refreshed in the 1950s, or at least as much as the rigid conventions it laboured under allowed. Its Scottish-born, Oxford-educated editor, John Douglas (JD) Pringle, was an elegant leader writer with liberal views who Henderson had poached from *The Times* in 1952. Pringle had brightened the leader page and wanted to refresh the *Sydney Morning Herald*'s content and appearance further but he was frustrated by the company's antiquated division of powers which allowed the editor to only control the leader and opinion pages – not the news pages – which as Pringle later said, were 'by far the most important part of any paper'.¹⁰² He left at the end of his contract in 1957.

In 1954, Fairfax had made another big move when it sold its Hunter Street site in the CBD – which the *Sydney Morning Herald* had occupied for nearly 100 years – for a record price, and also sold Associated Newspapers' Elizabeth Street building.[103] In December 1955, the company moved 2.5 kilometres south-west to the inner suburb of Ultimo, then considered the edge of the city proper. The new premises were situated on a massive site bounded by Broadway, Jones, Thomas and Wattle streets. The site was close to Central train station, but away from CBD traffic snarls and close to arterial roads. This was important because most newspapers were now distributed by road not train.

The Broadway building had none of the elegance of the old one – it was brutally functional and resembled two large boxes – but the company was now able to print the *Sydney Morning Herald*, the *Sun*, *Sun-Herald* and *Financial Review* all from the one building using the latest printing and typesetting technology. This gave them an edge over rivals for decades to come.

From 1955, the *Sun* was beating Ezra Norton's *Daily Mirror*. Norton's weekly scandal sheet, *Truth*, was also suffering due to the circulation war between Fairfax's *Sun-Herald* and Packer's *Sunday Telegraph*. At 61, Norton was nervous about his health. He had long been obsessed with his own mortality. He was also finding the expense of modern newspaper publishing too much to bear, and the 1955 strike had hurt financially. Most damning of all during an era of male dynasties, Norton had no male successor. His daughter, Mary, was three years old.[104] Norton's first wife had a son, whom Norton had adopted, but Dr John Stanley Norton was a 41-year-old medical practitioner, not connected with running newspapers, and Norton did not consider him a significant heir.[105]

HWT leaders had been discussing with Norton the prospect of buying him out, but in November 1958 Norton decided to go instead to Henderson, his occasional lunch companion, with whom he was on good terms.[106] Norton's *Daily Mirror* and *Truth* would be an odd fit with the august *Sydney Morning Herald*, but Henderson was again determined to keep the HWT out of Sydney and Packer out of the afternoon field.

Instead of purchasing Norton's company, Truth and Sportsman Ltd, outright and taking the opportunity to close the *Daily Mirror* and give the *Sun* a lucrative monopoly in Sydney's afternoon market (such as the *Herald* enjoyed in Melbourne), the Fairfax group set up a strange and duplicitous arrangement. In December 1958, a shelf company called O'Connell Pty Ltd acquired Norton's controlling interest in Truth and Sportsman and changed the company name to 'Mirror Newspapers Ltd'. This shelf company was owned by Fairfax's solicitors and financed through a subsidiary of John Fairfax Ltd.[107] The connection was one of 'the best-kept secrets in Sydney's financial circles' at the time.[108] It was also a convoluted way to avoid being accused of having a monopoly in the afternoon market, and of having reduced the diversity of owners yet again, from three Sydney owners down to two.

The Fairfax group had performed some corporate housekeeping that made it more agile and able to take up opportunities when they arose. Unlike other newspaper groups that had become public companies in the 1940s, Fairfax & Sons was still a private company in 1955. Its shares were owned by ten members of the Fairfax family, with Warwick Fairfax by far the largest shareholder. (He held three times more shares than the next family member.)[109]

In 1951, the family was pushed to consider moving to a public company structure after the Menzies government reduced the amount of tax paid on undistributed profits for public companies but not for private companies (and Menzies was unmoved by his nemesis' complaints about the policy). In late 1955, the move became inevitable when the company needed funds but its application for a large loan was unsuccessful. By April 1956, John Fairfax Ltd was incorporated as a public company. Half the issued shares went to Warwick Fairfax and his cousin Vincent Fairfax, and half were offered to the public. Warwick became chairman; Henderson was managing director; Vincent Fairfax was a director; and Warwick's 24-year-old son, James Fairfax, joined the board in May 1957.[110]

John Fairfax Ltd had authorised capital of £10 million and made a net profit of £354 000 in 1956. Although impressive, this was still less than half the profits of the HWT, which had started down its own expansionist path 30 years earlier under Keith Murdoch.[111] All of the large newspaper groups were now looking towards television as the new frontier and the next opportunity for growth, profits and influence.

CHAPTER 10
TAKING OVER TELEVISION

Newspaper owners and executives had worried about the introduction of radio in the 1920s, but television posed a much greater threat about 30 years later. After a trip to the United States in 1952 to study the new medium, a Fairfax executive warned his bosses that television 'hits harder [and] with more impact than any medium known to man'.[1] Fortunately for Australian newspaper owners, they had plenty of time to study and plan for television. By the time policymakers began to seriously consider introducing it to Australia in the late 1940s and early 1950s, television had been available to British and American audiences for more than 15 years.

In the United States especially, television was causing a social revolution. American households were already watching an average of 4.5 hours of television a day in 1950.[2] They no longer spent that leisure time at the cinema, listening to radio, or reading newspapers and magazines. Australia's press owners could see American and British newspapers were feeling the negative effects of television and they were determined to avoid the same fate. If television was going to cut into their newspapers' circulations and advertising revenue, they wanted to be the ones to wield the axe and reap the benefits.

PREPARING FOR TELEVISION

Between the mid-1930s and the late 1940s, most Australian newspapers reported on the development of television in generally negative terms. Years after it was well established in the United Kingdom and United States, Australian newspapers kept describing television as experimental technology likely to cause social problems.[3] But Associated Newspapers was more enthusiastic than most newspaper companies. Its first chairman, Hugh Denison, was a radio pioneer interested in new technology. Denison met with the chairman of the Baird company in London in the 1930s when it was the only company with a practical system of television (based on the work of Scottish electrical engineer, John Logie Baird). Around 1935, Denison visited a fully equipped television broadcasting station hidden beneath the glass Crystal Palace. It was the most extensive facility of its kind in Europe before it mysteriously burned down in a suspected act of industrial sabotage in 1936.

Associated Newspapers wanted to be the first to present a television broadcast in Australia. In 1939, it asked General Electric (GE) in London to install a television transmitter on the *Sun*'s roof in Sydney, but GE said that distance made that impossible.[4] World War II and Associated Newspapers' financial woes also stymied development but the company remained keen. Its next chairman, John Butters, was a distinguished engineer who was well placed to study television. He travelled to the United States several times in the early 1950s; in New York, he visited the most advanced television manufacturer in the world, Radio Corporation of America (RCA), and its National Broadcasting Company (NBC), one of the two largest television networks in the United States. Butters also studied television in the United Kingdom and France before sending staff on further tours of the United States and Europe.[5]

The HWT was also planning ahead. It brought out American television experts to Australia and sent several executives, including Jack Williams, overseas. On a 1952 trip to the United States, Lloyd Dumas wrote to Keith Murdoch to tell him the San Francisco *Chronicle* had invested US$2 million in a television station and made it all back in less than a year because demand for television advertising was so high. Dumas stressed that limited competition was the key, though. If too many television stations were competing 'the honeymoon would be over'.[6]

Newspaper owners and executives who considered themselves free-market enthusiasts were strongly attracted to television from the beginning because it was a field of competition limited by government. Television transmission took place over a radio spectrum that could fit only a limited number of channels, so broadcasters had to be licensed by the government. Which party was in government suddenly became of even more consequence to the newspaper groups.

Among the others, Fairfax, Consolidated Press and Rupert Murdoch were also investigating television. During his Adelaide years, Murdoch toured the world twice to look at television stations and make connections with program suppliers, especially in the United States.[7]

From their many overseas trips, Australia's press owners knew what they definitely did *not* want to see in Australia: British- and French-style public broadcasting that would lock them out of television. In the United Kingdom, the BBC had begun television broadcasting in August 1936, and in 1954, it still retained a monopoly on both radio and television. Originally, the big London newspapers had 'not only supported the case for public broadcasting but demanded it' to protect 'their advertising revenues from an alarming new form of competition'.[8] British newspapers were still protected from commercial advertising on radio and television in 1954.

The Australian newspaper proprietors took a different attitude, which was summed up by the chief executive officer of Associated Newspapers, Eric Kennedy, when he wrote to his superiors in 1953. Kennedy argued that Australian newspapers needed to 'control commercial television'. He called it 'the selfish motif': 'As publishers of newspapers, we have a considerable investment to guard … television will eat into the advertising revenues of newspapers' and provide 'very strong competition'.[9]

In other words, Australian newspaper executives did not fear television advertising, so long as they were the ones in control of it. Rather than British-style public broadcasting, it was the unbridled commercialism and profit-making potential of American television they wanted Australia's policymakers to emulate. The newspapers were also convinced that they needed to be in television from the beginning. Unlike radio, there would be few licences available and much less opportunity to get involved later. The first stations also quickly became embedded with audiences and advertisers, making it much harder for latecomers.

They could see that American newspapers had missed their chance to control television. Although American newspapers were involved in a quarter of US television stations in 1955, they were not the major players.[10] Between 1946 and 1955, three large radio networks had taken control of

American television – NBC, the Columbia Broadcasting System (CBS) and the American Broadcasting Company (ABC).[11] (The San Francisco *Chronicle*'s television station, KRON, that Dumas had mentioned, was an NBC affiliate.) Before they went into television, the three radio networks had absolutely dominated commercial radio in the United States. They were owned by electrical manufacturing and communications companies, including GE and Westinghouse, that originally went into radio in order to sell radio sets.[12]

As advertisers followed audiences over to television, the period between 1949 and 1959 proved disastrous for American newspapers. They could not raise their advertising rates to cover their rising costs because radio and television were providing such strong competition. During that ten-year period, 217 American daily newspapers disappeared, and more than 1200 American cities became one-paper towns.[13] Even the big-city newspapers were feeling the effects. After a visit to the United States in 1954, Associated Newspapers' accountant (who was also one of its directors), told Butters that New York's newspapers were regretting they did not get into television early, and the lesson he took home was that 'we should undoubtedly press to get a licence for ourselves'.[14]

Australia's big newspaper groups had a major advantage as they set about achieving that goal. Many of them were not only newspaper proprietors but also radio broadcasters. Being awarded key radio licences by the Lyons government in the 1930s had encouraged the newspaper industry to develop a firm grip over Australian radio. In 1952–53, 48 per cent of commercial radio stations were owned, or part-owned, by newspapers.[15] There were only two major radio networks in Australia, and newspaper groups were at the centre of both.

The HWT stations, including some of the most popular in the big capital cities, formed the core of the Major Broadcasting Network, while six other newspaper groups (the British Daily Mirror group, Fairfax, David Syme and Co, News Limited, WAN and Davies Brothers) were involved in the Macquarie Broadcasting Network. A proprietary company owned by its 18 member radio stations, the Macquarie Network also had about 40 cooperating stations, giving it a very wide reach across Australia.[16]

Although the Fairfax group was a newcomer in radio compared to the

TEXTBOX 10.1 Australia's two major commercial radio networks, 1954–55

The Macquarie Broadcasting Network was owned by its member shareholders:

New South Wales
2CA Canberra (2GB)
2GB Sydney (DMG 45%, Fairfax 14%)
2LF Young (DMG, 2GB)
2LT Lithgow (2GB, DMG)
2MW Murwillumbah
2PK Parkes (DMG)
2NM Muswellbrook
2NX Bolwarra
2WL Wollongong (DMG)

Victoria
3AW Melbourne (David Syme and Co*, 2GB)

South Australia
5DN Adelaide (2GB/News Limited)**

Western Australia
6IX Perth (WAN)
6MD Merredin (WAN)
6WB Katanning (WAN)
6BY Bridgetown (WAN)

Tasmania
7HO Hobart (Davies Brothers)
7LA Launceston

The Major Broadcasting Network was an association of stations;

New South Wales
2UE Sydney
(Associated Newspapers/Fairfax)
2KO Newcastle
2NZ Inverell
2GZ Orange

Victoria
3DB Melbourne (HWT)
3LK Lubeck (HWT)

South Australia
5AD Adelaide (Advertiser/HWT)
5MU Murray Bridge (Advertiser/HWT)
5PI Crystal Brook (Advertiser/HWT)
5SE Mount Gambier (Advertiser/HWT)

Queensland
4AK Oakey (Qld Newspapers/HWT)
4BK Brisbane (Qld Newspapers/HWT)

Western Australia
6CI Collie
6PR Perth
6TZ Bunbury

Tasmania
EX Launceston
7HT Hobart

NOTE DMG = British Daily Mirror group. Textbox shows both minor and majority interests.

* Through its quarter interest in 3AW, David Syme and Co also controlled 3CV Maryborough, which was linked with three Victorian stations (3HA, 3SH, 3TR).

** News Limited also fully owned 2BH Broken Hill, and had a stake in 5RM Renmark.

SOURCE ABCB, *7th Annual Report*, Canberra, Commonwealth of Australia, 1954–55.

HWT, it had purchased a substantial interest in 2GB Sydney, the nucleus of the Macquarie Network, in 1952. And, after taking over Associated Newspapers, it also controlled 2UE Sydney between 1953 and 1956. This meant it had a pivotal station in both of the major radio networks while the shape of Australian television was being determined.

The British Daily Mirror group was still the owner of the *Argus* throughout that crucial period and during the events described in this chapter. It had built up such a large stake in Australian radio – a chain of 12 stations, and substantial control of 2GB and the Macquarie Network – that a resolution of Parliament protesting so much foreign ownership of Australian radio led it to reduce its radio interests in 1952–53.[17] Even after that, the Daily Mirror group still owned 45 per cent of 2GB (in which it was a co-owner with Fairfax), and 2GB had shares in other stations in the Macquarie Network, including 3AW (which made the Mirror group also a partner of *The Age*).[18] Separately, the Daily Mirror group also kept hold of the *Argus*'s three country Victorian radio stations (3SR, 3UL and 3YB), and ran them as a mini-network.[19]

Because the Australian newspaper groups had developed – on a more modest scale – some of the skillset and experience of the American radio networks, they hoped they would be able to emulate their leap from radio into dominating commercial television. The Australian Federation of Commercial Radio Broadcasters was lobbying politicians in the early 1950s and telling them that commercial radio stations were 'better equipped than any other applicant' to start up Australian television, and overseas 'precedent has been to grant TV licences to experienced broadcasters'.[20] Ironically, it would be a newspaper group that had no radio station which would become most dominant in commercial television. Although Consolidated Press lacked broadcasting experience, Packer was confident, from as early as 1951, that his company would be awarded a television licence.[21] The necessary conditions for success had been sown years before.

SHAPING TELEVISION

In order to have any chance of controlling television from its outset, the newspaper groups had first needed Labor out of office. The matter had become urgent in the lead-up to the 1949 election because, in 1948, the Chifley government took steps to prohibit commercial participation in television, with Calwell leading the fight against commercial media. Then, six months before the election, Chifley announced the government was hastening to build a British-style national public television system. This provoked a fierce response from newspaper groups that were wanting to obtain a commercial television licence.[22]

The *Herald* argued on its front page that, unless private enterprise played a role, Chifley's television system would be expensive, unprofitable and inferior. The *Advertiser* called the government's policy an 'AIMLESS APPROACH TO TELEVISION'.[23] Packer's *Daily Telegraph* – whose parent company had applied for a commercial television licence during World War II, and would again in 1949 even though none had been advertised – suddenly did not want television to go ahead when Labor was in office. It warned readers that, if television came to Australia, 'Your children will refuse to do their homework', 'no one will talk to you' when the television is on, and friends and neighbours will drop in uninvited 'at the oddest hours' to watch your television.[24]

The newspaper groups' television hopes were deeply entwined with the outcome of the 1949 election. Calls for tenders to build television transmitters in each capital city, that would be controlled by the ABC, had already been published, and Calwell would probably be made minister for broadcasting if Labor won.[25] As noted in Chapter 5, most newspapers campaigned fiercely against Labor in 1949 and threw their full support behind Menzies and the Liberal Party. Menzies had made clear that he opposed Labor's plan for 'a Government monopoly' of television.[26] He was the newspapers' best chance to secure a stake in television from the outset, and they must have hoped that he would remember their strong support when it came time for television licences to be allocated.

Once Menzies was in office, the next step was to convince him to move forward with introducing television because Menzies was in no hurry. He disliked television and had said, 'I hope this thing will not come to Australia in my term of office.'[27] (It was rumoured that Menzies' aversion developed after he was subjected to a bruising live television interview on a 'meet the press'–style program in the United States.)[28] Aside from Menzies' personal views, the newspaper groups also believed the motion picture industry was using its influence in government circles to delay the introduction of television.[29]

In the early 1950s, people still paid to go to 'the pictures' sometimes four or five times a week, and the cinema industry was (rightly) concerned about television affecting cinema attendance.[30] The cinema industry had been one of the first in Australia to come under American control, and four heads of the powerful US cinema industry visited Australia in late 1952 to lobby politicians against television. The industry had a friend in Cabinet with Harold Holt believed to be lobbying on behalf of the cinema interests.[31] (Holt's father was a theatre manager and film producer, and his brother was a publicity director for Hoyts, owned by the American 20th Century Fox.)[32]

The newspapers had also unintentionally made the environment less conducive to action because they had been a bit too effective in attacking the Chifley government's plans for introducing television on the basis that it was too expensive. The Menzies Cabinet was worried about the public reaction if it spent taxpayers' money on a luxury item such as television when Australia was coming out of hard economic times and needed funds to develop the national economy and secure power supplies and food production.[33]

In April 1952, the Australian Federation of Commercial Radio Broadcasters met with Menzies in Canberra and told him that, rather than being a distraction from economic recovery, television would work as an 'incentive to production ... [because] the ordinary citizen would work harder for luxuries [like television and the products it advertised] than necessities'. They also warned Menzies that a 'Government monopoly would be open to abuse as a powerful political medium'.[34] In other words, if Labor was in office they might use public television against the conservatives.

Colin Bednall, managing editor and director of the *Courier-Mail* and its radio stations, was also dispatched to lobby Menzies as an agent of the press–radio owners. Bednall had been dazzled by television during a trip to the United States in 1952, and was on very good terms with Menzies (who was a friend of Bednall's in-laws). During World War II, they had spent time together in London, and Menzies was grateful to Bednall for the support the *Courier-Mail* had given him.[35]

They met at Lennon's Hotel in Brisbane. Menzies did not seem particularly impressed by Bednall's argument about the 'growth and power' of television, so Bednall changed tack and tried to convince him that he should at least get a commercial television system in place before the coming election, just in case Labor won (the same argument the commercial radio lobby was making). Menzies suggested that Bednall channel his enthusiasm into writing a series of articles to promote television.[36] Bednall did so, and Packer's *Daily Telegraph* and Murdoch's *News* enthusiastically published his case for television in December 1952. The Melbourne *Herald* headlined it, 'TELEVISION BRINGS A FULLER LIFE'. Bednall argued that Australia needed television and that only radio stations 'could safely afford the investment' of capital that would be required.[37]

In November 1952, Bednall wrote to tell Rupert Murdoch, 'For the last two years, I have been fighting hard behind the political scenes for recognition by the Federal Government of the rights of existing newspaper radio interests to participate in Television.'[38] Murdoch replied on 4 December 1952, 'The Government's television proposals seem to be in large part a great personal triumph for you … We have a great chance here.'[39] Two weeks earlier, the Postmaster-General, Larry Anthony (who had overall responsibility for postal, broadcasting and telegraph services in Australia), had said he was going to advise Cabinet to let private enterprise play a role in introducing television. But first, Menzies wanted to test the newspaper groups' loyalty and pliability.

In November and December 1952, Menzies' press secretary wrote to newspaper executives asking their radio stations to give Menzies free airtime for a series of broadcasts. Bednall, Butters and Jack Williams enthusiastically agreed. Menzies would be given ten minutes at peak listening time each week for three months.[40] (They hoped Evatt would not complain or demand equal time. He did both, but was ignored.)[41] Menzies' broadcasts, called 'Man to Man', went out across 40 radio stations just as the government was deciding how to proceed with television, and just as it was starting to campaign for the May 1953 half-Senate election. The newspapers also reproduced major talking points from the broadcasts as news.

Menzies had asked for a favour and major newspaper groups that were seeking television licences had complied (and would do so again when Menzies started a new round of 'Man to Man' broadcasts in July 1953, and then further series in 1954 and 1955).[42] After years of enduring fickle newspaper proprietors, Menzies knew the balance of power was tipping in his favour. Governments that could give, or take away, television licences would have a hold over television broadcasters they never had over newspapers.

After years of inaction on television, and while Menzies' broadcasts were still being heard across the nation, there was a sudden flurry of activity. In mid-January 1953, Menzies announced that a Royal Commission would be established to make recommendations on television. In early February, he announced the names of the six commissioners. Colin Bednall was one. Insiders said Bednall was the first commissioner appointed, and at Menzies' direct request.[43]

The Royal Commission began in February 1953 and reported in May 1954. But five days before it started hearing evidence, the Menzies government pre-empted its findings by amending the *Broadcasting Act* to institute a dual system of public and commercial broadcasting. This settled the major issue at stake. No matter what the Royal Commission reported, there would be no government monopoly on television. Private enterprise was welcome.

Legislating for a dual system was a form of insurance in case Labor won the next election, but it was also designed to take advantage of a split in Labor. Calwell and some other Labor MPs were determined to keep the party's greatest enemy, the commercial media, out of television. But other Labor members felt the medium had enormous political potential and they were hoping to own a television station, either in the party's own right, or in alliance with others. Labor's leader, Evatt, was in the latter camp. He believed that commercial participation in television was probably inevitable, and that it would be electorally unpopular, and probably unconstitutional, to try to stop it.⁴⁴

This split became public in November 1952 when Evatt said that a Labor government would probably rely on a joint national and commercial television system similar to radio broadcasting, while Calwell vowed that a Labor government would cancel any commercial licences granted under a non-Labor government.

Evatt's fatalistic attitude to commercial television may have been influenced by what was going in the United Kingdom. Even there, the concept of a public broadcasting monopoly had ended. In May 1952, the British government had announced that commercial television would be allowed in the United Kingdom in the future.⁴⁵ This had come about after the Conservatives had returned to power in 1951, and after a campaign to commercialise British television. The campaign was said to have been 'masterminded by the London branch of the [American advertising agency] J Walter Thompson' working with a 'well-organized minority' of Conservative Party backbenchers who were directly connected with broadcasting and advertising interests.⁴⁶ While many British newspapers still opposed commercial television, the campaign calling for its introduction had the support of London's *Daily Mirror* and the *Financial Times*.⁴⁷

The opening of British commercial television would create important new markets for American advertisers (and lucrative work for their advertising agents). The Sydney branch of J Walter Thompson hoped to achieve a similar result in Australia. It was an active lobbyist for the introduction of commercial television to Australia. The agency represented General Motors, Coca-Cola, Nestlé, Kraft, Ford and Unilever, among many other, mostly American, companies. J Walter Thompson had worked closely with Australian newspapers and their radio stations since 1930, including as a highly influential producer of sponsored radio programs that it made on behalf of its clients. These included the *Dad and Dave* show, *Lux Radio Theatre* promoting Lux soap, and programs featuring one of Australia's biggest radio stars, Sydney quizmaster Bob Dyer.⁴⁸ The advertising agency was also a politically active company that Calwell had accused of 'meddling in [Australian] politics'.⁴⁹

The newspaper companies were more concerned about Calwell's own potential meddling. The prospect of investing hundreds of thousands of pounds to set up television companies and infrastructure, only to then have Calwell rip up their television licences, was deeply disturbing to them. They intensified their lobbying efforts with Menzies and the postmaster-general. This included trying to stiffen Menzies' resolve by judicious use of opinion polls. In January 1953, the *Advertiser* reported 'GALLUP POLL: COMMERCIAL TV WANTED'.[50] In October 1953, the *Herald* headline was 'GALLUP POLL SAYS ... GIVE US COMMERCIAL TELEVISION FIRST'.[51]

A 'STACKED' ROYAL COMMISSION

To no-one's surprise, the long-awaited report of the Royal Commission on Television confirmed the desirability of a dual system of public and private television. As historian Ann Curthoys pointed out, the membership of the Royal Commission had been 'stacked to ensure a report favourable to the establishment of commercial TV'.[52] Five of the six commissioners were, as Bednall later noted, 'trusty and well-beloved' friends of the government (including himself).[53] Calwell expressed this in harsher terms. He said the royal commissioners had been 'hand picked' to support a commercial system of television that would back the Liberal Party in state and federal elections.[54]

Along with Bednall, the other 'friendly' commissioners included a NSW Liberal MP, Robert Christian (RC) Wilson, and an Adelaide accountant named Norman Smith Young. These three commissioners ensured 'commercial interests were guaranteed a sympathetic hearing', but especially newspaper and radio owners.[55] Aside from being a Liberal MP, Wilson was also a large shareholder in a radio broadcasting company called Country Broadcasting Services Limited which hoped to gain a television licence for country New South Wales (and it did in 1960). The two radio stations this company owned in New South Wales were among those that gave Menzies airtime for his 'Man to Man' broadcasts.

Norman Smith Young (later known as Sir Norman Young) was a pillar of the Adelaide establishment as a financial adviser to big South

Australian companies including Elder Smith, South Australian Brewing Co, and the Bank of Adelaide. Labor suspected that Young was also News Limited's auditor.[56] That is unclear, but after the Royal Commission, Young did become chairman of directors of Adelaide radio station 5DN (in which Murdoch had a stake), and he helped Murdoch prepare his application for an Adelaide television licence. Later still, Young became a director and chairman of News Limited.[57]

Harold Giddy thought he had his own inside man at the Commission. He considered Bednall an advocate for the HWT and kept demanding information from him about the Commission's deliberations.[58] This irritated Bednall who left Queensland Newspapers in January 1954 when the HWT's – and Williams' – hold over it was extended. Bednall started at the *Argus* two months later, where he wrote most of its licence application for GTV, then became GTV's general manager in early 1956.

In other words, Wilson, Young and Bednall all benefitted from the system of commercial television they promoted as commissioners. During the six months of the Royal Commission, Bednall's views and recommendations tended to line up strongly with the interests of the newspaper–radio groups. He also used his journalistic skills to ask sharp questions of witnesses whose testimony threatened their interests, including representatives from the ABC and two ministers of religion to whom he gave 'a terrible time' during questioning.[59]

While the Royal Commission was hearing evidence, newspapers were publishing headlines such as, 'NEWSPAPERS "IDEAL TO BEGIN TV"' and 'PAPERS "IDEALLY SUITED TO INTRODUCE TV"'.[60] Newspapers also stressed that they could be entrusted with the high cultural and moral responsibility of television after some witnesses to the Royal Commission expressed concerns about the impact of television on children and education. Newspaper executives were especially worried that someone who had actually *seen* American television – with its focus on guns, violence and crime – might give evidence.

The *Herald* made a valiant effort to head off such concerns by publishing a long article in which it admitted that American television had initially tried to attract viewers with 'poor taste' material, including programs 'overladen with sex, murder and violence', but argued this was just a 'passing phase'. The *Herald* claimed that, instead of gun violence, American stations were now broadcasting 'good music, dramas, programmes with literary or historical themes, and news transmissions'.[61] (Nineteen months after this *Herald* article, the US Senate Committee on Juvenile Delinquency wrote a report linking television programs with a rise in juvenile crime. It found the 'number of acts and threats of violence' on American television had increased, not diminished.)[62]

When Butters appeared before the Royal Commission in 1953, he laid out a long wish list on behalf of all the would-be television broadcasters. He said they did not want to share a television transmitter and did not want the ABC to begin first. They did not want program standards imposed. They did not want licence fees levied on television viewers, nor high taxes on gross revenues. They wanted ten-year licences with automatic renewal options. In a confidential statement to the Commission, Butters added further conditions. He said the newspaper groups wanted cheap licence fees, the elimination of sales tax and payroll tax, plus duty-free importations on equipment. They also wanted as few restrictions placed on commercial licence holders as possible.[63]

The Royal Commission's final report recommended three-year licences (but the government increased this to five years). Otherwise, its final recommendations were mostly in line with the newspaper groups' demands. The papers were well pleased, and the *Daily Telegraph* commended the report as 'thorough and wise'.[64]

The question of who would own Australia's television transmitters was settled in the newspapers' favour and it was a vital issue. In many countries, the physical assets for television were owned by the state and leased to commercial broadcasters. When the United Kingdom moved ahead with opening up commercial television in 1954, it set up a system where the television transmitters would be owned and operated by a public authority called the ITA (Independent Television Authority), and commercial franchisees would be contracted to supply programs to the ITA in return for the right to sell advertising.

The Australian newspapers did not want state-owned transmitters because that would make it easier for a future Labor government to carry out Calwell's threat to revoke commercial licences and nationalise television. Instead, they wanted to build and own their own television transmitters as that would make it nearly impossible to dislodge them from television. Even if they were not meeting their licence conditions, and some government wanted to cancel their licence, it would have to pay extensive compensation for the transmitter, or ask a new licensee to build another and that would leave unhappy voters either out of pocket or without a television channel.[65] No sane government was likely to do either.

Privately owned television transmitters meant Australia's television licensing system lacked 'the fundamental element that would make it work' – the ability to easily revoke a licence.[66] Rather than seriously scrutinising broadcasters' performance, Bednall later wryly observed that the Australian Broadcasting Control Board (ABCB) ended up mailing out broadcast licence renewals 'like birthday cards'.[67]

The technology chosen was also significant. The newspapers successfully lobbied for Australian television be developed in the Very High Frequency (VHF) band. This band was highly restricted; it could only fit seven channels at the time, and two of these were used by the Civil Aviation Department.[68] This physically protected the incoming licensees from competition. If the Ultra High Frequency (UHF) band had been chosen, it could have accommodated hundreds of television stations, including from 'trade unions, women's organisations, political parties, local government or students' but 'also other commercial interests who could have broken the big media companies' hold.[69] Even in the United States, UHF was part of the television system, and the Federal Communications Commission (FCC) used it to reserve channels for educational stations.[70]

Another victory for the newspapers was the way their argument that the public – not censors or regulators – should be the arbiter of good taste and suitable viewing, was influential in the final report. In the United Kingdom, the driving force had instead been the desire for quality and to avoid the 'low standards' of 'vulgar' American television.[71] When British commercial television began in September 1955, it was in the form of limited commercial competition conducted within a public service framework. There was only one commercial channel, Independent Television (ITV), and this was a network of independently owned regional companies that produced programs for the public authority (the ITA). ITV was modelled on the BBC, it had public service obligations and was required to produce programs of a 'high standard'. It could not focus on 'crude audience maximisation'.[72] ITV also faced strong regulation and periodic reviews and was subject to a special tax on its advertising revenues.[73] Australian commercial television was going to be far closer to the free-for-all style of American commercial television.

SCARING OFF COMPETITORS

Once a favourable television system was in place, the newspapers were eager to begin. 'NOW LET'S GET ON WITH TV', demanded the *Herald* in May 1954.[74] 'IT'S TIME THEY GAVE US TV', said the *Daily Mirror*.[75] They were growing impatient not only because the Royal Commission had taken 15 months to prepare its report, but also because they were increasingly confident they were first in line for licences.

In mid-1954, a few months before licence applications opened for Sydney and Melbourne, Dumas of the *Advertiser*/HWT told Butters of the non-aligned Associated Newspapers/Fairfax that, 'The Postmaster-General [Larry Anthony] seems very friendly to us all and realises that holders of television licences will have to be people who have both financial and programme resources. Newspapers and broadcasters are pretty considerably in his mind.'[76] Privately, the ABCB had also given the newspapers positive signals, but it had suggested they 'get together' with others, both commercial and social groups, because there were going to be more applicants than licences.[77]

In this competitive race for licences, being able to control the narrative, at a time when newspapers still could, was an extraordinary advantage. At every turn, the newspaper groups amplified concerns about the cost involved in pioneering television. This either scared off potential competitors or encouraged them to join up with the newspapers.

Packer's *Daily Telegraph* said that whoever started television would face 'big losses for 5 years'.[78] The *Sun* claimed that any television company would 'lose a good deal of money' at first.[79] The *Herald* piously declared that 'private enterprise is prepared to carry much of the cost and the risks', making it sound like whoever started the first television stations would be performing a public service rather than very likely making an enormous profit.[80]

Originally, there had been some genuine concern within the newspaper groups about the costs involved in starting up television. But those concerns had mostly dissipated by the early 1950s. Even as the *Herald* was presenting television as a risky endeavour, the newspaper companies' internal documents show they knew from the United States that television paid 'handsomely' so long as competition was limited. In their own words, growth in television advertising revenue in the United States had been 'phenomenal' at 270 per cent between 1950 and 1951, and the majority of American television stations had made a 'rapid' recovery from any losses.[81] There was likely to be far less commercial competition in Australia so the prospects were even better.

In July 1954, Murray Stevenson, the chief engineer of 2UE, advised Butters that, although performing the 'pioneering work' of television was costly, it was not as expensive as they had feared, and ultimate success was assured for the first licences in a metropolitan area. Even just holding a television licence would be of 'great value', probably around £1 million.[82] (That turned out to be a gross underestimate: a licence was worth £3.7 million by 1960 – around $115 million today.)

The Australian newspapers were so dominant in radio that they were less concerned about electrical manufacturers, communication companies or non-newspaper radio broadcasters as competitors for licences. One group they were keeping a sharp eye on, though, was AWA (Amalgamated Wireless (Australasia) Ltd). Australia's largest manufacturer of radio, telecommunications, television and audio equipment, AWA was also an experienced radio broadcaster. It owned eight radio stations in New South Wales, Victoria and Queensland and had shares in another 11. Allied with the powerful Marconi company, AWA also had the technical expertise. It was AWA (not Associated Newspapers) that had delivered the first experimental TV broadcast in Australia in February 1954 during the Queen's tour.[83]

In November 1954, the *Sydney Morning Herald* announced its parent company had joined with AWA, but also with the British Daily Mirror group (its partner in 2GB and the Macquarie Network), plus Email (a maker of electric meters, radios and fridges), in a new company called Amalgamated Television Services Pty Ltd that would apply for a Sydney television licence (Table 10.1). The *Sydney Morning Herald* brazenly declared to its readers, and any potential competitors, that Amalgamated Television had such vast experience and resources it 'could not be rivalled by any other group of interests'.[84]

The British Daily Mirror group had also joined with its 3AW partner, *The Age*, in a separate company, called General Television Corporation Pty Ltd, to apply for a Melbourne licence. More surprising was that its British rival had also arrived on the scene. Lord Rothermere's Associated Newspapers (publisher of the London *Daily Mail*) had joined up with Packer's Consolidated Press to apply for a Sydney licence, and also partnered with the HWT to apply in Melbourne. Two of the United Kingdom's three big national newspaper groups were fighting a proxy battle for a stake in Australian commercial television.

Both had capital to contribute, but Associated Newspapers (UK) was a particularly valuable partner because it had television experience. In 1954, the owner of the Conservative-supporting *Daily Mail* had applied for, and won, a contract to produce London's weekday television programs for ITV.[85] This led to charges of political bias by the Labour-supporting *Daily Mirror* which had not applied for a contract. Instead, the Daily Mirror group waited for the 'right time and the right price' before it became involved in television at home.[86] (The Daily Mirror group invested heavily in Associated TeleVision Ltd (ATV), one of the most profitable ITV program contractors, in April 1956. By then, it already had two Australian television licences in hand, although not yet on air.)[87]

The Australian newspaper companies had also recruited foreign electrical manufacturers, including the Dutch Philips Industries, and American and British filmmakers and cinema interests (Table 10.1). And they had teamed up with community groups that might otherwise have made waves at licence hearings or opposed television on cultural, religious or educational grounds. The churches were less of a problem in this regard than many had expected. Rather than opposing television on moral grounds, several churches had been trying to obtain a television licence for themselves since 1953.[88] The Church of England was instead promised a

TABLE 10.1 The Menzies government's award of metropolitan commercial television licences in Sydney and Melbourne, 1955 (and station ownership until 1987)

Area	Channel/station Major owner	Granted licence (year)	Television company name	Newspaper shareholders when licence awarded	Other shareholders	Began trans-mission
Sydney	TCN-9 (Packer) (1955-87)	1955	Television Corporation Ltd	Consolidated Press; Associated Newspapers, England (*Daily Mail*)	Philips Electrical; 2SM; Paramount Film Service; 2KY; Tivoli Circuit; Church of England; public shareholders.	16 Sept 1956
	ATN-7 (Fairfax) (1955-87)	1955	Amalgamated Television Services Pty Ltd	Sun-Herald-2UE group (Fairfax/Associated Newspapers); 2GB-Macquarie-Artransa group (*Daily Mirror* Newspapers Ltd (London))	AWA; Email; 2UW; several other companies and individual shareholders.	2 Dec 1956
Melbourne	HSV-7 (HWT) (1955-87)	1955	Herald-Sun Television Pty Ltd	Herald and Weekly Times; Associated Newspapers, England (*Daily Mail*)		4 Nov 1956
	GTV-9 Electronic Industries (Warner) (1955-60) David Syme & Co (1955-59) Packer family (1960-87)	1955	General Television Corporation Pty Ltd	David Syme & Co; *The Argus* and *Australasian* Ltd (*Daily Mirror* Newspapers Ltd (London))	Electronic Industries; Hoyts Theatres; Greater Union Theatres; Nilsen's Broadcasting Service (3UZ); 3KZ; Efftee Broadcasters (3XY); JC Williamson Theatres; Cinesound Productions.	19 Jan 1957

SOURCES ABCB, *7th Annual Report, 1954-55*, Commonwealth of Australia, Canberra, 1955 and other ABCB annual reports; newspaper and television company annual reports and multiple newspaper articles.

seat on the board of Television Corporation Ltd (the Packer bid), while the Anglican and Catholic archbishops of Sydney had an agreement to act in an 'advisory' capacity to Amalgamated Television.[89]

Because it had no radio broadcasting experience, Packer's Consolidated Press had also recruited two radio stations for its licence application – the NSW Labor Council's 2KY, and Catholic radio station 2SM. This also helped mitigate potential opposition on the grounds of Packer's anti-Labor bias or his questionable ethical record. But the AWU state secretary warned the NSW Labor Council that it was being naïve. He said, 'Labor will have no influence at all in such a set-up ... You can't win playing with Packer.'[90] He was right. Labor had negligible influence within Packer's television company, and when the government did not enforce licence conditions requiring that airtime be provided to political or religious groups, Packer abandoned promises he had made to several groups.[91]

The HWT's television company stood out from the others because it owned 85 per cent of Herald-Sun TV Pty Ltd (named after its Melbourne dailies). There was only one other shareholder, Rothermere's Associated Newspapers, and it had no representative on the board. It was a sign of the HWT's financial strength, but also its confidence about gaining a television licence, that it did not feel the need to recruit a cast of thousands.

By contrast, General Television Corporation in Melbourne had the most diverse ownership (Table 10.1). Ten groups were involved in it, including Electronic Industries, a local manufacturer of television sets and equipment, owned by Arthur Warner. Warner was a safe pair of hands on the Liberal side of politics. He was a sitting Liberal member of the Victorian Legislative Council, the Victorian Minister for Transport and also an influential member of the IPA. Warner freely acknowledged that one of his objects in applying for a television licence was to sell as many television sets as possible.[92]

THE FIRST LICENCES: SYDNEY AND MELBOURNE

Applications for two commercial television licences in Sydney, and two in Melbourne, opened in October 1954. Introducing competing stations at such an early stage of television was unusual. The United Kingdom had opened up one commercial channel, ITV, in 1955, and would not introduce a second until 1982, while commercial competition against the public broadcaster was introduced in Canada only in 1960, and New Zealand in 1989.

Critics felt the award of two licences was calculated to make sure there was enough space for both Fairfax and Consolidated Press in Sydney, and the HWT and David Syme and Co in Melbourne. That way, no major press group would be offended – except for Ezra Norton, and he was no friend of the Menzies government anyway.

By the time the applications for the licences were due, in January 1955, all the hard work had been done. Rivals had either been frightened off or brought into the tent. In 1953, there had been 82 unsolicited applications for commercial television licences.[93] By 1955, there were only eight applications for Sydney, and four for Melbourne. Of the Sydney applicants, five of the eight had no realistic chance, and neither did two of the four applicants for Melbourne. There were no practical alternatives to the newspaper companies. Much later, Bednall would call this a 'tragedy'.[94]

Government policy had ruled out licences solely for special interests, such as religious groups or political parties, so that eliminated three of the eight applications in Sydney, including TNP Dougherty and HV Evatt, who had applied as joint trustees of the AWU and the Labor Party. Evatt and Dougherty put in a flimsy one-page application. They had no financial backing and no plans for how they would produce content. The main benefit of putting in the application was that Evatt could appear before the licence hearings. He used that opportunity to make his concerns about media monopolies heard but it would not have surprised him that most of what he said was not reported in newspapers.

Transcontinental Broadcasting Corporation Ltd was another applicant that was ruled out because it was associated with 2KA Katoomba, 'Labor's voice on the air', in a bid organised by Evatt's friend, Alfred Paddison.[95] A final unrealistic applicant was LH Benson Greene, who had been certified insane in the 1930s, served time in prison, and been described as an 'arch schemer and humbugger'.[96]

An application by Associated TV Pty Ltd (CG Scrimgeour) was not a special interest group, and it had some practical experience because

Scrimgeour ran Pagewood Studios, which had made some films. But there was an element of doubt, or even impropriety, around Scrimgeour that the newspapers amplified. They reported he had lost his job in New Zealand in 1943, when he was controller of broadcasting, for defying the minister.[97] And there was talk of him having made a recording of a 'drunken orgy' (Scrimgeour said it was a farewell party for a staff member with some robust language).[98]

Of the three remaining, and realistic, contenders for the Sydney licences, Norton's Truth and Sportsman missed out, while Amalgamated Television (Fairfax–Associated Newspapers) and Consolidated Press were successful (Table 10.1). A month after Larry Anthony retired as postmaster-general in January 1956, he became a director of Philips Electrical Industries, Packer's partner in the company that had won a television licence while Anthony was the postmaster-general.[99] There were also rumours that the head of one company had boasted he paid out £100 000 on 'gifts' to make sure he got the licence.[100]

For the Melbourne licence, Evatt and Dougherty had put in another bid that also had no chance. Nor did an application by Vernon de Witt Margetts, furniture retailer and director of gospel music broadcaster 3AK. Margetts told the ABCB hearing he had no shareholders, no technical knowledge, and no programs, but devoted his 'life to our Lord Jesus Christ'.[101] The two remaining applicants for Melbourne – the HWT and General Television Corporation Pty Ltd (which included *The Age* and the *Argus*) – were therefore the guaranteed winners.

All of the newspaper groups that had pledged their support to Menzies at the 1944 dinner party had won a television licence. And all (except for the *Argus*) had editorialised for Menzies across the past four federal elections. Historian Cameron Hazlehurst argued the Menzies government used television licences as a way to guarantee the support and approval of powerful newspaper proprietors. He argued licences were 'a pay-off for past favours; they were part reward, and part payment in advance'.[102] But the beauty of it was that the government could legitimately claim it had no other choices for licensees. That was true, but only because all of the policy decisions about radio licences and the shape of television, plus all of the encouragement and inside information, had led to that outcome.

Realistically, it was probably only large overseas companies that would have the 'funds, courage and know-how' to take on the newspapers in television.[103] But the newspaper groups were again fortunate because foreign ownership was a hot topic. Neither the Menzies government nor the Labor opposition wanted to see a powerful new medium misused for 'propaganda' by foreign interests.[104] After granting the first four television licences, the ABCB required three of the four licensees to reduce the amount of foreign ownership in their syndicates. This forced Consolidated Press, Fairfax and David Syme and Co to take up a larger stake in their respective television companies than they had originally envisaged.[105] Although they had to scramble to find the extra cash, and that was a stretch for Fairfax and David Syme and Co especially, the foreign ownership limits meant the newspaper groups would now play an even larger role in television.

The licence rules specified that a single organisation was not permitted to own or control more than one television station in a capital city, and two stations in Australia. The control of any station could not be varied without the consent of the minister. The government also laid down 13 conditions for the licence holders including content standards, but these were mostly light touch, and the newspaper groups were pleased with the ABCB's attentiveness to their demands.[106]

The new licence holders met at the HWT boardroom and agreed to lobby for a low flat fee for a television licence, not one based on earnings or a percentage of revenue. They also demanded 'maximum freedom' from government regulation to pioneer television 'in their own way'.[107] Again, their demands were largely adhered to. According to internal Fairfax memos, the chairman of the ABCB, Robert Osborne, even showed the licence holders 'extremely confidential' documents that were going to be submitted to Cabinet and the newspaper companies' lawyers were able to change the wording of licence conditions until they were satisfied.[108] The newspaper groups had more control over television than probably even they had dared hope for back in the early 1950s, and they were not done yet.

CHAPTER 11
A LICENCE TO PRINT MONEY

Because Frank Packer could not compete with Fairfax or the HWT in newspapers, he was determined to outdo them in television. Packer insisted that TCN-9 Sydney be the first station to launch and his *Daily Telegraph* heavily promoted the start of television and conditioned its audience for the sort of television programming they would want. The paper especially hyped up TCN's historic opening night on 16 September 1956.[1] It was Australia's first regular television broadcast and Bruce Gyngell famously launched it by saying, 'Good evening and welcome to television'. (Such is the magic of television, many Australians believe they have seen footage of this event. What they have actually seen is Gyngell performing a re-enactment years later. In 1956, he spoke live and there was no videotape.)

There were only around 3000 television sets in New South Wales, but Packer's *Daily Telegraph* claimed that 100 000 viewers saw TCN's first broadcast in private homes, clubs and hotels, or even by looking through the windows of electrical shops and department stores.[2] The paper described scenes of immense excitement, including traffic jams, television parties and special trips to the city, as thousands lined up for a glimpse of television (Figure 11.1).

Just as historic as Gyngell's famous words, although much less well known, were Australia's first television advertisements, also broadcast on TCN-9 that night. The first was a 20-second advertisement for Rothmans cigarettes.[3] The second was for Vincent's APC. This was an analgesic powder similar to the better-known Bex, and also marketed towards women. Vincent's promised to cure headaches, pain, and all manner of ills (even depression, originally). It was banned in the 1970s because it contained an addictive painkiller that caused kidney damage and cancer. With hindsight, it seems a strange omen that the first two products commercial television advertised were both killing their consumers.

FIGURE 11.1 The *Daily Telegraph* hypes up the opening night of television and its TCN-9 station, 17 September 1956

SOURCE Mitchell Library, State Library of New South Wales.

TEXTBOX 11.1 Early television

Television developed slowly. At first, stations were broadcasting for limited hours. Expensive motion-picture film was the only medium on which television programs could be recorded. Otherwise, television had to be transmitted live (until videotape arrived in the late 1950s). That encouraged the growth of live variety, cooking and quiz shows, often filmed in hastily improvised studios by huge cameras that wobbled as they rolled across bumpy floors. Desperate for content, stations also played old newsreels and imported films repeatedly.

Television programming remained inconsistent and unpolished for years, but Australians flocked to it nonetheless. In Melbourne, where every daily newspaper had an interest in television, and they heavily promoted its programs and celebrities, the take-up of television was particularly fast. (In Sydney, it was 'only' three out of four newspapers.)

Magazines were also used to stimulate interest. Packer's *Women's Weekly* began publishing a television section. Rupert Murdoch started the first dedicated television magazine, *TV Week*, in 1957 (at first called *TV-Radio Week*). And Packer teamed up with an unlikely ally, the ABC. They merged their respective television publications into a rival, called *TV Times*.

Advertisers also flocked to television. Some of the first big television advertisers were McWilliams Wines, Tooth and Company beer, (the British) Rothmans cigarettes and Cadbury chocolate, and (the American) General Motors and Kraft Foods.[4]

The government had placed restrictions on advertising time. These were designed to protect viewers from having their programs interrupted by too many advertisements. But the restrictions also meant demand for advertising time exceeded supply, so commercial broadcasters were able to charge high prices, making television a very profitable industry.

Cigarette advertising was especially lucrative. Colin Bednall later argued that one of the many political favours that the Menzies government (followed by the Holt, Gorton and McMahon governments) did for the media companies was to refuse to ban cigarette advertising.[5] In the United Kingdom, a total ban on cigarette advertising on television began in 1965, but in Australia, cigarette advertising still appeared on television until 1976.

Predictably, Arthur Calwell was not impressed by commercial television. The month after television began, he rained on Packer's parade by announcing that Labor's policy was still to nationalise all radio and television services.[6] This ensured all of the newspaper groups that were investing big money in television would continue to see Labor as a serious risk to their interests. Calwell's threat to switch off commercial television was also out of step with the significant public interest in it.

Packer's insistence on launching first paid off. Fairfax's ATN-7 began 11 weeks after TCN-9 and lagged behind it in both popularity and profitability. David McNicoll said TCN-9 'got the jump' on the competition and they 'never caught up'.[7] To its credit, ATN-7 tried to invest in local content, but former television executive, Nigel Dick, said it 'was not very successful ... [because] the Fairfax Group had stretched its financial resources thinly'.[8] It made quite a few 'flops'.[9] Bednall believed that Rupert Henderson, despite his formidable skills in newspapers, did not understand television and 'made a mess of trying to run [it] in Sydney'.[10] Much like its parent newspaper, the *Sydney Morning Herald*, ATN-7 was considered 'large, genteel and a bit dull'.[11]

Packer, on the other hand, proved adept at using a cheap formula to satisfy popular taste. Although he had no previous broadcasting experience, he understood tabloid audiences. American commercial television had been built on the traditions of the popular press, including comic strips and press photographs, as well as popular cinema, stage variety and vaudeville.

Intellectually, the other companies also knew that commercial television was most profitable when it was pitched as entertainment for low-paid workers. The HWT had told the Royal Commission on Television that once television sets were sold at reasonable prices, 'television becomes primarily the entertainment of people in lower income groups'.[12] That was especially true in the United States, but even in the United Kingdom, the *Daily Mirror* told advertisers in 1952 that the 'working class' were the 'people with money to spend these days. Take a glance at the average council estate. See the television masts.'[13] Packer had more of a 'gut' feel for what all of this meant, and his approach proved influential in shaping the nature of Australian commercial television.

Packer ran his television operations on a shoestring basis, just as he did with the *Daily Telegraph*. The formula he used for TCN-9 focused on cheap American imports, especially programs with cowboys and crime-fighting, as well as local sport, quizzes and variety. When TCN's pre-on-air schedules were provided to the ABCB in 1956, they showed local content totals of between four to seven hours, very different from 'the 35 hours per week said to be in Packer's application for a licence'.[14] Packer's formula took TCN-9 to the top of the ratings figures and other stations imitated. In 1957, eight of the top ten most-watched television programs in Australia were from the United States or United Kingdom, including *I Love Lucy*, *Alfred Hitchcock Presents* and *The Mickey Mouse Club*. By 1959, ten out of ten were American, including *77 Sunset Strip*, *Wagon Train*, *Perry Mason* and *Leave it to Beaver*.[15]

Australian television was strangely flooded with westerns in particular. On 10 July 1958, viewers in Sydney could switch between TCN-9 and ATN-7 to watch an hour of 'western adventure' on *Western Theatre*, then *Kellogg's Wild West Show*, followed by *Western Time*, and then *Annie Oakley*.[16] Presumably, Calwell felt somewhat vindicated as he had predicted, before it began, that commercial television would be 'like imported comics and just as educational'.[17]

For American producers of programs, including CBS and NBC, Australia proved to be one of the top two markets in the world, along with Canada. The American producers were able to sell programs that had already paid their way on the American market to Australian television stations at bargain basement prices. Local producers wanting to tell Australian stories simply could not compete.[18] It would cost about 28 times as much to make a program in Australia compared to importing an American series.[19]

By 1960, commercial television was so swamped with cheap foreign content that the postmaster-general introduced a requirement that stations broadcast 40 per cent Australian content overall, and four hours in peak viewing time every month. Commercial stations routinely failed to meet the quota, and as author Sandra Hall noted, the ABCB proved 'extraordinarily timid' in dealing with the broadcasters.[20]

Bednall later voiced his disappointment – but probably not his surprise – that the 'rationale for programming' in Australia turned out to be 'delivery of the greatest number of viewing heads for commercial advertisers'.[21] It was all contrary to the promises the newspaper companies had made to the Royal Commission and in their licence applications. Then, they had talked up the educational and cultural benefits of television, predicting it would be used to televise 'lectures by famous educationalists' and 'demonstrations by world-famous scientists'.[22] They had promised to broadcast special educational films for children and to use television as an educational force rather than just for entertainment.[23] The HWT had stressed it would be broadcasting hours of religious, educational and quality children's programs every week, and developing 'wholesome, good, entertaining' programs to advance culture.[24]

It would take the 1963 Senate Select Committee on the Encouragement of Australian Productions for Television (known as the Vincent Report) to shame the commercial television stations into broadcasting more children's television and locally made programs. When HSV-7's *Homicide* began in 1964, it became the first locally-made program to rate in the national top ten.[25] That encouraged other local productions but Australian commercial television continued to rely on foreign content and it never became known for its lectures, plays, ballets or symphony orchestras. In 1966, *The Times* of London called Australian commercial television 'nasty, brutish and banal'. It blamed the Australian newspaper companies for that result. Stung by the criticism, the HWT paid for a full-page advertisement in *The Times* to defend itself.[26]

THE OTHER PIONEERS

In Melbourne, the HWT's HSV-7 had been the first to officially launch, on 4 November 1956, just in time for the Melbourne Olympics. Melbourne's three stations, HSV-7, GTV-9 and the ABC's ABV-2, scored an enormous coup when they were allowed to broadcast the Olympic Games (in GTV-9's case, as a test transmission, because it was not yet officially on air). Day and night coverage of Olympic events gave television an enormous boost, aided by heavy promotion in the commercial stations' respective newspapers and magazines.[27] Although many Melburnians were still having to watch through the windows of electrical shops, it was live television and, as the *Herald*'s Cecil Edwards noted, 'No newspaper could capture the thrill and the excitement; no words or static illustration could vie with the living, moving picture.'[28]

HSV-7 built on its Olympics coverage to develop a reputation for sporting coverage, especially Victorian Football League (VFL), but Bednall, now the general manager of rival GTV-9, was determined to beat his nemesis, Jack Williams. Ironically, GTV-9's gala opening night occurred on 19 January 1957, the same day the *Argus* closed. As the HWT was the new owner of the defunct paper's remaining assets, it had to sell the *Argus*'s shares in GTV-9 in order to remain compliant with the *Broadcasting Act* restriction on owning more than one television station in a capital city. The HWT sold the shares to Arthur Warner, which gave him a controlling interest in the station.

Warner had been leading GTV-9 anyway, because, although David Syme and Co originally had an equal stake (of 35 per cent), the company was still in its sleepy postwar phase under Oswald Syme. It had never shown much interest in the television company nor tried to exert any control. David Syme and Co had left it to Warner to be in charge and he, in turn, had given Bednall a fairly free rein to manage GTV-9. Bednall appreciated the independence even if he found Warner to be cunning and unscrupulous. (Stories abounded that Warner had built his fortune from unethical practices, including double-selling radio units to the government during the war.)[29]

Four decades later, Bednall was still described as 'Australia's most successful television boss'.[30] Under him, GTV-9 cultivated Australian talent, including a variety-quiz show, *In Melbourne Tonight* with Graham Kennedy, that became 'the biggest money spinner in Australian television'.[31] GTV-9 usually won the ratings, and Bednall felt it became the dominant station in Melbourne because it was more independent and more willing to take risks than stations under the close watch of domineering newspaper managers.[32]

HSV-7's first newsreader, Eric Pearce, would presumably have agreed. Pearce later recalled 'the aggressively close interest of commercial TV's masters, the newspaper magnates'. He described their attitude to television

TEXTBOX 11.2 Stars, opinions, images: Newspapers respond to television

Newspaper executives knew their papers would not be able to compete with television's 'on the spot', see-it-for-yourself coverage. After a visit to RCA in New York in 1954, an Associated Newspapers director recommended that, 'Probably the answer is to build up "star" writers so that the public will want to see what they thought about the event rather than a report of what took place.'[33]

Ahead of television's arrival, the newspapers sent senior journalists to affiliated radio stations to give commentaries, host programs and build up a public profile. And when television began, some of the first locally made programs that the newspaper-owned stations developed were designed to use the star power of television to sell newspapers.

These included programs with journalists starring as news commentators, including Eric Baume, who hosted *This I Believe*, broadcast on ATN-7 from the station's second day until 1958. Another popular format of the 1950s was to have a panel of journalists interviewing celebrities and politicians, including TCN-9's *Meet the Press*, GTV-9's *Face the Nation* and ATN-7's *Comment*.

A greater focus on individual journalists and columnists meant bylines began to be seen more regularly in newspapers. Proprietors and editors had traditionally frowned on them because they believed bylines spoiled the notion of the newspaper as 'monolithic [and] majestically aloof'.[34] There were also more practical reasons. Executives worried that a journalist with a 'name' would be more expensive, more liable to be poached by rivals, and also more sensitive about editorial direction because they had a personal investment in pieces that appeared under their name.

But bylines would now be used more regularly because they were part of 'the answer' to television. Newspapers could not rival television for immediacy, but they could provide background, context, analysis, commentary, opinion and interpretation.

The visual nature of television also led newspapers to place a greater emphasis on bold photographs; as technology improved, cameras became

> faster, more portable and more accurate. Press photographers were able to capture more intense, realistic images.
>
> There was also renewed emphasis on the still-popular comics. In 1951, there had been a corporate battle over Jimmy Bancks' 'Ginger Meggs' between Packer and Associated Newspapers. Packer won. After running in the *Sydney Sun* for 29 years, *Ginger Meggs* moved to Packer's *Sunday Telegraph*. In the 1950s, Fairfax's *Sun-Herald* had *Fatty Finn*, while in Melbourne, the *Sun News-Pictorial* had 'Bluey and Curley'. The most popular comics were widely syndicated throughout Australia.

as a mixture of 'suspicion, anxiety and disdain'.[35] Where GTV-9's modern studio was purpose-designed for live variety shows, the HWT's HSV-7 was crammed into an old newsprint warehouse in Dorcas Street, South Melbourne. Author Sandra Hall said HSV-7's building looked 'like an old-fashioned newspaper office and some said that, at times, it was run like one'.[36]

The Age was even more antiquated in its approach, and Warner, recognising that its managers had little interest in the television company and were averse to debt, shrewdly put out a share issue to increase GTV-9's capital. David Syme and Co's profits were down and its executives felt unable to afford to take up more shares, but they also went further and decided to reduce their existing shareholding in the television company. They sold nearly 80 000 shares to Warner.[37] Bednall thought it 'incredible' that *The Age* achieved equal status with Warner in GTV-9 then threw it away by selling him a large part of its holding at par.[38]

Of course, the other broadcaster in both Melbourne and Sydney was the public broadcaster, the ABC. The newspaper companies resented it as much in television as they had in radio, and for the same reasons. It was underpinned by government revenue but also, any loss of audience to the ABC, even for a half-hour program, meant a loss of advertising revenue for a commercial station. Packer argued in the *Sunday Telegraph* in 1957 that the country did not need a national broadcaster.[39]

The newspapers tended to ridicule the ABC from the start and gleefully reported how unpopular it was compared to the commercial stations (the ABC had only around 10 per cent of audience share in 1958).[40] They did not point out that, while the commercial channels were only lightly regulated and able to cater to a mass audience, the ABC's charter required that it educate and inform citizens. The ABC took its programming inspiration for this goal from the BBC but, unlike the powerful British public broadcaster, it was outnumbered by commercial channels from the beginning and denied a similarly central position in television.[41]

In the early 1970s, after Bednall had defected to the Labor side of politics, he advised the ABC's general manager to always assume that 'senior members of [newspapers'] editorial staffs have instructions to seek out, and give prominence to, any happening or statement likely to show the ABC in a poor light'.[42] That was still true of some newspapers 50 years later, when they were resenting competition from the ABC in yet another new medium, the internet, and in streaming television, too.

'SPINELESS': TV IN BRISBANE AND ADELAIDE

In 1957, it was time for television to move beyond Sydney and Melbourne. The ABCB called for applications for an unspecified number of television licences in Brisbane and Adelaide. Newspaper groups were now considered so formidable in television that there were no other applications. The three applicants for a Brisbane licence were Queensland Television Ltd, a syndicate that included Ezra Norton's *Truth* and *Sportsman*, the Fairfax group and General Television Corporation (Arthur Warner and David Syme and Co); Brisbane TV Ltd (the HWT through Queensland Press and the *Courier-Mail*); and Consolidated Television Qld (Packer/Consolidated Press).

In Adelaide, the three applications were from Consolidated Television South Australia Ltd (Packer/Consolidated Press); Southern Television Corp Ltd (Rupert Murdoch/News Limited); and Television Broadcasters Ltd (the HWT through Advertiser Newspapers Ltd).

Packer's applications for both cities were 'ill-prepared and hasty' with 'no solid basis whatsoever'.[43] Packer was less concerned about winning a licence and more concerned about making sure that two would be awarded in each city. He wanted to develop networking arrangements and spread the costs of buying and making programs across more than one station and city. Economies of scale were as crucial in television as they were in newspapers.

As an insurance policy, a year before Packer had met with the other Sydney and Melbourne licensees to 'carve up the network' in the event that only one licence was granted in both Brisbane and Adelaide.[44] Rupert Murdoch was not invited. Murdoch's biographer, George Munster, said the older media groups treated Murdoch like a 'country cousin'. But he saw television as the key to his future in the Australian media and the 'pursuit of a television licence' in Adelaide had become Murdoch's 'major preoccupation'.[45]

At the ABCB hearings, Murdoch pushed strongly for only one licence to be awarded in Adelaide. He presented himself 'as an unabashed advocate of monopoly'.[46] Lloyd Dumas, chairman of the *Advertiser*, also argued strongly for only one licence. Both wanted the same prize – a licence without a rival – because that guaranteed success for the sole station that would have all the city's television advertising.

Murdoch and Dumas used their newspapers to push their company's credentials and denigrate their opponent. The *Advertiser* delighted in publishing details of a brutal cross-examination in which Murdoch was forced to admit that he had given a different answer in a television interview to one he had given under oath, and that a front-page story in the *News* was misleading. Caught out, Murdoch had replied 'Yes, well, all right, sorry.'[47]

Murdoch's youth was highlighted by the QCs acting for rival bids. The *Advertiser*'s QC argued that Murdoch did not have the necessary experience in business or even 'in the ways of the world' to run both a newspaper and a television station. Another QC described Murdoch's 'over-enthusiasm to achieve his own ends', his 'impulsiveness' and 'an imperfect memory when it would appear to suit his purpose not to remember'.[48] The *Advertiser* published these exchanges in detail, while the *News* studiously ignored them.

Meanwhile, Rupert Murdoch told the ABCB hearings that Dumas had been appointed by his father to head the *Advertiser* in 1929 as Keith Murdoch's 'nominee', that Dumas had accepted the job on that basis, and the two had 'worked together for many years in the running of the *Advertiser*'. The point of this history lesson was, Murdoch claimed, that the *Advertiser*'s policy was still effectively controlled in Melbourne by the HWT.[49]

To rebut this, the *Advertiser*'s QC said that control over the *Advertiser* – which had been exercised by the Melbourne HWT syndicate of WL Baillieu, Theodore Fink and Keith Murdoch in the late 1920s – had 'just seeped away' as shareholdings were dispersed among families and descendants. He conceded the HWT owned 36.7 per cent of shares in the *Advertiser* but insisted that these were held 'for investment purposes without control in point of law'.[50]

Dumas claimed, 'In the whole of my experience, there has never been any control exercised by the *Herald*, or any attempt.'[51] But under cross-examination, Dumas could recall only two occasions since 1929 when the *Advertiser* had ever expressed a different policy to the HWT. The first was about a proposed flour tax during the Depression, and the second was over the 1944 government powers referendum.[52] The HWT's control also proved to be an issue in Brisbane where the HWT-affiliated applicant, Brisbane TV Ltd, was at pains to tell the inquiry that it was a 'Queensland company'.[53]

When the ABCB completed its report in July 1958, it expressed 'considerable doubt' about whether the Brisbane and Adelaide licences should be granted to companies affiliated with the HWT.[54] It said it was impressed by the case for a single commercial licence in both cities because of their small populations and concerns there might not be enough advertising revenue to support two licences. The ABCB recommended that fresh applications be called for a sole licence in each city and said it hoped this clarity would encourage local interests not aligned with the newspaper licensees to apply. The ABCB went further and recommended that new applicants 'should have no links to ownership with existing licensees and … undertake not to join networks'.[55]

Only Murdoch's company had no existing licence. The HWT, Fairfax and Packer groups would have been ruled out. But an election was due in four months, and the Menzies government was not keen on infuriating its most powerful media supporters. The government stalled for time. Then, in a shock move in September, the postmaster-general suddenly announced that the government had rejected the ABCB's recommendation. It gave no explanation. It ordered two licences be granted in each city, and that the ABCB quickly select them from the existing applicants.[56]

A fortnight later, after Parliament had been prorogued for the elections, it was announced that the HWT/Advertiser Newspapers and Murdoch/News Limited would be awarded the Adelaide licences (for ADS-7 and NWS-9 respectively). In Brisbane, the licences were awarded to the HWT/Queensland Press, and the company sponsored by Fairfax, Truth and Sportsman, and General Television Corporation (for stations BTQ-7 and QTQ-9 respectively) (Table 11.1).

Packer was happy because he had achieved the outcome he had sought – expanded networking opportunities.[57] The Fairfax group was also pleased because it was now directly involved in two stations, in Sydney and Brisbane. And the HWT was delighted because it now effectively had three television licences (in Melbourne, Brisbane and Adelaide), even though the *Broadcasting and Television Act* prohibited this. The ABCB said assurances had been given that the HWT would not exercise control over these other syndicates. It expressed doubts about that but said, given the government's directive to choose from the existing applications, 'we do not think ... we can carry the matter further'.[58]

As Bridget Griffen-Foley noted, 'a company that had been loyally supporting the Coalition both in Victoria and at the federal level [the HWT] was allowed to expand into television interstate', in two states.[59] Media academic, Trevor Barr, argued the Menzies government blatantly favoured the major media proprietors when it overturned the ABCB's original recommendations and it was a case of 'political interference'.[60] Murdoch would have agreed. Although happy to have gained a television licence in Adelaide, he was angry that there were two. Murdoch believed Menzies had interfered in the ABCB process, and his dislike of the prime minister intensified. When Arthur Calwell said the ABCB was a 'poor, spineless, useless instrumentality' that should be abolished because it had

TABLE 11.1 The Menzies government's award of metropolitan commercial television licences, 1958–60 (and station ownership until 1987)

Area	Channel/station Major owner	Granted licence (year)	Television company name	Newspaper shareholders when licence awarded	Other shareholders	Began trans-mission
Brisbane	**QTQ-9** Truth and Sportsman (1958) Fairfax (1958-80)	1958	Queensland Television Ltd	Truth and Sportsman; Amalgamated Television (Fairfax); General Television Corporation (Melb) (Diversified but Fairfax increasingly dominant after 1959)	NBC International; ATV Aust Pty Ltd; public shareholders.	16 Aug 1959
	BTQ-7 HWT (1958-82) Fairfax (1983-87)	1958	Brisbane TV Ltd	*Courier-Mail, Brisbane Telegraph* (Queensland Newspapers/Telegraph Newspapers/HWT) Associated Newspapers, England (*Daily Mail*) Northern Star (Lismore) Tweed Newspaper Co Ltd	AWA; Email; Television Corporation Ltd; Commonwealth Broadcasting Corp; public shareholders.	1 Nov 1959
Adelaide	**NWS-9** News Ltd (Murdoch) (1958-80)	1958	Southern Television Corporation Ltd	News Limited	ATV Australia; 2GB; Hume Broadcasters Ltd (5DN); public shareholders.	5 Sept 1959
	ADS-7 (later ADS-10) HWT (1958-87)	1958	Television Broadcasters Ltd	Advertiser Newspapers Ltd (HWT) Associated Newspapers, England (*Daily Mail*)	5KA; Philips Electrical; public shareholders.	24 October 1959

Area	Channel/station Major owner	Granted licence (year)	Television company name	Newspaper shareholders when licence awarded	Other shareholders	Began transmission
Perth	**TVW-7** Western Australian Newspapers (1958-69) HWT (1969-1971)*	1958	TVW Ltd	Western Australian Newspapers Ltd	Public shareholders.	16 October 1959
Hobart	**TVT-6** Davies Bros Ltd (1958-1963) HWT (1963-Jan 82)	1958	Tasmanian Television Ltd	Davies Brothers Ltd	Robert Nettleford Pty Ltd; 7HO; public shareholders.	23 May 1960
Canberra	**CTC-7** Federal Capital Press of Aust (1958-64) Fairfax (1964-1980)	1960	Canberra Television Ltd	*Canberra Times* (Federal Capital Press of Aust)	Canberra Broadcasters Pty Ltd (2CA); other shareholders	2 June 1962

* The HWT sold the bulk of WAN's shares in TVW Ltd to 56 different individuals/companies in order to comply with broadcasting ownership restrictions. Shares were spread widely but the HWT retained some shares in TVW into the 1980s (ABCB, *23rd Annual Report 1970-71*, Commonwealth of Australia, Canberra, 1971, p. 173; CPD (Senate), 16 February 1971, p. 23).

SOURCES ABCB, *11th Annual Report, 1958-59*, and *12th Annual Report, 1959-60*; other ABCB annual reports; multiple newspaper articles, including *Sydney Morning Herald*, 30 November 1979, p. 1, and 5 February 1983, p. 26; *The Age*, 10 May 1986, p. 25, and 5 May 1984, p. 21; Nick Herd, Networking TV, pp. 321-22 (but note, because ownership was complicated, deliberately so, and ownership sometimes hidden through layers of company holdings, some sources contradict each other.).

capitulated to a government that treated it 'like a doormat', Murdoch's *News* delighted in publishing Calwell's spray.⁶¹

A federal election was held six weeks after the announcement of the new television licences. The HWT papers gave full support to the Menzies government.⁶² So did Packer's *Daily Telegraph*.⁶³ Fairfax's *Sydney Morning Herald* was more qualified but concluded the government 'ought to be returned to office for safety's sake'.⁶⁴ But Murdoch's *News* was noticeably muted. As Munster noted, the *News* basically went 'as far as it could in opposing a certain winner' in 1958.⁶⁵

TELEVISION IN PERTH, HOBART AND CANBERRA

At the end of September 1958, the ABCB recommended that TVW Ltd be granted a sole commercial television licence for Perth (TVW-7), and Tasmanian Television Ltd the one licence for Hobart (TVT-6). Again, the licence winners were dominated by the daily newspapers in the two cities – the *West Australian* in Perth and the *Mercury* in Hobart. And by 1959, even Menzies' Cabinet was worried about 'the coercive activities' the newspaper-owned television stations were using around programming and networking.⁶⁶

When it came time to assess five applications for Canberra's sole television licence in 1959, the ABCB said it preferred local applicants not associated with existing stations. That had not stopped them applying by stealth. There were claims raised at the licence hearings that one applicant was a 'dummy' company with Packer behind it, and would essentially be a relay of TCN-9 from Sydney, while another applicant was 'bound hand to foot' to Fairfax's Amalgamated Television.⁶⁷

The winner was a third applicant, Canberra Television Ltd (for CTC-7). Federal Capital Press, publisher of the *Canberra Times*, was one of its two major shareholders. Yet again, a television licence had been handed to the local newspaper, but the Fairfax group was also involved in Canberra Television's other major shareholder, the local radio station, 2CA. Part of the Macquarie Network, 2CA was owned by 2GB (in which Fairfax still had a 14 per cent stake).⁶⁸ It was not as large or direct a stake as Fairfax's

Amalgamated Television had wanted, though. The manager of Canberra Television told the ABCB that Amalgamated Television's manager had demanded a 15 per cent shareholding, and threatened he would otherwise organise a local company to run against it for the licence and also refuse to give Canberra Television any programs if it won.[69]

PACKER GETS GTV-9

By the time CTC-7's licence conditions were announced in November 1960, newspapers were the controlling shareholders of commercial television licences in every capital city. Earlier that year, Arthur Warner had a heart attack and began to reduce his political and commercial commitments. Warner sold Electronic Industries to the British firm Pye Industries. Foreign ownership limits prevented Pye Industries from holding the controlling interest in GTV-9, so Warner had to sell those shares separately. Rupert Henderson offered £4 for each £1 share and thought he had a deal with Warner, but when Packer found out he rushed to Melbourne and offered Warner £6 per share.[70] Rupert Murdoch also put in an offer of £6 per share.[71]

When Warner told Henderson their deal was off, Henderson called him 'all the names under the sun', then said he would match Packer's offer, and sent Warner a deposit of £100 000.[72] Jack Williams also made an offer (which is curious because the HWT would not be allowed to own two stations in the one city; presumably, he expected to find a shelf company or friendly group to either take on the sale or mask it).[73] Although Warner had made a verbal agreement with Packer, he was again considering switching course. Packer's influential friend, Ian Potter, stepped in and told Warner he would be finished in Melbourne's business community if he backed out of the deal with Packer.[74] Potter also underwrote the share issue that allowed Packer to afford the £3.7 million purchase. Williams was reportedly consoled that at least GTV-9 went to Packer and not Rupert Murdoch.[75]

Warner had sold his shares at a colossal premium of 600 per cent. He rang Bednall and said, 'I have news for you. I have sold you out to Frank

Packer.' He then appeared at Bednall's house the next morning looking guilty. Warner said he regretted his decision and asked Bednall to contact Menzies and ask him to block the deal. Menzies laughed at that suggestion but he did get Packer to send Bednall a long telegram promising he would not interfere with the management of the station. (Menzies hinted he wrote the details of the telegram himself and convinced Packer to agree.)[76]

After the Postmaster-General's Department (PMG) approved the share transfer, Packer became the largest player in Australian commercial television. The reaction at GTV-9 was grim, for Packer's reputation as a tyrant boss was well known. One staff member fainted. Others quit. Bednall tried to reassure others by posting a note on the staff noticeboard saying he was not leaving and Packer 'sees no reason at all to interfere' with GTV.[77]

For the next few years, Packer mostly restrained himself from interfering, although Bednall had to protect Graham Kennedy from Packer's homophobic rants, and Packer complained that Bednall was spending too much money. In 1965, the government floated a proposal to place a levy on the gross revenue of television companies, Bednall thought Packer would use that as an excuse to interfere so he resigned. Bednall thought Packer's interference after he left plunged GTV-9 into 'mediocrity'.[78] But even mediocre television paid well, and especially after Packer realigned the network arrangements so the two Channel 9s were affiliated. 'ATN and HSV were furious', as some top-rating imported programs switched channels, and from then on, they were disadvantaged by Packer's dominance of the two most lucrative television markets.[79]

Packer took a leaf out of Warner's book and used capital raising and new share issues as a way of increasing his shareholding in GTV-9 at David Syme and Co's expense. By 1965, David Syme and Co's shareholding was down to 18 per cent. They felt there was little point remaining, and by 1967, they were out of television entirely.[80] The award of television licences had separated the newspaper groups that would do well in the future from those that would be left behind. Voluntarily abandoning television was a big mistake (Chapter 18).

MONEY AND POWER IN TELEVISION

Australia's major newspaper groups had been remarkably successful at taking control of commercial television. Ten of Australia's first 11 commercial television licences were awarded to newspaper-dominated groups. The eleventh had two newspapers involved, and one of those was the joint-largest shareholder with an electronics company. By 1960, it was a clean sweep. Newspaper companies were in control of all the commercial television stations in Australia. As HV Evatt pointed out, no other country had allowed newspaper companies 'to become the sole pioneers in the field of commercial television'.[81] It would have long-term consequences and change the nature of media power.

Despite all their scaremongering about financial losses, Packer's TCN-9 was making a declared profit by 1958 (and his creative accounting methods meant profits might have been made earlier). GTV-9 came close to making a profit after only one year, and HSV-7 was making a profit at the end of 1959.[82] Although the *Advertiser*'s ADS-7 in Adelaide had three times the amount of capital behind it as Rupert Murdoch's NWS-9, Murdoch's contacts and agreements in the United States were so good that NWS-9 became known for showing major new programs with little delay behind New York and London. It was making good profits in its second and third years of operation.[83] Fairfax's ATN-7 took the longest to make a profit.[84]

By the early 1960s, the newspaper groups' television stations were making a great deal of money.[85] In 1961, Labor's Eddie Ward complained that they were receiving special treatment from the Menzies government, because they were only paying a 'paltry £90,000-odd' in taxes, whereas the British government collected £10 million in tax from its commercial television operators.[86]

British commercial television had also become highly profitable. It was supposedly Roy Thomson (later Lord Thomson), the owner of the *Scotsman* and the ITV franchisee Scottish Television, who famously said that a television licence was a licence to print money. It may actually have been Cecil Harmsworth King (chairman of the Daily Mirror group).[87] But it may as well have been Frank Packer, as the conditions for profit were even better in Australia. In the United Kingdom, other newspapers had followed the *Daily Mirror*, the *Scotsman* and the *Daily Mail* into television, including the *News Chronicle*, the *Manchester Guardian*, the *News of the World* and the *Birmingham Post*, which had all invested in television companies.[88] By 1959, newspaper companies held around 25 per cent of the British television franchisees' share capital.[89] As with the American newspapers, this was nowhere near the level of control that the Australian newspaper groups gained over commercial television.

Promises the newspaper groups had made during the Royal Commission and licence hearings, that their television companies would have diverse ownership, and they would not tie up in networks, had been broken. The ABCB's foreign ownership limits had reduced diversity in the first instance by preventing foreign companies from investing as much as they wanted to in Australian television. And by 1959, the largest foreign investor, the British Daily Mirror group (which had invested nearly £2.5 million in Australian media since 1948), had sold out of the country entirely, or so it claimed (Chapter 14).[90]

The newspapers had increased their dominance further by buying out partners and acquiring shares previously held by members of the public.[91] By the end of the 1960s, Consolidated Press owned 100 per cent of both TCN-9 Sydney and GTV-9 Melbourne. Fairfax had lifted its ownership from 35 per cent of ATN-7 Sydney to 94 per cent. Rupert Murdoch increased New Limited's stake in NWS-9 Adelaide from 54 per cent to 72 per cent in 1967, and 100 per cent in 1968.[92]

Even in TCN-9's early years, when members of the general public had collectively held more shares in the station than Packer did, that did not stop him from treating it like a personal fiefdom.[93] David McNicoll recalled how Packer was hosting a dinner party and a guest teased him that his horse, Foresight, had slowed down over the last furlong of a race held at Randwick the day before. Packer phoned TCN-9 and told them to broadcast the race to prove his dinner guest wrong. 'We're in the middle of a John Wayne film', the poor technician said. But Packer insisted the movie be interrupted to play the race – twice. As McNicoll said, 'the poor bloody public'.[94]

Television licences concentrated an unhealthy amount of power in the hands of newspaper owners, and once embedded in television, they would be there for decades to come (Tables 10.1 and 11.1). Politicians would be treading even more carefully around powerful groups that were able to attack them across print, radio and television. But, at the same time, television licences also made the newspaper groups less powerful. Newspapers proudly proclaimed that their British forebears had broken free of state licensing of the press in the 1700s, but now they were licensed by the government to run television stations, and reliant on the government to renew their licences.

Through planning, licensing and regulatory decisions, a government could now severely affect the fortunes of the newspaper–television groups. Peter Robinson, who was editor of the *Australian Financial Review* for part of the 1970s, noted how this changed the relationship. He said, 'I am not suggesting that Australian newspaper proprietors before World War II did not play politics. Of course they did. But it was not until the introduction of commercial television into Australia that there was an overpowering motive of self-interest behind press relationships with politicians.'[95]

PART THREE

THE 1960s

CHAPTER 12
BRAWLING IN THE SUBURBS

The 1960s was an era of big, circulation-boosting stories, including the Vietnam War, the Beatles tour, the assassination of John F Kennedy, the disappearance of Menzies' successor, Harold Holt, and the moon landing. News gathering was becoming faster, more mobile, and more visual. The 'rivers of gold' classified advertising kept flowing. Overall, it appeared to be a prosperous time of growth, rising profits and optimism. But fault lines were starting to appear.

Around four million daily papers were being sold each day in the mid-1960s, a high per capita circulation by world standards, but circulation gains for most of the metropolitan dailies were only modest, and for some papers, non-existent. Even as immigration brought potential new readers, newspaper circulation was not keeping pace with population growth.[1] The newspapers' own research had identified 'a marked loss' in sales between 1949 and 1959, especially in Sydney, where papers had higher cover prices than in Melbourne.[2]

In capital cities around the country, families had moved away from the old inner suburbs dependent on public transport, had built their homes in the outer suburbs and were now driving to and from work. In Sydney, the removal of the city's tram network in the late 1950s (which had once been one of the largest in the world) had accelerated that trend and seen public transport use plummet while private car usage and traffic congestion grew.

With readers located further out in the suburbs, it had become more difficult to deliver their newspaper before breakfast, and there was also less time and opportunity for them to read it. Peak time for radio listening was now weekday mornings instead of late evening because so many people were in cars listening to the radio on the way to work. All of these factors had an impact on the morning newspapers.

Conditions were even more difficult for the afternoon papers because their circulation was more concentrated in the inner cities, so they were even more vulnerable to the forces of urban change. In the past, newspapers had located their offices on prime real estate in the heart of the city to be close to ports, transport and major news sites such as parliament, the courts and the stock exchange. What was once a strength was now becoming a problem. The afternoon papers had to print earlier just so they could get deliveries out by truck through inner-city traffic jams and onto the streets for sale, including out in the sprawling suburbs.

Television was also having an impact. Only ten years after it had been launched, 95 per cent of households in Sydney and Melbourne owned a television set. On average, Australian viewers were watching four hours of television a day, making them among the world's most committed television audiences.[3] Afternoon papers were bearing the brunt of this shift, too. In 1938, the *Herald* had boasted that 'evening time is reading time', but now most families were watching television at night.[4] People had once relied upon afternoon papers for same-day 'breaking news', but now they could see it on television. In Melbourne, Cecil Edwards had the misfortune of starting as the *Herald*'s editor in 1956 when television began. Watching with dismay as circulation declined, he estimated 'television cost [the paper] three years of normal growth'. As Edwards noted, 'Television competes for people's time in a way that radio never did. You can listen, or half-listen, to radio, and read at the same time. You cannot watch television and read.'[5]

Edwards gave the *Herald* a fresh look, inspired by American design principles. His revamp helped its circulation climb to more than 500 000 by 1964, a figure it was able to maintain between 1967 and 1971.[6] But the *Herald* had no direct competitor and a low cover price. Other afternoon papers were not so fortunate, and the signs from overseas were not good. After 25 years of television in the United Kingdom, including five years of commercial television, London's three afternoon papers were selling fewer copies in 1960 than they had in 1946. One of them, the *Star*, was forced to close that year.[7]

In the United States, the effects of television were leading many newspapers into financial peril.⁸ Australia's largest newspaper groups were protected from television's worst effects because they had such a large stake in it. In the 1960s, they would use the profits from television to fund an arms race of asset buying so they could diversify and bulk up to ward off predators and future-proof their companies. It was a sign of how much had changed that newspaper companies could no longer rely on their metropolitan newspapers alone. Rupert Murdoch was the first to identify one important new market to conquer, out in the growing suburbs of Sydney.

THE ONLY SON

It was becoming more apparent to the old newspaper barons that Rupert Murdoch had something unquenchable inside him. There was a drive and energy, plus an ability to handle risks, and an obsession with newspapers and making money that would last his long lifetime.

Like Warwick Fairfax and Frank Packer, Murdoch had the dynastic advantage of being an only son (although he had three sisters). Dynasties were more difficult to manage when there was competition between siblings (as the three men's own children would demonstrate). Also like his rivals, Murdoch had the freedom to forge his own path. All three heirs lost their fathers at an early age. Warwick when he was 26, Frank when he was 27, and Murdoch when he was only 21.

Keith's death was an immense personal tragedy for Rupert, who adored, perhaps even revered, his father. But in a business sense, Rupert would have had a very different career if his father had lived. Towards the end of his life, Keith had been unable to hand over the reins at the HWT even when his judgement was waning and his influence was proving detrimental. He would have been an even more domineering presence within the family company he had worked so hard to build. Keith would have been constantly looking over Rupert's shoulder and he would have been a restraining force on his son because Keith's judgement had declined, his tactics were from a bygone era, and because he cared about appearances, conventions and social approval where Rupert did not. It was Rupert's unleashed business style

– unimpeded even by the bonds of friendship – and his willingness to be openly ruthless, that were at the heart of his business success.

After his father's death, Rupert Murdoch had spent seven years learning the ropes in Adelaide. He was tougher as a result of his competition against the *Advertiser*, much wiser about financial and operations management, and the undisputed boss at News Limited. Despite the problems afflicting afternoon papers, Murdoch had managed to double the number of columns of advertising in the *News* in six years. By 1959, he had expanded News Limited so the company owned 50 per cent of a profitable Sunday paper in Adelaide, 60 per cent of South Australia's first television station (NWS-9), and had newspaper or magazine interests in all mainland states in Australia.[9] After gaining a television licence, News Limited's profits had jumped 75 per cent between 1958 and 1959.[10] At the start of the 1960s, Murdoch was ready to make his most audacious move yet – into Sydney – and he entered via the back door in a manoeuvre that focused on the suburbs and took Sydney's newspaper barons by surprise.

LIFE IN THE SUBURBS

Department store advertising was the backbone of metropolitan newspapers, especially the afternoon ones. But department stores, like the newspapers they advertised in, had achieved their success in urban cities built around extensive use of public transport. The rise of motor cars and suburban living was an even bigger threat to their existence. Many shoppers who previously headed into the city to visit department stores were now car owners discouraged by the lack of parking. City trading was suffering, while suburban retail trading was growing.[11] Some of the grand city stores of the past, such as Sydney Snow Ltd and Anthony Hordern & Sons, would not survive the 1960s. The department stores that did, such as David Jones, Myer and Grace Brothers, followed their customers out to the suburbs.

Grace Brothers in Sydney was one of the first to move to the suburbs. In 1933, it opened a new store in the growing western suburb of Parramatta where it was enthusiastically welcomed by the local paper, the *Cumberland Argus*, which called its store opening a 'gigantic step' for the suburb, and a 'radiant' and 'brilliant' presence.[12] Grace Brothers' advertisements would help boost the coffers of the *Cumberland Argus* for years to come. Although its new Parramatta store was a standalone one, the trend in the United States was for department stores to buy up large tracts of undeveloped land in the outer suburbs and build large complexes with multiple retailers and ample parking to cater for the car-driving demographic.

Australian retailers began to follow suit and Chadstone Shopping Centre, which opened in the south-eastern suburbs of Melbourne in 1960, was typical of the American-style 'one-stop-shopping' centre that aimed to lure motoring housewives from new residential estates. It had a three-level Myer department store, a supermarket, 72 other shops, and angled car parking that its advertising said was 'easier' for women who could not manage reverse parking.[13]

Grace Brothers rebuilt its Parramatta store in 1956 to include rooftop parking and a supermarket. In November 1961, David Jones opened a rival department store in Parramatta, which was followed by a huge Waltons, located near a Woolworths and a newly-enlarged Coles supermarket.[14] Off the back of all this development, the *Cumberland Argus* had grown fat with advertising, expanding from 16 pages in 1950, to up to 32 pages by 1961. Traditionally, suburban papers were considered the poor cousin of the much wealthier metropolitan papers, but now they were newly prosperous as a result of growth in suburban housing, shopping centres and secondary industry.

At this time, the vast majority of suburban papers were located in New South Wales and Victoria. Most were tabloid-sized weeklies (or bi-weeklies) filled with local news and advertising. They were normally paid for by advertisers and given away free, usually being hand-delivered to home letterboxes, local offices and factories on a Wednesday to encourage Thursday shopping. Suburban papers were once owned by small, independent local proprietors, but the same forces of consolidation that had affected the metropolitan dailies since the 1920s had also hit the suburban papers. Chain ownership had become more common. Parramatta was both the site of Australia's first suburban paper (which had begun in 1843), and also, by the late 1950s, the home of the largest suburban newspaper chain in the country.

In 1957, Cumberland Newspapers owned 21 suburban titles throughout greater western Sydney.[15] Its flagship paper was the *Cumberland Argus*. A young Sydney journalist named Earl Stanley White had launched a rival, the *Parramatta Advertiser*, in 1933, to cash in on Grace Brothers' arrival. When White's *Advertiser* took revenue away from the *Cumberland Argus*, it weakened it so much that he was able to purchase it in 1936. And as Sydney's population moved westwards, White used the two papers as a base to build up Cumberland Newspapers.

By 1960, the *Cumberland Argus* was boasting that its circulation was 'more than double that of any city newspaper'.[16] In the past, suburban papers had a bad reputation due to their lack of design and poor journalism. They were considered mediocre 'local rags' or 'throw aways' that were not much better than unwanted junk mail. But suburban papers had lifted their game by the 1950s.[17] They were also early adopters of offset printing technology, which gave them a major advantage in quality and agility over the metropolitan papers (which would have to rely on their hot metal letterpress production methods for decades yet).

Suburban papers prided themselves on giving excellent, personalised service to advertisers, and compared to the metropolitan papers, were offering better advertising rates and discounts. This was well received by department stores and major retailers that were less flush with cash than in the past due to competition from suburban trading, but also due to the rise of discount price retailers such as Coles. The suburbans promised that their local advertisements would 'Meet the housewives right where they live'.[18] And mass migration to the suburbs meant the suburban papers' residential and commercial real-estate advertising sections were also booming. All of this was eating into the advertising revenue of the metropolitan papers.

MURDOCH'S INVASION

Rupert Murdoch was the first major newspaper proprietor to invest big money into suburban papers.[19] In February 1960, he paid £1 million to acquire Cumberland Newspapers from Earl White, who did not know he was selling his company to Murdoch because Murdoch had been represented by a Sydney businessman in negotiations. By now, Cumberland Newspapers had 27 free suburban papers stretching from Hurstville in Sydney's south to Hornsby in the north, and the Blue Mountains in the west. It had its own premises, more than 500 employees, and one of the best equipped plants in the state, which it used to conduct a thriving job-printing business.[20] It was a valuable company in its own right but its strategic value was just as important to Murdoch.

Murdoch was aiming to take circulation and advertising away from Fairfax's and Packer's Sydney dailies. He immediately set out on a program of expansion, spending millions on new equipment, enlarging Cumberland's premises, broadening its papers' circulation areas and adding titles to the group. Only a month after he purchased the company, he added the *Bankstown Observer* (once owned by Bankstown's 'Mr Big', the notoriously corrupt Ray Fitzpatrick).[21] Cumberland Newspapers was now covering from Eastwood and Ryde out through Hurstville to Penrith and Katoomba, and claimed a circulation of almost half a million per week.[22]

Fairfax and Consolidated Press were so alarmed by this incursion into Sydney's suburbs that the two rivals joined forces. In April 1960, they established Suburban Publications Pty Ltd.[23] They were joint financial partners in this company, but the Packers were more active in terms of control and Clyde Packer, Frank's eldest son, became managing director.

The plan was to fight off Murdoch by publishing their own suburban papers in his territory using the idle time of the *Daily Mirror* presses at Kippax Street (owned by Fairfax via the contrivance of the O'Connell shelf company). But Murdoch counter-attacked, and in early May 1960, announced Cumberland Newspapers was going to start a free newspaper with a circulation of 75 000 in affluent North Sydney, that would go into 'every home from Kirribilli to Hornsby'.[24] This was prime territory for the *Sydney Morning Herald*, and it was a calculated blow that Murdoch sharpened by striking at Fairfax's reputation among its elite clients and readers. As Fairfax's treasurer, RP Falkingham, noted, Murdoch's *North Shore Times* 'hit at us three times' just in its first edition.[25]

Less than two weeks later, on 20 May, Henderson sold the *Daily Mirror* to Murdoch. Just three months after Murdoch had arrived in Sydney via Cumberland Newspapers, he owned one of Sydney's four daily metropolitan newspapers. This was a momentous event with long-term consequences that are explored later in this chapter and others, but there was also one immediate impact. The sale left the Packers scrambling to find alternative premises for Suburban Publications just weeks before it was due to launch a suburban paper to challenge Murdoch.

THE ANGLICAN PRESS BRAWL

Frank Packer was a harsh and remote father who used to dish out what younger son, Kerry, described as 'a lot of hidings'.[26] Frank considered both sons to be disappointments, but in the 1950s and early 1960s, Clyde was his favourite and heir apparent.[27] Kerry, as a child with polio, had spent time in an iron lung and been sent to Canberra to be looked after by a housekeeper and a 'grim' nurse. For four years, he did not see his father, and he saw his socialite mother only six times.[28] Even David McNicoll, who was very loyal to his boss, conceded that Frank was 'very tough on his boys', and especially on Kerry. According to McNicoll, Kerry was 'thought of almost as a dolt'.[29] Even his mother called him 'stupid'.[30] Later, Kerry's business ability would surprise many, but in the early 1960s, it was Clyde who was entrusted with important tasks.

Because he was on the board of Anglican Press, Clyde knew of a location where they might print suburban papers to push back against Murdoch. Anglican Press published *The Anglican*, a left-leaning weekly paper that was the official organ of 13 Church of England dioceses, and claimed its readers were 'solid, God-fearing citizens'.[31] The Anglican Press plant was situated on prime Sydney real estate in Queen Street, Chippendale, near Central railway station. It had a huge composing room suitable for setting suburban papers, and it was in receivership and up for sale. The Packers made an offer of £50 000 which was verbally accepted by the receiver. Clyde then unwisely revealed the deal to Francis James, the owner and editor of *The Anglican*, the night before the deal was to be signed.

Francis James was a well-known Sydney character, a gregarious eccentric who got around the city dressed in a flowing black opera cloak and a ridiculously large black hat. The son of an Anglican clergyman,

FIGURE 12.1 Frank Packer with his sons Clyde (left) and Kerry, pictured in 1962. The caption to the photograph helpfully pointed out that, 'Clyde is 6 feet 3 inches and 240 pounds; Kerry is 6 feet 2 inches and 215 pounds'.
SOURCE National Archives of Australia.

James had been a flying ace in World War II who was shot down and escaped from a prisoner-of-war camp in Germany before making a fortune from fishing trawlers off the west coast of Australia. He used to work for the *Sydney Morning Herald* where he famously composed his stories on a special writing desk in the back of his Phantom Rolls Royce, parked outside its office.

James did not own the Anglican Press premises, but he had influence with the bishops who did, and he convinced them not to sell to the Packers. The church company sacked the receiver who was about to sign the deal with the Packers, and James contacted Rupert Murdoch, who he knew would have a strong interest in stopping the Packers from gaining Anglican Press. Their verbal deal not honoured, the Packers decided to forgo legal niceties and forcibly, and illegally, seize the premises. Clyde, Kerry, their lawyer and some employees (including David McNicoll and journalist Donald Horne) showed up at Anglican Press around 7 pm on 7 June and demanded entry. The new receiver told them they could not enter so the Packer contingent went around the back and broke in.

After locking the front door from the inside, the receiver returned to his office to find Clyde sitting in his chair. The phone line had been cut so he could not call for help. Settling in for the night, the Packer contingent barricaded the windows and had a locksmith change the locks. At one point, Clyde grabbed the Anglican Press' one-legged general manager, John Willis, by the back of his collar and hauled him out the door onto the street. Francis James soon found out what was going on and phoned Murdoch. James offered to round up his old air force buddies but Murdoch insisted that this was a job for Frank Browne.

Browne was the sports editor of Murdoch's *Sunday Mirror* and an avowed enemy of the Packers. Browne was someone newspapers would dub a 'colourful identity' to avoid being sued. Although not always a reliable reporter of his own life, it seems that Browne had been in special forces roles in the military, and was also a former rugby player and professional boxer. In the gambling world he was known as a 'knuckleman' who carried a pistol and had worked protection for mafia mobs in Chicago.[32] As a journalist, Browne was best known for having been imprisoned for three months in 1955, alongside gangster Ray Fitzpatrick, his employer at the *Bankstown Observer*. They are the only people to have been jailed by the House of Representatives.[33]

Browne gathered what James described as 'four of the biggest bruisers' he had ever seen. They included Al Morgan, 'the best street fighter in Sydney', and two of his mates who were also regulars at illegal gambling den, Thommo's Two-up School.[34] Murdoch met the gang at the Sydney Town Hall at midnight, pressed several hundred pounds into James' hand to pay the others and then left for home. A *Daily Mirror* photographer had been stationed at the front of Anglican Press and Murdoch was being kept informed of events via two-way radio from the photographer's car.

BRAWLING IN THE SUBURBS 253

FIGURE 12.2 Clyde Packer throws the general manager of Anglican Press into the street during an infamous brawl over Sydney's suburban newspapers, *Daily Mirror*, 8 June 1960
SOURCES Newspix and the State Library of NSW.

Browne's mob arrived at Anglican Press around 1 am, armed with monkey wrenches and mallets. They made a fracas at the front and broke down the front door, while James climbed through a toilet window at the back. Once inside, a brawl ensued. Although they were outnumbered two to one, Browne and his 'bruisers' overpowered eight of the Packer entourage who hurriedly left the building. They had to pile into one car because the tyres of two other cars had been let down. At one stage, Browne had turned his attention to Kerry Packer. Like his father, Kerry had been a good amateur boxer, but Browne was a hardened professional who had been an enforcer for American gangsters. It was a very one-sided fight.

Both Packers were said to have been seriously injured that night. Clyde may have suffered broken ribs while Kerry was unconscious on his back in the middle of the street at one point. Browne later said, 'the Packer brothers were valiant [and] took their punishment like men, unlike David McNicoll' who disappeared when the fight began.[35] After the Packer party fled, James led his victorious group in a prayer of thanks for re-capturing the building.

Murdoch compounded the Packers' humiliation by publishing a front-page story in the next day's *Daily Mirror* headlined, 'KNIGHT'S SONS IN CITY BRAWL' (Figure 12.2). A large photograph showed a menacing Clyde throwing John Willis into the street. Other photographs on inside pages showed a battering ram being used on the door, and Kerry with a swollen eye, looking stunned.[36] Of course, the *Daily Mirror* did not explain Murdoch's interest in the events at hand. And James cheekily told a newspaper reporter who asked if there had been a brawl that, 'We have been holding a prayer meeting.'[37]

Anglican Press won a court order banning the Packers from the premises and requiring them to return documents taken that night from a steel safe that was forced open. Three employees brought actions against the Packers for assault which were settled out of court. Many years later, journalist Douglas Golding sold six suburban papers in Canberra to a syndicate headed by Kerry Packer. He 'did not remind [Kerry] we had already met – in Queen Street, Chippendale'. Golding had been on the end of the battering ram that hit Kerry full in the front when he opened the door.[38]

A BATTLE, THEN A TRUCE

Murdoch had won the battle for Anglican Press – from a safe distance – but he did not win the overall war in suburbia. The Packer–Fairfax-owned Suburban Publications was able to bring out its new paper, the *St George and Sutherland Shire Leader*, in Murdoch's distribution area as scheduled at the end of June 1960, by printing it at Consolidated Press. Packer, his sons and his chauffeur helped load 75 000 copies of the *Leader* which were taken from Consolidated Press to a triple garage that was hired for distribution and overseen by 'six large Italian gentleman, hired by Clyde from a nightclub in Double Bay' to ensure there was no further trouble.[39]

Later in June, the Packers bought the *District News* at Sutherland and incorporated it in the *Leader*. Their free paper was distributed throughout St George and Sutherland where it competed with three of Murdoch's suburban papers. In August, Suburban Publications started another new paper, the *Parramatta Mail*, to strike directly at Cumberland Newspapers in the west, where its flagship and money-spinner was now the *Parramatta Advertiser* (the *Cumberland Argus* having been merged into it in October 1962).

Suburban Publications then launched another two papers in the western suburbs: the *Northern Star* in Ryde, and the *Inner Western Times* at Burwood. Packer and Fairfax were fighting Murdoch in the north, south, east and west. It was an expensive and wasteful battle. Losses of many thousands of pounds were mounting up. In areas like the North Shore, residents were receiving four different suburban newspapers, and unwanted papers were littering gardens and blowing down the streets.[40]

In July 1961, Fairfax, Packer and Murdoch sat down to peace talks in Murdoch's office that went on for seven hours. Souter said the groups 'haggled ... like Spain and Portugal carving up the New World'.[41] They divided Sydney's suburban market between them and signed a seven-year territorial agreement. This was effectively a no-competition pact. Murdoch ceded Cumberland's papers in the St George area so that Suburban Publications could control there, while Suburban Publications handed over its papers in Parramatta, Ryde and Burwood so Cumberland Newspapers' *Parramatta Advertiser* could rule the west.[42] The no-competition agreement was extended several times and lasted nearly 12 years, until June 1973, just before the enactment of the *Trade Practices Act*, which would have made it illegal.[43]

Murdoch also made an incursion into Melbourne in 1961, using the same tactic of buying a suburban paper in his father's old domain. Murdoch purchased the *Dandenong Journal* in south-east Melbourne, an area that had seen rapid growth in factories, industry and housing. But the HWT had already quietly mounted a defence.[44] Unlike Murdoch, who had hidden his identity from potential sellers such as Earl White and aimed for complete takeover, the HWT dealt directly with individual proprietors. In return for loose equity in their companies, the HWT offered them interest-free loans to help keep them afloat and independent. As a result, the HWT was able to bind several groups of desirable suburban papers to it, including the Cheltenham-based Standard Newspapers, a chain of suburban papers focused on the Mornington Peninsula and the southern and south-eastern suburbs of Melbourne.[45]

Murdoch never became as large a presence in Victorian suburban papers as he did in New South Wales. This was partly because of the HWT's defensive manoeuvres, but also because of the independence of the Leader group of suburban papers (controlled by the Mott family), and because David Syme and Co built up its own chain of suburban papers under the banner of Age Suburban.

In the years ahead, Murdoch would over-expand in suburban newspapers and have to scale back due to financial losses, but in the 1960s he used them to achieve good profits and, the best result of all, to pressure Fairfax into selling him the *Daily Mirror*. He now had an afternoon daily in Sydney and the basis on which to stake a future claim in the country's largest television market. Murdoch understood just how vital a stepping stone the *Daily Mirror* was. After the sale was finalised at Fairfax headquarters, he danced a jig on the parquetry floor, then gleefully phoned Clyde Packer to rub it in.

A FATEFUL DECISION

Precisely what Henderson was thinking when he sold Murdoch the *Daily Mirror* is one of the great mysteries of Australian newspaper history. While Murdoch had applied some pressure when he entered Sydney's northern suburbs, why did Henderson think a solution to suburban competition was to sell Murdoch a metropolitan paper and make him an even larger, and more direct, competitor against Fairfax's *Sun*? The conventional explanation is that Henderson believed the debt incurred from purchasing the *Daily Mirror* would send Murdoch bankrupt. At this time, the old press barons and industry hardheads thought Murdoch was overconfident, overexposed to debt, and likely to burn out quickly.

Evidence of Henderson's thinking is contained in his correspondence with Lloyd Dumas of the *Advertiser*. Across the next two years, they watched, expecting that Murdoch's risky borrowing, his mysterious capital raising, and multiple purchases, would sink him. Five months after Murdoch bought the *Daily Mirror*, Dumas wrote to Henderson, 'I should think the next 12 months are going to be months of great anxiety for our young friend.'[46] In September 1961, Dumas predicted 'his cash will run out'.[47] In an excited note in October, Dumas said of Murdoch and News Limited, 'I think they are strained almost to breaking point.'[48] On another occasion, Dumas rhetorically asked Henderson, 'How long can [Murdoch] keep this up?'[49] Neither of them could possibly have known that the answer was 'for at least another 60 years'.

Henderson had some good reasons to want to be rid of the *Daily Mirror*. The remote control method of running it via a shelf company was not working well. The paper was losing money and circulation, and its sensational content was a concern. (The *Daily Mirror*'s last front-page story before Murdoch purchased it was a false one that claimed the Queen Mother was going to marry the treasurer of her household, a story denied emphatically by all parties concerned.)[50]

If Henderson and Fairfax had been more ruthless, they would simply have closed the *Daily Mirror* and let the *Sun* reap the benefits of no competition. Souter argued they did not do this because Fairfax directors genuinely believed, for the sake of the public interest, that it was important to have competition, and they did not want the company exposed to accusations of monopoly in the afternoon field.[51] This seems an extraordinarily prim view for the company to have taken. The HWT had already closed several competing papers with very little pushback, and it had happily withstood accusations of monopoly in Melbourne's afternoon field for decades, while collecting the financial benefits that provided.

But even their competitors acknowledged that the Fairfax family sacrificed financial opportunities because they sincerely believed in the public interest element of newspapers. So, if that was the case, and the *Daily Mirror* had to go to someone, then Murdoch made sense. He made a high offer for the paper that gave Fairfax a handsome profit of £500 000 at a time when money was needed for investment in television.[52] The deal also kept Fairfax's main rival, Packer, out of the afternoon field, preventing him from gaining the morning–afternoon combination that he desperately wanted. It also kept the HWT out of Sydney. In previous years, the HWT and Fairfax companies had a friendly relationship and a 'gentlemen's agreement' to keep out of each other's territory. But Henderson and Jack Williams did not get along, and Williams had his eye on the *Daily Mirror* and on entering Sydney.[53]

Compared to Packer and Williams, Murdoch seemed the least dangerous competitor. Henderson probably felt he had young Murdoch's measure. According to David McNicoll, there had been a dinner at Frank Packer's house not long after Murdoch acquired Cumberland Newspapers, at which Henderson rounded on Murdoch in 'cruel fashion' and told him he would be run out of Sydney, causing Murdoch to go white and be 'not far from tears'. (McNicoll felt that experience cemented Murdoch's determination to take on the 'big boys' of newspapers and beat them at their own game.)[54]

There would be other times when Henderson and Murdoch clashed, including in 1963, when Murdoch believed that 'old man' Henderson cost him a Sydney television licence (Chapter 13). But there was also a level of mutual admiration between them, and perhaps even paternal feeling on Henderson's part. Henderson had been on good terms with Keith Murdoch, and from an early age, Rupert had admired Henderson as a hardened newspaper veteran and sought his counsel. Intriguingly, in James Fairfax's autobiography, he raised the possibility that Henderson may have sold the *Daily Mirror* because he 'wanted to help the young emerging Murdoch on his way, a quixotic act of which he might have been capable'.[55]

The timing was also important as the sale happened just as Henderson was moving away from Warwick Fairfax and building his own, personal mini media empire (Chapter 14). Tensions had emerged over Warwick's new wife, Mary, who Henderson thought was dangerously ambitious and planned to interfere in the running of the company. Henderson acted in an unusually unilateral way over the sale of the *Daily Mirror*. He carried it out against Warwick Fairfax's expressed wishes, and despite objections from Fairfax's treasurer, RP Falkingham. Henderson pushed through the sale without the chairman's knowledge. Warwick Fairfax was at sea, on his way back from his ten-month honeymoon, and the first he knew of it was when he read about the sale in the ship's radio newspaper.[56]

Henderson and Mary Fairfax later became bitter enemies, so her comments must be viewed in that light, but she claimed in 1990 that Warwick was always suspicious about Henderson's motives, 'because no businessman in his right mind, without government intervention, sells a monopoly ... why did Mr Henderson sell a monopoly, a smart operator like him?'[57] The Packer camp was also stunned. David McNicoll said later, 'Henderson was supposed to be such a bloody brilliant man. By selling the *Mirror* to Murdoch he lost the game. Let Murdoch in. Oh, God. Crazy, crazy.'[58] It was a rare moment of gloating on that side because Henderson was a formidable opponent to McNicoll and Packer, frustrating them at nearly every turn.

Whatever the motivation, the sale meant the Murdoch family finally owned a Sydney metropolitan paper, nearly 40 years after Keith Murdoch had unsuccessfully tried to buy the *Evening News* in the early 1920s, and then had left Sydney well alone. Rupert Murdoch was only 29 years old. The deal had not only given him the *Daily Mirror* and *Sunday Mirror*, but also extensive printing plants in Sydney, Melbourne and Brisbane, commercial printing businesses in those three cities, and the weekly *Truth* papers (which were coyly described to News Limited shareholders as 'weekly papers' rather than by their sullied name).[59]

Murdoch's investments had mostly turned out to be good ones with high profits, and he used the money to fund further expansion. From 1954 to 1964, News Limited enjoyed the fastest growth of any major newspaper company. Its shareholder funds increased twenty-fold and its tangible assets and net profits around eighteen-fold.[60] Murdoch began to expand overseas, into Asia in 1962 with *Asia Magazine*, and then New Zealand in 1964, with the purchase of shares in the Wellington newspaper, the *Dominion*.[61]

Letting Murdoch into Sydney, and giving him a daily paper and Norton's old scandal sheets, are seen as constituting the worst mistake of Henderson's otherwise stellar career. Henderson could not have known how far Murdoch would take the opportunity, and some have argued that Murdoch's tabloid newspaper 'genius' would have broken through no matter what the Fairfax company did. But there were warning signs, and Henderson ignored them. Later, when he had to manage the intense competition between the *Sun* and the *Daily Mirror*, Warwick Fairfax would tell Henderson, 'Well, it's all your fault; you brought him into Sydney.'[62]

CHAPTER 13
OLD AND NEW TRICKS

When Murdoch arrived in Sydney to take up ownership of the *Daily Mirror* in 1960, a strange conversion was taking place across the railway tracks at Fairfax's Broadway headquarters. The *Sydney Morning Herald* had supported Menzies' Liberal Party during all six postwar elections between 1946 and 1958, but rows between former friends Warwick Fairfax and Robert Menzies over wartime newsprint rationing had left a legacy of bitterness. And moments of tension had been breaking out.

In 1954, Menzies had complained about the *Sydney Morning Herald*'s coverage to some of its reporters. When word got back to Henderson, he was outraged and wrote to Menzies firmly denying that the *Sydney Morning Herald* was 'engaged in some underhand campaign against you'.[1] In 1957, it was the Fairfax directors who felt victimised. They blamed the Menzies government's credit policy for causing a 'distressing' 28 per cent decline in the *Sydney Morning Herald*'s job advertisements.[2]

After Menzies endured months of what he considered to be 'acid ... personal attacks' from the *Sydney Morning Herald* that year, he told parliament it could no longer be considered a paper of record.[3] The next day, the paper responded that Menzies simply resented any criticism: 'he likes to "dish it out" but not to take it'.[4] In 1958, the *Sydney Morning Herald* had backed the Menzies government but said it would probably lose seats, and 'has only itself to blame'.[5]

Menzies believed the *Sydney Morning Herald* was running a vendetta against him that dated from the war years and had already continued for nearly two decades. Overlooking the paper's early – and periodic – support for him, he came to believe that the '*Sydney Morning Herald* has always detested me, a detestation which I heartily reciprocate.'[6] Menzies felt the paper, and its directors, scorned him because he 'was not born of wealthy parents' nor 'in Sydney'.[7] Hostilities were about to boil over.

PERSONAL OR POLITICAL?: THE 1961 ELECTION

The year 1960 had been a tough one for newspapers. In March, their nemesis, Arthur Calwell, had replaced HV Evatt as Labor leader. In November, the Menzies government slammed the brakes on an overheating economy so hard they induced a mini-recession. Trying to prevent out-of-control inflation, the government's 'credit squeeze' mini-Budget restricted bank credit, increased sales tax on motor cars by up to 40 per cent, and cancelled tax deductions on corporate debentures to discourage speculation on land and shares.[8] Advertising for real estate and motor cars collapsed. Unemployment jumped by more than two per cent, so job ads suffered too. *Newspaper News* calculated that press advertising 'nose-dived' by 1.8 million inches.[9]

The Fairfax group was appalled. Although the paper was a conservative bastion, and Calwell had been its number one enemy during the wartime censorship battles, it threw its resources behind him in 1961 in the hope that he could oust Menzies. The group had already given Calwell some discreet policy and public relations advice in 1958 but now, at Warwick Fairfax's direction, Henderson acted as a pseudo–campaign manager behind the scenes. Calwell was given direct support in the form of policy advice, speeches, press releases and cheap television time. And the old socialist warrior proved surprisingly open to receiving this help and to letting the advice of a conservative media company shape his economic policy. The prudish, press-hating Calwell and the womanising, capitalist-handmaiden Henderson (that 'Quilp-like creature'), even became firm friends.

Two of Fairfax's top journalists, Maxwell Newton and Lou Leck, prepared speeches for Calwell in a section of the office dubbed the 'Labor ward'. Both had trained as economists. They helped Calwell craft a moderate policy the *Sydney Morning Herald* could support for Calwell's budget reply in August 1961, and for his policy speech in November.[10] In the previous ten years, economic policy had become more central to politics, and also to journalism. Since 1951, the Fairfax group had published the *Australian Financial Review* (which became a bi-weekly in 1961). Originally, the *Financial Review* was launched as a defensive move to spoil Associated Newspapers' plan for a similar, business-focused newspaper, but Fairfax's directors, frustrated the Menzies government was not taking their economic advice, also hoped it might become an Australian version of the *Financial Times* of London. That paper had a reputation for influencing the British government's economic policies.

Since 1960, the *Financial Review* had been edited by Max Newton. Henderson had a high regard for the talented and dynamic, but also erratic, Newton. He once described Newton 'as the only person he had ever regarded as his equal'.[11] The quality and status of economic coverage had been elevated by Newton and the *Financial Review*, but also by the *Sydney Morning Herald*'s highly respected finance editor, Tom Fitzgerald, and 'the alcoholic genius', Jack Eddy, the finance editor of the Melbourne *Herald*.[12] In Sydney, which was rapidly becoming the financial capital of Australia, Newton and Fitzgerald had been strongly pushing for the Menzies government to 'open up the Australian economy'.[13]

Glenda Korporaal, a later deputy editor of the *Financial Review*, described this period as a time when key industries, such as car manufacturing, steel, clothing, footwear and textiles, existed under 'heavy protectionist barriers', when 'one of the main jobs of business leaders ... was to go to Canberra to lobby for continued protection' and '[b]usiness and the Liberal Party were joined at the hip of mutual interest'.[14]

Ahead of the 1961 election, both papers were highly critical of the Menzies government's limited and controlled economic policies. Anonymous columns also appeared in the *Sydney Morning Herald* that criticised Menzies personally, and were widely understood to have been written by Warwick Fairfax.[15] But when it came time to set out the paper's official stance, there was a split in the ranks. Although Henderson was helping Calwell, and was also personally critical of Menzies' economic policies, he argued the *Sydney Morning Herald* should be detached (as it had been in 1943). Henderson wanted the paper to avoid calling for the return of the Menzies government but to stick to its conservative tradition and not endorse Labor either.

After securing a promise from Calwell that nationalisation would not be raised during the life of the next parliament if Labor won, Warwick Fairfax insisted the paper endorse Labor.[16] Warwick wrote an editorial endorsing Labor and tried to get it published after Henderson left the office. The general manager, Angus McLachlan, was Henderson's deputy and knew where real power lay in the organisation. He insisted on calling Henderson. Over the telephone, Henderson argued with Fairfax but eventually gave in and let the editorial be published.[17]

In the 70 years since Labor had first campaigned for office in New South Wales, the *Sydney Morning Herald* had never advocated the election of a Labor government at either state or federal level. The paper's change of allegiance shocked its conservative readers. Warwick Fairfax was snubbed at his exclusive men's clubs. James Fairfax felt the disapproval of his social set. And Rupert Henderson's granddaughter still recalls how classmates at her North Shore school were forbidden to talk to her by their scandalised parents.[18]

A key editorial was headed, 'LABOUR [sic] PRESENTS THE BETTER CASE'. It argued the Menzies government had 'blundered' its economic policies, and although Labor's 'platforms and principles … are not acceptable to the [*Sydney Morning*] *Herald*', the party had done well under Calwell and should 'have its opportunity'.[19] In two other editorials, the *Sydney Morning Herald* defended its about-face by arguing that Menzies was actually the one who had changed, because he had 'turn[ed] towards socialism' and abandoned his party's 'Liberal principles'.[20] That the socialist bogey could be employed against Menzies – who had been using it relentlessly against Labor for over a decade – showed just how flexible that accusation had become.

Fairfax's *Sydney Morning Herald* and *Sun* were the only daily metropolitan papers in the country to endorse Labor (Table 13.1). The *Financial Review* also endorsed Calwell. The company's papers had all turned on Menzies in unison, as if directed from above. The *Sun* said Menzies had no plan. The *Financial Review* said his government had led the country into a 'shocking mess'. The *Sydney Morning Herald* called Menzies' complacency 'frightening'.[21]

Although new in Sydney, Murdoch plunged right into the city's robust

"As we've consistently said, Mr. Warwick, Menzies has brought us all to the brink of ruin."

FIGURE 13.1 Packer's newspaper ridicules Warwick Fairfax and Rupert Henderson for their antipathy to Menzies in a Les Tanner cartoon in the *Daily Telegraph*, 29 September 1961
SOURCE State Library of NSW. Reproduced with permission of the Tanner family.

tradition of stirring up newspaper rivals. His *Sunday Mirror* ran a front page showing a photograph of Calwell's car waiting for him outside Fairfax headquarters. The text was written as a jeering 'wedding notice' for Arthur Calwell and 'Rags' Henderson, described as the 'least glamorous [political wedding] of the season ... The flowers were pink, by request.'[22] Although Murdoch's Adelaide *News* had stood out among the other dailies for its criticism of the Menzies government during the 1958 election, Murdoch was now hopeful of obtaining a Sydney television licence. In 1961, his *News* and *Daily Mirror* backed Menzies in the final week of the campaign, saying Calwell did not 'match up'.[23]

Packer stood steadfast as always with Menzies, and chided the Fairfax group for its lack of gratitude (Figure 13.1). He could afford to be forgiving of the credit squeeze. Women's magazines, including the *Women's Weekly*, had suffered much less than newspapers, and Packer's *Daily Telegraph* had only about one-twelfth of the classified advertising volume of the

TABLE 13.1 The partisan support of major newspapers, 1943–72

Newspaper	1943	1946	1949	1951	1954
Labor victory shown in bold	**Curtin**	**Chifley**	Menzies	Menzies	Menzies
	Labor	**Labor**	Coalition	Coalition	Coalition
Sydney Morning Herald	Critical of both parties. Advocated a vote for new parties or independents	Con.	Con.	Con.	Con.
Daily Telegraph	Con.	Con.	Con.	Con.	Con.
Sun	Con.	Con.	Con.	Con.	Con.
Daily Mirror	Con.	**Lab.**	No endorsement	Con.	**Lab.**
Age	Advocated a vote for new parties/independents	Moderate support Con.	Con.	Con.	Con.
Argus	Con.	Con.	No endorsement	No endorsement	**Lab.**
Sun News-Pictorial	Con.	Con.	Con.	Con.	Con.
Herald	Con.	Con.	Con.	Con.	Con.
Courier-Mail	Con.	Con.	Con.	Con.	Con.
Brisbane Telegraph	Con.	Con.	Con.	Con.	Con.
Advertiser	Con.	Con.	Con.	Con.	Con.
News	Con.	Con.	Con.	Con.	Critical of both major parties
West Australian	Con.	Con.	Con.	Con.	Con.
Daily News	Con.	No editorial	Con.	No clear support	No editorial
Mercury	Con.	Con.	Con.	Con.	Con.
Canberra Times	No clear support	Moderate support for Con.	Con.	Con.	Con.
NT News					
Australian Financial Review					Con.
The Australian					

NOTE 'Conservative' refers to the Liberal Party of Australia (usually in coalition with the Country Party). The *Australian Financial Review* became a daily newspaper in 1963; endorsements are shown earlier as they are discussed in the text. The *NT News* became a daily in 1964; endorsements are shown from then.

Newspaper	1955	1958	1961	1963	1966	1969	1972
Labor victory shown in bold	Menzies Coalition	Menzies Coalition	Menzies Coalition	Menzies Coalition	Holt Coalition	Gorton Coalition	**Whitlam Labor**
Sydney Morning Herald	Con.	Con.	Lab.	Con.	Con.	Con.	Con.
Daily Telegraph	Con.	Con.	Con.	Con.	Con.	Con.	Lab.
Sun	Con.	Con.	Lab.	Con.	Con.	No editorial	Con.
Daily Mirror	Con.	Lab.	Con.	Lab.	Con.	Con.	Lab.
Age	Con.	Con.	Con.	Con.	Con.	Con. (with some criticism)	Lab.
Argus	Against anti-Communist Labor (DLP)						
Sun News-Pictorial	Con.	Con.	Con.	Con.	Con.	Con.	Con.
Herald	Con.	Con.	Con.	Con.	Con.	Con.	Con.
Courier-Mail	Con.	Con.	Con.	Con.	Con.	Con.	Con.
Brisbane Telegraph	Con.	Con.	Con.	No clear support	No clear support	No editorial	Con.
Advertiser	Con.	Con.	Con.	Con.	Con.	Con.	Con.
News	No clear support	No clear support	Con.	No clear support	Con.	Con.	Lab.
West Australian	Con.	Con.	Con.	Con.	Con.	Con.	Con.
Daily News	No editorial	No editorial	No editorial	No editorial	No clear support.	No editorial	No editorial
Mercury	Con.	Con.	Con.	Con.	Con.	Con.	Con.
Canberra Times	Con.	No clear support	No clear support	Con.	Con.	No clear support	No explicit support but more pro Labor
NT News					No clear support	No clear support	Lab.
Australian Financial Review	Con.	Con.	Lab.	Con.	No clear support	No clear support	No clear support
The Australian					Con.	Con.	Lab.

Sydney Morning Herald.²⁴ Just as Henderson was helping Calwell, Packer was helping Menzies by keeping tabs on the activities of other Sydney newspaper figures and reporting this intelligence back to Menzies.²⁵

Packer also sent his Canberra political correspondent to give Menzies advice. Alan Reid, known as the 'Red Fox' for his red hair and political cunning, was on his way to becoming a legendary political reporter (he covered politics for nearly 50 years, from 1937 to 1985). Reid worked for the grandfather, father and son (RC, Frank and Kerry), and demonstrated unshakeable loyalty to the Packer family. In 1954, Frank Packer had poached him from the Sydney *Sun* and smoothed things over so that Menzies would accept Reid and forgive his critical coverage of the Petrov affair.²⁶

Reid's election advice to Menzies was that he should restore his economic credibility after the credit squeeze and turn public opinion back to the government by making a pledge to restore full employment in 12 months. Menzies made the promise the next day. The *Daily Telegraph* gave this pledge enthusiastic coverage (whereas Fairfax's *Sun* said Menzies was simply repeating a projection Calwell had made a month ago).²⁷

The Menzies government won the election by two seats.²⁸ Reid, Packer and several Liberal politicians were convinced that Reid's advice had saved the government.²⁹ Packer's friend, Liberal MP Billy McMahon, was among them. He fervently believed that the support of the *Daily Telegraph* and *Sunday Telegraph* was 'decisive' in 1961, and McMahon became convinced that the *Telegraph*s' anti-Labor campaigns were the key to holding Sydney's suburbs for the Liberal Party throughout the 1960s.³⁰

Others had a different understanding of the election result in 1961. The Coalition had lost 15 seats but none in Menzies' home state of Victoria. DLP preferences in Melbourne had saved the Menzies government. The DLP-friendly HWT owned two of the three daily papers. Although the HWT had taken a financial hit, and its papers were more critical of Menzies than usual, the *Herald* concluded that 'Labor is not yet ready to lead the nation' (it would be another 23 years before the *Herald* felt Labor was ready for federal office, after 83 years of editorialising against it).³¹ Melbourne's third paper, *The Age*, had close links to Menzies, including through its editor, Menzies' friend, Keith Sinclair. Although it had also been deeply affected by the impact of the credit squeeze on classified advertising, *The Age* was far more forgiving than the *Sydney Morning Herald*.

All of the newspaper groups had reason to begrudge the Menzies government's credit squeeze but only John Fairfax Ltd editorialised against the government, and actively campaigned to remove it from office. This fact, plus the level of hostility directed towards Menzies personally, led many to suspect there must be more to it than just lost advertising revenue. This brings us to one of the most salacious, but unverified, stories of Australian newspaper history.

The strong rumour in the press gallery was that the hostility between Menzies and Warwick Fairfax 'stemmed from an affair Menzies had with Fairfax's wife'.[32] Ian Fitchett, who was the *Sydney Morning Herald*'s chief political correspondent during the critical period of 1960–61, told younger journalist Rob Chalmers that the affair was 'taken as fact by hundreds', including government staffers, senior public servants and Sydney's society set.[33] Mungo MacCallum, who was a member of the press gallery from 1969 to 1998, also found the rumour was considered fact by many journalists and staffers. The story was that Fairfax had 'belatedly' discovered that Menzies had an affair with his first wife, the vivacious Betty (Marcie Elizabeth, née Wilson, mother of James).[34] Peter Costigan, a past president of the Canberra press gallery and chief political reporter for the HWT, also believed that this alleged affair was the real reason why the Fairfax company campaigned against Menzies in 1961, and Alan Reid apparently also believed this.[35]

Those who revere Menzies' memory consider this rumour both false and distasteful. Gerard Henderson of conservative thinktank, the Sydney Institute, has pointed out that there is no evidence for it (although MacCallum responded by asking what evidence would there be for such a private event?).[36] Menzies' biographer, Allan Martin, and Vic Carroll, who was finance editor of the *Sun-Herald* in the early 1960s, were also sceptical.[37] In his memoirs, James Fairfax wrote that his mother and Menzies were 'lifelong friend[s]' but, alluding to the rumour, said he never felt there was 'any substance' to stories of a personal feud between his father and Menzies.[38]

Certainly, the timing of events seems odd. Warwick had separated from Betty in 1944, and they divorced in 1945. In 1959, he had divorced his second wife, Hanne, and married his third wife, Mary Symonds. If Warwick had only just found out about an affair with Betty, after a delay of more than 15 years and two further marriages, the impact of such a betrayal must surely have been dulled somewhat.

The rumoured affair may simply have been a way for outsiders to make sense of why a highly conservative newspaper so loathed Menzies that it embraced Calwell in 1961. Although many observers found it difficult to believe the feud was simply about economic policy and company profits, reading through Warwick's correspondence in the 1940s and the internal board minutes and file notes from 1961, it is clear there was genuine outrage and distress in the boardroom about the negative financial impact of Menzies government policies.

Whether the affair rumour was actually true is, of course, unlikely to ever be settled now, but it is true that it was a widespread belief in political and journalistic circles at the time. In March 1962, Menzies defended his government following its poor election result and mentioned that one factor was the *Sydney Morning Herald*'s campaign against him. Four days later, Labor MP Les Haylen, a former Packer journalist, stood up in parliament and gave a cutting review of Menzies' speech:

> Whenever he is trapped, [Menzies] becomes a ham actor … On Thursday last, he … started to talk about the tragic differences between himself and a powerful friend in Sydney … He decided to play Hamlet. He walked the gloomy battlements of his political humiliation, communing with his ghosts. He saw them everywhere, particularly on the editorial board and in the management of the *Sydney Morning Herald* … he descended into the famous graveyard scene, accompanied by his two gravediggers, the Treasurer (Harold Holt) and the Minister for External Affairs (Sir Garfield Barwick). When they dug up the skeleton of the Liberal Party of Australia, the Prime Minister took the skull in his hands and said, "Alas, poor Warwick! I knew [her] well!"[39]

Hansard actually recorded the last line as, 'I knew *him* well', but *Nation Review* journalists insisted that 'him' 'was not the pronoun that kept the House in uproarious laughter for two minutes'.[40]

STEEL CITIES

It is just as likely that the Fairfax company's red-hot anger towards Menzies in 1961 was not only a response to the credit squeeze but also a reaction to how the government was carving up country television licences. In November 1960, the government had thwarted John Fairfax Ltd's television ambitions in Newcastle and Wollongong. Newcastle, 170 kilometres north of Sydney, had long been an important region for the company. In the late 1910s, it sent Rupert Henderson there as the *Sydney Morning Herald*'s representative, and that was a large and important job even then. By the 1960s, Newcastle was even more significant. It had the fastest growing population of any Australian city outside the capitals. It was also the third biggest port in the country, the supplier of half the country's coal, and home to BHP's steelworks.[41] In 1957, David Jones had established a store in Newcastle, and where department stores went, big city newspapers often followed.

On top of all of those reasons, Newcastle was newly important because the city was about to gain a television station, and when it did, its television transmission area would overlap with Sydney's. Around 150 000 people who were current viewers of ATN-7 and TCN-9 would be able to receive a new station broadcasting from Newcastle.[42] Of the five applicants for Newcastle's sole television licence, one applicant was allied with Fairfax, another with Packer. Both were looking to defend their patch, but both had missed out. The licence for Newcastle's NBN-3 station went to Newcastle Broadcasting and Television Corporation Ltd. The publisher of the *Newcastle Morning Herald* and the *Newcastle Sun* had a stake in this company, but it was mostly owned by the Lamb family, owners of Newcastle radio stations 2KO and 2HD (and also 2UE Sydney).

The metropolitan newspaper groups had expected country areas to be their points of 'natural growth' in television as they could string stations into a network and save on production costs.[43] But the Menzies government wanted country television to be locally owned and independent of the existing licensees, which also had the advantage of giving Country Party interests and supporters the chance to gain licences in their areas.

Of the 13 country television licences awarded in November 1960, Packer had applied for three, and Fairfax for four. They had failed with all seven, including in the Illawarra/Wollongong area.[44] This was another strategically important region as the home of the Port Kembla Steelworks (a BHP subsidiary), another new David Jones store, and with the overlap between Wollongong's television transmission area and the Sydney stations even greater than in Newcastle.[45] The television licence was granted to Television Wollongong Transmissions Ltd, which launched the WIN-4 station.

Both Packer and Fairfax moved quickly to attempt to get around the Menzies government's policy of localism. In Newcastle, both sought to acquire Newcastle Newspapers Pty Ltd, part-owner of NBN-3 and publisher of the *Newcastle Morning Herald* and the afternoon *Newcastle Sun*. Sydney Wansey was the Bermuda-based heir to the estate which held a majority of its shares. He refused to sell to Packer.[46] After two frantic visits to Bermuda, the Fairfax group acquired a 45 per cent interest in Newcastle Newspapers in September 1961.[47]

When Fairfax's papers had lashed Menzies during the 1961 election, its freshly-acquired Newcastle papers had joined in along with all of the group's other newspapers. The *Newcastle Morning Herald* said a 'smug' Menzies, with his 'indomitable faith in his own political genius', refused to acknowledge his mistakes, and had used the 'mandate' given in 1958 'as a licence for arrogance'.[48]

Other owners of the Newcastle television station, and also of Wollongong's, were put under immense pressure to sell. In 1962, both country television companies complained to the PMG that they were having trouble obtaining popular overseas television programs. The minister discovered that Packer's TCN-9 and Fairfax's ATN-7 had told program distributors they would stop buying from them if they supplied programs to the Newcastle and Wollongong stations. The suppliers had taken the threats seriously and refused to supply NBN and WIN.

Without these popular programs, NBN-3 and WIN-4 could not compete. Most Wollongong and Newcastle viewers were able to receive the three Sydney channels clearly, so they could watch the programs on those stations instead. NBN and WIN suffered heavy financial losses.[49] The PMG imposed new licence conditions on TCN-9 and ATN-7 to try to stop them hobbling other stations, but they mounted a legal challenge in the High Court. They won in August 1963, and after that, any hope of obtaining the necessary overseas programs for WIN and NBN was gone. The stations' local shareholders started to sell out, including the Lamb family, which sold substantial interests in Newcastle Broadcasting and Television Corporation to Consolidated Press Ltd and News Limited in August 1963. The big newspaper–television companies were making a mockery of the government's attempts to keep them out of country television.[50]

REVENGE AND THIRD TELEVISION LICENCES

In 1961, the Menzies government had come very close to defeat. It had scraped into office with a one-seat majority in the House of Representatives, and lost effective control of the Senate, now requiring the support of either the DLP or independent senators. Despite this fragile position, the government began its new term freshly committed to a policy that would upset some of the largest media companies. It wanted to allocate new commercial television licences in Sydney, Melbourne, Brisbane, Adelaide and Perth, even though the ABCB had warned that new competition for advertising revenue was premature in Sydney and Melbourne, and unwise in Brisbane and Adelaide due to their smaller populations.[51]

There was a suspicion, including from within the Fairfax group, that new licences were a way of rewarding those who had been 'politically good' and punishing those who had been 'politically bad'.[52] Henderson and Dumas had been unsuccessfully lobbying Menzies to not proceed with new metropolitan stations.[53] But Menzies' most loyal media supporter, Packer, was lobbying for the charge. He would be affected if a third commercial television station began in Sydney and took advertising revenue away from TCN-9, but Packer expected to be more than compensated by the new opportunities in networking that would open up. Selling programs and program rights to smaller stations was a large part of Packer's business model. His company made up to five times more from on-selling programs than other broadcasters and he had been lobbying Menzies for years to bring in new licences for Brisbane, Adelaide and Perth.[54]

Murdoch also saw the policy as an opportunity. Although his Adelaide television station, NWS-9, would suffer from new competition, Murdoch was hopeful of obtaining the new Sydney licence. Sydney and Melbourne were the main game in television; that was the axis where the real money and power resided. Those two cities contained 65 per cent of the population.[55] Most overseas programs shown on Australian commercial television were purchased by the Sydney and Melbourne stations and then 'on sold' to stations in smaller cities. And 'practically all' of the television programs produced in Australia were made in Sydney or Melbourne.[56] As a small, single television station in Adelaide, NWS-9 had very little decision-making power, and as part of Packer's network, it was 'the tail on the dog'.[57]

In 1962, the Menzies government called for applications for third commercial television licences in Sydney, Melbourne, Brisbane and Adelaide, and a second one in Perth. None of the five new licences went to newspaper groups (Table 13.2). They were out of favour. The government had grown weary of watching them dominate the young television industry and poke loopholes in their licensing policies. Menzies was also broadly disenchanted with the press, especially Fairfax, after nearly losing office.

Melbourne's new licence for Channel O (as in 'oh', not zero; it later became Channel 10) went to Austarama, a wholly owned subsidiary of airline and road transport company Ansett Transport Industries. Ansett had no experience in broadcasting. Its founder and managing director, Reg Ansett, was a swashbuckling, risk-taking entrepreneur who had friends in Cabinet. At this time, he was considered 'the favoured son of the Menzies government'.[58] Ansett's company had been the overwhelming beneficiary of government subsidies for aviation, government-guaranteed loans, and the government's unusual two airlines policy (which protected Ansett from commercial competition).[59] Television was now another government-protected oligopoly to which Ansett was granted access.

The government did draw the line, though, at giving Ansett a second licence, as it had also applied in Brisbane. Universal Telecasters Qld (TVQ-0) was selected instead on the basis that it was a local company independent of licensees in other cities.[60] Ansett soon made a mockery of that principle, and of the whole licensing process, in what Sandra Hall called 'the era's most showy piece of financial footwork'. As soon as Universal Telecasters was listed on the Brisbane Stock Exchange, Ansett bought up nearly all its shares. And because the company's articles of association limited any one shareholder's total voting rights to 15 per cent, even though Ansett had clear financial control of Universal Telecasters, it technically was not in control of it. Ansett's transaction did not contravene the *Broadcasting and Television Act*, so an embarrassed government had to sign off on it.[61]

Ansett also had a 5 per cent shareholding in South Australian Telecasters Ltd, which was chosen to be the third Adelaide commercial station (SAS-10), and a 4.5 per cent shareholding in Swan Television Ltd, which was chosen as the second Perth station (STW-9).[62] The Menzies government had broken the newspaper companies' grip on commercial television but had created a new monster with Ansett either controlling, or an investor in, four of the five new licences.

Although the newspaper groups were no longer centre stage, they were still hovering in the background of new licensees. Dumas had written to Menzies in April 1962 warning him that the 'syndicate of respectable Adelaide citizens [making up South Australian Telecasters Ltd was] sponsored by Ian Potter … [and] Frank Packer was behind it'.[63] The winning applicant in Sydney was United Telecasters Sydney Ltd (TEN-10), and it had Fairfax fingerprints all over it. It was a consortium that included Fairfax friends, sugar giant CSR and the Bank of New South Wales, but also AWA and Email, which had originally been partners with Fairfax in ATN-7. AWA and Email had never been strongly committed to ATN-7 and had sold their shares to the Fairfax group in January 1961 at a profit of around five times what they had contributed to the project.[64]

Although they had only recently sold out of metropolitan television, AWA and Email had been given a second chance. Murdoch was furious that his rival application had been rejected. His bid had emphasised News Limited's Sydney subsidiaries, and he had carefully selected respectable partners.[65] Murdoch believed, from inside information, that his application was the frontrunner until it had been vetoed by Menzies. He interpreted this as punishment for his earlier support for Labor and his half-hearted endorsement of Menzies in 1961.[66] Years later, Murdoch said 'old man Henderson' confessed to him that the Sydney licence outcome had been predetermined. According to Murdoch's account of what Henderson confessed, Henderson and Menzies had done a deal in 1961, when Henderson bought AWA out of ATN-7, that Menzies would 'work it [that AWA] would get the next licence'. Murdoch said Henderson 'told me … how he fixed it'.[67] With United Telecasters running the third commercial station in Sydney, the Fairfax group had a new competitor but at least it included old friends. And Henderson had a special interest in AWA as it was a partner in the regional media empire he was building up for himself and his family (Chapter 14).

STRANGE BEDFELLOWS

Murdoch had entered Sydney newspapers via the backdoor of suburban papers in 1960. After missing out on Sydney's third commercial television licence, he applied the same strategy to television. When the company behind Wollongong's WIN-4 increased its capital in April 1963, it issued the new shares – amounting to one-third of the company – to Murdoch's Mirror Newspapers.[68] Murdoch then pumped money into WIN-4, and flew to the United States and bought up 2500 hours of first-release programs before Packer or Fairfax could bid on them.[69] These were new series of popular programs shown on TCN-9 and ATN-7. Because WIN-4 was within range of Sydney viewers, Murdoch's plan was to use the programs to entice Sydney viewers to buy an aerial that would receive WIN-4 and take away audiences – and advertisers – from the existing Sydney channels.

Murdoch later said this plan to turn WIN-4 into a Sydney station-in-exile probably would have failed if he was left to carry it out, but an under-pressure Packer acted rashly. He sold Murdoch a 25 per cent stake in TCN-9 in Sydney in order to secure the rights to those American programs for his stations.[70] This made Murdoch a substantial TCN-9 shareholder with a stake in Sydney television. And it made Packer and Murdoch mutually suspicious partners.

As more of the local shareholders sold out of WIN-4 and NBN-3, Packer, Murdoch, and also Fairfax, ended up coexisting in the Newcastle and Wollongong stations and running them as relay stations of their Sydney channels. Even Rupert Henderson's family company, Henderson

TABLE 13.2 Newspaper groups abandoned: The Menzies government's allocation of new commercial television licences, 1963–64

Area	Channel/station Major owner	Granted licence (year)	Company name	Original major shareholders	Began transmission
Sydney	TEN-10 Non-newspaper consortium (1963-79)	1963	United Telecasters Sydney Ltd	AWA; CSR, Email; Bank of New South Wales; NRMA; JC Williamson Theatres; NBC International (US); public shareholders.	5 April 1965
Melbourne	ATV-0 (later 10) Ansett (1963-79)	1963	Austarama Television Pty Ltd	Ansett Transport Industries (Austarama was a wholly owned subsidiary of Ansett)	1 Aug 1964
Brisbane	TVQ-0 Ansett (1964-80)	1964	Universal Telecasters Qld Ltd	Original application consortium was: CQBH Pty Ltd (Central Queensland Broadcasting Corporation Pty Ltd.), but Ansett acquired 49 per cent of the company's shareholding.	1 July 1965
Adelaide	SAS-10 Non-newspaper consortium (1964-80)	1964	South Australian Telecasters Ltd	Ansett; Adelaide Steamship Co; John Martin and Co Ltd; Master Butchers Ltd; South Australian Insurance Co Ltd; other minor shareholders and a public share issue in South Australia.	26 July 1965
Perth	STW-9 Non-newspaper consortium (1964-87)	1964	Swan Television Ltd	Ansett; Esanda Ltd; Thomson Television International Ltd (England); Queensland Insurance Co; other shareholders, including AMP; and a public issue of shares.	12 June 1965

SOURCES ABCB and Australian Broadcasting Tribunal annual reports and secondary sources, including *Canberra Times*, 6 May 1984, p. 3, and 7 January 1984, p. 18.

Holdings Pty Ltd, ended up owning a stake in WIN-4 and other NSW country television stations (Chapter 14). The newspaper groups had yet again skirted around government attempts to stop them taking over country television stations. Among their fellow NBN-3 shareholders were mining companies, including BHP, Conzinc RioTinto, North Broken Hill, Hamersley Holdings Ltd, Loloma Mining Corp, Mount Isa Mines and International Oils Exploration.[71] The newspaper groups were not the only ones protecting their interests.

THE 'FACELESS MEN': THE 1963 ELECTION

After missing out on the third Sydney television licence, Murdoch loathed Menzies.[72] When the next federal election was held in November 1963, just seven months after the licence decision, Murdoch's papers slammed the Menzies government's record of 'stagnation', 'muddle and slackness'. The *Daily Mirror* instead endorsed Calwell as a 'man of outstanding vision and skill', a leader with a 'vital personality and vigorous patriotism'.[73] ('Vigor' and 'vitality' were sought-after qualities. Calwell was 67 and Menzies about to turn 69.)

Murdoch had put aside the fact that Calwell despised his father, Keith (just as Fairfax and Henderson had put aside their previous differences with the Labor leader). Murdoch was still hedging his bets, though. Even as he lunched with Calwell two days before the election, and made a substantial donation towards Labor's campaign, Murdoch was also pushing for the deputy prime minister, John McEwen (leader of the Country Party), to replace Menzies.[74] The *News* stated that McEwen's 'vigor' and his pro-economic growth attitude almost made up for Menzies' shortcomings. It declared, 'If Mr McEwen was the leader, or even the prospective leader, the Government would be in no trouble.'[75] But McEwen was leader of the Country Party, not the Liberal Party, and an impractical choice on Murdoch's part. This was a sign of how politically 'naïve' and unconnected on the Liberal side Murdoch was at this stage.[76]

Over at Broadway, the Fairfax papers' marriage of convenience with Calwell had ended, much to the amusement of Consolidated Press

"Should old acquaintance be forgot . . ."

FIGURE 13.2 The *Daily Telegraph* was amused by Fairfax's reconciliation with Menzies. Calwell is shown being thrown out of the boardroom while the *Financial Review* and the *Sydney Morning Herald*'s finance editor, Tom Fitzgerald, have been caned and sent to the naughty corner, 25 November 1963.
SOURCE State Library of NSW. Reproduced with permission of the Tanner family.

(Figure 13.2). After the credit squeeze, the economy had recovered quickly, advertising revenue had jumped back, and Murdoch had been kept out of Sydney television. Warwick Fairfax was back dining with Menzies.[77] The chairman insisted, once again, on writing the *Sydney Morning Herald*'s election editorial without consulting Henderson. This time, the editorial abruptly directed the *Sydney Morning Herald* back to supporting Menzies. Henderson did not want the paper to swing back so quickly after 1961 and had a blazing row with Warwick. A previously strong relationship was now characterised by reduced trust and increased tension.[78]

Henderson was not the only one upset about the editorial. Three of the company's top journalists – Tom Fitzgerald, Max Newton and Lou Leck – continued to be concerned about Menzies' economic performance, and they contemplated resignation.[79]

The 1961 election was an aberration. The Fairfax company had been a strong supporter of the Liberal Party, if not Menzies personally, since the party's founding. Aside from editorial support, it quietly made regular financial donations to the Liberal Party, as well as donations of photographs and equipment.[80] At the same time, the *Sydney Morning Herald* always vehemently proclaimed its independence and impartiality. The paper's conflicted approach was beautifully summed up in a reply that Rupert Henderson sent to the New South Wales premier, the Liberal Party's Robert Askin, in 1969, after Askin complained about critical coverage. Henderson told Askin, 'you are entitled to assume we are supporting your party, but we do not, and could not, allow our policy or our views to influence the presentation of news. That must be impartial, objective, and free from comment.'[81]

Over at Frank Packer's *Daily Telegraph*, there were no delusions of impartiality. Packer's passionate support for Menzies, and his loathing of communism, unions and the Labor Party, flavoured the paper's comment and news coverage alike. Packer was 'a traditionalist, a Royalist, a conservative [and] a free enterpriser', and he had no hesitation in pushing his own agenda in his paper.[82] His best political weapon had once been Brian Penton. Now, it was the also strongly anti-communist Alan Reid. David McNicoll said Reid was a 'political animal' who lived and breathed politics.[83] Politicians went to Reid to find out what was going on in their own party as well as their opponents'. He was a political player, not just a reporter, and considered a master political strategist in his own right. He later boasted that Menzies regularly sought his views on issues of the day.[84]

Reid was especially valuable to both Packer and Menzies because his Labor sources were impeccable. He had been a Labor Party member, and a favourite of Ben Chifley.[85] But his exposé on BA Santamaria and the Groupers in 1954 had helped set in motion the Labor split and Reid had continued, since then, to advance Packer's anti-Labor campaigns. The Labor Party did not renew Reid's membership of its Canberra branch in 1957, and Calwell apparently did not speak to Reid for 12 years.[86]

In the club-like atmosphere of Canberra, Reid still maintained very good relations with other Labor contacts, especially Pat Kennelly, Fred Daly, Clyde Cameron, Allan Fraser, Les Haylen and, sometimes, Evatt.[87]

From them, Reid obtained inside information on the party that enabled him to write blow-by-blow accounts of Labor's turmoil, its closed meetings, secret decisions and party intrigue, which Reid and Packer used to great effect against Labor in the 1950s and 1960s. Reid said in 1971 that Packer 'never interfered with my copy during 15 years'.[88] There was no need. As Reid's biographers, Ross Fitzgerald and Stephen Holt, noted, 'There was no doubting the relish with which Reid served his master.'[89]

In 1962 and early 1963, Packer and Reid were worried about Menzies' election prospects. Public opinion polls had favoured Labor and Calwell throughout 1962, although missteps by Calwell in foreign affairs had dulled that advantage.[90] Reid, McNicoll and Packer were convinced that the *Daily Telegraph* had saved the Menzies government in 1961, and now they needed to save it again in 1963. An opportunity presented itself in March when the Labor Party's federal conference met at the Kingston Hotel in Canberra.

Neither Labor leader Arthur Calwell, nor his deputy Gough Whitlam, was a delegate to the conference which, at that time, consisted of six delegates from each state. But the conference was deciding an important question of policy that was troubling Labor's leadership: whether Labor should support moves by the Menzies government to allow US bases on Australian soil that could be used to control nuclear-armed submarines. Calwell and Whitlam were in favour of the bases. Both addressed the conference and then retired to Parliament House. After lengthy debate among the delegates, the final vote was cast at 1.45 am. By then, Calwell and Whitlam had returned to the Kingston Hotel and were waiting outside to discover the result.[91] Reid spotted them standing under a street lamp as conference delegates occasionally came out to confer and update them on progress inside.

Packer had given Reid a specific brief 'to depict the ALP conference in as unfavourable a light as possible'.[92] The two leaders huddled in the street presented a remarkable opportunity to visually show Labor as weak and vacillating. But a photograph was essential to make the point. A frustrated Reid could not manage to summon a staff photographer at that late hour, but he noticed one of the observers outside the hotel was a friend. His fellow trout fisherman, Vladimir Paral, worked as a scientific

FIGURE 13.3 Alan Reid kills Labor's election hopes with his 'faceless men' scoop in the *Daily Telegraph*, 22 March 1963
SOURCE State Library of NSW. Reproduced with permission of Newspix.

photographer at the John Curtin School of Medical Research. Reid asked Paral to rush home, get his camera and not to worry if his shots did not flatter the subjects. Paral quickly developed the photographs and Reid had them flown to Sydney on the first flight out of Canberra.[93]

The photographs were powerful because they showed Labor's leaders standing out on the street, in the dark, anxiously 'waiting for orders from their bosses' about what policy they would take to the electorate (Figure 13.3).[94] Reid's accompanying story also evoked weak, indecisive and undemocratic leadership. It described the party's leaders as beholden to federal conference delegates who were '36 virtually unknown men'. There were actually 35 men and one woman delegate whose names were freely available but the notion was simple, evocative, and soon caught on.

Building on the *Daily Telegraph*'s story, a fortnight later, Liberal Party backbencher Harry Turner used the phrase 'the 36 faceless men'. Then Menzies began using it regularly.[95] After it became clear that the charge was cutting through and hurting Labor's credibility, an early election was called. The Liberal Party ran newspaper advertisements and leaflets that pointed to Labor's 36 'faceless men ... not elected to Parliament nor responsible to the people'.[96] The implication that Labor's leaders were not in charge of party policy was devastatingly effective and the 'faceless men' episode was widely viewed as a significant factor in the Liberal Party's electoral success in 1963, and even in 1966.[97] Gough Whitlam called it 'a devastating blow' against Labor.[98] After the Menzies government was returned with an increased majority, Menzies wrote to Packer to thank him for his media outlets' 'tremendous loyalty and enthusiastic help'.[99]

MURDOCH'S PLAN B

Honeymoons were dangerous times for newspaper owners. While Warwick Fairfax was honeymooning, Henderson sold the *Daily Mirror*. While Murdoch was honeymooning in 1967, Packer diluted Murdoch's shareholding in TCN-9 down to insignificance by shifting stock between companies in a 'classic reverse takeover' manoeuvre.[100] A month later, Murdoch was forced to sell his TCN-9 holding to Packer at a considerable loss of $1.1 million.[101] Both of them had acted rashly, but Packer had the last laugh. Years before, Murdoch had already privately concluded that Frank Packer 'must be the biggest crook in Australian newspapers, but equally he is the cleverest'.[102]

Murdoch would have to wait years for another chance to get into television in Sydney. In the meantime, he had a new project to occupy him. Like his father before him, Murdoch dreamed of starting a British-style, high-quality national newspaper in Australia. It had also been a dream of Rupert Henderson, Colin Bednall and others.

Starting up any newspaper in the 1960s was not a prospect for the faint hearted. Even in the 1920s, when circulations were growing, production costs were lower, and newspapers had no competition from television, owners had needed deep pockets and steady nerves to wait out years of potentially ruinous losses until a metropolitan daily was established. Although Rupert's father was considered the best in the business, he had only ever bought existing metropolitan papers or merged them. He had never started one from scratch.

But the idea of launching a *national* paper, in a country the size of Australia, was considered even more foolhardy. As a later CEO of the HWT, John D'Arcy, pointed out, distributing daily newspapers just in the state of Queensland 'was the equivalent of *The Times* in London being delivered in Moscow daily at breakfast time'.[103] Australia's most profitable newspapers were all metropolitan based. They relied on the retail and classified advertisers in their city, and on the fact that distance prevented the newspapers in any other capital city from competing with them. There were also cultural factors to consider. How could one paper overcome parochialism and successfully cross state borders? How would it cover state politics or, just as importantly, different codes of football?

Conventional wisdom had it that Australia's geography and culture made a truly national daily impossible, just as it had proven to be in the United States. And yet, there was some precedent for national media, as the *Bulletin*, the *Australian Women's Weekly* and the ABC had shown. And, technically, in 1964, there were already two national daily newspapers. The *Daily Commercial News* had been published since April 1891. It was essentially a list of shipping movements but it had a surprisingly long life (108 years under its original name).

The second national daily was the *Financial Review*. After becoming a bi-weekly in 1961, and seeing off a challenge from Packer's short-lived *Australian Financial Times*, the *Financial Review* had become a daily in 1963. At first, it was difficult to convince readers to purchase five editions a week, but the increasing buoyancy of the stock market helped the financial paper survive as a daily.

Both of the existing national papers were specialist publications, but Murdoch wanted to create a national paper for a wide, general audience, and the mid-1960s seemed the right time to launch it. The economy was prosperous and there was a growing national mindset. Companies were continuing to move interstate, retail chains were growing, and national advertising was increasing, including on television. Australia's national capital seemed the logical place to launch a national newspaper, but Canberra was suddenly filled with newspaper activity.

THE END OF THE (MALE) LINE: THE *CANBERRA TIMES*

The *Canberra Times* was a newly attractive asset in the early 1960s because Canberra's population had doubled between 1953 and 1960, and the sole daily paper in the area had found an audience among the growing number of public servants, diplomats and interstate emigrants.[104] Advertising revenue had finally become lucrative, and the *Canberra Times*' 15 per cent stake in Canberra Television Ltd, which launched CTC-7 in June 1962, was also valuable.

Despite all of this growth and expansion, the *Canberra Times* was still being run like a family business on a shoestring, a cross between a country paper and a 'sweatshop'.[105] Arthur Thomas (AT) Shakespeare was the small, dour, no-nonsense figure who was head of the family. Thomas Mitchell Shakespeare, AT's father, and the founder of the paper, had six children, including four sons who all worked at the *Canberra Times*, but in one of those quirks of fate that could crush a dynasty in patriarchal times, the family had run out of male succession by 1958. AT had two daughters, but no male heir.[106] Even though Queen Elizabeth II had been on the throne for more than five years, in the Australian newspaper industry, only male descendants were considered capable of running a big media business. But the only male born to any of the *Canberra Times* founder's six children was AT's nephew, George Shakespeare Dowling. He was only five years old in 1958, lived in Dubbo, and his parents had no involvement with the paper.[107]

That year, Shakespeare approached Rupert Henderson at Fairfax. They knew each other well because both had joined the *Sydney Morning Herald* as cadets in 1915, and Shakespeare had worked there for ten years. Shakespeare believed Fairfax was the company that was most likely to allow the *Canberra Times* to remain as an independent, civic-minded paper focused on Canberra. He wrote to Henderson in 1958 and assured him that, if anyone threatened the *Canberra Times* or approached him to sell, he would call on Fairfax first.[108]

Because of Canberra's geographic proximity to Sydney, the Fairfax company was very interested in the *Canberra Times*. It was a point of vulnerability and a potential weapon that a canny rival like Murdoch could use against them. In mid-1962, Fairfax directors were also considering starting their own 'high quality' Canberra paper which 'eventually could become the national newspaper' of Australia.[109] As Murdoch had the same idea in mind, it was now a race to see who would get there first: the 66-year-old Henderson or 31-year-old Murdoch.

Fairfax acquired a site in the Canberra industrial suburb of Fyshwick in 1962 and erected a large building, ostensibly for printing standby editions of the *Sydney Morning Herald*, but Shakespeare correctly suspected that Fairfax intended to use it to launch a Canberra paper. Henderson had told the Fairfax board he was considering using the site to start an afternoon dummy paper to push Shakespeare to sell.[110] Murdoch turned to his suburban paper tactic yet again. One of Shakespeare's printers, Ken Cowley, had teamed up with a real estate agent, Jim Pead, in 1961 and started the *Territorial*, a free suburban bi-weekly. Murdoch quietly bought the *Territorial* and had Pead purchase a large property in Mort Street, the same street as the *Canberra Times*.

Shakespeare was now fielding overtures and threats from multiple angles. Recognising that the giants were closing in, he made a secret deal with Fairfax on 4 April 1963 to sell them one-eighth of the shares in his family's holding company for £60 000, with an option to buy the remainder in 1967, or earlier if a competitor arrived.[111]

In early 1964, Shakespeare was approached by both Consolidated Press and the HWT. He told Henderson of these offers. Shakespeare then ran into Murdoch at a party in King's Hall for the opening of Parliament on 25 February. Shakespeare asked Murdoch directly, 'What are you going to do with that land in Mort Street?' Murdoch replied, 'Run you out of business!' The group around them laughed, but Shakespeare did not. As soon as he left, he telephoned Henderson and gave Fairfax the signal to buy the remaining seven-eighths of the holding company for £600 000.[112]

On 1 May 1964, John Fairfax Ltd announced to Canberra's residents that it now owned the *Canberra Times*. It assured them the paper would be run independently and would 'in no way [be] an appendage of New South Wales or Sydney interests'.[113] The company told its *Sydney Morning Herald* readers that it wanted to develop the *Canberra Times* 'as a national daily newspaper based in Canberra'.[114] According to Max Newton, Murdoch was 'devastated', '[b]owling over a country rag like the *Canberra Times* was one thing, bowling over Rupert Henderson was another'.[115]

To ready for the battle, Fairfax poured money into the famously under-resourced *Canberra Times*, and John Pringle, former editor of the *Sydney Morning Herald*, was lured back from Fleet Street to edit it. For the first time, the *Canberra Times* was provided with a news editor, features editor, political correspondent in the press gallery, an economics editor, and a chief subeditor.[116] Fairfax even bought 50 houses in one day for new staff.[117]

Shakespeare relinquished the managing editorship of the paper but he remained chairman of its parent company until his death in 1975. The Fairfax company valued its reputation for honouring deals and for respecting long-standing traditions and family links.

Recognising the game had changed, Murdoch closed the *Territorial* on 21 May 1964 (Ken Cowley became one of his most trusted lieutenants). He then pushed ahead with his national paper.

MURDOCH'S BABY: THE *AUSTRALIAN*

Like Henderson, Murdoch originally planned to launch a Canberra paper that would go national only later, once it was established. But now that Fairfax had revitalised the *Canberra Times*, Murdoch had to quickly change focus and he made his new project a national paper from the start, about two years ahead of schedule.[118] When Murdoch launched the *Australian* in July 1964, it was the boldest move since Norton launched the *Daily Mirror* in 1941. And Norton had a wartime audience, lower costs, a much bigger market, and no transport problems. As academic and author Rodney Tiffen pointed out, Murdoch 'took a massive commercial risk … It was not clear that enough national advertising existed to sustain a [national] newspaper'.[119]

Murdoch wanted it to be a quality broadsheet for 'thinking men and women' that was printed in Canberra, and then distributed nationally.[120] All of those choices posed major problems. Back in 1957, Pringle had pointed out to Australian intellectuals longing for a local version of the British *Guardian*, that only about 2.8 per cent of the adult population in Britain read the 'serious "quality" newspapers'. If that was replicated in Australia, there would only be a total audience of 172 000 readers spread across a vast continent, only half of whom would be actual buyers, when a paper now needed a circulation of more than 200 000 to confidently survive because newspaper production costs were so high.[121] This statement drew attention to exactly the kind of problems Murdoch would be facing.

Murdoch hired Max Newton, who had left Fairfax after a series of arguments with management, to be the *Australian*'s first editor. But Murdoch also brought in a Fleet Street veteran, Stanley Cecil (Sol) Chandler, who had served as long-time deputy to Arthur Christiansen at the *Daily Express*, thus creating a degree of conflict over who was in charge. Planned for September, the *Australian* was rushed into print when Murdoch insisted it begin in July, only one day after its first dummy run.[122] Mistakes occurred in the rush, including the wrong date, which caused Murdoch to stop the presses.

The *Australian* took time to find its feet. It had a 'hotch potch' of content that reflected tensions between Newton and Chandler about how to balance its serious, intellectual focus, with lighter touches that reflected the entertainment values Murdoch prized in tabloids.[123] Chandler was soon dispatched to Melbourne to take charge of *Truth*.

The revitalised *Canberra Times* had damaged the *Australian*'s local prospects, and Canberra's population was so small it did not have enough buyers or advertisers to support a second newspaper. Most of the *Australian*'s sales would have to come from Sydney and Melbourne.[124] Trying to be both a local paper for Canberra and an authoritative national broadsheet at the same time was another tricky balancing act. The mismatch helped drive the paper to near closure in its first year, along with the decision to produce the paper from Canberra, which proved disastrous in terms of distribution.

Staff working out of the former home of the *Territorial* in Mort Street were producing three sets of matrices (or mats), the cardboard impressions of the pages from which the round stereo printing plates were made. They would pack one set for Sydney, and one for Melbourne, in aluminium suitcases, then drive them to Canberra airport by 11 pm so they could be printed on location in the major capital cities, ideally by 12.30 am.[125] But Canberra's foggy winters sometimes meant the airport was closed, or planes were grounded.

Murdoch famously stood on the tarmac at Canberra airport in his pyjamas on several occasions trying to convince pilots and officials that the fog was just a mist and they could take off.[126] If they could not be persuaded, the mats had to be driven by car to another airport, or even to Sydney, where copies could be made and then flown to other capitals. As a result of these disruptions, the *Australian* sometimes did not arrive in other capital cities until lunchtime, or not at all.

Murdoch and Newton had anticipated a daily circulation of 80 000 to 100 000.[127] But in 1965, circulation was around 61 000.[128] Newton later described the *Australian* as 'a wild idea, a mistake, a dream of such compulsion ... a once-in-a-lifetime chance', and also a 'rather shattering experience'.[129] Considered 'narcissistic' and with a touch of the 'mad genius' about him, Newton created an atmosphere that shocked reporters who were used to greater discipline and integrity, including encouraging the rigging of expenses and using the paper to promote shares he had an interest in.[130] Murdoch regarded the *Australian* as his baby; he had taken enormous financial risks on it and wanted to be deeply involved in its production. Newton felt that Murdoch 'rushing around, making up pages on the stone and carrying on' was a 'grave limitation', not a help.[131] Soon the two were arguing, and Newton was out after less than a year.

Newton's deputy, Walter Kommer, replaced him in March 1965. Kommer focused on production and commercial, while Adrian Deamer was poached from the *Sun News-Pictorial* and brought on as assistant managing editor in 1966. Deamer had a top newspaper pedigree. His father, Sydney, had been a legendary editor of the *Herald* and the *Daily Telegraph*. When he arrived, Deamer took on the bulk of responsibility for editorial and was essentially the *Australian*'s editor, in all but name, until he formally received that title in March 1969.[132]

Under Deamer, the *Australian* went from 'scrappy' to dynamic.[133] It became known as an exciting, innovative paper with quality content, enthusiastic staff, and growing circulation and influence. In the stuffy and provincial world of 1960s newspapers, the *Australian* was seen as a breath of fresh air with its serious coverage of business and international news, its liberal editorial line, and its willingness to tackle taboo topics.[134] It was blazing a trail for a new kind of reporting focused on national politics and policy at a time when readers had been socialised to be interested only in their own city.

The *Australian*'s prospects improved further in September 1966 when it became the first newspaper in the southern hemisphere to introduce facsimile transmission. New equipment, purchased from England, allowed a page to be made up at the Canberra office, then a proof pulled from that page was transmitted over the Post Office's telephone system so it could be printed out as a film negative at the printing centres in Melbourne and Sydney, giving a facsimile copy of each page for printing.[135] This liberated the paper from expensive hot-metal technology and improved its logistics and distribution.

The facsimile method was not enough to justify having the paper based in Canberra, though. In the Fairfax boardroom, Angus McLachlan told directors in June 1965 that Murdoch had sacked 40 employees and the paper had reduced its Canberra coverage. McLachlan said that, as far as Canberra was concerned, the *Canberra Times*' battle was nearly won.[136] In March 1967 it was over. Murdoch moved the *Australian* to Sydney where he segregated its staff in a chocolate factory, next door to the *Daily Mirror* in Surry Hills, to prevent any tabloid contamination of his quality paper.[137]

FOR LOVE OR MONEY?

Murdoch's motivation in starting up the *Australian* has been a source of much speculation. Some believed it was personal, that he had the idea in his head from his parents, and he was especially driven by a desire to please his mother, Dame Elisabeth. It was a way to make amends for his crass, lowbrow tabloids, especially *Truth*, which she found 'disgusting'.[138] She had reportedly told Murdoch to 'publish something decent for a change'.[139]

Others believed there was a more pragmatic motivation: that Murdoch wanted to own a paper that was read by premiers and prime ministers. He wanted to be politically influential in national politics in a way that his lightweight tabloids could never achieve. According to this theory, the *Australian* gave Murdoch credibility and respectability in political and business communities. It gave him the cachet and political access he needed to expand his business, including to win government-awarded television licences and approval for business mergers and takeovers.

The *Australian* was certainly not about making a quick profit. The venture nearly brought Murdoch undone. According to journalist Mark Day, who documented the paper's history on its 50th anniversary, in its first year 'the *Australian* lost $1.4 million, wiping out all profit from Murdoch's other enterprises'.[140] At other times, it racked up 'appalling' losses of more than $7 million annually.[141] Across the paper's first 20 years, Murdoch lost at least $30 million on it.[142]

At various times, News Limited directors, the Commonwealth Bank and others tried to convince Murdoch to cut his losses and close it, but Murdoch kept financially propping up the *Australian* for decades to come. The paper made its first (modest) profit only in 1985, 21 years after it was launched.[143] It was said that Reg Ansett and Sir Roderick Miller (a coal mine, shipping and breweries owner) gave substantial financial support to the *Australian* in its early years, and that it was difficult to find any criticism of them in Murdoch's papers as a result.[144]

By 1967, improved technology, tight control over costs, and the desertion of Canberra as a base, meant that losses were manageable. Some creative accounting also helped. The paper's costs and losses were spread around the group 'where they became tax deductions against other profits'.[145] Ultimately, the *Australian* survived the 1960s only because Murdoch insisted that it did.[146] Usually, in his approach to business matters, Murdoch was considered ruthlessly pragmatic and profit oriented, but the *Australian* was a clear exception. The paper was, as George Munster said, 'a personal monument' for Murdoch, that spelt out his 'loves, hates and manoeuvres' like nowhere else, and had to be propped up no matter the cost.[147]

CHAPTER 14
THE REALM OF THE BLACK PRINCE

While 33-year-old Rupert Murdoch was forging ahead with the *Australian*, his rivals were heading for retirement. In 1964, Rupert 'Rags' Henderson at Fairfax was 68, Jack Williams at the HWT was 63, and Frank Packer at Consolidated Press was 58. At the end of that year, Henderson would retire as managing director. He had worked at Fairfax for 49 years after joining the *Sydney Morning Herald* as a 19-year-old cadet in 1915.

A small man, whose clothes were always too big on him, Henderson had long bony fingers and thick glasses. He spoke in a 'rough, exaggerated reckless style' with great intensity and an 'amusing turn of phrase'.[1] He was known for being at his desk in his panelled fourteenth-floor Broadway office at all hours of the day and night. Within the industry, his energy and dedication were legendary. Admirers said that Henderson had an 'inviolable sense of loyalty' to the *Sydney Morning Herald* and the Fairfax family.[2] The company always seemed to come first, ahead of Henderson's family life and personal interests, which included reading, theatre and art collecting.

Frank Packer prized loyalty above almost any other attribute, and he thoroughly envied the Fairfaxes their shrewd and faithful defender.[3] A rather different view of Henderson's devotion was proposed by Max Walsh, though. A *Financial Review* journalist in the 1960s and later its editor, Walsh argued that Henderson 'mythologised' the Fairfax family and acted as such a 'wonderful steward' for them, because as long as the Fairfaxes were in charge, Henderson was really in control.[4]

Henderson had been carefully managing the family since his earliest days in the company. Insiders said it was Warwick Fairfax's mother, Lady Mabel Fairfax (née Hixson), who recognised the potential in Henderson, made sure that his talents were appreciated, and that he was sent to London as chief of the *Sydney Morning Herald*'s Fleet Street office from 1923 to 1926. His other important duty in London was to befriend and guide Warwick while the heir to the company was studying at Oxford. (Similar to how Keith Murdoch sent Rohan Rivett to mentor and watch over Rupert in London 25 years later.) When Warwick returned to Sydney after completing his studies, Henderson was not far behind.

Warwick, Mabel's only child, had been born nine years after she married James Oswald Fairfax. At a time when women were supposed to keep out of business matters, Lady Mabel had a reputation for being the 'real boss' at Fairfax, and especially after her husband dropped dead on the golf course in 1928. Mabel was watching through all of the main act of Henderson's career. She died, aged 93, in 1965, just ten weeks after Henderson retired as managing director.

If it was Mabel's handiwork to pair her shy, dreamy, intellectual son with the canny, street smart Henderson, the company owed her a debt. For generations, the Fairfaxes were known as honourable people with good values. They were philanthropic, cultured, believed in public service and contributed to Australian society. Warwick Fairfax, with his haughty grandeur, and the wily, determined Henderson, proved to be the right combination. Rupert Murdoch said in 1990, 'The modern Fairfax [company] was the creation of Rupert Henderson ... without him the family control would not have survived the 1950s.'[5]

Henderson was creative in solving problems, and had a remarkable memory and grasp of detail. He was also tough as nails. Hardened journalists and other media executives found him frightening and he seemed to enjoy his reputation as a hard man. He was just as formidable at home. His granddaughters, Helen and Judith, used to 'shake in [their] boots' when they went to visit him.[6] Irene Thirkell was Henderson's secretary for 40 years. 'Miss Thirkell', as she was always referred to within the company, said she saw her boss cry just once, in 1961, when 30-year-old David Lloyd Jones rang to tell Henderson he was dying of cancer.[7]

Although Henderson was considered hard, ruthless, and cunning 'as a rat', he also had a wicked sense of humour, and valued his reputation for integrity and being 'a man of his word'.[8] This was an enormous advantage when it came to making deals with other business leaders, and it helped him defeat Frank Packer on several occasions during their long rivalry. Packer gained the edge in television, but as journalist Errol Simper noted, Henderson 'stopped [Packer] buying the *Newcastle Herald*, the *Canberra Times*, Associated Newspapers. He stopped him getting the *Daily Mirror*, the *Sun*. In fact, Packer never laid a glove on Fairfax in the newspaper business.'[9]

Aside from his duties at Fairfax, Henderson held powerful roles in the industry, including as director of the international news agency Reuters, and chairman of AAP, Australian Newsprint Mills and ANPA. He developed a reputation for making on-the-spot decisions and solving industry problems as they arose. Even people who said they hated him tended to have the highest regard for his abilities.

When he retired, Packer's *Bulletin* announced his long-time rival's departure by mocking Henderson's short stature in a piece headlined, 'A BIG LITTLE MAN RETIRES'. Although the article lauded his abilities, it also called Henderson the 'Black Prince' of the Fairfax empire and described him as a man with a 'lonely, implacable veneer' that few had ever penetrated.[10] Henderson did have a private life, though, and before he was an industry titan, it had sometimes spilled out onto the pages of other newspapers.

HENDERSON AT HOME

In many respects, Rupert Henderson and his contemporary, Keith Murdoch, had parallel careers. Both rose from star political reporter, to heading their paper's London office, to company executive, to industry leader. But their private lives were very different. Keith Murdoch did not marry until he was 42 years old, and he was 45 when his son was born. Henderson married when he was 18, to Helene Mason, who had just turned 20. His son, Rupert William Geary (RWG) Henderson, known to all as 'Chips', was born seven months later.

Chips did not see much of his busy father, especially after his parents separated. When Chips was 17 years old and a champion sprinter at boarding school, his parents started bitter divorce proceedings which ended up in the Supreme Court. According to Helene, the final argument that caused Henderson to leave the marital home and move in with his mother occurred when Helene could not find him the morning paper to read at breakfast![11] In her petition, Helene and her sister described Henderson as 'very temperamental', 'very nervy' and 'rather bad tempered'.[12]

The divorce proceedings dragged on for five years. During that time, Henderson rose from the *Sydney Morning Herald*'s circulation manager to become secretary to the general manager. He was next in line for that role and could ill afford a scandal. He needed the divorce to be finalised. In May 1937, both the *Labor Daily* and *Truth* reported how Henderson sensationally told the court that he and another witness had observed Helene and a man named Maurice Fletcher in 'compromising circumstances', wearing 'night attire', in the bedroom of Fletcher's apartment in Manly, where she stayed overnight.[13] Henderson was represented in court by a King's Counsel and three other legal advisers. The divorce was granted. A brief notice, which listed Helene's adultery as the cause, appeared in the *Sydney Morning Herald*.[14]

This was 40 years before no-fault divorce and so adultery was still a common ground for divorce. It was not unusual for an aggrieved party to hire a private investigator, or for couples who wanted to divorce to resort to staging adulterous trysts for use as evidence in court. The Crown Solicitor seemed to suspect that Henderson and Helene were colluding in their evidence, but finally accepted that Helene had committed adultery.[15] It was not surprising that she might have started a new relationship, five years after Henderson had left. It was more surprising that that it did not come out in court that Henderson was known around Sydney as a womaniser. Perhaps it was either in gratitude, or by arrangement, that Henderson made sure Helene was taken care of for the rest of her life, not only financially but also in terms of her wellbeing.[16]

Another piece of unwanted publicity soon arose. Chips had started at the *Sydney Morning Herald* as a cadet journalist in 1934, but was prone to running a bit wild in his youth. In August 1938, two months after Henderson was promoted to general manager, Chips was arrested after police found him slumped in his car with blood running from his ear.

He told them, 'I am drunk – I am absolutely full to the neck.' This was reported in *Truth*, and on page three of the *Sun*.[17] A year later, Chips joined the Army just weeks after the outbreak of World War II. He served for four-and-a-half years. When Chips returned home, he went back to work at the *Sydney Morning Herald*.

Because he was a late-in-life father, Keith Murdoch had very little time before he died to integrate his son into the companies he had built up, but Henderson had plenty of time. Chips worked for the Fairfax company and its subsidiaries for 46 years, including as advertising manager of the *Sun* and *Sun-Herald*, and manager of Sungravure (Fairfax's magazine publishing company) between 1957 and 1970. He also served as a director of Amalgamated Television, Associated Newspapers and Canberra Television Ltd (CTC-7).[18]

Chips also worked with his father in running the family companies in regional media that Henderson built up. But the relationship between them was challenging, and sometimes strained. Chips was warm, charming and very popular at Fairfax, but he never had the talent or business skills of his father. No-one did. And that impossible standard must have been a difficult burden for Henderson's only son to carry. It was never a very warm or personable relationship between them. Chips always called him 'Father' or 'Rupert', never 'Dad'.[19] And Henderson was a domineering figure who cast a shadow over his son's family. Chips' daughter, Judith Cook, recalls of her home life that, 'If things were good with Rupert everything was good, [but] if [Chips and Rupert] weren't getting along, things were terrible.'[20] To complicate matters further, Henderson had a second family. After he and Helene had finally divorced in 1937, he had married Hazel Harris, the daughter of a Riverina orchardist, in 1939. When they married in New York, she was 26 years old, 17 years younger than Henderson. They had a daughter, Margaret, in 1946.

HENDERSON'S MINI-EMPIRE

Another career parallel that Henderson had in common with Keith Murdoch was that both built up a separate media empire for themselves and their family while they were building up a large public company for their employer. Keith went after expensive, politically influential daily metropolitan newspapers, but Henderson targeted quietly profitable and geographically valuable regional newspapers and television stations. His excursion into newspaper ownership began in 1945 when he formed a business partnership with Hanne Anderson, a Danish artist who had never owned a business. At the time, Hanne was Warwick Fairfax's 'attractive blonde companion'.[21] She became his second wife in 1948, after Warwick divorced Betty.

In 1945, Forbie Sullivan, one of two sisters who had inherited the Wagga *Daily Advertiser* from their father, went to Sydney to try to interest the Fairfax company in buying the paper but ended up meeting with Henderson instead.[22] After concerns were raised publicly about a big city newspaper company taking over provincial papers, Henderson purchased the paper in partnership with Hanne. Although Henderson insisted he was buying in a 'personal' capacity, disgruntled country newspaper owners were not convinced. They suspected the purchase was on behalf of the Fairfax company and that Hanne was in a relationship with, and a front for, Warwick Fairfax.[23]

In 1955, Henderson and Hanne acquired another regional paper after Arthur Shakespeare alerted Henderson that it was in financial difficulty.[24] The 100-year-old *Illawarra Mercury* in Wollongong, south of Sydney, was one of Australia's most important provincial newspapers and located in a region of importance to the Fairfax company. When Hanne and Warwick Fairfax divorced in 1959, it was Henderson who negotiated the divorce settlement with her in London. And he also bought out Hanne's half-share in their joint ventures.

Between 1960 and 1962, Henderson progressively obtained the *South Coast Times*, which also circulated in Wollongong. It was a shareholder in the WIN-4 Wollongong television licence that Fairfax had missed out on in 1960. In 1962, Henderson also purchased the *Goulburn Evening Post* (the only daily paper in Goulburn), and the *Berrima District Post*. His family-controlled holding company also bought the *Gosford Times* and absorbed it into another purchase, a paper called the *Central Coast Express*.[25]

The Fairfax company had missed out on country television licences in

1960, but Henderson was successful when he applied in his own right as a regional media owner in 1962. He was one of the original shareholders in Riverina Television Ltd which secured the licence for television station RVN-2 at Wagga Wagga. When the licence was awarded, the ABCB required that Henderson's shareholding in Riverina Television be reduced because his paper, the Wagga *Daily Advertiser*, could hardly be considered local given that it was owned by a Sydney newspaper manager who did not reside in Wagga.[26] But Henderson just built his stake back up over the next ten years, increasing it from 150 000 shares to 750 000.[27]

Henderson was also successful in 1962 as a shareholder in the company awarded a regional television licence in Albury on the Victorian border, Albury Upper Murray Television (AMV-4). In this venture, Henderson's partners included AWA, which had been a partner with Fairfax in Sydney television. After Henderson arranged for the Fairfax group to purchase AWA's shares in ATN-7 for a high price, AWA had gone into regional television with him.[28] Henderson's family company, Henderson Holdings, also had shares in AWA so he had a direct stake in making sure it prospered.[29] These facts add a new dimension to Murdoch's claim, discussed in Chapter 13, that Henderson did a deal with Menzies to make sure AWA got Sydney's third television licence.

When the Fairfax company had purchased Newcastle Newspapers in 1961, that had been the first step in building a 'geographical defensive perimeter' around Sydney to protect the 'crown jewels'.[30] Traditionally, the crown jewels were the *Sydney Morning Herald* and its classified advertising revenue, but now also included ATN-7 and its advertising. The defensive perimeter had been extended in 1964 with the purchase of the *Canberra Times* and its stake in CTC-7. Now, with Henderson owning media assets in Wagga Wagga, Wollongong, Goulburn and other parts of regional NSW, Sydney was protected on all sides.

THE (SECOND) LADY MACBETH OF FAIRFAX

If Mabel Fairfax brought Henderson close to her son Warwick, in Henderson's mind, it was Warwick's third wife, Mary, who pushed them apart. During the 1950s, while Henderson was busily expanding the Fairfax company, Warwick had been content to stay mostly in the background. He was pursuing his interests in art, travel, ballet and spirituality, plus writing plays and a book about metaphysics, and driving around town in a Phantom V Rolls Royce.[31] But Warwick's approach to the company had changed in the early 1960s. His friends and allies said Warwick was merely taking an active interest as befitted the majority shareholder and custodian of the *Sydney Morning Herald* legacy. Others, especially Henderson, felt an ambitious Mary was pushing Warwick forward.

In some sources, Mary Fairfax has been painted in almost caricature form, as a scheming, erratic, untrustworthy Lady Macbeth type. But there was an element of misogyny and antisemitism involved in her reception into the WASPish world of the Fairfaxes and their company. Mary was a Polish-born businesswoman from a Jewish family who owned several Sydney dress shops. She was smart, ambitious and frustrated. With her effusive manner and acute awareness of social position and status, she rubbed many people the wrong way, including Henderson.

Mary was 20 years younger than Warwick, and he seemed to dote on her and crave her approval. He also seemed to gain a new confidence and zest for life. This was interpreted by Henderson as the result of Mary possessing a sexual hold over Warwick. According to Max Newton, Henderson once said of Warwick that he 'goes out at night with the Jew bitch and comes in in the morning thinking he's fuckin Tarzan'.[32] This was consistent with other accounts of Henderson as being a sexist and racist bigot.

Mary and Warwick became known for hosting lavish parties at Fairwater, their mansion at Double Bay. She was described by her friends as a vivacious socialite and girlish 'party animal'.[33] Her enemies thought she was a hedonist and an insufferable social climber. It was reportedly Mary who pushed for her husband to be knighted. Menzies had knighted a high proportion of newspaper owners and executives, including Frank Packer in 1959 (something the ardent royalist had coveted for years). But Menzies never awarded that honour to his nemesis. In 1967, Warwick was knighted on the state (New South Wales) list.

Henderson thought Mary was dangerously ambitious. In a story he often told later to explain their feud, he met up with Warwick and

Mary Fairfax when they were in Europe taking their long honeymoon in 1959–60. According to Henderson, Mary asked to speak with him privately, told him she had 'a very strong influence' on her new husband, and said, 'Warwick trusts you. If you and I play our cards right, we can run the company.' Henderson had replied, 'Mrs Fairfax, I already run the company.'[34]

That had been true for years, but especially after Henderson had recently moved to limit Warwick's power as a way of blocking any influence Mary might seek to exert over the company via her husband. Although Fairfax was a public company, the Fairfax family still held the majority of its shares, around 53 per cent, and Warwick held almost two-thirds of the family's shareholding. A month before the wedding, Henderson had convinced him to transfer almost half of his Fairfax shares to his 26-year-old son James, ostensibly to avoid future death taxes. Because of this move, which became known as the 'Kinghaven arrangement', Warwick now had slightly fewer shares than his son James and cousin Vincent combined. He needed their support on the board, which still included Henderson, too. Mary Fairfax was furious. She knew he had done it to limit her influence and thought he had tricked her husband out of control of his own company.[35] Henderson's sale of the *Daily Mirror* to Rupert Murdoch strained relations further.

The Kinghaven arrangement was put into force in 1960–61, after Warwick's messy private life ended up in court. Mary had been married to a friend of Warwick's named Cedric Symons, when they had begun their affair. The disgruntled ex-husband had issued a Supreme Court writ against Warwick alleging the *Sydney Morning Herald* chairman had induced Mary to leave him and forced the breakup of their marriage. Henderson and James Fairfax (with the support of Vincent) insisted that Warwick temporarily resign as chairman in January 1961 in order to avoid embarrassing the company while the case was heard. Warwick felt the move was forced upon him and that it was a grab for power by Henderson and his son.[36] He was re-appointed in March when the case was settled out of court, but tension lingered even after the still-influential Lady Mabel had tried to repair relations between her son and grandson.[37]

Once back, Warwick was determined to play a more active role in the company. His editorial interventions later in 1961 during the election, and also in 1963, were evidence of that. Like Henderson, James did not approve of Warwick's interference in editorial and management matters. James had grown up with a sense of duty to the family business hanging over him, and he viewed it more as a matter of service than a burning personal ambition, or a way to assert authority or seek aggrandisement. He had been a director since 1957 and would be turning 32 in 1965. At an age where he would be expected to be playing a growing role in the family company, James was tending to side more with Henderson than with his own father.

THE BLACK PRINCE RETIRES

How to strengthen the *Sydney Morning Herald* was one of the areas of tension between Henderson and Warwick Fairfax. The jewel of the empire was losing sales to the *Daily Telegraph* in country areas, and not finding enough readers in the new housing estates around Sydney.[38] Advertisers were withdrawing advertisements from the paper's least popular days of the week.

To deal with the problem, Henderson considered starting a third morning paper, a tabloid with lots of pictures, to split the *Daily Telegraph*'s circulation and advertising. But Warwick worried this would just 'intensify the prejudice against broadsheet newspapers'. Henderson wanted to bring in new, young staff for the *Sydney Morning Herald*. But Warwick was against any 'drastic' reorganisation. Henderson argued the directors needed to wake up to changes in reading habits and make the *Sydney Morning Herald* a more popular paper. But Warwick wanted to protect its 'prestige' and 'status'.[39]

When Henderson talked vaguely of retiring in 1964, word got back to Warwick. Rather than asking Henderson to stay, the chairman encouraged him to set a date. Henderson felt he was 'being got rid of' even though he was the one who had raised the possibility. He accepted a retirement date of December 1964.[40]

Henderson performed one last big deal as managing director and it was a coup for the Fairfax company. In June 1964, he arranged for John Fairfax Ltd to purchase the Australian assets of Associated Television

Corporation Ltd (ATV). ATV was a British television company, one of the original 1955 ITV franchisees in the United Kingdom. In Australia, it owned the remnants of the Daily Mirror group's radio station chain as well as shares in several television stations.[41] Although the Daily Mirror group said it had sold out of Australian broadcasting completely in September 1958, it sold its Australian assets to the British television company that it had been heavily invested in since 1956. ATV was largely run by others (including one of the biggest names in British television, Lew Grade), but Hugh Cudlipp, chairman of the Daily Mirror group, had been on the ATV board since 1959.[42]

Henderson again beat Frank Packer to the prize of ATV. It was an important contest for Fairfax to win because ATV held shares in radio and television stations that Fairfax had substantial shareholdings in, including 2GB and ATN-7 in Sydney, but also QTQ-9 Brisbane, CTC-7 Canberra, WIN-4 Wollongong and RVN-2 Wagga Wagga. ATV's other assets included shares in six other radio stations, and shares in nine television stations in total.[43]

The deal cemented the Fairfax company's hold on key broadcasting assets, and netted it £3.8 million in tax-free capital gains over four years.[44] The radio assets were restructured into a public company called Macquarie Broadcasting Holdings, which controlled eight radio stations.[45] Macquarie would become a wholly owned subsidiary of John Fairfax Ltd in 1978.[46]

When Henderson began as managing director in 1949, Fairfax was a relatively small family company that published one morning newspaper. When he retired at the end of 1964, Fairfax was one of the largest financial groups in Australia. The share market valued the company at £40 million ($1.1 billion in today's money).[47] It owned seven newspapers (the *Sydney Morning Herald*, the *Sun*, the *Sun-Herald*, the *Australian Financial Review*, the *Canberra Times*, the *Newcastle Morning Herald* and the *Newcastle Sun*), as well as substantial interests in television, magazines, radio, news services and newsprint. Henderson had changed the nature of Fairfax from a newspaper company to a complex, multi-media conglomerate with a labyrinth of assets (Figure 14.1). In the eight years before Henderson retired, the company's profits had grown by 160 per cent, and the rate of

GROUP STRUCTURE

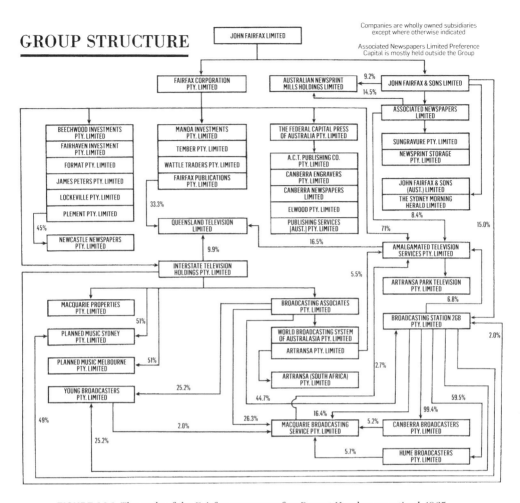

FIGURE 14.1 The scale of the Fairfax company after Rupert Henderson retired, 1965
SOURCE John Fairfax Ltd, *Annual Report 1965*, p. 2, Fairfax Media Business Archive, MLMSS 9894/13, Mitchell Library, State Library of New South Wales.

dividend it paid to investors (including the Fairfax family), had more than doubled.[48]

Although Henderson retired as managing director, he remained on Fairfax's board of directors until 1978, and continued to oversee important projects, including as chairman of ATN-7 until 1974, and chairman of Australian Newsprint Mills, Macquarie Broadcasting Holdings Ltd and Reuter Trustees, until 1978.[49] Henderson did not suffer the fate of early death caused by stress, over-work and unhealthy living that befell so many of his contemporaries. He lived to 90.

THE 'LITTLE GODS'

Henderson's ATV deal was yet another poke in the eye to the Menzies government's television ownership limits, and its policy for local television in regional areas. The deal had given Fairfax an additional 14.5 per cent interest in ATN-7 Sydney, 15 per cent in CTC-7 Canberra, and 10 per cent in QTQ-9 Brisbane. Fairfax had also taken possession of ATV's shares in six regional television stations.[50] In 1963, Menzies' Cabinet had already been concerned about the newspaper groups' 'stranglehold' on the young commercial television industry.[51] Ungrateful for the extraordinary largesse bestowed upon them during the first round of television licencing, the newspaper groups had continued to expand their dominance beyond their official licence allocations.

In 1960, the government had tried to restrain them by introducing a tighter definition of the concept of 'control' into the *Broadcasting and Television Act* 1956. But that only sparked what Sandra Hall called 'the golden age of media takeovers' – a period in which 'legislatory skill [ran] a bad second to corporate cunning'. Ansett's audacious takeover of the Brisbane licensee was a blatant example, but the newspaper groups had also, in quieter fashion, been using indirect shareholdings and other means to get around ownership restrictions.[52]

Despite the *Broadcasting and Television Act*'s limit on owning more than two television stations in Australia, by 1964 the HWT, Packer and Murdoch groups each held substantial shareholdings in six stations, and the Fairfax group in four. After the ATV deal, Fairfax had an interest in nine television stations.[53] The law deemed a person to be in control of a television licensee company if they controlled more than 15 per cent of voting rights, but the postmaster-general, Charles Davidson, noted the newspaper groups 'found no difficulty' circumventing that by amending their articles of association so no matter how big their shareholding was in a particular television company, their voting rights were limited to 15 per cent.[54]

In early 1963, Cabinet had approved in principle a plan that Davidson proposed for tightening ownership rules. But with its razor-thin majority of one in the House of Representatives, the government chose not to act against the newspaper groups until after the 1963 election, when it secured a far more comfortable majority of 21, and after the half-Senate election in 1964, where it secured an equal number of seats with Labor and the DLP held the balance of power.[55]

In 1965, the government added new ownership and control provisions to the *Broadcasting and Television Act*. This prohibited the holding of a 'prescribed interest' in more than two television stations in Australia, and more than one station within a capital city. As Keith Windschuttle explained, someone was deemed to hold a prescribed interest if they

> had direct ownership of 5 per cent of a television station, or an indirect ownership (by having a share in a company which itself had a share in the station) of 15 per cent. The ploy by Ansett and Fairfax of having effective ownership but only 15 per cent of formal voting rights, was outlawed.[56]

However, the government baulked at making existing licence holders conform to these new requirements. A 'grandfathering' clause was added which allowed companies to keep their existing interests in television as at 17 December 1964. According to Bednall, this clause was the result of a political deal done between the newspapers and deputy prime minister and Country Party leader, John McEwen, 'without the prior knowledge of the junior minister directly concerned', or indeed of Menzies. The prime minister was said to have been furious about it but unwilling to enrage the newspaper owners by retracting McEwen's promise.[57]

Labor MP Francis (Frank) Stewart argued the government was 'well aware that it has been tricked by these snide operators', yet none of the infringers would 'have to sell up any of their interests'. Stewart pointed out that the government had been forced to re-write its legislation 'twice in five years … in an attempt to curtail the activities of these people, who, for some reason or other, seem to be regarded as little gods because they happen to control our newspapers'.[58]

HENDERSON'S USEFUL RETIREMENT

The media companies and their expensive lawyers wasted no time in trying to find ways around the new legislation. One method was to invest their employees' pension funds in television shares.[59] MPs also suspected that 'nominee companies registered in Canberra' were being used to hide 'illegal control of dozens of television and radio stations'.[60] Shareholdings and ownership were being masked so effectively that it was difficult to untangle who owned what. But there was suspicion that Henderson's private assets were one way the Fairfax company was evading the ownership limits of the *Broadcasting and Television Act*.

After December 1964, the Fairfax company had been prohibited from obtaining any new shareholdings of more than 5 per cent in companies holding television licences, and even from increasing the shareholdings they had been allowed to keep under the grandfathering provisions. But there was a noticeable crossover between Rupert Henderson's private interests and those of his employer (Table 14.1). Adding to the sense of subterfuge, Henderson's family company, Henderson Holdings, had a paid up capital of only $2004, but had received a loan from the Fairfax company of $300 000.[61] Into the 1970s, questions were being asked in Parliament, and in Packer's *Bulletin* magazine, about whether the Henderson companies were being used by Fairfax to circumvent the ownership rules.[62]

The Fairfax company's ANZ bank manager, HE Hendy, also seemed to be involved in hiding television ownership. By 1968, Hendy owned shares in seven television stations through three different companies.[63] On paper, he was the sole owner of the three companies, which had an issued capital of just $14 between them, yet somehow owned nearly $1 million worth of shares in the five television stations that Fairfax also had an interest in.[64]

Questions were also asked in Parliament about the Elwood company. Previously owned by Fairfax, it was sold for a nominal amount in 1967, and ended up in the hands of Henderson's second wife, Hazel, and daughter, Margaret. Elwood had a capital of only $4 but had managed to buy hundreds of thousands of dollars' worth of shares in television companies. When critics decried the ongoing abuse of television ownership laws, government MPs replied by saying that their hands were tied. The

TABLE 14.1 Rupert Henderson's regional media empire, 1968–69

Region	Henderson family assets		Connection with John Fairfax Ltd*
	Newspapers	Television stations	
Wagga Wagga	*Daily Advertiser*	Riverina Television Ltd (RVN-2) (20 per cent)	Held shares in RVN-2 via 2LF radio station.
Albury		Albury Upper Murray Television (AMV-4) (15 per cent)	(5 per cent)
Wollongong	*Illawarra Mercury* *South Coast Times* (was folded into the *Illawarra Mercury* in May 1968)	The *South Coast Times* held shares in WIN-4.	In 1969, the Fairfax group bought Henderson's controlling interest in Illawarra Newspapers/South Coast Times Pty Ltd
			Television Wollongong Transmissions Ltd (WIN-4) (23 per cent)
Goulburn	*Goulburn Evening Post*		
Berrima	*Berrima District Post*		
Gosford	*Central Coast Express*		
Leeton	*Murrumbidgee Irrigator*	Murrumbidgee Irrigation Areas (MTN-9) (8 per cent)	
Canberra		Canberra Television Ltd (CTC-7) (5 per cent)	(32 per cent)
Brisbane		Queensland Television Ltd (QTQ-9) (0.5 per cent)	(70 per cent)

* Fairfax company shares include shares held by HE Hendy and the percentage of shares owned is a minimum as shares were also likely owned via other names/companies.

NOTE The relevant Henderson company names were: A & F Sullivan Pty Ltd, Henderson Holdings Pty Ltd and Elwood Pty Ltd.

SOURCE ABCB, *21st Annual Report, 1968-69*, Commonwealth of Australia, Canberra, 1969.

legislation could only look at who owned a company, not what loans were provided to it, and Henderson's wife and daughter had provided 11 statutory declarations to say they owned the shares.[65]

MOVING INTO MELBOURNE: FAIRFAX AND DAVID SYME

After Henderson retired in December 1964, 56-year-old Angus McLachlan, who had been news editor, 1937–49, and general manager since 1949, was considered the obvious choice to succeed him as managing director.[66] Where Henderson had been the Fairfaxes' aggressive action man, McLachlan had been Henderson's charming deputy who performed all the legwork that brought Henderson's rapid-fire decisions to life. The two had worked together daily for over 25 years, but McLachlan never addressed him as anything other than 'Mr Henderson'.[67]

Because McLachlan had witnessed Warwick Fairfax's growing ambition and interference, he insisted he would accept the position of managing director only on condition that he take his instructions from the board and not from the chairman. With Henderson looking on from his seat on the board, the stately and courteous McLachlan was responsible for Fairfax's most important deal of the 1960s.

In 1965, all of the major newspaper companies were keeping an unseemly watch on the health of 87-year-old Oswald Syme, the last surviving son of David Syme, in Melbourne. Although David Syme and Co had become a public company in 1948, the Syme trust beneficiaries retained control of an overwhelming majority of its shares. Four of the six board members were trustees of David Syme's estate.[68] The board was traditionally heavy with farmers and retired military officers, rather than directors with journalism, finance, or even corporate, experience.

Greg Taylor, who started at *The Age* in 1949 as a cadet, and later became its editor, said the company was 'being run like a corner grocer's store. None of them [the Syme management] had any business sense at all'.[69] The rights of the trust beneficiaries to collect their dividends seemed to be the board's paramount concern. In 1963, Warwick Fairfax told the

Fairfax board that *The Age* was 'badly run', but somehow it managed to maintain its classified advertising base nonetheless.[70] The Fairfax company understood just how valuable that advantage was.

Several newspaper companies were waiting to pounce because, once Oswald Syme died, *The Age* would be immediately vulnerable to takeover as David Syme's will had decreed that the trustees 'could not sell the paper or divide its assets' until all of his sons had died.[71] Upon Oswald's death, David Syme's estate would be divided equally among his 18 grandchildren. And, like the Shakespeare family, where once there had been a plethora of brothers, there was now a paucity of sons. Sixteen of the 18 grandchildren were women. With the exception of Kathleen Syme, who had taken it upon herself to be actively involved, women had generally been ignored in succession planning, and not socialised into the work of the newspaper. It was widely understood that most of David Syme's grandchildren and their spouses were more interested in cash than running a newspaper, and many had been waiting impatiently to sell their shares as soon as they could.

Oswald Syme's only surviving daughter, Nancy Neill, was one of the few grandchildren known to be concerned about protecting the paper and its future. Nancy's first husband, Hamish Macdonald, had been killed in Malaya during World War II. Their son, Chesborough Ranald Macdonald (known as Ranald), was appointed managing director of David Syme and Co in 1964, when he was only 26 years old. He had studied newspaper management and journalism at Cambridge and Columbia University, and spent three years as a junior reporter on *The Age*.[72]

Macdonald had a keen sense of *The Age*'s traditions as a once radically liberal paper under David Syme. Despite decades of faded glory and stagnation since then, the paper's independence was still the pride of Melbourne's intelligentsia and it was the city's only quality morning paper. But because *The Age* lacked a television station, it was in a vulnerable financial position. Macdonald wanted to organise a defence against takeover from the most likely predators: the HWT, Packer, and Macdonald's distant cousin, Rupert Murdoch (both were related to the Greene family of Toorak/Kew). Given what had happened to the *Argus*, keeping *The Age* from falling into the hands of its rival, the HWT, was a key goal. The HWT had already built up a stake in David Syme and Co of around 10 per cent, which was enough to make the Syme family nervous.

Nancy's second husband, Lieutenant-Colonel Edwin Hill Balfour (EHB) Neill, was Macdonald's stepfather and had succeeded his father-in-law, Oswald Syme, as chairman in October 1964. As a military man, grazier, and a Melbourne Club regular with little business ability, Neill was considered well qualified for *The Age*'s stuffy board. He was almost a caricature of a pompous, upper-class twit. Neill always wore a monocle on a chain, and a carnation in the lapel of his pin-striped suits.[73] His hobbies included polo and grouse hunting.

Former *Age* journalist Geoffrey Barker described Neill as a 'reactionary buffoon'.[74] His hasty-to-the-point-of-abrupt chairman's addresses summed up Neill's hands-off attitude to the position. When Arthur Calwell was introduced to Neill at an event, it was said that Calwell had remarked, 'Ah Colonel Neill of *The Age* is it – how's the circulation?' And Neill had replied, 'Excellent, thank you – I always keep myself very fit.'[75]

Oswald Syme's death would make the company prey, and a bidding war was already going on in the background, pushing up *The Age*'s share price. Ranald Macdonald and his stepfather considered many possible options for financing, but decided the best way to preserve *The Age* was to link up with another newspaper company.

Nearly 20 years earlier, David Syme and Co had been a private company short of cash. In 1947, it had asked the Fairfax company for help so that it could afford to extend and renovate its Collins Street premises. A partnership was proposed, but eventually rejected because the Fairfax company wanted the right to nominate the general manager, a position then held by a Syme.[76] Those earlier discussions with Fairfax made it seem a likely prospect. So did the good relationship between key leaders at both companies, and their shared sense of history as the descendants of newspaper families who had ruled over their respective cities for more than a century. The Fairfax family had become full owners of the *Sydney Morning Herald* in 1856, the same year the Syme family gained control of *The Age*.

Endearing himself to neither family, in 1964, Gough Whitlam, then deputy leader of Labor, told the National Press Club that monopoly control of the Australian press would not be so bad if it were run by those who had worked their way to the top. Instead, he said, control was inherited or nepotic. In the case of the *Sydney Morning Herald*, 'as with the Bourbons, it becomes respectable after three or four generations. And in the case of *The Age*, as with the Hapsburgs, you can marry into control or do it collaterally.'[77]

Fairfax and David Syme and Co also had common synergies between their flagship newspapers, such as their style, character, audiences and advertising. Of all the suitors on offer, Fairfax was the most likely to understand and respect the role of an independent, quality newspaper. In late 1964 or early 1965, Colonel Neill approached Warwick Fairfax and told him the Syme trust beneficiaries were keen to sell, including Neill, who admitted that he was personally short of cash. Long negotiations ensued, during which Angus McLachlan found Neill to be 'not much better than a snobbish phony'. Neill tried to extract a better deal for himself and his wife, and to keep that secret from the other trust beneficiaries. McLachlan concluded, 'it is money Neill is after, not the preservation of *The Age*'s independence and Syme influence'.[78] But those traditions were important to Macdonald.

Trying to unite the members of the divided Syme family in a plan took more than a year of negotiations. A very patient and persistent McLachlan was mainly responsible for the historic agreement. A secret deal was made under which Syme family members would receive cash up front and they would sell John Fairfax Ltd enough shares to make sure that more than 50 per cent remained in Fairfax and Syme hands, that *The Age* remained independent, and the Syme family retained managerial control.

To achieve these goals, a partnership agreement was devised. It included that both Fairfax and Syme appoint two representatives to a group that would meet before each meeting of shareholders. Fairfax agreed not to support any resolution that was not supported by the Syme representatives. In the event of disagreement, both parties would abstain. If that happened, the HWT, with the next largest bloc of votes at shareholders' meetings, would prevail. Because this was an intolerable prospect to both the Fairfax and Syme interests, it forced them to always compromise and vote together. Fairfax also accepted that the board of David Syme and Co would have three Fairfax members and three Syme members for as long as the Syme family held at least 10 per cent of the company. This meant Syme family members would remain equal partners with an 'equal voice' even if their holding shrank to as little as 10 per cent.[79]

Before this deal was concluded in December 1966, there were some last-minute attempts to foil it. The HWT chairman, Jack Williams, made phone calls to *Age* executives that were not returned. A telex sent by Packer via *The Age* reporters' room offering talks for a partnership was also ignored. And Murdoch sent a courier, who waited outside *The Age* office with a bid, but did not see Oswald Syme entering through a back door, so he gave the envelope to a Syme executive who put it in his pocket and did not get it out until the deal was done.

As Ranald Macdonald explained to the author, the other last-minute event that happened before the signing was that chairman Neill 'went and saw Warwick Fairfax in Sydney [and] instead of selling a third, he wanted to sell half'. That meant the same deal had to be extended to all the other members of the family before they signed. 'So we had to change all the forms the night before. [And] of course, they all sold [and] took the money. So we ended up with having a third' of the shares. This meant 'it was [more like a] 70/30' partnership in Fairfax's favour from the beginning, 'instead of 50/50'. That set up the potential for problems immediately, 'but at least it meant that the paper was independent'.[80]

The Syme board met at 5.30 pm on 13 December 1966 to approve the deal, and the partnership was announced that night, but only the bare bones of the arrangement were made public. Many details remained secret for another 15 years. *The Age*, once one of Australia's strongest, independent metropolitan newspapers, was now under the wing of the Fairfax group.

THE 'COMMITTEE OF ONE'

McLachlan's leadership of Fairfax was cut short when he suffered a heart attack in 1969. On doctors' advice, he resigned as managing director, but remained on the Fairfax board until 1980. McLachlan, along with

Henderson and Vincent Fairfax, wanted the company's treasurer, Robert Percy (RP) Falkingham, to be promoted to the role, but Warwick Fairfax took the opportunity to step into the breach. Although he was nearly 68 (the same age at which he had encouraged Henderson to retire), Warwick Fairfax acquired more control over day-to-day management. In addition to his chairman responsibilities, Warwick became an unusually constituted 'committee of one', in which he exercised all of the administrative and management powers of the board. To the frustration of many of his editors and fellow board members, he also began exercising his authority over editorial matters.

In 1965, McLachlan had convinced John Pringle to return as editor to restore some lustre to the *Sydney Morning Herald* and help it hold onto its 'more intelligent readers' who were being lured to the *Australian*.[81] Pringle's second stint as editor lasted from 1965 to 1970, and he had authority over the entire paper at last. He breathed life into it, but lost several battles over modernising it, and eventually incurred Warwick Fairfax's displeasure over some of his editorial decisions, especially over the Vietnam War (Chapter 20). Pringle left without a formal farewell in 1970.[82]

Warwick Fairfax was more strongly asserting his vision of how the company should operate. In his view, the Fairfax papers should all speak in unison, taking their lead from the *Sydney Morning Herald*, and its views should reflect his own. But he was a wealthy, Oxford-educated heir and knight who was over retirement age, and out of touch with the social changes of the 1960s and the growth of independent journalism.

Warwick tried to sideline Henderson, especially between 1969 and 1976. During that period, Henderson relied on James, Vincent, and Vincent's son, John B Fairfax, to try to restrain Warwick's more authoritarian instincts. Complicating future family and corporate relations, in December 1960, Warwick and Mary's son, Warwick Fairfax (Junior), had been born. This added another future heir to the family, with fateful results, although the final chapter of that family succession drama would not play out until the 1980s.

FROM RAGS TO RICHES: HENDERSON'S END

Henderson and Chips managed the family companies in regional television and newspapers in the 1970s, and newspapers in Griffith, Yass and Coleambally were added to the stable.[83] Regional television could be highly profitable when the stations had a monopoly in their area as they usually produced only news and sport, with all other programs purchased from the Sydney and Melbourne television networks at low rates.[84]

Where Keith Murdoch felt he was never adequately rewarded for his empire-building for the HWT, Henderson made sure that he was amply rewarded by Fairfax. One of Warwick Fairfax's relatives would point out to Henderson's granddaughters that, 'Your grandfather made our family very wealthy, but he made himself a lot of money too'.[85] Within the Fairfax family, it was noted with some chagrin that all of the assets Henderson acquired when he was managing director of Fairfax, with money borrowed from the Fairfax company, ended up in the Henderson stable instead of the Fairfax stable.[86] And Henderson made the company pay through the nose to get back assets they had funded him to purchase.

After Henderson's holding company closed the *South Coast Times* in May 1968, and folded it into the *Illawarra Mercury*, it had a newspaper monopoly in Wollongong. In 1969, the Fairfax group bought Henderson's controlling interest in the *Illawarra Mercury*. Although the shares were valued in the Henderson company's own books at $646 000, the Fairfax company paid $2.4 million for them, delivering a windfall for Henderson.[87]

And in 1983, Fairfax's Federal Capital Press purchased the two companies owned by Henderson that published the *Goulburn Post*, the *Highland Post* and the *Yass Post*. Henderson had lost neither his money-making ability nor his negotiating skills. He haggled over the final price. Just when it looked like a deal had been made for a sale price of $863 000, he walked away from negotiations, only to return and secure a final price of just over $1 million.[88]

By 1985, Henderson was sitting on a goldmine because the price of his family's country television shares had nearly doubled, and he had been able to increase his holdings over two decades through bonus issues, without having to put up any new cash. He sold his remaining 51 per cent shareholding in Riverina and North-East Victoria Television (operator of RVN-2 in Wagga Wagga and AMV-4 in north-eastern Victoria) to Koitaki Ltd and Paul Ramsay Communications, for $15 million, after playing the two groups off against each other. He made a profit of $14 million ($43 million in today's money). 'Not a bad return, is it?', the 89-year-old Henderson quipped to a reporter.[89]

Chips was not able to inherit any of these proceeds from the mini-empire that he helped build up. He had died four years earlier, in November 1980, aged only 65, predeceasing his father by five years. In September 1986, Henderson died at a Potts Point hospital, aged 90. His second family received everything that was left in the family companies, including the Wagga Wagga *Daily Advertiser*. In practice, this meant his daughter Margaret, because Henderson's wife, Hazel, died just two months after him. Although Henderson had been an executive for decades, and at one time was simultaneously a director of 15 companies, his death certificate listed his occupation simply as 'journalist'.[90] He had always insisted to business friends that he was a journalist first and foremost. Others felt he was the archetype of an old-fashioned media mogul.

CHAPTER 15

THE QUIET BARON OF FLINDERS STREET

Jack Williams, like Rupert Henderson, was feared and respected within the newspaper industry. He was also astute, hard working and very loyal to his company. Despite these similarities, or perhaps because of them, the two industry titans did not get along. As managing director of the HWT since 1953, Williams had been building it up, and sometimes competing against Henderson for the same assets. In 1966, Lloyd Dumas implored Henderson to try to restore the 'harmony' that used to exist between Fairfax and the HWT.[1] The future of both companies might have been different if their leaders had been able to work harmoniously in the 1960s.

In 1964, Williams became executive chairman of the HWT board and combined the duties of chairman and managing director. He was in complete control of the largest media group in the southern hemisphere. Williams was one of the most powerful men in Australia, but he was also the most private and self-effacing media baron. Journalist and editor Rohan Rivett said Williams had a 'total modesty, an almost obsessive desire to avoid the bright lights, to shun display of wealth, power and influence'.[2]

It was Rivett who dubbed Williams 'the quiet baron' and dared to drag him into the spotlight by writing a profile of him for the *Canberra Times*, but only after Williams had safely retired. Rivett described how their companies had battled 'night and day' for nine years in Adelaide when Rivett was editor-in-chief of the *News* between 1951 and 1960, and competing against the HWT's *Advertiser*. It was a heated battle, and the organisations' 'top brass' in Adelaide detested each other, but Rivett said Williams always found time before board meetings to stop in and see him, and there were: 'No salvos. No jibes. [Just a] real understanding sympathy. A positive, personal encouragement done with exquisite courtesy as of a great matador chatting amicably with a younger trier between bulls.'[3]

Rivett attended around a dozen newspaper proprietor conferences and said Williams stood out among the other press barons because he always kept 'his cool' and 'never "performed"'. But also because, whenever there were negotiations with the AJA over pay and conditions, Williams 'showed a liberal, broad-minded desire for a negotiation and a fair deal [for staff] that was seldom echoed by the Sydney proprietors'.[4]

The other newspaper barons had their stunts, yachts (Packer), Rolls Royces (Warwick Fairfax), art collections (Murdoch and Henderson), lavish properties, and 'glamourous personal companions to self-advertise', but Rivett said Williams just worked hard to quietly build a robust empire for the benefit of his employees and shareholders.[5]

Where Murdoch and Henderson both built up side dynasties for themselves and their families, Williams' acquisitions were all for the HWT. Cecil Edwards said the 'guiding star' of Keith Murdoch's life was always 'service to Murdoch'. He felt Murdoch was as ambitious for himself as he was for the HWT, whereas, with Williams, the HWT 'came first, its people a close second, and John Williams a very bad third'.[6]

Keith Murdoch enjoyed high society, collected fine art and period furniture. He was acquisitive, materialistic and bought prestigious real estate. Williams was humble, hated social vanity, and had little interest in possessions. He used his financial skill to carefully select blue-chip shareholdings. On paper, those shares made Williams a millionaire by the time he died, but people who knew him said that his gold AJA honour badge was his most prized possession.[7] Williams lived for years in what Edwards described as a 'tiny house'.[8] It was a two-storey terrace in Gipps Street, East Melbourne, just a 20-minute walk to the HWT office.

Although a Cold-War Catholic, Williams was more progressive on some issues than many others of his age, including his fellow media moguls. In 1965, Williams called for more Asian immigration to Australia and an end to the White Australia policy. He abhorred capital punishment and was concerned about poverty in developing countries.

Williams' reputation around the HWT office had hardened by the 1960s. He was still considered tough, gruff and introverted. Often uncommunicative, Williams could be harsh and 'autocratic'.[9] Many of the staff were terrified of him, although Joan Newman, who occasionally filled in as Williams' secretary, suspected his bark was worse than his bite.[10] His biographer, historian David Dunstan, says, 'Williams was a complex man … insecure personally, yet controlling, feared by those who worked for him, but compassionate and paternal in many of his dealings.'[11] Journalist Geoffrey Tebbutt said Williams was 'difficult, prickly, demanding and yet tolerant, helpful and understanding'.[12]

Rivett said in his profile that, 'in journalists' pubs around the country … even those who hate him, or say they do, never suggest that Williams did a dishonest or mean thing to another newspaperman [sic], employee or rival'.[13] Williams 'was not a sacking boss' like Frank Packer or Rupert Murdoch.[14] Ian Hamilton, who was state political reporter for the *Herald* in the late 1960s when Williams led the HWT, said, 'if you were one of the family, you were one of the family. They looked after people.' The saying around the office was 'you'd have to throw up on the editor's desk to get the sack'. One day, the theory was put to the test when the features page editor of the *Sun News-Pictorial* was called back from the pub to speak with the editor, Harry Gordon, and vomited on Gordon's desk. Even he did not get the sack.[15]

Williams' own drinking was less obvious than it had been in the 1940s, but he still kept the odd, late hours of the secret alcoholic, haunting the HWT building late at night. His alcoholism never impeded his enormous capacity for work, though. Williams was known for working incredibly long hours, seven days a week, for more than 40 years. His home life bore the brunt of that. In 1931, when he was 29, Williams had married Mabel Gwendoline Dawkins, 34, an accomplished artist. Their only child, John Irven Williams, was born in 1933.

The family atmosphere that Williams encouraged at the HWT was very real for him. He spent 49 years at the company. His older sister, Catherine Williams, spent 30 years there as a clerk, and was nearly 70 when she retired in 1963.[16] As Henderson did with Chips at Fairfax, Williams brought his son into the HWT to train as a journalist. And yet, there seemed to be no sense of dynasty in Williams.

John Dahlsen was the commercial solicitor for the HWT in the 1960s, and later a director of the company and its chairman. He says Williams saw himself as a CEO and did not believe that entitled to him to any further claim on the company: 'Jack, unlike Keith Murdoch, had no proprietorial ambitions nor any desire to build a shareholding, get control of the *Herald* or hand anything on to his son … His son was a journalist and received no [special] benefits.'[17]

Unlike Chips, John Williams did not stay in his father's company nor even in journalism. In 1960, when he was working as the HWT's special correspondent in South Vietnam, John was expelled by the government for criticising the Ngo Dinh Diem regime, which was notorious for its abuse of human rights. This perhaps inspired him to go on to work for the United Nations in Geneva and New York, including in senior roles at UNICEF.

A 'REPUBLIC OF MANAGEMENT'

When Jack Williams said in 1969, 'My first and last love is newspapers', he was not exaggerating.[18] The business was his life. It absorbed him immensely. Aside from his religion, he seemed to have no other interests. Leaving the HWT was so painful a process that it took Williams six years to retire in stages. His first retirement came at the end of 1967, when the 66-year-old Williams announced that he was retiring as managing director. He remained chairman of the board though, until his second retirement at the end of 1969.

By then, the HWT owned eight daily newspapers and published more than 12 magazines and weekly papers. It owned, or had a stake in, six television stations, and 17 radio stations (see Table 16.2).[19] Williams had mixed journalistic skills with drive and financial flair to build a media empire that, as Rivett noted, was 'bigger than anything Keith Murdoch ever dreamed of'.[20]

Williams had also fortified the HWT to protect it from predators, and the threat of takeover, by expanding the company's interlocking shareholding network, which was then considered one of the most developed in the world.[21] The largest shareholders in the HWT were Advertiser Newspapers Ltd and Queensland Press Ltd. In return, the HWT held 31 per cent of Advertiser Newspapers Ltd and 41 per cent of the capital of Queensland Press Ltd. (And as Cecil Edwards noted, 'only a purist would argue that' 30 per cent 'is not a controlling interest'.[22])

Williams had designed the basis of the scheme when he worked under Keith Murdoch. Now, he was using it to protect the company from Keith's son, and other rivals.

The interlocking shareholdings, along with the HWT's scattered shareholding register, had helped secure managerial control under Williams so the company was protected from external threat, but also 'intrusion from shareholder ranks'.[23] Packer's *Sunday Telegraph* said Williams had turned the HWT into a 'republic of management', in which power was vested in the company's managing executives and they maintained that power by keeping the shareholders happy.[24]

When Williams took over as managing director in 1953, shareholders had funds of more than $8 million in the HWT. When he retired as chairman in 1969, those funds exceeded $60 million, and the HWT was valued at $138 million ($1.7 billion in today's money), a 15-fold increase.[25] Williams had turned the HWT into a giant wealth-producing business. Profit in his first year in charge had been $787 000, and in his last year as managing director, was $5.5 million (both in 1967 dollars).[26] The HWT had few liabilities, extremely strong liquid assets and substantial reserves, both declared and 'hidden'.[27]

Williams recognised that journalism was a business, so share prices and dividends were seen as measures of success.[28] But the journalism mattered, too. Williams insisted that journalism always be clear, accurate and readable for the newspapers' 'mum and dad' audience out in the suburbs. When Fred Flowers, the chief of staff, asked Williams if they could order more chairs for the reporters' room because it was short about a dozen, Williams had replied, 'Not on your life! Reporters shouldn't be in the office. They should be out gathering news. No more chairs!'[29]

When Williams became managing editor in 1950, the circulation of the *Sun News-Pictorial* was 426 000 copies a day. When he first retired in 1967, it was 629 000. And the *Herald* had risen during that period from 416 000 to 501 000.[30] Both papers broke sales records in 1963 and 1964.[31]

John Dahlsen said 'Williams' accomplishments' in growing the HWT, were 'just as impressive as [Keith] Murdoch's but his contribution has been buried with the support of the Murdoch family; where Keith Murdoch is portrayed as the sole and only hero'.[32] On one occasion, though, Rupert Murdoch did implicitly acknowledge Williams' role. In 1980, Rupert said his father, Keith, 'built the foundations [of the HWT] rather than the empire itself'.[33]

Williams himself had contributed to the mythologising of his old mentor despite what he knew about Murdoch's conflicts of interest, and the sour ending to their relationship. He did this partly by his modesty and gift for silence, but also more overtly.

On the day after he retired as HWT chairman in 1969, Williams was interviewed in his office by an *Age* journalist who noted that a portrait of Keith Murdoch occupied pride of place on the wall. Williams told the journalist that Murdoch was 'the most able newspaperman this country had ever known', and said, 'We still call him the Boss here, you know'.[34] Murdoch had been dead for 17 years.

WILLIAMS' INFLUENCE

In the 1960s, the HWT owned the largest chain of newspapers that had ever been assembled in Australia, yet nobody spoke of a 'Williams press' in the way they had about a 'Murdoch press'. Williams had a much lower public profile but was also not known for interfering politically and editorially the way Murdoch had (Chapter 8). Dahlsen says Williams did not like staff or 'journalists becoming too friendly with politicians or senior business people. He believed you had to keep your distance ... a different philosophy to Keith'.[35]

Dahlsen says Williams 'was obsessed about giving all parties a fair go and their opportunities a fair case, particularly at election time', and 'never attempted to influence editorial decisions made by the affiliates in [other states]. He may have forewarned [them] of the *Herald* position and the reasons but each affiliate was free to make their own editorial positions. Some affiliates occasionally took different editorial positions.'[36] None, however, took independence as far as editorialising for Labor at federal elections during Williams' reign (see Table 13.1).

Under Williams, neither the light, bright *Sun News-Pictorial*, nor the more politically influential *Herald*, was a crusading paper. His motto was that reader service was more important. Rivett noted that only cruelty to children and animals, destruction of trees, and distaste for extremism seemed to inspire HWT campaigns in the mid-to-late 1960s.[37] The Melbourne papers' focus on small, local issues gave them the appearance of being non-threatening and almost apolitical.

Parks and new fountains would inspire campaigns, but Williams was particularly obsessed with trees. When journalist Ian Hamilton was on the *Herald*'s town hall round, the city council 'couldn't cut a branch off a tree without me knowing about it'.[38] Williams' other major preoccupations were beautifying the Flinders Street railway yards, and doing something about the ugly Gas and Fuel Towers, both of which were visible from his office window.

Outside of such micro-level, local issues, Williams seemed to remain 'aloof from involvement in the world of politics'.[39] But historian David Dunstan argues that perception was misleading; that Williams constantly broke his own edict about not getting too close to politicians, and enjoyed 'ingratiating himself with politicians' when he was in Queensland, and in Victoria.[40]

In Victoria, Williams had been part of Liberal premier Tom Hollway's notorious 'kitchen Cabinet' between 1947 and 1950, when Hollway essentially ran the state from his room at the Windsor Hotel, with Williams part of his small circle of gin-soaked advisers.[41] Williams was also a friend and drinking companion of Henry Bolte, who became a Liberal premier at the Victorian state election of 1955 after the Labor–DLP split destroyed the Cain Labor government. Williams would drink with Bolte most nights, including at the Imperial Hotel, across the road from Parliament House in Spring Street.

Bolte was kept in power by DLP preferences, and he dominated state politics until his retirement in 1972. The HWT papers' unrelenting critical scrutiny of the Labor Party, their unabashed support for Bolte, and allocation of space to the DLP and its causes, aided that outcome. The *Herald* and the *Sun News-Pictorial* strongly supported Bolte's push for population growth and industrial expansion and argued he was doing a good job in bringing large industrial projects to Victoria that were creating wealth and jobs.

Although Williams hated ostentatious displays of power and influence, he accepted a knighthood from the Bolte government in 1958. Five months later, the *Herald*'s editorial for the Victorian election said, 'the State has forged ahead in the past three years', and Bolte's party was the only option for a bright future.[42] At the 1961 state election, the *Herald*'s election-eve entreaty to 'STICK TO THE BOLTE TEAM' was placed on its front page.[43]

In 1972, Rivett said the HWT newspapers had given 'great ... service' to Bolte, his ministry, and his party, over many years.[44] Max Newton seconded that view, and in the 1970s, said of the seemingly apolitical stance of the Melbourne papers that:

> The PR operation by the ruling clique of Collins Street – Bolte and a few of his mates at the Melbourne *Herald* – is the most consummate, skilful job done for a long time. You have to take your hats off to the Melbourne *Herald* for the way they have been able to wash brains white for about a decade and a half. It was done with tremendous skill. It kept people's minds off the important and on the irrelevant and trivial. It served to consolidate the financial and political power of a group of people in this state [Victoria] as in no other way in Australia.[45]

The papers' strong support for Bolte was sometimes reciprocated (see also Chapter 18). Journalist Laurie Oakes was working at the *Sun News-Pictorial* in the 1960s and early 1970s, and recalls 'one of the rare times in journalism where someone tried to instruct me on how to write a story'. The Melbourne *Herald* had incorrectly recorded a federal Cabinet decision. The Cabinet had made no such decision. But 'I was told I should write a story backing up the *Herald* ... and I refused. The next day, I read the paper.' It said Henry Bolte, Premier of Victoria, had confirmed the *Herald*'s story. Oakes says, 'So that's how close they were to Henry.'[46]

One issue caused serious division, though. In 1962, Bolte wanted murderer Robert Tait sentenced to death, but Tait escaped the penalty after he was found insane. In 1965, Bolte told the *Bulletin* that he remained 'good mates' with Jack Williams and staff at the HWT 'even right through ... the Tait hanging business ... when they were all against me'.[47] In 1967, Bolte was even more determined that Ronald Ryan be hanged after a guard was killed during Ryan and Peter Walker's prison escape. Bolte again faced strong opposition from the HWT papers, and also from *The Age*, but he refused to back down.

The friendship between Williams and Bolte was never the same after Ryan's execution, but there was no permanent fracture in the HWT's support for the Bolte government. The 1967 state election was held three months after Ryan was hanged, and the *Herald* said the Bolte government should be returned because of its record of growth and its support for state aid to independent schools.[48] Independent schools essentially meant Catholic schools because they had 'more than 80 per cent of private school enrolments' in the early 1960s.[49]

School funding was a crucial issue for the DLP, the Catholic Church and its supporters. Bishops had been lobbying for funding for Catholic schools for years. Opponents argued state funding should not be provided to private religious schools. Days before the 1963 election, Menzies controversially announced the Coalition would fund science labs and other resources in Catholic and independent schools. Unlike the Melbourne *Herald*, the *Sydney Morning Herald* was railing against state aid to non-government schools, and described the policy as an 'open bid' for the preferences of the DLP.[50] Menzies relied on DLP preferences. So did Bolte: his 'policy was to keep "the DLP alive"'.[51]

Williams' friend Peter Norris was a key campaigner for state aid for Catholic schools. Like Williams, he was a committed Catholic of Irish background. Norris was a senior partner of the HWT's law firm, Corr and Corr Solicitors, which was also the Catholic Church's law firm. Norris had worked at Corrs since the 1940s. In 1951, he acted for John Wren, and tried to stop booksellers from selling Frank Hardy's novel, *Power Without Glory*, which, by implication, was highly critical of Wren but also the Catholic Church.

Age columnist Peter Thomson wrote that Norris 'loved his church and was its confidant and legal adviser'. *The Age*'s editor, Graham Perkin, called Norris the 'eminence grise of St Patrick's Cathedral' because he was such a principal adviser to the church.[52] Once granted, state funding to Catholic schools was expanded significantly in the 1960s and 1970s. Norris helped successfully fight off legal challenges to state aid that went all the way to the High Court.

Rather than being removed from politics, Williams' connections suggest the possibility that he was a quiet but influential powerbroker in Victorian state politics, and also in Catholic politics, at a time when Catholic politics mattered a great deal. But whatever influence he wielded, it was exercised personally and unobtrusively. Unlike Murdoch, Williams did not use the company's journalists as political envoys and weapons. And he did not publicly summon prime ministers to the building, nor try to claim credit for putting them in office.

Williams avoided any hint of dominance. In keeping with that, the HWT's Melbourne papers did not indulge in loud, crusading campaigns on big issues. And yet, they were the most dominant and influential newspapers in the state, and their quiet, steady conservatism helped encourage an unusually conservative political outlook that made Victoria the odd state out nationally.[53]

From the time of the Labor split in 1955, Victoria was the centre of the DLP's support and power. At first with the help of DLP preferences, the state became a Liberal Party bastion. Bolte's election in 1955 ushered in 27 years of Liberal governments in Victoria. At federal elections in the 1960s, DLP preferences also had an impact (Chapter 13).[54] And even after the DLP's support began to wane, Victoria remained unusually conservative. For example, Labor's failure to gain a similar swing in Victoria as it did in other states during the 1969 election cost the party victory and saved the Coalition government.[55]

THE HWT TURNS SOUTH

In the 1950s, the acquisition of Queensland Press was Williams' corporate triumph. In the 1960s, he led two additional coups that cemented his reputation as the biggest media builder in Australia. The first was in the south.

TEXTBOX 15.1 Colour on the page

Newspaper companies knew that colour television would be coming to Australia one day. It was already widespread in the United States by the mid-1960s, and in the United Kingdom by the late 1960s. An article in the *Canberra Times* in 1968 was optimistically headlined, '"NEWSPAPERS IN COLOUR" ANSWER TO COLOUR TV'.[56] But this was no easy answer.

It was still technically difficult to achieve good results with colour on the newspapers' letterpress printing presses. In April 1962, Sydney's *Daily Mirror* offered 'spot' or 'pick-out' colour – just one colour – for advertisers willing to pay extra to make their advertisements stand out. Its competitor, the *Sun*, followed a week later.[57] The daily newspapers could offer colour only on a very limited and irregular basis, and advertisers complained the quality was not as good as for magazines.

Because the competition from television was hurting magazines too, the popular magazines were publishing more colour pages. And they were able to achieve much better results than newspapers could because magazines had longer production times, smaller print runs and used offset printing presses.

The HWT came up with a way to introduce magazine-quality colour into its newspapers. In early 1956, it had installed a very advanced Rembrandt four-colour press at its commercial printery, called Herald Gravure (later Giganticolor), which was located in the Melbourne suburb of Hawthorn. The German-made press was the first of its kind in Australia, and one of only six in the world. It could print in colour on both sides of the sheet in one operation.[58] And its capacity was boosted by equipment from the *Argus*, whose own experiment with colour had been ground breaking but premature.

The HWT started to pre-print colour pages off-site at Herald Gravure and then transport the pages to its Flinders Street headquarters, where they were manually inserted into the newspaper. Using this method, the *Herald* became the first daily newspaper to include a four-colour gravure advertisement in September 1962.[59]

The company was able to use the same process for big news events. It pre-printed colour front and back covers in Hawthorn for special editions, including the Melbourne Cup and the VFL Grand Final. The covers were

> rushed back to Flinders Street where the black-and-white edition of the paper was placed inside. It took the *Herald* more than 40 hours to produce a wrap-around for the 1967 VFL Grand Final, so the method was used sparingly, but the quality was considered excellent and colour covers were seen as sure-fire sales boosters.[60]
>
> Herald Gravure's facilities were so advanced, and its colour advertisements proved so popular with major advertisers (especially car manufacturers and tobacco companies), that interstate newspapers began paying for Herald Gravure to pre-print colour advertisements for them and deliver the pages interstate.
>
> In 1967–68, Herald Gravure printed more than 52 million colour pre-prints for daily newspapers across Australia. It took on printing jobs only for interstate papers, not for competitors like *The Age* (which had to invest in its own colour printing facilities).
>
> Into the 1970s, Herald Gravure was still producing 90 per cent of total gravure colour in Australian newspapers and making an excellent profit for the HWT.[61] And colour television did not arrive in Australia until 1975. Newspapers had helped dampen desire before then by reporting that colour televisions were unreliable, 'too dear' and sometimes exploded.[62]

Williams had built closer contact with the Davies family, owners of Hobart's only daily newspaper, the *Mercury*, in 1957, when he sold them a near-new printing press, stereotyping plant and composing equipment, all prized assets stripped from the defunct *Argus*. The printing press was so big that the *Mercury*'s building had to be altered so it could fit. Although Davies Brothers Ltd also owned an interest in Hobart radio station 7HO, and in the city's only commercial television station, TVT-6, the company's profits were stagnant. In 1961, its revenue declined 16 per cent.[63] The following year, some Davies family members decided to sell their holdings.

In August 1962, the HWT purchased a 14.8 per cent shareholding in Davies Brothers. George Francis Davies (known as 'Bill' or 'GF') was the 51-year-old chairman of directors. A great-grandson of the paper's founder, he was the fourth generation of his family to run the newspaper. A strong advocate of private enterprise, which matched the HWT's world view,

Davies stayed on as managing director even as the HWT extended its grip on the company.

In 1963, the HWT increased its shareholding to 23 per cent. In 1964, it increased it again, to 49 per cent, and took full control.[64] Less than ten years after the Davies family had made Davies Brothers Ltd a public company, control had slipped from their hands. GF Davies remained managing director until December 1971, and chairman until 1985, but he was the last Davies on the board.

A NON-SUCCESSION PLAN

When Williams retired from the managing director role in 1967, he said he hoped to still make a contribution, but 'I have been long enough in this calling to know the dangers of trying to conduct the day-to-day editing or management from the sidelines.'[65] Williams had been the victim of Keith Murdoch's pseudo-'retirement' in the early 1950s, when Murdoch had continued 'to attend almost full-time in an office' nearby, and kept interfering and giving his successor unwanted advice.[66] Cecil Edwards noted this must be 'an occupational disease', though, because Williams did precisely the same thing, despite his vow not to.[67] Like Murdoch, Williams also stayed on as chairman and failed to anoint a clear successor.

No managing director was appointed to succeed Williams. Instead, four executives were supposed to jointly manage. Frank Daly was editor-in-chief, and remained in that post. Keith Macpherson, the assistant general manager, was promoted to general manager. Lyle Turnbull became deputy editor-in-chief, and Richard Sampson was the finance director.

Williams set up this new management structure to centre principally around Daly and Macpherson. Daly had worked under Williams at Queensland Newspapers in Brisbane between 1937 and 1945, when Daly was editor of the *Sunday Mail*. He had followed Williams to Melbourne and was editor of the *Sun News-Pictorial* from 1953 to 1965, editor of the *Herald* in 1966, and editor-in-chief from 1966.[68]

Keith Macpherson was the son of Duncan Macpherson, the first general manager of the *Sun News-Pictorial*. Three years after the death of his father, 18-year-old Macpherson had joined the HWT as a junior. A former Scotch College student, Macpherson began in the mailroom and moved up to the stationery store. One of his early jobs was cleaning the pens in Keith Murdoch's office. After studying to become an accountant, Macpherson joined the *Herald*'s accounts division, and in 1959 became the company secretary. Five years later, he was assistant general manager, before being promoted to general manager.[69]

John Dahlsen believes Williams may have set up this strange succession plan because he did not know who was going to be the better successor, 'so he put them both there to find out'. But he also suspects that, 'clearly, Williams created that situation of two people [to] divide and conquer [so] that he could maintain his influence. Because one of his problems was, like a lot of newspaper people, they can't let go.'[70] Still chairman, Williams absolutely dominated the board after he stepped down as managing director. The leadership group was being closely watched and expected to run the business under Williams' guidance.

TO THE WEST: WILLIAMS' LAST BIG DEAL

Newspaper managers in Sydney and Melbourne were all looking towards Western Australia in the late 1960s because the state had experienced rapid growth after mining export laws were changed. In 1938, when Australia's known reserves of iron ore were small, the export of ore had been prohibited. But, after years of lobbying by mining companies, including Western Mining Corporation and Rio Tinto, the Menzies government agreed to partially lift restrictions on the international sale of iron ore in November 1960.

Lang Hancock, an amateur geologist and the owner of two stations in the Pilbara region of Western Australia, had discovered enormous deposits of ore in the Turner River area in 1952. After the law change, Hancock and his partner, Peter Wright, signed an agreement with Conzinc Rio Tinto, the company formed by a 1962 merger between British Rio Tinto and Australia's Consolidated Zinc (whose key founders included WL Baillieu and WS Robinson). When the Menzies and Holt governments removed the remaining restrictions on exporting iron ore in 1965 and 1966, Western Australia was on its way to becoming the largest iron ore supplier in the world.

This mining-led boom had rapidly increased the state's population, industry and economy. The *West Australian*, as the only morning daily newspaper in the isolated capital city of Perth, was doing extremely well as a result. Between 1958 and 1968, the newspaper's circulation had increased by 33 per cent, double the growth achieved by any other morning paper in Australia.[71] The *West Australian*'s sales were the highest per capita of any daily newspaper in Australia. Its parent company, West Australian Newspapers (WAN), also published Perth's only afternoon paper, the *Daily News*, and it had gained three times the circulation increase of other afternoon metropolitan newspapers.[72]

WAN had become an extremely attractive takeover target. It had a stranglehold on Perth's daily press, so its papers carried a 'huge share of press advertising'. And they were read by 80 per cent of people in the state, so they were highly influential in a state crucial to Australia's economic future.[73] Aside from the newspapers, WAN had a controlling interest of 44 per cent in TVW-7, the top-rating television station in Perth. It also owned four radio stations in Western Australia, plus a transport company (Bays) and South West Printing and Publishing, which published country newspapers and performed job printing.

In four years, WAN's profits had doubled, and it had been investing its growing profits wisely. Its external investments were worth $8.4 million and included shares in ANM and in other media companies.[74] In 1969, WAN was expected to make $2 million profit.[75] It was so well off, it even had its own ship, the *Hiawatha*, which was used to entertain advertisers and dignitaries.

The giants were closing in on WAN, and the HWT was the obvious frontrunner. Since the 1920s, the HWT had had close links with WAN, including common shareholders from within the Baillieu family and other Collins House mining company interests (Chapter 1). Suspicions had continued that WAN was not as independent of Melbourne or the HWT as it claimed to be. In 1955, HV Evatt claimed the HWT controlled 'one or two [newspapers] in Perth'. The HWT responded that it 'does not own any interest in any paper in Western Australia'.[76] But several of the HWT's key shareholders still did. A WAN shareholder list from 1954 reveals that its major shareholders still included Baillieu family members and their investment companies, as well as Collins House companies.[77]

The HWT *did* own shares in WAN by 1969. It held about 2 per cent of WAN's capital.[78] And WAN had entwined itself into the HWT's interlocking shareholding structure: it held shares in the HWT, Advertiser Newspapers Ltd and Queensland Press.[79] As Williams put it, the HWT had 'always got on' well with the *West Australian*.[80] But the HWT would need to beat off fierce competition because other media companies were also involved in Western Australia and hoping to take advantage of the state's mining boom.

Rupert Murdoch owned the *Sunday Times* in Perth, and more than 20 country newspapers throughout Western Australia. Via subsidiary companies, he also owned all of the shares in radio stations 6KY Perth and 6NA Narrogin.[81]

Packer and his Melbourne friend Ian Potter were also very interested in Western Australia. Potter was playing a key role in putting together consortiums to develop the state's big mining projects. They kicked off the takeover race on 30 June 1969. A syndicate involving Packer, Potter and the lord mayor of Perth, Tom Wardle (who owned the 'Tom the Cheap' grocery chain), announced they would pay $12.6 million in cash for a 25 per cent shareholding in WAN. Potter's firm, Tricontinental Corporation, was the vehicle for this bid. Implausibly, Packer claimed from Sydney that their motivation was to keep WAN in local hands.[82]

At midnight that night, Rupert Murdoch told shareholders not to accept the Tricontinental offer. He proposed a merger of certain of his News Limited assets with WAN, and also promised that local control would remain in place. On this, and other details, his proposal was vague, though, and not much pursued. Murdoch was more focused on the United Kingdom at this time, and needed cash to expand there (Chapter 16). The HWT did not have that problem. It had a great deal of cash on hand. Williams responded by offering a very generous share swap of two HWT 50-cent shares for every single WAN 50-cent share. This added up to around $70 million in 1969, making it the most expensive takeover offer in Australian history, and especially because WAN had been valued at only $37 million.[83]

Murdoch could not compete. Packer was out, too, and Williams was said to be 'very annoyed' with him for trying to move in on WAN, as the two were normally friends.[84] Williams wanted to make sure that WAN's TVW-7 did not join Packer's Nine network (at this time, TVW-7 bought programs from both the HWT-dominated Seven network and Packer's Nine network). But the fight over Western Australian media was also about broader issues.

Communist paper, the *Tribune*, put it bluntly when it claimed the battle for WAN was a battle for control over the state's media that was being waged by mineral development companies associated with Tricontinental versus HWT shareholders, all of whom were 'big investors in Western Australia minerals'.[85] The oil refining group, Boral Ltd, held 35 per cent of Tricontinental's shares.[86] Boral had just signed an agreement with an American mining company for mineral exploration in Western Australia. Potter was 'intimately involved' in Boral's expansion in the 1950s and 1960s.[87] He had joined the board of Boral three months before he and Packer announced their bid. Tricontinental also held large shareholdings in BHP, which had been mining iron ore in Western Australia since 1951.

The HWT shareholders spanned both 'old' and 'new' parts of Collins House. There had been a split in the group dating from the late 1940s. The 'old' Collins House was still Melbourne based, but was no longer vigorous or expanding. Declining Broken Hill ore reserves meant its most dynamic part was now the Western Mining Corporation, which was reviving the West Australian goldfields after discovering nickel at Kambalda in 1965. It was one of several groups keen to explore the Pilbara area.[88]

But the frontrunner of the iron ore boom was Hamersley Holdings, which represented the breakaway part of Collins House. When WS Robinson was leading the Zinc Corporation in the 1940s, it had increased its London contacts, symbolically moved its office out of Collins House in 1949, and finally merged with Rio Tinto in 1962. Aged 74, Robinson had resigned from official positions at Consolidated Zinc in 1951, but was still keenly watching over Conzinc Rio Tinto until his death in 1963. Robinson had been on the WAN board from 1927 to 1937, and other directors on that board, as well as key editorial staff at the WAN newspapers, were still linked with him into the 1950s.[89]

Conzinc Rio Tinto owned 60 per cent of Hamersley Holdings, which became the largest iron ore mining company in Australia after it developed a huge open-cut mining operation in the Hamersley Range in the Pilbara region in the mid-1960s. Hamersley Holdings signed the agreements with Hancock and Wright in 1963, which enriched their divided families for generations to come.[90] Once allowed to export iron ore to Japan and other countries, Hamersley Holdings' profits and prospects soared.

The newly rich Hancock and Wright were also 'sniffing round' WAN.[91] They felt the *West Australian* and the Liberal–Country state government were not conservative enough, and were especially unhappy with the *West Australian*'s coverage of their Pilbara iron ore discoveries.[92] They continued a long tradition of Australian mining magnates who saw newspaper ownership as a way to try to influence public affairs. Two months before Packer and Potter started the takeover battle for WAN, Hancock and Wright began publishing the *Independent*, in April 1969. It was a Perth weekly newspaper (renamed the *Sunday Independent* in 1971) that was edited by the ever mobile Max Newton (who, in 1969, said he had started 'three or four new newspapers' during the past six years).[93]

The *Independent* was the first new paper in Western Australia for 60 years.[94] Local journalists dubbed it 'Hancock's *Herald*' because it was so obviously launched to help further its owners' mining interests, and so blatantly reflected their strong views, including their hatred of socialism and bureaucracy. (They converted the *Independent* into a daily in 1973, but the re-named *Independent Sun* lasted just four weeks as a daily paper.)

Like Packer and Murdoch, Hancock and Wright could not top the HWT's huge offer for WAN. Two other interested parties also dropped out. British newspaper owners, Lord Rothermere (son of Harold Harmsworth) and Lord Thomson (who said he had 'always had my eye on' WAN), were deterred by the preference for local control, and also by the WAN board's ability to block transfers.[95]

The HWT's $70 million offer was conditional on it obtaining 90 per cent of WAN's shareholdings. WAN's board tried to get the HWT to vary the proposal so that majority control could remain with the present shareholders, but the HWT would not budge. Williams hot-footed it to Perth on 5–6 July and talked the board into accepting the huge offer and surrendering local control.[96]

Once WAN was in the stable, the HWT's profits jumped by $3.6 million to $9.3 million in 1970.[97] The HWT now controlled more than 50 per cent of the circulation of Australia's daily newspapers.[98] When Williams died in 1982, he held shares in Hamersley Holdings Ltd and BHP.[99] When he had obtained those shares is not known.

THE FROZEN GIANT

After the WAN deal, the HWT looked almost invincible. It had an exceptionally strong financial position, and owned print and electronic media across Melbourne, Brisbane, Adelaide, Perth and Hobart (see Table 16.2). As a newspaper company, it owned far more broadcasting stations than would have been allowed in many other countries, including 'the USA, UK, Sweden, France, Italy, [and] West Germany'.[100] But because the HWT had the most assets, the amendments the Menzies government had made to the *Broadcasting and Television Act* in 1965 were affecting it the most (Chapter 14).

When the changes were made, Menzies was coming to the end of his long reign as prime minister and was more willing to take on the big media groups. Williams complained the HWT was not even consulted.[101] Dahlsen believes the law change was a reaction to how Williams was using the HWT's 'huge cash flow to acquire minority and blocking interests' in other companies and 'only some of these deals were known to the public … Had Jack not been restrained he would have achieved a monopoly.'[102] Dahlsen suspects Menzies felt he had to stop the growth and reach of the group, not because the HWT was unsupportive of his government, but because Menzies the lawyer could see power accumulating and felt he had to stop it. Dahlsen says today that 'Menzies was acting in the public interest in curbing the growth of [the HWT] … [It] was an oligopoly with massive media influence.'[103]

The practical effect of the law change was to freeze many of the investment shareholdings the newspaper companies had as of 17 December 1964. The HWT could not legally acquire additional interests in television, and could not invest as much as it would like in other companies, including the companies it was using to fortify itself against takeover. In a rare public intervention in 1968, Williams publicly called it 'a very bad law'.[104] He said it was also difficult to conform to because of the concept of 'indirect ownership'. He gave an example. If the HWT bought shares in BHP, and BHP then bought shares in Advertiser Newspapers Ltd, that would make the HWT in breach of the law because it now indirectly owned more shares in television. Williams said, 'An outside company in which we had no say whatever could make us lawbreakers – without our even being aware of it.'[105]

The HWT felt so aggrieved it challenged the constitutional validity of the legislation in the High Court in October 1966, but lost. The HWT lobbied the Menzies government (and successive governments) to wind back the changes, but Williams said he received 'a ton of sympathy and very patient listening and that's all'.[106]

HWT executives felt the company was now in a 'legal straitjacket'.[107] It could not buy 'a single share' in any of the companies involved in Williams' interlocking shareholdings, and the internal assessment was that this 'could be crippling. If some other interest – say, an overseas group – made a total takeover bid for the shares of any of these companies we would not be able to make a matching offer.'[108]

The HWT was a giant but it was a frozen giant with a fear of takeover. In the coming years, these factors would lead the company to adopt a defensive, conservative approach that would make it more vulnerable, not less.

Because the HWT had to be careful to avoid investing in other companies with Australian broadcasting licences, it expanded its investments overseas, but only on a small scale. In Papua New Guinea, where it had publishing links since World War II, the HWT acquired the country's two main newspapers – the *South Pacific Post* and the *New Guinea Times Courier* – and merged them into one publication in 1969, called the *Post-Courier*.

Domestically, the HWT tested the government's resolve to enforce the law when it purchased WAN. Because WAN had a 44 per cent stake in

TVW-7, the purchase put the HWT in contravention of the *Broadcasting and Television Act*, which prohibited it from obtaining an interest of more than 5 per cent. The postmaster-general instructed the HWT to dispose of the additional television shares. The HWT tried to get around the restrictions by selling shares to its WAN employees' pension fund, but in March 1970 the Gorton government introduced an amendment to prohibit that. It made the prohibition retrospective to stop those transactions, which the HWT correctly described as 'directed at us', but also as 'dictatorial' and 'unjust'.[109]

The HWT had to sell all but 25 000 of WAN's 600 000 shares in TVW-7, and also sell WAN's four radio stations.[110] Still jockeying for the best possible outcome, the HWT sold the radio stations to TVW-7, then put TVW-7 shares into 'friendly hands'.[111] The shares were sold to around 20 different companies and individuals, which included HWT-friendly companies such as Tasmanian Television Ltd and Silverton Securities Pty Ltd. WAN was no longer in control of TVW-7, but it continued to buy programs from the HWT-dominated Seven network, and later formally affiliated with it.[112]

To prevent the scenario Williams had outlined, where external companies might put the HWT in jeopardy, the HWT changed its articles of association in 1968 to give its directors special powers to refuse share registrations. These were 'radical powers ... very rare, if not unique' that could be used to force shareholders to sell shares if their holdings put the HWT in breach of the *Broadcasting and Television Act*.[113] Because those powers also helped protect the HWT from takeover, the *Financial Review* argued they helped 'make the [HWT] fortress impregnable'.[114]

But there was another problem, and it was coming from inside the fortress. The HWT's Melbourne rival, David Syme and Co, identified it in a top-secret report compiled in 1967. Shown only to a handful of executives and kept 'under lock and key', the report concluded that, although the HWT was a formidable competitor with many advantages, it was 'demonstrably weak' at senior management level. In a clear reference to Williams and his inadequate succession plan, the David Syme and Co report said that 'key [HWT] personnel are nearing retirement age and/or are suffering from ill health. Replacements for these personnel are difficult to identify.'[115]

In addition, the HWT had only one outside director, so it was prone to 'introspective' policies.[116] Even this 'outside' director was not very external. Brian Donaldson was a senior partner from the HWT's solicitor, Corr and Corr. When he died in 1972, two directors were appointed to the HWT board, and both were internal, deepening the drift toward introspection.[117]

There was a growing sense of stagnation. Adrian Deamer, who moved from the *Sun News-Pictorial* in Melbourne under Williams to the *Australian* under Rupert Murdoch in 1966, said that, for all his faults, Murdoch had an attitude of 'enthusiasm and buoyancy and life', whereas the HWT was 'becoming so complacent and uninteresting … it was just sort of churning over … [during a] period where utter complacency had set in'.[118]

David Syme and Co was not the only competitor who knew about Williams' 'ill-health'. In 1968, Vic Carroll of Fairfax attended the HWT's annual meeting. Afterwards, he wrote a confidential memo for Fairfax executives. Carroll said Williams seemed 'very nervous', could barely read his speech, and kept making mistakes. He was using 'words that were not there', then spending 'agonising moments' stumbling and trying to get back on track. He read so slowly and haltingly that everyone was relieved when he was finished, but a staff member then had to take the chairman aside to tell him he had forgotten to read the notice of the meeting and the proxies. Williams was unable to answer some questions and he was 'confused' and made errors during voting procedures. There was something wrong with his eyesight as well as his concentration.[119]

AT THE END

Williams remained chairman for another year after that meeting. That year, 1969, the *Herald* celebrated 100 years as an afternoon paper, but the media world had changed so much that television was now more profitable than the company's flagship newspaper.[120] Although responsible for the WAN takeover, years of heavy drinking and long working hours continued to take their toll on Williams' health. There were whispers among the HWT journalists that, 'Sir John Williams [was] mad', that he was 'in his dotage ... [and] putting on his toy hat and chasing fire brigades'. There were 'all these funny stories of [his] eccentricities'.[121]

Aged 68, Williams retired as chairman of the HWT board on the last day of 1969. He announced that Philip Jones would be the new chairman. The insipid succession plan Williams had put in place two years earlier had not produced a strong successor. Jones had emerged as a third contender because Williams was unhappy with Macpherson.

Jones was another accountant. From his schooldays, Jones had 'lived in a world of figures', moving from studying bookkeeping to accountancy, and then three years of law.[122] He had worked as a Treasury official in the 1940s, and joined the HWT as company secretary in 1951. Jones was the general manager between 1953 and 1963, joined the HWT board in 1957, and had been its vice-chairman since 1966.

Macpherson was sidelined and sent to Perth to become the managing director of WAN in August 1970.[123] Jones was a more malleable figure. Dahlsen describes him as 'a very weak individual. I was very unimpressed with him ... [Jones] came out of bureaucracy, he was a bureaucrat. [A] very limited individual. How he got to where he was in the *Herald* I'll never know.'[124]

Jones' malleability may have been his chief point of appeal for Williams who, even at this stage of his life and poor health, could not let go. After he retired as chairman, Williams stayed as a director on the HWT board. Dahlsen was working at Corr and Corr, which had such a close relationship with the HWT at this time that it was located in the *Argus* building owned by the HWT. Williams had an office in that building, too, and Dahlsen remembers how 'as soon as the [news]papers were published, first thing you had to do was race them up to his office. And he'd go through them with a fine tooth comb ... I've no doubt there were numerous telephone conversations that followed. Everyone knew that he was in the background vetting every blooming publication that came out. So his influence remained beyond his executive days.'[125]

Williams' third, and final, retirement as a director of the HWT came in 1973.[126] His wife, Mabel, died in October 1980. Around that time, Williams had a stroke. He also had diabetes. After he went blind, a friend used to visit Williams at his nursing home in East Melbourne to read him the newspapers. Williams died there in March 1982. The executor of his will was Peter Norris, his friend of more than 30 years. Corr and Corr (renamed Corrs Chambers Westgarth) remained the law firm used by the Catholic Church until 2022.[127]

Williams' will had been prepared by another senior partner of Corr and Corr, Alan Corr, a descendant of the law firm's founders. When it had been taken to Williams to sign in 1980, the once highly-skilled journalist could mark it only with a shaky 'X'.[128] As with Rupert Henderson, Williams' death certificate listed his occupation simply as 'journalist'.[129]

CHAPTER 16
THE NEW WORLD

In the first half of the 1960s, Menzies had established a dominance over the federal parliamentary press gallery similar to the one he held over his party. After more than a decade in office, his government tended to be reported as if it was immovable and part of the natural order. Encouraging a sense of lethargy, the top jobs in the press gallery were all held by men who had been in Canberra 'fifteen years or longer', some since the war years.[1] Nearly all of them worked for conservative newspapers, which were generally supportive of Menzies and rarely undertook any critical or investigative reporting.

The HWT's Melbourne papers were focused on the removal of trees and encouraging Victorians' infatuation with football. *The Age*'s chief political correspondent, John Bennetts, had a reputation for never having broken a story (Chapter 18). The *Daily Telegraph*, which had once been an active campaigner against red tape, government intrusion and inefficiency, had settled into years of predictable, uncritical promotion of Menzies. As Packer later admitted, the *Daily Telegraph* 'consistently supported [Menzies] from 1949, when he resumed power, until he retired in 1966'.[2]

The world was changing, though, and Menzies' retirement marked the end of an era. He retired in January 1966, aged 71, after a record 16-year term as prime minister. Labor was thoroughly in the electoral wilderness. The party had lost six federal elections since Menzies came to office, and there was only one state Labor government left (in Tasmania).[3]

Harold Holt replaced Menzies. The amiable Holt was 'hard-working and hard-playing'.[4] He had long political experience, having served in parliament since 1935, been Menzies' deputy for a decade, and treasurer for seven years.[5] Newspaper owners had wanted Holt sacked in 1961 for his 'credit squeeze' policies, but he had been working hard to win back their trust, including by being very accessible to the press.[6]

Just weeks after Menzies' retirement, another major change occurred as decimal currency was introduced to Australia. In Sydney, the cover price of the papers moved from sixpence to five cents. Melbourne's consistently cheaper papers converted from four pence to four cents, but that was still an increase in real terms, so circulation dropped. The *Sun News-Pictorial* recovered but the once indomitable *Herald* was showing signs of a more permanent shift away from afternoon papers.[7] And Australians were changing more than their newspaper buying habits as the 1960s, especially the latter years of the decade, were a time of immense social, cultural and political change, that challenged the newspapers to wake up.

A LANDSLIDE: THE 1966 ELECTION

During the 1960s, Australia was increasingly drawn into international conflicts driven by American anti-communism efforts. The Menzies government made the US alliance a high priority, including offering Australian combat troops for Vietnam 'before the US had even asked for them'.[8] The government introduced conscription in 1964, and formally committed a battalion to Vietnam in April 1965.

As Rodney Tiffen noted of this period, the 'majority of the Australian press' showed 'whole-hearted support for the government'.[9] Murdoch's *Australian* was the exception. With the blessing of Douglas Brass, the anti-war editorial director of News Limited, the *Australian* was 'the sole voice among morning papers' to editorialise against the government's commitment of troops.[10]

By contrast, the anti-communist Melbourne *Herald* consistently supported the war. So did the *Sydney Morning Herald*, which was unfailingly hostile in its coverage of anyone who raised doubts about Australia's involvement.[11] As Bridget Griffen-Foley noted, at the *Daily Telegraph*, 'there was no questioning whatsoever of Australia's commitment to Vietnam'.[12] The *Courier-Mail* told its readers the American alliance was crucial for Australia's national security.[13] The *Mercury* argued that, if Australia deserted its 'ally in the middle of the fight', it would be 'a "scab" nation'.[14] Non-participation would be a 'slap in the face' to the United States, said the *Canberra Times*.[15]

An appreciative US president, Lyndon B Johnson, visited Australia a month before the 1966 election. He attracted large and enthusiastic crowds, but dissent over the Vietnam War was growing. Newspapers were openly excited about the president's visit and tended to represent any protests against Johnson or the war as isolated incidents that were, the *Courier-Mail* said, 'unrepresentative of Australian feeling'.[16] The *Canberra Times*' description of anti-Vietnam protesters as 'organised ratbags' was fairly typical.[17] Tiffen argued that mainstream newspapers' coverage 'of anti-war dissent in Australia was consistently negative, with rarely any suggestion that it deserved serious consideration'.[18]

In Melbourne, two protesters threw bags of paint at Johnson's limousine as it drove through the streets. Terry Phelan, a press photographer for the *Sun News-Pictorial*, took a Walkley award-winning photograph that showed Johnson's bodyguard spattered with paint. The photograph was published prominently in some overseas newspapers, but Phelan's own newspaper – in his words – 'buried' it by publishing it as a small photograph on an inside page deep in the paper. Phelan believes that HWT management: 'didn't want to upset LBJ while he was here' and it was 'pretty weak of [them] … If they'd run it big on page one … they would've sold lots more copies of the paper … which is what you're supposed to be there for'.[19]

When a late November election was announced, Holt was still benefitting from LBJ's visit, but also from a perception that he was a fresh leader. His opponent, Labor's Arthur Calwell, was 70, as cantankerous as ever, and widely viewed as having stayed in the job too long. Labor's election campaign in October and November 'fell apart under the strains of Vietnam and tensions over the leadership' between Calwell and Whitlam, who was 20 years Calwell's junior and eager to succeed him.[20]

No daily metropolitan paper advocated a vote for Labor in 1966. Because the *Australian* had opposed the war in Vietnam, its readers and staff might have expected it to oppose the government's re-election, but Murdoch's political views and alliances were changing. He wanted the paper to back Holt.[21] After a three-week internal tussle, the *Australian*'s election-day editorial was headed, 'NO ALTERNATIVE TO THE HOLT GOVERNMENT'. Any lingering fondness for Calwell from 1961 was gone. The *Australian* said Labor's leadership was 'weak and old-fashioned'.[22] Consistent with the other daily papers, the *Australian* told readers that the Vietnam War 'helps stop the downward thrust of communism in Asia and helps guarantee our protection by the United States'.[23]

There was still widespread public support for Australia's involvement in Vietnam in 1966, and the Holt government won the election in a landslide. The number of Liberal Party members elected (61) set a postwar record, and the Coalition's two-party preferred vote, at 56.9 per cent, still stands as a record high.[24]

TABLOID WARFARE: *SUN* VERSUS *MIRROR*

When Henderson sold the *Daily Mirror* to Rupert Murdoch in 1960, he expected the young upstart to fail and to flee Sydney quickly, dragging a trail of debt behind him. But Murdoch put both money and determination into the *Daily Mirror*. Before the *Australian* was created, it was his personal flagship, his chance to prove that he could make it in one of the most competitive newspaper cities in the world.

Fairfax editor, John Douglas Pringle, described Sydney as a 'rough, boisterous, greedy city' where '"push" is a quality much admired'.[25] It suited Murdoch perfectly. He rolled up his shirtsleeves and revelled in the competition. Within two years, the *Daily Mirror*'s circulation had nearly caught up to Fairfax's *Sun*, which was still the 'dizzy sister' of the sober *Sydney Morning Herald*.[26]

Murdoch gave Zell Rabin, editor of the *Daily Mirror* from 1963 until his death in 1966 aged 34, an unusually free editorial hand. The paper was plumped up with more editorial matter, more stories about sex, crime, celebrity, sport and scandal. It was also heavily promoted and advertised. By early 1966, the *Mirror* was outselling the *Sun*.[27] The *Daily Mirror* maintained its frontrunner position for more than a decade, although often by only a slim margin, sometimes only 3000 to 8000 sales.[28] Afternoon papers were in trouble around the world, and with no prospect of great growth, the papers were locked in a grim battle to hold onto as many existing readers as possible.

Murdoch had originally thought about taking the *Daily Mirror*, especially the *Sunday Mirror*, upmarket, but soon abandoned that approach when he could not attract enough upmarket advertising.[29] Instead, the *Sun*–*Mirror* battle was fought as a brash tabloid war. Murdoch took the *Mirror* dramatically downmarket and the *Sun* followed as staff from the two papers competed fiercely for scoops, salacious headlines and photographs.

Afternoons in Sydney were punctuated by newspaper vendors shouting, 'The *Sun* or the *Mirrorrrr*', and the city's streets were lined with lurid posters tempting home-bound commuters to buy a paper to read about 'BIZARRE CITY DEATH', 'THREAT TO STRIP PUPIL', 'GUN BLAST WOMAN DIES AT WASHTUB', 'SEX ATTACK, BASHINGS, ROBBERY!'[30]

The street posters were crucial. Executives believed a sensational poster could lift the circulation of either paper by 10 000 copies.[31] They were notoriously misleading and sometimes downright dishonest. When movie star Elizabeth Taylor underwent throat surgery in 1961, the *Sun*'s street posters gave updates throughout the day: 'LIZ TAYLOR IN HOSPITAL', 'LIZ SERIOUS', 'LIZ GRAVE', and then the final edition: 'FILM STAR DIES'.[32] That last poster sold a lot of papers, but the film star in question was not Taylor but a little-known comedian named George Formby, whose death was mentioned in a small story on an inside page.[33]

Mark Day worked on the *Mirror* during the late 1960s and became its editor in 1974. He argued the public was in on the joke of the outrageous headlines and 'seemed to enjoy the game of "cheat" posters'.[34] The papers were aiming for entertainment and sales, not credibility, and the intense nature of their competition led to some legendary stories in the industry. One of the most famous was about Steve Dunleavy junior, who worked as a reporter on the *Daily Mirror*. His father, Steve Dunleavy senior, was a photographer at the rival *Sun*. When Dunleavy senior took some potential front-page pictures of lost hikers in the mountains, Steve 'slashed his old man's tyres', leaving him stranded in the mountains so the *Mirror* could be first with the story.[35] Three years later, Dunleavy senior had his revenge when he locked his son in a laundry to stop him scooping the *Sun* when police arrested the 'Kingsgrove slasher'.[36]

The papers' staff deliberately fed each other false leads to distract or slow down their opposition.³⁷ And the papers were never more than one edition behind in copying any scoop or new section their rival might print, whether it was a story, a consumer advice line, a medical advice column, or a lift-out racing form guide.³⁸ Ethics were not a consideration. Dunleavy junior said *Daily Mirror* reporters 'would do anything to get a story, literally anything. I lost count of the number of times I posed as a cop, a public servant or a funeral director.'³⁹

One of the papers' reporters was infamously said to have stolen a family photograph album from a grieving family. One of Murdoch's biographers, William Shawcross, wrote that, 'A doctor's coat was always hanging in the editor's room, available to any reporter assigned to call upon some person in hospital.'⁴⁰ In 1969, a freelance photographer posed as a doctor to get access to singer Marianne Faithfull as she lay in a coma in the intensive care unit of Sydney's St Vincent's Hospital after a drug overdose. The resulting photograph appeared on the front page of the *Sunday Mirror*.⁴¹

Pringle wrote in 1965 that the *Sun* and the *Daily Mirror* were 'two of the worst and most vulgar papers in the world'.⁴² The papers took a similar approach, but Murdoch's *Mirror* was more salacious. The *Sun* tended to aim for a more middle-class audience and was considered slightly more respectable. That gave it an advantage in terms of advertising, but not street sales, so the *Sun* was able to survive 'on a generally lower overall circulation because it sold much better in the Sydney metropolitan area, and particularly the more wealthy eastern and northern suburbs'.⁴³ Its reputation as a more family-oriented newspaper meant the *Sun* held onto national advertisers even as Murdoch was enticing retail advertisers to the *Mirror* and generally outperforming the *Sun* on promotions and luring younger readers.⁴⁴

There was a long history of newspapers publishing photographs of women's bodies to lure readers, including by running beauty contests in the 1920s. Even 'family' newspapers such as the *Herald* were publishing faux-innocent 'girl in bikini' photographs in the 1950s and 1960s. As historian Fay Anderson explained, the women shown in these 'hot weather' photographs were not professional models. Press photographers were instead scouting beaches and parks to find attractive young women, often in their teens, who were wearing bikinis or revealing clothes and were willing to be photographed.⁴⁵ The Sydney tabloids invested in a different genre by publishing studio photographs of professional female models in more revealing bikinis and poses. These were printed on page three, the second most important page in the paper, but sometimes on page one.

The 'page-three girl' was prominent in the *Daily Mirror* and the *Sun*, but also in *Truth* and the weekly *Australasian Post*. (Once a magazine with literary ambitions and quality photographs, the *Australasian Post* became a staple in barber shops around the country with content focused on sex, adultery and nudity, as well as gossip, weird stories and Australiana.)

The *Daily Mirror* page-three girls exposed more flesh than the *Sun*'s, but contrary to popular belief, the genre was not invented by Murdoch. When he took over the *Daily Mirror* in 1960, it already had a 'page-three girl', although there is some debate about which paper started it. Gavin Souter said the *Sun* began the practice of publishing a 'pretty girl on the left of page three' and the *Mirror* copied.⁴⁶ Another source argued the *Daily Mirror* introduced the feature first, in 1959 (the year before Murdoch bought the *Mirror*), and this feature became known as the '*Mirror* bird', and the *Sun* copied it.⁴⁷ Either way, Murdoch did not pioneer the 'page-three girl', but he did export and adapt it (as described later in this chapter).

Despite the seemingly no-holds-barred nature of their competition, the *Mirror* and the *Sun* did have some rules of combat to abide by. They had a range of agreements in place to contain costs, including agreed limits on sports coverage, and the use of colour, as well as an agreement (later broken) 'not to run lottery-type contests that have a low level of skill'.⁴⁸ The two groups also agreed not to use 'sex words' to promote their papers.⁴⁹ When the *Sun* put up a street poster on 7 September 1965 saying, '"RELIGIOUS MURDER": UNDIES SLASHED', Murdoch sent a copy of the poster to Fairfax executives to suggest it might have crossed the line.⁵⁰ But by the mid-1970s, his *Mirror* was publishing headlines about 'RAPE UNDER SPELL' and a 'SEX KILLING', so the agreement was terminated.⁵¹

Another agreement was about price. The traditional Sydney practice of price fixing had continued so the rival papers always had the same cover price in the 1960s. When they raised that price to seven cents in 1970, they announced the price rise on the same day, and implemented it simultaneously five days later. In July 1975, Murdoch would break this convention, too. Until then, the papers had the same cover price and much the same news and features (because they copied from each other), so they began using crossword games and prize competitions as a way to differentiate themselves and lure readers. The crossword puzzles of the 1960s gave way to extravagant prizes in the 1970s which 'escalated from one edition to the next, as one paper sought to outbid the other'.[52] Mark Day says:

> Rupert was always drilling us – never let them have an advantage. Make sure we have EVERYTHING that they have, then add more. The *Sun*, of course, adopted the same approach, so we were in ever-escalating duels, especially in promotions. A typical example would be when the *Sun* launched a competition to 'win a $250,000 house'. By the second edition, the *Mirror* had 'win a $250,000 house AND a car'. The *Sun*'s third edition matched the *Mirror*, so in the final edition the *Mirror* upped it to 'Win a $250,000 house with A CAR AND A BOAT'. The next day the *Sun* had a bigger boat ... and the *Mirror* got a bigger house.[53]

MURDOCH TAKES ON FLEET STREET

After honing his tabloid skills for so many years, from Perth's *Sunday Times* in 1954 to the *Daily Mirror* and *Truth* in the 1960s, Murdoch was ready to venture further afield. The HWT had invested overseas, in Papua New Guinea, and later Fiji, but Murdoch had a much bolder vision of overseas conquest. Australia was becoming too small for him because of the broadcast ownership restrictions, but also because Jack Williams and the HWT had devoured so many of the key pickings. It was said that Murdoch spoke with Williams in 1968, and proposed a vague plan to merge the interests of News Limited and the HWT and succeed Williams when the HWT chairman retired, but this plan was overruled by the HWT board, prompting Murdoch to look overseas instead.[54]

Concerns about News Limited's finances had evaporated by 1968. Murdoch's newspapers were making money (except for the *Australian*).

Truth, and to a lesser degree, the *Daily Mirror*, were especially bringing in revenue. In Melbourne, *Truth*'s circulation under Sol Chandler had shot up from 220 000 to 385 000, through a greater focus on football, and on what journalist Evan Whitton (who worked at *Truth* in the 1960s) described as mixing factual stories with soft porn.[55] News Limited's profits had also been boosted by increased revenue from television and radio, and even from record pressing through News Limited's Festival Records.[56] News Limited's headquarters had been transferred from Adelaide to Sydney.

Murdoch's Adelaide nemesis, Lloyd Dumas, wrote to Fairfax's RP Falkingham with undisguised resentment that Murdoch probably 'feels that he can survive anything' now.[57] News Limited's net profit had risen to a record $3.4 million in 1969, and his company was worth $52 million (about $655 million in today's money).[58]

A financially stable Murdoch set off to take on Fleet Street, still considered the heart of journalism, just as it had been when Murdoch's father had first tried to make it there as a journalist in 1908. In 1968, Rupert pounced on a British weekly called *News of the World*. It had begun in 1843, was published as a national Sunday paper, and was known for its shock-horror, titillating content, often based on crime news. Reflecting the 'old working-class habit of reading a newspaper only at the weekend', the Sunday papers were some of the highest circulating newspapers, not just in the United Kingdom, but in the world.[59] Although *News of the World*'s sales had halved in the previous 40 years, it was still Britain's most popular Sunday newspaper, and with a mammoth audience of six million readers, it had 'the biggest circulation in the western world'.[60]

Murdoch won control of *News of the World* in early 1969 after gaining the support of the Carr family, the paper's commercially naïve owners. He had triumphed after an acrimonious year-long struggle against the shadowy Czechoslovakian-born British media baron, Robert Maxwell. After Murdoch took over the *News of the World*, he reportedly broke a 'gentlemen's agreement' he had made with the Carr family, adding to a sense that he was brazen, ruthless and unwilling to play by the conventions of the British establishment.[61]

Back in Australia, Murdoch had needed the help of well-placed friends so he could transfer a substantial amount of his assets to the United

Kingdom to make his bid for the *News of the World*. This was still a time of strict foreign exchange controls when the Reserve Bank regulated capital flows in and out of Australia. Any final decisions on controversial transactions were made by the treasurer.

Previously secret Treasury files, released in 2008, revealed that News Limited sought permission in September 1968 to transfer $10 million to the United Kingdom (on top of $2 million which had been approved in July). The Reserve Bank and the Treasury department were strongly opposed. The department told treasurer William (Billy) McMahon that the benefits for Australia were only 'marginal'. There was also concern about how Australia's balance of payments would withstand such a large shift of capital out of the country.[62]

McMahon, who had a close friendship with Frank Packer but was no friend of Murdoch's, refused News Limited's request. Only intervention by the prime minister, now John Gorton, a Murdoch ally, allowed the transaction to go ahead and save the day for Murdoch. After McMahon was safely out of Canberra, Country Party leader and deputy prime minister John McEwen and Gorton had got together to look over the funds transfer application at the Kurrajong Hotel, while Murdoch reportedly waited in the garden. Gorton later said, 'I always liked Murdoch' and, referring to the money transfer, boasted, 'I started him on his way'.[63]

The previous year, 1967, had been a dramatic one in Australian politics. In February, Gough Whitlam had succeeded Calwell as Labor leader. On 17 December, Harold Holt disappeared while swimming at Portsea and Gorton became prime minister in January 1968. Murdoch had helped advance Gorton's prospects over McMahon's after his *Australian* published a series of articles highlighting McEwen's opposition to McMahon. McEwen privately told McMahon, 'I will not serve under you because I don't trust you.' Publicly, McEwen would only say that, 'Mr McMahon knows the reasons why'.[64]

Three days before the Liberal leadership vote, the *Australian* published a remarkable front-page story on 'WHY McEWEN VETOES McMAHON: FOREIGN AGENT IS THE MAN BETWEEN THE LEADERS'.[65] The story alleged that Murdoch's then-nemesis, the *Australian*'s former editor, Max Newton, was an agent of foreign influence and a threat to national security. The only basis for this claim was that Newton was undertaking some consulting work for the Japan Export Trade Organisation. Newton was close to McMahon, a connection which the article revealed, and the story was used to damage McMahon's leadership run. Murdoch had obtained the information for the story from McEwen, who had received it from ASIO.[66]

Packer badly wanted his friend McMahon to win, but his staff finally convinced him that McMahon had no chance in the face of McEwen's opposition and the climate of intrigue and criticism now swirling. McMahon dropped out. Acting on Packer's orders, David McNicoll rang the two main contenders remaining – Gorton and Paul Hasluck – to pressure them to keep McMahon on as treasurer. Fearful of getting Packer offside, Gorton was the more enthusiastic of the two about this unappealing prospect, so he got the nod from the Packer camp.[67]

Gorton, the compromise candidate, unexpectedly became prime minister in what Rodney Tiffen called Murdoch's 'first big political coup'.[68] The Liberal leadership was becoming a playing field for rival media empires to contest, and that would continue (Chapter 19).

A self-admitted 'bastard' by birth, Gorton was the son of a wealthy businessman and his mistress. A former RAAF fighter pilot, Gorton had been shot down during World War II, leaving him with facial injuries and a flattened nose that gave him a battered look. He did not seem to have any strong, specific policy ambitions, other than being a proud nationalist. Gorton was independent, a maverick known for his informality and his down-to-earth manner. The public perception of Gorton at this time was that he was authentic and direct. He was seen as a likeable, straight-talking, dinky-di Aussie with a larrikin streak and a love of the good life – drinking, gambling and women. Within his party, this contributed to a perception that he was unreliable.

Murdoch had his first ally–prime minister in office so he was not happy when *Truth* published a story, in January 1968, that painted Gorton as a thief.[69] *Truth* published details of an old court case that revealed how, when Gorton's father died, Gorton and his wife had cut his father's latest mistress out of his will. Gorton had transferred her shares to his wife, after signing his name as a witness to a signature the woman had made on a blank share transfer form years earlier, then making a false entry in the company's minute book.[70] *Truth* editor, Sol Chandler, received a telegram: 'RESIGNATION ACCEPTED, PLEASE VACATE OFFICE IMMEDIATELY. REPLACEMENT ARRIVES MONDAY. MURDOCH'.[71] Evan Whitton recalled that Chandler said, 'I'm out, boys. I made Murdoch a million, and he's sacked me.'[72] *Tribune* reported the sacking came after 'pressure on Murdoch by Prime Minister Gorton'.[73]

In the United Kingdom, Murdoch forged ahead with the newspaper purchased partly with profits from *Truth* and money transferred with Gorton's help. Murdoch had spiced up *News of the World*, including through a serialisation of Christine Keeler's autobiography in July 1969 that made him more enemies among the British establishment but built circulation. Four months later, Murdoch bought London's *Sun*, formerly the *Daily Herald*. The *Sun* had been losing money since it had changed its name in 1964, and its owners were planning to close it. It had a circulation of only 850 000 against the (London) *Daily Mirror* which was selling around five million copies.[74] The *Sun* was considered a born loser and a bad purchase, so Murdoch was able to buy it for a bargain price of around A$400 000.[75]

Murdoch poached the northern editor of the *Daily Mail* in Manchester, Larry Lamb, to become editor. The *Sun* was changed from a broadsheet to a tabloid that mixed sensation and irreverence with an anti-establishment edge that reflected the more permissive 1960s. The new *Sun*'s first edition, on 17 November 1969, was three hours late off the presses. Although rough, and noticeably rushed, it featured the 'exclusive' confession of a horse trainer who doped his own horses ('HORSE DOPE SENSATION'), a front-page picture of the 'rumoured' girlfriend of Prince Charles, and a serialisation of the racy book, *The Love Machine*. Within three days, 'the *Sun* had doubled its pre-Murdoch sale'.[76]

Commodifying the 'sexual revolution', Murdoch imported the 'page-three girl' he had inherited at the Sydney *Daily Mirror* and took off more of her clothes. The pictures became progressively more risqué, until in 1970, less than a year after he bought it, Murdoch's *Sun* had a bare-breasted model on page three, a daily feature that was used as a sales device for another 44 years, until 2015.

The disapproving *Times* pointed out that, 'This is an old way to create a new paper. Its formula is a simple one ... sex, sport and sensation.'[77] Under Murdoch and Lamb, that formula saw the paper's circulation build rapidly. Within 12 months, the *Sun* grew from selling 850 000 to 1.75 million copies a day.[78] By 1976, the *Sun* was selling more than three million a day, and challenging the (London) *Daily Mirror* as the highest-selling British daily.[79]

Murdoch's reputation as a proprietor who could revive dying newspapers was growing. He had a keen sense of pushing social conventions and taking into account local predilections. Darren Tindale, a former photographer at the *Sun News-Pictorial*, said, 'Australian readers would not have tolerated nudity at this time because they regarded themselves as more sophisticated.'[80] But in the United Kingdom, Murdoch found a large audience who wanted to buy a paper that had news and sport stories accompanied by bare-breasted women. His British papers also engaged in the relentless pursuit of stories about the British Royal Family and television celebrities, preferably stories that involved sex and scandal. Sex was a crucial selling point for Murdoch's British tabloids, along with what academic Brian McNair dubbed 'yuck journalism', stories with 'graphic coverage of the bizarre, the tragic and the pathetic'.[81]

The huge revenue that Murdoch made from his British newspapers helped prop up the *Australian* back home.[82] Mark Day noted that, by expanding to the United Kingdom, 'Murdoch had grown his pie to the extent that the *Australian*'s losses were no longer life-threatening.'[83] The London *Sun* especially became Murdoch's financial bedrock. In 1970, the British arm of Murdoch's company (called News International) was already making nearly double the profits of News Limited's Australian assets.[84] And in 1971, profits from the United Kingdom rose by 40 per cent.[85]

THE 1969 ELECTION

Holt had led his party to a spectacular win in 1966, but Gorton faced a more difficult electoral climate in 1969. Whitlam, a tall barrister with an imperious manner, had changed the nature of the contest with his strong verbal skills, intimidating intellect, and big policy ambitions showing up the inadequacies of Gorton's irreverent, larrikin image. Whitlam had also reformed the Labor Party, discarded outdated policies and was presenting a more modern image.

After two decades in office, the Liberal–Country Party Coalition was looking tired, and Gorton's lack of discipline and waning public popularity did not help its cause. He was increasingly seen as reckless and scandal prone. Since 1968, there had been much innuendo and speculation over Gorton's 22-year-old principal private secretary, Ainsley Gotto. In keeping with the ingrained sexism of the times, his colleagues were annoyed that he gave so much power to a young woman, and journalists seemed unable to accept that Gotto had been promoted on merit at such a young age. She was invariably described in news reports as a 'very attractive', 'shapely ... girl'.[86]

A second scandal concerned Gorton's late-night visit in November 1968 to the American Embassy with 19-year-old journalist Geraldine Willesee. Another young woman who was pioneering a path in a masculine world, and was being subjected to career-limiting innuendo, Willesee was employed by Australian United Press 'as the sole accredited female member of the federal parliamentary press corps'.[87] Gorton was at a press gallery dinner when he was summoned to the US Embassy to receive an important update about Vietnam, but he kept drinking and dancing for several hours, then decided to take a dance partner, Willesee, with him. He showed up at the embassy around 1 am, demanded admittance, and then kept drinking and chatting with Willesee at one end of the room while pointedly ignoring the US Ambassador.

During their conversations that night, Gorton delivered Willesee a genuine scoop – that he wanted Australia to withdraw from Vietnam. But her boss, Ken Braddick, ripped the page from her typewriter when she tried to file the story, tearing it up and telling her the conversation was off the record. Willesee was then sacked. She later wrote:

> For 40 years anyone within whispering distance has felt comfortable to ask for 'the real story' about that visit to the US embassy with John Gorton ... The questions have always been code for: did you bonk the prime minister? Well, no. I interviewed him. Got a good story, too. He wanted to bail out of the Vietnam War.[88]

Yet another scandal based on innuendo broke in March 1969 when it became public that a drunken and solo Gorton had visited the dressing room of 23-year-old singer Liza Minnelli, daughter of Judy Garland, at a Sydney nightclub in June 1968. Gotto, the US Embassy incident, and the dressing room visit, all made international headlines, as well as local news coverage. There was speculation that Gorton's more conservative enemies were working hard to promote the scandals.

Despite his private views on Vietnam, Gorton confirmed the Coalition's continued support for the United States' position. This meant voters in 1969 were given a stark choice on the issue because, although Labor was wary of making Vietnam the centrepiece of its campaign pitch, Whitlam pledged to end conscription and withdraw the Australian forces.

No daily metropolitan paper advocated a vote for Labor. *The Age* came closest. Although it backed the conservatives, it expressed reservations and gave Labor's policy platform a lot of positive attention (Chapter 18). Packer much preferred McMahon, but wanted the Coalition in office, so he and the *Daily Telegraph* supported Gorton. Packer even offered Gorton help with his policy speech and arranged for his 'best people' at GTV-9 to coach him on television technique, but Gorton showed up late, was rude to the staff and put in a terrible performance, lowering him even further in Packer's estimation.[89]

Murdoch was living in the United Kingdom, and preoccupied by the re-launch of the *Sun*, but he still kept a close eye on his Australian papers which reflected his support for Gorton. The issues where the Coalition was seen as stronger – Vietnam, defence and security – were described as the major issues of the campaign, rather than health, housing and education, where Labor was seen to have a strong advantage. The Adelaide *News* acknowledged that Whitlam had been the better performer during the campaign but told readers their vote was not about 'one man' but 'a whole government'. It argued Labor's policies were 'an attractive package', but asked what was the value of housing, health and education if 'we stand alone in the world, without friends, labelled as a nation that does not honor its commitments'?[90]

Murdoch's *Daily Mirror* made the same points and even used some of the same phrases.[91] His *Australian* also admitted that Gorton was 'no great shakes as a campaigner', but said 'thoughtful' and 'fair-minded' voters would back Gorton anyway because of defence and foreign relations. However, almost as an insurance policy, the editorial was headed 'NO DISASTER EITHER WAY'.[92] And the Murdoch outlets implied that Labor would be ready for office next time around if it 'fixed' its defence policy.

As a group, the newspapers were more supportive of Labor than they had been at any time since Curtin and World War II (not counting the aberration of Fairfax in 1961). Even the *Sydney Morning Herald* admitted that Whitlam had performed better than Gorton, and that Labor was 'more attractive and more responsible than it has been for many years', but it also concluded that Labor's defence and foreign policy was too 'radical [a] change of direction'.[93] Quietly in the background, the Fairfax group had offered the Liberal Party help with publicity.[94] The HWT papers, including the *Sun News-Pictorial* and the *Herald*, argued similarly that Australia's military commitments in Asia were the real issue of the election, that Australia should not 'ignore our responsibilities as an ally of the United States', and the government should be returned on that basis.[95]

Labor ran a strong campaign on domestic policy issues and made substantial gains at the 1969 election. It won more than half of the two-party preferred vote (50.2 per cent), recovered much of the ground it lost in 1966, and came very close to victory. It lost the election by only four seats.[96] DLP preferences, especially in Victoria, were seen as the major cause of Labor's defeat.[97] Thirty years later, Gorton acknowledged that he 'didn't like anything about Vietnam', and 'forces within his own party and a need to appease the [DLP], whose preferences helped the Liberals hold power, had kept Australia in the war'.[98]

The government's majority in the House of Representatives was reduced from 40 to only seven seats. The Labor Party was now seen as a viable contender for government and within striking distance of that goal, while Gorton was a wounded figure within his party, and seen to bear much of the blame for the poor result. His unorthodox behaviour had alienated colleagues, instability in the party had heightened, and a leadership challenge was looming, with help from the Packer group (Chapter 19).

FIGURE 16.1 Labor leader Gough Whitlam reads the *Sun-Herald* at his Cabramatta home with his daughter, Catherine, the day after the 1969 federal election, 26 October 1969

SOURCE Picture by George Lipman. Fairfax Syndication/Nine Publishing.

TELEVISION IN THE 1960s

Television had been around since 1956, but Gorton was said to be 'the first prime minister of the television age' (and that was unfortunate for him, as he was a weak television performer).[99] It had taken more than a decade for television to mature into a powerful news medium and a prime site for politics.

In the 1950s, television news had been 'scrappy'.[100] In 1959, news and weather accounted for only 2.8 per cent of television programming.[101] Bulletins were brief and dull. Although the ABC devoted twice as much time as commercial stations to broadcasting news, it took a very cautious and stuffy approach.[102] Throughout the Menzies years, the ABC stuck doggedly to a formula of only reporting official authorised facts, balanced out by a response from the Opposition, even though so much news during the tumultuous 1960s was coming from off-the-record leaks and briefings.[103]

During this era of big domestic and international stories, the ABC changed its approach and the commercial television stations noticed how popular news bulletins were, both with audiences and advertisers. They increased the length and frequency of news programs, improved their formats, and heavily promoted newsreaders who became the faces of their respective stations.

Technology also improved what was possible. Cameras and recording equipment were becoming more portable. Outside broadcast vans were being used to collect on-the-spot news. In 1962, coaxial cables linked major cities so simultaneous (or 'live') television broadcasts could occur. This meant that film of interstate news events no longer had to be flown by plane to other locations. And satellite technology developed so overseas news events could be shown in Australia. This was expensive technology, though, so it tended to be used only for big stories, and more towards the end of the 1960s.[104]

As television news coverage improved, newspapers suffered a loss of prestige and trust. When the ABCB undertook public opinion surveys in 1969, most people nominated television as the most believable medium. Newspapers were considered the least believable, especially in Sydney, where the tabloids were notoriously outrageous.[105]

As television was becoming more central to people's lives, politics was moving away from public halls, newspapers and the streets. Whitlam's speechwriter, Graham Freudenberg, said 1969 was the 'last [federal election] campaign that depended upon the ... eight o'clock public meeting ... in whatever city or town we were speaking'.[106] The next federal election was highly focused on television (Chapter 20).

Current affairs programs also contributed to politics being brought into the home via television. The ABC's weekly *Four Corners* program began in 1961, and helped enforce the notion that political interviews could be entertaining viewing. In 1967, the ABC launched *This Day Tonight*, a half-hour week-night television program with hard-hitting political interviews. At its peak, *This Day Tonight* was a ratings winner, and its focus on investigative reporting and confrontations with politicians shook up political coverage.[107]

Televised sports coverage was also improving in the 1960s. Viewers had greater access to live events, including horse racing, which had always been a bread-and-butter staple of newspapers. Cricket test matches, and boxing and wrestling programs, were drawing huge viewing audiences in the 1960s.[108] TCN-9 had begun the first integrated sports program, *Westinghouse World of Sport* in 1958, while HSV-7's version, also called *World of Sport*, began in Melbourne in 1959 as a two-hour Sunday program which was incredibly popular and ran for 28 years.[109]

Television's targeting of low-paid workers with sports, entertainment and news was having an impact on newspapers because they had relied on that demographic ever since the days of the 'penny press' in the 1860s.[110] Research conducted for Fairfax in 1960 found the 'industrial class' was turning off newspapers the most.[111] And research commissioned for *The Age* in 1968 confirmed that tabloid readers were by far the heaviest television viewers.[112] This was leading the tabloid papers, especially in Sydney, to become even more visual, attention-grabbing and salacious, in order to entice people to buy a newspaper when they could watch television for free at home. The 'serious' papers, on the other hand, were finding ways to monetise the benefits of a smaller, but more loyal and more affluent, audience (Chapter 18).

TEXTBOX 16.1 Radio in the 1960s

Like television, radio was becoming more of a competitor to newspapers. Rodney Tiffen noted how, in the second half of the 1960s, 'radio news started to resemble what we receive today'.[113] Portable tape recorders were allowing 'more interviewing of sources', there were more voices, and 'greater mobility and actuality in radio news'.[114]

A law change in April 1967 meant radio stations were legally allowed to broadcast live telephone interviews. This spurred the growth of talkback radio programs as listeners 'dialled in' to ask questions or make comments.[115] Radio hosts were also 'dialling out' to more regularly interview politicians and public figures on air.[116]

In 1967, the ABC began broadcasting *AM*, a morning current affairs radio program that journalist Max Walsh described as the electronic equivalent of a morning newspaper.[117] Through programs such as *AM*, as well as talkback interviews, radio was starting to generate news as well as reporting on it.

TEXTBOX 16.2 A new paper: The *Canberra News*

After years with no new entrants to the field, in 1969 two new metropolitan dailies were launched. But the conditions for new starters were now so difficult that neither lasted long. The disaster of David Syme and Co's *Newsday* in Melbourne is described in Chapter 18. In Canberra, the Fairfax group felt obliged to launch a new paper to protect its *Canberra Times* after Murdoch registered the name *Canberra Mirror*. Max Newton, who was printing several weeklies in Canberra, also seemed to be making plans to start an afternoon paper.[118]

In November 1969, Fairfax launched Canberra's first afternoon paper, the *Canberra News*. Because the paper was a defensive move, and afternoon papers no longer had strong prospects, the newspaper was given a modest budget. It had bikini girls on page three, but not enough local news, or enough reporters to collect such news.

The company expected losses for at least the first few years, but by 1974, the *Canberra News* had built up a circulation of just 13 000 and it had

> not been embraced by retailers either. It did not have enough advertising to pay its costs. Losses of $1.7 million had been incurred in four-and-a-half years, and it was on track to keep losing about $500 000 a year. The company blamed rising costs, especially wages.[119] But *Nation Review* journalists also suspected the *Canberra Times'* and *Canberra News'* administrative costs were both being tallied under *Canberra News* to paint the 'gloomiest possible accountant's picture' to justify its closure.[120]
>
> The paper was closed in July 1974. Fifty-five staff lost their jobs, including 23 journalists, although most were redeployed elsewhere in the company. Internally, John B Fairfax called its closure a 'disastrous failure'.[121]

THE SIZE OF THE GIANTS

After so many corporate manoeuvres in the 1960s, it is appropriate to pause at the end of the decade to take stock of the extraordinary size of the newspaper groups.

The HWT was the formidable industry leader. Across its subsidiaries, the HWT was making profits of more than $13 million (Table 16.1). This was more than some of its largest advertisers, including David Jones ($6 million) and Coles ($10 million), and almost as much as its long-standing ally, Myer ($15 million).[122] The HWT was making double the profits of Packer's company (even with lucrative revenue from the Nine network included), and three times the profits of the Fairfax group. Although there were large newspaper chains in the United States (such as Gannett Co Inc, Ridder Publications Inc and Knight Newspapers Inc), even at their peak, none of them came close to rivalling the HWT in market share. It was selling more than 50 per cent of Australia's metropolitan daily newspapers.[123]

From the 12 separate owners in 1945, only four major newspaper groups remained: the HWT, Fairfax, Consolidated Press and Rupert Murdoch's News Limited. Television licences had underwritten their growth. The only semi-independent owner left was David Syme and Co, owner of *The Age*, and only as the financially subservient junior in a partnership with Fairfax.

TABLE 16.1 The financial strength of the major newspaper groups, 1969

	Last group profit $m	Share market value $m
Herald and Weekly Times	6.30	137.9
Advertiser	2.32	40.2
Queensland Press	2.62	37.6
West Australian Newspapers	1.79	69.4
Combined HWT group total	*13.03*	*285.1*
John Fairfax	3.40	56.9
David Syme and Co	0.98	11.7
Consolidated Press Holdings*	3.01	30.3
Television Corporation*	3.45	48.3
News Limited	2.46	52.1

SOURCES Company annual reports and *Sydney Morning Herald*, 2 July 1969, p. 18, and 4 September 1970, p. 21.

* Consolidated Press Holdings (CPH) held 75 per cent of the capital of Television Corporation. CPH's stated group profit result covers 15 months.

The big four groups controlled daily newspapers, but also weekly papers, magazines, radio and television stations, newsprint production and cable news (Table 16.2). In terms of size, reach, influence and profits, they were truly 'media monsters'. And where the HWT was the mature giant of the industry, Murdoch's News Limited was the energetic up-and-comer, with the results of its rapid expansion becoming clearer.

In 1969, aside from metropolitan dailies, there were about 40 provincial daily papers, 400 weekly papers (including 13 metropolitan weeklies), plus hundreds of country and suburban papers.[124] There were still pockets of independence in Australia's print media, but the major newspaper groups had bought many suburban and country newspapers, and they would continue buying more in the 1970s.

As barriers to publishing had been reduced by the introduction of offset printing, new outlets had been growing. These included new suburban papers, but also student newspapers, and what was then dubbed 'the ethnic press': the many newspapers that catered for diasporic communities and non-English-speaking migrants. There were also new Indigenous, feminist, gay and lesbian publications. Not all of these were newspapers,

Table 16.2 The size of the media monsters: Their major interests and assets, 1969

Company	Daily metropolitan/national newspapers (Aust)	Radio stations	Television stations	Other publications and magazines*
Herald and Weekly Times (including as a major shareholder in Advertiser Newspapers; Queensland Press; WAN and Davies Brothers)	*Herald* *Sun News-Pictorial* *Advertiser* *Courier-Mail* *Telegraph* (Brisbane) *Mercury* *West Australian* *Daily News* (Perth)	3DB Melbourne 3LK Lubeck 3XY Melbourne 4AK Oakey 4BK Brisbane 4BH Brisbane 4AM Atherton 5AD Adelaide 5MU Murray Bridge 5PI Crystal Brook 5SE Mount Gambier 7HO Hobart 7EX Launceston 6IX Perth** 6BY Bridgetown** 6MD Merredin** 6WB Katanning**	HSV-7 Melbourne BTQ-7 Brisbane ADS-7 Adelaide TVT-6 Hobart TVW-7 Perth** FNQ-10 Cairns	*Sunday Mail* (Brisb) *Sunday Mail* (Adel) (jointly owned with News Ltd) *Weekly Times* *Sporting Globe* *Bendigo Advertiser* *Listener In-TV* Overseas: *Papua-New Guinea Post-Courier* *Nu Gini Toktok* (PNG)) Magazines: *Australasian Post* *Home Beautiful* *Your Garden* *Aircraft*
Fairfax	*Australian Financial Review* *Sydney Morning Herald* *Sun* *Canberra Times* *Canberra News* (until 1974)	3XY Melbourne 2NM Muswellbrook 2NX Bolwarra Through shareholdings in Macquarie Broadcasting: 2GB Sydney 2CA Canberra 2LF Young 2WL Wollongong 3AW Melbourne 4BH Brisbane 5DN Adelaide	ATN-7 Sydney QTQ-9 Brisbane CTC-7 Canberra NBN-3 Newcastle RTN-8 Richmond WIN-4 Illawarra AMV-4 Murray BTV-6 Ballarat DDQ-10 Darling Downs SDQ-4 Southern Downs	*Sun-Herald* (Sunday) *Newcastle Morning Herald* *Newcastle Sun* *Goulburn Evening Post* *Daily Advertiser* (Wagga) *Illawarra Mercury* Magazines: *Woman's Day* *Pix* *People* *Radio, Television and Hobbies*
David Syme and Co (in partnership with Fairfax)	*The Age* *Newsday* (until May 1970)	3XY Melbourne		*News* (Shepparton) *Seymour Telegraph* *Kyabram Free Press* *Tatura Guardian Press* Magazines: *Motor Manual* *Caravan World*

Company	Daily metropolitan/ national newspapers (Aust)	Radio stations	Television stations	Other publications and magazines*
Consolidated Press	*Daily Telegraph*	3AK Melbourne 2LF Young 2GZ Orange 2NZ Inverell 6PM Perth 6AM Northam 6KG Kalgoorlie 6GE Geraldton	TCN-9 Sydney GTV-9 Melbourne NBN-3 Newcastle WIN-4 Illawarra ECN-8 Manning River CBN-8 Tablelands CWN-6 Western slopes BTQ-7 Brisbane DDQ-10 Darling Downs SDQ-4 Southern Downs	*Sunday Telegraph* *Maitland Mercury* *Manning River Times* *Gloucester Advocate* Magazines: *Australian Women's Weekly* *Australian Magazine (AM)* *Bulletin* *Australian Home Journal* *TV Times* (in conjunction with the ABC)
News Limited	The *Australian* The *News* *Daily Mirror* *NT News*	2BH Broken Hill 4BH Brisbane 5DN Adelaide 6KY Perth 6NA Narrogin	NWS-9 Adelaide TEN-10 Sydney SAS-10 Adelaide TVW-7 Perth NBN-3 Newcastle WIN-4 Illawarra ECN-8 Manning River SES-8 South East SA GTS-4 Spencer Gulf BTW-3 Bunbury NEN-9 Upper Namoi GSW-9 Southern Agricultural	*Sunday Mail* (Adel) (jointly owned with the *Advertiser*) *Sunday Times* (Perth) *Sunday Mirror* (Syd) *Barrier Miner* *Centralian Advocate* *Wimmera Mail-Times* *Sunday Truth* (Brisb) *Truth* (Melb) Overseas: *Dominion* (NZ) *News of the World* (UK) *Sun* (UK) Magazines: *New Idea* *TV Week*

* Only select magazines and country papers are shown, not all are listed. Suburban newspapers are not listed.

** This table shows the position after the HWT acquired WAN in 1969. As explained in Chapter 15, the HWT would soon sell the four WA radio stations to TVW-7, and then sold most of WAN's shareholding in TVW-7 to others, but retained a 1.85 per cent share.

SOURCES ABCB, *21st Annual Report, 1968-69*, Commonwealth of Australia, Canberra, 1969; ABCB, Annual Report, 1969-70, Commonwealth of Australia, Canberra, 1970; HWT, *Annual Report 1969*; David Syme and Co, *Annual Report 1970*; News Limited, *Annual Report 1971*, and multiple other sources.

TEXTBOX 16.3 Taking over the country (papers)

In the 1960s, the metropolitan newspaper groups pushed out into the suburbs, but also into the regions. They took over country papers, changing the nature of a sector that had once been characterised by diverse, independent, locally-owned papers. Many of these papers were especially attractive because they held shares in their region's local television station.

In New South Wales, the Fairfax group bought the *Newcastle Morning Herald* in 1961 and *Illawarra Mercury* in 1969, while Rupert Henderson built up his own stable of country papers (Chapter 14). Packer's Consolidated Press also built up a chain of NSW papers starting with the *Maitland Mercury*, the oldest provincial paper in New South Wales, which it purchased in 1960. It used the *Mercury* as a base to acquire further papers between 1964 and 1978, including in Cessnock, Taree, Gloucester, Gosford and Forster.[125] In 1967, Consolidated Press also purchased an interest in Western Newspapers Ltd, the publisher of papers in Orange, Lithgow, Forbes and Parkes, and built up its stake until it was the major shareholder.[126]

In Victoria, the HWT bought the *Bendigo Advertiser* in 1963, which had begun publishing in 1853 and became a daily in 1856, when its first readers were prospectors on the Bendigo goldfields.[127] In 1974, the HWT acquired the even older *Geelong Advertiser* (1840). That gave the HWT two of Victoria's six provincial dailies.[128]

In Queensland, the HWT's Queensland Press acquired a stake in Provincial Newspapers (Qld.) Ltd in the 1970s, which owned a string of daily newspapers in south-east and central Queensland, including in Mackay, Rockhampton, Gladstone, Bundaberg, Maryborough, Ipswich, Warwick and Toowoomba, and some non-dailies, such as the *Nambour Chronicle* which became the springboard in 1980 for the *Sunshine Coast Daily*.[129]

Murdoch also bought up country papers. By 1971, he still had the *Barrier Miner* in Broken Hill, which he had inherited from his father, but had added the *Centralian Advocate* (Alice Springs), the *Wimmera Mail-Times* (Horsham), and 12 other regional papers, many in Western Australia.[130]

or regularly printed, but they highlighted areas where the metropolitan papers were failing to cater for diversity and failing to provide a plurality of views.

Although printing on a small scale was easier for new entrants, profit making and long-term survival were tougher, including for the mass scale newspapers. Although they still had the lion's share of press advertising, as well as circulations that were among the highest in the world, the economics of newspaper publishing had changed so much that the metropolitan newspapers could no longer exist without income from outside investments.[131] At a Fairfax board meeting in February 1968, directors were reminded that 'the falling profitability of newspapers was a worldwide trend and the only way to maintain earnings was to diversify'.[132]

Diversification had already been pursued so ferociously in the 1960s that – in addition to swallowing up assets across print, radio and television – the newspaper groups had also gone into business in printing, bookbinding, packaging, music, transport, travel and leisure. Advertiser Newspapers is a good example of this. It bought five outside businesses in South Australia between 1960 and 1966. Aside from publishing newspapers, running a television station and four radio stations, it was also making telephone directories, paper bags, computer stationery and flexible packaging, and performing commercial printing and courier delivery services.[133]

Even the HWT – with its massive-circulation metropolitan dailies in Melbourne, and papers unburdened by direct competition in several markets – was relying on interests other than newspapers to provide the bulk of its profits. The Australian newspaper groups needed the extra capital from outside investments in order to meet rising costs for newsprint and labour, research and promotions, building and production, and, especially, to afford developments in automation. Otherwise, the high costs of old-fashioned production methods threatened to destroy newspapers.

PART FOUR

THE EARLY 1970s

CHAPTER 17
THE MAGIC GARDEN OF COMPUTERS

In the 1960s, newspapers reported on spacecraft that could orbit the Earth and land humans on the moon. But their own technology, which they were using to make those reports, had effectively been invented in the 1400s. Since Johannes Gutenberg invented movable type around 1450, and William Caxton introduced a printing press to England in 1476, the only major refinements in newspaper production had been the rotary press and linotype machine. In the 1890s, newspaper production had been considered radically advanced because of those machines, but by the 1960s, newspapers had fallen behind other industries, especially the automotive and aviation industries, which were already using automation, computers and modern production methods.

Newspapers were trying to compete in speed and accuracy with television and radio using printing presses that had barely changed in the past 90 years. To remain attractive to readers, they were adding more features, sections, photography and advertisements, but their antiquated equipment was struggling under the weight of increased demand. Owners knew that if they did not invest in new technology to increase efficiency and speed up their processes, newspapers risked being priced out of existence. Greater mechanisation and automation were seen as the key ways to reduce costs and increase profits, but they also held out the advantage of reducing owners' dependence on skilled, unionised printing labour, which was always a point of industrial vulnerability (the strikes of 1944 and 1955 had not been forgotten).

In the 1970s, newspapers moved from 'hot metal' typesetting to 'cold type' photocomposition, and from journalists using typewriters to computers. The transition took decades to achieve so this chapter deviates from the chronological order of other chapters and charts the early steps towards automation through to the conclusion of those stages in the mid-1980s. These were years of radical change in newspaper buildings across the country as new technologies changed the nature of newspaper work, caused huge job losses, and sometimes led to strikes, violence and industrial sabotage.

HOT METAL AND PAPER SLIPS

To understand what newspaper owners were trying to change, it is important to consider how newspapers were produced in the 1960s. The main tool of journalism was a typewriter (often older than the reporter). Journalists would type out their story onto small, numbered slips of carbon copy paper that had been cut to fit into the reading frame of a linotype machine, perhaps fitting only one paragraph on each sheet. A subeditor would read over the typewritten sheets, edit them, make sure the story fit the column length available, then add a top sheet that specified the column width and type size in which the story should be set. This package of copy and instructions would go to the linotype operator.

The composing room where the linotype operators worked in smudged aprons was well described by journalist Michael Shmith as 'a space of steel, metal, lead and wet paper that looked like a cross between a hospital kitchen and an armaments factory, and smelt like a cross between a foundry and a weather shelter for saturated dogs'.[1] There, 500 years after Gutenberg and Caxton, each word of the journalist's story would be assembled using characters of movable type cast into lines and slotted into a special steel tray called a galley.

A revolutionary form of automation had already been introduced into this process in the 1890s. The linotype machine, as the name said, made a line of type. It was considered a wonder of the industrial revolution, something spectacularly complex and cutting-edge when it was introduced. A strange, cumbersome machine that weighed three-quarters of a tonne, it looked like a gigantic metal accordion with a network of complicated pulleys, two clanking metal arms and a keyboard attached (Figure 17.1). At the back, not far from the operator's face, was a pot of boiling metal.

The linotype operator used the keyboard at the front, which had

FIGURE 17.1 These linotype operators, working at the HWT building, Melbourne, in 1964, could produce about six lines a minute
SOURCE Newspix.

letters arranged by frequency rather than the 'qwerty' layout of a normal typewriter, to type in reporters' stories, line by line. The clunky machine behind the keyboard would then transport little moulds of lead from above, and cast them into a line of metal type (a 'slug') below in one action, using hot melted metal and spewing out clouds of lead fumes.

A skilled operator could cast about six lines a minute. If they made a mistake, they had to keep going and fill up the line. They would usually fill it by running their finger straight down the first lines on the keyboard, which produced the letters 'etaoin shrdlu'. If the subeditor and proofreader both missed this placeholder and it was not picked out, it went through to print, an error in the paper known as a compositor's 'gremlin'. (Searching the National Library's TROVE digitised archive of newspapers for 'etaoin shrdlu' (or the compositor's other favourite placeholder, 'cmfwypis'), yields thousands of gremlins, but given the tens of millions of articles on TROVE,

FIGURE 17.2 *Sydney Morning Herald* compositors preparing the paper on the stone, 1944. This was the first edition with news, rather than advertisements, on the front page.
SOURCE State Library of New South Wales.

the overall picture is one of highly skilled operators making relatively few errors, especially on the capital city dailies.)

Once the galley with type was ready, it was transferred to 'the stone', where the full page was being set by a compositor on a heavy frame (called a 'forme') working to the subeditor's design and layout instructions. (The place where the loose components of the page were assembled was still called 'the stone' after the marble and granite slabs used in monasteries for printing during the Middle Ages, even though stone slabs had disappeared centuries before.) All of the content the compositor was looking at was cast in metal with the face set in reverse for printing, so compositors had to be able to mirror read, and so did the subeditor, who was usually reading upside down as well from the other side of the table.

Because there was a high potential for errors in such a manually intensive process performed at high speed, and then read back-to-front, this led to another stage in the process, the proofreading. Working in pairs, proofreaders would check a practice-run proof and compare it with the original copy. (The proof was the source of the wet paper smell. Being damp improved the paper's absorbency as a giant roller moved across the type.) One reader would read aloud while the other marked any corrections on the proof. The linotype operator would have to set new lines of type to fix the errors, and the compositor would amend the page, and add any engravings of photographs, or display advertising, to complete the page forme.

When the page was ready, a sheet of papier-mâché was placed over the forme and pushed under a press to create a mould with a reverse impression of the page. This matrice or 'mat' was then curved, dried and trimmed before being placed in a casting machine that used it as a mould to cast a heavy, semicircular, metal stereo plate to go on the drum of the printing press. The stereo plates were made of an expensive alloy of lead, tin and antimony. In a space like a hell's kitchen of roaring furnaces, the metal would be melted down again for the next day's edition, but a percentage was lost each time during the process.

The amount of labour and metal involved up to this point was incredible. For printing, machines took over. Once the stereo plate was on the printing press, a web of paper from a long reel was fed through the press between an impression cylinder and the plate cylinder. As the plate was inked by a roller, the imprint of the page was transferred onto the paper when the two cylinders rolled together, making the term 'press' an apt one for describing letterpress printing. This all happened at very high speed on the newspapers' huge rotary presses.

THE PLAN

The *Daily Telegraph* had been the first newspaper in Sydney to install linotype machines in 1894. Directors were so worried about industrial sabotage by compositors who were then typesetting by hand that they installed 12 new linotype machines in a fenced-off area protected by armed guards. But there were no reports of sabotage or strife. It seems the compositors were philosophical about the technological shift, even though

> **TEXTBOX 17.1 The future of printing**
>
> To print from the photocomposition process, a whole page was photographed and a negative of the photograph was used to make the stereo plate for letterpress printing. But photocomposition worked even better when it was paired with web-offset printing.
>
> In offset printing, the printing plate was mounted on a cylinder that was immersed in ink. The ink was taken up by the exposed area before it was transferred to a second rubber cylinder which transferred the text (offset it) onto paper. Because rubber gripped the paper more snugly than a lead plate could, this produced a sharper image, and because offset printing could be operated by unskilled workers, it greatly reduced labour costs.
>
> The newspaper companies used offset printing at their suburban papers and commercial printeries. Many bought one or two offset printers to experiment at their daily newspapers around 1979–80, but rotary letterpress machines would remain the workhorses of the industry throughout the 1970s and 1980s. These machines were old and much modified, but they were robust, reliable and the daily newspapers had invested a fortune in them. The transition to full offset printing would not occur until the mid-1990s when News Limited and Fairfax both made an enormous investment in moving their metropolitan and national papers to offset printing at dedicated production plants. Letterpress then became redundant.
>
> In the interim, newspaper companies worked out a way to combine photocomposition with letterpress printing by using machines that converted pages of 'cold type' into plastic plates. These plastic plates were easier, cleaner and cheaper to produce than the old metal stereo plates. They were also about 40 times lighter, and gave better quality results.

the machines led to about 70 per cent of them losing their jobs.[2] In the 1960s and 1970s, newspaper owners were hoping their employees would be similarly compliant.

By the early 1970s, owners were envisioning a future where journalists would enter their stories onto computers, then called 'visual display terminals' (VDTs). The subeditor would edit that story on their own VDT, add headings and make corrections. The computer would align the story, instantly set it into the right column width, and send it to a typesetting computer which, instead of typesetting it with hot metal and linotype, would use photocomposition (or 'cold type'). In this method, the story would be printed as a photographic image on special photographic printing paper. It would then be cut and pasted (literally) onto a layout form designed by the subeditor, who would carefully check it over before it went off to be printed.

In this whole process, only the journalist and subeditor were involved before the page was ready to be made up. Eventually, the linotype operator, compositor and reader could all be eliminated. This would mean enormous savings in cost and time, but it would take years to get to this point and the newsroom would be the last production area to be tackled. In the early 1960s, newspaper companies were experimenting with some early forms of automation in the composing room but they were more focused on automating elements of production in the less industrially threatening areas of the newspaper office – clerical, administration and newspaper 'finishing'. These were the areas where low-paid, non-unionised women worked in large numbers.

CODE AND PUNCHED PAPER TAPE

The publishing room, where published newspapers were finished off, was the first area to be subject to extensive automation in the 1960s. Over the decades, it had already been downsized. Cutting and folding units added to printing presses reduced the number of workers who used to manually fold newspapers, and intricate systems of conveyer belts saved precious seconds in getting hot-off-the-press newspapers out for delivery.

The jobs targeted in the 1960s were the domain of the workers who grouped, wrapped and tied newspapers into bundles ready for distribution. The newspaper companies bought more efficient stacker machines, wire-tying machines, wrapping equipment and new conveyer systems. Tests on automating aspects of Fairfax's publishing room in 1962 gave such good results that Rupert Henderson, with characteristic exuberance, told the

> **TEXTBOX 17.2** Pneumatic tubes
>
> When editorial matter was produced on hard-copy paper slips, the shout of 'copy' or 'boy' would ring out through newspaper offices across the land. The position of the copy boy (and more commonly after World War II, the copy girl) was created to help manage the immense flow of paper circulating around a newspaper building. But an early form of automation was also introduced to speed up the process.
>
> Another wonder of the industrial age, pneumatic tubes were the instant messaging system of the late 19th century. They looked like pipes and used air pressure and vacuum suction to send copy and proofs between departments much faster than the nimblest messenger could carry them (Figure 17.3). Some newspapers were still using them for internal communication in the 1980s.
>
> Pneumatic tubes were also used in government buildings, hospitals, banks and department stores from the early 1900s. They were not just for internal communication. Under city streets, pneumatic tubes extended like octopus tentacles to connect the General Post Office (GPO) to other buildings, including the stock exchange and newspapers, to give them fast access to telegraph and cable messages received by the telegraph office at the GPO.
>
> In 1929, the Sydney *Sun* was one of the first newspapers to install a pneumatic tube to the GPO. It used to take a panting copy boy five minutes to run a telegram from the GPO to the *Sun*. Now, it arrived in 50 seconds by tube.
>
> The *Argus* became the first Victorian newspaper to be connected to the GPO in Elizabeth Street via pneumatic tube in 1934, and by 1938, five newspaper offices were connected to their local GPO, including the *Advertiser*, *Courier-Mail* and *West Australian*. Around 1944, the *Sydney Morning Herald*, *Daily Telegraph* and *The Age* were connected.[3] Many newspapers learned about the unconditional surrender that signalled the end of World War II through a telegraph message forwarded via pneumatic tube from the GPO.

FIGURE 17.3 A pneumatic tube delivery system used for *Sun* telegrams, Sydney, circa 1929. It is unclear if this image is showing the tubes at Associated Newspapers' building or the GPO.
SOURCE National Library of Australia.

board the savings on staff would be 'spectacular'.[4] Machines replaced 100 jobs in the publishing room by 1963.[5]

Much more gradually and cautiously, Fairfax was also introducing automation to the composing room by using teletype setting (TTS). TTS would prove to be a transitional stage on the path to full computer typesetting.

AAP had been using teletype since the mid-1940s as a much faster way of sending overseas news than Morse code.[6] Radio beams would carry the teletype message directly from an AAP operator in London or New York, as they typed, to the receiver at a newspaper office. Stock exchanges were also using teletype to send financial information directly to newspapers. When the service was extended in the 1950s, AAP and stock exchange news could be received at newspapers by a teletypesetter. This machine received each typed character of the message as a pattern of holes punched across the width of a strip of paper tape.

The big leap of TTS was that, rather than the linotype operator having to re-type all of the incoming stories, the punched paper tape could be fed directly into a reader on the linotype machine. This unit would automatically convert the holes back into words and drive the linotype machine to make its lead slugs. At around 14 lines per minute, it could drive the linotype at twice the rate a manual operator could.[7]

TTS operators could also use a keyboard on the unit to translate typewritten words into holes on paper tape so that corrections and alterations to line spacing were done electronically. This saved subeditors and linotype operators from the time-consuming task of having to manually hyphenate words and justify text so the right-hand margins of the newspaper column would be straight. This stage had always caused a bottleneck in the typesetting process.

TTS machines memorably sounded like machine-gun fire when they were operating. It took about a year to train a skilled TTS operator, and Fairfax was training many around 1959–60. By 1964, Fairfax had a large proportion of its type produced by TTS. Its processes were so advanced the HWT sent a representative to study them.[8] About three years after that visit, the HWT bought one TTS machine made by IBM in 1967, and another in 1968.[9]

Fairfax continued to forge ahead. It had been the trailblazer in adopting new technology for more than 80 years. Its huge volume of classified advertising always gave it the money and motivation to seek out the best equipment and processes. In 1967, Angus McLachlan told the *Sydney Morning Herald* chapel that he intended to proceed with computerised typesetting, although he did not indicate a date. Packer, unwilling to spend money on TTS, and later, photocomposition, proposed teaming up with Fairfax to share the costs involved, but Fairfax executives fobbed him off and proceeded on their own way.[10] By the end of the 1960s, the *Daily Telegraph*'s plant was looking especially antiquated and run down.[11]

The implications of TTS became clearer in 1967 when there was a newspaper strike in Sydney. Managers at the three daily newspaper companies had downgraded around 130 journalists to avoid having to pay them salary increases imposed by a new award.[12] The resulting strike began on 1 August and lasted for 16 days.[13] Although the strike was initiated by journalists, printers joined in to support their colleagues.[14] The 1967 strike lasted longer for Fairfax than those of 1944 and 1955, but the company withstood it much better because it used TTS.

Although thinner than usual, the *Sydney Morning Herald* and *Australian Financial Review* were published each day and did not miss a single edition. The *Sun* missed only one day.[15] Fairfax management estimated that the cost of the strike was only $70 000, and Henderson told the board this was 'a remarkably small price to pay' because the benefits from 'reduced production costs' would continue to grow.[16]

Fairfax, which had downgraded the most journalists, seemed to have made preparations to withstand a long strike. It had been secretly training non-union labour, including women, to use TTS machines.[17] This was against the company's agreement with the Printing and Kindred Industries Union (PKIU). (Another relic from the Middle Ages was that women could never be admitted to a printing chapel or composing room, a tradition that was used to maintain high wages.) Although the strike had been initiated by journalists, it was the printers who received the strongest message from it. Fairfax had shown that it could produce a newspaper without their skilled labour.

Privately, Fairfax executives boasted among themselves that overseas newspapers 'heard about our 1967 performance and sought details of how we did it'.[18] Presumably, these were British newspapers because the American newspaper industry was unlikely to need Australian advice about technology. About 60 of the United States' 1761 daily papers were already using photocomposition in 1963.[19] The transition was not being achieved without industrial protest, though. In New York, there was a 144-day printers' strike in 1962, which killed the *New York Mirror*, and threw thousands out of work. A strike over automation in 1965 saw the *New York Times* and six other newspapers disappear from newsstands for 24 days.

British newspapers were trying to introduce new technology but facing strong resistance from powerful printing unions. Many British papers were suffering crippling financial losses that would lead, in the 1970s, to mass staff sackings and the closure of newspapers.[20] Australian owners warned their workers not to stand in the way of technological progress or risk a similar fate.

COLD TYPE AND COMPUTERS: FAIRFAX'S EXPERIMENT

Fairfax was the first company in Australia to attempt an American-style transformation to computer typesetting. It had started experimenting in 1957 when it purchased an early cold-type machine, an Intertype Fotosetter, that could set about six lines a minute by using light to film a photograph of type characters. In 1969, Fairfax bought an improved Linofilm version that could set 20 lines per minute. The technology was improving rapidly now, and both machines were made obsolete when Fairfax purchased two Photon machines in 1971 that could set 100 lines per minute.[21]

The third generation of photosetting devices were even faster as they were more computer based. But no matter how advanced the machinery, it was the human element that employers were concerned about. To get to a point where the keystrokes made by journalists did not need to be duplicated by a compositor, or printed out and checked, but could directly drive the printing presses, journalists would have to be convinced to give up their trusty typewriters and hard-copy system for something as experimental and ephemeral as a computer.

In 1973, Fairfax's editorial manager, Tom Farrell, visited the *Detroit News*, then the United States' largest circulation afternoon newspaper, and AP in New York. Both had largely replaced typewriters with VDTs over the past two years. In December 1973, after Farrell returned to Sydney, he gave a lecture to Fairfax staff and a demonstration on a Singer 9400 VDT, which was set up for them to try.[22]

Many staff had never used a computer before, and the VDT was considered a remarkable novelty; a machine that combined a typewriter with a television screen. Farrell told staff not to fear they would lose their job, 'For us in this company, human beings come before technology'.[23] But Australian owners were reading tantalising reports of how American newspapers had been able to cut 50 per cent of their workforce after converting from hot metal to cold production.[24] By the mid-1970s, an estimated 85 per cent of North American dailies were being composed in cold type.[25] And computers were not just in American composing rooms, they were in newsrooms as well.

The *Detroit News* had an electronic system of more than 70 VDTs by 1974. The *Baltimore Sun*, the *New York Times* and the New York *Daily News* had transitioned their journalists to using VDTs.[26] During a 20-day printers' strike in New York in May 1974, the *Daily News* switched to full automation, and 35 staff, who were mainly secretaries and executives, published two million copies per day without printers.[27]

Many newspapers in Australia also had photocomposition facilities by then, but they were mainly used for advertising, especially display advertising, not editorial. When David Syme and Co moved into its new Spencer Street building in 1969 (Chapter 18), it had installed two phototypesetting machines alongside *The Age*'s 38 linotype machines.[28] Its Melbourne rival, the HWT, had purchased an American Fototronic 1200 phototypesetter in 1970, then added another two phototypesetters in 1974. The machinery was so evocative of some futuristic fantasy that HWT staff called the area where the machines were housed the 'Magic Garden'. Awe was tinged with contempt at the prospect of humans being replaced by machines.

Fairfax continued to be the main trailblazer in Australia. By April 1975, its *National Times* was being fully photocomposed, and the company was pleased with an advanced Digiset photosetting machine made by the German Siemens company.[29] New technology was increasing productivity and lowering costs even more 'spectacularly' than management had expected.

In December 1975, Fairfax announced an ambitious program of computerised newspaper production for its Broadway plant. The company selected a Dutch software firm Arsycom (an acronym of 'architects of systems using computers') to create its new computer-based cold type system. The system would cost Fairfax $7 million ($28 million in today's money) to implement between 1976 and 1981, nearly double the amount it initially budgeted for.[30]

Progress with phototypesetting moved quickly. By 1976, one-third of the composing room at Broadway was taken up by computers.[31] And by August 1977, cold typesetting was making up 17 per cent of the *Sydney Morning Herald*.[32] Tonnes of hot metal were still being used to produce the company's publications, but the use of photocomposition, which would soon be able to reduce typesetting time by up to 700 per cent, was growing.[33]

As in the United States, this meant job losses and industrial concern were inevitable. Printing was rich with hundreds of years' worth of skill and tradition. Printers served six-year apprenticeships, had their own language for technical terms, and a 'chapel' at every major newspaper (the traditional name for a meeting of compositors, essentially a union). There were also larger, formal printing unions, particularly the PKIU.

Printers traditionally enjoyed a strong industrial bargaining position at newspapers because, without them, production would stop. It was also the nature of the work. Owners needed newspapers to be produced quickly, and they needed the fastest, most skilled and reliable workers to achieve that. A forme, for example, had to be loaded just right. If it was bound too tightly, it could spring out under pressure. Too loose, it might fall apart. Either way, it would spoil the print run and could damage very expensive machinery.

Through a long history of industrial organising, including keeping out junior, non-union and female labour in order to keep wages high, compositors in the 1950s were earning up to double the average wage. Some were in the salary bracket of school principals and company directors.[34]

The Fairfax company was known for its special appreciation of typesetting and printing. The original Fairfax owner, John Fairfax, had been a printer, apprenticed aged 12 in England in 1817. Even as a wealthy newspaper owner, he insisted his sons serve a period learning in the composing room.[35] The company prided itself on having the most modern printing equipment, but also on the level of cooperation between its chapel and management. (As a mark of respect for the printer's trade, a stone rendering of Caxton's head formed the keystone in the doorway of the old *Sydney Morning Herald* building at Hunter Street.) But the gentle working conditions of the old Fairfax building, where tradition was valued and jobs were often handed down from father to son, had been replaced by a new focus on productivity at Broadway.

Fairfax employed hundreds of staff as compositors, linotype operators, 'sluggers' (who lifted out faulty lines of type), stone hands, linotype mechanics and readers. Now, all of their jobs were disappearing. Fairfax predicted 300 to 400 printers would be made redundant, saving the company between $4 and $5 million a year.[36]

Saving money, increasing speed, and reducing industrial vulnerability were all major motivations for technological change, but newspaper companies were also being pushed to change their old ways. American manufacturers stopped making hot-metal machines. Spare parts became scarce and expensive, and there was a shortage of skilled composing staff because would-be apprentices could see that hot-metal work was a dying trade.

Profits from television had protected the Australian newspaper groups from the financial plight of many newspapers in the United Kingdom and United States in the 1960s, but Australian companies still had to address rising costs and lower profitability from their newspapers or risk them dragging down the whole group. Fairfax's financial statements showed the scale of the problem. In 1976, television stations were contributing 42 per cent of the Fairfax group's after-tax profits. The company's five newspapers were contributing only 7 per cent, but were employing 48 per cent of its total staff.[37]

STRIKES AND PICKET LINES

In March and April 1975, there was a 25-day printers' strike at Fairfax over the imposition of cost-saving measures, especially the use of new rosters which cut back on overtime and penalty shifts. Although the strike was financially costly, and kept the *Sun* off newsstands for six issues, the AJA did not join in, and Fairfax management was again able to use TTS and non-union staff to prevent the strike from having a more crippling effect.[38]

Murdoch was watching and proceeding cautiously with new technology. Later, he would become known for aggressively taking on British printing unions in the mid-1980s, but in Australia in the mid-1970s, there were no abrupt mass sackings or manufactured confrontations with unions. And when conflict erupted in Melbourne, Murdoch broke with his fellow proprietors, not the strikers.

In August 1975, around 600 printers at the HWT and David Syme and Co went on strike for 13 days after industrial negotiations broke down over the introduction of TTS and further automation in printing work. The PKIU went on strike on 8 August, and picket lines were set up outside both newspaper buildings about a week later. AJA members did not join the strike, and crossed the picket lines to get to work.

When picketers tried to stop trucks from leaving to deliver newspapers, truck windows were smashed, several picketers were hurt, and seven were arrested outside *The Age*. The violence escalated as a picketer gripping the front of a lorry was driven at speed about 800 metres before he could jump off, and in the worst instance, a HWT truck driven by two executives was reportedly shot at, with rifle shot shattering both side windows.[39]

In order to avoid running the gauntlet of the picket line, the *Herald* was not published on 19 August – the first time the paper had not appeared in its 135-year history.[40] *The Age* and the *Sun News-Pictorial* made it out only after police linked arms and formed a 'human horseshoe' at each building to shield delivery trucks.[41]

The level of bitterness and hostility shocked the newspaper industry. Normally, Melbourne's newspaper world was so sedate it was described as 'bland and rather stuffy'. Both the HWT and David Syme and Co were known for valuing good relations with employees. Just a few years earlier, relations between the HWT's management and its printers had been described as 'almost suffocatingly paternalistic'.[42] The two Melbourne companies were among the last in the industry to retain 'closed shop', all-union printing labour, and this was at the crux of the dispute. Managers had decided to allow some department heads to be exempt from union membership. The PKIU knew this would severely reduce its effectiveness in negotiations over computer typesetting because, in the event of future industrial action, non-union department heads could continue working to produce the newspapers.[43]

The HWT and David Syme and Co tested their automated systems and machines under emergency conditions during the strike. The *Sun News-Pictorial* and the *Herald* were using computer-generated paper tape to feed linotypes, while *The Age* was using cold type, including optical character recognition and photocomposition. At both buildings, the technology worked well, and became faster and more efficient as the strike went on.

Murdoch privately assured the Melbourne proprietors they had his 'whole-hearted support', but then took advantage of the strike to (temporarily) fulfil his ambition to publish a daily paper in Melbourne.[44] With the cooperation of the printing unions, Murdoch revamped the bi-weekly *Truth*, renamed it the *Daily Truth*, and published it as a more family-friendly daily during the strike. Murdoch even offered the PKIU a free half page in the paper to publicise their complaints against their employers. Once the strike ended, *Truth* went back to its usual name, content and publishing schedule.

A year later, the scale of job losses ahead was becoming apparent at Fairfax, and the PKIU pressed for assurances about the redeployment of displaced staff. In September 1976, the company proposed that it would protect permanent PKIU employees' jobs until the end of 1981, including retraining employees affected by new technology. The PKIU counter-proposed a 35-hour week, a $20-a-week pay increase, and no forced retrenchments due to automation. When management refused to accept those terms, the PKIU called a 24-hour strike on 21 October 1976.[45]

The strike was extended, and ended up lasting 60 days, the longest the Fairfax company had experienced. James Fairfax, then deputy chairman, later recalled that Fairfax papers had been regularly publishing editorials chiding governments and industry for giving in to union pressure, 'and now we were being put to the test ourselves'.[46]

The strike involved more than 1400 production and maintenance workers and some strikers picketed the Broadway building. As in Melbourne, delivery of the papers was held up, there were near daily confrontations with delivery drivers, and verbal abuse sometimes escalated into physical violence. Five police officers were injured, and seven picket-line strikers were arrested.[47]

A *Sydney Morning Herald* editorial taunted the striking workers. It said the company was using new technology to produce 32 million newspapers without them, making the strike 'pointless'.[48] To ram home the point, on 1 December, Fairfax printed a 104-page edition of the *Sun*, the largest issue of an afternoon paper ever produced during a strike in Australia.[49] By then, a phototypesetter could set 2400 lines per minute, where it would have taken 400 linotype operators working simultaneously to achieve that speed.[50]

The strike was settled on 20 December after the company agreed to just one claim, that it broaden the definition of a 'temporary' employee. The settlement was an important victory for Fairfax, but ultimately for all of the newspaper proprietors because the PKIU had a long history of opposing arbitration of its claims but now, its position weakened, it agreed to accept arbitration by the Industrial Commission on the use of VDTs. This led to the all-important Cahill decision, which settled an important territorial dispute between the PKIU and several other unions.

In the old hot-metal system, editorial copy had been in the hands of the printers almost as soon as it left the subeditors' hands – and the PKIU wanted to keep it that way. It wanted printers to control entry of all copy directly into the typesetting system. This would mean journalists and clerical workers would have to type out content on a typewriter just so a printing employee could re-type it into the computer system. Fairfax, supported by the AJA and the Federated Clerks Union of Australia, wanted journalists and clerical workers to use VDTs to enter newspaper content directly. The dispute came before Justice Cahill of the NSW Industrial Commission and a decision was handed down in August 1977.

COMPUTERS IN THE NEWSROOM

Cahill ruled that Fairfax journalists and phone-room typists could input copy directly into the typesetting system via a computer without it needing to be re-keyboarded by printing workers. PKIU members would instead be responsible for entering any 'hard copy' material into VDTs, including display and classified advertisements submitted by mail or over the counter, plus any editorial material that arrived by mail, or was typed or handwritten.[51]

As Rod Kirkpatrick noted, 'Overnight, the machine compositors had lost 70 per cent of the work' they were previously responsible for.[52] When the Sydney printers accepted the Cahill decision, they effectively surrendered control over VDT usage, and printers in other states had to as well, or else face a daunting precedent. After the general principles of the Cahill decision were accepted by the main unions, they became the basis for the introduction of cold type around the country.

This paved the way for the introduction of VDTs to the newsroom, and spurred newspapers to invest in computers. In June 1977, 18 months after signing up for the Arsycom system, Fairfax had only 19 VDTs.[53] After the Cahill decision, it ordered 300 more, and the new VDTs were in place by the end of 1978.

In April 1979, News Limited began introducing VDTs connected to phototypesetting machines at its Sydney plant. The system was called Newscom and was rolled out at the *Australian* first, and then the *Sunday Telegraph* (Murdoch had acquired the *Daily Telegraph* and *Sunday Telegraph* in 1972; see Chapter 19).[54] By May 1979, News Limited had 43 VDTs in the reporters' room for the *Australian* and two on the production floor.[55]

News Limited was taking what Fairfax executives privately considered a 'very hard-nosed' approach to the Cahill decision by 'keep[ing] everything possible out of the hands of the PKIU', and News Limited seemed to have the full support of the AJA for that approach.[56] Relations between the PKIU and the AJA were at a low point during this period. Thousands of composing and printing jobs were being eliminated around the country and many printers believed the AJA had 'sold them out over VDTs'.[57] The alternative view was that printers had been holding publishers hostage, and holding back the industry, for too long, through intransigence and unreasonable demands.

The printers were now in a no-win situation. The more they went on strike, the more management advanced the use of technology. When there was a week-long industrial dispute at Fairfax in February 1979, the company's use of cold typesetting rose by 387 per cent.[58] That year was a pivotal one for the rollout of computers, not only at newspapers, but also in government, banking, communications and retail. It was estimated that 20 000 typists' jobs in Sydney alone were made redundant by computers in 1979.[59]

In Melbourne, the HWT was one of many companies boosting its use of computers. In 1979, its new System 5500 arrived. Compared to Fairfax, the HWT had taken its time to choose the best option. A team of three HWT staff had spent 18 months studying the best computer typesetting systems in the United States and Europe in 1976–77. The HWT signed a contract in 1978, two years after Fairfax had contracted Arsycom. The technology had already improved significantly.

The HWT ordered an American-made Mergenthaler Linotype System 5500. The system included three Linotron 606 phototypesetters that generated characters using moving rays of light from a cathode-ray tube, and more than 200 VDTs.[60] Unlike Arsycom, the Mergenthaler company had a long history of working specifically with typesetting and newspapers. The German–American inventor, Ottmar Mergenthaler, had invented the first linotype machine in 1884, and the Mergenthaler company had transitioned into phototypesetting in the 1950s, then into more advanced computerised typesetting.

Eight HWT staff, including programmers, had worked at Mergenthaler's Park Avenue headquarters in New York for nine months to make sure the system met HWT requirements and to learn how to train staff. Back in Melbourne, the HWT building was altered to set up an electronic composing room on the fourth floor. System 5500 was placed there when it arrived in 1979. Initially, it was used for non-daily publications, and after six months was fully producing two magazines, *Aircraft* and *Home Beautiful*, in December 1979. At first, re-trained TTS operators worked with journalists to key in the copy, but this shifted to journalists writing

FIGURE 17.4 The Herald and Weekly Times' Linotron 606 phototypesetter was capable of setting up to 3000 lines of type a minute
SOURCE HWT Ltd, *Annual Report*, 1979 (Newspix).

the copy directly on VDTs. The Cahill decision was one factor that enabled that shift; the other was an industrial agreement signed between the HWT and David Syme with the PKIU on 10 July 1979, after two-and-a-half years of negotiation.[61]

The use of computers was growing fast, but they were still novel and a source of industrial anxiety. From the United States came reports of journalists developing cataracts, headaches, visual fatigue and eye strain from using VDTs. Some studies suggested that anxiety, depression and radiation exposure were also connected with computer use.[62]

Concerns about health and safety prompted another strike in 1980 after the AJA made an ambitious claim for a $50 a week disability allowance for workers who had to operate VDTs (about $226 in today's money). On 12 May 1980, Justice Alley rejected this in favour of a mere $5 allowance. The AJA responded by immediately banning the use of VDTs by its members until a pay deal was reached. At News Limited, where VDT use was advanced, the company sacked 28 subeditors who refused VDT duty. One was also sacked at Fairfax for the same reason.[63] To protest these dismissals, the AJA went on strike on 13 May 1980. Within 48 hours, the strike extended to all metropolitan dailies, even though many were not yet using VDTs. This was the AJA's first national strike and it lasted 31 days.[64]

The main papers affected were the two national daily papers, the *Australian* and the *Australian Financial Review*, which missed publishing editions during the strike. Other publications were published as usual, and – because they were produced by executives, many of whom were former journalists – looked much the same to readers.[65] The strike ended when the AJA agreed to go back to the Arbitration Commission after employers promised to reinstate the sacked subeditors if journalists returned to work on VDTs. The Commission varied the original decision to provide for journalists using VDTs to receive an extra 6 per cent above their base rate.[66]

COMPUTER CRASHES AND GALLEY RATTLES

With journalists back at work, the number of pages produced by VDTs was steadily rising. Although the AJA called the introduction of computers in the newsroom the 'most traumatic and most radical change in journalism in living memory', most journalists adapted quickly and came to appreciate the ability computers gave them to quickly rewrite sentences, move them around, and correct misspellings.[67] Those advantages were only possible when the machines worked, though.

Early computers had plenty of teething problems. When News Limited's Newscom system was introduced, it did not have enough terminals, power or memory. It experienced constant crashes on a daily basis, leading to frequent union stop-work meetings. Warren Beeby was the *Australian*'s production editor and recalled in an interview with Mark Day:

> Boy, they were trying times ... It was a nightmare. The system ... frequently crashed ... We'd ring up and ask, 'How long will it be down?' They'd say, 'About two schooners.' All the staff would rush out the door to the pub, have their two schooners, then come back. I'm afraid some days after seven crashes, they'd all be pissed.[68]

There was a suspicion that some crashes were the result of deliberate industrial sabotage as staff had apparently worked out that the system was so sensitive a crash could be induced just by over-enlarging the font to dramatic sizes such as 144 point.[69] It took about a year to get a better, replacement system, which was introduced to the *Daily Telegraph* and the *Daily Mirror* in 1980.[70]

But Fairfax was having the worst issues and discovering that being an early adopter had its disadvantages. When Fairfax had contracted Arsycom to research all the computers and software available in the world in 1974, Arsycom had reported back that no off-the-shelf computer system could handle a newspaper the size of the *Sydney Morning Herald* with its huge classified advertising section, and only its own custom-built software was up to the task. Arsycom's system was fully operating at Fairfax by 1980, but it was essentially experimental. Aside from two Dutch newspaper companies, no other major newspaper in the world seems to have chosen it.

In September 1981, Arsycom's different systems were reconfigured to do both advertising and editorial work through a single system. Arsycom had worked well enough when it was just handling advertising, but it could not cope with editorial tasks as well. The system crashed regularly and copy was lost. In October 1981, it suffered a serious failure over four days.

Fairfax's VDTs had only 16K of memory. To put that into context, when the first generation Apple iPhone came out in 2007, people were carrying around a device in their pocket that had 8000 times more memory. Journalists could back up their work on a floppy disc but only if they could find one. There was around one floppy disc for every ten VDTs.[71] Nervous journalists resorted to printing out their work after every few paragraphs in case the system went down. There were only a few seconds of warning. Green lights in the ceiling would turn red, an alarm would go off and the system would crash.

By early 1982, around half of Fairfax's 200 journalists were working on VDTs, but constant crashes and breakdowns were leading to enormous stress and long hours to recover lost work.[72] Staff morale was suffering. At the *Sydney Morning Herald*, a frustrated subeditor put his boot through a VDT screen. Arsycom had become a white elephant, and in September 1982 a working group decided the system was beyond redemption. In February 1983, Fairfax announced that it was buying a replacement system from California-based Systems Integrated Inc (SII), one of the two largest suppliers of newspaper systems in the world. SII had successfully installed more than 300 terminals for the *Los Angeles Times* and the *Washington Post*, plus a smaller system for AAP in Australia.[73]

The announcement came just in time. In April 1983, Arsycom 'turned in its worst ever production performance' with 191 crashes in a single month, an average of 92 minutes of lost work time a day.[74] A trial version of the SII system arrived that month, and when it was fully installed in late 1983, it took only a few weeks for it to be working well. Fairfax journalist George Richards led the training team for the SII system and later described it as 'a beauty … [the] Rolls Royce of computer systems … it was so good they kept it on in classified until 2011. It lasted for twenty seven years. For a computer system that's amazing.'[75]

After the switchover, the weekly *Sun-Herald* went to cold type entirely, all content going through the SII system, on 1 January 1984. Six weeks later, on 17 February 1984, the *Financial Review* was the first of Fairfax's Broadway dailies to shift completely to cold type. At the end, a linotype machine was only being used to set the front page of the *Sydney Morning Herald*, until the 27 March 1984 edition, which was the first to be produced in full cold type and direct printing via polymer plates, with no hot metal.

Although Fairfax had started its transition earlier than any other company, newspapers with smaller circulations were able to move faster to cold type. This included provincial and suburban papers, but also the smaller-circulation capital city dailies such as Fairfax's *Canberra Times* and

TABLE 17.1 The transition from hot metal to cold type, 1977–84

The first edition produced using no hot metal	Newspaper
May 1977	*Canberra Times*
June 1977	*Mercury*
1980	*Advertiser*
July 1983	*The Age*
April 1983	*Sun News-Pictorial*
August 1983	*Herald*
February 1984	*Australian Financial Review*
March 1984	*Sydney Morning Herald*

NOTE Definitions of 'hot metal' use in production varied. As far as possible, this table shows the date of the first edition that used no linotype machines and no hot metal typesetting. Usually, the front and back pages, along with the sports sections, were the last to be switched from hot metal to cold type. Specific dates of this transition for papers owned by Mirror Newspapers/News Limited could not be located.

SOURCES Multiple newspaper articles and company annual reports.

the Hobart *Mercury*.[76] For the larger daily newspapers, full conversion to photocomposition occurred in the early 1980s (Table 17.1).

Between 1980 and 1982, David Syme and Co had installed a multi-million dollar computerised typesetting system for *The Age*. It was used for classified advertisements first, but on 19 July 1983 *The Age* was printed entirely, from front to back cover, in cold type. The HWT's Melbourne dailies had also had a smoother transition and beaten Fairfax's *Sydney Morning Herald*.[77]

System 5500 had been producing all of the HWT's magazines and 95 per cent of its weekly papers since 1981, and classified ads were switched progressively into the system that year, too. The big move had come after the editorial area on the third floor of the Flinders Street building was modified for total online operation with VDTs in early 1983. By then, the magic garden had grown to more than 300 computers connected to typesetters. It had cost more than $14 million ($47 million in today's money); including $7 million to buy the system and a further $5 million on building renovations.[78]

On 27 August 1983 at 5.26 pm, the last hot metal pages of the *Herald*

FIGURE 17.5 After three decades of transition, computers in the newsroom at the Herald and Weekly Times' Flinders Street building, 1986
SOURCE Newspix.

were produced in the composing room, a moment marked by a deafening galley rattle. And on 25 January 1984, the HWT produced its last newspapers using lead stereo plates. All of its publications were printed after that using photosensitive plastic plates, a further moment that marked the end of the age of molten metal.[79] The industry's linotype machines were mostly sold for scrap metal, with a few kept as museum pieces.

WHEN THE COMPOSING ROOM FELL SILENT

There were a lot of farewell functions at newspaper offices in the 1970s and early 1980s, as the last practitioners of hundreds of years of printing skill and tradition departed. The sights, sounds and smells of newspaper buildings were forever changed. The hot, gloomy, noisy composing rooms, with their simmering lead cauldrons, were gone. The boiler suits, aprons and dustcoats worn in the grimy world of ink and metal were no longer needed. The composing room was now a well-lit, quiet, clean and air-conditioned space, more like a normal, modern office in the business world.

Many in the industry missed the excitement of the old environment, including the distinctive symphony of linotypes jingling and TTS machines firing. But nobody missed the health and safety issues associated with constantly working around lead and hot metal. Even the linotypes, the machines Thomas Edison had called 'the eighth wonder of the world', contained asbestos and exposed operators and mechanics to serious health risks.

Newsrooms were quieter, too. The sound of typewriters clattering, and pings from carriage returns as they hit the end of each line, were replaced by muted clicks from computer keyboards. The floors of editorial offices were carpeted now, and no longer strewn with crumpled copy paper. The position of copy boy (or girl), which had been an entry-level job for generations of journalists, was largely gone by the 1980s.

Using computers shifted journalists' focus from content to production. Because they were compositors now, too, they spent more time at their desks, which did not fit with Jack Williams' conception of journalism (Chapter 15). There were many who missed the sensory world of newspaper production, including the old fraternity between workers. There was less conversation now that people stared into computer screens all day. But for newspaper proprietors, technology was seen as a godsend that had provided a pathway for printed newspapers to survive the era of electronic media.

CHAPTER 18
A NEW *AGE*

As the new decade dawned in January 1970, Melbourne's newspaper world looked suddenly alive. For the first time in 33 years, a new afternoon daily, *Newsday*, was being sold on the streets. And after 104 years, Melburnians could walk to a milk bar on Sunday and buy a locally produced Sunday paper, the *Sunday Observer*. From Mondays to Saturdays, the *Sun News-Pictorial* was a powerhouse, selling around 640 000 copies a day. And its rival, *The Age*, seemed reborn. It had a new building, a fresh look, and new energy and purpose.

The Age was reviving some of the passion and independence of its peak crusading years in the 1890s under David Syme. The paper was trying to leave behind its more recent past. As Mark Day argued, the industry view in the early 1960s was that *The Age*'s 'management was a Dickensian-era joke ... its content devoid of life. It was a subs' paper: reporters were harangued into writing to a deadly-dull, just-the-facts formula.'[1]

A SLEEPING PAPER

The Age had hibernated throughout the 1940s and 1950s. David's son, Oswald Syme, whose imminent death led the company to form a partnership with Fairfax in 1966 (Chapter 14), had been chairman since 1942 after the deaths of his older brothers. His tenure was a reminder that it was unrealistic to expect an heir would necessarily have the same drive, ability, or even interest, in newspapers that a parent had.

David Syme had been a gold prospector and a road contractor before he became a canny and hardened newspaper proprietor. But his wealth and success meant his youngest son had been raised to live the privileged life of a country gentleman. Oswald had been privately schooled in Hamilton. He was a member of all the right clubs – the Australian Club, the Melbourne Club, the Athenaeum Club and the Victoria Racing Club (VRC). Oswald was a kind man who wanted to be a farmer, not a newspaper proprietor.

His grandson, Ranald Macdonald, recalls a company story about his grandfather's approach. On a Friday soon after 64-year-old Oswald took charge in 1942, *The Age*'s editor, Harold Alfred Maurice (HAM) Campbell, handed him the next day's editorial to approve before the printers began. Syme was heading out the door, going to his sheep property in Macedon. He put the editorial in his pocket and said, 'Thanks, I'll look at it over the weekend', and then he left.[2] It was clear to everyone involved that this meant Oswald Syme was abrogating editorial control to Campbell.

Campbell essentially ran *The Age* from 1939 to his death in 1959, but he also used to delegate authority, in his case, to subeditors. Campbell often left the office before the paper rolled off the presses. Many staff who worked at *The Age* for years never actually met the 'invisible editor'.[3] Campbell could be seen at the Melbourne Club, though, lunching regularly with Melbourne's burghers. His friends included Menzies, and Menzies' Cabinet minister, John McEwen.

Once considered radical and independent, *The Age* had become rigid and dull by 1957, the year Campbell was knighted on the recommendation of the Menzies government. British journalist Martin Walker described *The Age* as having fallen asleep 'in the loyal embrace of the Liberal Party'.[4] And as historian Sybil Nolan said, 'When Menzies described *The Age* as his favourite newspaper, it merely confirmed for some observers that editorial sclerosis had set in.'[5] The paper's old-fashioned design and uncritical, establishment tone had alienated its once core readers among Melbourne's working class. By the end of the 1950s, *The Age* had the lowest home penetration of the top ten newspapers in Sydney and Melbourne.[6] Its circulation was less than a third of its competitor, the *Sun News-Pictorial*.[7] *The Age* had stagnant sales and no clout.

The drift continued under *The Age*'s next editor, Keith Sinclair, whose tenure was described as 'decent but dreary'.[8] Sinclair was another remote editor who, like his predecessor, seemed more interested in society and political hobnobbing than the daily business of putting out the paper. *The Age* feature writer, Roger Aldridge, said Sinclair 'hired me twice but he never spoke to me once'.[9] Sinclair was driven around in a black Humber limousine. The frosty editor allowed only a few staff into his office and insisted they put their jackets on first.[10] Along with the monocled Colonel Neill, *The Age* was an idiosyncratic and stuffy place (Chapter 14).

Sinclair was also close to Menzies, personally and politically. He would ask new *Age* recruits about their politics to try to weed out communists.[11] It went further than that. According to Macdonald, ASIO vetted new reporters when Sinclair was in charge. Sinclair denied this, but it was widely suspected, including at Fairfax, that *The Age* had an association with the security services.[12] And in Canberra, journalists suspected that John Bennetts, *The Age*'s chief political correspondent from 1960 to 1967, was ASIO's 'man' in the federal press gallery.[13]

Bennetts had been in the Army, was politically conservative, and 'had little sympathy for the Vietnam protest movement'.[14] Mike Willesee, who worked with Bennetts in *The Age*'s tiny Canberra bureau, said Bennetts 'never broke a story' but he did spend a great deal of time socialising with members of Cabinet, visiting dignitaries and intelligence contacts.[15] Bennetts and the *Daily Telegraph*'s equally pro-Menzies Alan Reid had a copy-swapping arrangement that meant Bennetts received watered-down versions of Reid's anti-Labor scoops.[16]

Bennetts' reporting was fully in keeping with *The Age*'s reputation for predictable coverage. Sinclair had a list of taboo subjects, and would not allow a staff cartoonist (something even the prim *Sydney Morning Herald* had had since 1944). Sinclair did defy members of the board and Premier Bolte on the issue of capital punishment, though, with *The Age* joining the HWT papers in opposing the executions of Robert Tait and Ronald Ryan.[17]

THE BEGINNING OF THE GOLDEN *AGE*

From the time Ranald Macdonald had become managing director of David Syme and Co in 1964, he had been on a mission to expand the company and revive *The Age* after decades of indifferent, amateurish leadership. One of the obstacles he faced was how financial conservatism and a short-term desire for cash had led to some terrible business decisions,

FIGURE 18.1 Ranald Macdonald, the great-grandson of David Syme, and managing director of David Syme and Co, 1979. Behind him is a statuette of Mercury, the Roman messenger god which symbolised *The Age*'s role in communication.

SOURCE Fairfax Syndication/Nine Publishing.

including selling the company's shareholdings in GTV-9 between 1959 and 1967 (Chapter 11).

Without television, *The Age* had been rendered the 'poor cousin' of the HWT's Melbourne papers.[18] *The Age* had no profits from television, and no strength to promote itself. The HWT cleverly used football as the linchpin for constant cross-promotion between Channel Seven (HSV-7), the *Sun News-Pictorial*, 3DB radio, and the company's regional papers, which made it a 'very strong empire' in Victoria.[19] Meanwhile, *The Age* had to pay for all of its broadcast advertising and sales promotion.

The Age's poor financial prospects had led Syme family members, including Macdonald, to enter the partnership arrangement with Fairfax in December 1966 (Chapter 14). Before signing off on that agreement, Macdonald had already convinced the board, in October 1966, that Sinclair had to go. Menzies had telephoned Colonel Neill and asked that his friend be reinstated. His plea was unsuccessful, but Sinclair did receive an extraordinarily generous compensation package, including three years' pay, a round-the-world trip and a black Humber.[20] A few months after he left the company, Sinclair was given a job working for the Liberal government as a media and public affairs adviser. That was an unusual career move for a former editor and taken as evidence of how close he was to the government.

Macdonald replaced Sinclair with Graham Perkin, previously the assistant editor. When Macdonald had started at *The Age*, he had worked under Perkin and 'learned his paper from the bottom up' by performing junior reporting tasks for three years alongside other reporters.[21] Macdonald had a great deal of faith in Perkin and the new editor set a different tone immediately. Unlike his predecessors, Perkin refused to join the Melbourne Club after he was promoted, lest it compromise his independence.[22]

With the support of Macdonald, Perkin was about to usher in a period marked by independence and progress that would come to be considered the 'golden era' of *The Age*. Perkin gave the paper a vigour it had lacked for decades. He hired talented staff, took on new issues and adopted new policies. *The Age* was given a fresh layout, with an emphasis on graphics and design. Its editorial columns had greater variation and more progressive views. Allan Barnes was sent to replace John Bennetts in Canberra. Perkin also hired a police rounds reporter, Jack Darmody, a former heavyweight boxer with contacts in the police and criminal worlds who 'turned *The Age*'s crime reporting on its head'.[23] Among his many other new appointments was *The Age*'s first cartoonist in 30 years, Les Tanner, who mercilessly lampooned Premier Bolte. Bold use of photographs, taken by skilled photographers, including Ray Blackburn, John Lamb and Bruce Postle, also helped transform *The Age*.

In 1967, Perkin established an Insight team to pursue investigative journalism. He borrowed the idea, and the name, from the British *Sunday Times*' investigative team which had been established in 1963 but expanded under the paper's next editor, Perkin's friend, Harold Evans. The *Sunday Times*' revelations about the thalidomide scandal and the Philby affair inspired Perkins and other editors around the world to devote more resources to investigative journalism.

'Quality' papers in Australia had previously left investigations and exposés to tabloids such as *Truth*, or back in their heyday in the 1920s, to the *Daily Guardian* and *Smith's Weekly*. The tabloid 'muckraking' approach focused on exposing personal scandals and individual examples of injustice, such as quack doctors, abortionists, corrupt police officers, con artists and massage parlour owners.²⁴ *The Age*'s Insight team was evidence of a stirring interest in using investigations to uncover broader political and social injustices.

The Insight team pursued investigations into many different topics, including state care homes, pyramid organisations and crooked Housing Commission land deals. At the same time, *Truth* was still doing its own muckraking. Alongside its usual fare of 'soft porn', it was breaking important stories under Sol Chandler, including Richard L'Estrange's exposure of the scandal of the *Melbourne–Voyager* collision, Evan Whitton's investigation of life on the pension in 1967, and Whitton's 1969 revelations of police extortion from abortion clinics.²⁵

The Age was also being influenced by competition at the other end of the quality spectrum. *The Age*'s management was genuinely worried about the *Australian* as a competitor when Adrian Deamer was editor.²⁶ With its elegant design and its intellectual edge, the *Australian* had shown up smug, old-fashioned papers accustomed to lazily pushing their views.

The *Sydney Morning Herald* had looked rigid and dour by comparison, and editor David Bowman recalled how its staff would begin their daily news conference with 'a sad admission that the *Australian* had found the dimensions in the day's news that everyone else had missed'.²⁷ The *Australian* forced all of its upmarket rivals to lift their standards. *The Age*, the *Sydney Morning Herald* and the *Financial Review* gave their journalists more freedom to interpret, comment and provide opinions. They were also focusing more on design and editing, broadening their news coverage, and taking more interest in foreign affairs.²⁸

At the middle level of the newspaper market, *The Age*'s direct morning rival in Melbourne, the *Sun News-Pictorial*, had no peer in Australia and was a formidable adversary. Per capita, it was probably the highest-selling weekday newspaper in the world. Although better known for its football coverage and photographs of cute animals than its political coverage, the paper nonetheless had a reputation for solid, serious reporting in tabloid style. Ranald Macdonald says the *Sun News-Pictorial* was a 'model tabloid' that was 'Melbourne's voice'.²⁹

The paper had moved beyond a fixation on trees. Harry Gordon had become editor in 1968, and under his direction, the *Sun News-*

Pictorial was demanding action on Victoria's appallingly high death toll from road accidents in late 1970. The paper's 'Declare War on 1034' campaign (the figure for the road toll that year) has been called the most successful newspaper campaign of the 20th century.[30] It encouraged the state government to adopt the world's first compulsory seat belt laws and paved the way for further action to prevent drink driving. A later editor of *The Age*, Michael Gawenda, said the *Sun News-Pictorial* 'under Harry Gordon was one of the world's great tabloids'.[31]

At a local level, new publications that had been made possible by the availability of offset printing were operating in *The Age*'s backyard and prodding it to change its style and its stance. Student and alternative press outlets were being animated by opposition to conscription, the Vietnam War and apartheid, and support for civil rights and the women's movement. In 1971, the free-distribution *Melbourne Times* developed out of the *Carlton News* (which had begun in 1969). An activist community newspaper, the *Melbourne Times* deliberately renounced editorial impartiality and ran campaigns on issues affecting inner-city life.[32] By promoting itself as the independent voice of Melbourne's inner suburbs, the *Melbourne Times* was challenging *The Age* in its heartland.

OUT OF THE MIDDLE

After a decade of commercial television pitching itself towards a working-class audience, upmarket papers were trying to build a dedicated audience at the other end of the spectrum in the late 1960s, but this was especially important for *The Age*. Because the *Sun News-Pictorial* had such a wide audience, *The Age* focused on building up a smaller, more affluent audience that it could charge advertisers a premium rate to reach. One sign that this strategy was working was that, between 1965 and 1971, *The Age* put up its advertising rates by 47 per cent.[33]

Newspapers were moving away from the middle, creating a sharper demarcation between 'quality' broadsheets and 'popular' tabloids. This was also happening in the United Kingdom, where sociologist Jeremy Tunstall argued that, after commercial television arrived in 1955, 'Television influences ... played a large part in destroying the middle-brow, middle-market, sector of the British national press.'[34] In the United States as well, a 'trend towards [more] "serious" papers' at the upper end of the market was occurring in the 1970s.[35]

Because overall newspaper circulation growth had stalled, newspapers could no longer promise to get advertisers extra readers, but they could promise to get them a better type of reader – one with a higher income. To attract this affluent audience, which also tended to be educated and interested in politics and world affairs, the upmarket papers promised journalism that was serious, responsible, comprehensive and analytical. This was expensive journalism to produce.

The *Australian Financial Review*'s base of elite readers from the business and financial sectors had expanded. The export of iron ore from Western Australia, the discovery of oil in the Bass Strait, and nickel in Kalgoorlie, had all been 'good for financial journalism'.[36]

The Age and the *Sydney Morning Herald* had a different business model that relied heavily on classified advertising. They ran on business margins that would be unthinkable in any other industry. In 1971, it cost seven cents to buy a copy of the *Sydney Morning Herald*, but Fairfax had already spent 19.3 cents to produce and distribute it.[37] Classified advertising made that business model possible. The *Australian*, which was also delivering 'quality' journalism, did not have many classified ads, and it was losing enormous sums of money.

Fortunately for *The Age* and the *Sydney Morning Herald*, classified advertising was growing as society was becoming more complex and mobile. There were sharp increases in employment, real estate and used car advertisements.[38] And television could not replicate this type of advertising or steal it away. While the *Sydney Morning Herald* and *The Age* already had a traditional stranglehold on classified advertising in their cities, classified advertising was becoming even more associated with them. As newspapers became more stratified, employers valued the gravitas of the venerable broadsheets even more and did not want to look for staff from among the readers of lightweight tabloids or blatantly downmarket papers.

Between 1961 and 1971, the *Sydney Morning Herald*'s advertising volume grew by an extraordinary 68 per cent.[39] The paper was breaking world records in 1970 and 1971 for the highest number of classified advertising columns.[40] In 1971, only the *New York Times* and the *Los Angeles Times* carried more classified advertisements, but they both published seven days a week while the *Sydney Morning Herald* published for only six.[41] During the 1970s, the *Sydney Morning Herald* and *The Age* were either the top two newspapers in the world for classified advertising, or else they were in the top four.[42] So *The Age* was also doing well, but Sydney had the most growth because it was overtaking Melbourne as Australia's financial and business centre.

With their affluent audiences, *The Age* and the *Sydney Morning Herald* were also carrying more display advertising for expensive cars, whitegoods, furniture, clothing, alcohol and travel. Due to the rise of chain stores and supermarket conglomerates, decisions about how to spend advertising dollars were being made 'by fewer people in fewer places' and, American-style, their decisions were increasingly made on the basis of data.[43] Among the Australian newspapers, *The Age* was at the forefront of researching its audience for advertisers, and to the point that it could tell them information such as '42 per cent of all *Age* readers purchased jeans' in the past year, or 50 per cent of 'big spending, heavy Scotch buyers' were regular *Age* readers.[44]

With so many more classified and display advertisements, the *Sydney Morning Herald* and *The Age* had to make sure they remained balanced between editorial and advertising or else risk turning off readers. So the papers were proportionately fattened with larger sport and lifestyle sections, glossy magazines, television guides, and new features aimed at high-spending suburban consumers, especially women. The 'sectional revolution' imported into Australia from the United States saw newspapers launch new sections called 'Lifestyle', 'Living', 'Style', 'Weekend' and 'Home'.[45]

The *Sydney Morning Herald* and *The Age* were landing on doorsteps with a mighty thud. Back in 1949, they were around 36 to 40 pages. In February 1970, the *Sydney Morning Herald* published its first 128-page issue, which included 980 columns of classified advertising.[46] Fairfax's presses were at their limit, and the company had to buy extra plant so it could print up to 144 pages.[47] Even big American newspapers were not attempting to regularly print that much.[48] (And Fairfax's *Sun-Herald* was even larger. Its 192-page edition in September 1970 was the largest tabloid ever produced in Australia at that time.)[49]

Because the papers were so heavy, people were more reluctant to buy them as a casual sale from a newsagency or newsstand. This meant *The Age* and the *Sydney Morning Herald* needed to attract loyal readers and subscribers who felt their worldview was being represented. They had to pay greater attention to their readers' views and interests.

Larger papers also meant that Fairfax and David Syme and Co had to invest in new technology to keep their production costs down (Chapter 17). Fairfax also spent money on improving the content and appearance of the *Sydney Morning Herald* and the *Financial Review*. As well as this, it launched a new weekly, the *National Times*, in February 1971. Designed to attract readers who wanted a serious, analytical Sunday newspaper, the *National Times* quickly became known for its long, narrative-style 'New Journalism' features, and its investigative journalism.[50]

At David Syme and Co, growing profits were ploughed into revitalising *The Age* and launching a companion paper (described below). It was too late to invest in metropolitan television, but David Syme and Co formed a suburban newspaper company, called Age Suburban, which owned 11 suburban papers by 1973. Many of these were in the west and north of Melbourne.[51] There was also a messy attempt to increase the company's holdings in radio.

In 1969, David Syme and Co bought a 50 per cent interest in Efftee Broadcasters Pty Ltd, the company that operated Melbourne commercial radio station 3XY. (The Liberal Party was the owner of the licence. They leased it, on a long-term basis, to Efftee Broadcasters.) Macdonald gave 3XY's general manager the 'green light' to play contemporary pop and rock (then a novel format for AM radio). Radio 3XY cornered the under-25s market, became 'the most profitable radio station in Australia and reigned at the top of the Melbourne ratings for a decade'.[52]

But David Syme and Co did not seem to factor in the ownership limits of the *Broadcasting and Television Act* (Chapter 15). The company was immediately forced to sell its 25 per cent shareholding in 3AW (Fairfax also owned a stake in 3AW, and because David Syme and Co was majority-owned by Fairfax, buying 3XY had put Fairfax/Syme over the limit of one metropolitan licence in one city.)[53] Then, in 1972–73, the Australian Broadcasting Control Board looked at the transaction again, and made David Syme and Co reduce its 50 per cent stake in 3XY to 15 per cent, interpreting that to be the maximum legally allowed.[54] (To make matters even more painful, in the long term, 3AW would have been the better investment because 3XY became a victim of the introduction of commercial FM radio in 1980 and the station closed in 1991. David Syme and Co had sold its shares in 1986.)[55]

Another sign of investment and expansion at David Syme and Co was visible on the western edge of Melbourne's CBD. The Fairfax partnership helped *The Age* pay for a much needed new building. When the deal was signed, *The Age* was still at its prime Collins Street address, across from the Town Hall, where it had been since 1879. Its building, never a single unit, had been patched up and added to at great cost over more than ten years,

FIGURE 18.2 The old *Age* building in Collins Street on the left in 1957, and on the right as it was when *The Age* moved out in 1969. After a new tower was built, the famous rooftop statue of Mercury was moved to the older building.

SOURCES For the 1957 image, Lyle Fowler. Courtesy State Library of Victoria. For the 1973 image, Wolfgang Sievers. Courtesy National Library of Australia.

including replacing a grand old building with a modern tower (Figure 18.2). But the production areas were still a 'grubby and gloomy old warren' with a notoriously cramped composing room.[56]

The premises were unsuitable for a modern newspaper. The overcrowded printing presses could produce a maximum of 80 pages, so *The Age* was having to refuse advertising. And traffic congestion and parking problems were holding up supplies and distribution because *The Age*'s loading dock could be accessed only by a narrow alleyway, called Manchester Lane, that was off busy Collins Street. Deliveries had to be taken in and out one truck at a time across a busy footpath and through increasing traffic jams. If the company wanted to start an afternoon paper to minimise its costs, which was one goal it had been exploring, it was going to be impossible from that site.

In January 1966, the company had purchased a site on the western edge of Melbourne's CBD at the corner of Spencer Street and what Aldridge called 'the dog end of Lonsdale Street'.[57] It was an unvisited, industrial part of the city fringe. *Age* columnist John Lahey described it as a neighbourhood of 'unloved warehouses and 7am sandwich shops'.[58] Fairfax money helped fund a new five-storey building for this site. Printing was transferred across in January 1968, and other staff moved in after the editorial spaces were finished in May 1969. The project had cost around $13 million ($160 million in today's money), and included a load-bearing roof so a helicopter could land on top of the building (although this never seems to have actually happened).[59]

In 1955, Fairfax's Broadway building in Sydney had raised eyebrows for its functionalist, box-like form, but it was positively ornate compared to *The Age*'s Brutalist brown-brick building (Figure 18.3). Melburnians debated whether it had overtaken Jack Williams' bête noire, the Gas and Fuel Towers, as the ugliest building in the city. But at least *The Age*'s unsightly new home had full air conditioning, modern amenities and ample space for delivery vehicles to get in and out. These were all crucial for producing more newspapers, but especially for afternoon papers which needed to be distributed quickly.

The search was now on for the best way to use the building's capacity. As Packer had known for years, it was now financially unviable to produce

FIGURE 18.3 The ugliest building in Melbourne? The new *Age* building in Spencer Street, 1969.
SOURCE Fairfax Syndication/Nine Publishing.

only a morning paper from a large plant. Since 1964, Macdonald had been keen to start up a Sunday paper as a stepping stone toward the longer term goal of launching an afternoon daily as a competitor to the *Herald*. Starting with a Sunday paper would give David Syme and Co experience in bringing out a tabloid under time pressure, and if it found a weekend audience, its readers could be transitioned into buying an afternoon tabloid during the week. If, on the other hand, the new Sunday paper failed, the losses would not be fatal, whereas those from a failed afternoon paper could be ruinous.[60] Plans progressed in 1967, but one big obstacle remained: Sunday papers were still illegal in Victoria.

MELBOURNE ON THE SABBATH

Sundays in Melbourne were very quiet during the 1960s. Shops were closed. Cinemas were shut during the day. There were no VFL games. It was even illegal to bake bread for sale. (In June 1967, 110 bakeries in Melbourne and

Geelong were raided in a hunt for illegal operators who were supplying fresh bread to milk bars on Sundays.)[61] And unlike every other mainland capital city, there was no Sunday paper.[62] Melburnians were expected to attend church and focus on their souls.

The *Sunday Observance Act* of 1677 was one of many archaic British laws that Victoria inherited. Where other states liberalised such laws, Victoria extended them. The Police Offences Statute 1865 prohibited trading on Sunday. (It also prohibited pigeon shooting on Sunday, and the beating of carpets or flying of kites in a public place on any day of the week if it caused annoyance.)

The prohibition on Sunday trading was presumed to include the publication, distribution and sale of newspapers, but in November 1889, the *Sunday Newspapers Act* was passed to remove any doubt. This was judged necessary because posters had appeared around the streets of inner-city Prahran promoting a forthcoming *Sunday Times*.[63] The would-be publisher was a 'man named [William Henry Leighton] Bailey' who came 'from Sydney and wanted to run a Sunday paper just the same as in Sydney', until he was stopped by god-fearing Victorian MPs, including the temperance leader (and next premier) James Munro.[64]

Another Sydney sinner, John Norton, dared to invade Melbourne in 1902 with his scandalous weekly. *Truth* was published on Sundays in Sydney and Brisbane, but had to be published on Saturday in Melbourne.[65] Norton despaired of what he called 'pumped up Victorian wowserism', which also prevented drinking in hotels on a Sunday. He cried, 'How long, oh Lord, how long?'[66]

Bizarrely, Victoria's laws to protect the Sabbath did not actually stop newspaper workers from working on Sunday, something they routinely did to put together Monday morning editions. To make matters more absurd, Sydney newspaper companies worked out that the Victorian government could not stop interstate papers from being sold in Melbourne because section 92 of the Australian Constitution prohibits the restriction of free trade between states.[67] So, in 1969, although newsagents were shut on Sundays in Melbourne and there was no home delivery or street sales, more than 100 000 interstate Sunday papers were being sold.[68] Melburnians could walk to their local milk bar, and along with their day-old bread, buy a copy of Fairfax's *Sun-Herald*, Murdoch's *Sunday Mirror*, or other Sunday papers that had been imported from Sydney and Adelaide overnight.

During the 1960s, Jack Williams could have lobbied his friend, Premier Henry Bolte, to change the law so Sunday papers could be produced and sold in Victoria, but Williams' religious convictions supported the prohibition on Sunday papers, and so did his financial acumen. The HWT produced a big Saturday afternoon *Herald* that was full of Myer ads, sports news, magazine and feature sections. A Sunday paper would eat into its audience and advertising revenue, as well as that of the HWT's Saturday *Sporting Globe*. Sunday papers were also more expensive to produce and distribute, and their profit margins were lower. If a rival started a Sunday paper, the HWT would have to compete, but it was not keen because it stood to lose money.[69]

The law change went the other way. In April 1966, Bolte's government passed the *Summary Offences Act*, which suddenly killed Macdonald's burgeoning plans for a Sunday paper 'with the stroke of a pen' because it included a clause specifically prohibiting the production of Sunday newspapers in Victoria.[70] Macdonald suspected this happened after '[Jack] Williams met with Bolte over three or four whiskies'.[71] Now, the penalty for publishing on a Sunday was a fine that escalated with each offence. By the third offence, the state could seize and sell all of the newspaper's plant and machinery, a drastic and chilling prospect.[72]

Even so, in December 1966, Macdonald publicly announced that *The Age* was considering starting either a Sunday newspaper or an afternoon daily. Either one would be a direct assault on the HWT, and Macdonald publicly talked up the potential for a 'full scale newspaper war'.[73] His team continued making secret plans for the future Sunday paper, an operation they codenamed 'Project 7'. The team wrote in 1967, 'Our competition is the Saturday *Herald*, which sells 600 000 copies … Our object with a Sunday paper is to dominate in this field. To do this, we must aim for 500 000 copies.'[74] Anything less would not be enough to survive and could put *The Age* at risk.

By 1968, Williams and Macdonald were both worried that Murdoch might enter the Sunday paper field in Melbourne, using his under-utilised Southdown presses at *Truth*'s headquarters in La Trobe Street. Accepting that a local Sunday paper was inevitable, the HWT started preparing to create one. HWT staff visited New York in 1968 to research Sunday papers, where they awkwardly crossed paths with *Age* staff who were there for the same reason.⁷⁵ *The Age* staff visited *Newsday*, an afternoon tabloid serving the Eastern counties in New York. It was known for its unusual status as a 'respectable tabloid', with a liberal stance and Pulitzer prize-winning journalism.

In Sydney, Fairfax executives had concerns about their Melbourne partner's plan for a Sunday paper, but they agreed to back it on the condition that, if the paper did not meet its forecast budget targets, it would be terminated.⁷⁶ Angus McLachlan sounded a warning to Macdonald that even Fairfax's *Sun-Herald*, with its record circulation and very high advertising revenue in Sydney, made relatively low profits because of intense competition. He pointed out that the HWT had 'immense financial resources' and would 'throw everything into the venture' to protect its dominant position in Melbourne.⁷⁷

But the Syme camp was so confident that they were privately assessing that the HWT's 'management is weak and fearful of this [Sunday] venture'.⁷⁸ On 28 December 1968, the front page of *The Age* announced '"*THE AGE*" TO BRING VICTORIA ITS FIRST SUNDAY NEWSPAPER'.⁷⁹ The paper said the Sunday edition was coming in the next six months. By early 1969, Macdonald's team had their Sunday tabloid ready to go.

It was called *Newsday* after the New York paper, but would not imitate its namesake's style. Instead, it was designed as a 'bright, breezy', popular tabloid, with a heavy emphasis on entertainment.⁸⁰ The rationale was that people wanted a Sunday paper suitable for a day of leisure, with content that was not 'heavy or difficult', a 'relaxing sort of paper' that could be read at a slower, weekend pace.⁸¹ The first dummy edition was published in February 1969. Macdonald publicly estimated a potential circulation of 400 000 to 500 000.⁸² At the HWT, a similar process of top-secret dummy runs was underway focused on publishing a *Sunday Sun* based on the *Sun News-Pictorial*.⁸³

With both companies ready to enter the Sunday field, the expectation was that the law would be changed 'as soon as they ask'.⁸⁴ That happened in March 1969 with an amendment to the *Summary Offences Act* 1966. This removed the legal obstacle but another obstacle was proving more difficult.

Macdonald had announced the Sunday paper before he had negotiated with the printing unions. That gave them the upper hand in negotiations, and by July, it was clear that printing workers and their unions would not agree to work on Saturday afternoons and evenings. This was the industry's traditional period of rest in Melbourne, and a time to watch the football. Even triple penalty rates could not tempt them.[85] It was also apparent that many authorised newsagents, controlled by the powerful Victorian Authorised Newsagents Association (over which the HWT had significant influence), were not willing to open up their shops or organise home delivery on their one day off a week.[86]

Macdonald had hired new staff for a Sunday paper that could not go ahead.[87] He went to the board and persuaded them to switch *Newsday* from a Sunday paper to an afternoon daily to compete against the *Herald*. This was possible because, under the company's existing agreement, it could ask workers to work for an afternoon paper but not a Sunday.

NEWSDAY

Newsday was switched from a planned Sunday paper to an afternoon one in the space of six weeks. The *Herald* had a 100-year head start as an afternoon paper. At a time when afternoon papers, weakened by television, were struggling or closing, it was one of the most secure, successful and respected afternoon papers in the world. The *Herald*'s daily sales for the six months to September 1969 were 504 140.[88] It had enjoyed the benefits of monopoly in Melbourne's afternoon field for 33 years. The last competitor to take it on, the *Argus*'s *Evening Star* (1933–36), had failed so badly that it had nearly brought down the *Argus* as well. In fact, the *Argus* had never fully recovered before it closed 21 years later.

None of those factors inspired confidence, but nevertheless the first edition of *Newsday* rolled off the presses on 30 September 1969 at Spencer Street. It was not designed as a counterpart to *The Age*, nor to appeal to *Age* readers who valued the paper's dignity and solidity. *Newsday* was instead a brazen tabloid with big headlines and photographs, aimed at a young audience. It was promoted as being 'with it' and 'modern', and it relied heavily on features and star columnists, including a 'groovy girl' columnist, and Dame Zara, widow of Harold Holt, solving readers' problems.[89]

The first edition's front page contained what former *Age* journalist Ben Hills called a 'nothing story about an upcoming visit by Princess Anne', and 'a scrappy report of a major rail disaster in northern Victoria'.[90] Among its other early stories were one on a pet shop selling carpet snakes, another on girls who lived in flats, and a centre spread on singer Tom Jones lying in bed.[91] It contained surprisingly little news and the back page did not even have sport (an odd omission in sports-mad Melbourne that was rectified within a fortnight).

Newsday was in trouble from the beginning. It sold 360 000 on its first day, but by the end of its first week, was selling only 100 000. That went steadily down to less than 70 000.[92] It was losing money from day one. *Newsday*'s editor Tim Hewat had been brought back to Australia after 20 years on Fleet Street, but was dispatched after only six weeks (probably a record for the sacking of a daily metropolitan editor). By imposing a foreign formula without regard for local preferences, *Newsday* seemed to repeat all of the mistakes of the *Argus* under its British owners. It looked like a poor imitation of a Fleet Street 'red-top', and that was what Hewat wanted. He told staff he wanted *Newsday* to be a 'shit paper, so low that the *Herald* couldn't fight us on its terms'.[93]

Perkin thought *Newsday* 'outraged readers' because it displayed a 'total unfamiliarity with Melbourne's character, standards and interests'.[94] He was given the task of trying to rescue it. More news was injected, and in what the *Bulletin* called 'a strange display of [a newspaper company] exposing its underpants in public', a double-page mea culpa advertisement in *The Age* admitted mistakes and implored readers to give the paper another chance.[95] A further change in direction took the paper toward something more like Murdoch's *Daily Mirror*, but it was all too late.

Because *Newsday* was never accepted by the Melbourne public, advertisers deserted it. The doomed paper was closed in May 1970 and the Syme board had to use $3 million to write off its losses.[96] In its seven-month publication life, *Newsday* had hardly made a dent in the *Herald*'s circulation. The *Herald* lost 50 000 readers when *Newsday* started, but it won them back within a couple of months and without making any major changes. By the time *Newsday* folded, the *Herald* was selling more copies than when *Newsday* had begun.[97] Safely restored to its monopoly position, the *Herald* raised its advertising rates.[98]

THE POLITICS OF PRESSURE

The HWT and David Syme and Co had both dropped their plans for a Sunday paper, but the law had been changed to allow Sunday publication, and Victoria's first legal Sunday paper appeared in June 1969. Published by the owner of the Greek newspaper *The Torch*, the *Sunday Post* lasted only seven turbulent weeks. In that brief time, it was sued twice: once by suppliers for not paying its bills, and once for libel by Bob Hawke, then an industrial advocate for the ACTU.[99]

Another Sunday paper appeared in September 1969. The *Sunday Observer* was established by Sydney transport company millionaire and anti-Vietnam activist, Gordon Barton. Journalist Valerie Lawson called him Australia's 'Great Gatsby'.[100] Barton was an unusually idealistic businessman and the founder of the Australia Party (a precursor to the Democrats). His *Sunday Observer* deliberately set itself apart from the mainstream newspapers, nearly all of which were still very supportive of Australia's involvement in Vietnam.

In December 1969, the *Sunday Observer* became the first newspaper in the world to publish shocking photographs of the US-led My Lai massacre of Vietnamese civilians. On 25 January 1970, the *Sunday Observer* published an advertisement from the Committee in Defiance of the *National Service Act*. (This was the Act that mandated that 20-year-old men, selected by a ballot of birthdays, be conscripted to serve in the Army for two years.) The advertisement included a photograph of two dead Viet Cong fighters. All Sydney daily newspapers had refused to publish it.[101]

Deep divisions had formed in Australia over the Vietnam War, with the strongest divide often between the business community, which tended to be highly pro-Vietnam, and young people (and their parents) who were part of the terrible lottery of the call-up for conscription.

The *Australian* had been paying serious, and critical, attention to the Vietnam War for years, but its own editorial position had been inconsistent. First, it was opposed to Australia's involvement in Vietnam in 1965. Then, it was supportive in 1966.[102] But in December 1969, the *Australian* had demanded the withdrawal of Australia's troops from Vietnam, becoming the first daily paper to 'speak for' the half of the country that was opposed to the military presence in Vietnam.[103]

The previous month, during the October 1969 election, *The Age*'s position had been very similar to that of other metropolitan dailies. It said it could not advocate a vote for Labor because the party's plan to abolish national service and pull Australian troops out of Vietnam by mid-1970 was 'short sighted and destructive'.[104] But *The Age* had focused a lot of positive attention on Labor's domestic policies.

The Age had supported Labor's health policies, its plan to abolish university fees and set up a schools commission, its promise to lift the pension, and its policies for housing and urban infrastructure and renewal. By directing readers' attention to those policies, *The Age* had helped promote Labor as a serious contender. Party insiders felt the paper helped achieve a big swing toward Labor in Victoria in 1969.[105] *The Age* had argued that Whitlam was the most impressive Labor leader since Chifley. It was not uncritical, though. It also called Whitlam a 'political prima donna with some extraordinary temperamental excesses'.[106]

As *The Age* was building a more affluent, educated audience, its political views were shifting, although more slowly and gradually than some might presume of the Perkin years. Melbourne was becoming the centre of protest against the Vietnam War. The Victorian federal Labor MP, Dr Jim Cairns, was the most prominent leader of the Vietnam Moratorium demonstrations of 1970 and 1971, which saw hundreds of thousands of Australians take to the streets to protest the war nationally, but with the largest attendance in Melbourne.

The *Australian* gave prominent coverage to the anti-war Moratoriums, which gained it readers and support from younger university-educated people.[107] Murdoch did not particularly like the *Australian*'s positive coverage of the Moratoriums, but he did not interfere.[108] And his Sydney *Daily Mirror* also supported the Moratoriums. Its front-page headline on 8 May 1970 was 'STOP THE WAR!'[109]

That was the day of the first national Moratorium demonstration in Australia. In the lead-up to that day, other major newspapers had been hostile. Conservative newspapers viewed the Moratorium as almost a form of terrorism, something outside the boundaries of democratic politics.

On 26 March, the Melbourne *Herald* said Cairns was on a 'perilous path' and had 'issued yesterday a strange and disturbing call to workers and students to "occupy the streets of Melbourne" on May 8'.[110] *The Age* also disapproved. On 30 March, an *Age* editorial said the planned Moratorium was 'irresponsible, potentially dangerous and ultimately futile'.[111] *The Age* said Cairns and his supporters 'have no right at all to stop the rest of the community going about its business' by obstructing city streets and 'inconvenienc[ing]' Victorians.[112]

Two days before the Moratorium, *The Age* asked if it was 'A matter of conscience or anarchy?'[113] And on the day of the Moratorium, *The Age*'s editorial was deeply ambivalent about the event, saying it was likely to lead to violence and 'is being conducted in the name of humanity. Whether it will advance that cause or not is, in any circumstances, arguable.'[114]

But the Moratorium on 8 May 1970 provided a massive display of public opposition to the Vietnam War. Nationally, up to 200 000 protesters were involved, including up to 100 000 in Melbourne.[115] The next day, *The Age* had changed its tune. It said the march was 'massive, colourful [and] peaceful … flooded central Melbourne in autumn sunshine like a tidal wave', and included 'Students … wharfies; middle-aged men in business suits; mini-skirted girls; workers in construction helmets'.[116]

A SUNDAY SPOILER

Before continuing with the events of 1971 in the next chapter, the fate of Melbourne's historic Sunday papers deserves a postscript. Barton ran the *Sunday Observer* for 18 months, but authorised newsagents (allied with the major newspaper groups) refused to open on Sundays or to organise home delivery for the paper, which crippled its prospects.

Barton's company used milk bars for sales instead and recruited its own network of newsboys and newsgirls. It also tried to split its losses by starting up a national Sunday paper, *Sunday Review*, in October 1970, to share the costs. But when Barton's losses hit $1.5 million, he pulled the pin on the *Sunday Observer* in March 1971.[117] Melbourne was left without a local Sunday paper again, although not for long.

Two weeks later, Max Newton picked up where Barton left off. Using the paper's presses and many of its staff, Newton started publishing the *Melbourne Observer* on Sundays. It was a very different paper to Barton's left-leaning, anti-war, anti-apartheid paper. Newton's version was a populist, right-wing 'red-top' paper that advertised brothels. Even Newton described it as a 'vulgar paper of entertainment'.[118] It had no real competition in that market because the similarly lecherous *Truth* was published on Saturdays.

The *Melbourne Observer* was rebranded in August 1973. It took up the old name, but still not the content or style, of the *Sunday Observer*. Its circulation was now 120 000. This, and a lingering fear that Murdoch would enter the Sunday market, motivated the HWT and Syme/Fairfax to join forces and reluctantly create a Sunday paper. A joint ownership agreement was signed in August 1973. It set strict limits that the jointly produced *Melbourne Sunday Press* (soon just the *Sunday Press*) could be a maximum of 48 pages with a maximum of 35 per cent advertising. And the partners hoped to sell only about 50 000 copies.[119]

Steve Foley, who was a Sunday paper editor in Victoria in the 1990s, characterised the *Sunday Press* as 'a low-budget "spoiler" intended to protect the more lucrative Saturday *Herald* and Saturday *Age* against hostile invaders (chiefly Murdoch)', but also each other.[120] The agreement prevented either group from publishing any other Sunday newspaper in Melbourne.

Because the venture was principally about stopping competitors from entering the market, the aims and budget of the *Sunday Press* were modest when it began in September 1973. Its chief-of-staff later described it as 'an uneasy little paper' where 'most of the staff seemed to be trying to get a job elsewhere'.[121] The *Sunday Press* was promoted little in its parent newspapers and its cover price was expensive (double the price of the *Sun-Herald* in Sydney). But Newton's *Sunday Observer* was priced even higher. At 45 cents, it was 15 cents more expensive than the *Sunday Press*, but Newton thought he was onto a winning formula. He said, 'Tits, trots, TAB and TV – that's what the mob wants'.[122] His *Sunday Observer* hit a peak circulation of 200 000 in 1974, but then started to decline.

Newton recognised that selling a paper 'which contained no news for 45 cents' up against the HWT and David Syme and Co, 'was too good to last'.[123] He was struggling with addiction at this time. Journalist John Sorrel, who considered Newton a 'wayward genius', found him one day on the office's kitchen floor, drunk and reciting 16th century poetry.[124] The paper was bankrupting Newton, and in 1977, he was sacked from his own companies by a receiver.

Suburban newspaper publisher Peter Isaacson purchased the *Sunday Observer* and ran it as a more financially responsible, commercially-oriented newspaper. But Sunday papers never took off in Melbourne in the way they did in other states. This was partly due to the lack of a Sunday paper tradition, partly by design on the part of established papers who wanted to protect their Saturday editions, and partly because newsagents did not open on Sunday.

By 1974, Sydney had three Sunday papers with a combined circulation of 1.8 million, but Melbourne's two small Sunday papers had a total circulation of only 250 000.[125] Nearly 14 years after the *Sunday Press* started, the Sunday newspaper market in Melbourne in 1987 was only a fifth the size of Sydney's, and a third of Brisbane's. It was smaller even than in Perth and Adelaide.[126] Presumably, Norton would have seen this as the long tail of Victorian wowserism.

CHAPTER 19
FRANK PLAYS POLITICS

Billy McMahon had missed out on the Liberal leadership to Gorton in 1968, but Frank Packer had not given up hope that his good friend would become prime minister. Packer and McMahon had attended the same school on Sydney's North Shore, and when Packer and EG Theodore started Sydney Newspapers Ltd in 1932, a 24-year-old McMahon had signed the paperwork.[1] McMahon was then working as an articled law clerk for the oldest law firm in Australia. Called Allen, Allen & Hemsley, it was a firm that Packer ended up keeping on retainer almost permanently, and McMahon was a partner there from 1939 to 1941.

McMahon did more than sign the paperwork for Sydney Newspapers, though; he also took up shares in it. His biographer, Patrick Mullins, said it was 'among the best investments that McMahon ever made'.[2] In the 1970s, Sydney Newspapers was one of a handful of companies the Packers used to keep tight control of Consolidated Press.[3]

Packer and his shareholder/lawyer had been brought closer together by their mutual doctor, George Halliday. An ear, nose and throat surgeon, Halliday fixed McMahon's hearing and also tended to Packer's ailments. According to David McNicoll, Halliday was convinced McMahon 'was one of the greatest men in Australia', and the doctor 'steered Packer to a political fixation about McMahon'.[4]

McMahon was an unlikely contender for such admiration. He was short, bald, and mercilessly lampooned by cartoonists for his large ears. He was also disliked and distrusted by many of his colleagues. But Packer's trusted political correspondent Alan Reid had also talked up McMahon's abilities and prospects to Packer.

Ever since the 'faceless men' episode in 1963, Packer had relied on Reid's judgement and his considerable journalistic talents. Reid set the tone for the *Daily Telegraph*, and his articles, columns and television appearances on Channel Nine were influential. Reid's press gallery colleague, Mungo MacCallum, said Reid's specialty was to take an example of minor internal party dissent within the Labor Party and 'blow it up' into 'something enormous', while he ignored, or minimised, more serious internal dissent in the Liberal Party.[5] MacCallum quipped the *Daily Telegraph*'s subeditors had a set of standing headlines kept at the ready for Reid's articles, including 'REBUFF TO WHITLAM', 'NEW ALP SPLIT LOOMS' and 'SETBACK FOR LABOR'.[6]

Since the mid-1950s, Reid's reports had contributed to a view of Labor as sinister and faction ridden. Journalist Laurie Oakes argued, 'There is no doubt [Reid] was a significant factor in keeping [Labor] in the wilderness for 23 years.'[7] (Even Reid acknowledged, years later, that it was democratically 'unhealthy' that his critical scrutiny of Labor was not balanced out by anyone performing equivalent scrutiny of the Coalition during that period. He did not address why he thought he could not possibly do both himself.)[8]

In Canberra, Reid was regarded as the embodiment of Packer, and an emissary and lobbyist for his boss. Reid was part of a select group that Packer liked, trusted, and paid handsomely. Long-serving Labor politician Clyde Cameron said the Packers had genuine affection for Reid and considered him a 'colleague' rather than an employee. According to Cameron, 'Reid influenced [the Packers] more often than they influenced him.'[9]

Probably no other journalist had such a close relationship with their proprietor. Just how close became a little clearer after Frank Packer died in 1974. It came to light that Cairnton Pty Ltd (named after the Packer residence), was one of two companies at the centre of a complicated web of interlocking family companies that safeguarded the Packer family empire. There were five directors of Cairnton Pty Ltd: Frank Packer, his sons, Clyde and Kerry, and Alan Reid and his wife Joan.[10] For Packer, who was very wary of outsiders, this hints at an extraordinary level of trust. It also suggests Reid had a vested interest in helping Packer's companies. When he was lobbying for Packer's interests, he was also furthering his own.

Reid's value, both as a reporter and a lobbyist, derived from his access to politicians. He would famously wait in King's Hall at Parliament House for hours each day at the same spot, leaning on a glass exhibition cabinet, where he had a view of people coming in and out of the building. Passing politicians would stop and give Reid information. They often received more information from him in return than they had given out. And they also received his canny advice and legendary discretion. Many of Reid's best contacts were still from within Labor, despite the damage he had inflicted upon the party, but Whitlam was not one of them. The Labor leader reportedly had no direct contact with Reid between 1966 and 1971.[11] Not surprisingly, denied the access that was his stock-in-trade, Reid disliked Whitlam. But he liked McMahon, who was an extraordinary source of top-level, secret information for Reid. The two were so friendly that Billy and his wife, Sonia, were the guests of honour at the wedding of Alan Reid's daughter in December 1971.[12]

THE GREATEST MAN IN AUSTRALIA

McMahon had married late in life, when he was aged 57. During his bachelor years, he had been a regular visitor to Packer's residence, Cairnton, in Bellevue Hill, around the corner from McMahon's home. Later, Packer enjoyed showing off Treasurer McMahon at dinner parties to impress his VIP guests.[13] Like Halliday, Packer became convinced that McMahon was going to be a big success. But Packer's judgement was declining, along with his health. Clyde Packer said of Frank's later years, 'My father was a drunk. Nothing he said after 9 pm could be taken seriously.'[14]

Despite ill health, Packer was still working long hours. He badgered his television executives after 9 pm with ludicrously out-of-touch suggestions, and continued to insist that he personally vet all political stories of significance in the *Telegraph*s (although he sometimes delegated this task to McNicoll).[15] Journalist Ian Moffitt said in 1971 that only a *Daily Telegraph* journalist 'with a death wish disregards what he wants', and the best his journalists could manage in terms of independence was to slip 'opposing opinions into stories' in 'disguised ways'.[16]

Although Packer had given Menzies unquestioning support for 16 years, he had been unleashed by Menzies' retirement in 1966 because Menzies had been in firm control of the Liberal Party, and had tended to keep Packer at a certain regal distance. With Menzies gone, the Liberal

Party was more fluid, and Packer had the prospect of exerting more influence, including the tantalising possibility of having a close friend (and shareholder) in the prime minister's office.

One sign that Packer felt unleashed was the way he had ignored Menzies during the Liberal Party leadership contest that followed Harold Holt's death in December 1967. Menzies had wanted Packer and McNicoll to support Paul Hasluck.[17] Once Packer had accepted that McMahon was not a viable contender, he had backed Gorton (Chapter 16). McNicoll had then treated Gorton as an 'honoured friend' until mid-1969.[18] After that, McNicoll started to run hot and cold on the prime minister.[19]

After the Liberal Party's poor showing in the 1969 election, relations between Gorton and Consolidated Press had deteriorated. Two weeks after polling day, Packer and Reid had encouraged McMahon to challenge for the Liberal Party leadership.[20] The *Daily Telegraph* backed McMahon strongly, and so did the *Sydney Morning Herald* (it did not like Gorton's centralist approach on states' rights). But Gorton hung on to the leadership with a thin majority after a partyroom vote. He then dropped McMahon from the Treasury, demoting him to minister for external affairs.

Outraged at this demotion, Packer's *Daily Telegraph* and the *Bulletin* had begun making more obvious attempts to destabilise Gorton's leadership. (Packer had acquired the *Bulletin* in 1960 and turned the once radical journal into 'a middle-of-the-road, not to say right-wing, news magazine'.)[21] Alan Reid was an enthusiastic political assassin. He disliked Gorton and was determined to drive him out. Gorton had not only demoted McMahon, but had also committed the unpardonable sin of refusing to 'take advice' from Packer and McNicoll, and presumably from Reid as well. Worse still, Gorton had boasted to others that he told Packer 'where to get off.'[22]

Gorton had alienated his more conservative Liberal colleagues, too, with his independent manner. He was sometimes impulsive, and did not always consult. Some of his key policy positions went against traditional Liberal values, and Gorton's work ethic was not always strong. He was sometimes embarrassingly ill-prepared.[23] Questions about his personal conduct also remained. Journalist Richard Walsh said Packer and David McNicoll had 'previously helped cover up the amazing Liza Minnelli affair [in 1968] but now no more'.[24]

FIGURE 19.1 Packer's man, William (Billy) McMahon, on the left, deposed Murdoch's man, John Gorton, on the right, in 1971. They are shown here outside (old) Parliament House in 1969. Gorton was Murdoch's first prime minister but Murdoch had abandoned him by 1971.

SOURCE National Archives of Australia.

Reid helped plan a strategy to bring down Gorton.[25] It would make use of the resources of the Packer group, including the *Daily Telegraph*, *Sunday Telegraph*, *Bulletin* magazine, Channel Nine television stations, and even a subsidiary book-publishing company. The pretext came in February 1971 when a series of stories began appearing in newspapers and on the ABC about tensions between Defence Minister Malcolm Fraser and the army authorities. (It seems McMahon was probably involved in leaking exaggerated accounts of these tensions, including to the *Daily Telegraph*).[26]

Fraser, another known leaker of information to Consolidated Press, gave his side of the story to *Bulletin* journalist Peter Samuel. Fraser claimed that an act of army insubordination designed to sabotage Australia's civil aid program in Vietnam was at the centre of the tensions. Reid then encouraged the head of the *Daily Telegraph*'s Canberra bureau,

Robert Baudino, to check Fraser's claims directly with Gorton. When Baudino did, the prime minister effectively sided with the chief of the general staff of the army, and did not defend his minister. The *Daily Telegraph*'s report emphasised Gorton's disloyalty to Fraser, and the *Bulletin* ran a piece the next day supporting Fraser's claims and putting pressure on Gorton.[27]

Encouraged by Reid, Packer decided on 4 March to publicly call for Gorton to go. On 7 March, Reid's story, 'RESIGN CALL TO FRASER', was on the front page of the *Sunday Telegraph*. It quoted unnamed Liberal MPs as saying they hoped Fraser would resign in order to bring on a leadership challenge to Gorton (the same outcome that Packer, Reid and McNicoll wanted). Inside the paper, an editorial written by McNicoll said it was 'time for a change of leader'.[28]

That night on *Meet the Press* on Channel Nine, Clyde Packer's recollection was that the episode was deliberately geared towards 'get[ting] McMahon in office'.[29] McNicoll hosted the program and his guests were all from Consolidated Press, including Reid. Ratcheting up the pressure on Fraser, Reid goaded that unless the minister for defence took a stand and resigned in response to Gorton's disloyalty, Fraser would be a 'puppet' and a diminished figure.[30] It was a very public, prime-time warning that, unless Fraser acted, he would no longer have the support of Consolidated Press, which would be a severe blow to his future leadership ambitions.

The next day, 8 March 1971, Fraser resigned from Cabinet. Reid took pleasure in believing that his statements on *Meet the Press* had been the catalyst.[31] Gorton believed similarly. He thought *Meet the Press* had done 'everything possible ... to play on Fraser's vanity and conceit'.[32]

On 9 March, Fraser gave a remarkable statement to the House of Representatives in which he said Gorton was 'not fit to hold the great office of prime minister'. Where other papers' headlines on 10 March made clear that this line was a quote from Fraser, the *Daily Telegraph*'s headline simply said, 'GORTON: NOT FIT TO HOLD OFFICE', as if it was a statement of fact.[33] While *The Age* and the *Sydney Morning Herald* were more factual in their news columns, their editorials also said Gorton should go.

The Age had already published an editorial the previous day that was an early call that the Liberal Party 'must have a new leader and the nation must have a new Prime Minister ... untarnished by the stink of personal enmity, disloyalty and self-seeking disregard for the national good'.³⁴ Now, on 10 March, *The Age*'s editorial said, 'We agree with Mr Fraser's damning assessment of the Prime Minister: he should not hold his great office.'³⁵ The *Sydney Morning Herald*'s editorial that day was headed 'CRISIS PRONE'. It said Gorton was an electoral liability who had shown 'all too clearly that he cannot manage a team or hold it together'.³⁶

From London, Murdoch had also abandoned Gorton. The *Australian*'s editorial was headlined 'GORTON MUST GO'.³⁷ One of its reporters, Alan Ramsey, had been writing critical accounts of the prime minister's actions, including one based on a conversation he had with Gorton. While Gorton was telling Parliament his recollection of that conversation, Ramsey had yelled out dramatically from the press gallery above, 'You liar!'³⁸

On the same day that so many editorials called for Gorton to be replaced, 10 March, the parliamentary Liberal Party met in Canberra. One of Gorton's detractors read one of the two damning *Age* editorials to the party meeting.³⁹ After patiently hearing out his critics, Gorton called for a vote of confidence in his leadership. The vote was tied 33 to 33, and Gorton resigned. McMahon defeated Billy Snedden for the leadership, and was soon sworn in as prime minister. To the surprise of his colleagues, Gorton stood for deputy leader and won it. This meant the party was still not unified. Most of McMahon's colleagues did not trust him, and he had an aggrieved deputy sitting at his shoulder who wanted him gone.

During a period of further tension in August 1971, as Gorton and his supporters hoped he could be rehabilitated back into the leadership, Alan Reid's book, *The Gorton Experiment*, was rushed into print by a Consolidated Press subsidiary, Shakespeare Head Press. The book reviewed Gorton's tenure as prime minister and cast him in a very poor light. It was widely viewed as a way to keep Gorton from challenging McMahon by reminding everyone of Gorton's faults so he could not stage a comeback. Murdoch's *Sunday Australian* invited Gorton to respond to the book in a series of paid articles. In the first piece, Gorton defended his tenure in office and described Reid as Packer's 'hatchet man'.⁴⁰

In an interview on the ABC's *PM* program on 9 August, Packer denied he was behind Reid's book and claimed, implausibly, that he hardly ever spoke to Reid. Packer did venture his opinion, though, saying that

'McMahon ought to get rid of Gorton out of the Cabinet'. He accused Gorton of breaking Cabinet confidentiality in the *Sunday Australian* piece, and said Gorton was 'a great embarrassment' who should retire from the post of deputy leader.[41] Within a week, McMahon had asked for, and received, Gorton's resignation from Cabinet.

The perception that Packer, Reid and Consolidated Press had 'set the scene' for Gorton's demise had taken hold in political and journalistic circles.[42] Rohan Rivett said a 'campaign of informed cleverness, brilliantly written, timed and executed has been mounted against Gorton' by the Packer group.[43] Labor's Kim Beazley Sr. told the House of Representatives that the 'Press king makers' had brought Gorton down because he 'refused to be a Packer Prime Minister'. Beazley said Packer now had a 'very good chance of owning [McMahon's] government'.[44] But it turned out to be one that was not worth owning.

THE WORST PRIME MINISTER

McNicoll helped McMahon become prime minister but later said that McMahon was 'hopeless', 'had a horrible nature', and only 'a bit of a brain'.[45] He was not the only one to criticise McMahon. Few Australian politicians have been so widely derided. In a survey of political scientists and political historians in 2010, McMahon was ranked the worst prime minister in Australia's history. When the survey was held again in 2020, it yielded the same result.[46]

The best that anyone seems to have said about McMahon was that he was shrewd, tenacious, hardworking and pragmatic. More commonly, it was said that he was vain, selfish and a pathological liar. He sounds uncannily like an earlier, Australian version of US President Donald Trump. Like Trump, McMahon seemed to have ambition unmatched by ability, and a level of insecurity and indecision that led him to spend inordinate amounts of time on the telephone seeking advice and counsel. McMahon was also reportedly so unethical, and so willing to use any means to advance his own interests, that he would cheat during friendly games of squash, just as Trump did at golf.[47]

Even though McMahon was a useful leaker of information, he was not well liked among journalists (Reid aside). This was partly because they regarded him as a 'fantasist', but also because McMahon was known for going above journalists' heads to complain, and for ringing up their editors and trying to influence coverage.[48] Over 40 years later, Laurie Oakes said:

> Billy McMahon was an extraordinary bloke. He was devious, nasty, dishonest. He once asked to borrow a tape recorder from the radio station I worked for. When we went to collect it later, he claimed it was his. I had to point to where it said 'Property of radio station 2SM' engraved on it. The fact that he was prime minister of this country was a disgrace.[49]

David Bowman, who later worked closely with McMahon to ghostwrite his potential autobiography, thought McMahon was 'a third-rate politician and that he could be PM is a damning indictment of the country. He is really a rather nasty bit of work … what an unpleasant little turd.'[50] Alan Ramsey thought McMahon 'was a devious, conniving, mendacious little man'.[51] McMahon's lack of integrity was notorious. Laurie Oakes said, 'When he was prime minister, [McMahon] rang me to tell me what happened in Cabinet – and the next minute, he reprimanded his Cabinet for leaking!'[52]

Packer had ignored Menzies' warnings. Menzies thought McMahon was a disloyal 'worm', 'a contemptible little squirt' and a 'dreadful little man'.[53] He despised how McMahon would 'sneak' down to the *Daily Telegraph* and *Sydney Morning Herald* staff and give them a 'ball [by] ball' description of Cabinet conversations.[54] In one account, after McMahon left a Cabinet meeting early, 'Menzies looked at the clock, sighed and said "oh dear, just in time for the final edition!"'.[55]

When the private papers of Menzies' preferred leadership candidate, Paul Hasluck, were opened by the National Archives of Australia in 2005, they contained Hasluck's written notes. He had described McMahon as 'a professional dealer in lies, a seller of government secrets in return for favours, one who had been disloyal to each prime minister with whom he had served, and an intensely ambitious man'. In another note, Hasluck had written in 1968 that McMahon was 'devious, dishonest, untrustworthy, petty, cowardly [and] a contemptible creature'.[56] Gorton's assessment was similar. He said McMahon was a 'lying little bastard' who had thwarted party policies, lied to state premiers and otherwise sought to sabotage the party to advance his own selfish interests.[57]

Once installed as prime minister, it quickly became obvious, even to Packer, that McMahon was out of his depth. He was unpopular and a poor communicator. McMahon dithered and was unable to deal with the problems of inflation, unemployment and currency crises. His government had painfully few achievements to its name. Gorton summed up the situation by saying that 'Packer thought [McMahon] was marvellous until he became prime minister and then didn't like him'.[58] And yet, there was still some satisfaction to be had at the thought of installing a prime minister, no matter how disappointing that prime minister turned out to be. In 1972, McNicoll boasted on ABC's *This Day Tonight* that it was 'indisputable' that he and Frank Packer had been largely responsible for Gorton losing the prime ministership and his replacement by McMahon.[59]

The head of the *Bulletin*'s Canberra bureau, Peter Samuel, claimed otherwise. He wrote an anonymous account for *Australian Quarterly* under the pseudonym 'Mr Y' that was published soon after the leadership change. 'Mr Y' dismissed suggestions of a top-down, orchestrated plot by Consolidated Press against Gorton, but he did point to Reid as a major player in events. According to 'Mr Y', Packer did not endorse some of the activities of his employees. This is an interesting perspective from an insider who was involved in events, but it is difficult to know which parts of it to believe because Samuel later admitted that about 10 per cent of the 'Mr Y' article was 'mischievous' and not true.[60]

Regardless of who was more culpable for the Packer group's anti-Gorton campaign – Reid (who might have influenced the Packers more than they influenced him on this issue) or Packer (who vetted all content of significance and whose edicts were disregarded only by those with a 'death wish') – it is still too simplistic to write off the Liberal leadership change in 1971 as purely the result of a 'Packer plot'. A media campaign has to be planted in fertile ground to bear fruit. Through his behaviour and decisions, Gorton played the starring role in his own demise. There was already public and party dissatisfaction with him. Key colleagues and other media outlets had also wanted Gorton out.

Outside of Consolidated Press, *The Age* editor Graham Perkin reportedly believed that an editorial he wrote (the one that was read to the Liberal Party meeting on 10 March), helped stiffen the resolve of timid backbenchers to replace Gorton.[61] This is a useful reminder of just how difficult it is to assess the impact of one specific example of media content, or even a larger media campaign. Did Perkin's editorial have more or less impact than the Baudino article that reported Gorton's disloyalty to Fraser? Did Reid's statement on *Meet the Press* have more impact than both? And what of the longer term impact of McMahon relentlessly leaking information that was very damaging to Gorton in the months leading up to March 1971? Those leaks, including to Consolidated Press, helped build up a picture of a scandal-ridden prime minister, and without that context, the Fraser–army imbroglio would not have been so wounding to Gorton.

The more solid basis for assessment is intention, rather than impact. And on this point, it is clear that Reid, Packer and McNicoll set out to depose a prime minister and replace him with a friend and company shareholder. Whether they were fully, or only partially, responsible for that outcome, or even just its timing, does not make such a deliberate attempt to abuse media power any less extraordinary.

AT MURDOCH'S TAJ MAHAL

Murdoch did not welcome the new prime minister. He 'loathed' McMahon and considered him an obvious Packer agent.[62] And McMahon's tenure also coincided with a downturn in the economy that exacerbated a rough patch for Murdoch's Australian assets. The circulation of Fairfax's *Sun* was drawing closer to his *Daily Mirror*. The *Australian* was still a financial drain. And the new *Sunday Australian*, launched in February 1971, was taking circulation away from the weekday and Saturday editions without boosting advertising enough to make money.

On the positive side, News Limited's headquarters on the corner of Kippax and Holt streets had been expanded and updated so the Sydney papers and the *Australian* could all be printed from the same presses, and all the staff could be in one building. That building now had five extra floors, modern art in the foyer, and the most sophisticated machinery in the production areas. Creating this 'Taj Mahal' of Australian newspaper buildings had cost more than $8 million, though.[63]

In mid-1971, News Limited senior executives told staff the company was under 'grave financial strain'.[64] Murdoch was dining with Whitlam and trying to draw closer to the Labor leader. He felt McMahon was not doing enough to make business conditions easier in the face of high inflation, unemployment and wage growth. Although Murdoch was usually based overseas now, and ruling his Australian assets as an 'absentee landlord', he returned regularly, and during one trip home, made another big decision.[65]

In July, Murdoch sacked Adrian Deamer, who had been editor of the *Australian* for three years and had played a major role at the paper for five. Rodney Tiffen called Deamer's editorship 'among the most successful … both professionally and commercially, in Australian journalism'.[66] Deamer had made the *Australian* a paper that others tried to imitate, and its circulation had nearly doubled in the three years to 1970.[67] But Murdoch was unhappy with the paper's political stance.

Under Deamer, the *Australian* was known for its 'liberal and outspoken' editorial line, including on Aboriginal land rights, the emerging women's movement, and the Vietnam War.[68] Murdoch had complained to Deamer that the paper criticised political leaders he supported, favoured black people over white, 'wanted to flood the country with Asians', and was 'unAustralian'. Murdoch also told him the *Australian* was 'too intellectual' and 'too political', all of which Deamer took to be a euphemism for 'too left-wing'.[69]

Deamer's sacking came after an *Australian* editorial in June 1971 criticised the McMahon government for its offer to fly the South African Springboks rugby union team (a symbol of its racist apartheid regime), around Australia in an air force plane for their tour. Deamer's sacking was further evidence that Murdoch was building 'a highly personalised business culture' centred on staff who were loyal, compliant and dependent upon him.[70]

After Deamer left, the *Australian* was directed to become less controversial and more middle-brow, but trouble came in other forms. In 1972, the paper was not published on 12 and 13 April due to strike action involving reading-room staff, one of the roles set to be replaced by new technology (Chapter 17). The *Australian* was not printed again on 22 April after a walkout by printing staff over a wage claim. In May, industrial conflict spread to the *Sydney Morning Herald* and the *Daily Telegraph* when their staff were asked to typeset for the *Australian*. The proprietors were worried that journalists would join the printers' strike, which could lead the AJA to form a permanent alliance with the PKIU. If that happened, it would weaken the proprietors' industrial bargaining position just as they were introducing major changes due to new technology. Murdoch told journalists on the *Australian* and *Sunday Australian* that if they went on strike in solidarity with the printers, he would close both unprofitable papers. The journalists did not strike, and the printers' claims were defeated.[71]

MURDOCH BUYS THE *TELEGRAPH*S

Murdoch had flown to Australia from London during the strike, which led him to have closer contact with the Packers than he normally would as they joined forces to try to stop wage increases and AJA-PKIU cooperation. Murdoch probably also sensed an opportunity. Sixty-five-year-old Frank Packer had conducted the *Daily Telegraph* for 36 years, and the *Sunday Telegraph* for 33 years. For the last six of those years, he had been flirting with the idea of selling them.[72] In that time, he had let their plant and equipment run down so the *Daily Telegraph*'s composing room was 'about the worst in Australia'; dirty – overcrowded and with antiquated machinery (Chapter 17).[73]

During the long editorship of James Kingston 'King' Watson from 1953 to 1970, the *Daily Telegraph* had lost some of its 'zing' and crusading style as Watson lacked the 'mercurial brilliance' of his predecessors, Brian Penton and Cyril Pearl.[74] The paper's format and views were also looking old fashioned. Between 1969 and 1971, the *Daily Telegraph*'s daily sales declined by 20 000.⁷⁵ It was losing a considerable amount of money, and the *Sunday Telegraph* was just breaking even.⁷⁶ The Packers had tried various ways to prop up the papers, including increasing the *Daily Telegraph*'s cover price in 1970. But in April 1972, they failed to convince Fairfax to increase the *Sydney Morning Herald*'s cover price in unison again.⁷⁷ The Packers had also failed to persuade the Fairfax group to increase Sunday advertising rates. And they had even canvassed the idea of Fairfax printing the *Telegraph*s on a contract basis.⁷⁸

There were few options remaining. The Packers had been left behind in newspapers. While the HWT, Fairfax and News Limited owned multiple daily metropolitan papers, Consolidated Press had only the *Daily Telegraph* (see Tables 16.1 and 16.2). It was an expensive asset as a stand-alone daily and the other owners were wondering how long Packer could hold on. His health was declining, and both of his sons seemed more interested in television.

Although Clyde Packer was the heir apparent, his younger brother Kerry was demonstrating a sharp business brain as deputy chairman of Consolidated Press Holdings Ltd and advertising director of Australian Consolidated Press Ltd. Journalists suspected that dyslexia was the reason for Kerry's lack of affinity with newspapers and his strong preference for television. Dyslexia was probably also the cause of his father and mother's cruel assessment of Kerry, in his youth, as the 'idiot son'.⁷⁹

By 1972, Kerry, and to a lesser degree, Clyde, wanted their father to sell the *Telegraph*s. In 1967, both Murdoch and Fairfax had offered to buy the *Daily Telegraph*, but Frank had refused.⁸⁰ He relished the ability the paper gave him to have a say on day-to-day issues, and to throw his weight around politically. But Frank was now more willing to negotiate, as the recent strike, looming wage demands and technological costs were worrying him.⁸¹

Observers suspected something was afoot on 31 May 1972 when the *Daily Telegraph* described McMahon, its company's chosen prime minister, as 'a nightmare to the Australian taxpayer and private enterprise'.⁸² It may have been an expression of genuine disappointment in McMahon, but it also seemed to be an attempt to court Murdoch, who was the Packers' guest at dinner that night. Afterwards, Kerry took Murdoch to a boxing match between middleweight champion Tony Mundine and American Denny Moyer. By coincidence, Sir Vincent Fairfax (Warwick's cousin) and his son, John B Fairfax, were sitting behind them, surprised to see their rivals together at one of the only boxing matches John B ever attended.[83]

Kerry drove Murdoch to his hotel after the match, and the two of them sat in the car outside and talked sale terms. They struck a deal, but Frank then had to be talked into it by his sons, with Kerry doing most of the persuading.[84] On Friday 2 June 1972, Frank formally agreed to the sale. He and Murdoch met on the Saturday. Their lawyers hammered out the details in Frank's offices at Castlereagh Street and then boarded a plane bound for Canberra to save tax on share transfers. The plane had to turn back, but the next day, the lawyers flew to Canberra where the contracts were signed on the Sunday.[85]

Murdoch had increased his bid until Packer could not resist. The final price was $15 million ($163 million today). This was to be paid mostly in cash, and it was just for the goodwill of the papers. No physical assets, such as plant or buildings, were included. How could Packer senior refuse such a generous offer for two proven loss-makers? Other newspaper groups were shocked by the price. It was considered outrageously high.[86] But the Packers felt they could no longer afford to have their presses idle for half the day, and Murdoch felt the same about his own situation. He wanted a popular morning paper in Sydney to go with his afternoon *Daily Mirror*, and buying an established paper was a much better proposition than starting a new one.

The newspaper industry was not surprised the Packers had finally sold the *Telegraph*s, but many had expected the HWT would be the buyer, or a British owner, probably Beaverbook, or even Fairfax.[87] Jack Williams was still a director on the HWT board, and at some point, he had tried to convince his fellow board members that the company should buy the *Telegraph*s, but the board had declined; a golden opportunity missed. That Murdoch was the buyer instead of the HWT, and that it all happened so quickly, caught the industry by surprise. Perhaps most shocked of all was Consolidated Press's editor-in-chief. McNicoll was overseas at the time of the sale, and the Packer sons had probably taken advantage of his absence so that McNicoll could not talk their father out of selling.[88]

The public announcement of the sale had been delayed because Packer childishly wanted to include a final, stinging attack on the Fairfax group and Murdoch would not allow it.[89] But once announced, the repercussions began to flow immediately. The next day, News Limited advised that its quality broadsheet, the *Sunday Australian* (which had stagnated at a circulation of 180 000, compared to Fairfax's *Sun-Herald* at 700 000), would be merged with the tabloid *Sunday Telegraph* (circulation 600 000).[90]

Sydney journalists braced themselves for job losses and a fierce circulation battle as Murdoch sought to claw back some of his $15 million. The immediate casualties were 13 *Daily Telegraph* editorial staff, 271 printers and 129 compositors.[91] The production job losses were high because the *Daily Telegraph*'s manual equipment needed more staff to run and service the old machines. News Limited did not need so many workers because it had the latest, and more automated, equipment.

Murdoch now controlled two of Sydney's three general morning papers (*Australian* and *Daily Telegraph*), one of its two afternoon papers (*Daily Mirror*), and two of its three Sunday papers (*Sunday Mirror* and *Sunday Telegraph*). Staff and machinery at the Kippax Street building had to print all five newspapers. Industry insiders wondered whether even Murdoch's modern presses could manage it. The presses would need to turn out the 560 000 print run of the *Sunday Telegraph* plus an estimated 450 000 *Sunday Mirror*s. Sunday 11 June was the first test, and the Kippax building passed. It managed to print 1.25 million papers, the greatest number printed at one plant in Australia on a single day.[92]

The *Daily Telegraph* had been eye-wateringly expensive, and the Commonwealth Bank had to step in as Murdoch's white knight yet again, but the morning–afternoon paper combination soon made it a sound investment. Murdoch was able to defray his production and operating costs across five papers. His presses were 'going flat out all the time'.[93]

Another flow-on effect of the purchase helped Murdoch make back some money. In the 1930s, his father had dreamed of making Australian newsprint a reality, and he helped pioneer the creation of Australian Newsprint Mills (ANM) in 1938. ANM was the sole Australian producer of newsprint, a company owned and controlled jointly by newspaper owners.[94] With little sentimentality about a venture that meant a lot to his father, in August 1972 Rupert Murdoch sold News Limited's large holding in ANM to Fairfax for an estimated $3.56 million to help pay for his purchase of the *Telegraph*s.[95] But the sale turned out to be even more beneficial than that for Murdoch.

In 1966, ANM had signed ten-year contracts with its customers. When inflation rocketed up in the early 1970s, those contracts placed ANM in a grave financial position, so its owner-customers voluntarily agreed to pay more for their newsprint to make sure that ANM survived. Because News Limited had no stake in ANM, it refused to join in with the voluntary price sacrifice. This aroused the fury of the rest of the industry, but for the next three years, as Fairfax's newsprint costs rose much faster than News Limited's, Murdoch saved about $6 million. That gave him a big advantage in the *Sun* versus *Daily Mirror*, and *Sydney Morning Herald* versus *Daily Telegraph*, battles.[96]

Another important flow-on effect was political rather than financial. Although the *Daily Telegraph* had become more critical of McMahon by mid-1972, it had previously been his biggest promoter and defender. With the coming election due to be won or lost in *Daily Telegraph*–reading suburban seats, the sale was very bad news indeed for McMahon. He firmly believed in the power of the *Telegraph*s to keep Labor out of office and now Packer had sold McMahon out to Murdoch, a man who hated the prime minister and did not bother to conceal it. (The previous year, Murdoch had introduced McMahon to a group of London newspaper owners as 'Billy the Leak'.)[97]

On the night the deal was made, Murdoch had phoned McMahon and Whitlam to inform them that he was the new owner of the *Telegraph*s. He told McMahon, 'I can promise, Prime Minister, that we will be as fair to you as you deserve.' Close by, Packer laughed and said, 'If you do that, you'll murder him'.[98]

When Packer and McMahon next saw each other, McMahon was despondent and said, 'Frank, I think that ends our prospects for the election.'[99] Mungo MacCullum wrote more plainly in *The Review* that the Liberals were 'scared shitless'.[100] Labor figures, on the other hand, were delighted that the sale had removed Packer, an avowed Labor enemy who always had his journalists present the party in the worst light possible.

In London, Murdoch was considered left-wing at this time because his *Sun* was supporting Harold Wilson's Labour Party. In Australia, Murdoch's political preferences had already veered from supporting Labor's Arthur Calwell, to the Country Party's John McEwen, to the Liberals' John Gorton, and now he was being seen around town with Labor's Gough Whitlam. Australian political insiders strongly suspected that Murdoch was pragmatic and transaction oriented, that he was motivated by profit and power, rather than any deep ideological attachment.

Murdoch drew on his tabloid magic to try to make the *Daily Telegraph* a more popular paper. It was given a facelift, including changing its old masthead to a more modern font. The paper promised a 'bright new look', better pictures, a women's page for 'the housewife and the young swinger', top sports writers, and a new astrology page.[101] Women in bikinis and skimpy outfits started appearing in large photographs, including on the front page.

According to a boardroom spy who was reporting back to the Fairfax group, News Limited planned for the *Telegraph*s to 'back Labor in the [forthcoming 1972] election, earning them good will and sales in the industrial areas'.[102] But Murdoch needed to retain the *Telegraph*s' existing readership, too. So instead of doing a sudden political U-turn, the papers became less combative and more apolitical in Murdoch's first five months of ownership, and their politically strident conservative editorials were dropped.[103]

David McNicoll had resigned as editor-in-chief of Consolidated Press when Murdoch bought the papers, but he remained close to the Packers and had a desk at Consolidated Press, where he resumed his old career as a columnist, this time with the *Bulletin*. A few months after the sale, McNicoll predicted that the *Daily Telegraph* would be very successful as a non-opinionated paper like the *Sun News-Pictorial*, and would 'put on a lot of circulation'.[104] In other words, McNicoll knew that his bosses' political obsessions, which he had helped Frank foist onto readers, had been to the detriment of the paper's popularity and viability. Under Packer, the *Daily Telegraph* had been around 40 000 buyers ahead of the *Sydney Morning Herald*. Under Murdoch, it lost readers at first, but by 1974 it had pulled ahead of the *Sydney Morning Herald* by 60 000 readers, and in 1975, by

70 000. The *Sydney Morning Herald* would have to work hard to narrow that gap.[105]

THE PACKER FAMILY BOWS OUT OF DAILY PAPERS

The sale of the *Telegraph*s left Australia with only three major newspaper owners: the HWT, Fairfax and News Limited. This was the most concentrated daily press market Australia had ever seen. The three groups controlled more than 98 per cent of all daily and Sunday newspapers sold in capital cities, and more than 90 per cent of daily newspapers sold across Australia.[106] In the early 1950s, Sydney had been the most turbulent and competitive market with four colourful owners battling it out, and now it was down to just two. Monopoly, or duopoly, had become the norm for daily papers in capital cities (Table 19.1).

Packer's group still had two very profitable television stations, TCN-9 Sydney and GTV-9 Melbourne, plus the Castlereagh Street premises, the *Women's Weekly*, the *Bulletin*, the *Australian Home Journal*, *TV Times* (with the ABC), radio interests in Melbourne and Perth, the *Maitland Mercury*, and other regional and suburban newspapers.[107] But by all accounts, Frank regretted the sale of the *Telegraph*s. Television was not the same, although a frustrated Frank tried to make it so. He began directing his heavy-handed political interventions at the television stations.

In August 1972, just months after the *Telegraph*s were sold to Murdoch, Frank ordered Clyde to keep the ACTU president, Bob Hawke, from ever appearing on any Channel Nine news or current affairs program again (Frank thought Hawke was a 'communist' who had the measure of Nine's interviewers). When Clyde told Mike Willesee that a segment with Hawke for *A Current Affair* had been vetoed by Frank and would not go to air, Willesee resigned. Clyde took a moment and then responded, 'Congratulations on your integrity. I've just completed my last official act as managing director. I resign too.'[108]

Clyde had been a member of the NSW Legislative Council for the Liberal Party and was no fan of either Labor or the unions. He said he felt his father was making poor decisions and trying to run the television

TABLE 19.1 Daily metropolitan newspaper ownership after the *Daily Telegraph* sale, 1972

	HWT	Fairfax	News Limited	Other
National		1 daily	1 daily	
Sydney		2 dailies, 1 Sunday	2 dailies, 2 Sundays	
Melbourne	2 dailies	1 daily (Syme-Fairfax)		Max Newton: 1 Sunday
Brisbane	2 dailies, 1 Sunday		1 Sunday	
Adelaide	1 daily, 1 Sunday*		1 daily, 1 Sunday*	
Perth	2 dailies, 1 weekend		1 Sunday	Lang Hancock and Peter Wright: 1 Sunday
Hobart	1 daily, 1 weekend			
Canberra		2 dailies		
Darwin			1 daily	

* A joint HWT-News Limited Sunday paper.

NOTE Does not count the *Sunday Australian* as a national paper as it was quickly merged into the *Sunday Telegraph* after the sale. Does not include *Truth* of which News Limited now owned less than 50 per cent.

companies like newspapers when 'the airwaves were publicly owned and television channels had a responsibility not to ram their own viewpoint down the public's throat'.[109] After decades of tight control and bullying, Clyde had finally had enough. He split from Frank completely and moved to the United States in 1976, never to return. Clyde later said, 'I suspect my father was as glad to get rid of me as I was to get rid of him.'[110] Clyde also said he thought Frank was a victim of 'the tycoon syndrome' where 'your personality becomes smaller and smaller … I think it's a gigantic cover up for inferiority.' Clyde thought his father was desperately shy and insecure but tried 'to cover up with bluster'.[111]

After Clyde resigned, Frank had the Nine Network broadcast two unprecedented prime-time editorials during the 1972 election campaign, both written by McNicoll. One began, 'It will not take the solid, middle-of-the-road voter long to work out which policy – Mr Whitlam's or Mr McMahon's – is the best for Australia and for him.' It painted Labor as unrealistic and immoral, while McMahon was steady and pragmatic. Despite complaints, including from Colin Bednall who knew it breached the impartiality requirements of the *Broadcasting and Television Act*, Packer correctly anticipated that the Australian Broadcasting Control Board would do little about it. A week later, TCN-9 and GTV-9 broadcast another editorial criticising Labor. It described Whitlam's policy speech as 'marijuana dreams', and Packer refused to broadcast Labor's reply. He gave nearly $20 000 worth of free advertising time to the DLP, and banned the *Bulletin* from publishing a feature on Margaret Whitlam.[112]

This was Frank's last opportunity to push his views during a federal election. He died in May 1974, aged 67. (His father and grandfather had both died in their fifties.) Menzies paid tribute to Packer by stating, oddly, that Packer was a 'real man' and that any of his faults were at least 'masculine' ones.[113] Menzies also acknowledged that Packer 'gave me support in difficult days'.[114] An otherwise glowing obituary in Packer's *Bulletin* put it differently. It said Frank was an 'unabashed partisan' and acknowledged that many viewed him as an 'anti-communist, anti-socialist zealot who misused his immense communications power to unfairly promote the cause of conservative politics in Australia'.[115]

Alan Reid, who had been one of Packer's key enablers in that project, was another career casualty of the sale of the papers to Murdoch. Reid sacrificed his newspaper career to stay with the Packers. They gave him a prominent slot at the *Bulletin* magazine and on the Channel Nine program *Federal File*, but he too mourned the loss of power and influence that came from a daily newspaper. Even ten years later, in 1982, Reid said that 'If Kerry would fire or retire me I'd be back to a daily [paper] like a shot.'[116] For Reid, the important difference was that 'a newspaper story has much more impact on politicians, [even though] the public reacts more to television'.[117]

THE NEWSPAPER GENE

Kerry Packer borrowed money to buy out Clyde's share of the estate, then he built that inheritance into a $7 billion empire by the early 2000s, one that was centred on television, magazines, gambling and tourism.[118] The television licences that Frank had obtained when his friend Menzies was in office had secured the family's wealth for generations. And yet, it was noticeable that, after Frank, each generation of sons rejected what their tyrannical father had treasured.

Kerry rejected newspapers for television. Kerry's son, James, rejected television for casinos. In 2008, James sold the Nine Network and Consolidated Press's magazines. That officially ended the Packer family's four-generation control of key parts of the Australian media. The family did not have the deep, abiding attachment to newspapers that Murdoch had. For all their bravado, the Packers had also been too risk-averse, too stingy and too timid to be successful in newspapers or in the media beyond Australia's shores.

CHAPTER 20
THE WHITLAM EXPERIMENT

The December 1972 election was held six months after Murdoch's purchase of the *Daily Telegraph*. The Liberal Party was facing its toughest federal election campaign since 1961. McMahon had inherited an economy with problems and, despite his economics degree and experience as treasurer, he had not found any solutions. Even friendly newspapers had dubbed the government's 1971 budget 'disastrous'.[1] Under McMahon, unemployment had hit a ten-year high, inflation was at a 20-year high, and productivity was suffering.[2]

The newspapers were feeling the effects of heavy cost increases and lower advertising revenue. But at least they had survived the 1960s. London had lost three daily papers since 1960. New York, which had eight daily newspapers in 1960, had only four by 1970.[3] Sydney, with only about a third of New York's population, had the same number of metropolitan daily papers (plus two national dailies as well).

Since World War II, only one of Australia's 16 capital city dailies had closed (the *Argus*). In part, this was because the newspaper industry had already been through a bruising period of consolidation in the 1920s and then the early Depression years. By 1941, there was not a lot of excess fat in the industry left to trim out; monopoly had already become the standard condition in capital cities other than Sydney and Melbourne (see Table 1.1). What the Australian newspaper industry had lost in the 30 years since was not newspapers but owners.

THE SURVIVORS

The industry had coalesced around three large newspaper groups. When McMahon and Whitlam thought about newspapers in 1972, and how they

TABLE 20.1 Australia's daily national and metropolitan newspapers, December 1972

Location	Title	Circulation*	Circulation growth or decline since 1945 %	Type of newspaper	Owner and major shareholders
National	Australian	136 000	n/a	Morning broadsheet	News Limited (Rupert Murdoch)
	Australian Financial Review	39 000	n/a	Morning compact (tabloid)	John Fairfax Ltd (Fairfax family)
Sydney	Sydney Morning Herald	274 000	–3	Morning broadsheet	John Fairfax Ltd (Fairfax family)
	Daily Telegraph	316 000	14	Morning tabloid	News Limited (Rupert Murdoch)
	Sun	309 000	18	Afternoon tabloid	John Fairfax Ltd (Fairfax family)
	Daily Mirror	312 000	4	Afternoon tabloid	News Limited (Rupert Murdoch)
Melbourne	Argus	Closed 1957			
	The Age	206 000	84	Morning broadsheet	David Syme and Co (John Fairfax Ltd (Fairfax family) *run in partnership with the Syme family)
	Sun News-Pictorial	648 000	98	Morning tabloid	Herald and Weekly Times Ltd
	Herald	498 000	59	Afternoon broadsheet	Herald and Weekly Times Ltd
Brisbane	Courier-Mail	260 000	66	Morning broadsheet	Queensland Press (Herald and Weekly Times Ltd)
	Telegraph	159 000	29	Afternoon tabloid	Queensland Press (Herald and Weekly Times Ltd)

Location	Title	Circulation*	Circulation growth or decline since 1945 %	Type of newspaper	Owner and major shareholders
Adelaide	*Advertiser*	217 000	70	Morning broadsheet	Advertiser Newspapers Ltd (Herald and Weekly Times Ltd)
	News	133 000	70	Afternoon tabloid	News Limited (Rupert Murdoch)
Perth	*West Australian*	218 000	132	Morning tabloid	Herald and Weekly Times Ltd
	Daily News	123 000	92	Afternoon tabloid	Herald and Weekly Times Ltd
Hobart	*Mercury*	53 000	83	Morning broadsheet	Davies Brothers Ltd (Herald and Weekly Times Ltd)
Canberra	*Canberra Times*	34 000	240	Morning broadsheet	John Fairfax Ltd (Fairfax family)
	Canberra News(a)	~13 000(b)	n/a	Afternoon tabloid	John Fairfax Ltd (Fairfax family)
Darwin	*NT News*	10 279	n/a	Morning tabloid	News Limited (Rupert Murdoch)

* Average daily paid circulation figures are from Goot, 1979, p. 5; and for the *NT News*, from the *Bulletin*, 12 January 1974, p. 12.

(a) The *Canberra News* would close in July 1974.

(b) Figures could not be located for 1972. The paper had a circulation of 13 000 when it closed in 1974 (Canberra Times, 20 July 1974, p. 1).

NOTE The name of the major company is listed rather than of subsidiary companies (such as Mirror Newspapers and Nationwide News as subsidiaries of News Limited, or WAN for the HWT). Advertiser Newspapers, Queensland Press and Davies Brothers are listed because, although the HWT was the majority owner, they were not technically subsidiary companies.

TEXTBOX 20.1 Television switches on in 1972

Television had become more adept at breaking news, live crosses and current affairs. Television stations were seeing such high ratings for their news bulletins that, in 1972, ATN-7 introduced an hour-long nightly news program. (In the early years of television, news bulletins had been just 15 minutes long.) The drama of the Gorton–McMahon years had also led to a greater focus on Canberra news specifically, and in 1972, for the first time, permanent television facilities were installed in Parliament House.

Although the ABC's ground-breaking current affairs programs had lost their edge by the early 1970s, Clyde Packer had backed Mike Willesee (a former ABC reporter and host) to create *A Current Affair* for the Nine Network. It had launched in 1971, and combined hard-hitting political interviews with show business flair, human interest stories and appearances by comedian Paul Hogan.

In the 11 months before the 1972 election, *A Current Affair* had become the first high-rating current affairs program on commercial television, and the first to be elevated to a prime-time slot. During the election, it was being broadcast at 7 pm, Monday to Friday, in Sydney, Melbourne, Brisbane and Adelaide.

In protest at his father's interference with *A Current Affair*, Clyde Packer had resigned from his family's television network in August 1972 (Chapter 19), but its host, the 'smooth ... good looking boy-next-door' Willesee, remained at Nine (until 1974).[4]

The program's success encouraged the commercial stations to invest more in current affairs. The Nine Network launched *Federal File*, a weekly political program with Alan Reid, ahead of the election. There were also morning programs, such as *Today*, which ran for two hours on ATN-7 and HSV-7, and combined news, light-hearted current affairs, entertainment and lifestyle.

There was more politics on television, including political advertisements, news reports and televised press conferences (which were sometimes given their own time slot in television schedules). On current affairs programs, political interviews were making headlines and winning ratings. Televised confrontations were starting to take the place of public meetings.

wanted to be represented in the press, they had to think about three men: Philip Jones, Warwick Fairfax and Rupert Murdoch. Of the 15 dailies that had survived since 1941, the HWT owned or controlled eight. Fairfax had four, plus the *Australian Financial Review* and the new (but doomed) *Canberra News* (Chapter 16). And Rupert Murdoch owned three (plus the *Australian* and the *NT News*) (Table 20.1). Twelve independent owners had been reduced to just three.

Newspaper audiences had shrunk, too. Since the days of Curtin's circus in the early 1940s, Australia's population had grown by around 77 per cent. Some newspapers had managed to achieve a similar growth in circulation, or even better, especially in Canberra and Perth, two cities that had experienced massive population growth (Table 20.1). But in Sydney, where the population had doubled, newspaper sales had not kept pace. Ominously, the *Sydney Morning Herald* was selling fewer copies in 1972 than it had in 1945. And the *Daily Telegraph* was selling only 14 per cent more than 30 years earlier. Perhaps Sydney had too many papers after all.

In Melbourne, where there were three daily metropolitan papers instead of four, and no competition in the afternoon market, total daily newspaper circulation had grown by 55 per cent since 1945, compared to only 8 per cent in Sydney. Although Melbourne had a smaller population, it was selling more daily newspapers than Sydney.

Afternoon papers were another cause for industry concern. None of the three afternoon papers in Sydney and Melbourne was keeping up with population growth. Despite (or perhaps because of) the many gimmicks the *Sun* and *Daily Mirror* were using to lure readers, the afternoon newspaper market in Sydney had grown by only 10 per cent since 1945, while Sydney's population had grown by 100 per cent. More people were turning to television news in the evening rather than of afternoon papers.

YOUNG GUNS IN THE GALLERY

Important changes had also been occurring in newspaper journalism, changes which were to Whitlam's advantage, not McMahon's, and which challenged the editorial influence of some proprietors. After *The Age*'s chief political correspondent in Canberra, John Bennetts, had retired in 1967, several other members of the old guard of press gallery reporters had also departed. Some of these men, mostly in their sixties, had been covering politics since World War II.

Kevin Power had left the same year as Bennetts. Power had been head of bureau for the *Daily Mirror* from 1944 and 'was a Catholic and an overt supporter of the DLP side of politics'.[5] Harold Cox, the Melbourne *Herald*'s Canberra representative since 1944, had retired in 1969, after serving in the press gallery since 1933. Ian Fitchett, who had been in the gallery since 1947 and the *Sydney Morning Herald*'s political correspondent since 1960, stopped covering daily news stories in 1970. 'Fitch' was one of the great characters of the gallery, and one of the few who had been able to hold his own in verbal sparring matches with Menzies.

These departures left Alan Reid as the doyen of the gallery. He was no longer at a daily newspaper, though, and Reid's interventions in 1971 to promote the hapless McMahon had been so overt, and so misguided, that they had created an impetus for change among the new breed of reporters who had arrived in the press gallery. They were in their twenties and thirties, tertiary-educated, intelligent, articulate and dogged.

The new generation included (in alphabetical order): Allan Barnes (*The Age*), Gay Davidson (*Canberra Times*), Michelle Grattan (*The Age*), Brian Johns (*Sydney Morning Herald*), Paul Kelly (*Australian, National Times*), Mungo MacCallum (*Australian, National Times, Nation Review*), Laurie Oakes (*Sun News-Pictorial*), Alan Ramsey (*Australian*), David Solomon (*Canberra Times, Australian*), Eric Walsh (*Daily Mirror*) and Max Walsh (*Australian Financial Review*).

Several among the new breed of reporters felt that Reid and others in the old guard had focused critically only on Labor even though, after Menzies retired, there had been leadership instability in the Liberal Party and a series of flawed leaders who had been brawling among themselves.[6] There was a new determination to exercise scrutiny over both parties, and this was not good news for McMahon.

Laurie Oakes had arrived in Canberra in January 1969. He was working for the *Sun News-Pictorial* after spending two years with the paper in Melbourne. Oakes later said that he and several others (including Allan

Barnes, Alan Ramsey, Brian Johns and David Solomon) deliberately 'set out to turn the spotlight on the machinations and movements, bickering, brawling and backstabbing in the non-Labor parties as well as the ALP'. Oakes said it was 'a conscious attempt to provide the balance we thought had been missing in political journalism partly because of Alan Reid's influence'.[7]

Ramsey later said that he felt Reid 'for all his ability and reputation, was owned, body and soul, by Frank Packer. He was the faithful family retainer.'[8] There was a longing for greater journalistic independence, although the extent to which this would be tolerated would vary between the media groups.

The new gallery reporters were less deferential to politicians than the old guard, and less socially connected to them within the village-like atmosphere of Canberra. Journalists were priding themselves on being more critical and not taking government statements at face value. They were also being more competitive among themselves.

Previously, reporters had operated through a news pool system that was actually called 'the Club', and individual reporters also had informal arrangements (as between Reid and Bennetts) to swap 'blacks' (carbon copies of their stories).[9] This had led to a sameness in coverage that the new breed of reporters was keen to break down. There was new competition for leaks, scoops and commentary.

With all of these changes, it seemed that Australian journalism was moving away from controlled, passive and pooled reporting, towards something more vibrant, individualised and probing. The growth of news and current affairs on television was one spur and another was the way upmarket papers had been shaking themselves free of stodginess and a 'just the facts' approach since the mid-1960s (Chapter 18).

Other factors that were encouraging a new energy, and a new sense of social/democratic purpose in journalism, were the turn towards investigative journalism, and the stance that American newspapers had taken against corrupt and dishonest governments. The *New York Times* had ignored President Richard Nixon's demands and printed the Pentagon Papers in 1971. Seven weeks before the 1972 election, the *Washington Post* had reported that the Watergate break-in had 'stemmed from a massive campaign of political spying and sabotage conducted on behalf of President Nixon's re-election and directed by officials of the White House'.[10] The paper would continue to wade through the lies and cover-ups to expose Watergate.

Another factor that had encouraged more critical journalism was the rise of insider newsletters written by, and often for, journalists. Since the late 1950s, these outlets had given journalists a chance to choose their own subjects and write their own views and insider accounts (at a time when their primary outlets would not have allowed them such autonomy). Tom Fitzgerald's *Nation*, which had been published in Sydney from 1958, was a fortnightly magazine for opinions, questioning, scepticism and probing when those qualities were in short supply in mainstream newspapers. *Nation* had a small circulation, never more than 12 000, but a cult following among subscribers who distributed it more widely.[11]

In July 1972, Gordon Barton bought out the debt-laden *Nation* from Fitzgerald and merged it with his national weekly paper, *The Review*. Published out of Melbourne, it had previously been called the *Sunday Review* (Chapter 18). The merger produced a new weekly newspaper, *Nation Review*, in July 1972. As Barton acknowledged, *Nation Review* had a 'profound lean to the Left'. But he exercised no editorial control over it, and said he was often embarrassed about things it published.[12] *The Age*'s Roger Aldridge said *Nation Review*'s 'witty, squalling, squabbling, libellous and libidinous antics were like a whiff of smelling salts' to the rest of the media.[13]

Aside from the trend towards critical journalism, Australian newsrooms were also catching up with second-wave feminism. Female journalists were being employed to report on wider and more interesting subject matter and were able to go beyond being social reporters in hats and gloves. Women's pages were disappearing at some papers, and at others were morphing into sections aimed at women *and* men, which had more generic names such as 'Accent' (which replaced the women's pages at *The Age* in 1967), and 'LOOK!' (which replaced the *Sydney Morning Herald*'s 'News for women' page in 1972).[14]

Although Warwick Fairfax would not allow the title 'Ms' to be used, the Fairfax group was nonetheless starting to slowly shake off its reputation for old-fashioned, prim sexism. John Pringle had hired more female journalists for the *Sydney Morning Herald* between 1965 and 1970. The number of female editorial staff at the paper doubled, from 15 in 1969 to 31 in 1973. It was still only one woman for every six men in the newsroom, but it was a start.[15] And as historian Barbara Lemon noted, Fairfax's *National Times* 'led the way in employing large numbers of women journalists and publishing articles that regularly tackled questions around women's right to work, equal pay, child care, contraception and abortion'.[16]

At Fairfax's *Canberra Times*, Gay Davidson was a trailblazer. In March 1971, she revealed to readers that she had been writing a political column under a pseudonym in order to disguise that a woman was writing it.[17] Davidson would officially become the *Canberra Times*' political correspondent in 1974. She also became the first woman to head a bureau in the federal parliamentary press gallery in 1975. When she had to ask permission to use a male toilet near her office, Davidson famously assured the decision makers that there would be 'no embarrassment' because most of the men would be 'facing the wall'.[18]

Davidson had been joined by another trailblazer in 1971, when Michelle Grattan arrived in Canberra as one of *The Age*'s political correspondents. Grattan was second last in *The Age* bureau's chain of command, but by 1976, was the paper's Canberra bureau chief. She remained its chief political correspondent in Canberra for 17 years.[19] Grattan became synonymous with *The Age*'s political coverage and famous for her work ethic, devotion to accuracy and unflappable nature. A future prime minister, Tony Abbott, called Grattan 'the toughest journalist you will ever encounter'.[20] (Fifty years after her arrival, Grattan was still covering politics from Canberra for the online outlet *The Conversation*, and her coverage was still regularly being reproduced in *The Age*.)

More female political reporters would join the new generation in the cramped, rabbit-warren-like accommodation they occupied in the (old) Parliament House roof, including Niki Savva, who arrived at the press gallery in 1972 as a junior reporter for the *Sun News-Pictorial*, and Anne Summers, who arrived in 1979 as a political correspondent for the *Financial Review* and soon became its Canberra bureau chief.

THE 'IT'S TIME' ELECTION

When Grattan arrived in Canberra in 1971, she found the place 'buzzing' with excitement.[21] There was an optimism around change and a pace to political life that meant there was no shortage of issues or events to cover. Party leaders were sometimes holding six or eight public events a day, from early breakfast to late at night.[22] By the time of the 1972 election, public and media interest in the campaign was high.

Whitlam was outlining new policies and expressing big ambitions for the country. He promised that Labor would establish a universal health insurance system, abolish university fees, raise the pension rate, abolish conscription, make preschool education available to every Australian child, and address community problems such as water supply and sewerage.

Labor's party structures had been revitalised, a factor which had helped restore public confidence in what was previously a divided and demoralised party, and helped rid it of the stigma of the 'faceless men' tag. Labor also had a well-functioning, professional electoral machine in place for the election and it unveiled a campaign strategy unlike anything previously seen in Australia.

Labor's heavily market-research–tested and television-focused campaign was centred around the campaign slogan 'It's Time' and was boosted by the star power of celebrity endorsements. Whitlam himself had a certain 'grandeur'. Smart, articulate and confident (some thought to the point of arrogance), he was very newsworthy. All of those qualities attracted the attention of many members of the gallery, some of whom were described as having a 'long romance' with the Labor leader.[23]

By contrast, McMahon was unpopular and a poor public speaker, who faced strong internal dissent and headed a divided party. According to Gallup polls, McMahon's approval rating had dropped from 55 per cent in April 1971 to 28 per cent in July 1972.[24] The press gallery had contributed to McMahon's declining public image by exposing his indecisiveness and insecurity, including as part of a growing interest in reporting on the behind-the-scenes aspects of politics. For example, in December 1972, Laurie Oakes reported McMahon's heavy reliance on advisers, saying he 'has not stirred out of Sydney without at least sixteen people with him', including speech writers, press officers and television experts.[25] Allan Barnes, in *The Age*, declared that 'Mr McMahon clutches these people to his bosom like a security blanket'.[26]

MURDOCH'S CAMPAIGN

Murdoch had put up with McMahon for the past 20 months after the Packer/Reid 'plot' of 1971. Now, the 1972 election was Murdoch's chance to play politics, and perhaps to be on the winning side this time, with all of the possible benefits of access and gratitude that might flow from that. Murdoch threw himself into campaigning for Labor with characteristic energy. Laurie Oakes and David Solomon believed he 'was an integral part of [Labor's] "It's Time" machine'.[27]

The night before Labor's campaign launch, Murdoch was with Whitlam on a boat cruise around Sydney Harbour. Doug McClelland, Labor's shadow minister for the media, was also on board. McClelland was an important addition to the gathering because Labor's platform included elements that were worrying newspaper/radio/television station owners.

Labor's plan to introduce a minister for the media brought up the unpleasant spectre of fights with Calwell during World War II. A Labor government was also likely to increase Australian content requirements for television, which would cost the stations money. There was also vague talk it might impose 'fairness' controls on radio and television.[28] But whatever Murdoch heard on the boat that night, he must have felt reassured that Labor's plans were no threat to his business interests. From that night on, his goodwill and support flowed to Labor.

Murdoch had already been meeting up occasionally with Whitlam since mid-1971, and considered himself to be, in his own later words, 'close to … or certainly very friendly to' the Labor leader at this point. A group of Whitlam's staffers had been tasked with making sure that Murdoch felt that way (in reality, Whitlam did not particularly like Murdoch, found him boring company, and preferred to keep him at a distance).[29]

For the rest of the campaign, Murdoch stayed in frequent contact with Labor's key strategists, especially Mick Young (the party's federal secretary) and Eric Walsh (Whitlam's press secretary). Walsh had previously worked for Murdoch for five years as the *Daily Mirror*'s political correspondent.[30] According to Adrian Deamer, Walsh had been more than just a political correspondent, 'he was a lobbyist and a backroom boy. He became Murdoch's sort of spy, you might say, in Canberra.'[31]

Walsh was one key link between Murdoch and Whitlam. Another was John Menadue, the general manager of News Limited. Menadue had previously been Whitlam's private secretary (1960–67), so the swapping of personnel between Whitlam's office and Murdoch's company had gone both ways. Walsh had helped arrange Menadue's move to News Limited, and the two liaised regularly during the campaign. They were close friends. (Alan Ramsey said Walsh and Menadue were part of a group known around Canberra as 'the Irish mafia' for their strong connections nurtured over long lunches.)[32]

Murdoch became so involved in Labor's campaign that he attended some strategy meetings, designed advertising, and donated around $75 000, mostly in the form of advertising space in his own publications.[33] Murdoch personally wrote some content, including a Labor press statement on releasing conscripts from prison.[34] He also made many suggestions to the Labor campaign team, though not all were acted upon. And just as Fairfax had done for Calwell in 1961, Murdoch directed a journalist to write an important speech for Whitlam. In this case, though, Whitlam's office discarded most of it.[35]

Murdoch also put his newspapers into service to campaign for Labor. One of his biographers, Simon Regan, said that Murdoch worked 12-hour days and 'sat in as virtual editorial director of his group of papers. He coordinated policy, dictated news stories' and editorials.[36] Murdoch later boasted, 'In 1972, I ran all of the election policies of my papers in Australia ... I wrote the leaders every day in the *Daily Mirror*.'[37]

Murdoch continued to favour the *Mirror* over his new acquisition, the *Daily Telegraph*, but Labor's case was in good hands at the *Telegraph*, too, where Alan Reid had been replaced by Richard Farmer. Murdoch had set Farmer the specific task of ridiculing the prime minister. Farmer (who later became a Labor strategist) said, 'That was my job: to make fun of [McMahon], wherever I could'.[38] The *Daily Telegraph* had transitioned from spending many years expressing a strongly pro-Liberal stance under Packer, through a few months of apolitical calm under Murdoch as its new owner, to now giving full support for Labor. 'LET'S GIVE WHITLAM A CHANCE', its editorial said on the eve of the election.[39] The *News* in Adelaide said 'Everybody stands to gain from a change [in government].'[40]

In the Murdoch papers, advocacy was not limited to editorials. News reports, often illustrated with a flattering portrait of Whitlam, were enthusiastic about Labor's policies. They tried to counter fears about Labor's economic credentials, fears that many newspapers, but especially the *Daily Telegraph*, had emphasised for decades. The Murdoch papers also drew attention to McMahon's many foibles. Eleven days before polling day, the *Daily Telegraph* said McMahon 'became angry and lost his composure yesterday … He seemed to wilt'.[41]

The *Australian* was a more sober paper, more intellectual and plugged into political and policy communities. It provided Murdoch with a bully pulpit to reach an influential audience. The *Australian* commended Labor's policy program as 'WHITLAM'S EXCITING PROPOSALS'.[42] It said 'Mr Whitlam's programme has vision', while 'Liberal policy is threadbare: its leadership is weary'.[43]

Murdoch was providing such strong support to Labor that an ABC television interviewer asked Whitlam if he, or the Labor Party, had made a secret deal with Murdoch. 'Certainly not', Whitlam replied.[44]

Murdoch was there at the beginning of the campaign, and he stayed to the end. Two days before polling day, he flew to Melbourne to have dinner with Whitlam, then he personally wrote the *Daily Mirror*'s editorial, endorsing Labor. Echoing Labor's campaign slogan, it said, 'The *Daily Mirror* believes it is time. Time for a change of government.'[45]

Murdoch later admitted that, 'We did some dreadful things to the other side [in 1972] … A lot more happened than even they managed to find out.'[46] He also said, 'I should have had more reserve, but I got emotionally involved. I allowed, with my eyes open, some of the journalists to go beyond being sort of partisans into almost being principals.'[47] It was passing the buck in the extreme to blame his journalists. Murdoch had played a very active role in campaigning for Labor and in directing his papers. Four days before the election, a frustrated McMahon called the Murdoch press 'rancid'.[48]

FAIRFAX'S FIGHTING WORDS

Whitlam had his own media problems. Although an enthusiastic Murdoch was on side, Labor still faced the opposition of the *Sydney Morning Herald*, the Sydney *Sun*, and all of the HWT's daily papers around the country. While Murdoch felt reassured by whatever he heard directly from Whitlam, McClelland and Labor's top advisers, there were many others in the newspaper industry and corporate world who remained nervous about Labor's policies. Business was worried about its plan to introduce a prices justification tribunal, direct government competition in the oil and pharmaceutical industries, and greater consumer protection.[49]

The Fairfax group was anxious about how Labor would approach newspapers and television. In editorials, the *Sydney Morning Herald* wondered aloud why Labor felt the need to have a minister for the media. During the campaign, Whitlam said a Labor government would give 'proper attention' to the media and the company's leaders were thoroughly spooked. In the next day's *Sydney Morning Herald*, the editorial told Whitlam directly that if he meant Labor intended to 'meddle' with the press, he could 'expect a first-class fight on his hands immediately'. The paper then launched into some unusually emotional hyperbole about how 'repugnant' it was for Labor to even consider acting as a 'totalitarian agent of control or manipulation'.[50]

In the lead-up to polling day, the *Sydney Morning Herald* published a flurry of editorials advocating a vote for the Coalition, including at least one editorial written personally by Warwick Fairfax. The paper stuck to its traditional lines of attack, arguing Labor was economically risky, weak on national security, beholden to militant unions, would trample states' rights, raise taxation and expand the bureaucracy. 'Why rock the boat?' asked the *Sydney Morning Herald*'s election-eve editorial.[51] Fairfax's Sydney *Sun* said Labor could not be trusted.[52]

When he was asked about these editorials, Whitlam responded that the Fairfaxes were 'an old-fashioned, autocratic family' who ran their paper in 'a feudal fashion'.[53] This was obviously an exaggerated taunt, but at the *Sydney Morning Herald*, Warwick Fairfax was still a 'committee of one' and he was increasingly exercising his dynastic authority. In April 1970, his stifling interference had caused the *Sydney Morning Herald*'s editor John Pringle to retire early and abruptly. Fairfax historian Gavin Souter said Pringle was 'by far the best editor the paper had ever had in all its hundred and thirty-nine years'.[54]

Warwick had been infuriated by an editorial about Easter that he felt was not religious enough, and another that had suggested Australia would one day become a republic.[55] The Vietnam War had also caused tension. While *The Age* had modified its stance on the Vietnam War as public opinion shifted, Warwick was determined that the *Sydney Morning Herald* should not budge. The *Sydney Morning Herald*'s editorial line supported conscription, the war and Australia's involvement in it. Although Pringle had promised to support the Fairfax board's view on Vietnam in 1965, he grew 'increasingly appalled' by the war. Pringle later said he felt, 'I was on the wrong side. And I was ashamed of it.'[56]

Guy Harriott had replaced Pringle as *Sydney Morning Herald* editor. The conservative Harriott was so stiff and formal that David McNicoll described him as 'ramrod-like'. Harriott's views were very much in line with Warwick Fairfax's so there was no longer any need for Warwick to discipline the editor, as he had regularly done with the more liberal-minded Pringle.[57] But the paper's circulation was suffering from their approach.[58] Warwick seemed to have little sense of the challenges and opportunities of the dawning era.

Whitlam's jibe about the Fairfaxes' 'autocratic' ways was not an accurate reflection of the company as a whole, though. Elsewhere in the group, pockets of independence and diversity were breaking out. The *Financial Review*'s support for the Coalition was implied rather than explicit, and Warwick Fairfax was irritated the paper did not show sufficient enthusiasm for McMahon.[59] In Canberra, where Labor's plans for an expanded bureaucracy would be welcomed, the *Canberra Times* avoided giving an explicit endorsement, but it did praise Labor's 'vision ... relentlessly developed' and Whitlam's 'methodical and disciplined' approach. And it said the McMahon government seemed to have run out of 'elan, of meaning, of inspired leadership'.[60]

But nowhere was the tussle for independence in the group more conspicuous than at *The Age*. John Fairfax Ltd had tightened its grip over its Melbourne asset after the *Newsday* disaster of 1969–70 (Chapter 18). Fairfax had been the controlling minority shareholder in David Syme and Co and it had lost money on that adventure. Fairfax managers and directors started paying more attention to *The Age* after that, and they increased Fairfax's stake in David Syme and Co. By July 1972, Fairfax held more than 50 per cent of the shares, making David Syme and Co technically a Fairfax subsidiary.[61]

As the election campaign began, *The Age* was no longer an independently owned Melbourne paper, but under the 1966 partnership agreement control of its management still remained with the Syme family in Melbourne (Chapter 14). That deal was now put to the test. And as journalist and editor Colleen Ryan noted, 'By today's standards, it was a tough deal' for Fairfax because even if Fairfax held '90 per cent of the shares' of David Syme and Co, it 'could not procure the passing of a resolution at a meeting of shareholders or directors which was opposed by the Syme minority' on the board.[62]

Warwick Fairfax wanted *The Age* to endorse McMahon just as he had personally in the *Sydney Morning Herald*. But *The Age* under Macdonald and Perkin had supported Labor's domestic policies in 1969, and the paper's opposition to Vietnam had hardened in 1971–72, which had moved *The Age* even closer to Labor's platform (Chapter 18). *The Age*'s public affairs reporter Bruce Grant had been allocated prime space in the paper since 1968, and he was writing lengthy pro-Labor articles. Grant was 'one of the earliest and strongest advocates for a change of government in 1972'.[63] Meanwhile, *The Age*'s former editor, Keith Sinclair, was working as McMahon's speechwriter–adviser during the campaign, a sign of just how much the paper had changed, politically, since he was in charge of it between 1959 and 1966.

Any desire Warwick Fairfax had to direct *The Age* editorially to back the Liberal Party for the election had to be tempered by caution about disrupting the paper's momentum. *The Age* was making money. It had renewed clout. It was influential with its opinion-shaping readership. Between 1971 and 1972, *The Age*'s circulation had grown by 12 000, more than any other metropolitan daily. In that same period, the paper that Warwick Fairfax was directing, the *Sydney Morning Herald*, had lost a further 1000 sales.[64]

The Age had shown there was money to be made in giving Melburnians a choice of political viewpoints by representing a soft left perspective. The 'soft' element of this was crucial. Unlike the *Argus* during its 'Red' years, advertisers did not judge *The Age* to be threatening. The paper was in demand from advertisers wanting to reach an affluent audience. In 1972–73, David Syme and Co boosted its profits by 53 per cent from the previous year.[65] In November 1972, Rupert Murdoch said *The Age* was one of the success stories of the era because it was packaging broadsheet news in a way that engaged younger readers of high income levels.[66]

The paper's commercial success fortified Perkin and Macdonald as they prepared for a showdown with the Fairfax directors. Aside from *The Age*'s editor and its managing director, its leader-writing staff and key reporters also wanted the paper to advocate a vote for Labor. There was uproar in the boardroom. Warwick Fairfax could not comprehend why Syme directors on the board would want to support Labor. He was probably under some pressure himself from politics and business figures. The Liberal Party president, Sir Robert Southey, had written to McMahon in March 1972, 'What influence has Warwick Fairfax? … whoever the real enemy is in *The Age*, and I think it is probably Perkin, he must be brought into line'.[67]

But Macdonald dug in on behalf of Perkin and editorial independence. A board meeting on 2 November ended with no resolution about which party *The Age* would endorse. By the time of the next meeting, on 28 November, the other directors had been blindsided. In the intervening days, *The Age* had made its position clear to readers through a series of editorials that supported Labor's policies. *The Age* editorial on the day the board met criticised McMahon's failure to modernise the Liberal Party, described his approach as one of 'indecision and lack of conviction', and said that Whitlam had turned 'the old Labor machine … to face the future'.[68]

The board had no choice but to begrudgingly accept that the paper would look ridiculous if it endorsed the Coalition now. Warwick Fairfax conceded.[69] But as a result of all the boardroom tension, *The Age*'s final editorial had to express its support for Labor in terms that were more 'limited and grudging' than Perkin had intended.[70] Nonetheless, the paper's support was on the record. The last time *The Age* had told its readers to vote Labor at a federal election was in 1937. Thirty-five years and 12 elections had passed since then.

THE HWT'S OLD WAYS

In editorials, the HWT papers conceded that Labor was putting forward appealing policies. Several of its papers even seemed to accept that Labor was going to win. But the *Herald* said the McMahon government 'should be given another term'.[71] And the *Sun News-Pictorial* cautioned against change 'for the sake of change'.[72]

In the late 1960s, Whitlam had neutralised state aid as a damaging national policy issue for Labor when he committed the party to providing federal aid to non-government schools. Deprived of its most galvanising cause, the DLP was running out of issues, electoral support and political influence. Although the party received only 6 per cent of the vote in 1969 (and it would receive only 5 per cent in 1972), the DLP was still being prominently reported in the HWT's Melbourne papers.[73]

Change was not something the HWT was well equipped for. In 1971, the average age of the HWT's board members was 67. Jack Williams had been with the company for 47 years, John Waters (former editor of the *Sun News-Pictorial*) for more than 50 years, and Archer Thomas (former editor of the *Herald*) for 48. In June 1972, Lyle Turnbull and Richard Sampson had been appointed directors to replace retiring members. Their appointments showed the company's ongoing preference for an internal-facing board. Turnbull was the editor-in-chief (Frank Daly had resigned in 1971). Although Turnbull was only 44, he had already been with the company for 26 years. Sampson was the company's finance director.

Accountants were still in charge at the HWT. Philip Jones was both chairman and managing director. Such a pairing of roles combined a great deal of power in one person, as it had with Williams, but was Jones the right person this time around? Continuing the tradition of Coalition governments knighting HWT leaders, Jones had received a knighthood in June 1971, but there was little sense of strong managerial and editorial drive at the HWT.

On the eve of the election, the 132-year-old *Herald* told the McMahon government that it needed 'rejuvenation'. It said the Liberal Party needed to promote talent, strengthen its leadership, appeal more to younger people and 'bring imagination and innovation, as well as experience, to its affairs'.[74] Could the HWT group take its own advice?

THE FUTURE

Labor was elected with a nine-seat majority in a historic victory. It had been 43 years since Labor had won an election from opposition, 26 years since Labor had won any federal election, and 23 years since Labor had been in government.[75] It was no landslide in terms of votes, though, with only a 2.6 per cent swing to Labor.[76] The landslide had occurred in 1969. It had not led to victory then, but it had paved the way for Labor's election win in 1972.

The election was also a historic moment for the newspaper industry. Murdoch, Perkin and Macdonald had broken the long tradition of an anti-Labor daily press during elections. Only twice in the past 50 years had Labor been supported at a federal election by two different proprietors (in 1954 it was the *Daily Mirror* and the *Argus* for Evatt; in 1929 it was *The Age* and the *Canberra Times* for Scullin, when Labor last won an election from opposition). Never before had the Labor Party enjoyed the support of five metropolitan dailies and one national paper (six metropolitan papers if we count the *Canberra Times* with its non-explicit editorial but still-visible support).

Murdoch was quoted as boasting that he had 'single-handedly put the present government into office'.[77] This assertion was ludicrous given the many factors involved in the rebuilding of Labor over the past five years. An alternative view was that Murdoch had switched to Labor when it was already on the ascendancy. The party had come close to victory in 1969, and McMahon's performance was so poor from March 1971 that he gave Labor every chance of success. Whitlam had felt confident he was going to win since late 1971.[78]

A suspicion that Murdoch had hitched himself to a sure-fire winner in 1972 was boosted by the fact that the biggest swing to Labor had occurred in Victoria, where he did not even own a daily paper.[79] For 17 years, Victoria had stood out from the rest of the country for never giving more than 44 per cent of its vote to Labor.[80] But the state's voting pattern was much closer to the other large states in 1972. Electorally speaking, Victoria had 'rejoined the nation'.[81]

Since 1969, *The Age* had helped make a vote for Labor respectable in Victoria, and Perkin was reputed to believe the paper's stance had contributed to Whitlam's victory.[82] It seems *The Age*'s editor was another who believed in the power of the press, and some journalists and political insiders tended to lean more towards his assumption of influence than Murdoch's (even though Murdoch controlled five daily papers compared to Perkin's one). Peter Blazey and Andrew Campbell, for example, argued *The Age*'s support was an 'important factor in Labor winning four outer suburban seats in Melbourne' that were crucial to Whitlam's victory.[83]

It was noticeable that in New South Wales, the state where Murdoch had most influence in 1972, there had been a larger swing toward Labor in 1969 (when he owned one Sydney daily and it had told voters to reject Labor) than in 1972 when Murdoch owned two dailies and both told their readers to vote Labor.

As always, the perception of influence was more important than the reality, though. And this was especially true in terms of the Australian political psyche. The lesson that Australian politicians took from 1972 was that Rupert Murdoch relished playing a kingmaker role (just as his father had in 1931), and had shown himself willing to turn the full firepower of his media assets in service of politicians he supported, and against those he opposed. Whether that had any decisive impact on the election result was unclear, but what politician wanted to take the risk of falling out of favour with a crusading media proprietor who owned a national newspaper, four daily metropolitan papers, four-and-a-half Sunday papers, more than 20 suburban papers and a television station?

The key question for media watchers now was whether Murdoch's support for Whitlam would last. Neither man was short of personal ego, and their relationship from this point on would depend upon what Murdoch wanted and expected from Whitlam, and whether he got it. Turbulent times lay ahead for the new Labor government because it was very ambitious, but it was also very inexperienced, and it was facing a hostile Senate. Internationally, the postwar golden age of the economy was coming to an end and the Australian economy would be coming under increasing pressure.

Two loud warnings had been sounded during the campaign, the first from the Murdoch camp. When the *Australian* had endorsed Labor on the eve of the 1972 election, it added a note of caution that implied the media company's support was conditional. The *Australian* said, because the party's vision was so bold, 'Labor party government will be an experiment, not a permanent commitment'.[84] The second warning came from within the Labor camp. ACTU president Bob Hawke told Whitlam at a campaign meeting, 'You're going to regret the day you got into bed with Rupert.'[85] The newspaper and the union leader were both right.

POSTSCRIPT

To the surprise of many in his social circles, one of Labor's election candidates in 1972 was Colin Bednall. The former journalist and media manager ran for the bayside seat of Flinders in Victoria, where television stars Graham Kennedy and Bert Newton handed out how-to-vote cards for him on polling day. In July, Bednall had been arrested in Tahiti, and deported, after criticising French nuclear tests in the Pacific. In December, Bednall polled well and gained an 11 per cent swing towards him in Flinders, but it was not enough to win the seat.[1]

Bednall had travelled a long way from his days as Keith Murdoch's protégé and Menzies' friend, and from his days as an anti-communist, free enterprise supporter and newspaper industry lobbyist. Bednall's defection to Labor meant he was not only being professionally shunned by Australian media owners, but also socially shunned by his Portsea and Melbourne Club set.

When he had been an editor and media manager, Bednall had used the power of the newspapers and radio stations at his command to campaign for favoured politicians and political positions. But as an outsider, he had come to see politics and the media from a very different perspective. Bednall said his social conscience had been moved by the poverty and inequality he saw in Hong Kong, where he had self-exiled to work in television after parting ways with Packer in the mid-1960s. When Bednall returned to Australia in 1969, he found the immense power of the press now appalled him.

Bednall argued the big media groups in Australia enjoyed 'legally and illegally, monopolies unparalleled anywhere in the world', with the possible exception of dictatorships in South America.[2] Bednall said that, in the United States and United Kingdom, it would be very difficult for a national leader to 'round up the mass media' because it was so varied and dispersed. But in Australia, a prime minister had to make only three telephone calls to have the Australian newspaper groups marshal 'their entire resources' across the nation, including daily newspapers, mass circulation magazines, chains of suburban free newspapers, regional papers, and radio and television stations. They could spread a message around the country 'in a dozen different ways' in a matter of only hours or days.[3]

In no other democratic nation was it possible to exercise such an extraordinary influence on public opinion with so little effort. And to make matters worse, there was no-one capable of challenging the dominance of the big groups. Commercially, they would crush a newcomer starting from scratch, but even extremely wealthy overseas companies could not realistically compete in Australia. Bednall had acted as a consultant for British and other overseas media companies. He told them to avoid Australia because the newspaper-radio-television companies owned too much and they used their media assets to cross-promote the different parts of their empires in a way that made them 'almost impregnable'.[4]

Bednall also told foreign owners to avoid Australia because its media groups were run by people who knew every political, editorial and legal dirty trick in the book: they suppressed information, manipulated politicians, ran political campaigns, distorted news and ruined opponents' reputations and livelihoods.[5] According to Bednall, the Anglo-Canadian newspaper publisher, Lord Thomson, investigated entering into Australian media but he decided to 'keep well clear', because, Thomson said, 'There are rough and tough characters there. Carry guns and things, you know.'[6] (It is very likely he said this around 1969 or 1970 and was thinking of Frank Packer and his associates.)

The newspaper industry that Bednall had been a part of when he was a decorated war correspondent in the 1940s was a very different place by the 1970s. The 'dynastic tyrants' – as Germaine Greer called the Fairfaxes and Murdochs – and the new managerial class at the helm of the HWT, had all cemented their positions and expanded their groups, but they were also beginning to show signs of struggling under the weight of social change, audience shifts and the new expectations of journalism.[7]

Over the next 30 years, there would be developments in media and communications that even the 'media monsters' could only delay but not hold back forever, including the internet. The newspaper groups would transform again. Even before the great digital disruption, one of the three media monsters would be swallowed up by a larger, bolder predator. Another would live on in a different form after a dramatic family conflict. And the third would become an international behemoth run by the most controversial media mogul in history. The seeds for all of those transformations had already been sown.

NOTES

Abbreviations

ABCB	Australian Broadcasting Control Board
ADB	*Australian Dictionary of Biography*
AFR	*Australian Financial Review*
ANU	Australian National University
ASIC	Australian Securities and Investments Commission
ATS	Amalgamated Television Services Pty Ltd
CPD	*Commonwealth Parliamentary Debates*
FMBA	Fairfax Media Business Archive (Mitchell Library)
HR	House of Representatives
HWT	Herald and Weekly Times Ltd
LA	Legislative Assembly
NAA	National Archives of Australia
NLA	National Library of Australia
PROV	Public Record Office Victoria
SMH	*Sydney Morning Herald*
SLNSW	State Library of New South Wales
SRSA	State Records of South Australia
UMA	University of Melbourne Archives
VPD	*Victorian Parliamentary Debates*

Introduction

1. Bednall, unpaginated typed version of unpublished autobiography, MS 5546/5, NLA. (There are three different versions of Bednall's unpublished autobiography manuscript in his files: a typed paginated version titled 'A Temporarily Undesirable Person' (box 5, folders 36–38) and an earlier unpaginated version, in both handwritten and typed formats, titled 'They Carry Guns and Things' (box 5, folders 42–44).
2. Morgan, 1993.
3. *News*, 9 July 1945, p. 3.
4. Mandle, 1997, p. 129.
5. Bednall, unpaginated typed version of unpublished autobiography, MS 5546/5, NLA.
6. ibid.
7. ibid.
8. Bednall, paginated typed version of unpublished autobiography, p. 372, MS 5546/5, NLA.
9. ibid., p. 206.
10. Bednall, unpaginated typed version of unpublished autobiography, MS 5546/5, NLA.
11. Bednall, paginated typed version of unpublished autobiography, p. 3, MS 5546/5, NLA.
12. *Courier-Mail*, 9 August 1941, p. 2 (but also syndicated across several other daily papers).

Chapter 1 At their peak

1. Younger, 1996, pp. 166–67.
2. *Young*, 2019, p. 83.
3. *Smith's Weekly*, 18 November 1939, p. 3.
4. Morgan et al., 2003, attachment 3.
5. *Workers' Star* (Perth), 12 November 1948, p. 4
6. Goot, 1979, pp. 5, 8.

7   *Sun News-Pictorial*, 22 March 1945, p. 7.
8   Cosgrove, 2011.
9   Young, 2019, pp. 430–31.
10 Morgan et al., 2003, attachment 2.
11 J Walter Thompson Pty Ltd, 'Recommendations for a newspaper publisher's cooperative campaign', July 1941, in Dumas Papers, MS 4849/box 11, NLA.
12 E.g. see *SMH*, 1 May 1945, p. 1.
13 *ibid.*; *Courier-Mail*, 7 February 1947, p. 4.
14 Joint Committee on Wireless Broadcasting, 1942, pp. 55–56.
15 Turnbull, 1947, p. 323; Inglis, 1987, p. 218.
16 The *Daily Commercial News and Shipping List* was also being published daily in Sydney but it did not contain journalism (as it would normally be defined). It was a four-page newspaper comprised of lists of shipping movements and aviation timetables plus related advertisements.
17 *Parliamentary Debates* (*Hansard*) (Senate), 27 November 1940, p. 167.
18 *Labor Call* (Melbourne), 12 December 1940, p. 15.
19 Edwards, 1972, p. 22.
20 Garden, p. 261.
21 *Herald*, 16 November 1945, p. 12.
22 Edwards, 1972, p. 116.
23 Goot, 1979, p. 5.
24 *Weekly Times*, 9 December 1942, p. 5: *The Stock Exchange Official Record*, November 1946, p. 364.
25 HWT, 'Annual Report to Shareholders', 1947, pp. 6–7, FMBA, MS 9894/1230, SLNSW; *Tribune* (Sydney), 25 June 1949, p. 6.
26 Morgan, 2008, p. ix.
27 Author interview with Gary Morgan, 7 October 2019.
28 *ibid*.
29 *Courier-Mail* (Brisbane), 10 September 1941, p. 4.
30 Goot, 2012.
31 Goot, 2010, p. 275.
32 *Herald*, 4 October 1941, p. 7.
33 Goot, 2012; Roberts, 2015, p. 232.
34 Buckridge, 1994, p. 235.
35 *Advertiser*, 9 May 1958, p. 5.
36 *Advertiser*, 21 February 1945, p. 2; Goot, 1979, p. 5; Advertiser Newspapers Ltd, p. 142.
37 Young, 2019, pp. 209–39.
38 *News*, 28 September 1945, p. 5 and 22 September 1944, p. 5.
39 Young, 2019, pp. 268–71.
40 E.g. *Tribune*, 5 April 1945, p. 3 and 1 May 1948, p. 7.
41 *Daily News*, 21 August 1941, p. 16; Goot, 1979, p. 5.
42 *Daily News*, 28 May 1940, p. 1 and 10 June 1946, p. 1.
43 *West Australian*, 10 July 1947, p. 20.
44 Young, 2019, pp. 274, 288–90.
45 Dunstan, 2012.
46 Technically, Associated Newspapers owned one paper and a third of another paper, as it owned the *Sun* and, in partnership with Consolidated Press, a third of the *Daily Telegraph*.
47 Speech notes for RA Henderson, 13 May 1948, in FMBA, MS 9894/1610, SLNSW.
48 *SMH*, 1 January 1948, p. 3.
49 The paper's classified advertising prices were raised twice in 1948–49, after three earlier price rises between 1945 and 1947 (*Sun*, 8 September 1949, p. 2).
50 G Lovett, 'Consolidated Press', 20 August 1953, McNicoll Papers, MS 7419/19.
51 Kearsley, undated; *The Review*, 20 August 1971, p. 1274.
52 Goot, 1979, p. 5.
53 *Tribune*, 23 May 1947, p. 3.
54 Morgan et al., 2003, attachment 1.

55 *Tribune*, 14 January 1947, p. 3.
56 David McNicoll interview with John Farquharson, 1997.
57 Souter, 1981, p. 280.
58 *Courier-Mail, 1933–1983: 50th Anniversary Souvenir*, p. 6.
59 *Daily Telegraph*, 23 November 1946, p. 11.
60 *Canberra Times*, 3 September 1976, p. 17.
61 Dobell, 1987, p. 47.
62 Lloyd, 2014.
63 'Metropolitan newspapers' document in Calwell Papers, MS 4738/36, NLA; *West Australian*, 10 July 1947, p. 20.
64 Baker, 2015; *Daily Telegraph*, 4 September 2015.
65 Walker, 1980a, p. 160; Hall, undated.
66 Cited in Walker, 1980a, p. 160.
67 Blair, 2005.
68 *West Australian*, 17 November 1979, p. 41. Between 1860 and 1877, Jane Syme, widow of David's brother Ebenezer, was an equal owner of *The Age* and took 50 per cent of its profits (Sayers, 1976).
69 Clarke, 2014, p. 495.
70 *Australasian Journalist*, 15 June 1927, p. 84.
71 Edwards, 1972, p. 55.
72 *Age*, 5 September 1977, p. 2.
73 Dunstan, 2018, p. 20.
74 Edwards, 1972, p. 26.
75 *Argus*, 25 August 1944, p. 4.
76 Bongiorno, 1996, pp. 25, 26, 50, 54.
77 Serle, 1990.
78 Goot, 1979, p. 5.
79 *Age*, 16 October 1948, p. 6.
80 Morgan et al., 2003, attachment 3.
81 *Courier-Mail*, 5 February 1988, pp. 8–9.
82 *Telegraph*, 30 September 1922, p. 16 and 12 June 1943, p. 8; *The Farmer and Settler* (Sydney), 5 November 1915, p. 4; *Queensland Times* (Ipswich), 8 January 1913, p. 6.
83 *Mercury*, 15 August 1949, p. 13.

Chapter 2 Curtin's circus
1 *SMH*, 9 October 1941, p. 8.
2 Clarke, 2020.
3 *Daily Telegraph*, 28 April 1945.
4 *Herald*, 4 October 1941, p. 4.
5 *Daily Telegraph*, 4 November 1941, p. 2.
6 HWT, *Annual Report*, 1947, pp. 6–7; *Herald*, 16 November 1945, p. 12.
7 Greenslade, 2020. Much depends of course on how 'genuine journalistic experience' is defined. Winston Churchill had worked as a war correspondent, for example.
8 Coatney, 2013 and Coatney, 2016, pp. 6-10.
9 See Isaacs, 2015; Walker, 1980b; *Newspaper News*, 1 August 1940, p. 2.
10 *Westralian Worker*, 9 January 1920. In 1922, he had written that 'The power of the press is greater than that of the Caesars of the school books or the statesmen of our existing Legislatures' (*Westralian Worker*, 17 March 1922, p. 4).
11 *CPD* (HR), 2 April 1941, p. 578.
12 Lloyd, 1988, p. 136.
13 *ibid.*, p. 125.
14 Quoted in Coatney, 2013, p. 74.
15 *Smith's Weekly*, 24 October 1942, p. 12.
16 Allan Fraser interview with Mel Pratt, 1975, NLA; *Daily Mirror*, 11 May 1976, p. 31.

17 Coatney, 2016, p. 91.
18 Roberts, 2015, p. 236.
19 Ward, 1981, pp. 52, 57.
20 Roberts, 2015, p. 235.
21 Lloyd, 1988, p. 155.
22 *Herald*, 4 February 1943, p. 4.
23 *ibid.*, 5 February 1943, p. 4.
24 *ibid.*
25 *Weekly Times*, 30 April 1942, p. 2.
26 Joe Alexander quoted in Griffen-Foley, 2003b, p. 13.
27 Quoted in Coatney, 2013, pp. 63–78.
28 Roberts, 2015, p. 234; *Herald*, 11 March 1942, p. 4.
29 *Herald*, 11 March 1942, p. 4 ; Roberts, 2015, p. 233.
30 Roberts, 2015, p. 234.
31 Younger, 2003, pp. 276–77; Ward, 1981, p. 66. See also Roberts, 2015, p. 241.
32 Griffen-Foley, 2003b, p. 14.
33 Young, 2019, pp. 523–25.
34 Younger, 2003, p. 257.
35 *ibid.*, p. 275.
36 *ibid.*, p. 260.
37 Roberts, 2015, p. 235.
38 *ibid.*
39 Lloyd and Hall, p. 150.
40 Day, 1999, p. 49.
41 Thompson, 1962, p. 67.
42 *ibid.*
43 Lloyd and Hall, 1997, pp. 99–100.
44 *ibid.*, p. 152.
45 Souter, 1981, p. 259.
46 Walker, 1980a, p. 203.
47 Hilvert, 1993; *Argus* (Melbourne), 5 April 1941, p. 1.
48 Walker, 1980a, p. 205.
49 *Newspaper News*, 1 October 1941, p. 5.
50 Hilvert, 1993.
51 Hasluck, 1970, p. 300.
52 Telegram from HV Evatt to RG Menzies, 10 July 1941, Menzies Papers, MS 4936, NLA.
53 Vickery, 2003, p. 197; Kiernan, 1976, p. 90.
54 Ward, 1981, p. 66.
55 Souter, 1981, p. 240.
56 *SMH*, 18 August 1942, p. 4.
57 Day, 1999, p. 478.
58 *Daily Telegraph*, 20 August 1942, p. 1; Day, 1999, p. 478.
59 *SMH*, 16 September 1942, p. 6.
60 Walker, 1980a, p. 215.
61 Mander, 1944, p. 20.
62 Meeting notes from 'Interview with Messrs Dedman and Ward, Sydney', 29 June 1942, FMBA, MLMSS 9894/102, SLNSW, pp. 1, 6.
63 Young, 2016a, pp. 144–45.
64 Mander, 1944, p. 25.
65 Lloyd, 2001, pp. 161–62.
66 *Herald*, 7 August 1943, p. 4.
67 Edwards, 1972, p. 108.
68 Young, 2019, p. 521.
69 Frank Chamberlain interview with Mel Pratt, 1972–73, NLA.
70 *Herald*, 24 July 1943, p. 3.

71 Frank Chamberlain interview with Mel Pratt, 1972–73, NLA.
72 Hazlehurst, 1989, p. 270.
73 *SMH*, 18 August 1943, p. 6 and 15 July 1943, p. 4.
74 Souter, 1981, p. 184.
75 *SMH*, 17 August 1943, p. 4.
76 *ibid.*, 21 August 1943, p. 8; 10 July 1943, p. 8 and 14 July 1943, p. 6.
77 Souter, 1981, p. 245.
78 Letter from RG Menzies to RA Henderson, 8 August 1943, Menzies Papers, MS4936, NLA.
79 Griffen-Foley, 1995, p. 66; Griffen-Foley, 2003a, p. 38; Buckridge, 1994, pp. 209–10, 213.
80 *Northern Star* (Lismore), 10 September 1943, p. 5.
81 *SMH*, 4 February 1954, p. 4.
82 Letter from K Murdoch to L Dumas, 23 August 1943, Dumas Papers, MSS 4849, folder 43, NLA; Goot, 2014, pp. 151–52; *Telegraph* (Brisbane), 19 August 1943, p. 2.
83 AJA Victoria District Committee, Melbourne, meeting of 18 March 1944, AJA Victorian branch records (1993.0133), 74/32/6, UMA.
84 Lloyd, 1988, p. 155.
85 Coatney, 2016, p. 93.
86 Report of meetings, 15 and 16 August 1943, Dumas Papers, MSS 4849/box 11/folder 71, NLA.
87 Roberts, 2015, p. 236.
88 Letter from L Dumas to K Murdoch, 25 August 1943; Letter from L Dumas to K Murdoch, 28 August 1943; Letter from L Dumas to K Murdoch, 31 August 1943; Memo from S Stephens to L Dumas, 6 September 1943, Dumas Papers, MSS 4849/11/71, NLA.
89 *Herald*, 23 August 1943, p. 4.
90 Telegram from A Calwell to K Murdoch, 19 November 1943, Calwell Papers, MS 4738/36/4, NLA.
91 Letter from K Murdoch to A Calwell, 19 November 1943, Calwell Papers, MS 4738/36/4, NLA.
92 Zwar, 1980, p. 94.
93 Ward, 1981, p. 65.
94 Goot, 2014, p. 150.
95 *Newspaper News*, 1 June 1944, p. 3.
96 Letter from W Fairfax to RG Menzies, 23 September 1943, Menzies Papers, MS4936/1, NLA.

Chapter 3 The press and the 'Cocky' go to war
1   *CPD* (HR), 13 November 1941, p. 415.
2   Macintyre, 2015, p. 264.
3   Kiernan, 1976, p. 75.
4   *Herald* (Melbourne), 19 March 1935, p. 5. (The original article, quoting W Kent Hughes' remarks approvingly, was published in the *Herald*, 1 March 1935, p. 18.)
5   *CPD* (HR), 20 May 1942, p. 1392.
6   *ibid.*, 21 May 1942, p. 1458.
7   *Daily Telegraph*, 21 May 1942, p. 1.
8   Calwell, AN Smith lecture: 'The Australian Labor Party and the Press', delivered at the University of Melbourne, 30 July 1959, p. 4; *Sun*, 2 May 1945, clipping in Calwell Papers, MS 4738, NLA.
9   Freudenberg, 1993.
10 Frank Chamberlain interview with Mel Pratt, 1972–73, NLA.
11 *ibid.*
12 Calwell, 1972, p. 90.
13 *CPD* (HR), 19 March 1941, p. 128.
14 Calwell, 1972, p. 89; Telegram from C Buttrose to *Advertiser*, 25 March 1941, Dumas Papers, MS 4849, NLA.
15 Calwell, 1972, p. 90.
16 Anonymous, 'Sir Keith Murdoch', Calwell Papers, MS 4738/36, NLA. (No author was listed but it may have been written by Gavin Casey, deputy director of the Department of Information and a state censor who had previously been a journalist at Perth's *Daily News*.)

17 Walker, 1980a, p. 213.
18 E.g. Mander, 1944, pp. 28–29, 32–33.
19 Roberts, 2015, p. 242; *Daily Telegraph* (Sydney), 16 December 1943, p. 7.
20 Hilvert, 1984, p. 175. (The order was withdrawn on 1 February after the *Daily Telegraph* gave a clear undertaking that it would abide by censorship regulations.)
21 Hasluck, p. 409.
22 Walker, 1980a, p. 214.
23 Hilvert, 1984, pp. 175–76.
24 E.g. *SMH*, 26 February 1944, p. 9.
25 *CPD* (HR), 7 March 1944, p. 1019.
26 Walker, 1980a, p. 217.
27 Souter, 1981, p. 243.
28 Penton, 1947, p. 59.
29 *ibid*., p. 59.
30 Day, 1999, pp. 534, 536.
31 *Daily Telegraph*, 23 April 1944, p. 1.
32 *Daily Examiner* (Grafton, NSW), 13 April 1944, p. 2.
33 Souter, 1981, p. 244.
34 Griffen-Foley, 1999, p. 129.
35 Penton, 1947, p. 67.
36 Griffen-Foley, 2000, p. 148.
37 Vickery, 2003, p. 209.
38 Griffen-Foley, 2000, pp. 148–49; *Sun* (Sydney), 17 April 1944, p. 3.
39 Hilvert, 1984, p. 179.
40 Souter, 1981, pp. 245–46.
41 *ibid*., p. 244. See also Penton, 1947, pp. 72–73.
42 Whitington, 1971, p. 180.
43 Penton, 1947, p. 68.
44 Souter, 1981, p. 246.
45 *ibid*., p. 247.
46 *Daily Telegraph*, 2 June 1945, p. 12.
47 *ibid*., 29 April 1944, p. 7.
48 Penton, 1947, p. 102; *Daily Telegraph*, 17 April 1944, p. 2; *SMH*, 17 April 1944, p. 1.
49 *Daily Telegraph*, 17 April 1944, p. 1; *Daily Telegraph*, 17 April 1944, p. 2.
50 Whitington, 1971, p. 182.
51 Hilvert, 1984, p. 179.
52 *CPD* (HR), 24 November 1944, p. 2144. In *Be Just and Fear Not*, Calwell said (p. 90) he made this decision at 3 am but other accounts suggest it was probably earlier in the night.
53 RA Henderson statement in 'Newspapers – censorship, defence and statement of claim', A472 W20951B, NAA; Whitington, 1971, p. 183.
54 Griffen-Foley, 1999, p. 129.
55 Penton, 1947, pp. 75–76; Whitington, 1971, p. 182.
56 *Daily Telegraph*, 18 April 1944, p. 9.
57 *Labor Call* (Melbourne), 27 April 1944, p. 8.
58 *Daily Telegraph*, 18 April 1944, p. 3.
59 *ibid*., 18 April 1944, p. 9; *Herald* (Melbourne), 19 April 1944, p. 3. One of the student demonstrators, Neil McInness, later became a journalist.
60 *Labor Call* (Melbourne), 27 April 1944, p. 8.
61 Souter, 1981, pp. 248–49.
62 Hilvert, 1984, pp. 8, 180.
63 *ibid*., p. 180.
64 Vickery, 2003, p. 212.
65 Hilvert, 1984, p. 181; Souter, 1981, p. 248; *Daily Telegraph*, 18 April 1944, p. 1.
66 Souter, 1981, p. 76.

NOTES TO PAGES 72–82 471

67 *CPD* (HR), 24 November 1944, p. 2144.
68 Calwell, 1972, p. 91.
69 Macintyre, 2015, p. 265.
70 *Townsville Daily Bulletin*, 20 April 1944, p. 3; *Newspaper News*, 1 May 1944, p. 1.
71 Hilvert, 1984, pp. 184–85.
72 *Sun* (Sydney), 17 March 1940, p. 1.
73 Calwell, 1972, p. 91.
74 Penton, 1947, p. 70.
75 Calwell, 1972, pp. 91–92; *Newspaper News*, 1 July 1944, p. 6.
76 Souter, 1981, p. 249.
77 *Newspaper News*, 1 June 1944, p. 1; *SMH*, 19 May 1944, p. 3.
78 *Daily Telegraph*, 21 April 1944, p. 5.
79 Hilvert, 1984, p. 188.
80 *Daily Telegraph*, 21 May 1944, p. 7.
81 *SMH*, 22 April 1944, p. 2.
82 *Newspaper News*, 1 May 1944, p. 1.
83 *ibid.*, 1 June 1944, p. 2.
84 *Daily Telegraph*, 29 April 1944, p. 7.
85 Cabinet brief: 'Urgent and necessary measures for the reform of the daily press: Agenda no 673; copy no: 19', Calwell Papers, MS 4738/268/1208, NLA.
86 John Frith interview with Shirley McKechnie, 1994, NLA. Australians recognise 'cocky' as an abbreviation for 'cockatoo'.
87 *CPD* (HR), 24 November 1944, p. 2144.
88 *Daily Telegraph*, 25 November 1944, p. 1.
89 *ibid.*, 29 August 1945, p. 5.
90 Kiernan, 1976, p. 104.
91 Souter, 1981, p. 251.
92 *SMH*, 14 March 1946, p. 1.
93 Letter from A Calwell to K Murdoch, 26 March 1945, Calwell Papers, MS 4738/36, NLA.
94 Letter from K Murdoch to A Calwell, 27 March 1945, *ibid*.
95 Letter from A Calwell to K Murdoch, 3 April 1945, *ibid*.
96 Edwards, 2018, p. 375.
97 *Daily Telegraph*, 18 May 1945, p. 6.
98 Kiernan, 1976, p. 105.

Chapter 4 New beginnings
1   *Daily Telegraph*, 22 May 1944, p. 1.
2   *SMH*, 13 September 1944, p. 4.
3   Souter, 1981, p. 252.
4   Hagan, 1966, p. 274.
5   Lloyd, 1988, p. 238.
6   Souter, 1981, p. 253; *Tribune* (Sydney), 8 June 1988, p. 6; Lloyd, 1988, p. 239.
7   Souter, 1981, p. 256.
8   *Herald*, 13 October 1944, p. 3; *Tribune*, 8 June 1988, p. 6; *Argus*, 10 October 1944, p. 3; *Canberra Times*, 9 October 1944, p. 3.
9   *Tribune*, 8 June 1988, p. 6; Souter, 1981, p. 253; *Telegraph* (Brisbane), 9 October 1944, p. 3.
10 *Herald*, 13 October 1944, p. 3.
11 *ibid.*; *Tribune*, 8 June 1988, p. 6; Lloyd, 1988, p. 240.
12 Griffen-Foley, 2000, p. 155.
13 Smith, undated a.
14 Souter, 1981, p. 258.
15 *SMH*, 19 January 1945, p. 5.
16 *Daily Telegraph*, 5 April 1945, p. 18 and 7 June 1945, p. 7.
17 *Herald*, 6 June 1947, p. 8, and 8 February 1943, p. 1.

18   Griffen-Foley, 2000, p. 151.
19   Aimer, 1979, p. 218.
20   *Herald*, 17 May 1943, p. 6.
21   Zwar, 1980, p. 124.
22   Kennedy, 1981; *Barrier Miner*, 15 April 1954, p. 1.
23   Aimer, 1979, p. 218.
24   Bertram, 1989, p. 5; Aimer, 1979, p. 218.
25   *Herald*, 17 May 1943, p. 6; Aimer, 1979, p. 218.
26   *Herald*, 22 July 1943, p. 7, and 25 August 1943, p. 8.
27   Macintyre, 2015, p. 147.
28   *Advertiser*, 26 July 1941, p. 9; *Argus*, 10 April 1943, p. 12; *Daily Telegraph*, 20 August 1943, p. 12; *SMH*, 26 August 1944, p. 5 and 17 December 1943, p. 7; *Canberra Times*, 20 December 1943, p. 2; *Australian Worker*, 22 December 1943, p. 2.
29   Blainey and Hutton, 1983, p. 218.
30   *Argus*, 2 July 1943, p. 8; *SMH*, 12 November 1943, p. 3; Blainey and Hutton, 1983, p. 223.
31   Younger, 1996, p. 442.
32   Eather and Cottle, 2012, p. 168.
33   *SMH*, 8 May 1943, p. 11.
34   *ibid.*, 15 July 1943, p. 4.
35   Mander, 1944, p. 81.
36   *Courier-Mail*, 7 October 1941, p. 8; *Argus*, 2 October 1943, p. 6.
37   *Canberra Times*, 1 August 1941, p. 6; *Daily Telegraph*, 25 May 1946, p. 16.
38   Spearritt; *Smith's Weekly*, 15 May 1943, p. 13; *Border Morning Mail* (Albury), 7 May 1943, p. 3.
39   *Daily Commercial News and Shipping List*, 23 January 1943, p. 2; *SMH*, 8 May 1943, p. 11; *Tribune*, 1 October 1947, p. 8 and 19 April 1945, p. 3.
40   *Labor Call* (Melbourne), 27 April 1944, p. 8; *Daily Telegraph*, 20 April 1944, p. 5; Aimer, 1979, p. 219; Macintyre, 2015, p. 268.
41   Bertram, 1989, p. 9.
42   Griffen-Foley, 2001a, p. 27.
43   *ibid.*, p. 24.
44   *SMH*, 24 March 1944, p. 7; Griffen-Foley, 2003b, pp. 12, 15.
45   Souter, 1981, p. 271; *Canberra Times*, 29 September 1985, p. 25.
46   Souter, 1981, p. 271.
47   *ibid.*; *Canberra Times*, 29 September 1985, p. 25; Bramston, 2019, p. 109.
48   Liberal Party of Australia, undated.
49   *Daily Telegraph*, 31 August 1944, p. 8.
50   *ibid.*, 3 October 1944, p. 4.
51   *Sun*, 20 October 1944, p. 6; *Herald*, 17 October 1944, p. 5.
52   *SMH/DT/Sun/DM*, 19 October 1944, p. 2, and 18 October 1944, p. 3.
53   Souter, 1981, p. 272.
54   *Sun*, 29 November 1944, p. 5.
55   *SMH*, 8 December 1944, p. 4; *Daily Mercury* (Mackay), 24 November 1944, p. 3; *Tribune*, 17 September 1946, p. 6; *West Australian*, 25 November 1944, p. 8; *Border Chronicle* (Bordertown), 11 August 1944, p. 6.
56   *Daily Telegraph*, 9 August 1944, p. 8 and 24 November 1944, p. 1.
57   *Argus*, 24 November 1944, p. 3.
58   *SMH*, 23 November 1944, p. 2 and 24 November 1944, p. 2.
59   Melbourne Steamship was an important company in Melbourne and had two representatives on the National Bank board sitting with Harold Giddy (*Tribune*, 27 September 1947, p. 1).
60   Henderson, 1994, p. 86.
61   Macintyre, 2016, p. 283.
62   *ibid.*, p. 87.
63   *SMH*, 15 December 1944, p. 2.
64   *Sun*, 15 December 1944, p. 4 and 21 December 1944, p. 4.

65 *Daily Telegraph*, 15 December 1944, p. 8.
66 Macintyre, 2016, p. 210.
67 Letter from RA Henderson to Chairman of the Liberal Party of Australia, 19 April 1945, FMBA, MLMSS 9894/512, SLNSW; Letter from General Manager, John Fairfax & Sons to Secretary, Liberal Party (NSW), 25 October 1949, FMBA, MLMSS 9894/512, SLNSW.
68 Younger, 2003, p. 315.
69 Allan Fraser interview with Mel Pratt, 1975, NLA.
70 Cox typescript reports, MS 4554, NLA.
71 Letter from RA Henderson to J Curtin, 1 April 1944, FMBA, MLMSS 9894/512, SLNSW.
72 *ibid.*, 15 November 1944, FMBA, MLMSS 9894/512, SLNSW.
73 *SMH*, 22 Jan 1945, p. 2.
74 Souter, 1981, p. 236.
75 *SMH*, 2 July 1945, p. 2.
76 Day, 2001, p. 237.
77 Souter, 1981, p. 237.
78 Dobell, 1987, p. 53.
79 Souter, 1981, p. 237.
80 Cox typescript reports, MS 4554, NLA; McMullin, 2001, p. 258; Day, 2001, p. 257.
81 Waterson, 1993.
82 Day, 2001, p. 255.
83 Waterson, 1993; *Daily Examiner* (Grafton), 9 December 1949, p. 1.
84 Crisp, 1963, p. 111.
85 *Daily Examiner* (Grafton), 9 December 1949, p. 1.
86 Crisp, 1963, pp. 110–11.
87 *News*, 16 August 1946, p. 5.
88 *Herald*, 30 November 1945, p. 4.
89 *SMH*, 27 November 1945, p. 5; *Daily Telegraph*, 26 November 1945, p. 9.
90 Macintyre, 2016, p. 205.
91 *Daily Telegraph*, 27 September 1946, p. 8.
92 Griffen-Foley, 2000, p. 172.
93 *SMH*, 23 September 1946, p. 2.
94 *Herald*, 27 September 1946, p. 1.
95 *Mercury*, 24 September 1946, p. 3.
96 Bramston, 2019, p. 122; Hazlehurst, 1979, p. 304.
97 *Herald*, 13 August 1947; *Courier-Mail*, 14 August 1947.
98 Correspondence between Murdoch and Menzies, dated 2, 5, 8 and 16 September 1947, in Menzies Papers, MS 4936/1/20/172, NLA.
99 *Courier-Mail*, 10 December 1947, p. 1.
100 Goot, 1979, p. 5.
101 Griffen-Foley, 2000, p. 169.
102 *SMH*, 5 December 1947, p. 7.
103 Younger, 2003, p. 290.

Chapter 5 Banking on the press
1 Curtin, 1940, JCPML00421/2, John Curtin Prime Ministerial Library.
2 McMullin, 2001, p. 252; Macintyre, 2015, p. 284.
3 *Kyogle Examiner* (NSW), 19 September 1947, p. 3.
4 *SMH*, 24 October 1947, p. 5.
5 Young, 2019, p. 14
6 Clarke, 1962, p. 13.
7 *SMH*, 18 May 1899, p. 3; *AFR*, 28 May 1999, p. 22; *Smith's Weekly*, 20 July 1946, p. 4.
8 *SMH*, 31 October 1952, p. 4.
9 *ibid.*, 6 July 1950, p. 5.
10 Clarke, 1962, p. 13.

11   Yule, 2012; *AFR*, 28 May 1999, p. 22.
12   Yule, 2012, p. 69; correspondence cited in Ward, 1981, p. 69.
13   Wheelwright, 1957, p. 174; *Herald*, 24 April 1944, p. 10; *Labor Call* (Melbourne), 3 March 1921, p. 6; Rawling, 1939, pp. 34, 42, 18.
14   Younger, 2003, p. 340.
15   Zwar, 1980, pp. 83–84. Will and three codicils of Keith Murdoch, PROV.
16   Walker, 1980a, p. 221.
17   Blainey and Hutton, 1983, pp. 217, 230; Martin, 1999, p. 20.
18   Eather and Cottle, 2012, p. 166; Brett, 2003, p. 91.
19   *AFR*, 26 October 1994, p. 6.
20   *Nation*, 7 November 1959, p. 16.
21   *AFR*, 16 August 2021, p. 3.
22   *Argus*, 23 January 1945, p. 6; *Canberra Times*, 15 July 1967, p. 15; Yule, 2021.
23   Martin, 1999, p. 20.
24   Macintyre, 2015, p. 287.
25   *Daily Telegraph*, 15 March 1945, p. 12.
26   Macintyre, 2015, pp. 429–30.
27   *SMH*, 23 August 1947, p. 2.
28   *Daily Telegraph*, 23 August 1947, p. 18. Note: some sources said it was 19 words, others said 44 words.
29   Edwards, 1972, p. 165.
30   *Sun*, 22 August 1947, p. 2.
31   Blainey and Hutton, 1983, p. 230.
32   *Sun*, 30 August 1947, p. 1.
33   Eather and Cottle, 2012, pp. 171–72.
34   *Daily Telegraph*, 14 March 1945, p. 15.
35   Eather and Cottle, 2012, p. 165.
36   *ibid.*, pp. 165–66.
37   Allan Fraser interview with Mel Pratt, 1975, NLA.
38   *Telegraph* (Brisbane), 16 October 1947, p. 2.
39   *SMH*, 4 September 1987, p. 11.
40   Crisp, 1963, pp. 419–21.
41   Allan Fraser interview with Mel Pratt, 1975, NLA.
42   *SMH*, 26 August 1947, p. 1.
43   *ibid.*, 18 August 1947, pp. 1, 2.
44   *Telegraph* (Brisbane), 24 October 1947, p. 2; *Herald*, 23 August 1947, p. 15; *Courier-Mail*, 18 August 1947, p. 1; *West Australian*, 23 August 1947, p. 9; *Argus*, 9 September 1947, p. 17.
45   *Telegraph* (Brisbane), 14 October 1947, p. 2; *SMH*, 19 August 1947, p. 2; *Argus*, 22 August 1947, p. 2 and 20 September 1947, p. 2.
46   Kerr, 1996.
47   *SMH*, 24 October 1947, p. 5.
48   E.g. *SMH*, 21 August 1947, p. 2 and 26 August 1947, p. 2.
49   Letter from JB Chifley to RA Henderson, 11 November 1946, FMBA, MLMSS 9894/511, SLNSW.
50   *Herald*, 22 August 1947, p. 4.
51   Ward, 1981, p. 67.
52   Abjorensen, 2017; Brett, 2003, p. 118.
53   Macintyre, 2015, p. 433.
54   Letter from J Butters to F Packer, 5 July 1946, FMBA, MLMSS 9894/103, SLNSW.
55   G Lovett, 'Consolidated Press', report sent to Ezra Norton on 20 August 1953, McNicoll Papers, MS 7419-19, SLNSW.
56   Lloyd, 1985, p. 224.
57   Letter from L Dumas to J Williams, 1 November 1941, Dumas Papers, MS 4849, NLA.
58   J Walter Thompson Pty Ltd, 'Recommendations for a newspaper publisher's cooperative campaign', July 1941, in Dumas Papers, MS 4849/11, NLA.

59 *Tribune*, 30 November 1945, p. 4.
60 Younger, 2003, p. 292.
61 MEAA, 2017; Lloyd, 1985, pp. 227–34.
62 Six Baillieus plus their allied companies, such as Assets Pty Ltd, were on News Limited's shareholder list in 1949 (News Limited, GRS/513/11, file 74/1922, SRSA).
63 Edwards, 1972, p. 99.
64 Bednall, handwritten unpaginated version of unpublished autobiography, Bednall Papers, MS 5546/5, NLA; *Age*, 19 May 1975, p. 8.
65 *Herald*, 9 December 1949, p. 7.
66 Reid, 2021. The Daily Mirror group also published the popular *Sunday Pictorial*.
67 *Guardian* (London), 14 October 1952, p. 4 and 21 April 1956, p. 12.
68 Crisp, 1961, p. 266.
69 *Advertiser*, 28 June 1949, p. 3; *Herald*, 27 June 1949, p. 3; *Daily Telegraph*, 27 June 1949, p. 7.
70 *Advertiser*, 26 March 1949, p. 1.
71 Letter from K Murdoch to C Bednall, 19 July 1949 and letter from C Bednall to K Murdoch, 21 July 1949, Bednall Papers, MS 5546, NLA.
72 *Daily Telegraph*, 25 June 1949, p. 15.
73 ibid., 27 June 1949, p. 7.
74 *Cobram Courier* (Vic), 19 August 1949, p. 1.
75 *West Australian*, 26 August 1949, p. 13.
76 Crisp, 1961, pp. 265, 267.
77 *Westralian Worker* (Perth), 9 December 1949, p. 8; *Age*, 8 December 1949, p. 2; Crisp, 1961, p. 265.
78 *Worker* (Brisbane), 30 August 1948, p. 9.
79 *West Australian*, 14 June 1948, p. 6.
80 Younger, 2003, p. 302.
81 Page, 2003, p. 65.
82 Younger, 2003, p. 301.
83 ibid., p. 314.
84 Dunstan, 1990, p. 188.
85 Macintyre, 2022, p. 222.
86 *Herald*, 7 April 1949, p. 9; Lee, 1994, p. 503.
87 *Herald*, 9 April 1949, p. 9.
88 *Herald*, 16 April 1949, p. 1; 18 April 1949, p. 1; 20 April 1949, p.1 and 21 April 1949, p. 1.
89 Sharpley, 1949.
90 Sharpley, 1949, front cover.
91 Younger, 2003, p. 314.
92 McQueen, 1977, p. 66.
93 Macintyre, 2022, p. 222.
94 McQueen, 1977, p. 66; Deery, 2012.
95 Deery, 2012.
96 McQueen, 1977, p. 66.
97 Younger, 2003, p. 315.
98 *Herald*, 9 December 1949, p. 4; *Age*, 8 December 1949, p. 2; *SMH*, 7 December 1949, p. 2; *Daily Telegraph*, 9 December 1949, p. 1.
99 Bednall, unpaginated autobiography, Bednall Papers, MS 5546, NLA.
100 Ward, 1981, p. 74.
101 McMullin, 2001, p. 266.
102 Macintyre, 2015, p. 434.
103 Blainey and Hutton, 1983, p. 233.
104 *Courier-Mail*, 5 December 1949, p. 2; Young, 2019, pp. 374–99.
105 *Balonne Beacon* (Queensland), 30 April 1942, p. 2.
106 Macintyre, 2015, p. 461; Young, 2003.
107 Young, 2003, p. 102.
108 McMullin, 2001, p. 266.

109 Freudenberg, 2001, p. 88.
110 Macintyre, 2016, p. 210; Freudenberg, 2001, p. 88.
111 *News*, 9 December 1949, p. 1; *Courier-Mail*, 5 December 1949, p. 2.
112 *Herald*, 7 December 1949, p. 1.
113 *Advertiser*, 7 December 1949, p. 1.
114 *Courier-Mail*, 7 December 1949, p. 1 and 9 December 1949, p. 7.
115 *Argus*, 7 December 1949, p. 5 and 8 December 1949, p. 3. See also Crisp, 1961, pp. 113–15.
116 *Mercury*, 22 April 1950, p. 10.
117 Younger, 2003, p. 316.
118 Letter from R Henderson to JB Chifley, 1 October 1946, and 12 December 1949, FMBA, MLMSS 9894/511, SLNSW.
119 Crisp, 1961, p. 264.
120 *ibid.*, p. 415.

Chapter 6 Newspapers fight the Cold War
1 Younger, 1996, p. 248.
2 Bednall, handwritten unpaginated autobiography, Bednall Papers, MS 5546, NLA; *Herald*, 25 January 1954, p. 3 and 10 April 1954, p. 15.
3 Memo from A McLachlan to RAG Henderson, 13 July 1954, FMBA, MLMSS 9894/922, SLNSW.
4 Macintyre, 2016, p. 205. (See also Murphy, 2000, p. 219.)
5 *ibid*.
6 Sungravure, 'House memo', 13 January 1960, FMBA, MLMSS 9894/357, SLNSW.
7 *Newspaper News*, 1 August 1956, p. 1.
8 *ibid*.
9 Davies, 2006, p. 40.
10 Schultz, 1998, p. 41. See also Gifford, 1997.
11 *Courier-Mail*, 20 June 2020, supplement, p. 9.
12 Associated Newspapers, 'Graded list as at 31 August 1953', FMBA, MLMSS 9894/1728, SLNSW.
13 *Sun*, 7 January 1954, p. 7 and 13 January 1954, p. 27; *SMH*, 4 July 1998, p. 6.
14 Hall, undated.
15 Clarke, 2014, p. 496.
16 *SMH*, 28 April 1990, Spectrum, p. 69.
17 *ibid.*, 14 December 1996, p. 147; Younger, 1999, pp. 412–14.
18 Lemon, undated; *SMH*, 28 April 1990, Spectrum, p. 69.
19 Speech notes, RA Henderson, 7 October 1959, FMBA, MLMSS 9894/1610, SLNSW.
20 Associated Newspapers, 'Staff list', 1 September 1953, FMBA, MLMSS 9894/1728, SLNSW.
21 HWT, *House News*, September 1944, reproduced in Younger, 1996 (without page numbers).
22 *Age*, 18 March 2009, p. 26.
23 Edwards, 1972, p. 114.
24 Chadwick, 1989, p. xxvi; *SMH*, 21 October 1950, p. 3.
25 Whitington, 1971, p. 131.
26 Younger, 2003, pp. 320, 329.
27 Letter from RG Menzies to C Bednall, 8 May 1953, Bednall Papers, MS 5546, NLA.
28 Davies, 2006; Gifford, 1997, pp. 22–23.
29 Letter from Bednall to unnamed correspondent, 8 August 1973, Bednall Papers, MS 5546/1/1, p. 7.
30 Gifford, 1997, p. 26.
31 Young, 2015.
32 Murphy, 2016, pp. 368–71; Haigh, 2022, pp. 339–40.
33 Associated Newspapers, 'General review of trading accounts, 1949', p. 5, FMBA, MLMSS 9894/934, SLNSW.
34 Letter from K Murdoch to L Dumas, 10 July 1952, Dumas Papers, MS 4849, NLA.
35 Telegram from K Murdoch to RG Menzies, 16 March 1951, Murdoch Papers, MS 2823, NLA.

36 Letter from R Henderson to RG Menzies, 8 June 1951 and letter from RG Menzies to R Henderson, 28 June 1951, FMBA, MLMSS 9894/511, SLNSW.
37 *Daily Telegraph*, 5 July 1951, p. 4.
38 Letter from K Murdoch to RG Menzies, 15 August 1951, Murdoch Papers, MS 2823, NLA.
39 'Import committee reports', 26 October 1955, 'Newsprint imports', (A4940-C146-1337105), NAA.
40 'The prime minister: Newsprint', 26 October 1955, (A4940-C146-1337105), NAA.
41 Bramston, 2019, p. 243.
42 Murphy, 2016, p. 367.
43 Zwar, 1980, p. 107.
44 *Tribune*, 15 November 1946, p. 1; Macintyre, 2022, p. 157.
45 *Herald*, 9 January 1951, p. 4 and 26 April 1951, p. 4; *Daily Telegraph*, 11 January 1951, p. 8.
46 Zwar, 1980, p. 124.
47 *ibid.*, p. 107.
48 *ibid.*, p. 108.
49 *Herald*, 20 October 1950, p. 4.
50 *Argus*, 21 September 1951, p. 2.
51 Younger, 2003, p. 323.
52 *SMH*, 21 September 1951, p. 2.
53 *Daily Telegraph*, 21 September 1951, p. 1.
54 *Age*, 21 September 1951, p. 2.
55 Chadwick, 1989, p. xxvii.
56 Griffen-Foley, 2003b, p. 46.
57 *Daily Telegraph*, 25 October 1954, p. 2; 14 May 1954, p. 9; 12 May 1954, p. 9; 27 November 1953, p. 8; 25 April 1953, p. 7; 23 February 1953, p. 11; 6 June 1952, p. 8; 4 July 1952, p. 1; 12 February 1951, p. 12 and 22 February 1952, p. 7.
58 Lloyd, 2002.
59 Edwards said, when he read it, he wanted to make it the paper's lead story but chose not to because wartime economies made it too difficult to change the planned edition (Edwards, 1972, p. 96).
60 *Smith's Weekly*, 8 March 1941, p. 14.
61 Younger, 2003, p. 285.
62 Zwar, 1980, p. 125.
63 *Age*, 2 May 1951, p. 5.
64 Macintyre, 2022, p. 194.
65 Zwar, 1980, p. 110.
66 US Department of Commerce report cited in *Kalgoorlie Miner*, 26 January 1954, p. 7 and *Daily Telegraph*, 13 September 1954, p. 8.
67 *Western Mail*, 6 March 1952, p. 7 and an example is *Herald*, 28 September 1954, p. 2.
68 Griffen-Foley, 2000, pp. 157, 183; Kearsley, undated.
69 Prior, 2015.
70 *Cairns Post*, 24 October 1951, p. 7.
71 Roberts, 2015, p. 264.
72 *West Wyalong Advocate*, 4 October 1951, p. 8.
73 *Herald*, 18 June 1951, p. 4.
74 *Courier-Mail*, 6 February 1952, p. 2; Richardson, 1988.
75 *Workers' Star*, 25 June 1948, p. 4.
76 Roberts, 2015, p. 264.
77 Letter from K Murdoch to C Bednall, 4 August 1952, Bednall Papers, MS 5546, NLA.
78 Report from Harold Cox, 8 September 1953, Cox Papers, MS 4554, NLA.
79 *Advertiser*, 6 March 1954, p. 4.
80 Manne, 2004, p. 87.
81 Report by Harold Cox, 19 April 1954, Cox Papers, MS 4554, NLA.
82 *West Australian*, 30 July 1954, p. 4.
83 *Canberra Times*, 27 July 2002, p. 3.
84 Report by Harold Cox, 19 April 1954, Cox Papers, MS 4554, NLA.

85 Oakes, undated a; letter from RG Menzies to RA Henderson, 27 April 1954, FMBA, MLMSS 9894/511, SLNSW. (The article appeared in the *Sun-Herald* on 25 April.) See also Murray, 1970, p. 149.
86 Murphy, 2016, p. 318; *News*, 10 September 1954, p. 1.
87 Allan Fraser interview with Mel Pratt, 1975, NLA.
88 Murphy, 2016, pp. 317–18, 338.
89 *Argus*, 9 December 1955, p. 4.
90 Costar, Love and Strangio, 2005, p. vii.
91 Murray, 1970, pp. 179–81.
92 Gardiner, 2005; see later chapters on the role of Alan Reid.
93 *NT News*, 5 May 1978, p. 18.
94 *Denmark Post* (Albany, WA), 5 April 1951, p. 3; *Newcastle Sun*, 26 June 1952, p. 8.
95 Kirkpatrick, 2005, pp. 56–57.
96 *NT News*, 5 May 1978, p. 18.
97 *ibid.*, 11 February 2012, p. 23.
98 *NT News*, 5 May 1978, p. 18.

Chapter 7 Death and betrayal in Melbourne

1 Younger, 2003, p. 330.
2 HWT, 1952, p. 13.
3 Younger, 1999, p. 437.
4 *Bulletin*, 13 April 1982, p. 58.
5 Dunstan, 2012.
6 Younger, 2003, p. 329; *Bulletin*, 4 December 1979, p. 98.
7 Zwar, 1980, p. 106.
8 Bednall, unpaginated typed autobiography, NLA, MS 5546/3.
9 Dunstan, 2012.
10 Dunstan, 2012; David Dunstan, interview with the author, 26 February 2021.
11 Bednall, handwritten unpaginated autobiography, MS 5546/3, NLA.
12 Dunstan, 2012.
13 Bednall, handwritten unpaginated autobiography, MS 5546/3, NLA.
14 Younger, 2003, p. 327.
15 Bednall, handwritten unpaginated autobiography, MS 5546/3, NLA.
16 Young, 2003, p. 332.
17 Hudson, 1993.
18 Younger, 2003, pp. 311–12.
19 Shawcross, 1992, pp. 72–73.
20 Letter from secretary of Consolidated Press Ltd to chairman of Associated Newspapers, 5 March 1946, FMBA, MLMSS 9894/103, SLNSW.
21 Younger, 2003, p. 345.
22 Zwar, 1980, p. 120.
23 Younger, 2003, p. 338.
24 Zwar, 1980, p. 118.
25 Younger, 2003, p. 352.
26 Zwar, 1980, p.121.
27 *ibid*.
28 *Canberra Times*, 29 September 1985, p. 25; Younger, 2003, p. 335.
29 Zwar, 1980, p. 121.
30 Younger, 2003, p. 344.
31 Roberts, 2015, p. 259.
32 Edwards, 1972, p. 145.
33 Dumas, 1969, p.158.
34 Roberts, 2015, p. 259.
35 Souter, 1981, p. 279.

36 Younger, 2003, pp. 326, 9.
37 Zwar, 1980, p. 107.
38 Younger, 2003, p. 336.
39 ibid., p. 333.
40 Letter from K Murdoch to L Dumas, 10 July 1952, Dumas Papers, MS 4849, NLA.
41 ibid.
42 ibid.
43 Calwell, 1972, p. 92.
44 Younger, 2003, pp. 342, 345.
45 Bednall, handwritten unpaginated autobiography, Bednall Papers, MS 5546/3, NLA. Note: Bednall says this occurred the day before Murdoch died.
46 ibid.
47 Younger, 2003, p. 344.
48 Young, 2003, p. 344; Bednall, handwritten unpaginated autobiography, Bednall Papers, MS 5546/3, NLA.
49 Dunstan, 1990, p. 148.
50 Younger, 2003, p. 348.
51 Dunstan, 2012.
52 Bednall, handwritten unpaginated autobiography, Bednall Papers, MS 5546/3, NLA.
53 Lever, 2012a.
54 It should be noted that the details of these final days of corporate intrigue remain unclear. Another version of events has it that Murdoch's *Argus* talks were not entirely secret and that he had proposed to the HWT board that, as the *Argus* was going to be sold, the HWT should finance him to purchase it (as they had with the *Courier-Mail*) because that would appear to be a separate company but the HWT could then quietly have near total domination of Melbourne's daily newspaper market. On this version of events, Williams opposed that proposal on grounds of conflict of interest and that is why Murdoch tried to have him sacked. These two versions are not entirely incompatible, though, because Murdoch's plan may have been secret until Williams became aware of it and that could have prompted Murdoch to propose that the HWT finance him.
55 *Courier-Mail*, 8 October 1952, p. 1.
56 Younger, 2003, p. 351.
57 Hetherington, 2004, p. 102
58 Edwards, 1972, p. 145.
59 *Daily Telegraph*, 7 June 1997, p. 34. (Note: Younger, 2003, p. 350 says 50 per cent.)
60 Will and three codicils of Keith Murdoch, PROV.
61 Letter from R Murdoch to C Bednall, 4 December 1952, Bednall Papers, MS 5546, NLA.
62 Lever, 2012a.
63 Younger, 2003, p. 352.
64 Wolff, 2010, p. 70; Bednall, handwritten unpaginated version of unpublished autobiography, Bednall Papers, MS 5546/3, NLA.
65 Lever, 2012a.
66 ibid.
67 ibid.
68 ibid.
69 *Bulletin*, 4 December 1979, p. 98.
70 Will and three codicils of Keith Murdoch, PROV
71 Letter from C Bednall to R Murdoch, 25 November 1952, Bednall Papers, MS 5546, NLA.
72 The other main partner in CWL was Victorian hotel and racehorse owner Patrick Cody, who also died in 1953.
73 Young, 2019, pp. 293–94.
74 *Courier-Mail*, 50th anniversary souvenir, 1983, p. 15.
75 Telegram from K Murdoch to C Bednall, 24 September 1945, Bednall Papers, MS 5546/1/4, p. 3.
76 *Age*, 9 January 1982, p. 12.

77 Letter from K Murdoch to C Bednall, 8 August 1950, MS 5546, NLA.
78 Bednall, handwritten unpaginated autobiography, Bednall Papers, MS 5546/3, NLA.
79 *ibid*.
80 *ibid*.
81 *ibid*.
82 *Courier-Mail*, 27 October 1953, p. 3.
83 *Advertiser*, 9 January 1984, p. 6; *SMH*, 24 December 1983, pp. 25-6.
84 *Age*, 9 January 1982, p. 12.
85 *Daily Telegraph*, 5 November 1953, p. 3.
86 Bednall, handwritten unpaginated autobiography, Bednall Papers, MS 5546/3, NLA.
87 Dunstan, 1990, p.150.

Chapter 8 Jack Williams: Empire builder, *Argus* killer?

1   *Argus*, 19 January 1957, p. 1.
2   Bednall, paginated typed version of unpublished autobiography, p. 5, MS 5546/5, NLA.
3   *Age*, 27 November 1952, p. 6 and 27 November 1954, p. 6; *Courier-Mail*, 26 November 1953, p. 12.
4   Dunstan, 1990, p. 149.
5   Dunstan, 2012.
6   *ibid*.; John Dahlsen, interview with the author, 26 July 2021.
7   Edwards, 1972, p. 147.
8   *ibid*., pp. 148.
9   Golding, 2012, p. 136.
10 David Dunstan, interview with the author, 19 March 2021; David Dunstan, email to the author, 15 June 2022.
11 *ibid*.
12 HWT, *House News*, October 1983, p. 11.
13 *Courier-Mail*, 50th anniversary souvenir, 1983, p. 15.
14 *Newspaper News*, 2 May 1955, p. 1.
15 Letter from K Murdoch to L Dumas, 10 July 1952, Dumas Papers, MS 4849, NLA.
16 Goot, 1979, pp. 18–19.
17 Statement on Queensland Press, 26 August 1956, FMBA, MLMSS 9894/409, SLNSW.
18 *Age*, 9 January 1982, p. 12.
19 D'Arcy, 2005, p. 10. See *Courier-Mail*, 50th anniversary souvenir, p. 15.
20 HWT, 'Shareholders' funds 1956–1965', 025740710, ASIC.
21 Bodycomb, undated.
22 Younger, 1999, p. 312.
23 Ranald Macdonald interview with the author, 10 January 2022.
24 Tipping, 1966; Younger, 1999, p. 316.
25 Younger, 1996, p. 42, 47.
26 *Grafton Argus and Clarence River General Advertiser*, 9 September 1910, p. 5; *Freeman's Journal* (Sydney) 6 October 1910, p. 36.
27 Dunstan, 2012.
28 Younger, 1996, p. 249
29 Dunstan, 1990, p. 149.
30 David Dunstan, email correspondence with the author, 25 February 2021.
31 *Herald*, 20 November 1958, p. 1 and 21 November 1958, p. 1.
32 David Dunstan phone interview with the author, 26 February 2021.
33 Wheelwright, 1957, p. 174; Rawling, 1939, p. 69.
34 *Tribune*, 25 June 1949, p. 6. See also *Herald*, 23 May 1934, p. 5; *Argus*, 20 December 1933, p. 5.
35 Wheelwright, 1957, p. 174; Rawling, 1939, p. 69.
36 *Herald*, 24 June 1954, p. 4 and 12 October 1953, p. 7.
37 *AFR*, 14 November 1968, p. 17.
38 Yule, 2012, p. 363; Blainey, 1969, pp. 281–82.

39	Wheelwright, 1957, p. 174; Featherstone, 1976.
40	Cannon, 1986, pp. 170, 23; *Bendigo Advertiser*, 14 September 1903, p. 4; Clarke, 1962, p. 15; Campbell, 1963, p. 263.
41	Clarke, 1962, p. 15.
42	Younger, 2003, p. 195; *Herald*, 24 January 1955, p. 3; *Tribune*, 5 February 1958, p. 8.
43	Cannon, 1993, pp. 52–53.
44	Edwards, 1972, p. 26.
45	Dunstan, 2003, p. 11; see also Dunstan, 1990, p. 148.
46	Inglis, 1987, p. 220.
47	Murray, 2005, p. 30.
48	Clarke, 1962, p. 10.
49	Murray, 2021, p. 178.
50	Murray, 2005, p. 30.
51	Bob Murray, interview with the author, 2022; Murray, 2005, p. 32.
52	*Age*, 2 November 1950, p. 3.
53	Murray, 2021, p. 165.
54	Bednall, handwritten unpaginated version of unpublished autobiography, MS 5546/5, NLA.
55	Richards, 1997, p. 165.
56	*Argus*, 19 June 1950, p. 3.
57	*ibid*., 15 June 1950, p. 1.
58	*ibid*., 13 May 1950, p. 1.
59	*ibid*.
60	Young, 2016c, p. 8; and McQueen, 2014, p. 96.
61	Jenkins, 2003, p. 19.
62	Murray, 2005, p. 32.
63	Young, 2016c, p. 8.
64	Letter from K Murdoch to C Bednall, 4 August 1952, MS 5546, NLA.
65	Bednall, handwritten unpaginated version of unpublished autobiography, MS 5546/5, NLA.
66	Griffen-Foley, 2000, pp. 194–95.
67	*ibid*., p. 195.
68	Younger, 2003, p. 342.
69	Cec Wallace in Porter, 2003, p. 43.
70	Letter from K Murdoch to C Bednall, 4 August 1952, MS 5546, NLA.
71	*Mercury*, 3 October 1953, p. 42; *West Australian*, 26 September 1953, p. 3; *SMH*, 28 September 1953, p. 4.
72	Bednall, handwritten unpaginated version of unpublished autobiography, MS 5546/5.
73	*ibid*.
74	*ibid*.
75	Letter from H Cudlipp to C Bednall, 15 April 1954, p. 3, Bednall Papers, MS 5546/1, NLA.
76	Bednall, handwritten unpaginated autobiography, MS 5546/5.
77	Letter from C Bednall to J Patience, 8 September 1954, Bednall Papers, MS 5546, NLA.
78	Bednall, handwritten unpaginated autobiography, MS 5546/5.
79	Goot, 1979, p. 5.
80	Murray, 2005, p. 31.
81	*Newspaper News*, 23 August 1963.
82	Clarke, 1962, p. 10; *Argus*, 19 January 1957, p. 1.
83	Dunstan, 2003, p. 12.
84	Usher and Murray, 2003; Williams, 2008, p. 122.
85	Dunstan, 2003, p. 12; Usher, 2007, p. 162.
86	Bob Murray, interview with the author, 2022.
87	Usher, 2007, p. 162.
88	Hills, 2010, p. 175.
89	Murray, 2005, p. 34.
90	*Tribune*, 12 June 1957, p. 3.

91 *Argus*, 28 May 1954, p. 4.
92 Dunstan, 2003, p. 12.
93 *Canberra Times*, 18 January 1957, p. 3.
94 *Age*, 11 May 1979, p. 7.

Chapter 9 On the move in Adelaide and Sydney
1   Shawcross, 1992, p. 62; *Canberra Times*, 29 September 1985, p. 25.
2   Shawcross, 1992, pp. 64–65.
3   Macintyre, 2015, p. 462.
4   Christiansen, 1961.
5   Shawcross, 1992, p. 80; *Guardian*, 'Sir Edward Pickering', 9 August 2003.
6   *Age*, 21 November 1979, p. 14.
7   *Mail*, 21 November 1953, p. 1.
8   Letter from K Murdoch to L Dumas, 10 July 1952, Dumas Papers, MS 4849, NLA.
9   Shawcross, 1992, p. 67.
10 Inglis, 2002; *Canberra Times*, 7 October 1977, p. 2.
11 *Australian*, 25 October 1975, p. 22.
12 *Mail*, 21 November 1953, p. 1.
13 Shawcross, 1992, p. 84.
14 *ibid*.
15 *ibid*., p. 86.
16 Young, 1991, p. 150.
17 *SMH*, 28 October 1954, p. 4.
18 Shawcross, 1992, p. 90.
19 *ibid*., p. 89.
20 *AFR*, 28 July 2011, p. 66.
21 *SMH*, 11 June 1953, p. 5; Shawcross, 1992, p. 88.
22 Munster, 1987, p. 285.
23 TelevisionAU, 2006.
24 Shawcross, 1992, pp. 90–91.
25 Lever, 2012c.
26 Kirkpatrick, 2005.
27 Munster, 1987, p. 55.
28 *ibid*., pp. 87, 100; Cameron, 1990, pp. 154–55.
29 Cameron, 1990, pp. 154–55.
30 Lever, 2012c; Whitton, 2016a.
31 Munster, 1987, p. 54; *Nation Review*, 6 December 1976, p. 1043.
32 *Advertiser*, 10 January 1987, p. 1.
33 Lord, 1983, p. 167.
34 Young, 1991, pp. 150–51; Shawcross, 1992, p. 100; *Canberra Times*, 7 October 1977, p. 2.
35 Lever, 2012c.
36 Shawcross, 1992, p. 78.
37 Menadue, 1999, p. 90.
38 Shawcross, 1992, p. 87.
39 Bowman, 1988, p.164.
40 Buckridge, 1994, p. 309; *Daily Telegraph*, 28 September 1950, p. 1.
41 Griffen-Foley, 2000, p. 179.
42 Young, 1991, pp. 53–55.
43 Griffen-Foley, 2000, p. 181.
44 Lever, 2012a.
45 Griffen-Foley, 2000, p. 187.
46 *Daily Telegraph*, 7 March 1953, p. 1.
47 Souter, 1981, p. 327.
48 Alan Reid, 'Recalls salad days', *Focus*, November–December 1979, p. 4.

49 David McNicoll interview with John Farquharson, 1997, NLA.
50 *ibid.*
51 *ibid.*
52 Stone, 2000, p. 68.
53 David McNicoll interview with John Farquharson, 1997, NLA.
54 Yule, 2006, pp. 218–19; see also Griffen-Foley, 2000, p. 210.
55 Yule, 2006, pp. 218–19.
56 *Worker* (Brisbane), 8 August 1955, p. 2.
57 *Argus*, 13 July 1955, p. 5; *Canberra Times*, 13 July 1955, p. 1.
58 Van Heekeren, 2014, pp. 441–42.
59 *Worker* (Brisbane), 8 August 1955, p. 2; Van Heekeren, 2014, p. 441.
60 Van Heekeren, 2014, p. 442.
61 Griffen-Foley, 2000, pp. 189–90.
62 Whitington, 1971, pp. 131, 134.
63 David McNicoll interview with John Farquharson, 1997, NLA.
64 *Cootamundra Herald*, 31 July 1950, p. 2.
65 Radi, 1996.
66 Younger, 2003, p. 326.
67 Letter from K Murdoch to L Dumas, 10 July 1952, Dumas Papers, MS 4849, NLA; Younger, 2003, p. 340.
68 'Strictly confidential: Notes on conference …', 2 October 1956, and 'Notes on [2nd] conference], 11 October 1956, FMBA, MLMSS 9894/410, SLNSW.
69 *Smith's Weekly*, 24 June 1950, p. 5.
70 'Strictly confidential: Notes on conference …', 2 October 1956, and 'Notes on [2nd] conference], 11 October 1956, FMBA, MLMSS 9894/410, SLNSW.
71 *Canberra Times*, 22 October 1964, p. 24.
72 *Argus*, 5 September 1951, p. 10.
73 Souter, 1981, p. 275.
74 'Issue of ordinary shares', 1953, p. 2, FMBA, MLMSS 9894/923, SLNSW.
75 'Statement by John Butters', 4 September 1953, p. 6, FMBA, MLMSS 9894/923, SLNSW.
76 *SMH*, 8 December 1949, p. 10; Strictly confidential 'Statement by John Butters', 4 September 1953, p. 4, p. 6, FMBA, MLMSS 9894/923, SLNSW.
77 Associated Newspapers, Annual report 1950, FMBA, MLMSS 9894/12, SLNSW; *Advertiser*, 24 November 1951, p. 10.
78 Souter, 1981, p. 302.
79 Denison, 2004, p. 99.
80 *Truth* (Sydney), 6 April 1941, p. 24.
81 *Bulletin*, 9 January 1965, p. 13.
82 'Associated Newspapers trading profit and loss statement', FMBA, MLMSS 9894/54, SLNSW.
83 Griffen-Foley, 2000, pp. 195–96.
84 Younger, 1996, p. 251; Letter from J Butters to H Giddy, 4 September 1953, FMBA, MLMSS 9894/1230, SLNSW.
85 Carroll, 2007.
86 Souter, 1981, p. 303; 'Statement by John Butters', 4 September 1953, p. 6, FMBA, MLMSS 9894/923, SLNSW.
87 'Statement by John Butters', 4 September 1953, p. 6, FMBA, MLMSS 9894/923, SLNSW.
88 *ibid.*, p. 8.
89 Souter, 1981, p. 305.
90 'Issue of ordinary shares', 1953, pp. 3–6, FMBA, MLMSS 9894/923, SLNSW; *Australian*, 9–10 November 1991, p. 27.
91 Griffen-Foley, 2000, p. 196.
92 *Sunday Telegraph*, 5 May 1974, p. 45.
93 David McNicoll interview with John Farquharson, 1997, NLA.
94 Letter from R Henderon to C Ogilvy, 3 February 1955, FMBA, MLMSS 9894/924, SLNSW.

95   Souter, 1981, p. 316.
96   *Bulletin*, 9 January 1965, p. 13.
97   Denison, 2004, p. 99.
98   *Newspaper News*, 1 October 1956, p. 2.
99   *SMH*, 12 March 1995, p. 34.
100 *Sun*, 16 October 1953, p. 1.
101 *Sun-Herald*, 12 October 2003, p. 61.
102 Milliken, undated.
103 *Advertiser*, 2 December 1954, p. 8; *SMH*, 11 January 1954, p. 1.
104 Lawson, 2000.
105 Norton left his adopted stepson only 4 per cent of his assets when he died in 1967 (Hall, 2008, pp. 227, 285).
106 Souter, 1981, p. 342.
107 *ibid.*, p. 343.
108 *Canberra Times*, 6 January 1967, p. 6.
109 Souter, 1981, p. 264.
110 *ibid.*, pp. 318, 320.
111 John Fairfax Ltd, Annual report 1956, p. 12, FMBA, MLMSS 9894/13, SLNSW; Associated Newspapers Annual report 1956, FMBA, MLMSS 9894/1230, SLNSW; *Argus*, 3 December 1956, p. 8 and 10 November 1956, p. 20.

Chapter 10 Taking over television
1   WA Whitlock, report on television, October 1952, FMBA, MLMSS 9894/65, SLNSW.
2   Bednall, handwritten unpaginated version of unpublished autobiography, Bednall Papers, MS 5546/5, NLA; Madrigal 2018.
3   C-Scott, 2018, pp. 138–39.
4   F Daniell, 'Memorandum re television', 13 June 1935, and General Electric Co to J Butters, 24 August 1939, FMBA, MLMSS 9894/931, SLNSW.
5   Correspondence in FMBA, MLMSS 9894/924/64, SLNSW.
6   Letter from L Dumas to K Murdoch, 30 June 1952, Dumas Papers, MS 4849, NLA.
7   Munster, 1987, p. 45.
8   Bednall, draft article for the IPA, 25 May 1964, p. 3, Bednall Papers, MS 5546/1/4; see also Paulu, 1956, p. 51.
9   E Kennedy, report on television, 16 March 1953, FMBA, MLMSS 9894/924/68, SLNSW.
10   *Argus*, 5 February 1955, p. 13.
11   A fourth major player – the DuMont network – had declined.
12   Emery et al., 2000, p. 272.
13   'Why newspapers are having trouble', *US News and World Report*, 16 January 1959; Calwell, 1959, p. 12.
14   Letter from RA Irish to J Butters, 19 July 1954, FMBA, MLMSS 9894/924/68, SLNSW.
15   ABCB, 1952–53, p. 26. This included regional newspapers and other types, not just the metropolitan dailies.
16   *ibid.*, p. 10; *Truth*, 20 January 1952, p. 39.
17   ABCB, 1952–53, p. 8.
18   ABCB, 1954–55, p. 9.
19   Until May 1957 (*Canberra Times*, 29 May 1957, p. 2).
20   Australian Federation of Commercial Broadcasting Stations, 'The case for commercial TV licences', undated (but circa 1952), 'Television: RG Casey', (M3299-99-2), NAA.
21   Tully, undated.
22   Curthoys, 1986, pp. 128–29.
23   *Herald*, 14 June 1949, p. 1; *Advertiser*, 18 June 1949, p. 2.
24   *Daily Telegraph*, 15 June 1949, p. 8.
25   Hall, 1976, p. 15; Armstrong, 1975, p. 67.
26   *Herald*, 19 December 1949, p. 12.

27 Inglis, 1983, p. 193; Gorman, 1998, p. 49.
28 Bednall, handwritten unpaginated version of unpublished autobiography, MS 5546/5, NLA.
29 BW Graham, 'Confidential: Television report', 8 November 1954, pp. 1–2, FMBA, MLMSS 9894/346, SLNSW.
30 Bednall, handwritten unpaginated version of unpublished autobiography, MS 5546/5, NLA.
31 ibid.
32 Hancock, 1996.
33 BW Graham, 'Confidential: Television report', 8 November 1954, pp. 1–2, FMBA, MLMSS 9894/346, SLNSW.
34 'Notes on deputation to prime minister', 4 April 1952, FMBA, MLMSS 9894/931, SLNSW.
35 Hazlehurst, 1979, pp. 216–17; letter from RG Menzies to C Bednall, 8 May 1953, Bednall Papers, MS 5546, NLA.
36 Bednall, handwritten unpaginated version of unpublished autobiography, MS 5546/5, NLA.
37 *Herald*, 20 December 1952, p. 4.
38 Letter from C Bednall to R Murdoch, 25 November 1952, Bednall Papers, MS 5546, NLA.
39 Letter from R Murdoch to C Bednall, 4 December 1952, *ibid*.
40 Telegram from C Bednall to J Butters, 17 December 1952, and telegram from J Ridley to John Butters, 18 December 1952, FMBA, MLMSS 9894/931, SLNSW.
41 Telegram from HV Evatt to J Butters, 20 April 1950, FMBA, MLMSS 9894/931, SLNSW.
42 *CPD* (HR), 6 August 1958, p. 121.
43 Mandle, 1997, p. 133.
44 *SMH*, 18 February 1953, p. 1.
45 *Guardian* (London), 16 May 1952, p. 7.
46 Barnouw, 1990, p. 229; Crisell, 2002, pp. 82, 84.
47 Crisell, 2002, p. 84.
48 Crawford, 2005; Griffen-Foley, 2009, pp. 214–15.
49 *Canberra Times*, 17 July 1946, p. 2. The newspapers also used J Walter Thompson to run their own public relations campaigns (e.g. J Walter Thompson Pty Ltd, 'Recommendations for a newspaper publisher's cooperative campaign', July 1941, in Dumas Papers, MS 4849/11, NLA).
50 *Advertiser*, 22 January 1953, p. 4.
51 *Herald*, 14 October 1953, p. 5.
52 Curthoys, 1991, p. 155.
53 Bednall, handwritten unpaginated version of unpublished autobiography, MS 5546/5, NLA.
54 *SMH*, 27 February 1953, p. 4.
55 Curthoys, 1986, p. 141.
56 *CPD* (HR), 18 April 1963, p. 750.
57 Young, 1991, pp. 145–46, 149, 151–53; *National Times*, 26–31 May 1975, p. 56.
58 Bednall, unpaginated typed version of unpublished autobiography, MS 5546/5, NLA.
59 Mandle, 1997, pp. 133–34.
60 *Advertiser*, 10 April 1953, p. 3; *Sun News-Pictorial*, 10 April 1953, p. 3.
61 *Herald*, 4 July 1953, p. 5.
62 *Press-Courier* (California), 10 February 1955, p. 24.
63 *Sun*, 9 April 1953, p. 5; 'Private and confidential: statement by the chairman of directors of Associated Newspapers Ltd and Radio 2UE (Sydney) Pty Ltd [John Butters] to the Royal Commission on Television', 9 April 1953, pp. 6, 12, FMBA, MLMSS 9894/924, SLNSW.
64 *Daily Telegraph*, 10 May 1954, p. 8.
65 Curthoys 1986, pp. 153–54; Hall, 1976, p. 17.
66 Herd, 2012, p. 33.
67 Letter from C Bednall to unnamed correspondent, 8 August 1973, p. 8, Bednall Papers, MS 5546/1/1, NLA.
68 *Barrier Miner*, 10 May 1954, p. 2; 'For Cabinet: Television, submission no. 103', 23 March 1959, p. 8, (A5818-vol 3-Agendum 104-TV), NAA.
69 Letter from C Bednall to EG Whitlam, December 1973, NLA, Bednall Papers, MS 5546/1/5; Bednall, unpaginated typed version of unpublished autobiography, MS 5546/5, NLA.

70   Barnouw, 1968, p. 295.
71   *Guardian* (London), 1 July 1954, p. 2.
72   Goodwin, 1998, p. 13.
73   Curran and Seaton, 2018, p. 254.
74   *Herald*, 10 May 1954, p. 4.
75   *Daily Mirror*, 1 April 1954 (clipping in 'Television: RG Casey', M3299-99-2, NAA).
76   Letter from L Dumas to J Butters, 30 July 1954, MLMSS 9894/924/64, NLA.
77   Memo from R Doutreband to J Butters, 29 July 1954, MLMSS 9894/924/64, NLA.
78   *Daily Telegraph*, 9 April 1953, p. 7.
79   *Sun*, 1 February 1955, p. 5.
80   *Herald*, 27 February 1953, p. 4.
81   Report by M Stevenson, February 1951, FMBA, MLMSS 9894/924/68, SLNSW.
82   Memo from M Stevenson to J Butters, 9 July 1954, FMBA, MLMSS 9894/924/64, SLNSW; *Advertiser*, 16 February 1955, p. 6.
83   *Argus*, 28 July 1951, p. 14; ABCB, 1955–56, pp. 11–12; F Daniell, 'Memorandum re television', 13 June 1935, FMBA, MLMSS 9894/931, SLNSW.
84   *SMH*, 6 November 1954, p. 1.
85   *Observer* (London), 31 May 1953, p. 2; *Daily Telegraph* (London), 23 November 1954, p. 18; *Sunday Dispatch* (London), 21 June 1959, p. 11.
86   Dudley Edwards, 2003, p. 266.
87   *Guardian* (London), 21 April 1956, p. 12.
88   *Courier-Mail*, 9 February 1953, p. 3 and 28 March 1953, p. 6.
89   *Newspaper News*, 1 February 1955, p. 2.
90   *Tribune*, 19 January 1955, p. 9.
91   Griffen-Foley, 2000, p. 207. (His station would, however, give airtime to Labor enemy BA Santamaria. A five-minute slot on Channel 9 became 'Point of View' which ran for nearly 30 years.)
92   Costar, 2002; *Age*, 22 January 1955, p. 4.
93   *Sun News-Pictorial*, 13 March 1953, p. 10.
94   Bednall, unpaginated typed version of unpublished autobiography, MS 5546/5, NLA.
95   *Daily News*, 10 December 1938, p. 3.
96   *Truth*, 13 March 1949, p. 16.
97   *Argus*, 16 February 1955, p. 10.
98   *Daily Telegraph*, 24 August 1943, p. 11.
99   As did Eddie Ward – *CPD* (HR), 9 May 1956, p. 1901; Brodrick, 1993.
100 *Tribune*, 27 April 1955, p. 8.
101 *Herald*, 21 January 1955, p. 3.
102 Cited in Curthoys and Merritt, 1986, p. 153.
103 Bednall, IPA draft article, 25 May 1964, NLA, Colin Bednall papers, MS 5546, box 1, folder 4, p. 3; Bednall, handwritten unpaginated version of unpublished autobiography, NLA, MS 5546, box 5, folders 42–44.
104 *SMH*, 31 October 1951, p. 8.
105 *Newspaper News*, 2 May 1955, p. 1; ABCB, 1954–55, pp. 29–34.
106 Telegram from A McLachlan to RG Osborne, 6 May 1957, and memo to RA Henderson, 20 September 1955, FMBA, MLMSS 9894/685, SLNSW.
107 Minutes of meeting held at HWT, 1 September 1955, FMBA, MLMSS 9894/685, SLNSW.
108 Letter from GC Remington to HW Chester, 31 August 1955, FMBA, MLMSS 9894/685, SLNSW.

Chapter 11 A licence to print money
1   Bye, 2006; *Daily Telegraph*, 15 September 1956, p. 4.
2   *Newspaper News*, 1 October 1956, p. 1; Television Corporation Limited, 1971.
3   *ibid*.
4   Report on television, FMBA, MLMSS 9894/924/66, SLNSW.

5   Bednall, paginated typed version of unpublished autobiography, p. 6, MS 5546/5, NLA.
6   Curthoys, 1986, p. 152.
7   David McNicoll interview with John Farquharson, 1997, NLA.
8   Dick, 2015, p. 82.
9   *TV Week*, 21–27 April 1960, p. 32.
10 Bednall, unpaginated typed version of unpublished autobiography, MS 5546/5, NLA.
11 *SMH*, 16 September 1991, p. 13.
12 Submission by the HWT (W Dunstan, General Manager) to the Royal Commission on Television, undated but circa 1953–54, p. 23, FMBA, MLMSS 9894/357, SLNSW.
13 Advertisement for the *Daily Mirror*, *Guardian* (London), 14 October 1952, p. 4.
14 Dick, 2015, pp. 64–65.
15 Beilby, 1981, pp. 11, 15.
16 *ABC Weekly*, vol. 20, no. 28, 9 July 1958, p. 35.
17 *Age*, 30 April 1956, p. 5.
18 Barnouw, 1990, p. 234.
19 Bonney, 1987, p. 47.
20 Hall, 1976, p. 5.
21 Bednall, unpaginated typed version of unpublished autobiography, MS 5546/5, NLA.
22 *Sun News-Pictorial*, 12 March 1953, p. 9.
23 *Advertiser*, 9 May 1958, p. 7.
24 *Herald*, 24 January 1955, p. 3; *Sun*, 25 January, 1955, p. 11.
25 Groves, undated.
26 HWT full page advertisement, *The Times*, 24 April 1966, FMBA, MLMSS 9894/411, SLNSW.
27 *Age*, 23 November 1956, pp. 7, 14, and 18 January 1957, p. 16.
28 Edwards, 1972, p. 158.
29 Bednall, unpaginated typed version of unpublished autobiography, Bednall Papers, MS 5546/5, NLA.
30 Mandle, 1997, p. 136.
31 Bednall, unpaginated typed version of unpublished autobiography, Bednall Papers, MS 5546/5, NLA.
32 Hall, 1976, p. 25.
33 Letter from RA Irish to J Butters, 19 July 1954, FMBA, MLMSS 9894/924/68, SLNSW.
34 Edwards, 1972, p. 199.
35 Beilby, 1981, p. 92.
36 Hall, 1976, p. 33.
37 Cabinet 'Submission Number 103', 17 March 1959, A5818-vol 3-Agendum-104-TV, NAA.
38 Bednall, unpaginated typed version of unpublished autobiography, Bednall Papers, MS 5546/5, NLA.
39 *Sunday Telegraph*, 18 August 1957, p. 7.
40 E.g. *Advertiser*, 29 April 1958, p. 6.
41 Inglis, 1983, pp. 194–96; Dick, 2015, p. 34.
42 Letter from C Bednall to TS Duckmanton, 2 November 1969, Bednall Papers, MS 5546/1/4.
43 *Age*, 31 May 1958, p. 9.
44 Griffen-Foley, 1999, pp. 220, 221.
45 Munster, 1987, pp. 44–45.
46 ibid., p. 46.
47 *Advertiser*, 9 May 1958, p. 7.
48 ibid., 28 May 1958, p. 5.
49 ibid., 9 May 1958, p. 5.
50 ibid., 30 May 1958, p. 5.
51 ibid., 10 May 1958, p. 5.
52 *Herald*, 9 May 1958, p. 7.
53 ibid., 21 May 1958, p. 3.
54 *SMH*, 14 October 1958, p. 3.
55 Munster, 1987, p. 46.

56 Griffen-Foley, 2003b, pp. 71–72.
57 And his company, Television Corporation Ltd, also had a small stake in the HWT's Brisbane TV Ltd.
58 *Age*, 14 October 1958, p. 3.
59 *ibid.*, p. 72.
60 Barr, 2000, p. 11.
61 *News*, 14 October 1958, p. 10.
62 *Herald*, 20 November 1958, p. 1.
63 *Daily Telegraph*, 21 November 1958, p. 1.
64 *SMH*, 21 November 1958, p. 2.
65 Munster, 1987, p. 47.
66 'Cabinet minute, 25 August 1959, Decision no. 408', A943-408-Cabinet Control over growth, NAA.
67 *Canberra Times*, 25 November 1959, p. 1, 5 December 1959, p. 3, and 12 December 1959, p. 3.
68 ABCB, 1959, p. 10.
69 *Canberra Times*, 20 November 1959, p. 3.
70 Griffen-Foley, 2000, p. 231.
71 *Bulletin*, 13 July 1960, p. 21.
72 Letter from A Warner to 'Charles', 7 July 1960, FMBA, MLMSS 9894/375, SLNSW.
73 *ibid*.
74 Griffen-Foley, 2000, p. 231; Yule, 2006, p. 219.
75 *Bulletin*, 13 July 1960, p. 21.
76 Bednall, unpaginated typed version of unpublished autobiography, Bednall Papers, MS 5546/5, NLA.
77 Bednall, All staff memo, 12 July 1960, Bednall Papers, MS 5546/1/4.
78 Bednall, unpaginated typed version of unpublished autobiography, Bednall Papers, MS 5546/5, NLA.
79 Hall, 1976, p. 26.
80 Ranald Macdonald, telephone interview with the author, 17 March 2021; ABCB, 1961, p. 28; ABCB, 1968, p. 116.
81 *CPD* (HR), 3 May 1956, p. 1770.
82 Hall, 1976, pp. 23, 25, 33; Windschuttle, 1988, p. 103.
83 ABCB, 1959, p. 27; News Limited, Annual report and balance sheet 1960; Shawcross, 1992, p. 55.
84 'ATS balance sheets and accounts as at 30 June 1958', and 'ATS balance sheets and accounts', 27 December 1964, FMBA, MLMSS 9894/352, SLNSW.
85 Hall, 1976, p. 36.
86 *CPD* (HR), 18 April 1963, p. 753.
87 *Manchester Guardian* (London), 8 July 1958, p. 1.
88 *Observer* (London), 13 July 1958, p. 13.
89 *ibid.*, 20 September 1959, p. 7; Black, 2005, p. 566.
90 It had sold its Australian newspaper, radio and television interests as well as the HWT shares it had gained from its sale of the *Argus* in 1957 (*Guardian* (London), 4 June 1959, p. 13).
91 Cabinet Minutes, 10 April 1959, decision no. 129, A4943-86, NAA.
92 *CPD* (HR), 11 November 1971, p. 3443; *SMH*, 23 August 1962, p. 7; *Canberra Times*, 11 March 1967, p. 14, and 1 September 1967, p. 14; *SMH*, 1 October 1968, p. 18; ABCB, 1969, p. 139.
93 Cabinet 'Submission Number 103', by CW Davidson, 17 March 1959, A5818-vol 3-Agendum-104-TV, NAA.
94 David McNicoll interview with John Farquharson, 1997, NLA.
95 McQueen, 1977, p. 61.

Chapter 12 Brawling in the suburbs

1 HWT full page advertisement, *The Times*, 24 April 1966, FMBA, MLMSS 9894/411, SLNSW; Goot, 1979, p.10; Tiffen, 2015, p. 68. Note: estimates range from 3.5 million to 4 million papers being sold each day.

2 Sungravure, 'House memo', 13 January 1960, FMBA, MLMSS 9894/457, SLNSW.
3 Australian Screen; Bednall, IPA draft article, 25 May 1964, pp. 1–2, 4, Bednall Papers, MS 5546/1, NLA.
4 *Herald* advertisement, *Newspaper News*, 1 August 1938, p. 11.
5 Edwards, 1972, pp. 157, 159.
6 Goot, 1979, p. 6.
7 Belson, 1961.
8 Minutes of the 389th meeting of directors of John Fairfax Ltd, 16 February 1967, FMBA, MLMSS 9894/3, SLNSW; Lindstrom, 1960.
9 *Canberra Times*, 27 February 1960, p. 3.
10 Rupert Murdoch, Chairman's address to annual general meeting, 28 October 1960, FMBA, MLMSS 9894/410, SLNSW; Munster, 1987, p. 287.
11 'Clive Ogilvy statement', 24 June 1953, p. 14, FMBA, MLMSS 9894/3957, SLNSW.
12 *Cumberland Argus and Fruitgrowers Advocate*, 6 April 1933, p. 4.
13 Anderson, undated.
14 *Cumberland Argus*, 27 November 1957, p. 14, and 17 January 1962, p. 1.
15 *Newspaper News*, 13 December 1957.
16 *Cumberland Argus*, 13 January 1960, p. 1.
17 *Newspaper News*, 2 February 1962, p. 2; Richardson, 2014, pp. 86–87.
18 *Newspaper News*, 6 March 1959, and 29 April 1960, p. 5.
19 Frank Packer and Ezra Norton had previously invested in a small way in suburban papers in the Eastern suburbs. Ezra Norton had wanted Cumberland Newspapers but Murdoch outbid him (*Newspaper News*, 4 March 1960, p. 1; *Daily Telegraph*, 25 February 1960; *Nation*, 12 March 1960, p. 12).
20 *Newspaper News*, 4 March 1960, p. 1; Rupert Murdoch, Chairman's address to annual general meeting, 28 October 1960, FMBA, MLMSS 9894/410, SLNSW.
21 Moore, 2008.
22 *Newspaper News*, 1 April 1960, p. 1.
23 Souter, 1981, p. 346.
24 *Newspaper News*, 4 May 1960.
25 Souter, 1981, p. 345.
26 Griffen-Foley, 2000, p. 166.
27 *Sun-Herald*, 1 August 1993, pp. 12–13.
28 Griffen-Foley, 2000, p. 146.
29 David McNicoll interview with John Farquharson, 1997, NLA.
30 *SMH*, 18 April 1998, Extra, p. 7.
31 Country Press Co-operative Company of Australia, 1961, p. 47.
32 *Bulletin*, 9 March 1982, pp. 56, 60; Souter, 2007.
33 Moore, 2008, pp. 197–212; Tiffen, 2010.
34 Letter from FG Rix to L Murdoch, 19 September 1997, reproduced in Chenoweth, 2014.
35 Presnell, 2014.
36 *Daily Mirror*, 8 June 1960, p. 3.
37 Newspaper clipping 'Fight over office', 8 June 1960, newspaper title not recorded, FMBA, MLMSS 9894/1097, SLNSW.
38 Golding, 2012. In addition to sources cited above, other sources used to describe the Anglican Press brawl are: *Daily Mirror*, 8 June 1960, pp. 1–5; *Canberra Times*, 9 June 1960, p. 10; *Sun-Herald*, 1 August 1993, pp. 12–13; Chadwick, 1989, p. xxx.
39 *Sun-Herald*, 1 August 1993, p. 13.
40 *Century*, 29 July 1960, p. 3.
41 Souter, 1981, p. 347.
42 *ibid.*; Munster, 1987, p. 60; *SMH*, 18 July 1961, p. 9.
43 Souter, 1981, p. 348; Bright, 1974, p. 187.
44 'Business manager' memo to CR Macdonald, 28 November 1973, FMBA, MLMSS 9894/25, SLNSW.

45 *Age*, 11 April 1989, p. 17; *Advertising News*, Golden Anniversary Book, 1978, pp. 34–36.
46 Letter from L Dumas to R Henderson, 26 October 1960, FMBA, MLMSS 9894/410, SLNSW.
47 Letter from L Dumas to R Henderson, 22 September 1961, *ibid*.
48 Letter from L Dumas to R Henderson, 31 October 1960, *ibid*.
49 Letter from L Dumas to R Henderson, 4 October 1961, *ibid*.
50 *Newspaper News*, 27 May 1960, p. 1.
51 Souter, 1981, p. 342; *SMH*, 15 March 1988, p. 7.
52 Souter, 1981, p. 364.
53 Dunstan, 2012.
54 *Bulletin*, 24 January 1984, p. 78.
55 Fairfax, 1992, p. 69.
56 *SMH*, 22 December 1990, p. 6; Souter, 1981, p. 369.
57 *SMH*, 22 December 1990, p. 6.
58 John Farquharson interview with David McNicoll, 1997, NLA.
59 Rupert Murdoch, Chairman's address annual to general meeting, 28 October 1960, FMBA, MLMSS 9894/410, SLNSW.
60 *Newspaper News*, 13 November 1964, p. 3.
61 *Daily Mirror*, 9 November 1970.
62 *SMH*, 15 March 1988, p. 7.

Chapter 13 Old and new tricks
1 Letter from R Henderson to RG Menzies, 30 April 1954, FMBA, MLMSS 9894/511, SLNSW.
2 Minutes of the 41st meeting of directors of John Fairfax Ltd, 28 March 1957, p. 3, FMBA, MLMSS 9894/1, SLNSW.
3 *CPD* (HR), 15 October 1957, p. 1355; *Canberra Times*, 16 October 1957, p. 1.
4 *SMH*, 16 October 1957, p. 4.
5 *SMH*, 21 November 1958, p. 2.
6 Fitzgerald, 2008, p. 89.
7 *Canberra Times*, 12 April 1981, p. 7; *SMH*, 22 April 2006, p. 27.
8 Munster, 1987, p. 63.
9 *Newspaper News*, 17 August 1962, p. 1.
10 Speech notes, FMBA, MLMSS 9894/513, SLNSW.
11 Waterford, undated.
12 *Age*, 25 September 2004, p. 12.
13 *AFR*, 25 November 2013, p. 18.
14 *Australian*, 24 March 2022, p. 21.
15 *Sunday Mirror*, 19 November, 1961, p. 1.
16 Fairfax, 1992, p. 77.
17 Souter, 1981, p. 382.
18 Judith Cook, telephone interview with the author, 2021.
19 *SMH*, 21 November 1961, p. 2.
20 *ibid*., 30 November 1961, and 5 December 1961, clippings in FMBA, MLMSS 9894/513, SLNSW.
21 *Sun*, 6 December 1961, p. 38; *AFR*, 28 November 1961, p. 2; *SMH*, 16 November 1961, clipping in FMBA, MLMSS 9894/513, SLNSW.
22 *Sunday Mirror*, 19 November, 1961, p. 1.
23 *Daily Mirror*, 7 December 1961, p. 30.
24 *Newspaper News*, 17 August 1962, p. 1.
25 Griffen-Foley, 2001a, p. 29.
26 Fitzgerald and Holt, 2010, pp. 100–01.
27 *Sun*, 7 December 1961, p. 38.
28 After allocating a Speaker.
29 *Canberra Times*, 2 May 1974, p. 2.
30 Fitzgerald and Holt, 2010, p. 147; *AFR*, 6 June 1972, p. 1.
31 *Herald*, 8 December 1961, p. 4.

32 Chalmers, 2011, p. 46.
33 *ibid.*, p. 48.
34 MacCallum, 2006.
35 Kirkman, 1996, p. 9; MacCallum, 2006.
36 *Crikey*, 2006a; MacCallum, 2006.
37 *Crikey*, 2006b.
38 Fairfax, 1992, pp. 19–20.
39 *CPD* (HR), 6 March 1962, p. 479.
40 *Nation Review*, 18–24 May 1978, pp. 10–11.
41 *Age*, 6 March 1967, p. 4.
42 *SMH*, 15 April 1962, p. 34.
43 *AFR*, 4 September 1972.
44 Their allied companies' licence applications had been unsuccessful, but they did have some minor holdings, via subsidiaries, in the winners (*SMH*, 9 November 1960, p. 10; *Canberra Times*, 9 November 1960, p. 1).
45 *SMH*, 15 April 1962, p. 34.
46 *ibid.*, 27 September 1961, p. 4.
47 To get around the provision in Newcastle Broadcasting and Television Corporation Ltd's articles that prevented any non-Newcastle-based owners, Wansey claimed publicly that he 'personally bought' Newcastle Newspapers' NBN shares. In reality, Fairfax loaned him the money, hid the transaction via Bank of New South Wales Nominees and then paid out the loan. Wansey was rewarded with a position as chairman of Newcastle Newspapers. John Fairfax Ltd acquired the remaining 55 per cent of the company in 1977. (Souter, 1981, pp. 352–53; *SMH*, 27 September 1961, p. 4.)
48 *Newcastle Morning Herald and Miners' Advocate*, 8 December 1961, p. 2.
49 *SMH*, 18 October 1963, p. 14.
50 Cushing, 2000.
51 Munster, 1987, pp. 63, 65; *CPD* (HR), 18 April 1963, p. 699.
52 *Nation*, 24 March 1962, p. 8.
53 Memo from AH McLachlan to RA Henderson, 16 August 1963, FMBA, MLMSS 9894/413, SLNSW.
54 *ibid.*; *CPD* (HR), 18 April 1963, p. 699; *SMH*, 15 April 1962, p. 9.
55 Johnston, 1967, p. 200.
56 Brown, 1989, p. 42.
57 *Age*, 30 September 1980, p. 16.
58 Easdown and Wilms, 2002, pp. 44, 21; *Canberra Times*, 10 April 1963, p. 1; *CPD* (HR), 18 April 1963, p. 699.
59 Fahey, 2007.
60 ABCB, 1964, pp. 45–46.
61 Hall, 1976, p. 42.
62 ABCB, 1964, p. 50; *Canberra Times*, 23 April 1964, p. 3.
63 Letter from L Dumas to RG Menzies, 17 April 1962, FMBA, MLMSS 9894/413, SLNSW.
64 *CPD* (HR), 18 April 1963, p. 697.
65 Including pastoral company, Elder Smith Goldsborough Mort, and American Broadcasting–Paramount Theatres, two churches and two trade unions. In Perth, a consortium that had included Western Press – a subsidiary of Murdoch's News Limited – was also rejected.
66 Dobell, 1987, p. 93; Chadwick, 1989, p. xxxi (but note: Chadwick states Ansett was awarded the Sydney licence in 1963 but it was United Telecasters).
67 Bowman, 1988, p. 76.
68 *Canberra Times*, 24 April 1963, p. 37; ABCB, 1963, p. 34.
69 Chadwick, 1989, p. xxxi.
70 Hall, 1976, p. 43.
71 'Newcastle Broadcasting and Television Corporation Limited: Share portfolio', 2 January 1969, FMBA, MLMSS 9894/1099, SLNSW.
72 Lever, 2012d.

73 *Daily Mirror*, 29 November 1963, p. 28.
74 Chadwick, 1989, p. xxxi; Calwell, 1972, p. 93.
75 *News*, 29 November 1963, p. 21.
76 Adrian Deamer interviewed by Stewart Harris, 1993, NLA, p. 20.
77 Chadwick, 1989, p. xxxi.
78 Fairfax, 1992, p. 71; Souter, 1981, pp. 368–69.
79 Fairfax, 1992, pp. 77–78.
80 Letter from General Manager, John Fairfax & Sons, to Secretary, Liberal Party (NSW), 25 October 1949; Letter from Secretary, John Fairfax & Sons, to Secretary, Liberal Party, 10 October 1950; Letter from E Holt to A McLachlan, 3 May 1951; Letter from RA Henderson to DS Aarons, 20 November 1961; Letter from DS Aarons to RA Henderson, 27 September 1962; FMBA, MLMSS 9894/512, SLNSW.
81 Letter from RA Henderson to RW Askin, 21 October 1964, FMBA, MLMSS 9894/512, SLNSW.
82 *SMH*, 2 May 1974, p. 7.
83 *Bulletin*, 15 September 1987, p. 45.
84 *ibid.*, 7 May 1985, p. 3; *West Australian*, 3 September 1987, p. 27.
85 *SMH*, 4 September 1987, p. 11.
86 *ibid.*, 9 November 1985, pp. 41, 45.
87 Fitzgerald and Holt, pp. 122–23; *SMH*, 3 September 1987, p. 8.
88 *Australian*, 14 August 1971, pp. 14–15.
89 Fitzgerald and Holt, 2010, p. 169.
90 Munster, 1987, p. 62.
91 *Australian*, 5 January 2013, p. 18.
92 *Canberra Times*, 22 March 2013, p. A021.
93 *Australian*, 29 May 2010, p. 4.
94 Liberal Party pamphlet, 'Mr Calwell and the faceless men', 1963.
95 CPD (HR), 3 April 1963, p. 350; *Canberra Times*, 24 April 1963, p. 3.
96 Liberal Party pamphlet, 'Mr Calwell and the faceless men', 1963.
97 Scalmer, 2001, pp. 100–01; *SMH*, 3 September 1987, p. 8.
98 Kelly, 2001, pp. 108–09.
99 Griffen-Foley, 2001a, p. 30.
100 *AFR*, 15 June 1967, p. 8.
101 *SMH*, 11 July 1967, clipping in FMBA, MLMSS 9894/426, SLNSW.
102 Shawcross, 1992, p. 79.
103 D'Arcy, 2005, pp. 12–13.
104 Macrotrends, 2022.
105 *Canberra Times*, 3 February 2021, p. 28.
106 *SMH*, 13 October 1975, p. 11; *Canberra Times*, 20 September 1976, p. 3.
107 *Canberra Times*, 21 April 2000, p. 11.
108 Souter, 1981, p. 354.
109 Minutes of the 226th meeting of John Fairfax Ltd, 19 July 1962, FMBA, MLMSS 9894/1, SLNSW FMBA, box 1.
110 Minutes of the 220th meeting of John Fairfax Ltd, 17 May 1962, *ibid*.
111 Souter, 1981, p. 355; Munster, p. 75.
112 *ibid.*; *Australian*, 17 May 2014, p. 6.
113 Souter, 1981, p. 356.
114 *SMH*, 1 May 1964.
115 *Australian*, 17 May 2014, p. 6.
116 Munster, 1987, p. 75.
117 Souter, 1981, p. 357.
118 Goot, 2015, p. 9.
119 Tiffen, 2009.
120 Goot, 2015, p. 9.
121 *Newspaper News*, 1 July 1957, pp. 3, 14, 20.

122 *Australian*, 17 May 2014, p. 6.
123 Cryle, 2008, pp. 6–7.
124 Day, undated.
125 Cryle, 2008, p. 7.
126 *Times* (UK), 5 June 1972, clipping from FMBA, MLMSS 9894/407, SLNSW.
127 Cryle, 2008, p. 7.
128 Letter from L Dumas to RP Falkingham, 5 March 1965, FMBA, MLMSS 9894/410, SLNSW.
129 Maxwell Newton, 'It was a wild idea, a mistake, a dream of such compulsion … a once-in-a-lifetime chance', *Australian*, 15 July 1989 (newspaper clipping, page unknown); Transcribed from tape recording of Maxwell Newton's address to the Advertising Club, 16 April 1969, FMBA, MLMSS 9894/407/WAN, SLNSW.
130 Anonymous, interview with the author.
131 Newton, Advertising Club address, *ibid*.
132 Adrian Deamer interview with Stewart Harris, 1993, NLA.
133 *ibid*.
134 Tiffen, 2009.
135 *Newspaper News*, 16 September 1966, p. 1.
136 Minutes of the 331st meeting of directors of John Fairfax Ltd, 22 June 1965, FMBA, MLMSS 9894/2, SLNSW.
137 Adrian Deamer interview with Stewart Harris, 1993, NLA; Cryle, 2008, p. 243.
138 Hills, 2010, p. 226.
139 Tiffen, 2014, p. 22.
140 *Australian*, 17 May 2014, p. 6.
141 *Bulletin*, 24 January 1984, p. 74; Adrian Deamer interview with Stewart Harris, 1993, NLA.
142 Munster, 1987, p. 73.
143 *Australian*, 15 July, p. 16.
144 *Vogue*, May 1972, pp. 70–71, 100.
145 *Australian*, 17 May 2014, p. 6.
146 For a summary of the debate on when and for how long it made profits, see Goot, 2015, p. 6.
147 Munster, 1987, p. 73.

Chapter 14 The realm of the Black Prince
1 *Australian*, 12 October 1978, p. 7.
2 *AM*, 6 October 1953, clipping in FMBA, MLMSS 9894/1610, SLNSW.
3 *Bulletin*, 9 January 1965, p. 13.
4 *ibid.*, 5 May 1981, p. 78.
5 *SMH*, 8 November 1990, p. 15.
6 Judith Cook, telephone interview with the author, 2021.
7 *SMH*, 21 November 1995, p. 15.
8 *Bulletin*, 9 January 1965, p. 13.
9 *Australian*, 9–10 November 1991, p. 27.
10 *Bulletin*, 9 January 1965, p. 13.
11 *Henderson v Henderson*, Supreme Court of NSW, SARANSW, (AF00167759, AF00167760).
12 Petition of restitution of conjugal rights, 10 June 1932, Supreme Court of NSW, SARANSW, (AF00167759, AF00167760).
13 *Labor Daily* (Sydney), 8 May 1937, p. 4; *Truth*, 9 May 1937, p. 21.
14 *SMH*, 8 May 1937, p. 10.
15 *Henderson v Henderson*, Supreme Court of NSW, SARANSW, (AF00167759, AF00167760).
16 Judith Cook, telephone interview with the author, 2021; *Truth* (Sydney), 26 December 1937, p. 16.
17 *Truth* (Sydney), 16 October 1938, p. 26.
18 'Minutes of meeting of the directors of ATS', 20 July 1962, p. 1, FMBA, MLMSS 9894/348, SLNSW.
19 Judith Cook, telephone interview with the author, 2021.

20 ibid.
21 Fairfax, 1992, p. 22.
22 Souter, 1981, p. 424.
23 *Scone Advocate*, 8 November 1946, p. 4; *SMH*, 26 October 1946, p. 5, and 17 September 2011, p. 23.
24 Kirkpatrick, 2000, pp. 298–99.
25 ibid.
26 ABCB, 1963, p. 38.
27 *Age*, 9 May 1985, p. 24.
28 *CPD* (HR), 18 April 1963, p. 697.
29 Amalgamated Television Services (ATS) return, undated (circa 1964), FMBA, MLMSS 9894/365, SLNSW.
30 Carroll, 2007.
31 Griffen-Foley, 2007a.
32 *Melbourne Observer*, 50th anniversary souvenir, 11 September 2019, p. 37.
33 *SMH*, 30 August 1997, p. 97.
34 *Age*, 15 December 1990, p. 4.
35 Ryan, 2013, p. 13.
36 Fairfax, 1992, p. 73.
37 Souter, 1981, p. 372.
38 Minutes of the 264th meeting of directors of John Fairfax Ltd, 11 July 1963, FMBA, MLMSS 9894/2, SLNSW.
39 Minutes of the 274th meeting of directors of John Fairfax Ltd, 17 October 1963; Minutes of the 287th meeting of directors of John Fairfax Ltd, 5 March 1964; Minutes of the 328th meeting of directors of John Fairfax Ltd, 18 May 1965, FMBA, MLMSS 9894/2, SLNSW.
40 Souter, 1981, p. 402.
41 ATV had set up an Australian subsidiary, ATV (Australia) Pty Ltd, to manage its Australian broadcasting assets.
42 Dudley Edwards, 2003, p. 303.
43 *Canberra Times*, 30 June 1964, p. 18; ABCB, 1965, pp. 12–13, 43.
44 Fairfax, 1992, p. 69.
45 ABCB, 1969, p. 143.
46 Souter, 1981, pp. 359, 363–65.
47 *Bulletin*, 9 January 1965, p. 13.
48 John Fairfax Limited, Annual Report 1957, p. 3; John Fairfax Limited, Annual Report 1960, p. 4; John Fairfax Limited, Annual Report 1965, p. 4.
49 *SMH*, 11 October 1978, p. 7.
50 *Canberra Times*, 21 September 1965, p. 14; *CPD* (HR), 25 May 1965, p. 1803; ABCB, 1964, p. 33.
51 *Canberra Times*, 1 January 1994, p. 8; *CPD* (HR), 25 May 1965, p. 1803.
52 Windschuttle, 1988, pp. 106–07.
53 Armstrong, 1975, p. 500; ABCB, 1965, pp. 44–46.
54 *Canberra Times*, 1 January 1994, p. 8; *CPD* (HR), 25 May 1965, p. 1803.
55 *Canberra Times*, 10 December 1963, p. 3 and 1 January 1994, p. 8; Barber and Johnson, 2014.
56 Windschuttle, 1988, pp. 107–08. See also Hall, 1976, p. 41.
57 Bednall, handwritten unpaginated version of unpublished autobiography, Bednall Papers, MS 5546/5, NLA; Armstrong, 1975, p. 501.
58 *CPD* (HR), 25 May 1965, p. 1805–06.
59 E.g. the HWT in relation to TVW Perth and Fairfax with CTC Canberra ('Cabinet minute, 10 December 1969, decision no. 44', NAA A5873-44, Cabinet-Broadcasting and TV Act-1).
60 Bednall, typed version of unpublished autobiography, p. 9, Bednall Papers, MS 5546/5, NLA.
61 Amalgamated Television Services (ATS) return, undated, FMBA, MLMSS 9894/365, SLNSW.
62 *Bulletin*, 3 February 1973, pp. 52–53.
63 ABCB, 1969, p. 151.
64 *Bulletin*, 3 February 1973, p. 52; Souter, 1981, p. 322

65 *CPD* (HR), 7 March 1972, p. 485; *CPD* (Senate), 20 April 1972, p. 1322.
66 *SMH*, 13 August 1996, p. 33, and 3 September 1996, p. 14.
67 Souter, 1981, p. 407.
68 David Syme and Co, Prospectus, 1950, FMBA, MLMSS 9894/149, SLNSW.
69 Hills, 2010, p. 89.
70 Minutes of the 274th meeting of directors of John Fairfax Ltd, 17 October 1963, FMBA, MLMSS 9894/2, SLNSW.
71 Nolan, 2001, p. 4.
72 Souter, 1981, p. 414; Tidey, 1998, p. 3.
73 *Herald*, 28 February 1969, page unknown, clipping in FMBA, MLMSS 9894/25, SLNSW.
74 Barker, 2012.
75 *Nation Review*, 29 November–5 December 1974, clipping in FMBA, MLMSS 9894/24, SLNSW.
76 Souter, 1981, p. 415.
77 *Newspaper News*, 11 December 1964, p. 8.
78 Hills, 2010, p. 233.
79 Tidey, 1998, p. 10; Chadwick, 1989, p. xxxiii.
80 Ranald Macdonald interview with the author, 2015.
81 Pringle cited in Goot, 2015, p. 17.
82 *Canberra Times*, 12 April 1981, p. 7.
83 Kirkpatrick, 2000, p. 298.
84 Brown, 1989, p. 43.
85 Judith Cook, telephone interview with the author, 2021.
86 John B Fairfax interview with the author, Sydney, 2019.
87 Souter, 1981, p. 425.
88 Kirkpatrick, 2000, p. 298.
89 *Age*, 9 May 1985, p. 24; *SMH*, 9 May 1985, p. 24, and 14 June 1985, p. 16.
90 Death certificate, RAG Henderson, NSW Registry of Births Deaths and Marriages, 21800/1986.

Chapter 15 The quiet baron of Flinders Street
1   Letter from L Dumas to RA Henderson, 7 January 1966, FMBA, MLMSS 9894/410, SLNSW.
2   *Canberra Times*, 10 January 1970, p. 15.
3   *ibid.*
4   *The Review*, 20 August 1971, p. 1275.
5   *Canberra Times*, 10 January 1970, p. 15.
6   Edwards, 1972, pp. 107, 146–47.
7   *Bulletin*, 6 February 1957, p. 10.
8   Edwards, 1972, pp. 146–47.
9   Dunstan, undated.
10 Joan Newman, telephone interview with the author, 19 March 2021.
11 David Dunstan, email to the author, 15 June 2022.
12 Edwards, 1972, p. 147; Younger, 1999, p. 43; Dunstan, 2012.
13 *Canberra Times*, 10 January 1970, p. 15.
14 David Dunstan, email to the author, 15 June 2022.
15 Ian Hamilton, telephone interview with the author, 2022.
16 File note, 1 June 1965, FMBA, MLMSS 9894/410/HWT, SLNSW.
17 Dahlsen, 2019, p. 56.
18 *Age*, 1 January 1970, p. 6.
19 As with Fairfax, there is always the chance that not all of the company's interests in television were declared.
20 *Canberra Times*, 10 January 1970, p. 15.
21 Finance and Development Department of David Syme and Co, 1967.
22 Edwards, 1972, p. 146.
23 Finance and Development Department of David Syme and Co, 1967, pp. 7–11, 15.
24 *Sunday Telegraph*, 10 December 1967, p. 122.

25 *Papua New Guinea Post-Courier*, 18 December 1970, p. 33; *Sunday Telegraph*, 10 December 1967, p. 122. See also Table 16.1.
26 *Sunday Telegraph*, 10 December 1967, p. 122.
27 Finance and Development Department of David Syme and Co, 1967, pp. 27–29; *Bulletin*, 19 January 1963, p. 51.
28 With thanks to David Dunstan for sharing his expertise on Williams and for supplying drafts and other papers that make this point and others discussed in this chapter.
29 HWT, *House News*, HWT, October 1983, p. 11.
30 Goot, 1979, pp. 5–6.
31 Younger, 1996, p. 272.
32 Dahlsen, 2019, p. 54.
33 Rupert Murdoch interviewed by Derryn Hinch, 3AW, 26 November 1980, transcript in FMBA, MLMSS 9894/416, SLNSW.
34 *Age*, 1 January 1970, p. 6.
35 John Dahlsen interview with the author, Carlton, 2019.
36 Dahlsen, 2019, p. 57.
37 *Canberra Times*, 10 January 1970, p. 15.
38 Ian Hamilton, phone interview with the author, 2022.
39 Younger, 1999, p. 438.
40 David Dunstan, phone interview with the author, 26 February 2021.
41 Costar, 2006, pp. 227–41.
42 *Herald*, 27 May 1958, p. 4.
43 *ibid.*, 14 July 1961, p. 1.
44 *Canberra Times*, 17 July 1972, p. 2.
45 *Melbourne Observer*, 50th anniversary souvenir, 11 September 2019, p. 37.
46 Laurie Oakes, interview with the author, Canberra, 2019.
47 *Bulletin*, 25 December 1965, p. 19.
48 *Herald*, 26 April 1967, p. 4.
49 Ryan and Watson, 2004, p. 3.
50 *SMH*, 21 November 1963, p. 6.
51 Dunstan, 2007.
52 *Age*, 31 October 1994, p. 16.
53 During the 1960s, on a two-party preferred basis, the vote for Labor in Victoria was an average of 5 percentage points lower than the national average, and nearly 7 points lower than Labor's vote in NSW (AEC, 2022).
54 Crisp, 1970.
55 *Age*, 4 December 1972, p. 7.
56 *Canberra Times*, 29 November 1968, p. 7.
57 *Newspaper News*, 27 April 1962, p. 1.
58 Younger, 1996, p. 288; *Bulletin*, 29 February 1956, p. 16.
59 Finance and Development Department of David Syme and Co, 1967, p. 8.
60 McQueen, 2014, p. 96.
61 Newspaper clipping headed '*Argus* profit doubles', unknown source, 11 January 1968, FMBA, MLMSS 9894/1095, SLNSW; *Canberra Times*, 11 January 1968, p. 20; *SMH*, 11 January 1969, p. 16; *Papua New Guinea Post-Courier*, 27 November 1972, p. 8.
62 *Canberra Times*, 20 September 1966, p. 15, and 3 July 1970, p. 5.
63 *ibid.*, 31 January 1962, p. 9.
64 Bester, 2014, p. 277.
65 Younger, 1999, p. 437.
66 Edwards, 1972, p. 145.
67 *ibid.*
68 *Age*, 30 June 1981, p. 6.
69 *Courier-Mail*, 31 December 1980, p. 7; *Age*, 21 November 1979, p. 15; *Australian*, 13 December 1993, from biography clippings, NLA.

70 John Dahlsen, interview with the author, Carlton, 2019.
71 Ian Potter and Co, 'Fortnightly review', 31 July 1969, FMBA, MLMSS 9894/1234, SLNSW.
72 WAN Ltd, Annual report and accounts 1968, in FMBA, MLMSS 9894/407/WAN, SLNSW.
73 *Advertising News*, 28 October 1977, pp. 19–20.
74 *News*, 26 May 1958, p. 3; Ian Potter and Co, 'Fortnightly review', 31 July 1969, FMBA, MLMSS 9894/1234, SLNSW; WAN Limited, Managing editor's address, 3 November 1961, FMBA, MLMSS 9894/413/WAN, SLNSW.
75 Memo from RB Falkingham to W Fairfax, 1 July 1969, FMBA, MLMSS 9894/407/WAN, SLNSW.
76 *Argus*, 5 December 1955, p. 5.
77 Plus individual investors such as Furza Brady, a wealthy Perth bookmaker, racehorse owner and former jockey who lived to 101. (WAN shareholder list 1954, ASIC Doc 025053342.)
78 *SMH*, 1 July 1969, p. 17.
79 WAN Ltd, Annual report and accounts, 1968, FMBA, MLMSS 9894/407/WAN, SLNSW.
80 *Canberra Times*, 10 July 1969, p. 19.
81 ABCB, 1970, p. 147.
82 *Daily Telegraph*, 1 July 1969, p. 15.
83 Cable from 'Kennedy' to V Carroll, 1 July 1969, FMBA, MLMSS 9894/407/WAN, SLNSW; *SMH*, 2 July 1969, p. 18.
84 Memo from A Cragg to L Leck, 7 July 1969, FMBA, MLMSS 9894/407/WAN, SLNSW.
85 *Tribune*, 9 July 1969, p. 8.
86 *SMH*, 1 July 1969, p. 17.
87 Yule, 2006, pp. 125.
88 *SMH*, 4 February 1968, p. 7; *Age*, 24 May 1969, p. 15.
89 Young, 2019, pp. 270–72. Robinson's interest in newspapers included repeatedly trying to convince Oswald Syme to sell *The Age* to him in 1950; on at least one occasion he was acting on behalf of an unknown third party (Nolan, 2001, pp. 6–7).
90 Boyce, 2001.
91 Cable from 'Kennedy' to V Carroll, 2 July 1969, FMBA, MLMSS 9894/407/WAN, SLNSW.
92 *Bulletin*, 7 December 1968, p. 85.
93 Transcribed tape recording of Maxwell Newton's address to the Advertising Club, 16 April 1969, FMBA, MLMSS 9894/407/WAN, SLNSW.
94 *Canberra Times*, 12 October 1973, p. 7.
95 Cables from 'Kennedy' to V Carroll, 30 June 1969 and 3 July 1969, FMBA, MLMSS 9894/407/WAN, SLNSW.
96 *ibid*.
97 HWT, Annual report 1970, FMBA, MLMSS 9894/1099, SLNSW.
98 *CPD* (Senate), 8 April 1970, p. 595.
99 'Inventory of assets', Supreme Court Victoria, probate document in the will of John Francis Williams, 28 May 1982, VPRS 28/P12, unit 129, item 904/598, PROV.
100 Letter from C Bednall to EG Whitlam, December 1973, Bednall Papers, MS 5546/1/5.
101 HWT, 'Chairman's address', 8 December 1965, in in HWT documents, ASIC (doc 025740710).
102 Dahlsen, 2016, p. 36.
103 *ibid.*, p. 37.
104 *Canberra Times*, 23 November 1968, p. 16.
105 HWT, 'Chairman's address', 8 December 1965, in HWT documents, ASIC (doc 025740710).
106 *AFR*, 5 December 1968, p. 26.
107 'Comment on the new *Television Act* 1965', Dahlsen papers, box 3, 1983/BTA folder.
108 *ibid*.
109 *Canberra Times*, 10 December 1970, p. 33.
110 Younger, 1999, p. 480.
111 Memo from RP Falkingham to W Fairfax, 1 July 1969, p. 1, FMBA, MLMSS 9894/407/WAN, SLNSW.
112 *Age*, 12 May 1979, p. 25.

113 *AFR*, 13 November 1968, p. 73.
114 *ibid.*, 14 November 1968, p. 17.
115 Finance and Development Department of David Syme and Co, 1967, p. 1.
116 *ibid.*, p. 78.
117 *Age*, 15 June 1972, p. 18.
118 Adrian Deamer interview with Stewart Harris, 1993, p. 5, NLA.
119 Memo from V Carroll to AH McLachlan, 5 December 1968, FMBA, MLMSS 9894/410, SLNSW FMBA.
120 *Canberra Times*, 23 November 1968, p. 16.
121 Laurie Oakes, interview with the author, Canberra, 2019.
122 Younger, 1999, p. 480.
123 *Australian*, 13 December 1993, page unknown, biography clipping, NLA.
124 John Dahlsen, interview with the author, Carlton, 2019.
125 *ibid*.
126 Dunstan, 2012.
127 The relationship was reportedly ended due to discomfort about continuing to defend the church against child abuse claims (*AFR*, 12 August 2022, p. 34).
128 Will of John Francis Williams, 28 May 1982, VPRS 28/P12, unit 129, item 904/598, PROV.
129 Death certificate of John Williams, (no. 7358/82), Victorian Registry of Births, Deaths and Marriages.

Chapter 16 The new world
1 Dobell, 1987, p. 63.
2 *AFR*, 6 June 1972, p. 1.
3 Up to December 1966. Then it was seven elections Labor lost (Barber and Johnson, 2014; Santamaria, 1969, p. 36).
4 Hancock, 1996.
5 Hancock, 2001, p. 284.
6 Hancock, 1996.
7 HWT, 'Directors' report 1966, [ASIC] doc 025740710.
8 Rickard, 1996, p. 208.
9 Tiffen, 1990, p. 137.
10 Tiffen, 2014, p. 92.
11 *Bulletin*, 5 May 1981, p. 78.
12 Griffen-Foley, 2001a, p. 32.
13 *Courier-Mail*, 25 November 1966, p. 1.
14 *Mercury*, 25 November 1966, p. 4.
15 *Canberra Times*, 25 November 1966, p. 2.
16 Curran, 2015, p. 76. For an example of the excitement, see *SMH*, 22 October 1966, p. 6.
17 *Canberra Times*, 25 November 1966, p. 2.
18 Tiffen, 1983, p. 184.
19 Young, 2016b, p. 74.
20 Freudenberg, 1993.
21 *Tribune*, 20 March 1968, p. 3.
22 *Australian*, 26 November 1966, p. 8.
23 *ibid*.
24 AEC, 2022.
25 Pringle, 1965, p. 199.
26 *Bulletin*, 18 August 1962, p. 21.
27 Tiffen, 2014, p. 20.
28 Goot, 1979, p. 6.
29 Munster, 1987, p. 62.
30 Souter, 1981, p. 523; *Bulletin*, 25 February 1967, p. 10.
31 Minutes of the 360th meeting of directors of John Fairfax Ltd, 12 April 1966, p. 906, FMBA, MLMSS 9894/2, NLA.

32 Hinch, 2004, p. 58.
33 It was not, as listed in one source, the actor William Boyd.
34 'Tabloid war stories', *Australian*, 11 May 2000.
35 *SMH*, 4 October 1990, p. 4.
36 *Age*, 13 March 1982, p. 155.
37 Hinch, 2004, p. 62.
38 Souter, 1981, p. 525.
39 *SMH*, 4 October 1990, p. 4.
40 *AFR*, 28 July 2011, p. 66.
41 Anderson, 2016, p. 213.
42 Pringle, 1965, p. 117.
43 *AFR*, 15 March 1988, p. 36.
44 Minutes of the 391st meeting of directors of John Fairfax Ltd, 7 March 1967, FMBA, MLMSS 9894/3, NLA.
45 Anderson, 2016, pp. 200–03.
46 Souter, 1981, p. 525.
47 Anne-Marie Willis cited in Anderson, 2016, p. 202.
48 News Limited–Fairfax agreement, FMBA, MLMSS 9894/407, NLA.
49 *ibid*.
50 *Sun* street poster, 7 September 1965, FMBA, MLMSS 9894/410, NLA.
51 Letter from B Hogben to GH Wilkinson, 7 September 1976, MLMSS 9894/407, NLA.
52 *SMH*, 4 October 1990, p. 4.
53 Mark Day, email correspondence with the author, 19 July 2021.
54 *Sunday Times* (London) magazine, 21 April 1974, (page unknown), newspaper clipping, NLA.
55 *Canberra Times*, 27 March 1968, p. 13; Whitton, 2016b; Whitton, 1987.
56 *B&T*, 23 October 1969, p. 18.
57 Letter from L Dumas to RP Falkingham, 15 January 1965, FMBA, MLMSS 9894/410, NLA.
58 *SMH*, 2 July 1969, p. 18.
59 Hood, 1972, p. 77.
60 *SMH*, 26 October 1968, p. 13; *Age*, 7 January 1969, p. 9.
61 *Bulletin*, 1 July 1986, p. 84.
62 *Canberra Times*, 2 August 2008, p. 1.
63 Mullins, 2018, p. 272.
64 *ibid*., pp. 242, 244.
65 Chadwick, 1989, p. xxxiii.
66 Munster, 1987, p. 86.
67 Mullins, 2018, p. 246; David McNicoll interview with John Farquharson, 1997, NLA.
68 Tiffen, 2014, p. 108.
69 Whitton, 1987; Whitton, 2016b; *Truth*, 13 January 1968, pp. 1–2.
70 *Truth*, 13 January 1968, p. 2.
71 Whitton, 1987. See also *Tribune*, 3 April 1968, p. 4.
72 Whitton, 1987.
73 *Tribune*, 7 February 1968, p. 2. But note, Rodney Lever (2009) believed the reason for the sacking was that Chandler had run 'a series of salacious stories' about 'merchants of Little Collins and Bourke Streets' who had been donors to Dame Elisabeth Murdoch's charities for many years, and that she insisted that Rupert sack Chandler. If true, it was a rare intervention on her part.
74 *Bulletin*, 29 November 1969, p. 69; *Guardian* (London), 15 November 1999, p. 74.
75 *Canberra Times*, 28 September 1983, p. 33.
76 *Guardian* (London), 15 November 1999, p. 74.
77 *ibid*.
78 *Australian*, 10 November 1970, p. 12.
79 *AFR*, 25 October 1976, p. 2.
80 Anderson, 2016, p. 203.
81 McNair, 1994, pp. 145–46.
82 Letter from L Dumas to RA Henderson, 6 March 1967, FMBA, MLMSS 9894/410, SLNSW.

83 *Australian*, 17 May 2014, p. 6.
84 *Age*, 28 April 1971, p. 14; News Limited, *Annual Report 1970*, p. 8.
85 *Guardian* (UK), 7 April 1972, p. 15.
86 *Age*, 17 February 1968, p. 13.
87 Fitzgerald and Holt, 2010, p. 204.
88 *Daily Telegraph*, 25 October 2015, p. 22.
89 Griffen-Foley, 2000, p. 291.
90 *News*, 24 October 1969, p. 20.
91 *Daily Mirror*, 24 October 1969, p. 2.
92 *Australian*, 25 October 1969, p. 20.
93 *SMH*, 24 October 1969, p. 2.
94 Letter from G Robertson to L Leck, 4 September 1969, FMBA, MLMSS 9894/512, SLNSW.
95 *Herald*, 24 October 1969, p. 4; *Sun News-Pictorial*, 24 October 1969, p. 8.
96 Barber and Johnson, 2014.
97 Reid, 2018, p. 125.
98 *Herald-Sun*, 30 December 1998, p. 17.
99 Tiffen, 2017, p. 112.
100 Rawson, 1961, p. 102.
101 Hastie, 2013, p. 95.
102 UNESCO, 1963, p. 83.
103 Dobell, 1987, pp. 80–81.
104 Hastie, 2013, pp. 99–100.
105 *Canberra Times*, 30 December 1971, p. 2.
106 Freudenberg, 2000, p. 92.
107 Turner, 2003.
108 Beilby, 1981, pp. 114–17.
109 *Age*, 26 March 1959, p. 21, and 13 February 1994, p. 34.
110 Young, 2019, pp. 71–73.
111 'Comments on the attached tables [Anderson analysis]', 8 January 1960, MLMSS 9894/357, SLNSW.
112 The Age ASRB Survey, July 1968, p. 31, FMBA, MLMSS 9894/210, SLNSW.
113 Tiffen, 2015, p. 69.
114 *ibid*.
115 Gould, 2007.
116 Gould, 2007; Griffen-Foley, 2007b.
117 Max Walsh quoted in Dobell, 1987, p. 88.
118 Souter, 1981, p. 359.
119 *SMH*, 20 July 1974, p. 2.
120 *Nation Review*, 2–8 August 1974, pp. 1351–52, FMBA, MLMSS 9894/576, SLNSW.
121 JB Fairfax, 'Report on the *Canberra Times*', August 1977, p. 34, FMBA, MLMSS 9894/577, SLNSW.
122 *SMH*, 29 Jan 1969, p. 17, 16 July 1970, p. 29, and 11 September 1970, p. 30.
123 Bogart, 1982, p. 62.
124 *ibid.*, 28 October 1969, p. 15, and 19 April 1971, supplement, p. 1.
125 *Daily Telegraph*, 15 June 1967, p. 27; Kirkpatrick, 2000, pp. 294–95.
126 *Canberra Times*, 28 November 1967, p. 15.
127 *Age*, 11 December 1963, p. 8.
128 Two of the six remaining by 1979 (*Canberra Times*, 21 November 1979, p. 2).
129 Kirkpatrick, 2014 and 1994a.
130 News Limited, *Annual Report 1971*, News Limited, Sydney.
131 *SMH*, 28 October 1969, p. 15; Minutes of meeting of directors of John Fairfax Ltd, 12 March 1968, FMBA, MLMSS 9894/2, SLNSW.
132 Minutes of meeting of directors of John Fairfax Ltd, 15 February 1968, FMBA, MLMSS 9894/2, SLNSW.
133 *Advertiser*, 13 January 1979, p. 17.

Chapter 17 The magic garden of computers

1. Shmith, 2011.
2. Hagan, 1966, p. 104; *PKIU State News*, vol. 4, June 1972, p. 1; *Daily Telegraph*, 28 April 1894, p. 4.
3. *Sun*, 1 December 1929, p. 2; *Argus*, 10 May 1934, p. 8; *West Australian*, 10 September 1938, p. 20; *Commonwealth of Australia Gazette*, 30 March 1944, p. 740, and 27 April 1944, p. 899.
4. Minutes of the 220th meeting of John Fairfax Ltd, 17 May 1962, FMBA, MLMSS 9894/1, SLNSW.
5. Memo by RP Falkingham, 14 March 1963, FMBA, MLMSS 9894/778, SLNSW.
6. *SMH*, 17 May 1946, p. 4.
7. *SMH*, 14 April 1981, p. 46.
8. Letter from RA Henderson to RR Macartney, 7 May 1964, in MLMSS 9894/407, SLNSW.
9. *AFR*, 1 July 1968, p. 45.
10. Minutes of meeting of directors of John Fairfax Ltd, 18 October 1967, MLMSS 9894/3, SLNSW.
11. *ibid*.; *PKIU State News*, vol 4, June 1972, p. 1.
12. Myrtle, undated, p. 10. Griffen-Foley, 2000, pp. 281–85.
13. Striking journalists revived *The Clarion* (the name used for the strikers' paper in 1955), publishing it for three editions on 9, 10 and 16 August (Myrtle, undated, p. 21).
14. *Canberra Times*, 17 August 1967, p. 13.
15. Myrtle, undated, p. 18.
16. Minutes of the meeting of directors of John Fairfax Ltd, 17 August 1967, FMBA, MLMSS 9894/3, SLNSW.
17. Myrtle, undated, p. 17.
18. 'THF' (Tom Farrell), 'Report', 31 May 1972, FMBA, MLMSS 9894/994, SLNSW.
19. *Wausau Daily Herald* (Wisconsin, US), 15 June 1963, p. 8.
20. *Canberra Times*, 29 July 1975, p. 10; *SMH*, 15 November 1976, p. 6.
21. Souter, 1981, p. 559.
22. John Fairfax Ltd, *Staff News*, December 1973, p. 5.
23. *ibid*.
24. *Press and Sun-Bulletin* (US), 22 July 1973, p. 27.
25. Cryle, 2008, p. 4; Genesove, 2000.
26. Joint publication between David Syme and Co, the HWT and unions, 'The changing world of newspapers', 1977, FMBA, MLMSS 9894/25, SLNSW.
27. *SMH*, 8 May 1974, p. 4; Griffin, 1984, p. 43.
28. *Age*, 14 May 1969, p. 3, and 19 July 1983, p. 11.
29. Souter, 1981, p. 561.
30. John Fairfax Ltd, *Annual Report 1976*, pp. 36–37, FMBA, MLMSS 9894/13, SLNSW; Fairfax, 1992, p. 104.
31. *ibid*.
32. 'Diary no. 1', pp. 98, 105, FMBA, MLMSS 9894/1728, SLNSW.
33. Genesove, 2000.
34. Hagan, 1966, pp. 237, 294–95.
35. *Australian Town and Country Journal*, 30 June 1877, p. 13.
36. *Canberra Times*, 14 April 1983, p. 15; Fairfax, 1992, p. 104
37. *SMH*, 15 November 1976, p. 6.
38. Souter, 1981, p. 562; *SMH*, 8 April 1975, p. 1; *Age*, 5 April 1975, p. 5.
39. *AFR*, 21 August 1975, p. 11; Buchanan.
40. *Tribune*, 26 August 1975, p. 5.
41. Buchanan, 2013.
42. *AFR*, 21 August 1975, p. 11.
43. *Age*, 22 August 1975, p. 3.
44. Memo from RP Falkingham to W Fairfax, 19 August 1975, FMBA, MLMSS 9894/416, SLNSW.
45. Souter, 1981, p. 564; Fairfax, 1992, p. 105.
46. Fairfax, 1992, p. 105.
47. *Canberra Times*, 13 November 1976, p. 1; *SMH*, 13 November, 1976, p. 1.

48 *SMH*, 9 December, 1976, p. 6.
49 'Diary no. 1', p. 68, FMBA, MLMSS 9894/1728, SLNSW.
50 *Canberra Times*, 20 May 1977, p. 3; John Fairfax Ltd, *Annual Report 1976*, pp. 36–37.
51 Kirkpatrick, 1994a, p. 262; Souter, 1981, p. 567.
52 Kirkpatrick, 1994a, p. 262.
53 'Diary no. 1', p. 98, FMBA, MLMSS 9894/1728, SLNSW.
54 Cryle, 2008, pp. 10–11, 14.
55 Letter from F Brenchley to MS Walsh, 30 May 1979, FMBA, MLMSS 9894/416, SLNSW.
56 *ibid*.
57 Cryle, 2008, p. 16.
58 'Diary no. 2', p. 214, FMBA, MLMSS 9894/1728, SLNSW.
59 *Age*, 27 March 1979, p. 32.
60 Younger, 1996, p. 199.
61 HWT, *House News*, Winter 1979, pp. 3, 4–5, and Summer 1979, p. 3, and October 1983, p. 3.
62 *Newsweek*, 13 August 1979, FMBA, MLMSS 9894/723, SLNSW; *The Journalist*, March/April 1981, p. 4.
63 Souter, 1981, p. 569. Note: some other sources say it was 26 subeditors at News Limited.
64 Souter, 1981, p. 569; Cryle, 2008, p. 15.
65 'Diary no. 2', pp. 275–76, FMBA, MLMSS 9894/723, SLNSW; *Age*, 15 May 1980, p. 1. (The AJA produced *The Clarion* again, but it was not created as a general newspaper to rival the employers' product (as in 1944 with the strikers' publication, *The News*). It was more narrowly focused on presenting the strikers' case.)
66 *SMH*, 19 May 1980, p. 3; David Syme and Co Ltd, *Annual Report 1980*, p. 19.
67 Souter, 1981, p. 568.
68 *Australian*, 4 June 2014, p. 14.
69 Cryle, 2008, pp. 12–13.
70 Letter from F Brenchley to MS Walsh, FMBA, MLMSS 9894/416, SLNSW; News Corporation Ltd, *Annual Report 1980*, 1981, p. 2; *Australian*, 4 June 2014, p. 14.
71 *SMH*, 15 August 1978, p. 25.
72 *Tribune*, 3 March 1982, p. 4.
73 'Diary no. 3', pp. 378, 390, FMBA, MLMSS 9894/1728, SLNSW.
74 *ibid*., p. 397.
75 Knight, p. 10. f.
76 *Canberra Times*, 20 May 1977, p. 3; JB Fairfax, Report on the *Canberra Times* 1977, August 1977, FMBA, box 577, p. 5; Mercer, 1999, p. 23.
77 David Syme and Co Ltd, *Annual Report 1980*, p. 4.
78 *Age*, 1 December 1981, p. 38; HWT, *House News*, 30 August 1978, p. 3, and October 1983, p. 9; Jones Grice and Co, 'Report on the company', 2 July 1980, Dahlsen Papers.
79 HWT, *House News*, October 1983, p. 9; 'Diary no. 3', p. 419, FMBA, MLMSS 9894/1728, SLNSW.

Chapter 18 A new *Age*

1 *Australian*, 22 May 2010, p. 7.
2 Ranald Macdonald, telephone interview with the author, 17 March 2021.
3 Hills, 2010, p. 153.
4 Walker, 1982, p. 293.
5 Nolan, 2014, p. 12.
6 'Anderson Analysis', 6 January 1960, FMBA, MLMSS 9894/357, SLNSW.
7 Goot, 1979, p. 6.
8 Barker, 2012.
9 Hills, 2010, p. 176.
10 *ibid*., p. 184.
11 *ibid*., p. 177.
12 'Diary no. 3', p. 416, FMBA, MLMSS 9894/1728, SLNSW; Hills, 2010, p. 410.

13 Bennetts denied this, too, but after leaving the paper, he became a military intelligence officer (Waterford, 1993; Hills, 2010, p.402).
14 Waterford, 1993.
15 Hills, 2010, pp. 157, 335.
16 *ibid.*, p. 334.
17 *ibid.*, pp. 180–82.
18 Ranald Macdonald, telephone interview with the author, 17 March 2021.
19 Ranald Macdonald, interview with the author, Flinders, 10 January 2022; EHB Neill, 'Memo', p. 4, 27 November 1967, MLMSS 9894/24, SLNSW.
20 Hills, 2010, p. 248.
21 Ranald Macdonald, interview with the author, Carlton, 12 May 2015; *Age*, 16 October 2004, supplement, p. 11.
22 Blazey and Campbell, 1974, p. 204.
23 *Age*, 16 October 2004, supplement, p. 11; *SMH*, 1 April 2006, p. 53.
24 McKnight, 1999.
25 Whitton, 1985, p. 124; Carson, 2020, p. 121–22.
26 Ranald Macdonald, interview with the author, Flinders, 10 January 2022.
27 Tiffen, 2014, p. 299. See also Minutes of the 389th meeting of directors of John Fairfax Ltd, 16 February 1967, FMBA, MLMSS 9894/3, SLNSW.
28 *Age*, 8 August 1969, p. 8; Goot, 2015, p. 17.
29 Ranald Macdonald, interview with the author, Flinders, 10 January 2022.
30 Smith, undated b.
31 *ibid*.
32 Nichols, 2005, p. 41/9; *AFR*, 7 November 1975, p. 2.
33 *Nation*, 29 April 1972, p. 11; *Age*, 16 October 1971, p. 17.
34 Tunstall, 1981, pp. 20–21.
35 Skelton, 'The *Sunday Age*: Appendix 3', April 1982, FMBA, MLMSS 9894/658, SLNSW.
36 Ryan, 2013, pp. 24–25.
37 *SMH*, 19 April 1971, 140th anniversary supplement, p. 4.
38 David Syme and Co, 'Managing Director's report to the board ... 21 May 1974', FMBA, MLMSS 9894/25, SLNSW.
39 *Advertising and Newspaper News*, 28 May 1971, p. 14.
40 Fairfax, Staff newsletter no. 39, 28 January 1971, FMBA, MLMSS 9894/195, SLNSW; Souter, 1981, p. 560.
41 *SMH*, 8 December 1971, p. 26.
42 *Age*, 6 October 1969, supplement, p. 3; *SMH*, 18 May 1968, p. 23; *Guardian*, 18 February 1995, p. 38; *SMH*, 19 April 1971, 140th anniversary supplement, p. 4; *Advertising and Newspaper News*, 28 May 1971, p. 14.
43 Bogart, 1982, p. 64.
44 *Advertising News*, 25 July 1975, p. 16, and 8 August 1975, p. 4.
45 Bogart, 1982, p. 64.
46 Fairfax, Staff newsletter no. 6, 19 February 1970, FMBA, MLMSS 9894/195, SLNSW.
47 *ibid.*, no. 9, 19 March 1970.
48 'Overseas visit 1973', 2 August 1973, FMBA, MLMSS 9894/994, SLNSW.
49 Fairfax, Staff newsletter no. 230, 16 October 1979, FMBA, MLMSS 9894/195, SLNSW.
50 Carson, 2020, p. 122.
51 'Business manager' memo to CR Macdonald, 28 November 1973, FMBA, MLMSS 9894/25, SLNSW; *Age*, 16 August 1973, p. 42.
52 *BRW*, 12 July 1991, p. 62.
53 *ibid.*; *Age*, 27 September 1969, p. 18, and 3 December 1981, p. 54.
54 *Age*, 29 September 1973, p. 19.
55 *ibid.*, 26 September 1991, p. 36.
56 Barker, 2012.
57 *Age*, 16 October 2004, supplement, p. 11.

58   Chandler, 2020.
59   *Age*, 6 October 1969, supplement, p. 2.
60   Edwards, 1972, p. 203; 'Notes on Project Seven', circa end 1968, p. 4, FMBA, MLMSS 9894/658, SLNSW.
61   *Age*, 5 June 1967, p. 3.
62   Edwards, 1972, p. 202.
63   *Prahran Telegraph*, 25 September 1889, p. 3.
64   *The Tocsin* (Melbourne), 13 July 1899, p. 2; *Table Talk*, 25 July 1901, p. 27.
65   In Perth, it was published on Saturday too (publication days for 1914–18, as per TROVE).
66   *SMH*, 22 March 1988, p. 17; *Bulletin*, 5 June 1984, p. 47.
67   *Sunday Age*, 16 August 2009, p. 13.
68   *Newspaper News*, 10 January 1969, p. 2.
69   Edwards, 1972, pp. 202–03.
70   Ranald Macdonald, interview with the author, Carlton, 12 May 2015; *VPD* (LA), 5 April 1966, pp. 3206–07.
71   Ranald Macdonald interview with the author, Carlton, 12 May 2015.
72   'Report to planning committee by Project 7 Committee', pp. 7–8, FMBA, MLMSS 9894/658, SLNSW.
73   *Canberra Times*, 15 December 1966, p. 20.
74   *Sunday Age*, 16 August 2009, p. 13.
75   Letter from P Michelmore to AH McLachlan, 25 September 1968, FMBA, MLMSS 9894/24, SLNSW.
76   Memo dated 23 December 1968, and memo from RP Falkingham to AH McLachlan, 11 December 1968, FMBA, MLMSS 9894/658, SLNSW.
77   Letter from AH McLachlan to CR Macdonald, 29 July 1968, FMBA, MLMSS 9894/658, SLNSW.
78   Report on 'Age Sunday paper', 11 December 1968, p. 4, FMBA, MLMSS 9894/658, SLNSW.
79   *Age*, 28 December 1968, p. 1.
80   'Report to planning committee by Project 7 Committee', p. 1, FMBA, MLMSS 9894/658, SLNSW.
81   'Editorial', project 7 committee report, p. 2, FMBA, MLMSS 9894/658, SLNSW.
82   *AFR*, 11 March 1969, clipping in FMBA, MLMSS 9894/658, SLNSW.
83   Tidey, 1998, p. 12. Note: there is not universal agreement about this. Some other sources believed the plan was for a *Sunday Herald*.
84   Report on '*Age* Sunday paper', 11 December 1968, p. 4, FMBA, MLMSS 9894/658, SLNSW.
85   Edwards, 1972, p. 202; *Bulletin*, 5 July 1969, p. 8; Hills, 2010, p. 378.
86   *Sunday Age*, 16 August 2009, p. 13.
87   Hills, 2010, p. 378.
88   Tidey, 1998, p. 13.
89   Edwards, 1972, p. 203; *Age*, 2 October 1969, p. 2; *Bulletin*, 20 September 1969, p. 20.
90   Hills, 2010, p. 378.
91   *Age*, 1 October 1969, p. 6.
92   Edwards, 1972, p. 204; *Bulletin*, 29 November 1969, p. 26.
93   Hills, 2010, p. 381.
94   *ibid.*, p. 380.
95   *Bulletin*, 29 November 1969, p. 26.
96   Souter, 1981, p. 495. The losses were not deadly because the company received income tax benefits of $1.2 million on its *Newsday* losses (David Syme and Co Ltd, *1970 Annual Report*).
97   Edwards, 1972, p. 204; Hills, 2010, pp. 379–80; HWT, *Annual Report 1970*, p. 12.
98   Chadwick, 1989, p. xxxiii.
99   *Age*, 30 July 1969, p. 10; *Bulletin*, 19 April 1969, p. 42.
100 *SMH*, 9 April 2005, p. 39.
101 *Tribune*, 4 February 1970, p. 5.
102 In October 1969, it called Labor's plan to end national service 'cheap politics' (*Australian*, 25 October 1969, p. 20).

103 Munster, 1987, p. 88. See also Tiffen, 2014, p. 93.
104 *Age*, 25 October 1969, p. 11.
105 Moss Cass, interview with the author, Carlton, 11 November 2013.
106 *Age*, 23 October 1969, p. 7, and 25 October 1969, p. 11.
107 Adrian Deamer, interview with Stewart Harris, NLA, 1993, p. 23.
108 *ibid.*, p. 53.
109 *Daily Mirror*, 8 May 1970, p. 1.
110 *Herald*, 26 March 1970, p. 6.
111 *Age*, 30 March 1970, p. 7.
112 *ibid.*
113 One of the anti-Moratorium viewpoints presented was from BA Santamaria (*Age*, 7 May 1970, p. 6).
114 *Age*, 8 May 1970, p. 7.
115 *ibid.*, 19 September 1970, p. 9.
116 *ibid.*, 9 May 1970, p. 1.
117 *ibid.*, 13 June 1989, p. 12.
118 *Farrago*, 4 June 1975, page unknown, reproduced at <https://www.melbobserver.com.au/wp/2019/01/06/too-bloody-bad-if-anyone-mangled/>.
119 Draft agreement, addressed to CR Macdonald, 21 August 1973, FMBA, MLMSS 9894/25, SLNSW.
120 *Sunday Age*, 16 August 2009, p. 13.
121 *Age*, 10 December 1989, p. 21.
122 *Bulletin*, 7 September 1974, p. 32.
123 *Farrago*, 4 June 1975, page unknown, reproduced at <https://www.melbobserver.com.au/wp/2019/01/06/too-bloody-bad-if-anyone-mangled/>; Newton, 1993, p. 219.
124 Newton, 1993, p. 212.
125 *Bulletin*, 7 September 1974, p. 30.
126 *SMH*, 10 October 1979, p. 14, and 30 May 1987, p. 36.

Chapter 19 Frank plays politics
1 Griffen-Foley, 2001b, p. 502.
2 Mullins, 2018, pp. 32–33.
3 *Tharunka* (NSW), 7 April 1976, p. 9.
4 David McNicoll interview with John Farquharson, 1997, NLA; Mullins, 2018, p. 147.
5 *The Review*, 10–16 June 1972, p. 948; Fitzgerald and Holt, 2010, p. 256.
6 Fitzgerald and Holt, 2010, p. 256.
7 *SMH*, 4 September 1987, p. 11.
8 *ibid.*
9 *ibid.*, 3 September 1987, p. 8.
10 *AFR*, 2 May 1974, pp. 1, 4.
11 Fitzgerald and Holt, 2010, p. 236.
12 *ibid.*, p. 252.
13 Griffen-Foley, 2000, p. 290.
14 Stone, 2000, p. 61.
15 *ibid.*, p. 65; 'Mr Y', 1971, pp. 2–7; *The Review*, 20 August 1971, p. 1274.
16 *Australian*, 14 August 1971, pp. 14–15.
17 Mullins, 2018, p. 246.
18 *The Review*, 20 August 1971, p. 1275.
19 Giffen-Foley, 2000, p. 291.
20 *ibid.*, p. 292.
21 *Canberra Times*, 2 May 1974, p. 2.
22 *The Review*, 20 August 1971, p. 1275; Griffen-Foley, 2000, pp. 276–77.
23 Tiffen, 2017, pp. 113–14.
24 *The Review*, 20 August 1971, p. 1274.

25 *SMH*, 4 September 1987, p. 11.
26 Mullins, 2018, pp. 397–99.
27 Griffen-Foley, 2000, p. 303.
28 Fitzgerald and Holt, 2010, p. 233; Holt, 2008.
29 This was Clyde Packer's recollection later (Stone, p. 59).
30 Griffen-Foley, 2000, p. 384; Lloyd, 1988, p. 247.
31 Fitzgerald and Holt, 2010, p. 234; Peter Samuel, interview with Mel Pratt, 1973, NLA, p. 73.
32 Mullins, 2018, p. 380.
33 *Daily Telegraph*, 10 March 1971, p. 1.
34 *Age*, 9 March 1971, p. 9.
35 *ibid.*, 10 March 1971, p. 9.
36 *SMH*, 10 March 1971, p. 6.
37 Munster, 1987, p. 90.
38 Lloyd, 1988, p. 247.
39 Possibly the 9 March one (Hills, 2010, p. 416).
40 Griffen-Foley, 2000, p. 305.
41 *The Review*, 20 August 1971, p. 1274.
42 *Australian*, 20 May 2002, p. 9; see also *Canberra Times*, Monday 20 September 1976, p. 42.
43 *The Review*, 20 August 1971, p. 1275.
44 *CPD* (HR), 15 March 1971, p. 839.
45 David McNicoll interview with John Farquharson, 1997, NLA.
46 Strangio, 2021.
47 Mullins, 2018, p. 162.
48 *ibid.*, p. 506; Lloyd, 1988, p. 249; Hawkins, 2012.
49 *In the Black*, 2016.
50 Williams, 2018.
51 *SMH*, 28 July 2007, page unknown (no page number provided on Factiva).
52 *ibid.*, 21 November 2015, p. 4.
53 Williams, 2018.
54 Bramston, 2019, pp. 160–61.
55 Golding cited in Hawkins, 2012.
56 *Age*, 4 June 2005, p. 9.
57 *ibid.*
58 *Herald-Sun*, 30 December 1998, p. 17.
59 *Canberra Times*, 13 July 1972, p. 3.
60 'Mr Y', 1971, pp. 2–7; Peter Samuel interview with Mel Pratt, 1973, NLA, p. 73.
61 Hills, 2010, p. 416.
62 Alan Ramsey, 'Past catches up with party gofer', *SMH*, 28 July 2007, page unknown (Factiva database); Griffen-Foley, 2003b, pp. 188–89.
63 *Melbourne Observer*, 11 June 1972, p. 6; *Australian*, 10 November 1970, p. 12; *Jobsons Investment Digest*, 28 July 1971, p. 6.
64 Memo from author unknown to T Farrell, 30 June 1971, FMBA, MLMSS 9894/415, SLNSW.
65 Munster, 1987, pp. 95, 89.
66 Tiffen, 2014, p. 299.
67 Goot, 1979, p. 6; Cryle, 2003, pp. 139–45.
68 Armstrong, undated.
69 *Age*, 30 December 1986, p. 12.
70 Menadue, 1999, p. 96.
71 *SMH*, 18 May 1972, p. 1; Cryle, 2008, p. 124; *The Review*, 10–16 June 1972, p. 948; *Canberra Times*, 11 May 1972, p. 8.
72 *Nation*, 10 June 1972, p. 5.
73 PKIU *State News*, vol 4(5), June 1972, p. 1.
74 Griffen-Foley, 2002.
75 Goot, 1979, p. 6.

76 PKIU *State News*, vol 4(5), June 1972, p. 1; *Newspaper Newsletter*, 9 June 1972, p. 1.
77 Letter from F Packer to RP Falkingham, 5 April 1972, FMBA, MLMSS 9894/411, SLNSW.
78 Memo from general manager to W Fairfax, 18 May 1970 and 8 October 1970, FMBA, MLMSS 9894/411, SLNSW.
79 ABC, 2014.
80 *Advertising News*, 7 January 1972, p. 11.
81 *ibid.*, 4 August 1972, page unknown, clipping in FMBA, MLMSS 9894/411, SLNSW.
82 *Canberra Times*, 3 June 1972, p. 3.
83 John B Fairfax, interview with the author, Sydney, 2019.
84 Griffen-Foley, 2000, pp. 316–17.
85 *Nation*, 10 June 1972, p. 5; *Canberra Times*, 8 June 1972, page unknown, clipping in FMBA, MLMSS 9894/411, SLNSW.
86 *Newspaper Newsletter*, 9 June 1972, page unknown, clipping in FMBA, MLMSS 9894/411, SLNSW; *Melbourne Observer*, 11 June 1972, p. 6.
87 *Advertising News*, 4 August 1972, page unknown, clipping in FMBA, MLMSS 9894/411, SLNSW.
88 *ibid*.
89 *Newspaper Newsletter*, 9 June 1972, page unknown, clipping in FMBA, MLMSS 9894/407, SLNSW.
90 *Canberra Times*, 6 June 1972, p. 9; *Melbourne Observer*, 11 June 1972, p. 6.
91 PKIU *State News*, vol 4(5), June 1972, p. 1.
92 *The Review*, 10–16 June 1972, p. 948.
93 *Advertising News*, 4 August 1972, page unknown, clipping in FMBA, MLMSS 9894/411, SLNSW.
94 Young, 2019, pp. 473–75.
95 *Canberra Times*, 23 August 1972, p. 25.
96 Merrilees, 1983, p. 298.
97 *The Review*, 10–16 June 1972, p. 948.
98 *Melbourne Observer*, 11 June 1972, p. 6; Chadwick, 1989, p. xxxv.
99 Griffen-Foley, 2000, p. 313.
100 *The Review*, 10–16 June 1972, p. 948.
101 *Daily Telegraph*, 30 July 1972.
102 Confidential memo, author unknown to RP Falkingham, 9 June 1972, FMBA, MLMSS 9894/415, SLNSW.
103 Munster, 1987, p. 98.
104 *Advertising News*, 4 August 1972, page unknown, in FMBA, MLMSS 9894/411, SLNSW.
105 Goot, 1979, p. 6; George Patterson, 'Status of the Media' figures outlined in McAllister et al., 1997.
106 *Canberra Times*, 5 August 1974, p. 2.
107 PKIU *State News*, vol 4(5), June 1972, p. 1.
108 *AFR*, 10 April 2001, p. 5.
109 *Australian*, 8 November 1973, p. 6.
110 *ibid*.
111 *SMH*, 28 October 1984, p. 17.
112 Chadwick, 1989, p. xxxv; McQueen, 1977, p. 89; Mullins, 2018, p. 583; Griffen-Foley, 2003b, pp. 195–96.
113 *SMH*, 2 May 1974, p. 12.
114 *Australian*, 2 May 1974, p. 3.
115 *Bulletin*, 11 May 1974, p. 13.
116 *Age*, 22 May 1982, p. 5.
117 *Bulletin*, 25 October 1975, p. 26.
118 *SMH*, 11 January 1979, p. 13, and 6 December 1978, p. 23; *Age*, 29 May 1979, p. 21.

Chapter 20 The Whitlam experiment
1 *Herald*, 1 December 1972, p. 4.
2 Hawkins, 2012.

3   This refers to English-language daily papers (Day Hochwald, 1988, p. 27).
4   *Bulletin*, 4 December 1971, p. 17.
5   Chalmers, 2011, p. 105.
6   Laurie Oakes interview with the author, Canberra, 2019; Dobell, 1987, p. 55.
7   *SMH*, 4 September 1987, p. 11.
8   Fitzgerald and Holt, 2010, p. 203.
9   *Bulletin*, 12 June 1965, p. 29; *Canberra Times*, 2 September 1986, p. 5.
10 *Washington Post* (US), 10 October 1972, p. 1.
11 *Age*, 2 December 1989, Books Extra, p. 9; Inglis, 1989.
12 *AFR*, 23 February 1976, p. 1; Olds, 2015, p. 45.
13 *Age*, 16 October 2004, supplement, p. 11.
14 *Australian Women's Weekly*, 11 August 1982, p. 38; *Age*, 22 April 1983, p. 3
15 Souter, 1981, p. 473.
16 Lemon, undated.
17 *Canberra Times*, 11 March 1971, p. 3.
18 Clarke, 2014; *Canberra Times*, 30 September 1969, p. 1, and 13 August 1985, p. 3.
19 *Age*, 18 November 1987, p. 26; *Australian*, 17–18 April 1993, page unknown, clipping.
20 Oakes, undated b.
21 Dobell, 1987, p. 117.
22 Michelle Grattan, interview with the author, Canberra, 2019.
23 *Age*, 13 June 1977, p. 7.
24 *SMH*, 4 August 1972, p. 3.
25 *Advertiser*, 2 December 1972, p. 5.
26 *Age*, 10 November, p. 9.
27 Oakes and Solomon, 1973, p. 275.
28 *Advertising News*, 8 December 1972, p. 4.
29 Munster, 1987, p. 99; Hocking, 2008, pp. 385–86.
30 Griffen-Foley, 2003b, p. 189.
31 Adrian Deamer interview with Stewart Harris, 1993, NLA, p. 35.
32 *SMH*, 19 March 1988, p. 35.
33 Tiffen, 2014, p. 109.
34 *SMH*, 17 October 1999, p. 53.
35 Griffen-Foley, 2003b, p. 199.
36 Regan, 1976, p. 97.
37 Bowman, 1988, p. 100.
38 Mullins, 2018, p. 583.
39 *Daily Telegraph*, 1 December 1972, p. 1.
40 *News*, 1 December 1972, p. 2.
41 *ibid.*, 22 November 1972, p. 3.
42 Munster, 1987, p. 101; *Australian*, 14 November 1972, p. 8.
43 *Australian*, 1 December 1972, p. 1.
44 *SMH*, 29 November 1972, p. 3.
45 *Daily Mirror*, 1 December 1972, p. 2.
46 Mullins, 2018, p. 585.
47 *ibid.*, pp. 585–86.
48 *Canberra Times*, 29 November 1972, p. 1.
49 *Advertising News*, 8 December 1972, p. 1.
50 *SMH*, 7 November 1972, p. 6.
51 *ibid.*, 1 December 1972, p. 6.
52 *Sun News-Pictorial*, 1 December 1972, p. 2.
53 *Canberra Times*, 29 November 1972, p. 1.
54 Milliken, undated.
55 Souter, 1981, pp. 430–39.
56 Milliken, undated.

57 Souter, 1981, pp. 207, 464–66.
58 Pringle had it up to between 285 000 and 295 000. In 1972, it was down to 274 000 (Goot, 1979, p. 6).
59 Souter, 1981, p. 480.
60 *Canberra Times*, 30 November 1972, p. 2, and 2 December 1972, p. 2.
61 Fairfax statement to the Sydney Stock Exchange, 14 June 1972, FMBA, MLMSS 9894/24, SLNSW.
62 *AFR*, 19 June 2012, p. 60.
63 *Age*, 19 September 1974, p. 4. (Perkin sacked Grant on the eve of the election when he found out that he was one of the organisers of an influential open letter, published in newspapers around the country, that advocated a vote for Labor. It was signed by leading citizens, including Kenneth Myer, chairman of the Myer emporium, and others who were not normally considered Labor supporters. Later, Grant was appointed high commissioner to India by the Whitlam government.)
64 Goot, 1979, p. 6; *Age*, 21 August 1989, p. 1.
65 *SMH*, 2 March 1974, p. 85.
66 *Australian*, 16 November 1972, p. 10.
67 *Tribune*, 1 December 1976, p. 9.
68 *Age*, 28 November 1972, p. 9.
69 Hills, 2010, p. 431; Bowman, 1988, p. 153.
70 Barker, 2012.
71 *Herald*, 1 December 1972, p. 4.
72 *Sun News-Pictorial*, 2 December 1972, p. 8.
73 Crisp, 1970, p. 65; Henderson, 1975, p. 78. After the election, Rohan Rivett stood up at an HWT shareholder meeting and asked why the company's papers devoted a disproportionate amount of space to the DLP (*Age*, 14 December 1972, p. 17).
74 *Herald*, 1 December 1972, p. 4.
75 *News*, 1 December 1972, p. 2.
76 Hocking, 2012, p. 3.
77 Shawcross, 1992, p. 162.
78 Tiffen, 2014, p. 108.
79 ibid., p. 118; *Age*, 4 December 1972, p. 7.
80 In two-party preferred terms (AEC).
81 *Age*, 3 December 1972, p. 7.
82 *Nation Review*, 14 May 1973, clipping in FMBA, MLMSS 9894/1625, SLNSW.
83 Blazey and Campbell, 1974, p. 203.
84 *Australian*, 1 December 1972, p. 1.
85 Chadwick, 1989, p. xxxv.

Postscript
1 *Age*, 4 December 1972, pp. 5, 10.
2 Letter from C Bednall to unknown correspondent, 8 August 1973, Bednall Papers, MS 5546/1, NLA.
3 Bednall, typed version of unpublished autobiography, p. 3, Bednall Papers, MS 5546/5, NLA. When Bednall was writing, Packer still owned the *Daily Telegraph* so he said four phone calls, but by 1972, it took only three to reach daily metropolitan newspaper owners.
4 Letter from C Bednall to J Spigelman, 11 July 1974, Bednall Papers, MS 5546/1, NLA.
5 Bednall, typed version of unpublished autobiography, p. 19, Bednall Papers, MS 5546/5, NLA.
6 ibid.
7 *Age*, 20 January 1972, p. 2.

BIBLIOGRAPHY

ARCHIVES AND MANUSCRIPT MATERIAL

Australian Securities and Investments Commission (ASIC)
HWT, 'Shareholders' funds 1956–1965', (025740710).

John Curtin Prime Ministerial Library
John Curtin, policy speech, 28 August 1940, Perth (JCPML00421/2).

John Dahlsen papers
John Dahlsen papers relating to the HWT, provided to the author.

Mitchell Library, State Library of New South Wales
David McNicoll Papers, MLMSS 7419.
Fairfax Media Limited Business Archive (FMBA), MLMSS 9894.

National Archives of Australia (NAA)
'Newspapers – censorship, defence and statement of claim', (A472 W20951B).
'Newsprint imports', (A4940-C146-1337105).
'Television: RG Casey', (M3299-99-2).
'Seventh Menzies Ministry – copies of Cabinet submissions and associated decisions (first series) [1958–1961]', (A5818-vol 3-Agendum 104-TV).

National Library of Australia (NLA)
Colin Blore Bednall Papers, MS 5546.
Arthur Augustus Calwell Papers, MS 4738.
Erle Harold Cox typescript reports, MS 4554.
Lloyd Dumas Papers, MS 4849.
Robert Menzies (Sir) Papers, MS 4936.

NSW Registry of Births Deaths and Marriages
Death certificate of RAG Henderson, 21800/1986.

Parliament of Australia
Commonwealth Parliamentary Debates (CPD) (Hansard).
Joint Committee on Wireless Broadcasting, *Report of the Joint Committee on Wireless Broadcasting*, Commonwealth Government Printer, Canberra, 1942.

Public Record Office Victoria (PROV)
Will and three codicils of Keith Murdoch, 473/792 (VPRS 28/P4, unit 693, item 473/792); and 455/344 (VPRS 7591/P2 unit 1583, item 455/344).
Probate and administration file of John Francis Williams, (VPRS 28/P12, unit 129, item 904/598).

State Archives and Records Authority of New South Wales (SARANSW)
Supreme Court of NSW, *Henderson v Henderson* (AF00167759, AF00167760).

State Records of South Australia (SRSA)
News Limited (GRS/513/11, file 74/1922).

University of Melbourne Archives (UMA)
Australian Journalists' Association (AJA), Victorian branch records (1993.0133).
AJA Victoria District Committee, Melbourne, meeting of 18 March 1944, AJA 74/32, box 6, UMA.
William Sydney (WS) Robinson Papers, (2001.0070).

Victorian Registry of Births, Deaths and Marriages
Death certificate of John Williams, (no. 7358/82).

INTERVIEWS AND TRANSCRIPTS

Calwell, Arthur, 'The Australian Labor Party and the press', AN Smith lecture, University of Melbourne, 30 July 1959.
Cass, Moss, interview with the author, Carlton, 11 November 2013.
Chamberlain, Frank, interview with Mel Pratt, 4 August 1972 and 19 January 1973, ORAL TRC 121/39, NLA.
Cook, Judith, telephone interview with the author, 21 May 2021.
Dahlsen, John, interview with the author, Carlton, 19 November 2019, and telephone interview, 26 July 2021.
Deamer, Adrian, interview with Stewart Harris, 8–9 November 1993, ORAL TRC 2984, NLA.
Dunstan, David, telephone interview with the author, 26 February 2021, and 19 March 2021.
Fairfax, John B, interview with the author, Sydney, 9 September 2019.
Fraser, Allan, interview with Mel Pratt, 18 February and 7–11 April 1975, ORAL TRC 121/66, NLA.
Freudenberg, Graham, interview with John Farquharson, 8–9 March and 13–14 June 2000, CTRC 3994, NLA.
Frith, John, interview with Shirley McKechnie, 30 April–1 May 1994, ORAL TRC 3056, NLA.
Grattan, Michelle, interview with the author, Canberra, 23 August 2019.
Hamilton, Ian, telephone interview with the author, 1 August 2022.
Macdonald, Ranald, interview with the author, Carlton, 12 May 2015 and Flinders, 10 January 2022; and by telephone, 27 February 2020 and 17 March 2021.
McNicoll, David, interview with John Farquharson, 22 May and 12 June 1997, ORAL TRC 3591, NLA.
Morgan, Gary, 'Women, the media, and people from other countries who have made Victoria – 1851 to Today', The Victoria Day Council 2008 La Trobe Lecture, Parliament of Victoria, 5 July 2008.
Morgan, Gary, interview with the author, East Melbourne, 7 October 2019.
Murray, Robert, interview with the author, Hampton, 16 June 2022.
Oakes, Laurie, interview with the author, Canberra, 26 August 2019.
Samuel, Peter, interview with Mel Pratt, 4 October 1973, ORAL TRC 121/47, NLA.

OFFICIAL RECORDS

Parliament of Australia
Commonwealth Parliamentary Debates (CPD) (Hansard).

PUBLISHED WORKS, THESES AND UNPUBLISHED MANUSCRIPTS

ABC (Australian Broadcasting Corporation), *Packer's Road*, April 2014, <https://www.abc.net.au/interactives/kerry-packers-road/>.
ABCB (Australian Broadcasting Control Board), *5th Annual Report, 1952–53*, Commonwealth of Australia, Canberra, 1953.
——, *7th Annual Report, 1954–55*, Commonwealth of Australia, Canberra, 1955.
——, *8th Annual Report, 1955–56*, Commonwealth of Australia, Canberra, 1956.

——, *11th Annual Report, 1958–59*, Commonwealth of Australia, Canberra, 1959.
——, *13th Annual Report, 1960–61*, Commonwealth of Australia, Canberra, 1961.
——, *15th Annual Report 1962–63*, Commonwealth of Australia, Canberra, 1963.
——, *16th Annual Report, 1963–64*, Commonwealth of Australia, Canberra, 1964.
——, *17th Annual Report, 1964–65*, Commonwealth of Australia, Canberra, 1965.
——, *20th Annual Report, 1967–68*, Commonwealth of Australia, Canberra, 1968.
——, *21st Annual Report, 1968–69*, Commonwealth of Australia, Canberra, 1969.
——, *22nd Annual Report, 1969–70*, Commonwealth of Australia, Canberra, 1970.
Abjorensen, Norman, 'How Australia's banks were almost nationalised', *The New Daily*, 16 June 2017, <https://thenewdaily.com.au/finance/finance-news/2017/06/16/chifley-bank-nationalisation/>.
Advertiser Newspapers Ltd, *125 Years of the Advertiser*, Adelaide, 1983.
AEC (Australian Electoral Commission), 'House of Representatives: Two party preferred results 1949 – present', 20 July 2022, <https://www.aec.gov.au/elections/federal_elections/tpp-results.htm>.
Aimer, Peter, 'Menzies and the birth of the Liberal Party' in Cameron Hazlehurst (ed.), *Australian Conservatism: Essays in Twentieth Century Political History*, ANU Press, Canberra, 1979, pp. 213–37.
Anderson, Fay, 'Chadstone Shopping Centre', *eMelbourne*, undated, <https://www.emelbourne.net.au/biogs/EM00323b.htm>.
——, '"The talent": Visual narratives of women, children and celebrity' in Fay Anderson and Sally Young (with Nikki Henningham), *Shooting the Picture: Press Photography in Australia*, Miegunyah Press, Melbourne, 2016, pp. 191–216.
Armstrong, David, 'Adrian Deamer', Melbourne Press Club, undated, <https://halloffame.melbournepressclub.com/article/adrian-deamer>.
Armstrong, Mark, 'The regulation of commercial radio and television broadcasting in Australia', Master of Laws thesis, University of NSW, September 1975.
Australian Screen, 'Australian film and television chronology', National Film and Sound Archive of Australia, undated, <https://aso.gov.au/chronology/1960s/>.
Baker, Jeannine, 'Marginal creatures: Australian women war reporters during World War II', *History Compass*, vol. 13, iss. 2, 2015, pp. 40–50.
Barber, Stephen and Sue Johnson, 'Federal election results 1901–2014', 17 July 2014, <https://www.aph.gov.au/About_Parliament/Parliamentary_Departments/Parliamentary_Library/pubs/rp/rp1415/FedElect>.
Barker, Geoffrey, 'The more things change …', *Inside Story*, 25 June 2012, <https://insidestory.org.au/the-more-things-change/>.
Barnouw, Erik, *A History of Broadcasting in the United States: The Golden Web, 1933 to 1953*, Oxford University Press, New York, 1968.
——, *Tube of Plenty: The Evolution of American Television*, Oxford University Press, New York, 1990.
Barr, Trevor, *Newmedia.com.au: The Changing Face of Australia's Media and Communications*, Allen & Unwin, Sydney, 2000.
Beilby, Peter (ed.), *Australian TV: The First 25 Years*, Thomas Nelson Australia, Melbourne, 1981.
Belson, William A, 'The effects of television on the reading and the buying of newspapers and magazines', *Public Opinion Quarterly*, vol. 25, no. 3, 1961, pp. 366–81.
Bertram, Michael, 'A history of the Institute of Public Affairs', MA thesis, University of Melbourne, August 1989.
Bester, Damian, '*Mercury* (Hobart)', in Bridget Griffen-Foley (ed.), *A Companion to the Australian Media*, Australian Scholarly Publishing, Melbourne, 2014, pp. 276–77.
Black, Lawrence, 'Whose finger on the button? British television and the politics of cultural control', *Historical Journal of Film, Radio and Television*, vol. 25, no. 4, 2005, pp. 547–75.
Blainey, Geoffrey, *The Rush that Never Ended: A History of Australian Mining*, Melbourne University Publishing, Melbourne, 1969.
—— and Geoffrey Hutton, *Gold and Paper 1858–1982: A History of the National Bank of Australasia Ltd*, Macmillan, Melbourne, 1983.
Blair, Sandy, 'Howe, Ann (1802–1842)', *ADB*, supplemental volume, 2005, <https://adb.anu.edu.au/biography/howe-ann-12994>.

Blazey, Peter and Andrew Campbell, *The Political Dice Men*, Outback Press, Melbourne, 1974.
Bodycomb, John, 'Sectarianism', *eMelbourne*, undated, <https://www.emelbourne.net.au/biogs/EM01347b.htm>.
Bogart, Leo, 'Newspapers in transition', *The Wilson Quarterly*, vol. 6, no. 5, 1982, pp. 58–70.
Bongiorno, Frank, *The People's Party: Victorian Labor and the Radical Tradition, 1875–1914*, Melbourne University Press, Melbourne, 1996.
Bonney, Bill, 'Commercial television: Regulation, technology and market forces', in Ted Wheelwright and Ken Buckley (eds), *Communications and the Media in Australia*, Allen & Unwin, Sydney, 1987, pp. 40–57.
Bowman, David, *The Captive Press*, Penguin Books, Melbourne, 1988.
Boyce, Gordon, 'Multilateral contracting in Australian mining: The development of Hamersley Iron, 1961–1966', *Enterprise & Society*, vol. 2, no. 3, 2001, pp. 543–75.
Bramston, Troy, *Robert Menzies: The Art of Politics*, Scribe, Melbourne, 2019.
Brett, Judith, *Australian Liberals and the Moral Middle Class*, Cambridge University Press, Melbourne, 2003.
Bright, Greg, 'Suburbans: The Sydney battle', *Politics*, vol. 9, no. 2, 1974, pp. 186–88.
Brodrick, Lloyd, 'Anthony, Hubert Lawrence (Larry) (1897–1957)', *ADB*, vol. 13, 1993, <https://adb.anu.edu.au/biography/anthony-hubert-lawrence-larry-9371>.
Brown, Allan, 'The restructure of Australian commercial television', *Journal of Media Economics*, vol. 2, no. 1, 1989, pp. 41–54.
Buchanan, Rachel, 'I buried the lead', 18 September 2013, <https://rachelbuchanan100.wordpress.com/2013/09/18/i-buried-the-lead/>.
Buckridge, Patrick, *The Scandalous Penton: A Biography of Brian Penton*, University of Queensland Press, Brisbane, 1994.
Bye, Susan, 'TV Memories, the *Daily Telegraph* and ton: "First in Australia"', *Media International Australia*, vol. 121, iss. 1, 2006, pp. 159–73.
Calwell, Arthur, *Be Just and Fear Not*, Lloyd O'Neil, Melbourne, 1972.
Cameron, Clyde, *The Confessions of Clyde Cameron 1913–1990, as told to Daniel Connell*, ABC Enterprises, Sydney, 1990.
Campbell, EW, *The 60 Rich Families Who Own Australia*, Current Book Distributors, Sydney, 1963.
Cannon, Michael, *The Land Boomers*, Lloyd O'Neil, Melbourne, 1986.
—— (ed.), *Hold Page One: Memoirs of Monty Grover, Editor*, Loch Haven Books, Melbourne, 1993.
Carroll, VJ, 'Henderson, Rupert Albert Geary (1896–1986)', *ADB*, vol. 17, 2007, <https://adb.anu.edu.au/biography/henderson-rupert-albert-geary-12621>.
Carson, Andrea, *Investigative Journalism, Democracy and the Digital Age*, Routledge, London, 2020.
Chadwick, Paul, *Media Mates: Carving up Australia's Media*, Macmillan, Melbourne, 1989.
Chalmers, Rob, *Inside the Canberra Press Gallery*, ANU E-Press, 2011.
Chandler, Jo, 'After the Nine-Fairfax deal, who will shape Melbourne like *The Age* once did?', *Mumbrella*, 28 July 2020, <https://mumbrella.com.au/after-the-nine-fairfax-deal-who-will-shape-melbourne-like-the-age-once-did-532128>.
Chenoweth, Neil, 'When Kerry met your father', 6 May 2014, <https://neilchenoweth.com/2014/05/06/when-kerry-met-your-father/>.
Christiansen, Arthur, *Headlines All My Life*, Heinemann, London, 1961.
Clarke, Duncan, *Meet the Press*, Coronation Press, Melbourne, 1962.
Clarke, Patricia, 'Women in the media' in Bridget Griffen-Foley (ed.), *A Companion to the Australian Media*, Australian Scholarly Publishing, Melbourne, 2014, pp. 495–98.
——, 'In the days of print: Four women journalists in World War II', *Australian Journal of Biography and History*, no. 4, 2020, <https://press-files.anu.edu.au/downloads/press/n7724/html/01_pclarke.xhtml?referer=&page=5; https://adb.anu.edu.au/biography/knox-sir-errol-galbraith-6991>.
Coatney, Caryn, 'John Curtin's forgotten media legacy: The impact of a wartime prime minister on news management techniques, 1941–45', *Labour History*, vol. 105, 2013, pp. 63–78.
——, *John Curtin: How He Won Over the Media*, Australian Scholarly Publishing, Melbourne, 2016.
Cosgrove, David, 'Long-term patterns of Australian public transport use', Australasian Transport Research Forum, Adelaide, 28–30 September 2011.

Costar, Brian, 'Warner, Sir Arthur George (1899–1966)', *ADB*, vol. 16, 2002, <https://adb.anu.edu.au/biography/warner-sir-arthur-george-11967>.
——, 'Tom Hollway: The bohemian', in Paul Strangio and Brian J Costar (eds), *The Victorian Premiers, 1856–2006*, Federation Press, Sydney, 2006, pp. 227–41.
——, Peter Love and Paul Strangio (eds), *The Great Labor Schism: A Retrospective*, Scribe Publications, Melbourne, 2005.
Country Press Co-operative Company of Australia, *Press Directory of Australia and New Zealand*, 12th edition, Sydney, 1961.
Crawford, Robert, 'Selling or buying American dreams?: Americanization and Australia's interwar advertising industry', *Comparative American Studies*, vol. 3, no. 2, 2005, pp. 213–36.
Crikey, 'Was Australia's longest serving PM a philanderer?', *Crikey*, 2 November 2006a, <https://www.crikey.com.au/2006/11/02/was-australias-longest-serving-pm-a-philanderer/>.
——, 'Rumours of Menzies's philandering greatly exaggerated', *Crikey*, 6 November 2006b, <https://www.crikey.com.au/2006/11/06/rumours-of-menziess-philandering-greatly-exaggerated/>.
Crisell, Andrew, *An Introductory History of British Broadcasting*, 2nd edition, Routledge, London, 2002.
Crisp, LF, *Ben Chifley: A Biography*, Longmans, Melbourne, 1963.
——, 'The DLP vote 1958–1969 – and after', *Politics*, vol. 5, no. 1, 1970, pp. 62–66.
Cryle, Denis, 'Addressing the nation: In search of Adrian Deamer', *Journal of Australian Studies*, vol. 27, iss. 78, 2003, pp. 139–45.
——, *Murdoch's Flagship: Twenty-Five years of the* Australian *Newspaper*, Melbourne University Publishing, Melbourne, 2008.
C-Scott, Marc, 'The prelude to television in Australia', *Historical Journal of Film, Radio and Television*, vol. 39, no. 1, 2018, pp. 132–46.
Curran, James, 'Beyond the euphoria: Lyndon Johnson in Australia and the politics of the Cold War alliance', *Journal of Cold War Studies*, vol. 17, no. 1, 2015, pp. 64–96.
—— and Jean Seaton, *Power Without Responsibility*, 8th edition, Routledge, London, 2018.
Curthoys, Ann, 'The getting of television: Dilemmas in ownership, control and culture 1941–1956' in Ann Curthoys and John Merritt (eds), *Better Dead than Red: Australia's First Cold War 1941–1956*, vol. 2, Allen & Unwin, Sydney, 1986, pp. 126–54.
——, 'Television before television', *Continuum: Journal of Media and Cultural Studies*, vol. 4, no. 2, 1991, pp. 152–70.
—— and John Merritt (eds), *Better Dead than Red: Australia's First Cold War 1941–1956*, vol. 2, Allen & Unwin, Sydney, 1986.
Cushing, Nancy, 'Lamb, John (1885–1974)', ADB, vol. 15, 2000, <https://adb.anu.edu.au/biography/lamb-john-10773>.
Dahlsen, John, 'Submission: Options to Strengthen the Misuse of Market Power Law', 10 February 2016, Treasury, <https://treasury.gov.au/sites/default/files/2019-03/C2015-061_Dahlsen_John.pdf>.
——, 'Murdoch down under: A truer story', 27 November 2019, unpublished paper provided to the author.
D'Arcy, John, *Media Mayhem: Playing with the Big Boys in Media*, Brolga Publishing, Melbourne, 2005.
Davies, David R, *The Postwar Decline of American Newspapers, 1945–1965*, Praeger Publishers, Westport, CT, 2006.
Day, David, *John Curtin: A Life*, Harper Collins, Sydney, 1999.
——, 'John Joseph Curtin', in Michelle Grattan (ed.), *Australian Prime Ministers*, New Holland, Sydney, 2001, pp. 216–37.
Day, Mark, 'The journey begins', *Australian*, undated, <www.theaustralian.com.au/50th-birthday/the-journey-begins/story-fnlk0fie-1226873772279>.
Day Hochwald, Eve, 'Cold type: Computerized typesetting and occupational subcultures in the New York City newspaper industry', PhD thesis, City University of New York, New York, 1988.
Deery, Phillip, 'Sharpley, Cecil Herbert (1908–1985)', *ADB*, vol. 18, 2012, <https://adb.anu.edu.au/biography/sharpley-cecil-herbert-14879>.
Denison, James L, *Building a Nation: Hugh Robert Denison KBE: Patron and Patriot*, James L Denison, Sydney, 2004.
Dick, Nigel, 'Media Mavericks: The history of free-to-air television', PhD thesis, University of Melbourne, Melbourne, 2015.

Dobell, Graeme, 'Watchers from the gallery: The Federal Parliamentary Press Gallery, 1901 to 1982', Bachelor of Arts (Journalism) thesis, RMIT, Melbourne, 1987.
Dudley Edwards, Ruth, *Newspapermen: Hugh Cudlipp, Cecil Harmsworth King and the Glory Days of Fleet Street*, Secker & Warburg, London, 2003.
Dumas, Lloyd, *A Full Life*, Sun Books, Melbourne, 1969.
Dunstan, David, 'Twists and turns: The origins and transformations of Melbourne's metropolitan press in the nineteenth century', *Victorian Historical Journal*, vol. 89, no. 1, 1989, pp. 5–26.
——, 'The *Argus*: The life, death and remembering of a great Australian newspaper', in Muriel Porter (ed.), *The Argus: The Life and Death of a Great Melbourne Newspaper*, RMIT Publishing, Melbourne, 2003, pp. 31–34.
——, 'Bolte, Sir Henry Edward (1908–1990)', *ADB*, vol. 17, 2007, <https://adb.anu.edu.au/biography/bolte-sir-henry-edward-12227>.
——, 'Williams, Sir John Francis (1901–1982)', *ADB*, vol. 18, 2012, <http://adb.anu.edu.au/biography/williams-sir-john-francis-15864>.
——, 'John Williams', Melbourne Press Club, undated, <https://halloffame.melbournepressclub.com/article/john-williams>.
Dunstan, Keith, *No Brains at All: An Autobiography*, Viking, Melbourne, 1990.
Easdown, Geoff and Peter Wilms, *Ansett: The Collapse*, Lothian Books, Melbourne, 2002.
Eather, Warwick and Drew Cottle, 'The mobilisation of capital behind "the Battle for Freedom": The Sydney banks, the Institute of Public Affairs (NSW) and opposition to the Australian Labor Party 1944–49', *Labour History*, vol. 103, no. 1, 2012, pp. 165–87.
Edwards, Cecil, *The Editor Regrets*, Hill of Content, Melbourne, 1972.
Edwards, John, *John Curtin's War: Volume 2*, Viking, Sydney, 2018.
Emery, Michael, Edwin Emery and Nancy L Roberts, *The Press in America: An Interpretive History of the Mass Media*, Pearson, Needham Heights, MA, 2000.
Fahey, Charles, 'Ansett, Sir Reginald Myles (Reg) (1909–1981)', *ADB*, vol. 17, 2007, <https://adb.anu.edu.au/biography/ansett-sir-reginald-myles-reg-12142>.
Fairfax, James, *My Regards to Broadway*, Angus & Robertson, Sydney, 1992.
Faulkner, John and Stuart Macintyre (eds), *True Believers: The Story of the Federal Parliamentary Labor Party*, Allen & Unwin, Sydney, 2001.
Featherstone, Guy, 'Smith, Louis Lawrence (1830–1910)', *ADB*, vol. 6, 1976, <http://adb.anu.edu.au/biography/smith-louis-lawrence-4610>.
Finance and Development Department of David Syme and Co, 'Confidential: Survey of Australian newspaper companies: The HWT', March 1967, FMBA, MLMSS 9894/1099, SLNSW.
Fitzgerald, Julian, *Inside The Parliamentary Press Gallery: Seeing Beyond The Spin*, Clareville Press, Canberra, 2008.
Fitzgerald, Ross and Stephen Holt, *Alan 'the Red Fox' Reid: Pressman Par Excellence*, NewSouth Publishing, Sydney, 2010.
Foyle, Lindsay, 'James (Jimmy) Charles Bancks', Australian Cartoonists Association, undated, <http://www.cartoonists.org.au/stanleys/halloffame/bancks_jimmy>.
Freudenberg, Graham, 'Calwell, Arthur Augustus (1896–1973)', *ADB*, vol. 13, 1993, <http://adb.anu.edu.au/biography/calwell-arthur-augustus-9667>.
——, 'Victory to defeat: 1941–49', in John Faulkner and Stuart Macintyre (eds), *True Believers: The Story of the Federal Parliamentary Labor* Party, Allen & Unwin, Sydney, 2001, pp. 76–89.
Garden, Don, *Theodore Fink: A Talent for Ubiquity*, Melbourne University Press, Melbourne, 1998.
Gardiner, Greg, 'The eye of the storm: Mainstream press representations of Dr Evatt and the Split' in Brian Costar, Peter Love and Paul Strangio (eds), *The Great Labor Schism: A Retrospective*, Scribe Publications, Melbourne, 2005, pp. 162–77.
Genesove, David, 'The adoption of offset presses in the daily newspaper industry in the United States', no. 7076, NBER Working Papers from National Bureau of Economic Research, Inc, 2000.
Gifford, Peter, 'Aspects of Australian newspaper journalism and the Cold War, 1945–1956', PhD thesis, Murdoch University, Perth, 1997.
Golding, Douglas, 'Confessions of a journalist: The night I hit Kerry Packer with a six by four', *Eternity News*, 11 October 2012, <https://www.eternitynews.com.au/archive/confessions-of-a-journalist-the-night-i-hit-kerry-packer-with-a-six-by-four/>.

Golding, Peter, 'Just a chattel of the sale', in Jim Usher (ed.), *The Argus: The Life and Death of a Great Melbourne Newspaper*, Australian Scholarly Publishing, Melbourne, 2007, pp. 104–36.

Goodwin, Peter, *Television Under the Tories*, British Film Institute, London, 1998.

Goot, Murray, 'Newspaper circulation in Australia, 1932–1977', Media Centre Paper no.11, Centre for the Study of Educational Communication and Media, La Trobe University, Melbourne, 1979.

——, '"A worse importation than chewing gum": American influences on the Australian press and their limits – The Australian Gallup Poll, 1941–1973', *Historical Journal of Film, Radio and Television*, vol. 30, no. 3, 2010, pp. 269–302.

——, 'Morgan, Roy Edward (1908–1985)', *ADB*, vol. 18, 2012, <https://adb.anu.edu.au/biography/morgan-roy-edward-15763>.

——, 'Labor's 1943 landslide: Political market research, Evatt, and the public opinion polls', *Labour History*, vol. 107, no. 1, 2014, pp. 149–67.

——, 'Fifty years of the *Australian*', *Media International Australia*, vol. 157, no. 1, 2015, pp. 5–27.

Gorman, Lyn, 'Menzies and television: A medium he "endured"', *Media International Australia*, vol. 87, 1998, pp. 49–67.

Gould, Liz, 'Cash and controversy: A short history of commercial talkback radio', *Media International Australia*, no. 122, February 2007, pp. 81–95.

Greenslade, Roy, 'Boris Johnson is the ultimate purveyor of fake news', *Guardian*, 24 February 2020, <https://www.theguardian.com/politics/2020/feb/23/boris-johnson-is-the-ultimate-purveyor-of-fake-news>.

Griffen-Foley, Bridget, '"Four more points than Moses": Dr HV Evatt, the press and the 1944 referendum', *Labour History*, no. 68, 1995, 63–79.

——, *The House of Packer: The Making of a Media Empire*, Allen & Unwin, Sydney, 1999.

——, *Sir Frank Packer: The Young Master*, Harper Collins, Sydney, 2000.

——, 'The press proprietor and the politician: Sir Frank Packer and Sir Robert Menzies', *Media International Australia*, no. 99, May 2001a, pp. 23–34.

——, 'Sir Frank Packer and the leadership of the Liberal Party, 1967–71', *Australian Journal of Political Science*, vol. 36, no. 3, 2001b, pp. 499–513.

——, 'Watson, James Kingston (1908–1978)', *ADB*, vol. 16, 2002, <https://adb.anu.edu.au/biography/watson-james-kingston-11979>.

——, '"A civilised amateur": Edgar Holt and his life in letters and politics', *Australian Journal of Politics and History*, vol. 49, no. 1, 2003a, pp. 31–47.

——, *Party Games: Australian Politicians and the Media from War to Dismissal*, Text Publishing, Melbourne, 2003b.

——, 'Fairfax, Sir Warwick Oswald (1901–1987)', *ADB*, vol. 17, 2007a, <https://adb.anu.edu.au/biography/fairfax-sir-warwick-oswald-12475>.

——, 'Talkback radio and Australian politics since the summer of 1967', *Media International Australia*, no. 122, February 2007b, pp. 96–107.

——, *Changing Stations: The Story of Australian Commercial Radio*, UNSW Press, Sydney, 2009.

Griffin, Tony, 'Technological change and craft control in the newspaper industry: An international comparison', *Cambridge Journal of Economics*, vol. 8, no. 1, 1984, pp. 41–61.

Groves, Derham, 'Television', *eMelbourne*, undated, <https://www.emelbourne.net.au/biogs/EM01477b.htm>.

Hagan, J, *Printers and Politics: A History of the Australian Printing Unions, 1850–1950*, ANU Press, Canberra, 1966.

Haigh, Gideon, *The Brilliant Boy: Doc Evatt and the Great Australian Dissent*, Scribner, Sydney, 2022.

Hall, Sandra, 'Elizabeth Riddell', Melbourne Press Club, undated, <https://halloffame.melbournepressclub.com/article/elizabeth-riddell>.

——, *Supertoy: 20 Years of Australian Television*, Sun Books, Melbourne, 1976.

——, *Tabloid Man: The Life and Times of Ezra Norton*, Fourth Estate, Sydney, 2008.

Hancock, IR, 'Holt, Harold Edward (1908–1967)', *ADB*, vol. 13, 1996, <https://adb.anu.edu.au/biography/holt-harold-edward-10530>.

——, 'Harold Edward Holt' in Michelle Grattan (ed.), *Australian Prime Ministers*, New Holland, Sydney, 2001, pp. 272–84.

Hasluck, Paul, *The Government and the People, 1939–41*, Australian War Memorial, Canberra, 1970.
Hastie, Madeleine, 'Free-to-air: A history of Sydney's commercial television programming, 1956–2012', unpublished PhD thesis, Macquarie University, Sydney, 2013.
Hawkins, John, 'William McMahon: The first treasurer with an economics degree', *Economic Roundup*, iss. 2, 2012, <https://treasury.gov.au/publication/economic-roundup-issue-2-2012-2/economic-roundup-issue-2-2012>.
Hazlehurst, Cameron, *Menzies Observed*, Allen & Unwin, Sydney, 1979.
Henderson, Gerard, 'Democratic Labor's last hurrah', *Australian Quarterly*, vol. 47, no. 1, 1975, pp. 77–89.
——, *Menzies' Child: The Liberal Party of Australia, 1944–1994*, Allen & Unwin, Sydney, 1994.
Herd, Nick, *Networking: Commercial Television in Australia*, Currency House, Sydney, 2012.
Hetherington, John, 'Keith Murdoch: The man in the paper mask', in Matthew Ricketson (ed.), *The Best Australian Profiles*, Black Inc., Melbourne, 2004, pp. 99–124.
Hills, Ben, *Breaking News: The Golden Age of Graham Perkin*, Scribe Publications, Melbourne, 2010.
Hilvert, John, *Blue Pencil Warriors: Censorship and Propaganda in World War II*, University of Queensland Press, Brisbane, 1984.
——, 'Edmund Garnet (1883–1959)', *ADB*, vol.13, 1993, <http://adb.anu.edu.au/biography/bonney-edmund-garnet-9538 Bonney>.
Hinch, Derryn, *The Fall and Rise of Derryn Hinch*, Hardie Grant Books, Melbourne, 2004.
Hocking, Jenny, *Gough Whitlam: A Moment in History*, Miegunyah Press, Melbourne, 2008.
——, *Gough Whitlam: His Time*, Miegunyah Press, Melbourne, 2012.
Holden, W Sprague, *Australia Goes to Press*, Melbourne University Press, Melbourne, 1962.
Holt, Stephen, 'Mr Y and Mr Gorton', *Quadrant*, vol. 52, iss. 10, 2008, p. 44.
Hood, Stuart, *The Mass Media*, Springer, London, 1972.
Hudson, WJ, 'Casey, Richard Gavin Gardiner (1890–1976)', *ADB*, vol.13, 1993, <http://adb.anu.edu.au/biography/casey-richard-gavin-gardiner-9706>.
HWT (Herald and Weekly Times), 'Keith Murdoch: Journalist' (booklet), HWT Ltd, Melbourne, 1952.
In the Black, 'Laurie Oakes reflects on 50 years of Australian political journalism', 3 January 2016, <https://www.intheblack.com/articles/2016/03/01/laurie-oakes-reflects-on-50-years-of-australian-political-journalism>.
Inglis, KS (Kenneth Stanley), *This is the ABC: The Australian Broadcasting Commission 1932–1983*, Melbourne University Press, Melbourne, 1983.
——, 'Press, radio and television', in Ann Curthoys, AW Martin and Tim Rowse (eds), *Australians From 1939*, Fairfax, Syme & Weldon Associates, Sydney, 1987, pp. 215–37.
——, *Nation: The Life of an Independent Journal, 1958–1972*, Melbourne University Press, Melbourne, 1989.
——, 'Rivett, Rohan Deakin (1917–1977)', *ADB*, vol. 16, 2002, <https://adb.anu.edu.au/biography/rivett-rohan-deakin-11533>.
Isaacs, Victor, 'Labour dailies', Australian Society for the Study of Labour History, 2015, <https://labourhistorycanberra.org/2015/05/labour-dailies/>.
Jenkins, Ken, 'Color was one of our great disasters', in Muriel Porter (ed.), *The Argus: The Life and Death of a Great Melbourne Newspaper*, RMIT Publishing, Melbourne, 2003, pp. 19–20.
Johnston, RJ, 'Population growth and urbanization in Australia, 1961–6', *Geography*, vol. 52, no. 2, 1967, pp. 199–202.
Kearsley, Bob, 'Frank Packer', Melbourne Press Club, undated, <https://halloffame.melbournepressclub.com/article/frank-packer>.
Kelly, Paul, 'Caucus under Whitlam: 1967–75' in John Faulkner and Stuart Macintyre (eds), *True Believers: The Story of the Federal Parliamentary Labor Party*, Allen & Unwin, Sydney, 2001, pp. 105–21.
Kennedy, BE, 'Gepp, Sir Herbert William (Bert) (1877–1954)', *ADB*, vol. 8, 1981, <https://adb.anu.edu.au/biography/gepp-sir-herbert-william-bert-6298>.
Kerr, Joan, 'John Eric Frith', 1996, Design and Art Australia Online, <https://www.daao.org.au/bio/john-eric-frith/biography/>.
Kiernan, Colm, 'Arthur A Calwell's clashes with the Australian press 1943–1945', *University of Wollongong Historical Journal*, vol. 2, no. 1, 1976, pp. 74–111.

Kirkman, Deborah A, *Whither the Australian Press Council?: Its Formation, Function and Future*, Australian Press Council, Sydney, 1996.

Kirkpatrick, Rod, 'Ghost of caution haunts house of Dunn: The rise and fall of a Queensland newspaper dynasty (1930–1989)', PhD thesis, University of Queensland, Brisbane, 1994a.

——, 'Six dynasties that ended with a whimper, not a bang', *Australian Studies in Journalism*, vol. 3, 1994b, pp. 109–29.

——, *Country Conscience: A History of the New South Wales Provincial Press, 1841–1995*, Infinite Harvest Publishing Pty Ltd, Canberra, 2000.

——, 'How a Communist rag in Darwin became a paper for Mount Isa', *PANPA Bulletin*, June 2005, pp. 56–57.

——, 'Provincial Newspapers (Qld) Ltd', in Bridget Griffen-Foley (ed.), *A Companion to the Australian Media*, Australian Scholarly Publishing, Melbourne, 2014, pp. 371–72.

Knight, Alan, 'Journalism redefined', in Alan Knight (ed.), *Challenge and Change: Reassessing Journalism's Global Future*, UTS E-Press, Sydney, 2013, pp. 1–30.

Lawson, Valerie, 'Norton, Ezra (1897–1967)', *ADB*, vol. 15, 2000, <https://adb.anu.edu.au/biography/norton-ezra-11260>.

Lee, David, 'The 1949 federal election: A reinterpretation', *Australian Journal of Political Science*, vol. 29, no. 3, 1994, pp. 501–19.

Lemon, Barbara, 'Women journalists in Australian history', *The Australian Women's Register*, <http://www.womenaustralia.info/exhib/cal/intro.html>.

Lever, Rodney E, 'The *Australian* was a stuff-up from the start', *Crikey*, 20 July 2009, <https://www.crikey.com.au/2009/07/20/the-australian-was-a-stuff-up-from-the-start/>.

——, 'How Rupert Murdoch took over the *News*', *Independent Australia*, 8 September 2012a, <https://independentaustralia.net/australia/australia-display/how-rupert-murdoch-took-over-the-news,4479>.

——, 'Rupert Murdoch in black and white', *Independent Australia*, 12 September 2012b, <https://independentaustralia.net/australia/australia-display/rupert-murdoch-in-black-and-white,4492>.

——, 'What went wrong at the *Australian*: An insider's account', *Independent Australia*, 30 August 2012c, <https://independentaustralia.net/business/business-display/what-went-wrong-at-the-australian-an-insiders-account,4445>.

——, 'Rupert Murdoch's crazy house', *Independent Australia*, 15 September 2012d, <https://independentaustralia.net/politics/politics-display/rupert-murdochs-crazy-house,4501>.

Liberal Party of Australia, 'Our history', undated, <https://www.liberal.org.au/our-history>.

Lindstrom, Carl E, *The Fading American Newspaper*, P Smith, Gloucester, MA, 1960.

Lloyd, Clem J, *Profession – Journalist: A History of the Australian Journalists' Association*, Hale & Iremonger, Sydney, 1985.

——, *Parliament and the Press: The Federal Parliamentary Press Gallery 1901–88*, Melbourne University Press, Melbourne, 1988.

——, 'Rise and fall of the United Australia Party', in JR Nethercote (ed.), *Liberalism and the Australian Federation*, Federation Press, Sydney, 2001, pp. 134–62.

——, 'Rodgers, Donald Kilgour (1906–1978)', *ADB*, vol. 16, 2002, <https://adb.anu.edu.au/biography/rodgers-donald-kilgour-11553>.

—— and Richard Hall, *Backroom Briefings: John Curtin's War*, National Library of Australia, Canberra, 1997.

Lloyd, Justine, 'Women's pages in Australian print media from the 1850s', *Media International Australia*, vol. 150, no. 1, 2014, pp. 61–65.

Lord, Peter, *125 Years of The Advertiser*, Advertiser Newspapers, Adelaide, 1983.

McAllister, Ian, Malcolm Mackerras and Carolyn Brown Boldiston, *Australian Political Facts*, 2nd edition, Longman Cheshire, Melbourne, 1997.

MacCallum, Mungo, 'Menzies, Fairfax and that affair: Mungo MacCallum replies', *Crikey*, 3 November 2006, <https://www.crikey.com.au/2006/11/03/menzies-fairfax-and-that-affair-mungo-maccallum-replies/>.

Macintyre, Stuart, *Australia's Boldest Experiment: War and Reconstruction in the 1940s*, NewSouth Publishing, Sydney, 2015.

——, *A Concise History of Australia*, Cambridge University Press, Melbourne, 2016.
——, *The Party*, Allen & Unwin, Sydney, 2022.
McKnight, David, 'The investigative tradition and Australian journalism 1945–1965' in Ann Curthoys and Julianne Schultz (eds), *Journalism: Print, Politics and Popular Culture*, University of Queensland Press, Brisbane, 1999, pp. 155–67.
McMullin, Ross, 'Joseph Benedict Chifley' in Michelle Grattan (ed.), *Australian Prime Ministers*, New Holland, Sydney, 2001, pp. 248–68.
McNair, Brian, *News and Journalism in the UK*, Routledge, London, 1994.
McNicoll, David, *Luck's a Fortune*, Sun Books, Melbourne, 1979.
McQueen, Humphrey, *Australia's Media Monopolies*, Widescope, Melbourne, 1977.
——, 'Colour in print media' in Bridget Griffen-Foley (ed.), *A Companion to the Australian Media*, Australian Scholarly Publishing, Melbourne, 2014, pp. 96–97.
Macrotrends, 'Canberra, Australia metro area population 1950–2022', 10 August 2022, <https://www.macrotrends.net/cities/206175/canberra/population>.
Madrigal, Alexis C, 'When did TV watching peak?', *The Atlantic*, 20 May 2018, <https://www.theatlantic.com/technology/archive/2018/05/when-did-tv-watching-peak/561464/>.
Mander, AE, *Public Enemy, The Press*, International Book Shop Pty Ltd, Melbourne, 1944.
Mandle, WF, 'Colin Bednall, 1913–1976', *Australian Journal of Communication*, vol. 24, no. 3, 1997, pp. 129–44.
Manne, Robert, *The Petrov Affair*, Text Publishing, Melbourne, 2004.
Martin, AW, *Robert Menzies: A Life, vol. 2, 1944–1978*, Melbourne University Press, Melbourne, 1999.
MEAA (Media Entertainment Arts Alliance), 'A proud history at the forefront of Australian journalism', 8 December 2017, <https://www.meaa.org/news/meaa-media-aja-history/>.
Menadue, John, *Things You Learn Along the Way*, David Lovell Publishing, Melbourne, 1999.
Mercer, Peter, *Media Tasmania: Two Centuries of Printing and Communications*, Davies Brothers Limited, The Mercury Print Museum, Hobart, 1999.
Merrilees, William, 'Anatomy of a price leadership challenge', *The Journal of Industrial Economics*, vol. 31, no. 3, 1983, pp. 291–311.
Milliken, Robert, 'John Douglas "JD" Pringle', Melbourne Press Club, <https://halloffame.melbournepressclub.com/article/j-d--pringle>.
Moore, Andrew, 'Mr Big, the Big Fella and the Split: Fault lines in Bankstown's Labor politics, 1955', *Labour History*, no. 95, 2008, pp. 197–212.
Morgan, Gary, Michele Levine and Marcus Tarrant, 'The power of newspaper editorial and advertising (we have some good news and some bad news)', News Limited Conference, Old Parliament House, Canberra, 16 June 2003.
Morgan, Patrick, 'Bednall, Colin Blore (1913–1976)', *ADB*, vol. 13, 1993, <https://adb.anu.edu.au/biography/bednall-colin-blore-9469>.
'Mr Y', 'A Packer plot?', *Australian Quarterly*, vol. 43, no. 2, June 1971, pp. 2–7.
Mullins, Patrick, *Tiberius with a Telephone: The Life and Times of William McMahon*, Scribe, Melbourne, 2018.
Munster, George, *A Paper Prince*, Penguin Books, Melbourne, 1987.
Murphy, John, *Imagining the Fifties: Private Settlement and Political Culture in Menzies' Australia*, UNSW Press, Sydney, 2000.
——, *Evatt: A Life*, NewSouth Publishing, Sydney, 2016.
Murray, Robert, *The Split: Australian Labor in the 1950s*, Cheshire, Melbourne, 1970.
——, 'The strange decline and death of the *Argus*', *Quadrant*, May 2005, pp. 28–35.
——, *Sandbelters: Memories of Middle Australia*, Arcadia, Melbourne, 2021.
Myrtle, John, 'Rethinking Australian journalism in the 1960s: The 1966–67 work value case and the Sydney newspaper strike', undated, <http://honesthistory.net.au/wp/wp-content/uploads/FINAL-1788-Myrtle-Newspaper-Strike-Rethink.pdf>.
Newton, Sarah, *Maxwell Newton*, Fremantle Arts Centre Press, Fremantle, 1993.
Nichols, David, '"Boiling in anger": Activist local newspapers of the 1960s and 1970s', *History Australia*, vol. 2, no. 2, 2005, pp. 41/1–41/16.
Nolan, Sybil, 'Half a century of obscurity: *The Age*, 1908–1964', Australian Media Traditions Conference, Central Queensland University, Yeppoon, 14–15 June 2001.

—— , 'Age', in Bridget Griffen-Foley (ed.), *A Companion to the Australian Media*, Australian Scholarly Publishing, Melbourne, 2014, pp. 12–14.
Oakes, Laurie, 'Alan Reid', Melbourne Press Club, undated a, <https://halloffame.melbournepressclub.com/article/alan-reid>.
—— , 'Michelle Grattan', Melbourne Press Club, undated b, <https://halloffame.melbournepressclub.com/article/michelle-grattan>.
—— and David Solomon, *The Making of an Australian Prime Minister*, Cheshire, Melbourne, 1973.
Olds, David, 'Rediscovering *Nation Review*', PhD thesis, Flinders University, Adelaide, 2015.
Page, Bruce, *The Murdoch Archipelago*, Simon & Schuster, London, 2003.
Paulu, Burton, *British Broadcasting: Radio and Television in the United Kingdom*, University of Minnesota Press, Minneapolis, MN, 1956.
Penton, Brian, *Censored!*, Shakespeare Head, Sydney, 1947.
Porter, Muriel (ed.), *The Argus: The Life and Death of a Great Melbourne Newspaper*, RMIT Publishing, Melbourne, 2003.
Presnell, Max, 'James Packer dust-up a family tradition', *SMH*, 9 May 2014, <https://www.smh.com.au/sport/racing/james-packer-dustup-a-family-tradition-20140510-zr8f7.html>.
Pringle, John Douglas, *Australian Accent*, Chatto & Windus, London, 1965.
Prior, James Anthony, 'America looks to Australia: Richard Casey's campaign in the United States, 1940–1942', PhD thesis, University of Wollongong, Wollongong, 2015.
Radi, Heather, 'Jackson, Alice Mabel (1887–1974)', *ADB*, vol. 14, 1996, <https://adb.anu.edu.au/biography/jackson-alice-mabel-10597>.
Rawling, James N, *Who Owns Australia?*, Modern Publishers, Sydney, 1939.
Rawson, DW, *Australia Votes: The 1958 Federal Election*, Melbourne University Press, Melbourne, 1961.
Regan, Simon, *Rupert Murdoch: A Business Biography*, Angus & Robertson, Sydney, 1976.
Reid, Alanah, 'A history of the *Daily Mirror*', *Historic Newspapers*, 2021, <https://www.historic-newspapers.co.uk/blog/daily-mirror-history/>.
Reid, Richard, '1969: Our politics are no longer frozen' in Benjamin T Jones, Frank Bongiorno and John Uhr (eds), *Elections Matter: The Federal Elections that Shaped Australia*, Monash University Publishing, Melbourne, 2018, pp. 116–34.
Richards, Huw, *The Bloody Circus: The Daily Herald and the Left*, Pluto Press, London, 1997.
Richardson, Nick, 'From "rags" to "riches": The evolution of the Australian suburban newspaper', *Media International Australia*, vol. 150, February 2014, pp. 83–88.
Richardson, Peter, 'Robinson, William Sydney (1876–1963)', *ADB*, vol. 11, 1988, <http://adb.anu.edu.au/biography/robinson-william-sydney-8247>.
Rickard, John, *Australia: A Cultural History*, Longman, London, 1996.
Roberts, Tom DC, *Before Rupert: Keith Murdoch and the Birth of a Dynasty*, University of Queensland Press, Brisbane, 2015.
Ryan, Chris and Louise Watson, 'The drift to private schools in Australia', Centre for Economic Policy Research, ANU, Canberra, September 2004, <https://rse.anu.edu.au/researchpapers/CEPR/DP479.pdf>.
Ryan, Colleen, *Fairfax: The Rise and Fall*, Miegunyah Press, Melbourne, 2013.
Santamaria, BA, 'Struggle on two fronts: The DLP and the 1969 election', *Australian Quarterly*, vol. 41, no. 4, 1969, pp. 33–42.
Sayers, CE, 'Syme, David (1827–1908)', *ADB*, vol. 6, 1976, <https://adb.anu.edu.au/biography/syme-david-4679>.
Sayers, Stuart, 'Campbell, Sir Harold Alfred Maurice (1892–1959)', *ADB*, vol. 13, 1993, <https://adb.anu.edu.au/biography/campbell-sir-harold-alfred-maurice-9681>.
Scalmer, Sean, 'Crisis to crisis: 1950–66', in John Faulkner and Stuart Macintyre (eds), *True Believers: The Story of the Federal Parliamentary Labor Party*, Allen & Unwin, Sydney, 2001, pp. 90–104.
Schultz, Julianne, *Reviving the Fourth Estate*, Cambridge University Press, Melbourne, 1998.
Serle, Geoffrey, 'Syme, Sir Geoffrey (1873–1942)', *ADB*, vol. 12, 1990, <https://adb.anu.edu.au/biography/syme-sir-geoffrey-8732>.
Sharpley, Cecil, 'I was a communist leader' [booklet], *Herald*, Melbourne, 1949.
Shawcross, William, *Murdoch: The Making of a Media Empire*, Simon & Schuster, New York, 1992.

Shmith, Michael, 'Long way from hot metal', 31 May 2011, *The Age*, <https://www.theage.com.au/national/victoria/long-way-from-hot-metal-the-changing-face-of-newspapers-20110530-1fcvt.html>.
Smith, Michael, 'Bertram Lindon "Don" Whitington', Melbourne Press Club, undated a, <https://halloffame.melbournepressclub.com/article/don-whitington>.
——, 'Harry Gordon', Melbourne Press Club, undated b, <https://halloffame.melbournepressclub.com/article/harry-gordon>.
Souter, Gavin, *Company of Heralds: A Century and a Half of Australian Publishing*, Melbourne University Press, Melbourne, 1981.
——, 'Browne, Francis Courtney (Frank) (1915–1981)', *ADB*, vol. 17, 2007, <https://adb.anu.edu.au/biography/browne-francis-courtney-frank-12259>.
Spearritt, Peter, 'Snow, Sir Sydney (1887–1958)', *ADB*, vol. 12, 1990, <http://adb.anu.edu.au/biography/snow-sir-sydney-8570>.
Stone, Gerald, *Compulsive Viewing*, Viking, Melbourne, 2000.
Strangio, Paul, 'Who were Australia's best prime ministers? We asked the experts', *The Conversation*, 2 August 2021, <https://theconversation.com/who-were-australias-best-prime-ministers-we-asked-the-experts-165302>.
TelevisionAU, 'https://televisionau.com/feature-articles/tv-week', 12 July 2006, <https://televisionau.com/feature-articles/tv-week>.
Television Corporation Limited, 'Fifteen years of leadership' (booklet), Sydney, circa 1971.
Thompson, John, *On Lips of Living Men*, Lansdowne Press, Melbourne, 1962.
Tidey, John, 'The last Syme: Ranald Macdonald's impact on *The Age*, 1964–1983', *Australian Journalism Monographs*, no. 2, 1998, pp. 1–29.
Tiffen, Rodney, 'News coverage of Vietnam' in Peter King (ed.), *Australia's Vietnam: Australia in the Second Indo-China War*, Allen & Unwin, Sydney, 1983, pp. 165–87.
——, 'The war the media lost' in Gregory Pemberton (ed.), *Vietnam Remembered*, Weldon Publishing, Sydney, 1990, pp. 110–37.
——, 'The *Australian* at forty-five', *Inside Story*, 14 July 2009, <https://insidestory.org.au/the-australian-at-forty-five/>.
——, 'Nine-tenths of the law', *Inside Story*, 3 June 2010, <https://insidestory.org.au/nine-tenths-of-the-law/>.
——, *Rupert Murdoch: A Reassessment*, UNSW Press, Sydney, 2014.
——, 'From punctuated equilibrium to threatened species: The evolution of Australian newspaper circulation and ownership', *Australian Journalism Review*, vol. 37, no. 1, 2015, pp. 63–80.
——, *Disposable Leaders: Media and Leadership Coups from Menzies to Abbott*, NewSouth Publishing, Sydney, 2017.
Tipping, Marjorie J, 'Cavenagh, George (1808–1869)', *ADB*, vol. 1, 1966, <https://adb.anu.edu.au/biography/cavenagh-george-1887>.
Tully, Helen, 'TV arrives in Australia in September 1956', National Film and Sound Archive of Australia (NFSA), undated, <https://www.nfsa.gov.au/latest/60th-anniversary-television>.
Tunstall, Jeremy, 'The British press in the age of television', *Sociological Review*, vol. 29, iss. 1, supplement, 1981, pp. 19–35.
Turnbull, Clive, 'Journalism' in Clinton H Grattan (ed.), *Australia*, University of California Press, Berkeley, CA, 1947, pp. 314–25.
Turner, Graeme, '"Popularising politics": *This Day Tonight* and Australian television current affairs', *Media International Australia*, vol. 106, no. 1, 2003, pp. 137–50.
UNESCO, *Statistics on Radio and Television, 1950–1960*, UNESCO, Paris, 1963.
Usher, Jim, 'Mirror executives acted without conscience' in Jim Usher (ed.), *The Argus: The Life and Death of a Great Melbourne Newspaper*, Australian Scholarly Publishing, Melbourne, 2007, p. 162.
—— and Bob Murray, 'The *Argus*: A brief history', in Muriel Porter (ed.), *The Argus: The Life and Death of a Great Melbourne Newspaper*, RMIT Publishing, Melbourne, 2003, p. 3.
Van Heekeren, Margaret, 'Strikes', in Bridget Griffen-Foley (ed.), *A Companion to the Australian Media*, Australian Scholarly Publishing, Melbourne, 2014, pp. 441–42.
Vickery, Edward, 'Telling Australia's story to the world: The Department of Information 1939–1950', PhD thesis, Australian National University, Canberra, 2003.

Walker, Martin, *Powers of the Press: The World's Great Newspapers*, Quartet Books, Melbourne, 1982.
Walker, Robin B, *Yesterday's News: A History of the Newspaper Press in New South Wales from 1920 to 1945*, Sydney University Press, Sydney, 1980a.
——, 'The fall of the *Labor Daily*', *Labour History*, no. 38, 1980b, pp. 67–75.
Ward, Michael, 'Sir Keith Murdoch: The Flinders Street broker', BLitt thesis, Australian National University, Canberra, 1981.
Waterford, Jack, 'Max Newton', Melbourne Press Club, undated, <https://halloffame.melbournepressclub.com/article/max-newton>.
——, 'Bennetts, Richard John (1925–1978)', *ADB*, vol. 13, 1993, <https://adb.anu.edu.au/biography/bennetts-richard-john-9492>.
Waterson, DB, 'Chifley, Joseph Benedict (Ben) (1885–1951)', *ADB*, vol. 13, 1993, <https://adb.anu.edu.au/biography/chifley-joseph-benedict-ben-9738>.
Wheelwright, Edward Lawrence, *Ownership and Control of Australian Companies*, Law Book Company of Australasia, Sydney, 1957.
Whitington, RS, *Sir Frank: The Frank Packer Story*, Cassell Australia, Melbourne, 1971.
Whitton, Evan, 'Getting it in: The life and times of a newspaperman', *Men's Journal Quarterly*, Summer 1985, pp. 123–27.
——, 'Amazing scenes', [book excerpts reproduced] at *Networked Knowledge*, 1987, <http://netk.net.au/Whitton/Amazing5.asp>.
——, 'Rupert Murdoch: Our part in his evil upfall', *Tasmanian Times*, 13 June 2016a, <https://tasmaniantimes.com/2016/06/rupert-murdoch-our-part-in-his-evil-upfall/>.
——, 'How Rupert Murdoch went bad', *Networked Knowledge*, 26 July 2016b, <http://netk.net.au/Whitton/Whitton14.pdf>.
Williams, Evan, 'Hot metal days', *Quadrant*, January–February 2008, pp. 121–23.
Williams, Stephen, 'Billy McMahon: A hopeless, forgettable PM', *Independent Australia*, 2 December 2018, <https://independentaustralia.net/politics/politics-display/billy-mcmahon-a-hopeless-forgettable-pm,12160>.
Windschuttle, Keith, *The Media: A New Analysis of the Press, Television, Radio and Advertising in Australia*, Penguin, Melbourne, 1988.
Wolff, Michael, *The Man Who Owns the News: Inside the Secret World of Rupert Murdoch*, Broadway Books, New York, 2010.
Young, Norman, *Figuratively Speaking*, N Young, Adelaide, 1991.
Young, Sally, 'A century of political communication in Australia, 1901–2001', *Journal of Australian Studies*, vol. 78, 2003, pp. 97–110.
——, *The Persuaders: Inside the Hidden Machine of Political Advertising*, Pluto Press, Melbourne, 2004.
——, 'Reading between the lines of Canberra news', *The Age*, 1 December 2015, p. 37.
——, 'Media power and photographs' in Fay Anderson and Sally Young (with Nikki Henningham), *Shooting the Picture: Press Photography in Australia*, Miegunyah Press, Melbourne, 2016a, pp. 141–64.
——, 'International events and the view from Australia' in Fay Anderson and Sally Young (with Nikki Henningham), *Shooting the Picture*: *Press Photography in Australia*, Miegunyah Press, Melbourne, 2016b, pp. 65–87.
——, 'Press photography in Australia, 1880–2015' in Fay Anderson and Sally Young (with Nikki Henningham), *Shooting the Picture: Press Photography in Australia*, Miegunyah Press, Melbourne, 2016c, pp. 1–24.
——, *Paper Emperors: The Rise of Australia's Newspaper Empires*, NewSouth Publishing, Sydney, 2019.
Younger, Ronald Michel, 'Let's go to press: The saga of Melbourne's longest running newspaper and its place in the community', unpublished manuscript, undated (circa 1996).
——, 'Profiles', unpublished document detailing profiles of HWT personnel (circa 1999).
——, *Keith Murdoch: Founder of a Media Empire*, Harper Collins, Sydney, 2003.
Yule, Peter, *Ian Potter: A Biography*, Miegunyah Press, Melbourne, 2006.
——, *William Lawrence Baillieu: Founder of Australia's Greatest Business Empire*, Hardie Grant Books, Melbourne, 2012.

——, 'Potter, Sir William Ian (1902–1994)', *ADB*, vol. 19, 2021, <https://adb.anu.edu.au/biography/potter-sir-william-ian-19778>.

Zwar, Desmond, *In Search of Keith Murdoch*, Macmillan, Sydney, 1980.

INDEX

Page numbers referring to images are in *italics*. Page numbers referring to tables are in **bold**.

2BH Broken Hill 11, 176
2CA Canberra 11, 200, 234
2GB Sydney 11, 123, 171, 200, 201, 212, 234, 302
2GZ Orange 200
2HD Newcastle 271
2KA Katoomba 216
2KO Newcastle 200, 271
2KY 215
2LF Young 200
2LT Lithgow 200
2MW Murwillumbah 200
2NM Muswellbrook 200
2NX Bolwarra 200
2NZ Inverell 200
2PK Parkes 200
2SM 215
2UE Sydney 11, 200, 201, 212, 271
2WL Wollongong 200
3AH Hamilton 11
3AK 217
3AW Melbourne 11, 200, 201, 213, 405–406
3DB Melbourne 11, 114, 123, 160, 200
3LK Lubeck 200
3SH Swan Hill 11
3SR Shepparton 11, 201
3TR Sale 11
3UL Warragul 11, 201
3UZ 11
3XY Melbourne 405–406
3YB Warrnambool 11, 201
4AK Oakey 11, 200
4BK Brisbane 11, 200
5AD Adelaide 11, 200
5DN Adelaide 176, 200, 208
5MU Murray Bridge 200
5PI Crystal Brook 200
5SE Mount Gambier 200

6BY Bridgetown 200
6CI Collie 200
6IX Perth 11, 200
6KY Perth 331
6MD Merredin 11, 200
6NA Narrogin 331
6PR Perth 200
6TZ Bunbury 200
6WB Katanning 11, 200
7HO 11, 200, 327
7HT Hobart 200
7LA Launceston 200

AAP *see* Australian Associated Press
Abbott, Tony 449
ABC 221, 227
    ABV-2 224
    AM 359
    Four Corners 357
    news coverage in Menzies years 357
    newspapers, rhetoric against 227–28
    PM 425
    programming 228
    This Day Tonight 358, 428
    war coverage 10
ACTU 414
Adelaide Steamship Co 89, 94
ADS-7 (ADS-10) 231, 232, 237
Advertiser
    1946 election campaign 95
    Chifley's television system 202
    control over 230
    Keith Murdoch sale of shareholding 109–10
    monopoly position 19
    News, competition against 148, 246, 316
    Rupert Murdoch bid for control 181
    Sunday Advertiser launch 177
    radio stations 11

INDEX 525

television licences in Adelaide 229–30
Advertiser Newspapers Ltd 13, 365
    HWT stake 19–20, 319
    Rupert Murdoch offer 181
    WAN and 331
advertising
    The Age 30–31, 41, 133
    American companies, by 135
    Argus 172, 174
    Chifley government controls 115
    cigarettes 221
    classified 403–404
    department store 246
    HWT 17
    News 178
    newspapers 7, 12, 123–24, 243, 262, 403–404, 457
    radio 10, 123
    suburban papers 247–48
    Sydney Morning Herald 22–23
    television 199 *see also* television
    women's magazines 187–88, 265
Advocate 163
The Age
    1943 election 47
    1944 referendum 87
    1961 election 268–69
    1969 election 354
    1972 election 456–58, 460
    advertising 29, 30–31, 402, 457
    anti-Catholicism 163
    Argus closure, impact 174
    Australian as competitor 401
    buildings *406*, 406–408, *408*
    cartoonist 400
    Chifley opinion of 113
    circulation and sales 30, 397, 456–57
    classified advertising 30–31, 403, 404
    crime reporting 400
    David Syme and Co ownership 11, 14, 30–31
    display advertising 404
    early 1970s rebirth 396, 400
    editorial sclerosis 396–97
    Fairfax partnership agreement 311–12, 399, 406–407
    financial problems 399
    Grattan and 449
    Insight team 400–401
    investigative journalism 400
    Labor's domestic policies, support for 415
    links to Menzies 268
    location 30
    Macdonald as managing director 309–310, 311, 398–400, 408, 411, 456–57
    Menzies and 397–98
    old building *406*
    old-fashioned aura 396–97
    Perkin as editor 400
    photography 400
    political views, shift in 415
    predictable coverage reputation 398
    'sectional revolution' 404–405
    security services association 398
    Sinclair as editor 397–99
    subscribers 405
    Sun News-Pictorial as rival 401–402
    Sunday papers in Melbourne 408–14
    Syme management 308–309, 396–97
    taboo subjects under Sinclair 398
    target audience 402, 405
    television and 213, 217, 227, 399
    Vietnam Moratoriums 416
    Vietnam War 415
    vulnerability to takeover 309–310
    Warwick Fairfax and 456–58 *see also* Fairfax, Warwick
    'worker's paper' reputation 30
Age Suburban 256, 405
Aircraft 388
Albury Upper Murray Television 298
Aldridge, Roger 397–98, 448
Alexander, Joe 35, 39, 51, 60
Allen, Allen & Hemsley 419
Alley, Justice 390
Amalgamated Television Services Pty Ltd 212–13, 215, 234, 235, 296
    Sydney television licence application 213, 217
American Broadcasting Company 199
AMV-4 Albury 298, 315
Anderson, Fay 345
The Anglican 250
Anglican Press 250
    The Anglican 250
    brawl 250–54
    Packers and 250–54

premises 251–52
receivership and sale 250
Ansett, Reg 274–75, 291, 304
Ansett Transport Industries 274
Anthony Hordern & Sons 246
Anthony, Larry 204, 217
Anti-Communist Labor Party *see* Democratic Labor Party (DLP)
Arbitration Commission 390
Argus 40, 132
    1949 election 116
    advertising 29–30
    anti-Catholic 163
    Bednall as editor 2, 169, 171–72, 208
    British Daily Mirror group ownership 110–12, 146–47, 158, 167–68, 201
    building 29
    changes 169
    closure 158, 172–74, 225
    colour printing presses 169–70, 171, 173
    communism charges against staff 168–69
    conservatism to left-wing shift 167–68
    Curtin government support 33
    decline in fortunes 30
    Evening Star 412
    financial problems 169–72
    HWT deal 172–74
    Labor politics and 168
    magazine 12
    news coverage 29
    Packer proposals 170, 172
    pneumatic tube use 376
    radio stations 11
Armstrong, Alfred Norman 'Jack' 179
Asia Magazine 260
ASIO 131, 350, 398
Askin, Robert 280
Associated Newspapers Ltd
    commercial banks link, 1940s-early 1950s 100, **101**, 102
    Daily Telegraph see Daily Telegraph
    Fairfax and 188, 191–93, 201
    financial problems 190
    founder 112
    industrial action and 64–65, 79, 81, 93
    IPA links 86, 88
    magazines 12, 125, 187
    Packer and 108, 190–92

    radio interests 10, 11, 200
    Robert Clyde Packer as managing editor 23
    Sydney newspaper ownership, 1945 14, 24, 26, 31–32
    television 197, 198, 211, 212, 214, 217
Associated Newspapers (UK) 213, 215
Associated Television Pty Ltd (ATV) 213, 216–17
    Fairfax purchase of Australian assets 301–302, 304
    shareholdings in Australia 302
Athenaeum Club 397
ATN-7 (Fairfax) 214, 222, 271, 276, 298, 302, 303, 304
    attempts to hobble other stations 272–72
    Comment 226
    Fairfax interest 238, 304
    news programming 444
    profit 237
    This I Believe 226
    Today 444
    westerns 223
ATV-0 274, 277
Austarama 274
Australasian Post 12
    'page-three girls' 346
Australia and New Zealand Bank Ltd 306
    Fairfax group link 1940s-early 1950s 101
Australia Party 414
Australian
    1966 election 342–43
    1969 election 354–55
    1972 election 453
    Canberra production 288–90
    Canberra Times and 288, 290
    circulation 289
    competition to other papers 401
    Deamer and 289–90, 401, 430
    facsimile transmission 290
    financial support sources 291
    industrial action 390, 431
    losses 291, 347, 403
    McEwen/McMahon story 349–50
    Newton and Chandler tensions 288
    motive for startup 290–91
    national distribution 287–89

INDEX 527

political influence, potential in 290–91
political stance 430, 431
potential readership 288
quality newspaper 287–88, 313
Rupert Murdoch's choices 287–88
Sydney, move to 290
trailblazing under Deamer 289–90
Vietnam Moratoriums 415–16
Vietnam War 341, 415–16
Australian-American Association 134–36
Australian defence policy and 136
Australian-American Co-operation Movement 134
Australian Associated Press (AAP) 1, 22, 294, 378
Australian Broadcasting Commission (ABC) see ABC
Australian Broadcasting Control Board (ABCB) 210, 211, 218, 223, 229, 406, 439
Brisbane and Adelaide television licences 230–31
foreign ownership limits 238
Perth, Hobart and Canberra television licences 234–35
Australian Club 397
Australian Consolidated Press (ACP) see Consolidated Press
Australian Federation of Commercial Radio Broadcasters 201, 203
Australian Financial Review 188, 239, 263, 284, 292, 446, 449
1961 election 263, 264
1972 election 455
Australian, impact 401
financial journalism 403
industrial action 390
Australian Financial Times 284
Australian Home Beautiful 12
Australian Iron and Steel 86
Australian Journalists Association (AJA) 35, 51, 79, 317, 384
The Clarion 186
code of ethics 109
industrial action 79, 186, 390
The News 80–81
PKIU and 387–88
Australian Labor Party (ALP) see Labor Party

Australian Mutual Provident Society (AMP) 86, 94, 101, 118, 190
Australian National Airways Ltd (ANA) 89
Australian Newspaper Proprietors' Association (ANPA) 45, 46, 59, 61, 109, 130, 294
Australian Newsprint Mills Ltd (ANM) 17, 22, 294, 303, 434–35
'Australian Public Opinion Polls (The Gallup Method)' 18
Australian Quarterly 428
Australian United Press 41, 353
Australian Woman's Day 12, 143
Home, merger with 187
Australian Women's Weekly 11, 12, 23, 186, 265, 284
circulation and profits 187, 188
influence 187
Australian Workers' Union 186
AWA (Amalgamated Wireless (Australasia) Ltd) 212, 275–76, 298
AWU (Australian Workers' Union) 215, 216

Baillieu, Clive 100
Baillieu family 20, 37, 94, 100, 110, 166, 330, 331
Baillieu, Maurice H (MH) 'Jac' 18, 152
Baillieu, William Lawrence (WL) 15, 100, 166, 230, 329
Baird, John Logie 197
Bancks, Jimmy 227
Bank of Adelaide 208
HWT link 1940s-early 1950s 101
Bank of New South Wales 99–100, 102, 106, 275
Fairfax group link 1940s-early 1950s 101
Bankstown Observer 249, 252
Barker, Geoffrey 310
Barnes, Allan 400, 446–47, 451
Barr, Trevor 231
Barrier Miner 143, 176, 364
Bartholomew, Harry Guy 111, 168, 169
Barton, Gordon 414, 416–17, 448
Baudino, Robert 424, 429
Baume, Eric 24, 226
This I Believe 226
BBC 198, 211, 228
Beatles' tour of Australia 243

Beaverbrook, Lord 85, 176
Beazley Senior, Kim 426
Bednall, Colin
    ABC, advice to 228
    ABCB, on 210, 223–24, 439
    Argus, at 2, 169, 171–72, 208
    autobiography 2–3
    Calwell and 150–51
    career overview 1–4
    cigarette advertising 221
    GTV-9 manager 2, 208, 225, 227, 235–36
    Henderson, on 222
    Keith Murdoch and 1–2, 110, 111, 117, 136, 144, 145, 150–51, 154–55
    Labor candidacy in 1972 462
    'media monsters' description 1, 462–63
    Menzies and 127, 129, 145, 203–204, 235–36, 305
    Packer and 2, 3, 172
    political shift in views 462–63
    pro-television articles 204
    Royal Commission on television 205, 207–208, 223–24
    Rupert Murdoch and 153, 154, 204
    Williams and 157
    Wren and 154, 155–56
Beeby, Warren 390–91
Bendigo Advertiser 364
Bennetts, John 340, 398, 400, 446
Berrima District Post 297
Birmingham Gazette (UK) 175
Birmingham Post (UK) 238
Blackburn, Ray 400
Blainey, Geoffrey 104
Blazey, Peter 460
Bolam, Silvester 111
Bolte, Henry 322, 410
    DLP support 325
    HWT support for 322–23
    Robert Tait case 323–24, 398
    Summary Offences Act 1966 410, 412
Bongiorno, Frank 30
Bonney, Edmund Garnet (EG) 43–44, 45, 57–59, 63–64, 67
    concession on censorship 74
    newspaper seizures for censorship breaches 67–71

Boral Ltd 332
Bowman, David 401, 427
Bowman, Maud Hamilton 166
Braddick, Ken 353
Brass, Douglas 131, 134, 341
Brisbane TV Ltd 228, 230
British commercial television 237
British Daily Mirror group
    Argus, closure of 167–73
    Argus, purchase of 110–12, 147, 158, 201
    Australia, selling out of 238
    King as chairman 146–47
    radio stations/investments 112, 171, 199, 200, 201, 302
    television 212–13
British newspaper industry 1, 109
    Royal Commission into 109, 110
    Rupert Murdoch and Fleet Street 348–49, 351
    technology and union resistance 380
Broadcasting Act 54, 225
Broadcasting and Television Act 1956 231, 275, 304
    abuse of laws 306
    amendments impacting HWT 334–35
    dual system of public and commercial broadcasting 205
    freezing of investment shareholdings 334–35
    grandfathering clause for existing interests 305
    impartiality requirements 439
    ownership restrictions 225, 231, 305, 405–406
    prescribed interest definition 305
Broken Hill Proprietary Ltd (BHP) 84, 93–94, 99, 100, 140, 271, 278, 332, 334
Broken Hill South 86
Brown, George 140
Browne, Frank 252, 254
BTQ-7 231, 232
Bulletin 284, 294, 306, 323–24, 413, 428, 436, 439
    Gorton destabilisation 422–24
    Henderson's retirement coverage 294
Burton, Dr John 140
Butters, John 93, 190–92, 193, 197, 204, 211, 212

INDEX 529

wishlist for potential television
    broadcasters 209

Cadbury 221
Cairns, Dr Jim 415, 416
Cairnton Pty Ltd 420
Calwell, Arthur 57
    1961 election 262
    1963 election 278, 281
    1966 election 342
    ABCB and 231, 234
    anti-commercial television 205–207,
        209–210, 222
    Archbishop Mannix, links to 165–66
    background 55–56
    biographer 55
    cartoon by Frith 75
    censorship battles 55–75
    character 55–56
    communist leader condemnation 115
    Curtin on 54–55
    Department of Information changes
        57–58
    deputy Opposition leader 129
    Henderson and 76
    Keith Murdoch and 55, 56–58, 150, 278
    Labor leader 262, 349
    libel actions 55
    minister for information 54–57
    order-to-submit 58–59, 63
    press reform plan 74
    press, relationship with 35, 52, 54,
        55–56, 76–77, 82, 102, 108, 113, 170,
        265, 310
    suit for damages 75–76
Cameron, Clyde 180, 280, 420
Cameron, Heather 26, 27–28
Campbell, Andrew 460
Campbell, Harold Alfred Maurice (HAM)
    44, 127, 397
Canberra conference 87
    anti-Labor groups 88–89
Canberra Mirror 359
Canberra News 359–60
    launch by Fairfax 359–60
Canberra Press Gallery
    ('The Circus') 35, 36
    1972 election 450–59
    censorship tensions 44
    changes in 445–47
    'the Club' 447
    McMahon unpopularity 450–51
    Menzies dominance over 340
    new generation 445–47
    women 449
Canberra Television Ltd 234–35, 285
    Fairfax involvement 234–35
Canberra Times 26, 27, 234, 285–87, 326,
    446, 449
    1972 election 455–56
    advertising revenue 285
    Consolidated Press interest in 286
    Fairfax acquisition 286–87, 298
    HWT interest in 286
    Rupert Murdoch interest in 286
    Shakespeare and Fairfax deal 286
    Vietnam War support 341–42
    Williams profile 316
Carlton and United Breweries (CUB) 15
Carlton News 402
Carroll, Vic 269, 337
Casey, Richard 95, 135, 145
Catholic Church Property Insurance
    Company 165
Catholic Social Studies Movement ('the
    Movement') 115, 163–64
Catholic Weekly 186
Catholic Worker 115
Catholicism 162–66
    school funding 324
Cavenagh, George 163
Caxton, William 369, 370
Censorship Advisory Committee 59
Centaur 41
Central Coast Express 297
Centralian Advocate 364
Chadstone Shopping Centre, Melbourne
    247
Chalmers, Rob 269
Chamberlain, Frank 48–49, 56
Chancellor, Christopher 148
Chandler, Stanley Cecil (Sol) 288, 348, 351,
    401
Channel 9 236, 420 *see also* GTV-9; TCN-9
    1972 election 439
    A Current Affair 437, 444
    anti-Labor editorials 439
    Federal File 439, 444

Meet the Press 424, 429
Channel O (Melbourne) (Channel 10) 274, 277
Chifley, Ben 50, 77, 78, 92–93, 98, 119, 175, 280
    1949 election campaign 117–19
    background in newspapers 93
    bank nationalisation 103–105
    commercial television policy 202
    death 129
    economy restraints 98, 115
    Lang claims against 119
    opinion on press 112–13
Chifley government
    1949 election 112–19
    bank nationalisation plans 98, 99, 102–107, 117
    industrial unrest 93–94, 118
    newsprint shortages 96–97
    press campaign against bank plans 104–106
Chifley, Patrick 93
Christiansen, Arthur 1, 176, 288
Christie, Vern 179
Chronicle (US) 197
Church of England 213–14
Clarke, Duncan 173
Clinch, Lindsay 193
Coca-Cola 135, 206
Cohen family 166
Cold War 134
    consumerism 124
    domesticity ideal 126
    family values 126
    Labor Party split 115, 139–40, 163–65, 280, 322
    newspapers' role in 124
    Petrov affair 136–39
    politics 127–29
Coleman, John 140
Coles 84, 247, 248, 360
Coles, George 84
Colgate-Palmolive 135
Collins House 15–16, 19, 20, 83, 86, 88, 100, 102, 136, 166, 330, 331, 332
Colonial Mutual 101
Colonial Sugar Refining Company (CSR) 86, 99, 275
    connection with banks 99

colour printing 169–71, 326–27
    Herald Gravure four-colour press 326–27
    HWT 326–27
    magazines 11–12, 187
Columbia Broadcasting System (CBS) 199, 223
comic strips 7–9, 227
Commercial Bank of Australasia 100
Commercial Banking Co of Sydney 99, 100
    Fairfax group link 1940s-early 1950s 101
commercial banks
    Fairfax family connection 99–100
    Labor complaints 98–99
    metal banks 100
    newspaper and bank links, 1940s-early 1950s **101**
    newspapers and 99–107, 117
    opposition to Labor nationalisation 104–107
    political role 98
    sugar banks 99–100
Commonwealth Bank 98, 102, 103, 104, 179
    misrepresentations on Labor policy 104–105
    Rupert Murdoch and 179, 181, 434
communism, fear of 81, 82, 94
Communist Party 81
    Menzies' proposed ban 131–33
    Newsletter printery 80, 186
    public concerns about communism 117, 118
    Royal Commission into activities 115
    Sharpley claims 113–15, 117
Communist Party Dissolution Act 132
    High Court challenge 132
Consolidated Press
    assets 437
    Associated Newspapers and 108, 190–92
    British Daily Mirror group and 170
    censorship battles 63, 64, 67–68, *68*
    Commonwealth peace officers 67
    Consolidated Television Qld 228
    Consolidated Television South Australia Ltd 228
    country papers 364

INDEX 531

industrial action 186
radio stations 10, 215
suburban papers 255–56
Suburban Publications Pty Ltd 249, 255–56
takeover threat 184–85
Telegraphs, decline in 431–32
Telegraphs, sale of 433–34
television 198, 201, 213, 216, 218
women's magazines 11, 23
Consolidated Television Qld 228
Consolidated Television South Australia Ltd 228
Consolidated Zinc 15, 329, 332
consumerism 123–24, 404
The Conversation 449
Conzinc Riotinto 278, 329, 332–33
Cook, Judith 293, 296
Corr, Alan 339
Corr and Corr Solicitors (Corrs Chambers Westgarth) 324, 337, 338
Costigan, Peter 269
Cottle, Drew 104
Country Broadcasting Services Limited 207
Country Party 33, 47, 48, 49–50, 92, 182, 278
Courier-Mail 2, 15, 95, 127, 143, 144
  'Day by Day' 25
  John Wren to John Williams, from 154–57
  Keith Murdoch ownership 108, 148, 152–53
  1949 election 116, 117
  Vietnam War support 341–42
Cowley, Ken 286, 287
Cowra detention centre breakout 75
Cox, Harold 92, 106, 132, 136, 137–38, 446
Crisp, LF 93
Cruden Investments Pty Ltd 146, 181
CTC-7 Canberra 233, 234, 285, 296, 298
  Fairfax interest 302, 304
Cudlipp, Hugh 170–71, 173, 302
Cumberland Argus 246–48
  circulation 248
Cumberland Newspapers 248–49, 255, 258
  acquisition by Rupert Murdoch 248–49
  coverage 249
  expansion 249
  no-competition agreement 255–56

strategic value 249
Curthoys, Ann 207
Curtin government 32, 33, 44, 73
  1943 election 46–52
  aviation nationalisation 89
  banks policy 98
  company taxation increase 33–34
  industrial disputes 78–80, 89
  newspaper criticism 45–47, 78, 91
  newspaper support 32, 33, 49–50
Curtin, John 33, 50, 53, 57, 59
  access to journalists 35–36
  alignment with US article 133–34
  censorship responsibility 44–45
  death 92
  full-time press secretary, appointment of 35
  health 91–92
  journalism background 34–36
  journalists' opinions of 35–36
  Keith Murdoch and 37–38, 41–42
  press conferences 35, *36*
  US visit 60, 73
CWL Pty Ltd 154, 162

Dahlsen, John 318–19, 320–21, 329, 334, 338
Daily Advertiser (Wagga Wagga) 297, 298, 315
Daily Commercial News 284
Daily Express (UK) 1, 176, 288
Daily Guardian 400
Daily Herald (UK) 81 *see also Sun* (UK)
  change to *Sun* 351
  Rupert Murdoch purchase 351
Daily Mail (UK) 1, 213, 238, 351
Daily Mirror
  1946 election 95
  1949 election 116
  1961 election 265
  1963 election 278, 280
  1969 election 354
  1972 election 452, 453
  Anglican Press brawl 252, *253*, 254
  censorship battle 69, *69*
  circulation 343
  colour printing 326
  crossword games/prize competitions 347

downmarket 344
ethics 345
Fairfax group and 194–95
false leads to rivals 344–45
Henderson negotiation for 194–95
launch 13, 24, 287
Mark Day as editor 344, 347
Norton ownership 3, 24, 111, 194–95
outrageous headlines 344
'page-three girls' 346
price fixing 346–47
promotions 347
revenue from 348
rules of combat with *Sun* 346
Rupert Murdoch, sale to 249–50, 256, 257–59, 283, 300, 343
street posters 344
strikes 79, 81–82, 185–86
tabloid warfare versus *Sun* 343–47
Vietnam Moratoriums support 416
Zell Rabin as editor 343
Daily Mirror (UK) 110–11, 206, 238, 351
left-wing paper 111–12
Daily News 15, 20–21, 330
Daily Telegraph
1943 election 49, 50
1946 election 94–95
1958 election 234
1961 election 265, 268, 281
1963 election 281–83
1969 election 354
1972 election 452–53
1944 referendum 86–87
advertising 265–66
Associated Newspapers partnership 23, 24
cartoons 265, *279*
censorship and 44, 58–59, 60–75
Chifley's television system 202
communism dangers 82, 94, 133
Curtin and 33, 35, 36, 45, 59
daily sales 431–32
Evatt and 50, 133
'faceless men' scoop 281–82, *282*, 283
Gorton destabilisation 423–24
industrial action 81–82, 140
job losses after sale 434
Liberal Party support 87–88, 90, 94–95
linotype machines 373–74
Menzies, on 33, 49, 87–88, 102–103, 265–66
money losses 432
old-fashioned 431–32
Packer and 23, 49, 87, 183–84
Penton as editor 23, 55, 182
plant and equipment rundown 431
Reid's articles 419–20
Rupert Murdoch changes to 436
sales 436–37
Stalin's death 183–84
strike 185–86
taxation coverage 183
TCN debut, promotion of 219, *220*
television 204, 211
'Town Talk' 25
Watson editorship 431
Daly, Frank 164, 328, 458
Daly, Fred 280
Dandenong Journal 256
D'Arcy, John 162, 284
Darling, Harold 84, 85, 89
Darmody, Jack 400
David Jones department store 85–86, 163, 246, 360
Newcastle 271
Parramatta 247
Wollongong 272
David Syme and Co *see also The Age*
3XY radio station 405–406
Age Suburban 256
computerised typesetting system 393
Efftee Broadcasters Pty Ltd interest 405
Fairfax group and 308–11, 360, 406, 456
General Television Corporation 228
Neill as chairman 310–11, 312
HWT secret report 336
HWT stake 310, 311
Newsday 359, 396, 411–14
Macdonald as managing director 309–310, 311, 398–400, 408, 411, 456–57
partnership agreement with Fairfax 311–12
printers' strike 384
profits from *The Age* 457
public company 308
radio stations 11, 199, 405–406

suburban papers 256
Sunday paper plans 408, 410–12
Syme trust beneficiaries control 308, 311
technology 381, 405
television 216, 218, 225, 227, 236
unions and Sunday paper 412
David Syme Trust 28, 308
Davidson, Gay 446, 449
Davidson, James Edward 19
Davies Brothers Ltd 327–28
Davies, David R 124
Davies family 13, 31, 199
    Hobart *Mercury* ownership 327
Davies, George Francis ('Bill') 327–28
Davies, John 31
Day, Mark 291, 344, 347, 352, 391, 396
Deakin, Alfred 34, 88, 177
Deamer, Adrian 289, 337, 401, 430–31, 452
Deamer, Sydney 25, 289
decimal currency, introduction of 341
Dedman, John 45–46, 86
Democratic Labor Party (DLP) 115, 139, 163–65, 174, 322, 439
    1961 election 273
    impact on Labor Party 139–40
    preferences direction 139, 325, 355
    school funding 324
    Victorian support and power 325
Denison Estates 11
Denison, Hugh 112, 152, 197
Denison, James L 190
department stores
    decline in the city 246
Detroit News 381
Dick, Nigel 222
The Dominion 260
Donaldson, Brian 337
Donnelly, Phyllis 129
Dougherty, TNP 216, 217
Dowling, George Shakespeare 285
Drakeford, Arthur 51
Dulux 15
Dumas, Lloyd
    Advertiser Newspapers role 19
    Elder Smith and Co director 93–94
    Henderson and 257, 316
    Keith Murdoch and 19, 51, 144, 148, 149–50, 152, 197
    Menzies and 127, 273, 275

Rupert Murdoch and 152–53, 177–78, 181, 229–30, 257, 348
television and 211, 229–30, 273, 275
Williams and 108–109, 149–50
Dunleavy junior, Steve 344, 345
Dunleavy senior, Steve 344
Dunlop Rubber 15
Dunstan, David 159 –60, 164, 168, 173, 174, 318, 322
Dunstan, Keith 25, 157, 158, 159, 164
Dunstan, William 143, 148, 159
Dutch Philips Industries 213
Dyer, Bob 206
Dyer, Louise 166

Eather, Warwick 104
Eddy, Jack 263
Edison, Thomas 395
Edward Wilson Trustees 30
Edwards, Cecil
    Argus description 29, 167–68
    Curtin's US speech 133–34
    Herald revamp 244
    Keith Murdoch, opinion of 39, 47–48, 110, 148, 152, 317
    television as competition for newspapers 225, 244
    Williams, opinion of 159, 317, 328
Efftee Broadcasters Pty Ltd 405
Eggleston, Frederic 40
Elder Smith and Co 94, 208
Electronic Industries 215
    sale 352
Elliott, Sydney 112, 168, 169
Elwood company 306, 308
Email 212–13, 275
English, Scottish & Australian Bank Ltd (ES&A) 100
    HWT link 1940s-early 1950s 101
Evans, Harold 400
Evatt, Dr Herbert Vere (HV) 44, 64, 132, 330
    1943 election 50
    1954 election 138
    cartoon *107*
    censorship principles 73
    commercial participation in television views 205–206, 237
    Communist Party referendum 133

534 MEDIA MONSTERS

erratic behaviour 129, 131, 138
Keith Murdoch and 40
leadership of Labor Party 129, 131, 138–39, 262
legal ability 72–73
negative press coverage 133, 137, 138–39
Petrov affair, impact 138
Sydney Morning Herald support 50
television licence applications 216, 217
Evening News 142
Evening Star 30
EX Launceston 200

'14 powers' referendum 86
   Menzies' opposition to 87
   press support and opposition 86–87
Fadden, Arthur 33, 47, 48, 92, 183
Fairfax & Sons *see* Fairfax group
Fairfax, Betty (Marcie Elizabeth, née Wilson) 269–70, 297
Fairfax group 10, 12, 13, 22–23, 31, 90, 195, 216, 218
   1961 election 262, 269
   1963 election 279, 301
   anxiety about Labor and Whitlam 454
   Arsycom 382, 387, 388, 391–92
   Associated Newspapers merger 192–93, 201
   buildings, sale of 194
   Canberra News 359–60
   Canberra Times and 285–87
   commercial bank links, 1940s-early 1950s **101**
   computer problems 391
   country papers 364
   country television licences 271–72, 297
   Daily Mirror, sale to Rupert Murdoch 249, 257–60, 283
   David Syme and Co, relationship with 310–11
   expansion 188, 190–94
   family connection to banks 99–100
   group structure 1965 **303**
   Henderson and 292–93, 306
   incorporation as public company 195
   Macquarie Broadcasting Holdings 301–302, 303, 304
   Norton deal 194–95
   partnership agreement with David Syme and Co 311–12
   printers' strike 384, 385–86
   public company structure 195, 300
   Queensland Television Ltd 228
   radio shareholding 123, 199, 201
   share market value in 1964 302
   SII computerised system 392
   Suburban Publications Pty Ltd 249
   technology, use of 378–83, 405
   television, preparing for 198
   TEN-10 275
   typesetting and printing tradition 383
   VDTs 391–92
   Warwick Fairfax and *see* Fairfax, Warwick
   Woman's Day 188
Fairfax, Hanne (née Anderson) 270, 297
Fairfax, James 195, 259, 264, 269, 300, 385–86
   Henderson and 301
   transfer of shares to 300
Fairfax, James Oswald 293
Fairfax, James Reading 99–100
Fairfax, John 71, 86, 99, 163, 383
Fairfax, John B 313, 360, 433
Fairfax, John Hubert 101
Fairfax, Lady Mabel (née Hixson) 292–93, 298, 300
Fairfax, Mary (née Symonds) 259, 270, 298–300
   Henderson and 259, 299–300
   marriage to Cedric Symons 300
   reputation 299
Fairfax, Vincent 101, 195, 300, 313, 433
Fairfax, Warwick *189*, 263
   1950s 299
   1961 election Labor endorsement 264, 300–301
   1972 election 454–56
   approach to family company 299–301, 313
   Associated Newspapers meeting 192
   censorship battles 59, 64, 70
   'committee of one' 313, 455
   editorials 103, 264, 300–301, 313, 454
   first wife's alleged affair 269–70
   Henderson and 42, 259, 260, 262, 279, 293, 300, 301, 313
   insensitivity example 92
   IPA, criticism of 85–87, 187

INDEX 535

'Kinghaven arrangement' 300
knighthood 299
managing director and chairman 313
Mary Fairfax and 299–300
Menzies and 33, 49, 52–53 261, 263, 269–70, 28–79
'A Political Observer' articles 49, 85
Press Censorship Advisory Committee 44–45, 59
role in Fairfax 22
shareholding in company 195, 300
Sun-Herald 193
transfer of shares to son James 300
UAP revelations 83
Fairfax, Warwick (Junior) 313
Faithfull, Marianne 345
Falkingham, RP 249, 259, 313, 348
Fallon, Clarrie 108
Farmer, Richard 452
Farrell, Tom 381
Federal Capital Press 234, 314
Federal Communications Commission (FCC) 210
federal elections, 1943–73
partisan support of major newspapers **266–67**
Federated Ironworkers' Association 186
Fenston, Esmé 187
Festival Records 348
Financial Times 206, 263
Fink, Catherine 16
Fink family 16, 166
Fink, Theodore 230
Fisher, Andrew 34
Fitchett, Ian 269, 446
Fitzgerald, James 88
Fitzgerald, Ross 281
Fitzgerald, Tom 263, 279, 448
Fitzpatrick, Ray 249, 252
Fletcher, Maurice 295
Flowers, Fred 160, 320
Foard, Dulcie 125
Foley, Steve 417
Ford Co 206
Forde, Francis 73, 92
Formby, George 344
Fraser, Allan 35, 104, 105, 280
Fraser, Colin 149
Fraser, Malcolm 423

army authorities, tensions 423–24
Gorton and 424
Freudenberg, Graham 118, 358
Frith, John 74–75, 80
cartoon use by Liberal Party *116*

Gallup, George 17–18
Garland, Judy 354
Gawenda, Michael 402
Geelong Advertiser 364
General Electric (GE) 135, 197
General Motors 135, 206, 221
General Television Corporation Pty Ltd 213, 215, 217, 228, 231
Gepp, Sir Herbert 83
Giddy, Harold 145
bank connections 85, 100, 101, 106, 154
HWT board 85, 100, 101, 160, 190–91, 208
Keith Murdoch's death 151, 152–53, 179
Gifford, Peter 129
Ginger Meggs 227
Godling, Douglas 254
Gollan, Ross 35, 76, 91–92, 120
Goodyear 135
Gordon, Harry 318, 401–402
Gorton government 336
Gorton, John 349, 357, 422, *423*
1969 election 352–55
abandonment by newspapers 424–25
calls for resignation 424–25
deputy leader 425–26
destabilisation by Consolidated Press 422, 423–24, 428–29
Fraser, disloyalty to 423–24
Liberal colleagues and 422, 429
public perception of 350
Reid's book on 425
Rupert Murdoch and 349–51, 354–55, 436
scandals 353–54, 422
Gosford Times 297
Gotto, Ainsley 353
Goulburn Post 297, 314
Grace Brothers 246
suburbs, move to 246–47, 248
Grade, Lew 302
Grant, Bruce 456

536 MEDIA MONSTERS

Grattan, Michelle 446, 449, 450
Great Depression 13, 19, 24, 26, 30, 98, 108
Greene, LH Benson 216
Greene, Rupert 175
Greer, Germaine 463
Griffen-Foley, Bridget 67, 231, 341
Grover, Monty 166
GTV-9 2, 171, 208, 214, 224, 354, 437
 Australian Consolidated Press ownership 238
 Australian talent 225
 Bednall management of 2, 208, 225, 235–36
 Face the Nation 226
 gala opening night 225
 In Melbourne Tonight 225
 Packer acquisition 235–36
 profit 237
 sale of shares 227, 235, 399
 studio 227
 ratings 225
Guardian 34, 238, 288
Gutenberg, Johannes 369, 370
Gyngell, Bruce 219

Hall, Sandra 223, 227, 274, 304
Halliday, George 419
Hamersley Holdings 278, 332–33, 334
Hamilton, Ian 318, 322
Hancock, Lang 329, 333
Hansen-Rubensohn 118
Hardy, Frank 155, 168, 324
 Power Without Glory 155, 168, 324
Harmsworth, Alfred *see* Northcliffe, Lord
Harmsworth, Harold *see* Rothermere, Lord
Harriott, Guy 455
Hasluck, Paul 350, 422, 427
Hawke, Bob 414, 437, 461
Haylen, Les 270, 280
Hazlehurst, Cameron 217
Heinz 135
Henderson, Gerard 90, 269
Henderson, Hazel (née Harris) 296, 306, 315
Henderson, Helene (née Mason) 294–95
Henderson Holdings Pty Ltd 276, 278, 296–98, 314–15
 country television shares 314–15
 loan from Fairfax company 306

Henderson, Margaret 296, 306, 315
Henderson, Rupert Albert Geary ('Rags') *191*, 280, 375–76, 379
 1961 election 263–64
 achievements for Fairfax 302–303
 Associated Newspapers, merger 190–93
 attributes 292, 293–94, 295
 Bednall's view of 3, 222
 Calwell and 55, 61, 63, 64–65, 76, 262, 265, 268
 Canberra Times see Canberra Times
 censorship 40, 61, 63, 64–70, 73
 Chifley, opinion on 119–20
 country papers 364
 country television licence 298
 Curtin and 91–92
 Daily Mirror, sale to Rupert Murdoch 249, 257–60, 283
 death 315
 divorce 295
 energy and dedication 292
 Fairfax group/family and 22–23, 188, 193, 195, 292–93
 family companies 276, 278, 296–298, 314–15 *see also* Henderson Holdings Pty Ltd
 granddaughters Helen and Judith 293
 home, at 294–96
 industrial action 81
 industry roles 294
 Keith Murdoch, views on 37
 last deal as managing director 301–302
 London 293
 loyalty 292
 Mary Fairfax and 259, 299–300
 Menzies and 50, 88, 130, 261, 273, 275–76
 mini-Empire 296–98, **307**
 newspaper ownership 297–98
 Newton, opinion of 263
 Packer and 294
 post-retirement 303, 314–15
 retirement 292, 293, 294, 301–303, 306–308
 Rupert Murdoch and 258–59, 275–76
 second family 296
 son Chips, relationship with 296
 strike response 81
 television licence fix 276

INDEX 537

tensions with Warwick Fairfax 42, 259, 279, 301
unwanted publicity 295–96
Warner and 235
wartime 'sacrifices' 46
wealth from family companies 314–15
Henderson, Rupert William Geary (RWG) 'Chips' 294–96, 318, 319
   Fairfax, career at 296
   family companies 314, 315
   father, relationship with 296
Hendy, HE 306
Herald 33, 35, 58, 142, 211–12, 412, 446
   1943 election 51–52
   1946 election 95
   1949 election 113–19
   1961 election 268
   1972 election 458
   1944 referendum 87
   1961 state election 323
   American television article 208–209
   Bolte, support for 322–24
   Calwell action against 55
   Catholic connection 163
   Chifley's television system 202
   circulation 244
   colour printing 326–27
   communism dangers 82, 115, 164–65
   Communist Party disclosures 114–15
   Communist Party referendum 132–33
   Curtin cartoon 41, 42
   Curtin's US alignment policy 133–34
   Edwards as editor 244
   Keith Murdoch articles 38–42, 47–48, 51, 135–36
   Lang claims about Chifley 119
   opinion polls 18
   price of 161
   pro-American enthusiasm 135–36
   reputation 16–17
   Rupert Murdoch cadetship 175
   sales records 320
   Vietnam War support 341
   Williams as editor-in-chief 143
   Williams as financial writer 21
Herald-Sun TV Pty Ltd 215
Herald and Weekly Times (HWT) 13–16
   1949 election 116
   1958 election 234

1969 election 355
1972 election 454, 458–59
Adelaide newspapers, stake in 19–20
advertising 17
Archbishop Mannix, reporting on 165
Argus deal 172–74
articles of association 336
Associated Newspapers and 190–92
Bendigo Advertiser 364
board and management 16–17
Brisbane 21
Brisbane TV Ltd 228
British Daily Mirror group 112
cadet reporter training 109
campaigns 322
Catholic connections 163–66
colour printing 326
commercial bank links, 1940s-early 1950s **101**
computers 388
Davies Brothers, shareholding in 327–28
electronic composing room 388–89
expansion 162
family atmosphere 318
Flinders Street building *161*
freezing of investment shareholdings 334–35
Geelong Advertiser 364
High Court challenge to Menzies legislation 335
home, at 16–17
influence of Williams 321–25 *see also* Williams, John (Jack)
interlocking share arrangement 153, 319–20, 331
'introspective policies' 337
Keith Murdoch lobbying through 38
Keith Murdoch's connection, change in 145–46, 147–49
Keith Murdoch's death 151–53
Labor banking policy, opposition to 106–107
Labor-DLP split 165
largest shareholders 319
legislation contravention 335–36
legislative amendments impacting 334–35
Linotron 606 phototypesetter *389*
magazines 12

market share 360
media holdings 319
metal banks connection 100
News Limited majority stake sale 110
newsroom computers 393–94, *394*
opinion polls 17–19
ownership 110
post-Keith Murdoch 158–62
post-Williams management structure 328–29
printers' strike 384
profits 360
protection from takeovers 319–20
Queensland Newspapers 21, 156–57
Queensland Press 162
radio 10–11
'republic of management' 320
Rupert Murdoch and 153
shareholders 15, 165–67
staff loyalty 149
suburban papers 256
Sunday papers 410–12
System 5500 393–94
taxation increase, impact 34
technology 381
television licences 162, 217, 224, 228
television, preparing for 197
value of 320
Victorian politics 322–23
WAN and 20
weaknesses 336–37
West Australian Newspapers Ltd (WAN) and 20–21, 330–34
Williams as executive chairman and managing director *see* Williams, John (Jack)
Hetton Bellbird Collieries 93
Hewat, Tim 413
High Court
    Labor bank legislation 103, 107, 117
    Labor Privy Council appeal 117
    newspaper suppression case 71–74
Highland Post 314
Hills, Ben 413
Hoe and Crabtree 169
Hoey, Tom 70
Hollway, Tom 322
Holt, Edgar 35–36, 60
Holt government 329

landslide 1966 election win 343
Holt, Harold 203, 243, 340, 342, 413, 422
    disappearance 349
Holt, Stephen 281
Home magazine 12
    Woman's Day merger 187
Home Beautiful 388
Hordern, Anthony 89
Horne, Donald 252
Hoskins, Cecil 86
Howe, Ann 27
Howe, George 27, 99
HSV-7 (Herald-Sun TV Pty Ltd) (HWT) (Melbourne) 162, 214
    Homicide 224
    profit 237
    sporting coverage 225, 358, 399
    studio 227
Hughes, Billy 34, 36, 47, 52
Hutton, Geoffrey 104

Illawarra Mercury 297, 314, 364
Illawarra/Wollongong area 272
Independent 333
Independent Television (ITV) (UK) 210–11, 213
Industrial Commission 81, 386
    Cahill decision 386–87, 389
Inner Western Times 255
Inside Canberra 140
Institute of Public Affairs (IPA)
    bank nationalisation opposition 104, 117
    council members 83, 84–85, 102
    establishment of 83
    first chairman 84
    'Looking Forward' manifesto 89–90
    NSW, in 85–86
    origins 83
    pro-American enthusiasm 135
    purpose 83–84
International Oils Exploration 278
Isaacson, Peter 418
ITA (Independent Television Authority) (UK) 209, 210

J Walter Thompson 206
Jackson, Alice 187
James, Francis 250–52, 254

Japan Export Trade Organisation 350
Jarrett, Pat 125
JB Were 102
Jenkin, Percy 43
John Fairfax Ltd *see* Fairfax group
Johns, Brian 446–47
Johnson, Boris 34
Johnson, President Lyndon B 342
Jones, Charles Lloyd 85–86
Jones, David 85
Jones, David Lloyd 293
Jones, Philip 338, 445, 458–59
journalism
    changes in 445–47
    computers and 390–92, 395
    insider newsletters 448
    investigative 400–401, 447–48
    newspaper audiences and 108–109
    second-wave feminism 448–49
    tabloid 'muckraking' approach 400–401
    training and accuracy 109
    US, in 447–48
    'women's pages' 124–25, 448
Journalists' Club 186

Kater, Norman 86
Keane, Senator 51
Keeler, Christine 351
Kelly, Dalziel 145
Kelly, Paul 446
Kelly, TH 86
Kemp, Charles Denton (CD) 83, 90, 135
Kennedy, Eric 59, 63, 81, 88, 134, 198, 236, 462
Kennedy, Graham 225
Kennedy, John F 243
Kennelly, Pat 280
Keon, Stan 168
Kerr, William 163
Kiernan, Colm 55, 77
Kiernan, Thomas 178–79
King, Cecil Harmsworth 2, 3, 111, 146–47, 169, 170, 171–72, 237
Kirkpatrick, Rod 387
Knox, Edward Ritchie 99
Knox, Errol 33
Knox, Sir Edward 99
Kodak 135
Koitaki Ltd 315

Kommer, Walter 289
Korporaal, Glenda 263
Kraft Foods 206, 221

Labor Daily 35, 64, 295
Labor Party 33–34
    1954 election 136–37
    1966 election 342–43
    1969 election 354–55
    1972 election 450–61
    commercial press bias against 20, 24, 30, 31, 35, 51, 52–53, 55, 102, 108, 112–13
    commercial television policy 202
    federal conference 1963 281
    'It's Time' slogan 450
    leadership changes 129
    Reid articles 420
    significance of 1972 election win 459–61
    split 115, 139–40, 163–65, 280, 322
    television policy, differences in 205–206
    victory in 1972 election 459–61
    Whitlam reforms 353
Labour Council 81
Lahey, John 407
Lamb family 271, 273
Lamb, John 400
Lamb, Larry 351
Lang, Jack 119
Latham, Chief Justice 72
Lawson, Valerie 414
Leck, Lou 262, 279
Lemon, Barbara 449
L'Estrange, Richard 401
Lever, Rodney 153, 179
Liberal Party 87–89, 102
    1946 election 94–95
    1949 election 116–19
    1969 election 422
    1972 election 441
    cartoon election campaign pamphlet *116*
    election advertising campaign 118
    formal launch 90
    Gorton leadership vote 425
    leadership vote after Holt's disappearance 349–50
    press support 89, 90, 94–95, 261

provisional constitution 90
Loloma Mining Corp 278
London Bank of Australia 100
Lyons government 10
Lyons, Joe 34, 37, 136

MacArthur, General Douglas 21, 40
MacCallum, Mungo 269, 420, 435, 446
Macartney, James 20
McClelland, Doug 451, 454
McConnan, Leslie 84–85, 102, 104, 117, 135
Macdonald, Hamish 309
Macdonald, (Chesborough) Ranald 399, 405
    The Age traditions 309, 310, 311
    ASIO connection to *The Age* 398
    Fairfax group negotiations 312
    managing director of David Syme and Co 309, 398–401
    1972 election 456–57
    Oswald Syme story 397
    Sunday paper in Melbourne 408, 410–12
    see also Newsday
    Warwick Fairfax and 456–57
Macdougall, Jim 25
McEwen, John 278, 305, 349, 350, 397, 436
Macintyre, Stuart 90, 115, 123
McKell, William 72
Mackinnon, Lauchlan 110
McLachlan, Angus 91, 264, 290, 308, 379
    managing director of Fairfax 308, 311–13, 411
McMahon, Billy 268, 349–50, *423*, 460
    1972 election 450–59
    economic issues 441
    Gorton's assessment 428
    Hasluck on 427–28
    journalists' views of 427
    leadership, winning 425
    Packer and 349, 350, 419, 421–22, 435, 439
    prime minister, as 426–29
    Reid and 421
    Rupert Murdoch and 435
    sale of *Telegraphs*, impact 435
    unpopularity 428, 450
McMahon, Sonia 421
McNair, Brian 352
McNicoll, David 281, 433, 455
    Anglican Press brawl 252, 254
    editor-in-chief Consolidated Press 184, 187, 436
    Gorton and 422, 424, 428, 429
    Henderson and Keith Murdoch story 258, 259
    McMahon, opinion of 426
    Packer and 25, 184–85, 187, 192, 238, 250, 350, 419, 421
    Reid, on 280
    television 222, 439
    'Town Talk' 25
Macpherson, Duncan 329
Macpherson, Keith 328–29, 338
Macquarie Broadcasting Holdings 302, 303, 304
Macquarie Network 11, 199, 200, 201, 212, 234
    member shareholders, 1954-55 200
McQueen, Humphrey 114
McWilliams Wines 221
magazines 265
    1950s, in 187–88
    colour printing 326
    newspapers and 11–12
    television and 221
Mail 176, 177
    industry dirty linen 177–78
Maitland Mercury 364
Major Broadcasting Group 199, 200
    member shareholders, 1954-55 200
Manchester Guardian see Guardian
Manne, Robert 137
Mannix, Archbishop Daniel 139, 163–64, 165, 173
    HWT shareholder 165
Mansell, Horace 63–64
Mant, Gilbert 70–71
Marconi company 212
Margetts, Vernon de Witt 217
Martin, Allan 269
Maxwell, Robert 348
Meeking, Charles 87
Melbourne
    Sunday newspapers 408–412, 414, 416–18
    Victorian legislation 409
Melbourne City Council 103
Melbourne Club 163, 397, 400

Melbourne Observer 417–18
Melbourne Olympic Games 224
Melbourne Steamship 94
Melbourne Sunday Press 417–18
Melbourne Times 402
Menadue, John 452
Menzies governments 40, 43, 44
    1961 election 273
    1963 election 278–83
    conscription 341
    country television licences 271–72, 304
    credit policy 261, 262–63, 265, 268–69
    international sale of iron ore restrictions 329–30
    metropolitan commercial television licences, 1958-60 **232-33**
    opinion on Arthur Fadden 48
    ownership restrictions for television stations 304–305
    Petrov affair 137–38
    referendum on Communist Party ban 132–33
    school funding 324–25
    television licences, use of 217
    third television licences 273–76, **277**
    US alliance as priority 341
    US bases in Australia 281
Menzies, Robert 1, 33, 35, 37, 47, 49, 50, 52–53, 78, 397
    1946 election 94–95
    1950s elections press support 127, 139, 266–67
    1954 election 137
    1961 election 262–70, 270
    alleged affair 269–70
    Bednall and 204, 236
    biographer 269
    communism fears, exploitation of 127
    Communist Party ban 131–33
    federal parliamentary press gallery and 340
    Keith Murdoch and 87, 88, 95–96, 107, 113, 119, 127, 130, 131–32, 136
    knighthoods awarded by 299, 397
    Labor banking legislation and 102–103, 105, 117
    legislative changes affecting media groups 334–35
    'Looking Forward' manifesto 89–90
    McMahon, views on 427
    'Man to Man' radio broadcasts 204–205, 207
    newspaper groups, test of loyalty for 204–205
    newspaper proprietors, relationship with 87–89
    political dominance 1950s 129
    press secretary 87
    rehabilitation by press 116–17
    Reid's election advice to 268
    retirement 340
    return to UAP leadership 83
    Rupert Murdoch and 181–82
    Sydney Morning Herald attacks 261
    television and 202–204, 207
    Warwick Fairfax and 261, 269
Mercury 11, 31
    1946 election campaign 95
    Davies family ownership 327
    television licence in Hobart 234
    Vietnam War support 341
Mergenthaler, Ottmar 388
Miller, Sir Roderick 291
Miners' Federation 118
Minnelli, Liza 354, 422
Mirror Newspapers Ltd 195
moon landing 243, 369
Moore, Thompson 166
Morgan, Al 252
Morgan, Roy 18–19, 31
Mott family 256
Mount Isa Mail 179
Mount Isa Mines 278
'the Movement' *see* Catholic Social Studies Movement ('the Movement')
Moyer, Denny 433
Mullins, Patrick 419
Mundine, Tony 433
Munro, James 409
Munster, George 180, 229, 234, 291
Murdoch, Elisabeth 39, 146, 151, 152, 290
Murdoch, Keith 39, 125, 161, 170–71, 317, 320
    1943 election 47
    1944 referendum 87
    all-party national government calls 37
    anti-censorship warrior 40–41, 43, 44, 56–57, 59

anti-communism 131
anti-Curtin sentiment 37–39, 41, 47–48, 50–51
banks and 100, 106
Bednall and 1–3
biographers 37–38, 40, 52, 90, 127, 132
Calwell and 55, 56–59
Communist Party intrigue story 113–14
conscription support 37–38
daughters 152
death 142, 151, 245
health 143, 146
HWT, connection 16, 19, 42, 145–46, 147–49, 320
independent newspaper group, building 109–10
IPA and 83, 85, 89
legacy 152–54
lobbying through papers 38
magazines and 187
Menzies and 33, 87, 88, 95–96, 107, 113, 119, 127, 130, 131–32, 136
negotiations for *Argus* merger 146–47, 150–51
opinion polls 17–18
political influence, rise and fall 36–42, 51–52
pro-American enthusiasm 134–36
public administration career 40, 134
Queensland Newspapers shareholding 15
Rupert Murdoch and 175–77
staff relations, approach 144–45, 149
succession plan 144, 145–51, 153
WAN 20
will 152–53, 155
Williams and *see* Williams, John (Jack)
World War II ideas 37
Wren, partnership with 21, 93, 108, 110, 150, 154–56
Murdoch, Rupert (Keith Rupert) 19, *39*, 145–46, 147, 170, 172, 235, 293, 312, 445
1961 election 265
1963 election 278
1966 election 342–43
1972 election 451–54, 459–60
Adelaide, television licences in 228–30
Advertiser control bid 181
Anglican Press and 251–54
ANM holding, sale to Fairfax 434–35
Australian see Australian
biographers 178–79, 229, 345, 452
'Boy Publisher' 176–78
British tabloids content 352
business style 245–46
Canberra *Territorial*, purchase 286, 287
competitors' beliefs about 257–58
country papers 364
Daily Mirror, purchase of 249–50, 256–59
Dumas, circulation war with 178
dynastic advantage 245
early newspaper experience 175–76, 246
expansion of News Limited 178–79, 260
financing 179
first dedicated television magazine 179, 221
Fleet Street 348–49, 351
Gorton and 349–51, 354
growing reputation as proprietor 352
Henderson and 258–59, 275–76
impact of father's death 152–54, 245–46
learning experiences 179
McMahon, opinion of 429, 430, 451
Melbourne, move into 256
Menzies and 139, 181–82, 231, 278
national newspaper launch 283–84 *see also Australian*
overseas expansion 347–49
Oxford 175–76
Packer and 431–33
political views 139, 181, 430, 436
portrayal by competitors 229
Queensland Newspapers sale 152–53
suburban papers, investment in 248–49, 255–56
Sydney, move into 246, 257–60, 276
Sydney television strategy 276, 283
tabloid techniques 178–79
TCN-9 stake 276, 283
Telegraphs, purchase of 433–35
television, preparation for 198
third TV licence opportunities 274
West Australian interests 331
Whitlam and 430, 436, 451–52, 461
Williams and 321
Murphy, Frank 51
Murray, Robert 169

Mussen, Gerald 19
Myer department store 246, 247, 360

Nambour Chronicle 364
Nation 448
Nation Review 270, 360, 446, 448
National Advocate 93
National Archives of Australia 427
National Bank of Australasia 84–85, 94, 100, 102, 106, 117, 152, 179
  HWT link 1940s-early 1950s 101
National Broadcasting Company (NBC) (US) 197, 199, 223
National Library of Australia 2
  TROVE 371
National Press Club 310–11
National Security Act 84
National Service Act 414
National Times 382, 405, 446, 449
National Union 83, 84
NBN-3 (Newcastle) 271, 276
  mining companies 278
  Packer, Rupert Murdoch and Fairfax coexistence 276–77
Neill, Lieutenant-Colonel Edwin Hill Balfour (EHB) 310–11, 312, 398, 399
Neill, Nancy 309
Nestlé 206
New Broken Hill Consolidated 88
New Guinea Times 335
New Idea 176
NSW Labor Council 215
New York Times 447
Newcastle
  Fairfax group 271
  significance of 271
  steelworks 271
  television station 271
Newcastle Broadcasting and Television Corporation Ltd 271
  overseas television programs 272–73
  sale of interests to Consolidated and News Limited 273
Newcastle Morning Herald 271, 272, 364
Newcastle Newspapers Pty Ltd 272, 298
  Packer and Fairfax attempts to acquire 272
Newcastle Sun 271, 272
Newcastle-Wallsend Coal 86

Newman, Joan 318
News (Adelaide) 1, 19–20, 138
  1958 election 234
  1961 election 265
  1963 election 278
  1969 election 354
  1972 election 453
  Advertiser, competition against 316
  Keith Murdoch and 108, 110, 116, 139, 146, 148
  News Limited 176
  Rivett and 178
  Rupert Murdoch and 178, 246
  Stuart rape trial campaign 180
  television, case for 204
News Chronicle (UK) 238
News Limited
  1963 election 278–83
  1972 election 436, 452
  Australian see Australian
  British newspaper profits 352
  expansion under Rupert Murdoch 178–79, 181, 260, 348–49, 361
  Festival Records 348
  finances 19, 257, 347–48, 429–30
  Fleet Street 348–49
  headquarters 348, 429–30
  HWT and 110, 153
  job losses 434
  Murdoch family trust 152, 154
  Newscom system 387, 390–91
  major interests and assets, 1969 363
  metropolitan newspaper ownership, 1972 438, 442, 443
  newsprint costs 435
  offset printing 374
  overseas expansion 260, 347–49, 351–52
  profits 178, 348
  public company 13
  radio 11, 201
  request for overseas capital movement 349
  Rupert Murdoch inheritance 146, 152–54, 175, 176–77, 153–54, 246, 248
  Southern Television Corp Ltd 179, 228
  technology 387, 390
  television 179, 231, 232, 246, 275
  VDTs 387

News of the World 238, 348
   Carr family ownership 348
   Rupert Murdoch and 348–49, 351
Newsday 359, 396, 411–14
   design 411, 412–13
   early stories 413
   losses 413–14
   switch from Sunday to afternoon paper 412
   tabloid 413
newspaper groups/industry
   1960s circulation-boosting stories 243
   1970s economy and 441
   1972 election result, significance 459–61
   Adelaide 19–20
   afternoon papers 244, 445
   alternative press outlets 361, 365, 402
   antiquated technology 369
   banks and *see* commercial banks
   Brisbane 21, 31
   British Royal Family, promotion of 126
   'butterfly department'/'hen coop' 124–25
   bylines 226
   censorship rebellion 67–71
   circulation 243–44
   Cold War coverage 127, 129
   columns 25
   comics 7, 9, 227
   concentrated press market 437
   country papers, takeover of 364
   Curtin government support 33
   daily metropolitan newspapers, 1945 **14–15**
   declining audiences 445
   democracy and 463
   diversification 365
   dominance in 1950s 123
   duopoly 437
   economics of publishing 365
   factors impacting 243–44
   family values 126
   financial strength, 1969 **361**
   four major groups 360–61
   industrial action/strikes 78–82, 369, 379, 384–86, 388, 431
   labour demands 130
   legislative amendments impacting 334–35
   mechanisation and automation 369
   media and communications developments 463–64
   media monsters, interests and assets, 1969 **362–63**
   Menzies' free radio broadcasts 204–205
   newsboy break *128*
   newspaper prices 161
   newsprint shortages 7, 9, 10, 12, 17, 22, 27, 32, 38, 49, 51, 74, 96–97, 119, 126, 130
   partisan support, 1943-72 **266–67**
   photographs 226–27
   politics and the press 52–53, **266–67**
   population growth 243
   power of 462–63
   price fixing 346–47
   production of *see* newspaper technology
   Protestant-Catholic sectarianism 162–63
   'quality' broadsheets and 'popular' tabloids, sharper demarcation 402–403
   radio 199
   sales 7, 9, 12, 243
   size of groups 360–63, 365
   strikes and picket lines 384–86
   suburbs, growth in 243, 246–48 *see also* suburban papers
   Sunday papers in Melbourne 408–14
   Sydney 21–24, 346–47
   tabloid warfare 343–47
   target audiences 403
   technological changes 369–70 *see also* newspaper technology
   television and *see* television
   unpopularity concerns 108–109
   wartime censorship issues 43–46
   Western Australia 20–21
   women in 26–28, 124–26, 449
Newspaper News 43, 262
newspaper ownership 13–16, 19–26, 127, 317
   anti-communism 127
   British Daily Mirror Group 110–12, 146–47, 158
   censorship battles 57–58, 60–64
   changes in 108–12
   commercial television 197–98 *see also* television

INDEX 545

composite paper 79–80, *80*, 81–82
daily metropolitan newspaper ownership post-*Telegraphs* sale **438**
daily national and metropolitan newspapers, December 1972 **442–43**
foreign 463
honeymoons 283
industrial action response 79–80
Menzies and 33
'one-in, all-in' principle 79–80
Packer family, end of control 440
political leanings 33, 35, 47–52, 82, **266**–**67**
power of 462–63
pro-US views 134
public broadcasting and 198
'special pleading' by 13
the survivors 441
Telegraphs 433
newspaper technology
    automation experimentation 375, 378
    automation introduction in 1890s 370–71
    cold typesetting 380–82, 392–93
    composing rooms, silence 394–95
    compositors 372
    computer crashes 390–94
    computer typesetting 380–82, 392–93
    computers 374–75, 387–90
    copy boys/girls 376
    distribution bundles 375
    errors 372–73
    Fairfax as trailblazer 378–82
    gremlins 371–72
    health and safety concerns 389–90
    hot metal to cold type transition, 1977-84 **393**
    industrial action and 379, 384–86, 388, 390
    industrial anxiety 389–90
    industrial organising 382–83
    job losses 383, 385, 387, 388
    labour and metal 373
    letterpress printing 374
    linotype machines 373–74, 388
    linotype operators 370–71, *371*, 372–73, 375
    newspaper production in 1960s 370–75
    newsroom, computers in 387–90

    offset printing 361, 374, 402
    photocomposition 374, 375, 380, 381, 382, 392–93
    photosetting devices 380
    pneumatic tubes messaging system 376, *377*
    printing presses 369, 373
    printing skills and traditions 382
    proofreading 372–73
    publishing room 375, 378
    stereo plates 373
    'the stone' 372
    teletype setting (TTS) 378–79, 384, 388
    trade unions 382
    TTS operators 378
    typewriters 370, 380–81
    UK 380
    US 380, 381
    visual display terminals (VDTs) 374–75, 381, 387, 390
Newton, Bert 462
Newton, Maxwell 262–63, 279, 287, 299, 323, 333, 349–50, 359, 417
    first editor of *Australian* 288–89
Nixon, President Richard 447–48
Nolan, Sybil 397
Norris, Peter 324–25, 339
North Australian Workers' Union 140
North Broken Hill 278
North Shore Times 249
Northcliffe, Lord 57, 110–11
Northern Standard 140, 141
Northern Star 255
Northern Territory News (*NT News*) 140–41
    funding 140–41
    purpose 140
    Rupert Murdoch acquisition 179
Norton, Ezra 27, 32, 81, 146, 216
    British Daily Mirror group talks 111
    Calwell, friendship with 56
    censorship issues 64–65
    character 23–24
    Daily Mirror ownership 3, 24, 287 *see also Daily Mirror*
    Fairfax deal 194–95
    finances 194
    health 194
    industrial action impact 186
    male successor, lack of 194

television 217, 228
Truth see Truth
Norton, John 409
Norton, Dr John Stanley 194
Norton, John 23
NWS-9 231, 232, 237, 246, 274
    News Limited stake 238

Oakes, Laurie 323, 420, 427, 446–47, 450–51
O'Connell Pty Ltd 195
Old Guard 85
opinion polls 17–19, 95–96, 114, 137, 207, 450
Osborne, Robert 218

Packer, Clyde 185, 249, 250, *251*, 252, *253*, 254, 256, 421, 424, 432, 437–39, 444
Packer, Frank 32, 50, 52, *251 see also*
    Consolidated Press
        1961 election 265
        1969 election 354
        Adelaide, television licences in 228–29
        Anglican Press brawl 250–54
        Argus proposal 170
        Associated Newspapers and 23, 24, 108, 190–92
        Australian-American Association involvement 135
        Australian Women's Weekly and 187
        Bednall and 2, 3, 172
        Brisbane, television licences in 228–29
        Calwell, clashes with 55, 61–64, 67, 75
        censorship battles 58–64, 67, 71, 73
        Consolidated Press takeover threat 184–85
        country television licences 271–72
        death 439
        dominance in television markets 236
        father, as 250, 438
        GTV-9 235–36
        Henderson and 293–94, 302
        ill health 421, 432
        industrial action due to 186
        influence 182–85
        knighthood 299
        loyalty to 292
        McMahon and 349, 350, 419, 421–22, 428, 432, 435
        Menzies and 33, 49, 87, 88, 127, 182, 265, 268, 273, 280–81, 283, 340, 421–22, 439
        national broadcaster, argument against 227
        newsprint allocations 97
        political interference 97, 268, 439
        pro-American enthusiasm 134, 135
        Reid and 268, 280–81, 419–21, 425–26
        Rupert Murdoch and 258, 276, 283, 431–33
        suburban papers 255–56
        TCN-9 'classic reverse takeover' manoeuvre 283
        Telegraphs, sale to Rupert Murdoch 432–34
        television and 201, 214, 215, 219, 222–23, 227, 228–29, 231, 234, 235–36, 238, 271–72, 273, 304, 437
        Theodore and 23
        third TV licence opportunities 273
        TV Times 221
        West Australian interests 331, 333
        Williams and 150
Packer, James 440
Packer, Kerry 250, *251*, 254, 432–33
    television over newspapers, preference for 432, 440
Packer, Robert Clyde (RC) 23
Paddison, Alfred 216
Pagewood Studios 217
Papua New Guinea
    HWT acquisitions 335
Paral, Vladimir 281–82
Parramatta Advertiser 248, 255
Parramatta Mail 255
Patience, Jack 112, 147
Paul Ramsay Communications 315
Pead, Jim 286
Pearce, Eric 225–26
Pearl, Cyril 63, 431
Pearson, Drew 25
    'Washington Merry-Go-Round' 25
Penton, Brian 23, 55, 75, 82, 182, 183, 280, 431
    cadet training program 109
    censorship battles 58–59, 60, 63, 65–66
Perkin, Graham 324, 400, 413, 429, 456–58, 460

INDEX 547

Perth Gazette 27
Petrov Episode 136–39
Petrov, Evdokia 137
Petrov, Vladimir 137
Phelan, Terry 342
Philips Electrical Industries 217
Pix 12
Playford, Premier Thomas 180–81
Police Offences Statute 1865 (Victoria) 409
Port Kembla Steelworks 273
Port Phillip Herald see Herald
Post-Courier 335
Postle, Bruce 400
Postmaster-General's Department (PMG) 236, 272
    licence conditions for TCN-9 and ATN-7 273–73
Potter, Ian 102, 185, 235, 331, 332
Power, Kevin 446
Press and Broadcasting Censorship order 73
Press Censorship Advisory Committee 44–45
Pringle, John Douglas (JD) 131, 138, 193, 287–88, 343, 345, 449, 455
    return to editorship of *Sydney Morning Herald* 313
    Warwick Fairfax editorial interference 455
Printing Industry Employees' Union of Australia (PIEUA) 79, 183–84
    The News 80–81
Printing and Kindred Industries Union (PKIU) 379, 384–86, 431
    AJA and 387–88
    Cahill decision 386–87, 389
Provincial Newspapers (Qld.) Ltd 364
Pye Industries 229

Qantas 89
QTQ-9 Brisbane 231, 232
    Fairfax interest 302, 304
Queensland Newspapers 11, 15, 102, 110, 146, 151, 208 *see also* Queensland Press, 328
    CWL Pty Ltd shareholding 154, 156
    Keith Murdoch stake 152–54
    sale to HWT 156–57
Queensland Press 160, 162, 364

    HWT shareholdings and capital 319–20, 325
    shareholders 162
    WAN and 331
Queensland Television Ltd 228

Rabin, Zell 343
radio
    1960s, in 359
    major commercial networks 1954-55 200
    newspapers and 10–11, 199
    ownership 10–11
    peak listening time 243
    sponsored programs 206
Radio Corporation of America (RCA) 197
Radio and Hobbies 12
Ramsey, Alan 425, 427, 446–47, 452
Ratcliffe, John 183
Regan, Simon 452
Reid, Alan 'Red Fox' 138, 268, 280, 398, 419, 422, 439, 444, 446, 452
    access to politicians 420–21
    'faceless men' scoop 282–83, 419
    The Gorton Experiment 425
    Gorton strategy 423–24, 426, 428
    Labor credentials 280–81, 421
    value to Packer 280–82, 419–20, 447
Reid, Joan 420
Reuters 148, 294, 303
The Review 448
Richards, Arthur 25
Richards, George 392
Ricketson, Staniforth 102
Riddell, Elizabeth 27, 124–25
Riddle, Duncan (DJ) 149
Rio Tinto 15, 329, 332
Riverina and North-East Television Ltd 298, 315
Rivett, Rohan 177, 180–81, 316, 322, 323, 426
    Williams, on 316–17
Roberts, Tom 40
Robertson, Connie 125
Robinson, Peter 239
Robinson, William Sydney (WS) 20, 88, 136, 329, 332
Rodgers, Don 35, 41, 87, 92, 133
Roman Catholic Trusts Corporation 165

Roosevelt, President Franklin D 17, 58
Rothermere, Lord 1, 3, 111, 213, 333
Rothman's cigarettes 219, 221
Rowe, Septimus 86
Royal Commission into banking 98
Royal Commission into Communist Party's activities 115
Royal Commission on espionage 138, 139
Royal Commission on Stuart case 180–81
Royal Commission on Television 3, 205, 222
    diversity promises 238
    dual system recommendation 207
    newspaper coverage 208
    ownership of transmitters 209–10
    recommendations 209
    stacked membership 207–11
    technology 210
    Ultra High Frequency (UHF) band 210
    Very High Frequency (VHF) band 210
    victories for newspapers 207, 209–11
    wishlist for commercial television 209
Royal Insurance 101
Rubensohn, Solomon (Sim) 118
RVN-2 Wagga Wagga 298, 302, 315
Ryan, Colleen 456
Ryan, Ronald 324, 398

St George and Sutherland Shire Leader 255
Sampson, Richard 328, 458
Samuel, Peter 423, 428
Santamaria, Bartholomew Augustine (BA) 115, 139, 280
SAS-10 Adelaide 275, 277
Savva, Niki 449
Schulz, Julianne 124
Schwarz, Mark 100
Scotsman 237, 238
Scottish Television 237
Scrimgeour, CG 216–17
Scullin government 37, 41, 98
Scullin, James 34, 44, 45
Scully, Frank 165
Seamen's Union 93
Senate Select Committee on the Encouragement of Australian Productions for Television (Vincent Report) 224
Shakespeare, Arthur Thomas (AT) 26, 28, 285–87, 297
    approach to Henderson 285

    Consolidated Press approach 286
    HWT approach 286
Shakespeare Head Press 425
Shakespeare, Thomas Mitchell (TM) 26, 285
Sharkey, Lance 70
Sharpley, Cecil 113–15, 117
Shawcross, William 345
Shmith, Michael 370
Silverton Securities Pty Ltd 336
Simper, Errol 294
Sinclair, Keith 268, 397–98, 456
    Menzies and 398, 399–400
Smith, Arthur Norman 152
Smith, Fred 41
Smith, Louis Lawrence 166
Smith's Weekly 27, 126, 400
Snedden, Billy 425
Snow, Sydney 85, 86
Solomon, David 446–47, 451
Souter, Gavin 88, 257–58, 346, 455
South Australian Brewing Co 208
South Australian Telecasters Ltd 275
South Coast Times 297, 314
South Pacific Post 335
South West Printing and Publishing 330
Southdown Press 176, 178
Southern Television Corporation Ltd 179, 228
Southey, Sir Robert 457
Sparrow, GE 44
Sporting Globe 410
Spowers, Allan 110
Stalin, Joseph 183
Standard Newspapers 256
Starke, Justice 71
Stevenson, Murray 212
Stewart, Francis (Frank) 305
Stuart, Rupert Max 180
STW-9 Perth 275, 277
suburban papers 246–48
    advertising 248
    chain ownership 247
    Consolidated Press 249–50, 255
    Leader group of 256
    Melbourne 256
    reputation 248
    Rupert Murdoch and 248–49, 255, 256
    technology, early adoption of 248
Suburban Publications Pty Ltd 249

INDEX 549

Fairfax/Consolidated Press establishment
of 249–50, 255
no-competition agreement 255–56
suburbs
growth in 243, 246–48
newspapers and advertising 246–47
retail trading, growth of 246
Sullivan, Forbie 297
Summers, Anne 449
Sun 24, 45, 46, 125, 138, 194, 211, 257, 264, 268, 296
1972 election 454
advertising 345
censorship battle, joining 64
colour printing 326
'Contact' 25
costs of 190
Daily Mirror and, competition 260, 346
ethics 345
false leads to rivals 344–45
outrageous headlines 344
'page-three girls' 346
pneumatic tube installation 376
price fixing 346–47
promotions 347
rules of combat with *Daily Mirror* 346
street posters 344
strikes 79, 81–82, 185–86
tabloid warfare 343–47
Sun (UK)
circulation increase 352
financial bedrock 352
'page-three girls' 351–52
Rupert Murdoch purchase 351–52
tabloid style 351–52
Sun-Herald 269, 296
competitor to *Sunday Telegraph* 193
Fatty Finn 227
merger of 2 papers 193
size 405
Sun News-Pictorial 1, 31, 58, 144, 147, 318, 328, 446, 449
1943 election 48
1972 election 458
'Bluey and Curley' 227
Bolte, support for 322–24
competitors 28–29
front page *8*
Gordon as editor 401–402

HWT and *see* Herald and Weekly Times (HWT)
newsprint shortages 17
'A Place in the Sun' column 25
rival to *The Age* 401
road death toll campaign 402
sales 7, 320, 396
Victory in the Pacific celebrations *9*
Vietnam War protest photo 342
Williams and *see* Williams, John (Jack)
'women's pages' 125
Sunday Advertiser 177–78
Sunday Australian 425–26
merger with *Sunday Telegraph* 434
Sunday Herald 188
merger with *Sunday Sun* 193
Sunday Independent 333
Sunday Mail 328
Sunday Mirror 252, 259, 265
Sunday Newspapers Act 1889 (Victoria) 409
Sunday Observance Act 1677 (Victoria) 409, 412
Sunday Observer 396, 414, 416–17
anti-Vietnam War stance 414
My Lai massacre photographs 414
Sunday Post 414
Sunday Press 417–18
Sunday Review 417 *see also Nation Review*
Sunday Sun 79, 188, 190
merger with *Sunday Herald* 193
Sunday Telegraph 23, 190, 193, 227, 432
censorship front page *62, 63*, 65
Ginger Meggs comic 227
merger with *Sunday Australian* 434
Sunday Times 178–79, 331, 400
birthplace of Murdoch journalism 178–79, 347
Sungravure 296
Sunshine Coast Daily 364
Swan Television Ltd 275
Sydney Gazette 27, 99
Sydney Morning Herald 9, 13, 31, 78, 188, 222, 251, 446
1950s changes 193
1943 election 47, 49–50
1946 election 95
1958 election 234
1961 election 262–64, 270, 280, 300–301

1963 election 278–79, 301
1969 election 355
1972 election 454
advertising losses 301
Amalgamated Television Services Pty Ltd announcement 212–13
anti-Catholicism 163
attacks on Menzies 49–50
Australian, impact 401
Canberra Times and 285–86, 298
cartoon use by Liberal Party 116
censorship battles 44, 59, 61, 65–67
classified advertising 403–404
'Column 8' 25
communism, dangers of 82
Curtin and 33, 35
Daily Telegraph as competitor 301, 346–37
display advertising 404
Fairfax family 22–23 *see also* Fairfax group
first Labor endorsement 264
Harriott as editor 455
Henderson and *see* Henderson, Rupert Albert Geary ('Rags')
industrial action 79–81
IPA 85
Labor banking policy, opposition to 105–106, *107*
Menzies and 261–62, 278–79
publication of Curtin's medical conditions 91–92
reputation 22–23
'sectional revolution' 404–405
state aid to non-government schools 324
strike 185–86
subscribers 405
Vietnam War support 341
Warwick Fairfax articles/editorials 42, 49, 85, 103, 300–301, 313
women's supplement 125
Sydney Newspapers Ltd 419
Sydney Snow Ltd 246
Syme, David 28, 30, 308, 396–97
 will 309
Syme, Kathleen 28, 309
Syme, Oswald 30, 225, 308–309, 310, 396–97
 lack of interest in *The Age* 397

Symons, Cedric 300
Systems Integrated Inc (SII) 392

Tait, Robert 323–24, 398
Tanner, Les 400
 cartoon by 265
Tasmanian Television Ltd 234, 336
Taylor, Elizabeth 344
Taylor, Greg 308
TCN-9 Sydney (Packer) 214, 219, 271, 273, 276, 437
 attempts to hobble other stations 272–73
 Australian Consolidated Press ownership 238
 Daily Telegraph coverage of debut 219, 220
 first Australian television advertisements 219
 local content 223
 Meet the Press 226
 Packer sale of stake to Rupert Murdoch 276
 Packer's formula 222–23
 profits 237
 ratings 223
 sports 358
 westerns 223
Tebbutt, Geoffrey 109, 318
Telegraph 31, 52, 160
Telegraph Newspaper Company Ltd 160–61
Television
 1950s traditional values 126
 1960s, in 357–58
 Adelaide 228–34, 277
 advertisers 221
 advertising 199, 206, 212, 219, 221
 American producers and Australia 223
 Australian content 223
 believability as medium 357
 Brisbane 228–34, 277
 Canberra 233, 234–35
 celebrities 226
 churches 213, 215
 children's programs 224
 cinema industry concerns 203
 colour 326, 327
 competitors, scaring off 211–15
 costs of starting up 212

INDEX 551

country television licences 271
current affairs 358, 444
diversity of ownership, lack of **214**, **232**, 237–39
early 221
first advertisements 219
first licences: Sydney and Melbourne 215–18
foreign ownership issues 218, 235, 238
Hobart 233, 234
Labor policy 202
licence holder conditions 218
licence rules 218
licences 197–98, 211, 271
live transmission 221
local producers and content 223, 224
magazines, use of 221
Melbourne **214**, 215–18, 277
Melbourne Olympic Games 224–25
Menzies government award of licences Sydney and Melbourne 1955 **214**
Menzies government's allocation of new licences, 1963-64 **277**
metropolitan commercial television licences, award of **232–233**
money and power in 237–39
news and weather 357
news bulletins ratings 444
newspaper bylines and 226
newspapers and 3, 196, 202, 211–18, 225–27, 234, 237–39, 244–45, 274, 276, 278, 304–305, 357–58, 383
ownership restrictions 304, 305, 306–308
Perth 233, 234, 277
pioneers 224–28
politics, impact on 358
popular formats 226
preparing for 196–99, 226
profit conditions 237–38
programming 221, 223–24
public broadcasting 198, 202, 227 *see also* ABC
restrictions on advertising time 221
Royal Commission *see* Royal Commission on Television
satellite technology 357
shaping 202–207
social revolution in US 196

sporting coverage 224–25, 358
Sydney **214**, 215–18, 277
tabloid audiences 222, 358
taxes collection from commercial stations 237
technology improvements 357
ten most-watched programs 1957 223
transmitters, ownership of 209–10
UK 206, 209, 210–11, 216, 222, 237–38, 244–45
US 198–99, 222, 244–45
Vincent Report 224
westerns 223
Television Broadcasters Ltd 228
Television Corporation Ltd 215
Television Wollongong Transmissions Ltd 272
  overseas television programs 272–73
TEN-10 Sydney 275, 277
Territorial 286, 287
Theodore, Edward Granville (EG) 23, 63, 87, 93, 108, 184, 419
Theodore, John (Jack) 108, 184–85
Theodore, Ned 184
Thirkell, Irene 293
Thomas, Archer 143, 458
Thomson, Lord 237, 333, 463
Thomson, Peter 324
Tiffen, Rodney 287, 341, 342, 350, 359, 430
The Times 224, 284, 351–52
Tindale, Darren 352
Tooth and Company beer 221
The Torch 414
Tout, Sir Frederick 100, 101
Trade Practices Act 256
Transcontinental Broadcasting Corporation Ltd 216
Tribune 24, 332, 351
Tricontinental Corporation 331, 332
Truman, Harry S 113
Truth 24, 79, 111, 186, 194, 217, 228, 259, 288, 290, 295, 348, 400, 401, 409
  Gorton story 350–51
  investigative journalism 401
  'page-three girls' 346
Truth and Sportsman Ltd 194, 195, 217, 228, 231
Tunstall, Jeremy 402–403
Turnbull, Clive 168

Turnbull, Lyle 328, 458
Turner, Harry 282
TV Guide 179
TVQ-0 Brisbane 274, 277
TV-Radio Week 179
TV Times 221
TV Week 221
TVT-6 233, 234, 327
TVW-7 233, 234, 330, 332, 336
TVW Ltd 234

Unilever 206
Union Trustee Co 101
United Australia Party (UAP) 37, 49–50, 52
  Consultative Council 83, 85, 86
  formation 47
  Menzies' return as leader 83
  'National Service Group' 47
  new political party, as *see* Liberal Party
  revelations 83
United States
  Australian 'double taxation' laws 135
  Curtin policy 133–34
  economy boom in 1950s 134–35
  investment in Australia 135
  Keith Murdoch and 134–35
  Senate Committee on Juvenile Delinquency 209
United Telecasters Sydney Ltd 275, 276
Universal Telecasters Qld 274–75
Usher, Jim 173

Victoria Racing Club 397
Victorian Authorised Newsagents Association 412
Victorian Chamber of Manufactures 83
Victorian Football League (VFL) 225
Vietnam War 243, 341, 455, 456
  dissent/protests 342, 402, 414–15
  divisions in Australia 414–15
  Geraldine Willesee scoop 353
  Gorton Coalition support 354
  My Lai massacre photographs 414
  newspaper support 341, 355
  President Johnson visit 342
  Sunday Post 414
  Vietnam Moratorium demonstrations 415–16

Vincent Report 224
Vincent's APC 219

Waddell, Dr Graham 65
Waine, Cecil Scott 86
Walker, Martin 397
Walker, Peter 324
Walsh, Eric 446, 452
Walsh, Max 292, 359, 446
Walsh, Richard 422
Wansey, Sydney 272
Ward, Eddie 46, 82, 99, 237
Ward, Michael 37–38
Wardle, Tom 331
Warner, Arthur 215, 225, 227, 228, 235–36
Washington Post 447–48
  Watergate reporting 447–48
Waters, John 144, 458
Waterside Workers Federation 132
Watson, Chris 34
Watson, James Kingston 'King' 431
West Australian 15, 20, 112, 333
  1946 election campaign 95
  circulation and sales 330
  television licence in Perth 234
West Australian Newspapers (WAN) 11, 13, 15, 20–21, 199
  assets 330
  bank connections 102
  board members 332–33
  circulation increase 330
  Hiawatha 330
  HWT and 20–21, 330–34, 335–36
  investments 330
  mining magnates' interest 333
  Packer bid for 331–32
  profits 330
  radio stations 330
  Rupert Murdoch proposal 331–32
  takeover target, as 330–32
  television 330
Western Australia
  growth 329
  mining boom 329–30, 332
Western Mining Corporation 329, 332
Western Newspapers Ltd 364
Western Press Ltd 178
Westralian Worker 34
White Australia policy 317

INDEX 553

White, Earl Stanley 248, 248–49, 256
White, Eric 140, 179
Whitington, Don 49, 82, 140, 179, 182
Whitlam, Catherine 356
Whitlam, Gough 281, 283, 310–11, 342, 356, 421
    1969 election 352–53
    1972 election 439, 450–59
    Fairfax family, views on 455
    Labor leader 349
    Rupert Murdoch and 430, 435, 436, 451–52, 461
    Vietnam War policy 354
Whitlam, Margaret 439
Whitton, Evan 348, 351, 401
Willesee, Geraldine 353
Willesee, Mike 398, 437, 444
Williams, Catherine 318
Williams, John Irven 318–19
Williams, John (Jack) 108–109, 159, 170–71, 181, 187–88, 190–91, 204
    absorption in newspapers 319
    accomplishments at HWT 320–21
    alcoholism 144, 318, 337
    Argus deal 172–74
    Bednall and 155–57, 208
    biographer 318
    Catholicism 162–66, 317, 324, 325, 410
    character 316–18, 325
    death 339
    early journalism career 142–43
    editorial style 321–22
    executive chairman of HWT 312, 316–19, 328–29, 337–38
    health problems 337–39
    Henderson and 316
    home life 318
    HWT 3, 126, 155–57, 158–62, 258, 292, 316–19, 321–25, 347, 458
    influence on HWT 321–25
    industry reputation 316, 317–18
    journalism principles 320
    Keith Murdoch and 21, 142–45, 147, 148–51, 152, 153, 317, 320–21, 433
    knighthood 323
    managing director of HWT 158–66, 316–19, 320, 328
    media management 160, 162
    other newspaper barons, comparison 317
    Packer and 150
    politicians and 322
    preoccupations 322
    progressive views 317
    Queensland Newspapers sale to HWT 156–57
    Queensland Press acquisition 156–57, 325
    'quiet baron' 316
    'republic of management' 319–21
    retirement stages 319, 321, 328, 338
    staff management 132, 159–60, 317, 318
    succession plan 328–29, 336, 338
    Sun News-Pictorial 320
    television 197, 225, 235, 334–35
    trees, obsession with 322
    Victorian politics and 322, 325
    WAN and 330–34
    will 339
Williams, Justice 71
Williams, Mabel Gwendoline (née Dawkins) 318, 338
Williams, William 18
Willis, John 252, 253, 254
Wilson, Earl 25
    'It Happened Last Night' 25
Wilson, Edward 110
Wilson, Harold 436
Wilson, Robert Christian (RC) 207
Wimmera Mail-Times 364
WIN-4 272, 276, 297, 302
    new shares issue to Mirror Newspapers 276
    Packer, Rupert Murdoch and Fairfax coexistence 276–77
Winchell, Walter 25
    'On Broadway' 25
Windschuttle, Keith 305
Winter, Samuel Vincent 163
Wollongong
    television licence 272
Woman 12, 125, 187
women
    admission to printing chapel/composing room, ban 379
    newspaper industry, in 26–28, 124–26, 449

'page-three girls' 346, 351–52
photographs for papers 345–46
second-wave feminism 448–49
sexism 353, 449
Woolworths 86
Workers Star 136
World War II 1, 4, 17
    censorship 7, 32, 40–41, 43–46, 54–74
    magazine sales 11
    newspaper sales/circulation 7, 9, 12, 14–15, 17, 19–20, 21, 30–31
    newsprint rationing 7, 10, 12, 17, 22–23, 27, 30, 38, 96, 261
    radio 10

women in newspaper offices 26–28
Wren, John 2, 21, 93, 108, 110, 150, 154–57, 168, 324
    links to Archbishop Mannix 165
    reputation 154–55, 156
Wright, Peter 329, 333

Yass Post 314
Young, Mick 451–52
Young, Norman 183, 207–208
Younger, Ron 90, 127, 164

Zinc Corporation 88, 140, 166, 332
Zwar, Desmond 132